Applied Linguistics and the Learning an
Foreign Languages

Advisory Editor: Pieter A.M. Seuren

D0917452

BAK
4-86
50

Applied Linguistics and the Learning and Teaching of Foreign Languages

Theo van Els
Theo Bongaerts
Guus Extra
Charles van Os
Anne-Mieke Janssen-van Dieten

Translated by R.R. van Oirsouw

Edward Arnold

Wingate College Library

100464

© Wolters-Noordhoff bv 1984

First edition published in 1977 by
Wolters-Noordhoff bv, Groningen, under the title
Handboek voor de Toegepaste Taalkunde
Revised English language edition first published in Great Britain 1984 by
Edward Arnold (Publishers) Ltd, 41 Bedford Square, London WC1B 3DQ

Edward Arnold (Australia) Pty Ltd, 80 Waverley Road, Caulfield East,
Victoria 3145, Australia

Edward Arnold, 300 North Charles Street, Baltimore, Maryland 21201, USA

English translation by R.R. van Oirsouw © Edward Arnold (Publishers) Ltd 1984

British Library Cataloguing in Publication Data

Applied linguistics and the learning and
    teaching of foreign languages.
    1. Language and languages—Study and
    teaching   2. Applied linguistics
    I. Els, Theo van
    407'.1   P53

    ISBN 0-7131-6422-0

All rights reserved. No part of this publication may be reproduced, stored in a
retrieval system, or transmitted in any form or by any means, electronic,
photocopying, recording, or otherwise, without the prior permission of Edward
Arnold (Publishers) Ltd.

Text set in 10/11½pt Times Compugraphic
by Colset Private Limited, Singapore
Printed and bound by Richard Clay (The Chaucer Press) Ltd, Bungay, Suffolk

Contents

Foreword

The present book is a completely revised and updated version of a handbook originally written in Dutch by four members of the same team of authors (T. van Els *et al.*, *Handboek voor de Toegepaste Taalkunde. Het leren en onderwijzen van moderne vreemde talen*, Groningen, Wolters–Noordhoff, 1977). The contents and plan of the book have been greatly inspired by the courses on the learning and teaching of second/foreign languages that we have been teaching to university students over a number of years. An important section of the student population that attend our courses prepare for the foreign language teaching profession. The courses are intended to provide prospective teachers and researchers in this area of applied linguistics with essential theoretical background information.

Although all chapters of the book have been written by individual members of our team, we like to think of the book as a joint undertaking for which we accept joint responsibility. Continuous mutual consultations, over the years, about the various teaching programmes and many critical discussions of earlier versions of the texts have led to a high degree of consensus on the contents and form of the book. The editorial finishing touch was applied by, mainly, Theo Bongaerts and by Theo van Els.

It is impossible to name all those who in the long history of this book have contributed to its completion. We owe a great debt of gratitude to many, not in the least to those who have reviewed the previous Dutch edition. We wish to thank Pieter Seuren, who urged us to prepare the English version, Rob van Oirsouw, who, as the translator of this book, was charged with the almost impossible task of merging five different styles into one, and Bert Weltens, who compiled the *Index of Persons* and the *Index of Subjects*. Thanks are also due to the publishing house of Wolters–Noordhoff (Groningen) for their co-operation. And finally we would like to thank all colleagues at the Department of Applied Linguistics in Nijmegen who in one way or another helped administratively to complete the manuscript.

Theo van Els
Theo Bongaerts
Guus Extra
Charles van Os
Anne-Mieke Janssen-van Dieten

Nijmegen/Tilburg
June 1983

Acknowledgements

The publishers would like to thank the following for permission to include copyright material:

Harcourt Brace Jovanovich Inc. for fig. 3.10 © 1977, reprinted by permission of the publisher; Harvard University for fig. 3.9 reprinted by permission; Instituut voor Toegepaste Sociologie for fig. 9.1; E. Kellerman for fig. 4.13; Longman Group Limited for figs. 10.1, 10.2, 10.3; University of Michigan for figs. 4.8, 4.9, 4.10, 4.14, 5.11, 5.12, 5.13; Gunter Narr Verlag for fig. 5.7; Newbury House Publishers Inc. for figs. 5.8, 5.9, 5.18; Georg Olms Verlag for fig. 10.6; Oxford University Press for fig. 4.7; Roskilde Universitetscenter for fig. 5.17 and Springer Verlag for figs. 5.3, 5.4, 5.5.

Part I
The Field of Study: A First Outline

1

Introduction

The juxtaposition in the title of this book of 'applied linguistics' and 'the learn-ing and teaching of foreign languages' is intended to suggest that, although the two terms are not synonymous, the area of applied linguistics that concerns us here, i.e. that of the learning and teaching of foreign languages, constitutes, in our opinion, the most important area within the extensive field of applied linguistics.

In the title of the Dutch edition, the book is called a 'handbook'. There are two reasons for this. First of all, we wanted to indicate that in this publication we aim to cover all the subparts of this area which we consider to be most relevant. Secondly, we wished to emphasize that we also intend this book to be a reference book and an introduction to other publications in the field. With this last consideration in mind we have included many bibliographical references.

Foreign language teaching (FLT) is a matter of considerable social impor-tance. There is a great demand for it, and in many countries FLT forms an important part of the educational facilities provided. Such provisions include not only all forms of regular education, from primary schools to universities, but also company courses, evening classes and summer schools, to mention a few other types of (usually adult) education. The frame of reference for our dis-cussion of the learning and teaching of foreign languages is that particular part of regular school education in which children from 10 to 16 come into contact with FLT for the first time; in other words, we shall mainly be talking about secondary education and, in some cases, about the higher grades in primary education. But our frame of reference ought to be narrowed down even further. The FLT that we have in mind is the type where the teaching takes place in a dif-ferent linguistic environment from that of the language to be learned: we will be focusing on L2 learning in an L1 environment, on *foreign* language learning, therefore, rather than *second* language learning. Our preference for this particular frame of reference is of course closely related to the fact that this book originated in the Netherlands, where most teaching of languages other than the mother tongue concerns the teaching of foreign languages in schools. FLT in schools is very important in the Netherlands and rests on a long and fertile tradition. We believe that what is said in this book about this particular area of FLT will apply to a considerable extent, *mutatis mutandis*, both to many other areas of FLT and to second language teaching.

We will, therefore, not devote separate attention to the teaching of second languages. In chapters of the second part of this book second language *learning* figures several times, but what separate attention is devoted to it must be seen in the light of our treatment of foreign language learning and FLT.

The times when it was fairly generally believed that teaching, including FLT, could hardly be subjected to scientific investigation, have passed. To make a sweeping generalization, one might say that in the past the research interest in FLT was focused exclusively on the language itself, and that it is only in the last few decades that the educational and psychological aspects of FLT have begun to attract their share of research attention. In many countries this development can undoubtedly be accounted for by changes in FLT needs and objectives. In the Netherlands, for instance, the incorporation of three foreign languages in the curricula of many types of secondary schools is no longer taken for granted, and other languages besides English, German and French are being introduced. Related to these changes in needs is the discussion that has been started about the traditional objectives of the teaching of each individual language. These changes in needs and objectives have prompted research into the most efficient teaching methods in different educational settings. It was realized that this necessitates fundamental research into foreign language learning processes. The L1 and L2 learning research that had developed independently of FLT provided a useful frame of reference.

We have written this book for those who have an interest in theories about the learning and teaching of foreign languages. We intend the book specifically for the following three categories of readers: (future) teachers of foreign languages, (future) researchers in this area of applied linguistics, and those who train (future) teachers and researchers. Independently of the question of how much each of these three categories should know about the subject, there is by no means full agreement on which knowledge is relevant. It is generally accepted that theories in this area are based on linguistics, psycholinguistics, sociolinguistics and educational theory. The actual content of teaching programmes in this area of applied linguistics varies from place to place, and different handbooks tend to emphasize different aspects. Not all handbooks assume the same amount of knowledge about the disciplines mentioned above. We expect our readers to have some personal experience in learning a foreign language. We also expect them to be familiar with the basic concepts of theoretical and descriptive linguistics, but we do not assume familiarity with psychological research.

This book contains the information that we consider essential for those who train future teachers of foreign languages, and for (prospective) researchers in this area of applied linguistics. Teachers will find that the book contains more information than is strictly necessary for their day-to-day teaching; for them, it is intended to be a work of reference and guide to further study to improve their day-to-day teaching. The preceding sentence might be taken to suggest that we have practical advice to offer to teachers. We do not provide any made-to-measure, directly applicable suggestions with regard to teaching. What we wish to offer is the theoretical background which is essential for diagnosing problems and without which effective therapy can only be achieved accidentally. Without a theoretical foundation a foreign language teacher can only gratefully, but helplessly, accept the suggestions for solving his practical problems offered by others.

We have already indicated that this book deals with only one area of the discipline of applied linguistics, be it the most important one. Moreover, within the area we have selected, we will not discuss all aspects, and not every aspect will be discussed equally exhaustively. We will pay more attention to oral than to written skills, for instance, to cater for the changing insights into the goals of (initial) FLT. Some aspects of the area selected will not be dealt with separately, although other writers in the field may have done so. The most conspicuous absentees are probably translation, the teaching of literature and the teaching of culture.

Only a subpart of all the aspects of translation are relevant within our framework. Translation can certainly play a useful role in training and testing language skills, but these are only two of the many aspects that would have to be dealt with in a separate discussion of translation. Translation as a discipline in its own right, the various ideas about what translation is from a philological, linguistic or sociolinguistic point of view, and the problems involved in training professional translators are matters which are too remote from what will concern us here.

Neither will we be concerned with the pedagogical questions raised by the teaching of literature. Traditionally, the teaching of literature has two main objectives, namely developing the appreciation of literature and engendering knowledge of literary theories, schools and works. The question of what the objectives of the teaching of literature could be is only very indirectly connected with the objectives of teaching language skills. In other respects, too, especially where the teaching of the two components mentioned above is concerned, there is no link to the framework of our discussion. The didactic procedures for developing appreciation and knowledge of literature are not only very different with respect to each other, they are also entirely different from the type of didactic procedures required for foreign language learning. Neither are these strategies specific: both apply, in comparable fashion, to the teaching of L1 literature, and they each exhibit a number of similarities to the teaching of other subjects, such as art and history.

Insofar as culture is a part of FLT proper, it will receive some mention in the chapters on objectives (9) and content selection (10); we do not, however, discuss it as an autonomous subpart with its own objectives and didactic procedures. In those cases where culture is taught in schools as an autonomous and independent subject, the didactic procedures used differ, as in the teaching of literature, from those used in teaching foreign language skills, but are at the same time not specific for the teaching of culture only.

We were in considerable doubt as to whether or not to treat research questions in our field of study in a separate chapter. Eventually we have decided not to. First of all, even if we had inserted a separate chapter on research, we would still have had to scatter the information on actual research projects and their findings over the rest of the book, to discuss them in conjunction with the relevant aspects of our field of study. Secondly, in a general introduction to applied linguistics such as we aim to offer in this book, a systematic treatment – be it elementary – of all basic questions of empirical research does not seem to be called for. For such matters as choice of research design, selection and matching of groups of subjects, controlling of variables and statistical analysis of research data the reader had better consult introductory handbooks of empirical research in the social sciences. What aspects of applied linguistic research are touched upon, we have spread over the other chapters. In chapter 2 the question is discussed whether research in the field of applied linguistics is necessarily applied in its orientation or can also be fundamentally orientated, and in chapter 7 the 'autonomy' of this field of research is gone into. A number of specific aspects of second and foreign language learning research are dealt with in chapter 5 (5.1.1.), in particular features of research design pertaining to period of data collection (longitudinal versus cross-sectional design), informants (single or multiple case-studies versus experiments with larger groups of subjects), and data collection procedures (naturalistic observation versus experimental tasks). In chapter 3 (3.2.1.) we compare our field with respect to the nature of data and procedures of data collection with the field of linguistic research. And although our treatment of language proficiency testing is in the first place geared to the use of such tests in FLT, much of it is equally applicable to the use of proficiency tests in applied linguistic research, especially such matters as reliability and validity of tests and discrete point versus integrative skill testing.

Our discussion of our field of study is contained in 15 chapters which are grouped into three parts. Part I contains, besides this Introduction, a chapter which aims to clarify the contents, methods and practical relevance of applied linguistics for the field of FLT, on the basis of a discussion of a number of questions of a terminological kind.

In Part II, chapters 3 to 6, we deal with what insights linguistic research, but especially psycholinguistic and sociolinguistic research, has provided on language behaviour, first language learning, second and foreign language learning, and learner characteristics.

Part III opens with a pivotal chapter on what relevance the various source disciplines may have for our field of applied linguistics. It is followed by a chapter surveying the historical development of FLT, which should provide the information that enables the reader to see the subsequent chapters in the right perspective. The rest of the chapters of Part III deal with the various aspects that can be distinguished in the didactic cycle. These are: the defining of aims and objectives; the selection of course content; the gradation of course content; didactic procedures; the use of media; textbook selection; and testing. Particularly in these chapters the restriction of our field of study to FLT in the stricter sense will be apparent.

2
Applied linguistics

2.1 Introduction

In the introduction to this book we have indicated that the subject matter which we shall discuss in this book, viz. the learning and teaching of foreign languages, is by many referred to as 'applied linguistics', although as a matter of fact it is only one of many sub-areas of applied linguistics. Some elucidation of why this is so seems appropriate at this point; this primarily terminological elucidation will also serve to illustrate some typical aspects of scientific endeavour within the field. We aim to achieve this by first of all dealing with a few aspects directly concerned with the two component parts of the term 'applied linguistics', then by dealing with the historical background of the term, and lastly, by comparing our interpretation of this area of research with that of others.

2.2 Analysis of the term

Many researchers have written at length on what the term 'applied linguistics' means. This fact alone could be taken to demonstrate that a purely semantic definition of the field will fail; if the field indeed were what the combination of the words 'applied' and 'linguistics' means, then the terminological problem would have been solved a long time ago. For although one can in principle distinguish at least some different types of applied science (see Back 1970:20 ff.), and although researchers are not agreed on what linguistics actually is, this issue would not have been the subject of so many books and articles in the past 25 years, if a purely semantic solution would have been sufficient to settle it. The problem, however, has always been that the semantic path is not the only path to the definition of the term 'applied linguistics' (see Corder 1972:10).

2.2.1 'Applied'

In all applied sciences the aim is to achieve or help to achieve goals which are outside the actual realm of the sciences themselves. Applied linguistics is, therefore, not the same as linguistics; neither is it a subsection of linguistics. Applications of sciences can be divided into a number of types. Back (1970:20 ff.) distinguishes three types of applied science, for which he gives examples from the field of linguistics:

(1) The methods and results from one branch of science are used to develop insights into another branch of science; among the examples from linguis-

tics which Back (1970:27) cites are philology and stylistics.

(2) The methods and results from a branch of science are used to solve practical social problems; FLT can be cited as an example.

(3) The application itself; under this interpretation the teacher who teaches his classes is actually involved in applied linguistics.

The term 'applied linguistics' is hardly ever used for type 3 applications. It is usually reserved for type 2 applications, as can be seen from the following definition by Corder (1974:5):

> Applied linguistics is the utilization of the knowledge about the nature of language achieved by linguistic research for the improvement of the efficiency of some practical task in which language is a central component.

The type 1 applications Back cites, philology and stylistics, are no longer referred to as applied linguistics. With sociolinguistics and psycholinguistics the case is different. In so far as they are not seen as genuine (sub)branches of linguistics, they come under applications of linguistics as cited under (1). For this reason, they have in the past often been grouped under the heading of 'applied linguistics', a practice which is sometimes still encountered (see 2.3.1.). There is, however, a tendency to narrow down the term 'applied linguistics', so as to exclude psycholinguistics and sociolinguistics, because in these disciplines the role of linguistics is very different from its role in the 'practical task' we are discussing here, namely FLT.

Some other practical tasks which Back (1970:28 ff.) mentions belong to the same category as FLT: translation, speech pathology, language policy and terminology. Kühlwein (1979) gives a similar list of areas within applied linguistics and lists the relevant literature for each individual area (see also Kühlwein and Barrera-Vidal 1977, Barrera-Vidal and Kühlwein 1977). All this gives us rather a long list of different 'practical tasks' which could be called 'applied linguistics'. In this respect, too, some researchers attempt to reach full agreement on what the *scope* of applied linguistics is. But like Kaplan (1980:VII), we doubt whether this is really necessary. It is, however, crucial to establish what in all these cases is meant by 'applied'. Is it the *method* of scientific research that we have to consider as characteristic of applied linguistics? Does applied linguistics, in its slant towards the improvement of 'the efficiency of a practical task', base itself solely on research of an applied nature, and is research of a more fundamental nature irrelevant or impossible? Some people tend towards the latter position, or even take a firm stand on it. To Galisson and Coste (1976:40), applied linguistics is a 'trait d'union indispensable entre la théorie et la pratique' – they are dealing with applied linguistics in the sense in which we use it in this book – and they characterize this intermediary position as follows:

> elle ne s'adonne pas à la recherche fondamentale (la linguistique lui fournit ses bases théoriques) et elle ne débouche pas sur la consommation (la méthodologie approprie à la classe les matériaux qu'elle sélectionne).

Another literal interpretation of the word 'applied' – or at least seemingly so – as a term for research in this area can be found in the following frequently quoted and discussed passage from Corder (1973:10):

> The application of linguistic knowledge to some object – or applied linguis-
> tics, as its name implies – is an activity. It is not a theoretical study. The
> applied linguist is a consumer, or user, not a producer of theories.

Many people (see e.g. James 1980:5) have interpreted Corder as saying that
applied linguistics is 'not a science in its own right, but merely a technology
based on "pure" linguistics'. Before James, Roulet (1973:33), Hüllen
(1974:14), Spillner (1977:155) and Widdowson (1979a:1) have argued emphatically that applied linguistics is indeed a science in its own right. In various places
in the *Edinburgh Course in Applied Linguistics* applied linguistics is characterized, following Corder, as a 'problem-oriented discipline', as opposed to
'theory-based' linguistics (see also Ingram n.d.). In a later discussion, Corder
himself makes it clear that he uses the term *applied* linguistics because the
applied linguist's 'objective is not to increase our understanding of the nature of
human language' (Corder 1978:81). In our opinion, however, which we assume
is shared by Corder, this does not mean that it is not necessary to develop
theories within the field of applied linguistics.

The fact that applied linguistics does not primarily aim to contribute to the
development of linguistics does not mean that no such contributions of applied
linguistics exist. Studying the way in which the L2 learning process can be
influenced through teaching, for example, will regularly cast a different light on
the theories about language structure, language learning and language use as
developed by theoretical linguists (see also Ferguson 1971b:105, Wardhaugh
and Brown 1976:5). Furthermore it is the case that although the primary aim of
applied linguistics may not be the development of theoretical linguistics, applied
linguists may still do research which properly speaking comes under the heading
of theoretical linguistics.

2.2.2 'Linguistics'

If one uses the term 'applied linguistics' in connection with the study of learning
and teaching foreign languages, one finds that not only the first part of the term
needs to be defined, but also the second, since a literal interpretation of this
second term can only lead to the conclusion that theoretical linguistics is the only
discipline at the basis of applied linguistics.

Applied linguistics has, in the past, indeed sometimes based itself solely on
findings from theoretical linguistics. The position then was, essentially, that in
order to be able to teach a language all one needed to know was how the language in question is structured. An FLT method such as the grammar/
translation method (see chapter 8) is a clear example of such a position. Well
known structuralist linguists like Charles C. Fries also had a deep-rooted confidence in the support that could be provided by theoretical linguistics (see
Engels 1968:5). Later on we shall see that the term 'applied linguistics' first
became very popular in Fries' circle, not unexpectedly so.

In later years, we find repeated warnings against this dependence of FLT on
developments within theoretical linguistics (see Johnson 1969:236, Bender

1979:7). Generally speaking, one can say that the assumption of a unilateral dependence has been abandoned, although not as long ago as Kühlwein (1979:157) would have us believe. Of course, there have been some researchers in the past who realized that theoretical linguistics alone would not suffice as a basis for FLT. One of the main exponents of the Reform Movement (see chapter 8), Henry Sweet, stated as early as 1899 that knowledge of 'the psychological laws on which memory and the association of ideas depend' is also an important source of inspiration for FLT, together with theoretical linguistics (Sweet 1964²:37). A large number of authors of the last few decades express their conviction that there is more than one discipline at the basis of FLT. In addition to linguistics and its subdisciplines, one often finds psychology, sociology, pedagogy and education mentioned (see Van Teslaar 1963:51, Halliday *et al.* 1964:169, Spolsky 1970:144, Szulc 1976:109, James 1980:6).

Not many experts these days are of the opinion that theoretical linguistics provides all the information necessary for FLT. For a number of them this is a reason to reject the term 'applied linguistics' altogether. They either look for a different term to cover what we have called 'applied linguistics' (see 2.3.2.), or they try to narrow down the field to such an extent that theoretical linguistics remains as the only relevant contributor; the latter position will be discussed below. But before we embark on this discussion we would like to point out that there are also people who think that the final solution to the terminological problem lies in interpreting the term linguistics in the widest possible sense: they hold that the field may be called applied linguistics if linguistics is understood to cover not only research into the structure of language, but also into the psychology and sociology thereof. It remains far from clear to us, however, how these experts (compare Brumfit 1980 and Richards 1975) would incorporate the important contribution of a discipline such as the science of education under the heading of linguistics.

But let us return to those who wish to narrow down the field of applied linguistics to the point where the name of the field can be derived literally from the second part: 'linguistics'. Especially in Great Britain, and in particular within what could be called the 'Edinburgh School of Applied Linguistics', one will find many people, among them the leading figure of this 'school' Pit Corder, who have tried for years to solve the terminological problem in this way, which, it seems to us, is rather forced. As can be seen in various places in the *Edinburgh Course in Applied Linguistics* and from the numerous publications by Corder on this subject, it is not the case that they expect theoretical linguistics to provide the solution to all FLT problems; educational policy, educational sociology, educational economics and general pedagogy are explicitly and emphatically mentioned. But the principles of disciplines other than linguistics – in the broadest sense – are not considered to belong to the domain of the applied linguist. This leads Corder (1973:13) to distinguish three levels of decision-making in the total language teaching operation; levels which can be characterized by questions of the following type:

(a) whether, what language and whom to teach?
(b) what, when and how much to teach?
(c) how to teach?

Corder singles out level (b) as the applied linguist's domain, because it is at this level that the contribution of linguistics will be most useful; levels (a) and (c) are allotted to politicians and teachers, respectively. It is our opinion, however, that the integration of principles from educational and didactic sciences cannot be left to politicians and teachers, who are mainly concerned with practical problems, but that these principles, too, have to be 'translated' like those of linguistics, by a 'theoretician' for them to be applicable to FLT.

What is essential is that one and the same FLT theoretician attempts to integrate the principles of the various source disciplines into a 'theory' of FLT. For want of a better name (see 2.3.2.) this theoretician is still often referred to as an applied linguist. In his work, which will always be of an interdisciplinary nature, language will always be central, and linguistics will usually be the most important source discipline. We say 'usually' because this may vary from case to case; we shall see later on that linguistics has more to contribute to the solution of problems connected with selection of teaching material than to the solution of certain problems in teaching methodology. Our objection to the way Corder sets out the area of applied linguistics, which is also supported by Politzer (1972:3 ff.), is that the contribution of other disciplines to FLT does not receive enough attention, or is not sufficiently integrated (see also chapter 7). For our position we will have to be excused a certain lack of terminological precision: we will not make the definition of the field subordinate to a semantically pure interpretation of the term 'applied linguistics'.

2.3 History of the term

In this section, we wish to give a brief historical survey of the use of the term, and discuss some of the proposals which have been made over the years to replace the term by one better suited to the field.

2.3.1 The term 'applied linguistics'

Back (1970:34 ff.) gives some examples from the nineteenth and early twentieth century which indicate that applications of linguistics were thought of before the term 'applied linguistics' came to be used. For it is a fairly recent term, and at first used specifically in connection with FLT, at least in Western Europe and the US. Apparently, it first came to be widely used in the US, some 20 or 30 years ago. Back (1970:50) quotes it from the title of Kandler (1952). In this interpretation, one also finds the term in e.g. Haas (1953), Cárdenas (1961), Lado (1957), and Politzer (1960). Mackey (1966:197) claims that it originated in around 1940.

Engels (1968:5) tells us that applied linguistics was recognized as an independent subject in the University of Michigan as early as 1946. It is, therefore, likely that the term originated there and then; it is certainly the case that its use was propagated from there. The English Language Institute of this university, under the guidance of Charles C.Fries and Robert Lado, occupied itself with teaching English to foreigners. From this Institute originates the well known journal

Language Learning, subtitled *Journal of Applied Linguistics* from its first (1948) issue. It was the first journal in the world to have the term 'applied linguistics' in its title, which the editors themselves point out in volume 17 (1967). Incidentally, they also point out a very early use of the term in the subtitle of Lockhart (1931).

The fact that the term in itself seemed to confer some sort of status has certainly contributed to its popularity. According to Mackey (1966:197) its use was propagated by people who clearly wanted to be known as *scientists* and not as *humanists*: by applying linguistics it was thought that the scientific status of the natural sciences, which had brought such great technological progress, would be conferred upon linguistics as well. Back (1970:42) and Van Ek (1971:332) also point out that a lot of status was attached to the term itself. Besides the argument mentioned by Mackey, the fact that within FLT it was especially the linguists who had contributed so greatly to the language courses that had been designed for the US army during World War II by the *American Council of Learned Societies* also played a role. Linguistics came very much into vogue, people started using the term 'linguistic method', and it was almost inevitable that 'applied linguistics' became popular as a near-synonym for FLT (see Moulton 1965:74).

People have not only tried to restrict the use of the term specifically to FLT. In a number of countries, especially Russia, applied linguistics exclusively meant automatic translation: a use which now seems to have vanished completely. The fact that the great expectations people had of this particular branch of applied linguistics have largely failed to materialize will certainly have contributed to its disappearance.

From a historical point of view it is interesting that the initiators of the *Association Internationale de Linguistique Appliquée* (AILA) considered these two areas, FLT and automatic translation, to be the main interest of applied linguistics when AILA was founded in Nancy in 1964. Until AILA started publishing its own AILA Bulletin in 1970, they used the two journals *T.(ranslation) A.(utomatique) Informations* and *IRAL* (see Strevens 1966:63 ff.). The latter journal first appeared in 1963, and it is sometimes forgotten that its full title has always been: *International Review of Applied Linguistics in Language Teaching*. AILA, however, interprets the term 'applied linguistics' in a broad sense in the world conferences it organizes every three years, and this broad interpretation also shows in the approximately 25 international societies for applied linguistics which are affiliated to AILA. It has been noticeable, however, that certainly during the last few AILA conferences (Stuttgart 1975, Montreal 1978 and Lund 1981) the emphasis has been mostly on the learning and teaching of foreign languages and on related areas such as L1 and L2 learning.

2.3.2 Alternative terms

In order to avoid the objections that can be raised against narrowing down the use of the term 'applied linguistics' to learning and teaching foreign languages, alternative terms have been suggested by some; others, in want of a decent alternative, prefer to speak simply of the 'scientific study of foreign language teaching', like Wilkins (1972b:197).

The first example of such an alternative term can be found e.g. in the work of William F.Mackey. In 1966 Mackey published an article entitled: 'Applied Linguistics: Its Meaning and Use' (see Mackey 1966), of which a slightly revised version was published in 1973 under the title of: 'Language Didactics and Applied Linguistics' (see Mackey 1973). The change in the title relates to the two short paragraphs which have been added towards the end. In these two paragraphs Mackey argues that since the problems of FLT are not central to either linguistics or psychology, a 'science of language didactics' should be developed. Of this science, he says the following:

> language didactics could make use of such disciplines as phonetics, descriptive linguistics, semantics, pedagogy, comparative stylistics, psycholinguistics, mathematical linguistics, psychometry, and any other science or technology which may help to solve its basic problems (Mackey 1973:13).

Girard (1972a:14) also prefers the term 'language didactics', and in some languages one finds variants of the Greek version thereof, for instance in many Italian publications and also in the Polish journal *Glottodidactica*, which first appeared in 1966 and has the English subtitle: *An International Journal of Applied Linguistics*.

One objection to 'language didactics' may be that the term is not specific enough, because it could incorporate both FLT and L1 teaching. Especially in German-speaking countries one finds advocates of the term 'foreign language didactics' ('Fremdsprachendidaktik', see e.g. Müller 1975, Schröder 1973a, Szulc 1976).

Dissatisfaction with the term 'applied linguistics' for the study of FLT has led in the Federal Republic of Germany to a popular if somewhat lengthy term 'language teaching and learning research' ('Sprachlehr- und -lernforschung'). Bausch (1974) uses as an argument in favour of this term the fact that it mentions the subject of research itself and not just one of the disciplines on which the research is based. Against it, the same objection could be raised as has been raised against 'language didactics', namely that it could include both FLT and L1 teaching.

This very same objection holds again for the new term introduced by Spolsky (1978b), 'educational linguistics'. A far more serious objection is that this term, like 'applied linguistics', suggests that it is based on one discipline only, namely linguistics. Spolsky recognizes that objection, but nevertheless fails to conclude from this that his suggestion is, therefore, superfluous.

2.4 Other surveys of the field

When we devote some space to the way in which other researchers have provided surveys of applied linguistics, then of course we do not mean surveys relating to the entire field that could be taken to constitute applied linguistics, nor to any random selection from it, such as Ebneter (1976) and Bouton (1978) respectively.

Among the surveys which have restricted themselves to FLT, there is a further group of publications which should not be compared to this book, and those are guides containing practical suggestions which can be applied in classroom practice, such as Hunfeld and Schröder (1979) and Broughton *et al.* (1980). In chapter 1 we have already established our position with respect to practical suggestions and advice to teachers.

This book should be compared with publications such as Mackey (1965), Allen and Corder (1973–1975) and Allen and Davies (1977) (together: *The Edinburgh Course in Applied Linguistics*), Spolsky (1978b) and Brown (1980).

The book resembles Mackey (1965) where the treatment of pedagogical aspects is concerned (part III). In addition, we give more attention to a systematic discussion (in chapter 7) of the source disciplines to see in how far they contribute to the field of applied linguistics as we conceive it. This we share with the *Edinburgh Course*, but the *Edinburgh Course* also contains an introduction to linguistics and is internally less coherent, partly because one volume consists of a collection of readings from outside the Edinburgh School, and partly because the contributions from the Edinburgh School itself were all conceived as independent articles, albeit especially written for the Course.

Spolsky (1978b) indicates in the introduction that he intends to give systematic coverage to the same (new) field that we are dealing with in this book, but, as Stern says in his 1980 review of the book, it remains too much a collection of articles which were written earlier, and because of this important areas within the field are neglected, such as the educational side.

Brown (1980) is closest in set-up and approach to what we aim to achieve in this book. However, he, too, pays less attention to educational matters, such as objectives, selection and gradation, media and teaching methods. He presents 'a comprehensive and up-to-date grasp of theoretical foundations of foreign language teaching', and outlines 'an integrated framework' thereof. That he deems it necessary to focus primarily on theories of teaching and learning and leaves the educational aspects untouched does not mean that his conception of what the field comprises is fundamentally different from ours.

Part II
Learning Second and Foreign Languages

3
Language behaviour and language learning

In this chapter we wish to put the subsequent chapters of part II and part III into perspective: a discussion of its main theme, learning and teaching a second or foreign language, will relate both directly and indirectly to our present knowledge of, and ideas about, language behaviour and language learning in general.

'Perspective' is the key word in this chapter. We can only touch upon a number of questions concerning language behaviour and language learning which we consider central to our discussion. For the rest, we shall restrict ourselves to a mention of the most important survey studies. For language behaviour, these surveys may be psycholinguistically or sociolinguistically oriented: for the first category, we refer to Clark and Clark (1977), Foss and Hakes (1978), Palermo (1978), Slobin (1979²) and Hörmann (1981), while for the second category, we refer to Dittmar (1976), Edwards (1979) and Hudson (1980).

In our discussion of *language behaviour* (3.1.) we shall pay attention to a structural approach to the phenomenon of 'language' as opposed to a procedural or functional approach (3.1.1.), and to a few of the consequences of these differences in approach for what is considered relevant data for a theory of language behaviour (3.1.2.).

In our discussion of *language learning* (3.2.), we shall touch upon a number of different theories about how children (are able to) learn a language. The theoretical orientations will be, in that order: a behaviouristic one (3.2.1.), a mentalistic one (3.2.2.), and a procedural one (3.2.3.). This discussion will conclude chapter 3 and at the same time introduce two central chapters in this book on L2 learning, namely chapters 4 and 5.

3.1 Language behaviour

3.1.1 Grammar and language behaviour

Language is the most important medium of human communication. It is both unique to the species and universal within that same species: only humans can learn to make use of verbal communication, and all humans can learn it. This makes human behaviour essentially different from animal behaviour: language behaviour is one of the most characteristic forms of human behaviour. It presupposes both sender (speaker or writer) and receiver (listener or reader) of verbal information. The former uses an auditory or visual code to communicate with the latter, schematically represented in fig. 3.1.:

Fig. 3.1   Schematic representation of language behaviour

Depending on the nature of the channel (auditory or visual) and the direction of communication (sender or receiver) we can distinguish the following four variants of language behaviour:

	Language production	Language comprehension
Oral language behaviour	speaking	listening
Written language behaviour	writing	reading

Fig. 3.2   Variants of language behaviour

In a number of respects, oral and written language behaviour are very different phenomena. We shall discuss these differences at the end of 3.1.1.

The concept of 'communication' presupposes an intention to communicate. Fig. 3.1., however, only depicts the sending and receiving of verbal information, not how the speaker proceeds from intention to production of verbal information, nor what the listener does with the information he has received. Speakers develop a speech plan with specific intentions, and then execute this plan in the shape of temporally organized speech. Listeners identify this speech stream in a specific way (as a question, promise, command, declaration, etc.), and then use this interpretation in a specific way (for instance by answering a question, or carrying out a command). These different steps in language behaviour can be represented as follows:

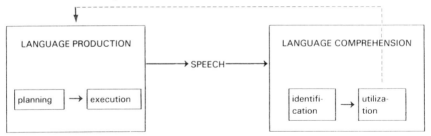

Fig. 3.3   Four steps in language behaviour

Take a sentence like

(1) Where are my keys?

Execution of this sentence will require the speaker to plan it first (he decides, in context Y, to produce a sentence about keys, more specifically a question, more specifically, a WH-question, more specifically, a WHERE-question). In executing such a speech plan, all sorts of things may go wrong, which is manifested in e.g. speech errors such as:

(2) Where is eh where are my keys?
(3) Where are my ka my keys?

Examples (2) and (3) show self-correction (with repetition) at the morphological and phonemic levels, respectively.

The listener, in his turn, has to identify sentence (1) as a WHERE-question, and subsequently to utilize the information it carries as adequately as possible (in this case, for instance, by replying with *I don't know* or by revealing where the keys are). However, the listener may not utilize the speaker's question adequately, by answering, for instance:

(4) Yesterday
     (sentence identified as WHEN– instead of WHERE–question)
(5) No
     (sentence identified as yes/no question instead of WH-question)
(6) I see
     (sentence identified as statement rather than as question)

As will be clear from sentence (1), an utterance will often lead to turn-taking, i.e. speaker and listener changing roles (hence the dotted line in fig. 3.3.). In reality, the steps outlined in fig. 3.3. are not always consecutive: planning and execution may, for instance, coalesce in time, or run into each other. A detailed and systematic discussion of the procedures of planning, execution, identification and utilization of speech is presented in Clark and Clark (1977).

Speech is based on a linguistic code. Both speaker and listener must be thoroughly acquainted with this code; verbal communication would otherwise be impossible. The linguistic code consists of a series of hierarchically ordered units, represented in fig. 3.4.:

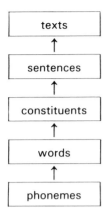

Fig. 3.4   Hierarchical structure of the linguistic code

All of these linguistic units exhibit a large number of universal characteristics. Each language, for instance, has vowels and consonants, and phonemes with distinctive features and distributional characteristics. Furthermore, each language has function words and content words (see e.g. Clark and Clark 1977:22) and can change certain content words into other content words (through such morphological procedures as conjugation, declension, derivation and composition). At the constituent level, one can distinguish between nominal and verbal constituents in all languages, and comparable syntactic relations hold between these two types of constituent (such as subject, object, and predicate). At the sentence level, it is possible in any language to perform various types of speech acts (e.g. questions vs. statements, direct vs. indirect speech acts) or to relate sentences to each other through coordination or subordination. And lastly, sentences may be combined into texts (e.g. monologues or dialogues). Within such a text there are, in turn, countless opportunities for referential or implicational use of language, for instance:

(7a) Speaker A: Charles has put the telephone under the tea-cosy
(7b) Speaker B: Is *that where* he's decided to put *it*?
(8a) Speaker A: Hugo writes poetry
(8b) Speaker B: Charles is quite intelligent *too*

Analogous to the hierarchical structure of the linguistic system as represented in fig. 3.4., language production and language comprehension can be viewed as processes of linguistic input and output consisting of the procedures set out in fig. 3.5. These are not autonomous, but hierarchically organized component procedures: comprehension of texts presupposes comprehension of sentences, while production of sentences presupposes production of words, etc. Another characteristic of language behaviour is the automaticity with which these component procedures are executed in the correct order: language behaviour is to a considerable extent automatic behaviour.

Psycholinguistic research into language behaviour covers all the levels listed in fig. 3.5. The higher the level of these procedures is, the less automatic the

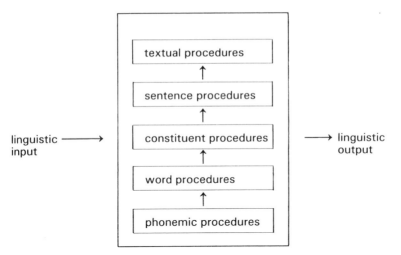

Fig. 3.5   Hierarchical description of language behaviour

language behaviour will be, and decision times will be longer. Also, theories tend to be less developed: much more is known about the comprehension and production of phonemes than about the comprehension and production of texts. It is also worth pointing out that within psycholinguistic research into the language behaviour of adults the bias has always been towards comprehension rather than towards production, while in research into the language behaviour of children, the reverse is the case.

At the most elementary level, that of phonemic procedures, we already find quite complex behaviour in the production and comprehension of language. Research into language production in this area has, in the last few years, focused mainly on speech errors, while research into language comprehension has focused mainly on errors in identifying sounds and on reaction times. At the word level, psycholinguistic research has traditionally occupied itself with word association and word recognition. Research into recognition of semantic relations between words is of a more recent period. Psycholinguistic research at the sentence level has, in the 1960s, mostly been inspired by the rise of transformational-generative grammar (see the correspondence hypothesis, to be discussed below), and concerns itself with the production, comprehension and retention of sentences, ranging from simple to extremely complex. Lastly, at the textual level, research has been conducted into the role of presuppositions in verbal communication, and, more generally and more recently, into the structure of descriptions and conversations.

Language production and language comprehension processes are so complex because the creative possibilities at each of the levels mentioned in fig. 3.5. are infinite (only phonemes are a closed class in all languages): people are capable of always producing and comprehending new words, constituents, sentences and texts. That children manage to develop this creative ability within a relatively short period of time, and almost without explicit information on language, has for centuries been an object of wonder and inquiry.

Although Jespersen (1904, 1967[13]), among others, has pointed out that speakers and listeners should never be ignored in the study of language, linguistics has, in the past, very much avoided real language users. Both De Saussure (1916) and Bloomfield (1933) have only marginally paid attention to language behaviour phenomena. The object of the study of linguistics has traditionally been taken to be mainly or even exclusively the study of grammar: here the interest is primarily in the linguistic code itself and not in the use of that code in verbal communication processes.

The main paradigm for the study of grammar has, since Chomsky (1965), been that of transformational-generative grammar, and the focus has been mainly on syntax. By 'generative' Chomsky means that on the basis of a finite rule system one can construct an infinite number of sentences. This rule system will yield only 'well formed' sentences. In this connection, Chomsky distinguishes between 'competence' and 'performance'. Competence is the ability to speak and understand a language, while performance is the actual application of this ability in language behaviour. In short: competence indicates what people *are able to do*, while performance indicates what people *actually do*.

Chomsky next poses that statements on the structure of language are 'indirect' statements on the structure of language behaviour. This is known as the correspondence hypothesis, and it exists in a strong and in a weak version. The weak version states that the distinction between surface and deep structure in sentences, and the notion of constituent structure, are based on some sort of psychological reality. The strong version states that the structure of the actual processes of sentence production and sentence comprehension are isomorphic to a transformational derivation by means of linguistic rules: the more transformations it takes, the harder a sentence will be to produce and/or understand.

The weak version is less easy to contest and is successfully used in theories of language behaviour. So much evidence against the strong version has been found, however, that it has generally been abandoned. The time factor plays no role whatsoever in transformational derivations describing the underlying structures of sentences. Time is, however, crucial to any inquiry into production and comprehension of language: both processes take time, and the amount of time required can give valuable indications about the degree of difficulty of what is being said or heard.

What Chomsky means by saying that statements on the structure of language are indirectly statements on the structure of language behaviour has always remained vague. The basic idea of the distinction we have drawn between grammar and language behaviour is that these two concepts differ essentially in what is considered to be relevant data for a theory. Statements about the systematicity of language behaviour require an approach to the phenomenon of language which differs essentially from what Chomsky considers necessary and sufficient. In the rest of this chapter we shall therefore make a distinction between the study of grammar (G) and the study of language behaviour (LB).

Within the study of LB, various areas of interest can be observed, which can be divided into studies with a psycholinguistic and studies with a sociolinguistic orientation.

Within sociolinguistics one finds a distinction between microsociolinguistics and macrosociolinguistics, or interactional and correlational sociolinguistics respectively. In interactional sociolinguistics attention is mainly focused on those factors which play a role in verbal interaction processes (speaker/listener relation, function and subject of conversation, etc.) while correlational sociolinguistics focuses on correlations between characteristics of the language of social groups on the one hand, and non-linguistic social characteristics of these groups on the other.

Within psycholinguistics the language behaviour of the individual is the main object of inquiry. Although psycholinguistics and interactional sociolinguistics have certain areas in common (for instance, their interest in speech acts and conversational structure), the approach to language behaviour of psycholinguistics is primarily a processing one, while that of interactional sociolinguistics is a functional one. In very general terms, we can describe the object of inquiry of psycholinguistics as: the processes involved in (the development of) the comprehension and production of language. Within production and comprehension of language, and the development of both forms of language behaviour, we can draw further distinctions, such as:

* speech vs. writing;
* first (native) language vs. second language;
* normal vs. impaired language behaviour.

In this chapter, however, our primary aim is not to devote attention to different approaches within the study of LB, but to the differences in approach between the study of G and LB. Chomsky (1965:3) made the following widely cited statement:

> Linguistic theory is concerned primarily with an ideal speaker-listener, in a completely homogeneous speech community, who knows its language perfectly and is unaffected by such grammatically irrelevant conditions as memory limitations, distractions, shifts of attention and interest, and errors (random or characteristic) in applying his knowledge of the language in actual performance.

This interpretation can only be acceptable if we read 'linguistic theory is concerned primarily with' as meaning 'a theory of grammar is concerned with': what is irrelevant in the study of G need not be irrelevant in the study of language.

Chomsky's conception of linguistics contains several abstractions:

(1) the notion of an 'ideal' speaker-listener, who 'knows' the language of his speech community perfectly, and is not influenced by memory limitations, distractions, shifts in attention and interest, and accidental or systematic 'errors';
(2) an abstraction away from the distinction between speakers and listeners;
(3) the 'completely homogeneous' speech community;
(4) text (relations between sentences) and context (situations in which sentences are used) are abstracted away from;
(5) finally, an abstraction away from the distinction between oral and written language behaviour is made.

Within the study of LB, the fundamental interest is in precisely those areas of language which the study of G abstracts away from.

Concerning the first abstraction, that of the 'ideal' speaker-listener we can remark that within the study of LB, real speakers and listeners are the starting-point for research. What Chomsky calls 'grammatically irrelevant conditions' (memory limitations, 'errors', etc.) are, from a language behavioural point of view, important determining factors in verbal communication, and, therefore, important objects of study. Furthermore, 'errors' are a prime source of information on a process which is given much attention in psycholinguistics, namely the process of language learning.

Concerning the second abstraction, that of the distinction between speakers and listeners, there is most certainly a parallel between production and comprehension in that in the former there is a translation of ideas into language, whereas in the latter there is a translation of language into ideas. Although speaking and understanding are based on the same medium, we cannot conclude from this that both activities are based on the same mental processes. In fact, planning and execution of speech are based on mental processes which differ from those of identification and utilization of speech (see fig. 3.3.). Furthermore, these activities require different organs; articulatory organs, for instance, are only used in speaking. That there are essential differences between the processes of production and comprehension will also be clear from the fact that people can often understand speech which they cannot produce (e.g. pronunciation variants within a language, or differences in degree of proficiency in languages other than the native language), whilst only in exceptional circumstances do they produce speech which they cannot understand. This asymmetry between production and comprehension is also prominent in language learning processes: both L1 and L2 learners understand many linguistic elements (sounds, words, constituents, sentences and texts) long before they can produce them.

Concerning the third abstraction, that of the 'homogeneous speech community', one should remark that although this abstraction may be necessary within Chomsky's conception of grammar, it is seen as a contradiction in the study of LB. Homogeneous speech communities do not exist and heterogeneity is a functional characteristic of any speech community. Following De Saussure, Chomsky has drawn a sharp distinction between diachronic and synchronic linguistic phenomena, and at the same time, identified the notion of *structure* with that of *homogeneity* (there may, of course, also be structure in heterogeneity). As a result of this, one finds that within the study of G processes of linguistic change and linguistic variation receive rather peripheral status. Within the study of LB, however, there is a central interest in both these phenomena. Linguistic change manifests itself in linguistic evolution within generations, and within individuals it manifests itself in both L1 and L2 learning. Linguistic variation manifests itself in differences between language users (user-related differences) and between situations of language use (use-related differences). As we have mentioned before, language learning processes are an important object of study within psycholinguistics, while sociolinguistics focuses not only on linguistic variation but also on the relation between (synchronic) linguistic variation and (diachronic) linguistic change.

Concerning the fourth abstraction, that of sentences in isolation, we can remark that the study of G aims to give a description of the structure of all possible well formed sentences of a language and shows little or no interest in the structure of texts (monologues or dialogues). This abstraction away from texts, however, is not possible in studying LB: language behaviour nearly always relates to the production or comprehension of sentences in texts. Within the study of LB, for instance, attention is devoted to (the development of) textual skills in general, and to the structure of conversation in particular.

The study of G, however, does not only abstract away from the text, but also from the (non-verbal) context. Sentences such as

(9)   The great rush for the new spring fashion has started
(10)   Boys don't cry

may have completely different functions. Sentence (9) may be a statement (one shopper remarking to another that C & A is very busy today), or an exhortation (as a slogan on the shop-windows of C & A to attract customers). Sentence (10) may be a statement, or a command (you should not cry). This particular type of ambiguity in utterances will be obscured if sentences are taken out of their situational context. In interactional studies of language behaviour the functions which sentences, or rather speech acts, can fulfil, play a central role. Speaking is considered a form of human action, and speakers expect listeners to recognize the function of an utterance and to act accordingly.

The fact that neither text nor context is taken into consideration in the study of G has the following remarkable consequences:

- on the one hand, certain ambiguities are ignored, because sentences are presented independent of their context (e.g. examples 9 and 10);
- on the other hand, certain other ambiguities are highlighted in sentences which in context would not be ambiguous.

An example of the latter is the classic example of

(11)   They are hunting dogs

The two readings of this sentence may be represented as follows:

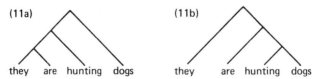

Sentence (11) will, however, not be ambiguous in context: *they* is a pronoun which will have been preceded by a specifying noun.

Concerning the fifth and last abstraction, that of no distinction between oral and written language behaviour, we have already remarked that oral and written language behaviour exhibit a number of very different characteristics:

- first of all, oral language behaviour often takes the form of dialogues, in which speaker and listener will take turns: a case of direct verbal interaction. In written language behaviour, however, there often is considerable distance

in time and space between reader and writer;
- decision procedures in oral language behaviour differ considerably from those in written language behaviour; the possibilities for self-correction in the formulation and interpretation of writing, for instance, differ considerably from those present in speech;
- linguistic and paralinguistic conventions are different for speech and writing. Statements without a subject, for instance, are quite frequent in speech (*don't know, can't see, won't*), but are considered 'ungrammatical' in writing. Such important characteristics as suprasegmentals (stress, intonation) and facial expressions and gestures are completely absent from written language. Furthermore, the possibilities for expressing attitudes towards linguistic conventions are different: a speaker may or may not deviate from conventions where sentence construction, lexical choice, and pronunciation are concerned, while a writer may or may not be unconventional in e.g. style or spelling. Readers and listeners, in their turn, will to some extent interpret each bit of writing or speech on the basis of their own attitudes towards these conventions;
- finally, children master oral language skills before they master written language skills. Reading and writing skills are acquired largely in school. Very often, written language behaviour is seen as 'derived from' oral language behaviour. Both types of language behaviour have their own, specific characteristics, however.

3.1.2 Observations in the study of grammar and language behaviour

In 3.1.1. we have dealt with five aspects of language which are abstracted away from in the study of G and which are considered to be important topics in the study of LB. These differences in approach are reflected in the type of data each approach considers relevant for its theory.

Relevant data in the study of G are linguistic intuitions; more especially, the linguist's *own* judgments on his or her *own* idiolect. Because the rule system which grammarians attempt to devise may only yield grammatical sentences, judgments on the grammaticality of sentences play a crucial role in the study of G. Furthermore, judgments on word stress or sentence stress are also relevant. In all these judgments, usually only one informant supplies the data, and this informant is most commonly the researcher himself. There are, however, no fundamental objections either against the former or against the latter.

In studying LB, the relevant data is the language behaviour of others. A distinction is often drawn between 'primary' and 'secondary' language behaviour (see e.g. Levelt and Kempen 1979). By primary language behaviour we mean the variants of language behaviour listed in fig. 3.2., and by secondary language behaviour intuitions (judgments) about language are meant. The notion of intuition must be interpreted very broadly here: it includes not only judgments on the structure of language (e.g. grammaticality judgments, word-stress judgments, judgments on syntactic relations between words in a sentence, etc.), but also judgments on language users (e.g. research into attitudes towards language). In all these studies of primary and secondary language behaviour (with the exception of single case studies, see 5.1.1.) more than one informant is involved, and there is a fundamental distinction between researcher and informant. In language learning research this distinction is not only a fundamental one, but also an inevitable one: while descriptions of adult language are usually given in the shape of grammars based on intuitions, child language is usually described in terms of grammars of production (see e.g. descriptions of two-word sentences in child language). The former type of grammar is based on what adults 'know', while the latter type of grammar is based on what children 'do'. Both types of grammar are based on fundamentally different data (see also Levelt 1974:10). It has become clear from a number of very diverse studies of language development that comprehension develops earlier than production (see Clark and Clark 1977:298-9), and that both these types of primary language behaviour precede intuitions of judgments (especially grammaticality judgments) about language.

Insofar as empirical research into grammaticality judgments has been carried out, it has been found that such judgments cannot be seen as the independent and stable entities which grammarians usually assume them to be. Levelt (1974:14-21) calls it 'a dangerous practice in linguistics to conclude from the lack of psychological information on the process of linguistic judgment that intuitions are indeed reliable', and discusses the following factors which may influence grammaticality judgments on sentences:

- the situational context of linguistic presentation;
- presentation of a sentence in isolation, or in contrast with other sentences;
- use of unnatural and distracting example sentences (the so-called 'unclear cases');
- the linguist as his own informant (bias through theoretical expectations);
- conventions of written language as supposed standards.

Labov (1975) is a classic discussion of different types of observations ('facts') in linguistics. He discusses such factors as we have mentioned above affecting the stability of grammaticality judgments, on the basis of, *inter alia*, Spencer (1973).

We can summarize the above discussion as follows:

- relevant data in the study of G are judgments on what people (usually linguists) *know intuitively* about language (usually their own idiolect);
- relevant data in the study of LB is what people (hardly ever linguists) *actually do* with language.

That in the study of LB more than one informant is preferred has additional consequences. Unlike in the study of G, in the study of LB there is a strong interest in quantitative data and research techniques which are generally used in behavioural research (see e.g. Meyers and Grossen 1978[2], Agnew and Pyke 1978[2], Ferguson 1981[5]).

If the language behaviour of informants is the basis for a theory, the first question which arises is how the researcher obtains data about this behaviour. Behavioural research may or may not be conducted in natural situations, depending on whether or not the researcher wishes to manipulate certain variables. Either extreme (no manipulation vs. total manipulation) is very difficult to carry out: on the one hand, it is characteristic of natural situations that observers are usually absent, on the other hand, it is impossible entirely to control or manipulate language behaviour. Moreover, there is a continuum of degrees of manipulation, rather than a distinction that can be clearly delimited.

Nevertheless, one may distinguish between the following two types of behavioural research:

(1) naturalistic observations: yield data on what informants do in situations which are as near to natural as possible;
(2) experiments: yield data on what informants do in situations which are as controlled as possible.

Naturalistic observations pose several problems: usually, they are time-consuming and not very goal-directed, and yield a massive quantity of data which are difficult to order. Sometimes, however, it is the only way to gain insight into behaviour (e.g. the structure of spontaneous conversation, or very early child language use). Experiments are usually less time-consuming and more goal-directed; they can provide more information on specific aspects of behaviour, using fewer data. However, one of the problems of experiments is that manipulations by the researcher may lead to sometimes extremely unnatural behaviour.

The choice between these two research strategies is determined first of all by the research objectives. Broadly speaking, sociolinguists exhibit a preference for naturalistic observation, while psycholinguists traditionally prefer experiments.

In experimental research into language behaviour four steps are usually distinguished:

(1) *theory*: a more or less coherent body of ideas;
(2) *hypothesis*: a prediction, derived from (1), that under certain controlled conditions a specific type of language behaviour will emerge;
(3) *observation*: registration of language behaviour under controlled conditions;
(4) *interpretation*: (2) is confirmed or rejected: in the latter case a new hypothesis and/or a new theory is required.

This method relies essentially on the testing of hypotheses. Naturalistic research, on the other hand, one usually engages in in order to generate hypotheses, and for that reason it often precedes experimental research. In the next chapters, we shall discuss data on language behaviour and language learning which have been obtained both through experimentation and through naturalistic observation.

3.2 Language learning

Language learning is based on the development of the hierarchy of skills listed in fig. 3.5. in section 3.1.1. Research into language learning at all of these levels (of which most recently textual, and especially discourse development) has increased enormously in the last 20 years. Dale (1976[2]) and De Villiers and

De Villiers (1978) give an excellent outline of these developments.

As we have already indicated at the beginning of chapter 3, we shall limit our-selves in this book to a discussion of a few central issues, to serve as background to our later discussion of the learning and teaching of a second/foreign lan-guage. To give just one example: one cannot separate a discussion of the audio-lingual method of language teaching (see 8.3.2.3.) from certain, in this case behaviouristic, ideas about how people learn languages.

For the theory of language learning, the development from a *behaviouristic* to a *mentalistic* psychology has been of crucial importance. Behaviourist theories base themselves exclusively on observable behaviour in the description and explanation of learning behaviour, while mentalistic theories base themselves on the structure and mechanisms of the mind for such descriptions and explana-tions. Behaviouristic ideas about language learning are based mainly on a theory of learning, in which the focus is mainly on the role of the environment, both verbal and non-verbal. Mentalistic ideas about language learning are based mainly on theoretical linguistic assumptions, in which the focus is on the innate capacity of any child to learn any language.

Behaviouristic and mentalistic ideas about language learning have led researchers to take extreme positions. A recent reaction to these extreme posi-tions is a procedural approach to language learning. This *procedural* approach, *while maintaining a mentalistic outlook*, exhibits a renewed interest in the struc-ture and function of children's linguistic input, and has caused a shift in the dis-cussion, away from innate versus learned linguistic ability, and towards the children's cognitive capacity to discover structure in the language around them and to put these discoveries to use. We shall now discuss these three approaches to the process of language learning.

3.2.1 A behaviouristic approach

Behaviourist or connectionist learning theories describe and explain behaviour using an SR-model. A connection is established between a stimulus or stimulus situation (S) and the organism's response (R) to this stimulus. In behaviourist psychology, the emphasis is on behaviour which may be learned by both humans and animals. That such behaviour will be limited to only the most elementary types of learning is seen as an argument in favour of its fundamental character: the more general the learning theory is, the more valuable it is. Because the theory has to explain the (learning) behaviour of all animate beings, no allow-ance is made, in the explanation of human behaviour, for such non-observable, specifically human factors as plans, intentions, attitudes, etc. Indeed, the elimination of such concepts is considered to be a prerequisite for a scientific analysis of behaviour.

The main representative of this approach to the study of (learning) behaviour is Skinner (1957). Skinner put rats in a cage with two levers. If the rat pressed the first lever, a morsel of food would drop into the cage. If the rate pressed the second lever, it would get itchpowder thrown over it. It turned out that rats are capable of learning: after a number of tries they systematically pressed the first lever. On the basis of this type of animal behaviour, Skinner defined the notion of *reinforcement*. If a certain action repeatedly leads to a positive or negative result, the odds of recurrence or non-recurrence of this action will increase. Skinner speaks of positive reinforcement, if the action recurs more frequently and of negative reinforcement if the action is not repeated. If an action is seen as a response to a certain stimulus, *positive reinforcement* could also be defined as: increase in the probability of occurrence of a response to a stimulus as a result of the fact that this response, being correct, is rewarded. *Negative reinforcement*, then, can be defined as a decrease in the probability of occurrence of a response as a result of the fact that this response, being wrong, is punished. The term 'reinforcement', incidentally, is often used exclusively in the sense of positive reinforcement. From the observation, systematization and prediction of animal responses to stimuli in laboratory experiments Skinner wants to draw conclusions about human behaviour. To Skinner a theory of language learning should be derived from a general behaviourist learning theory.

Skinner (1957) is a well known attempt at analysing language behaviour by tracing the factors influencing this behaviour. These factors are described in terms of stimulus and response. Each utterance follows on some sort of verbal or non-verbal stimulus; in the latter case, there is a stimulus situation causing somebody to respond with an utterance. Language behaviour can, according to Skinner, only be studied through observation of the world around the language user; that is, through observation of external factors. One important external factor in the language learning process is the *frequency* with which a certain utterance is used in the child's environment. In the behaviourists' view, children imitate the language of their environment to a considerable degree, and *imitation* is a strong contributing factor in the language learning process. A consequence of this is that the frequency with which words and structures occur in the language of the environment, will influence the language development of the child. In addition, *reinforcement* is needed to arrive at a higher level of language proficiency. Parental approval is an important type of reinforcement in the language learning process: when a child produces a grammatically correct utterance which is understood by its environment, approval from the parents may serve as reinforcement for such an utterance. In this way, the environment encourages the child to produce grammatical utterances, while not encouraging ungrammatical utterances.

3.2.2 A mentalistic approach

Chomsky (1959), in an extensive discussion of Skinner's (1957) *Verbal Behavior*, delivers the first serious attack on these behaviourist ideas about language learning. Chomsky argues that human behaviour is considerably more complex than animal behaviour. Moreover, certainly language behaviour is so specific to humans that it could never be explained through animal behaviour. According to Chomsky, a description of language behaviour cannot be just a description of external stimuli and concomitant responses, but it primarily has to be a description of the innate ability of human beings to learn a language. Chomsky discusses Skinner's theoretical concepts point by point and questions their relevance by demonstrating that the conclusions Skinner draws from laboratory experiments with animals cannot lead to conclusions about human behaviour, let alone language behaviour. Chomsky furthermore calls Skinner's speculations premature in the sense that little can and should be said about the language learning process before we have gained a better understanding of the linguistic system that is learned.

Chomsky's (1959) Skinner-review heralds a revolution in ideas about language learning; a revolution which took place in the 1960s. Until that time, most attention had been paid to external linguistic factors. After 1960, the contribution of the main factor in the learning process, the child itself, began to play a more and more dominant role. This revolution was strongly influenced by the rapid rise of a new development in linguistics which can also be traced back to Chomsky: transformational–generative grammar (TG) was a source of inspiration for all sorts of experiments in language learning research.

In TG it is assumed that the ability to learn languages is innate. The so-called Language Acquisition Device or LAD enables the child to make hypotheses about the structure of language in general, and about the structure of the language it is learning in particular. This is not a conscious process. The hypotheses the child subconsciously sets up are tested in its use of language, and continuously matched with the new linguistic input which the child obtains by listening to what is said in its immediate environment. This causes the child's hypotheses on the structure of language to be changed and adapted regularly: the child develops its rule system through a process of systematic changes towards the adult rule system.

This view of the language learning process, therefore, stresses the *mental* activities of the language learner himself, and strongly questions the relevance of such external factors as imitation, frequency of stimulus, and reinforcement. We shall discuss a few of the arguments used (see also De Villiers and De Villiers 1978:199–209, Slobin 1979[2]:100–4).

Imitation

Children quite regularly imitate words and structures which adults in their environment use. Much more frequently, however, we find that their utterances deviate from the language used by adults. These deviations are, furthermore, systematic. Systematic deviations from the language of adults are strong evidence against any theory which seeks to reduce the learning of language to imitative behaviour:

- in morphological differentiation countless instances of overgeneralization (= extension of the domain of a certain linguistic rule) occur; e.g. such forms as *mouses, mans, comed, goed*. Such innovations on the part of the child cannot be traced back to imitation, but are indications of rule governed behaviour, in this case based on the following principles:

> for noun + more than one: use noun + /s/
> for verb + past: use verb + /ed/

- in spite of the frequency with which negative and interrogative sentences occur in its linguistic environment, the language learning child goes its own way and does not merely imitate what it hears. Clark and Clark (1977:347–51), for instance, distinguish between three developmental stages for negative sentences:

Negative sentences	Observations
(a) Sentence-external Neg: Neg = *no* or *not*	*No sit there* *Wear mitten no*
(b) Sentence-internal Neg: Neg = *No(t)* or 'unanalysed' *don't, can't, won't*	*That no fish school* *You can't dance*
(c) Command of essentials of adult Neg system: 'analysed' Neg	*Paul didn't laugh* *That was not me*

Fig. 3.6   Stages in the development of negative sentences

- from countless experimental imitation tasks it has become clear that children's realizations will systematically deviate from the adult norm, often in the shape of deletion of function words (articles, prepositions, auxiliaries, etc.) or word endings (noun plurals, verb past, etc.); e.g.:

Adult norm	Children's imitations
(12) *Lassie doesn't like* *the water*	*He no like water*
(13) *Does Johnnie want a cat?*	*Johnnie want cat?*
(14) *The cat is being chased* *by the dog*	*Cat chasing dog*

Fig. 3.7   Deviations from the norm in children's imitations

In examples (12) and (13), the child has not yet mastered the *do*-construction, and in example (14) the sequence Noun–Verb–Noun is interpreted as an SVO-sentence. In none of these cases could one argue for pure imitation. Rather than trying to reproduce all they hear, children creatively 'filter out' those elements they themselves can already handle.

Frequency of stimulus

The following considerations demonstrate that the frequency of words and structures used in the child's environment has considerably less influence on its language development than behaviourist theory tends to suggest:

- overgeneralization of rules in past-tense formation occurs especially in those verbs which are frequent in adult language use, the so-called 'irregular verbs' (see Ervin 1964). Precisely because they are so frequent in adult language use, these verbs resist regularization. In spite of this high frequency, however, children often do not imitate such verbs, but produce systematic innovations such as *comed* and *goed*;
- function words and word endings show relatively little variation in English (e.g. the two articles *a(n)/the*, or the past tense of verbs, *-ed*), and they are at the same time quite frequent in adult language use. Nevertheless, they do not emerge until late in the language development of the child. In nearly all cases, the units in question are short and inconspicuous (they are usually monosyllabic, sometimes even monophonemic, and they are generally unstressed); therefore, they may initially be not very salient to the child;
- R. Brown (1973), in a longitudinal multiple case study, investigated the acquisition order of 14 so-called 'grammatical morphemes' (word endings and function words). It turned out that the acquisition order for these grammatical morphemes was quite similar for all children. It is remarkable, however, that this order of acquisition hardly correlates with the frequency of these forms in the linguistic input provided by the parents. Parental frequency, therefore, cannot be said to predict order of acquisition.

Reinforcement

Behaviourists see parental approval as one of the most important types of reinforcement in the language learning process:

- the hypothesis that reinforcement will lead to dominance of grammatically correct sentences is based on the assumption that parental approval and disapproval are dependent on the grammatical acceptability of the child's utterances. Brown *et al.* (1968), however, observed that in most cases parental approval and disapproval were not dependent on the grammatical acceptability of an utterance, but on its truth value. Parental approval will, therefore, encourage both grammatical and ungrammatical utterances, and cannot be seen as reinforcement for grammaticality;
- even if the child only uses a very primitive linguistic system, communication, especially with its parents, is possible. The child will, however, start to produce more complex utterances at a later stage, without parental disapproval of its earlier, primitive utterances.

3.2.3 A procedural approach

In his rejection of Skinnerian behaviourism, Chomsky concludes that we need a theory of grammar which will establish the formal properties of grammar. This, however, leaves us with the following problem:

> Although such a study, even if successful, would by no means answer the major problems involved in the investigation of meaning and the causation of behaviour, it surely will not be unrelated to these (Chomsky 1959:56).

What Chomsky is in fact saying in this passage is that a linguistic theory which establishes *what* is learned, does not, *ipso facto*, establish the actual operation of the process of learning. However, this gap between the 'what' and 'how' of language learning is one that will have to be bridged by any theory proposing to explain the process of language learning. The debate between behaviourists and mentalists about whether the ability to learn languages is innate or learned has, in fact, been a fruitless one, mainly concerned with a mutual belittling of assumptions. Where behaviourists ignored the contribution of the child itself in the learning process, mentalists have practically denied that linguistic input and environment play a role in this process, and have generally paid very scant attention indeed to the actual course language development takes. That both internal and external factors play a role in the development of language has been argued as early as 1907, by Stern and Stern (1907), quoted in Blumenthal (1970:87):

> In his form of speech, a child learning to speak is neither a phonograph reproducing external sounds nor a sovereign creator of language. In terms of the content of his speech, he is neither a pure associative machine nor a sovereign constructor of concepts. Rather, his speech is based on the continuing interaction of external impressions with internal systems.

The *procedural* approach to language development in which this interaction between internal and external factors is once again central, is of a more recent date. The starting-point in this approach, which remains a mentalistic one, is children's *cognitive* capacity to discover structure in the language around them. Both children's comprehension and production of language are seen as based on a continuously expanding and changing system of discovery procedures. Such a procedural approach can be represented as follows:

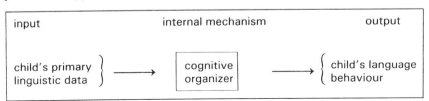

Fig. 3.8   The input/output system in language development

The output cannot be explained unless the following two questions are dealt with in considerable detail:

- what is the structure and function of the input?
- what does the child's cognitive organization consist of, that it causes these differences between input and output?

We shall consider these two questions at the end of this chapter.

Structure and function of children's linguistic input

In the mentalistic approach to language learning one of the assumptions was originally that children's linguistic input is completely unstructured. Under this assumption, there is no difference between what is said to children and what is said to adults; both contain ungrammatical utterances, false starts, slips of the tongue, and other kinds of speech errors. A result of this assumption was that there was hardly any interest in the actual linguistic input children receive.

This situation changed, mainly after 1970. While Brown and Bellugi (1964) had already pointed out that parental speech to young children consists of short, syntactically well formed, semantically simple and repetitive utterances, it was especially after 1970 that the picture of children's linguistic input became more refined. De Villiers and De Villiers (1978:194–5), citing many sources, summarize our knowledge of differences between adult–child and adult–adult speech as follows:

Type of difference	Observations
Phonological differences	Higher pitch and exaggerated intonation
	Clear enunciation, slower speech, and distinct pauses between utterances
	Phonological simplification, distinct consonant-vowel combinations, and frequent syllable re-duplication
Syntactic differences	Shorter and less varied utterance length (MLU), shorter mean preverb length
	Almost all sentences well-formed and intelligible
	Many partial/complete repetitions of own or child's utterances, sometimes with expansion
	Fewer disfluencies or broken sentences
	Many constituents uttered in isolation
	Transformationally less complex
	Fewer verbs per utterance, fewer coordinate or subordinate clauses, fewer embeddings
	Rarity of modifiers and pronouns, more content words and fewer functors
	Subject nouns or pronouns and auxiliary in *yes/no* questions often deleted
	More imperatives and questions to young children, particularly occasional questions
	Increasing number of declaratives with increasing age of child
Semantic differences	More limited vocabulary use, but with unique words for objects and many diminutives
	Reference invariably to the here and now; words have concrete referents and there are few references to the past
	Different level of generality in naming objects
	More limited range of semantic relations
Pragmatic differences	More directives, imperatives, and questions
	More deictic utterances

Fig. 3.9   Differences between adult-child and adult-adult speech (taken from DeVilliers and DeVilliers 1978, 194–5)

While recent studies continue to extend this impressive list, we may conclude that there are quite considerable differences between adult-child and adult-adult speech, and that adult-child speech is also much more structured or 'adapted' than was commonly assumed.

Nevertheless, such descriptions of the structure of children's linguistic input do not answer the question of what the function of this input is. Clark and Clark (1977:329-30), in this connection, ask the following central questions:

- are the modifications adults make necessary for learning?
- even if they are not necessary, are these modifications at least helpful?

A satisfactory answer to these questions is as yet not available, partly because naturalistic research into these questions remains a problem.

Children's cognitive organization of language

Even if modifications in children's linguistic input are helpful to learning, we are left with the problem of how to explain the differences between children's input and output (see fig. 3.8.).

Although there are as yet no detailed models for the description of children's cognitive organization of language, especially Slobin (1973) has, on the basis of data from a large number of unrelated languages, formulated a number of 'operating principles', which have attracted a lot of attention and have come to play an important role in the literature on language learning. Clark and Clark (1977:339-42) have reordered and reformulated these operating principles as follows:

SEMANTIC COHERENCE:

(a) Look for systematic modifications in the forms of words
(b) Look for grammatical markers that indicate underlying semantic distinctions clearly and make semantic sense
(c) Avoid exceptions

SURFACE STRUCTURE:

(d) Pay attention to the ends of words
(e) Pay attention to the order of words, prefixes, and suffixes
(f) Avoid interruption or rearrangement of linguistic units

Fig. 3.10 Operating principles used by language learners (taken from Clark and Clark 1977, 340)

Drawing on Slobin and Clark and Clark, we shall illustrate fig. 3.10. with some examples. The first three principles are concerned with the mapping of ideas onto language, whereas the last three principles deal with the segmentation problem (i.e. how to divide up the continuous speech stream into separate and meaningful linguistic units).

Principle A helps children to grasp the fact that word stems may be slightly modified to express important differences in meaning. Languages with a rich morphological system allow all sorts of changes with respect to conjugation, declension and derivation of words, as, for instance, in English:

conjugation: *I jump*, *I jump/ed/*, *he jump/s/*
declension: *the cat*, *the cat/s/*, *the cat/'s/ food*
derivation: *teach*, *teach/er/*

These changes are minimal from a segmental and suprasegmental point of view (i.e. restricted to one syllable or even one phoneme, and restricted to unstressed speech units). The child is only prepared to use these forms in its speech after an initial period in which these forms did not appear.

Principle B accounts for the late acquisition of ø-marked adult categories. Children prefer not to mark a semantic category with ø, but with some overt form. In Russian, children use masculine or feminine /-ov/ for all plural genitive nouns, replacing the feminine plural genitive. Arabic nouns have singular -marking for numerals over 10, but Egyptian children tend to use plural noun forms with all numerals. Also, in forms which may undergo contraction or deletion, both tend to be initially absent in children's speech, as, for instance, English *I will* before *I'll*, or *The pen which he used* before *The pen he used*. In scanning utterances, children search for overt cues to underlying meaning.

Principle C accounts for overextension of category marking. This has been extensively demonstrated for morphological development, as, for instance, in English *breaked, goed, mouses, mans* etc., for *broke, went, mice, men*. Rules applicable to larger classes are developed before rules for special cases.

Principle D draws on evidence from many languages that final markers are more salient for children than initial markers, and tend to be acquired earlier, e.g.:

English /ing/ before *BE. . . .ing*
French negator *pas* before *ne. . . .pas*
Dutch past participle /t/ before *ge. . . .t* (*kookt* before adult *gekookt* = boiled, *loopt* before adult *gelopen* = walked, *opruimt* before adult *opgeruimd* = cleared up).

Principle E helps children to keep track of the order of elements within words, and of the order of words within sentences. English children rarely, if ever, make mistakes like *ed-cook, es-fish, car the, school at, be will sick*. Also, this principle helps children to interpret NVN sequences as SVO utterances (which, in the case of passive sentences, turns out to be the wrong strategy).

Principle F, finally, leads English children to produce utterances such as:

Where I can go?	for:	*Where can I go?*
I know what is that	for:	*I know what that is*
The man was running	for:	*The man who was*
and fell down		*running fell down*

Furthermore, this principle is responsible for reducing discontinuous morphemes to continuous ones (see examples Principle D).

The study of such operating principles should be elaborated and refined for both first and second language learning, and, as Slobin has repeatedly pointed out, from a cross-linguistic perspective. Thus we may hope to gain a better understanding of what is easy or difficult for language learners, and why.

4

Second language learning (1): contrastive analysis and error analysis

4.1 Historical perspective

Learning a second language can take place in many different ways:

- L1 and L2 may be learned simultaneously or successively;
- In the latter case, L2 may be learned at various ages: it may be learned by children, adolescents or adults;
- L2 may be learned in either an L1 or an L2 environment; in the former case, L2 is usually learned through instruction, while in the latter case, L2 is learned through verbal contact with native speakers in a 'natural' environment (often in combination with L2 instruction);
- Lastly, L2 learning may relate to the development of various linguistic skills (e.g. oral vs. written, or productive vs. receptive skills).

McLaughlin (1978a: 72-3) speaks of successive L2 learning, if the L2 is introduced after the age of about three. Although this is of course an arbitrary boundary, we can note the following interesting paradox: although most people learn an L2 after they have learned their L1, research into L2 learning has traditionally focused on simultaneous learning of L1 and L2. The early work of Leopold (1939-1949) is a striking example of this. An excellent survey of the literature on simultaneous learning of L1 and L2 is given by McLaughlin (1978a: 72-98). Hatch (1978: 23-88) discusses some case studies. In this chapter, we shall focus on successive L2 learning.

The above mentioned distinction between L2 learning in an L1 environment (via instruction), and L2 learning in an L2 environment (through verbal contact with native speakers in a 'natural' environment), has given rise to a large number of different terms being used in the literature. We have listed the most current ones in fig. 4.1. The distinction between 'learning' and 'acquisition' is sometimes also used to indicate L2 development of adults and children respectively.

In Krashen's 'monitor model' (see Krashen 1977) the distinction between 'acquisition' and 'learning' is used to indicate differential processes in adult L2 use. The term 'acquisition' is used to refer to subconscious learning which is not influenced by explicit instruction about the L2 rule system or about errors against the L2 rule system. 'Learning', on the other hand, is a conscious process which is the result of explicit instruction about (errors against) the L2 rule system.

Krashen's monitor model has not remained uncriticized. McLaughlin

L2 learning in L1 environment	L2 learning in L2 environment
guided learning	unguided learning
tutored learning	untutored learning
formal learning	informal learning
	spontaneous learning
	natural(istic) learning
foreign language learning	second language learning
learning	acquisition

Fig. 4.1   Different terms for different L2 learning conditions

(1978b), for example, has pointed out a number of vague notions, contradictions and the absence of convincing empirical evidence. Krashen's (1979) response to McLaughlin has not convinced everyone. Krashen's distinction between '(subconscious) acquisition' and '(conscious) learning' remains the main problem. Felix (1981), for example, has shown there to be important similarities between L2 learning in a 'natural' environment and L2 learning in an instructional setting. Furthermore, one frequently finds mixed forms of L2 learning where the L2 is learned both in school and through exposure to the L2 in a 'natural' environment (it is especially these mixed forms which make it so difficult to isolate and measure the effects of teaching).

Concerning the difference between 'foreign language learning' and 'second language learning' it can be observed that a 'foreign' language may linguistically be closely related to the L1 and therefore not be all that 'foreign' (e.g. German learned by Dutch children in Dutch schools); on the other hand, a 'second' language may be linguistically quite unrelated to the L1 (e.g. Dutch learned by Turks in the Netherlands). Furthermore, the language learned may well be a third, or even fourth, rather than a 'second' language.

In conclusion: from the L2 learner's point of view, the distinctions in fig. 4.1. are premature, to say the least. In all cases, the L2 learner displays cognitive activities in his language behaviour, and it is, as yet, far from clear if, and in how far, these cognitive activities differ under different L2 learning conditions. We shall, therefore, in the following discussion use the terms 'L2 learning' and 'L2 learner' in a sense which is neutral with respect to the distinctions drawn in fig. 4.1.

It is necessary, however, to differentiate between the structure/order of L2 learning processes on the one hand, and the speed/success thereof on the other:

- the *structure/order* of L2 learning processes is determined to a large extent by general cognitive abilities and shows remarkable similarities under highly dissimilar L2 learning conditions: in all cases, L2 learners are faced with a similar task (which is to develop a hierarchically structured system of subskills), and seem to be using comparable operating principles (see 3.2.3. and 4.3.2.) to carry out that task;
- the *speed/success* of L2 learning processes, on the other hand, varies strongly between individuals, and is determined by social and psychological conditions of the L2 learner and his environment (see also 5.3.)

From a historical point of view, research into L2 learning has witnessed a number of shifts in emphasis and the developments in this area have been extremely rapid. Before 1970, L2 learning was almost exclusively related to teaching. The (implicit) assumption was that the L2 learner would learn what he was taught and would learn nothing that he was not taught. The focal point was a discussion of teaching methodology. Although hardly anything was known about L2 learning, assumptions about the 'best method' of teaching were numerous (see ch. 8). After 1970, the L2 learner himself became more and more the centre of attention. A central tenet of this type of research is that empirical data and theories about L2 learning should constitute an essential element in any discussion about the organization of teaching. This development is illustrated by the title of Oller and Richards (1973): *Focus on the Learner*. This shift in emphasis not only significantly increased the interest in natural L2 learning (in an L2 environment), but also provided the link with the research into L1 learning which had developed much earlier (see Ervin-Tripp 1974: 111–12 for some reflections on traditional differences in interest between L1 and L2 learning research). In research into L1 learning, deviations from the adult norm are interpreted as inevitable and systematic stages in the language learning process, whereas the tradition in L2 learning research is for deviations from the L2 norm to be interpreted as mere 'errors' (see 4.3.).

In this connection, it can be pointed out that research into successive L2 learning is, in a number of ways, more complex than research into L1 learning. This complexity is a result of at least the following three factors:

(a) There already exist L1 skills and intuitions about language: what role do these skills and intuitions play in L2 learning?
(b) Whereas L1 learning takes place during social interaction in a natural environment (usually the family), L2 learning can take place at all ages and in various learning conditions. Does this still allow for a general theory of L2 learning?
(c) Lastly, L2 learning is hardly ever as successful as L1 learning: what are the causes of success, or lack of success, in L2 learning, and what makes a 'good language learner'?

Hakuta and Cancino (1977) give an interesting survey of the ways in which our perspective on the learner has changed over time. They distinguish four different approaches: *contrastive analysis, error analysis, performance analysis* and *discourse analysis. Contrastive analysis* differs from the other three approaches in so far that it does not actually take the L2 learner into account. This approach is based on the similarities and differences that exist between two (or more) languages, at the same time taking into account a number of axioms about L2 learning behaviour. *Error analysis* focuses on the L2 learner; this approach consists of empirical research into the nature and causes of deviation from the L2 norm. *Performance analysis* is a new approach in so far that the focus of attention is no longer on deviations from the L2 norm at a given point in time, but on L2 learning behaviour as a whole. The approach to L2 learning is a procedural one, and addresses questions such as what an L2 learner can and cannot do in subsequent stages of L2 development. In *discourse analysis*, the focus is mainly on the use of L2 in conversation. In this type of research, it is not the sentence which is the highest level of description, but the text (i.e. a coherent body of sentences), and attention is also paid to the structure and function of the L2 input provided by native speakers for L2 learners (foreigner talk).

These changes in our perspective on the L2 learner will guide our discussion in chapters 4 and 5: we shall successively discuss the four approaches mentioned above. For a detailed and partly annotated bibliography of this entire field covering the period from 1967 to 1978, see Gutfleisch *et al.* (1979, 1980).

4.2 Contrastive analysis

As a general definition of contrastive analysis (henceforth CA) we shall use the following: systematic comparison of specific linguistic characteristics of two or more languages. Usually one finds the term 'contrastive linguistics' used as a synonym for contrastive analysis; the former term probably originates from Whorf (1941). Bibliographies of CA can be found in Hammer and Rice (1965), Thiem (1969), Selinker and Selinker (1972), Bausch (1977), Palmberg (1976, 1977), and Siegrist (1977). A recent survey of CA can be found in James (1980).

A number of fundamental and applied objectives have traditionally been attributed to CA, which we shall discuss in the following paragraphs:

(a) Providing insights into similarities and differences between languages;
(b) Explaining and predicting problems in L2 learning;
(c) Developing course materials for language teaching.

4.2.1 First objective of CA: providing insights into similarities and differences between languages

The first object can be interpreted as an attempt at establishing linguistic universals and language-specific characteristics of languages. Originally such contrastive research was done within the historical linguistic tradition. When William Jones in 1786 compared Greek and Latin with Sanskrit, he discovered systematic similarities between these languages. In the course of the nineteenth century, more and more comparative linguistic studies appeared. As, within languages, sounds form a strongly closed system in comparison to higher units, such as words and sentences, and are for that reason more amenable to exhaustive description and comparison, research concentrated mainly on phonological relations and phonological evolution (e.g. the sound laws of Verner and Grimm). Linguistic family trees were drawn up. The most important branches of the Indo-European tree are traditionally represented as in fig. 4.2. Of course any such representation of the relationship between languages is a gross oversimplification of reality. On the one hand, languages share more characteristics in some linguistic domains than others; on the other hand, fig. 4.2. entirely ignores different registers within languages.

The rise of the Prague School made the search for historical relationships between languages unpopular; a sentiment expressed as follows in Mathesius (1936:95):

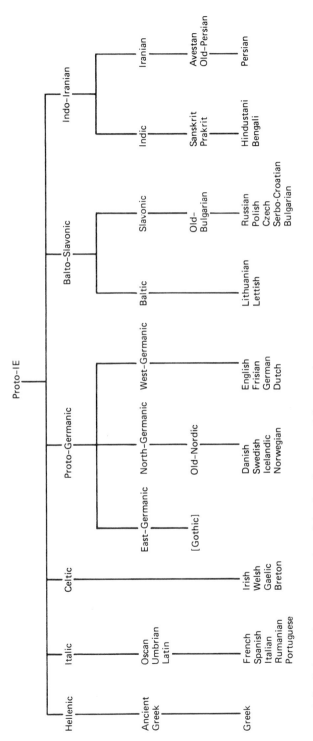

Fig. 4.2 Schematic representation of the development of the most important branches of the Indo-European family (currently spoken languages are listed at the end of each vertical branch)

A systematic analysis of any language can be achieved only on a strictly synchronic basis and with the aid of analytical comparison of languages of different types without regard to their genetic relations.

This constraint, however, does not solve all the problems connected with comparison between languages. Even if we no longer ask the question of which criteria could be used to establish (lack of) linguistic relationship, then the question of what it is that can be compared in two different languages still remains.

Languages are not structurally isomorphic. Often there is divergence or convergence between Li and Lj; we speak of divergence for the L2 learner when there are more structural elements available in the target language for expressing specific meanings than can be found in the source language, while the opposite holds true in the case of convergence. There are countless examples of divergence and convergence at the lexical level; compare, for instance, the following possibilities in German and English:

(1)   Uhr — watch
             clock
             hour

(2)   schlagen — beat
                 strike

(3)   du
       Sie — you
       ihr

Furthermore, there may be lexical gaps in one of the languages. This is often the case with words which express socio-cultural or technical aspects typical of a particular language community which can only be described with great difficulty in another language; compare:

(4)   Verzuiling (= Dutch for 'denominational segregation')

Convergence and divergence can also occur at a morphosyntactic level; compare, for example, Turkish and English:

(5)   He waited — bekledi
                  beklemiş

Where English has the regular past tense suffix /ed/, Turkish distinguishes between definite past tense /dI/ (used if the speaker knows, as a result of personal observation, that the reported event has taken place), and a narrative past tense /mIş/(used if the speaker has not himself witnessed the reported action.)

Comparison of a category (or class of categories) in Li with a category (or class of categories) in Lj first of all presupposes a criterion of equivalence. An often used criterion at the sentence level is that of 'translational equivalence'; Marton (1972:199) remarks:

The relation of equivalence holds between a sentence in one language and a sentence in another language (. . .) if each of them is an optimal translation of the other in a given context.

It remains unclear, however, in how far such an 'optimal comparison' concerns or ought to concern structural (semantic and/or morphosyntactic?) or functional (text- or context-related?) language features. In other words, the question of *what* we are comparing is dependent on the question of *how* we are comparing, and the answer to the latter question is determined by the model of linguistic description used. A 'tertium comparationis' is needed to be able to compare structures in Li and Lj: an abstract linguistic model which can be used as a basis for indicating how a certain linguistic category should be represented in Li and Lj.

A contrastive description of (categories of) Li and Lj will therefore have to be based on the same model of description. Coseriu (1972) is of the opinion that traditional, structuralist and transformational-generative grammars are in principle all equally useful, provided that they are 'explicit enough'. Krzeszowski (1972:75) and Slama-Cazacu (1976:190–1) share this opinion that contrastive analysis is not tied to any one specific model of description. There is, however, something peculiar about this position: on the one hand, not all models of linguistic description will always generate equally satisfactory descriptions, on the other hand any form of linguistic description, including contrastive analysis, will have to answer the question why model Mx is to be preferred to model My.

Especially Stegeman (1979:22–40) and James (1980:35–60) discuss in great detail the inadequacies of traditional, structuralist and transformational-generative grammars for contrastive purposes. Although traditional grammar has been very useful as a tool for describing countless aspects of especially Indo-European languages, the descriptions are not sufficiently explicit, the terminology is not unequivocal enough, and generalizations are often missed.

As a reaction to the intuitive methods of the traditional grammarians, structuralist grammarians based their grammar on actual speech performance: the utterances of native speakers of many languages were transcribed, segmented, and classified. The sentence was chosen as the highest unit of description. This led to heated debates about the possibility or impossibility of isolating sentences in a corpus of spoken language, and about the distinction between 'sentences' and 'non-sentences'. Furthermore, the same criticism as was levelled earlier at the traditional grammars also applies to a structuralist model of description.

Transformational-generative grammar has avoided the structuralist problems of defining the concept of 'sentence' by rejecting the corpus as a data base in principle. 'Data' in transformational-generative grammar means the intuitive judgments of competent native speakers about the grammaticality of sentences in a language (see also 3.1.2.). A (generative) grammar has to be capable of generating all possible grammatical sentences of a language and can, therefore, not be restricted to some corpus of utterances. In addition to structuralist contrastive grammars such as Moulton (1962) and Kufner (1962), we can register the first attempts at developing a contrastive generative grammar (henceforth CGG). The best known examples of these early attempts are

Stockwell and Bowen (1965) and Stockwell *et al.* (1965). The possibilities offered by CGG have also been investigated by König (1970), DiPietro (1971), Krzeszowski (1971), Raabe (1972) and Oksaar (1972). The criterion for comparability of contrasts between sentences in Li and Lj is no longer the surface structure of sentences, as will become clear from Krzeszowski (1971:38):

> Equivalent constructions have identical deep structures even if on the surface they are markedly different.

Stockwell *et al.* (1965) try, within the transformational-generative model of that period, to compare the derivational structures of Spanish and English sentences, thereby setting an example which was followed by many. In most studies, two derivations are considered identical when they consist of *the same number* of *identical* rewrite or transformational rules *in the same order*. Of the following two sentences, English and French respectively,

    (6a) The old man has bought a formidable dog
    (6b) Le vieil homme a acheté un chien formidable

the derivation is as follows:

Sentence 6a	Sentence 6b
(1) S → NP + VP	(1) same
(2) NP → Art + Adj + N	(2) same
(3) VP → V + NP′	(3) same
(4) V → Aux + MV	(4) same
(5) NP′ → Art + Adj + N	(5) NP′ → Art + N + Adj

Only in the last derivational rule a divergent pattern between the two sentences shows up. Similar attempts at comparing deep structures of sentences in various languages have been undertaken by Corder (1973:233–44) and, in greater detail, Van Buren (1974).

Krzeszowski (1979:12–15) has formulated the following five postulates to characterize a CGG (see also Van Buren 1976):

(a) If L1 . . . . Ln is a set of natural languages, CGG must recursively enumerate sentences in any Li and Lj. This means that for every sentence the grammar must decide whether or not the sentence has been generated either by Gi or by Gj, where Gi and Gj are generative grammars of Li and Lj, respectively.

(b) For each sentence in Li and Lj, CGG must assign one or more structural descriptions. Each ambiguous sentence must receive as many structural descriptions as there are in which it can be disambiguated.

(c) For each pair of sentences in Li and Lj, CGG must determine whether these sentences are equivalent. Equivalent sentences will have identical parts in their structural descriptions.

(d) For each pair of sentences in Li and Lj, CGG must specify those parts of the equivalent structural descriptions which are identical and those which are not. In other words, CGG must note the level of derivation at which the first diversification (= contrast) occurs. This level constitutes the border between identical and non-identical rules across Li and Lj. All the subsequent rules are by definition non-identical.

(e) For each pair of pairs of sentences in Li and Lj, CGG must determine which of the two pairs is more similar, i.e. diversified at a lower level of derivation. Sentences which are 'more similar' will share a larger number of identical rules employed in their derivations.

Postulates (a) and (b) define the notion of 'generative' grammar in a general sense, while postulates (c), (d) and (e) relate to contrasting languages. A further important criterion for a CGG according to Krzeszowski is that it should be based on text grammars rather than on sentence grammars. Restricting the generative capacity of the grammar to the boundaries of the sentence – as sentence grammars do – would allow for too much ambiguity. A large number of ambiguities could be removed if larger contexts were taken into consideration. CGG, then, is to enumerate contextually equivalent sentences in Li and Lj.

Although a CGG does not fall victim to quite a number of the objections raised earlier against traditional grammars, some new problems do emerge.

First of all, the notion of deep structure underwent so many changes in the subsequent versions of transformational-generative grammar that many reformulations of the criterion of equivalence in contrastive studies were necessary. Besides contrastive grammars based on generative syntax such as Krzeszowski (1979) we also find semantically based studies; Schwarze (1978) deals with contrasts between German and Italian in terms of case grammar, and Stegeman (1979) opts for a 'functional contrastive syntax' for his sentence-based comparison of German and Dutch.

Furthermore, the status of intuitive judgments on equivalence is doubtful. In fact, CGG uses two criteria for equivalence of pairs of sentences (compare also Krzeszowski 1979:11):

(a) a *formal* judgment of equivalence: this is given on the basis of a derivational comparison of the deep structures of two sentences;

(b) an *intuitive* judgment of equivalence: this is given on the basis of translation by competent bilingual informants.

The theory (a) has to provide an explanation for the intuitive translational competence of bilinguals (b). Bouton (1976), however, points out that competent bilinguals appeared to consider some structures mutual translations of each other when they were derivationally different.

Finally, the notion of 'competent bilingual' is also controversial. Lehiste (1971) found there to be considerable variation in the reliability of grammaticality judgments of 46 adult bilinguals (L1 = Estonian, L2 = English) on a list of 91 English tag-questions. All subjects were long-term residents of the US and Canada. Given that the empirical status of the intuitive judgments of monolingual native speakers is controversial (see e.g. Spencer 1973), the status of bilinguals' judgments can only be even more controversial.

4.2.2 Second objective of CA: explanation and prediction of problems in second language learning

Languages differ. This observation cannot only be linguistically corroborated, but it will also be confirmed by any L2 learner. The importance of the objective of CA cited under (a) in the introduction of 4.2. is often motivated by pointing out the importance of the second objective, listed there under (b). Nevertheless, (b) is as fraught with problems as (a) is. If one assumes that (b) is derived from (a), then one equates linguistic difference with learning problem. This equation has persisted from the earliest stages of CA onwards (compare Rusiecki 1976). Especially in the first few volumes of *Language Learning*, one can find many contrastive studies which are based on just this equation. One of the most notable publications in this connection is *Languages in Contact*, by Weinreich (1953). Weinreich was interested in language behaviour of bilinguals in communities where two languages are used alternately. Weinreich (1953:1) provides the classic definition of interference:

> Those instances of deviation from the norms of either language which occur in the speech of bilinguals as a result of their familiarity with more than one language, i.e. as a result of language contact.

In other words, Weinreich studied interference phenomena (at a phonological, morphosyntactic and lexical level) in contact situations where familiarity with more than one language is given. Weinreich furthermore introduces the following assumption (p.l.):

> The greater the difference between the two systems, i.e. the more numerous the mutually exclusive forms and patterns in each, the greater is the learning problem and the potential area of interference.

Weinreich's assumption has since come to be generally accepted as a principle of explanation for L2 *learning* (see Dulay and Burt 1974d for a critical discussion). Lado (1957:vii) cites the following objective for comparing languages:

> (. . .) the comparison of any two languages and cultures to discover and describe the problems that the speakers of one of the languages will have in learning the other.

Lado (1957:72), for that matter, made the following reservation:

> The list of problems resulting from the comparison of the foreign language with the native language (. . .) must be considered a list of hypothetical problems until final validation is achieved by checking it against the actual speech of students.

Unfortunately, the empirical validation of these claims was not recognized as a serious goal for research until 10 years later. Especially Lado's book led to a flourishing of contrastive linguistic research; compare Stockwell (1957) and Schachter (1959). Under the general editorship of Charles Ferguson the Center for Applied Linguistics in Washington started a *Contrastive Structure Series* in which English was compared with the major European languages taught in American schools. Volumes relating to German (Moulton 1962, Kufner

1962), Spanish (Stockwell and Bowen 1965, Stockwell *et al*. 1965) and Italian (Agard and DiPietro 1965a, 1965b) were published, and studies relating to French and Russian were prepared, but remained unpublished.

Although Lado (1957) already advocated empirical validation of the assumption that comparison between languages can predict learning problems, and although Stockwell (1957) questioned this assumption, it was not until Alatis (1968) that the first real change took place. One aspect which is continually highlighted in Alatis (1968) is the analysis of *errors* made by L2 learners: either seen as a parallel to CA research, or as an independent topic of research. At the same time, however, CA started to spread from the US, and more especially from the Center for Applied Linguistics, to other parts of the world (Rusiecki 1976:32). In the Far East and in various European countries, CA centres were set up, where the language of the native country was compared to English. The main European projects are shown in fig. 4.3.

Languages compared	Project location	Project researchers	Reported in
Finnish and English	Jyväskylä	Sajavaara and Lehtonen	*Jyväskylä contrastive studies* 1975- (Department of English, University of Jyväskylä)
German and English	Stuttgart	Nickel	*PAKS-Arbeitsberichte* 1967- (Cornelsen-Velhagen & Klasing, Bielefeld)
Hungarian and English	Budapest	Nemser and Tamas	*Working papers on the Hungarian-English contrastive linguistics project* 1972- (Linguistic Institute of the Hungarian Academy of Sciences)
Polish and English	Poznán	Fisiak and Zabrocki	*Papers and studies in contrastive linguistics* 1973- (University of Poznán and Center for Applied Linguistics, Washington)
Rumanian and English	Bucharest	Chitoran and Slama-Cazacu	*Bulletins of the Romanian-English comparative analysis project* 1971- (Bucharest University Press)
Serbo-Croatian and English	Zagreb	Filipović	*The Yugoslav Serbo-Croatian/ English contrastive project: reports, studies and pedagogical materials* 1969- (Center for Applied Linguistics, Washington, and Zagreb University)

Fig. 4.3   The major European CA projects

The projects listed here are not exclusively limited to CA, but also pay attention, in various degrees, to error analysis (see 4.3.) and to developing course materials for teaching (in all cases English as L2). This brings us to the third objective of CA as mentioned at the beginning of section 4.2.

4.2.3 Third objective of CA: developing course materials for language teaching

This objective can in turn be viewed as derived from the objective mentioned under (a) and (b) at the beginning of section 4.2., and is first stated in Fries (1945:9):

> The most effective materials (for teaching an L2) are those that are based upon a scientific description of the language to be learned, carefully compared with a parallel description of the native language of the learner.

Twenty years later this objective was still held to be as valid as it was before, as can be concluded from Ferguson's general introduction to the *Contrastive Structure Series* (compare Stockwell and Bowen 1965:V). In retrospection, it is surprising how readily it was assumed that CAs could be converted into teaching programmes. Van Buren (1974:280) gives the following warning in this connection:

> (. . .) the establishment of an adequate theoretical foundation for contrastive analysis must precede any attempt to show how the results of such analysis might be applied in the foreign language classroom. It seems certain, however, that the chain of connections between contrastive linguistic theory and what happens in the classroom will be rather complex, and that it must contain at least three major links: The highly technical analysis itself, the conversion of this analysis into a form which can be easily understood by non-specialists, and, finally, the conversion of the simplified statement into materials that can be used in the classroom.

Although CA is as old as FLT itself, attempts at converting descriptive data from CA into teaching programmes have by no means always been successful. Neither has there been systematic research into the effect of teaching methods based on CA; it has never been demonstrated that course materials based on CA are more effective than other materials based on different principles. Lastly, the realization that linguistic difference cannot be equated with learning problem has made people reticent to implement this last objective of CA.

4.2.4 Conclusion

On balance, we can say that CA has lost much of its initial appeal. The lack of perspective in the implementation of the objectives of CA is summarized in a clear fashion in Oller (1979c). The reactions to this lack of perspective tend to vary.

Some people suggest maintaining objective (a), and jettisoning objectives (b) and (c). CA could then contribute to translation theory, the description of particular languages, language typology, and the study of language universals. Within the framework of one of the European projects mentioned earlier, Fisiak *et al.* (1978:7) formulate this neutral position as follows:

> The present grammar is not a *pedagogical* (i.e. applied) *contrastive grammar.* It is not interested in setting up hierarchies of difficulty or explicitly defining areas of potential interference. It does not interpret linguistic facts in pedagogical terms. It is entirely neutral towards any type of application.

Others advocate maintaining objective (a) and a weakened version of objective (b): *some* L2 learning problems can be explained or predicted on the basis of linguistic differences between L1 and L2. We shall discuss this weaker version of objective (b) in 4.3. To the question of the (direct) applicability of linguistic findings we shall return in chapter seven.

4.3 Error analysis

This section consists of three parts. First of all, we shall give a brief historical survey of the notion of 'error'; secondly, a survey of the literature on descriptions and explanations of errors, and lastly, we shall consider some of the limitations of error analysis (henceforth EA), in sub-sections 4.3.1., 4.3.2., and 4.3.3. respectively.

Often, a series of successive steps is distinguished within EA (compare Nickel 1972a:11–15). This series of steps in its most complete form looks as follows:

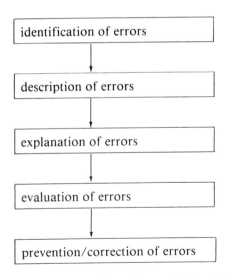

Errors cannot always be easily identified. First of all, the notion of 'error' presupposes a norm, and norms, in their turn, are dependent on, amongst other things, the medium (spoken or written language), the social context (formal or informal), and the relation between speaker and hearer (symmetrical or asymmetrical). Furthermore, it is quite possible for something which seems an error in isolation to be perfectly acceptable in context, and *vice versa*. In this chapter, we shall limit ourselves to two objectives of EA, namely description and explanation of errors. Aspects of two further objectives of EA, evaluation of errors, which relates to the assessment of error gravity (by native speakers, L2 teachers, or by the L2 learner himself), and correction of errors will be discussed in 12.2.5. Like CA, EA is often carried out with the aim of finding an application for its results.

4.3.1 The concept of 'error'

In 3.2.3. we have formulated the two core questions for research into language learning as follows:

What is it that is learned?
How does learning take place?

The first question concerns the product, the second the process of language learning. The answer to the second question, however, is strongly dependent on how the first question is answered, since what takes place in the learner's head is not open to direct observation. Hypotheses about the learning process are therefore usually inferred from the learner's language products.

That language learning cannot be reduced to a process of continuous imitation of language data provided by the environment has already been demonstrated in 3.2.2. After 1960, more and more studies appeared in which the language behaviour of children was characterized as the (subconscious) application of rule systems deviating strongly from the rule systems which adult speakers use. In 3.2.3. we have given the following schema to represent this view:

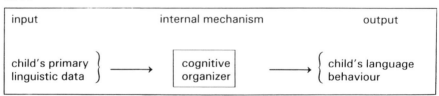

Fig. 4.4   The input/output system in language development

The 'creative errors' a child makes necessitate a distinction between *input* and *intake*. What the language learner does with the primary linguistic data we have described in 3.2.3. in terms of operating principles.

This approach to deviations from the (adult) norm dealt a heavy blow at the notion of 'error', since 'error' presupposes the norms of adult speakers. Deviations from these norms are now considered to be inevitable, necessary and systematic stages in the language learning process, and are taken to constitute (subconscious) hypotheses by the child about the language to be learned. In other words, after 1960 the child obtains the status of active participant in the language learning process.

In L2 learning, learners also regularly produce deviations from the L2 norm. Traditionally, such deviations did not receive much attention: they were labelled as 'errors' and were hardly considered outside publications on teaching. In these publications they were regarded as regrettable by-products of L2 learning which could and had to be avoided as much as possible with the help of efficient teaching. It was generally felt that L2 learners would only learn what they were taught and would learn nothing that they were not taught. The audiolingual method considered pattern drills especially useful as a remedy against possible errors (see 12.2.5.). If errors occurred, in spite of the teaching, this was invariably attributed to interference from L1. Consequently, the linguist's main contribution was expected to be in the area of CA.

At the end of the 1960s, people began to question one of the main objectives of CA, namely the explanation and prediction of L2 learning problems. People began to realize more and more that this approach left the L2 learner out of consideration. The fact that there was no empirical basis for CA in turn resulted in more attention being paid to EA.

From the above it can be observed that there exists a remarkably long distance in time between developments in the theory of L1 and L2 learning. While the notion of 'error' was jettisoned for the former after 1960, this same notion became popular in L2 learning research after 1970.

4.3.2 Description and explanation of errors

As we have remarked before, there is a very close connection between the notion of 'error' and the notion of 'interference' in the early literature on the subject. Interference is a notion which derives from skill research in psychology; Bilodeau (1966) is a standard work on the history of skill research and those factors which impede or facilitate the learning of skills. The central question is under what conditions the learning of new skills is impeded or facilitated by skills already learned. As nearly all new skills are learned on the basis of existing skills, skill research has traditionally shown a keen interest in the phenomenon of *transfer*. A distinction is usually made between *pro-active* and *retro-active* transfer. Pro-active transfer is the transfer of existing skills onto new skills, and retro-active transfer is transfer of new skills onto existing skills.

In both cases, transfer may be *positive* or *negative*. Positive transfer, or *facilitation*, is transfer of a skill X which facilitates the learning or has a positive influence on the command of a skill Y because of similarities between both skills. Negative transfer, or *interference*, is transfer of a skill X which impedes the learning or has a negative influence on the command of a skill Y because of differences between both skills. We therefore distinguish, in fig. 4.5, between four types of transfer, on the basis of direction and effect of transfer. The disadvantage of the terms 'positive' and 'negative' transfer is that they imply a value judgment; they are not purely descriptive. It should also be mentioned that the notions in figure 4.5 are subject to considerable terminological confusion in much of the available literature; for a discussion see Rattunde (1977).

It is difficult to determine precisely where and when the notion of transfer entered into linguistics. In section 4.2. we have already pointed out the important role of Weinreich (1953) in the development of the notion of interference. CA is based on the assumption that L2 learners will tend to transfer structural

	Positive transfer	Negative transfer
Pro-active transfer	pro-active facilitation	pro-active interference
Retro-active transfer	retro-active facilitation	retro-active interference

Fig. 4.5   Four types of transfer

L1 features to their L2 utterances. From this, we can conclude the interests of contrastive analysts to focus on pro-active interference rather than on retro-active interference (see, however, Jakobovits 1969), and on production rather than on comprehension of language. Wardhaugh (1970) contributed to the empirical status of CA; he distinguished between the following two claims:

- a strong (*a priori*) claim: L2 learning problems can be *predicted* on the basis of linguistic differences between L1 and L2;
- a weak (*a posteriori*) claim: *some* observed L2 learning problems can be *explained* on the basis of linguistic differences between L1 and L2.

The strong claim has generally been made under the following two assumptions:

- The chance of L2 learning problems occurring will increase proportionally to the linguistic differences between L1 and L2: linguistic differences give rise to *interference*;
- The chance of L2 learning problems occurring decreases proportionally to the absence of linguistic differences between L1 and L2: absence of linguistic differences gives rise to *facilitation*.

As has been pointed out before (see e.g. Gass 1979:329), the 'weak claim' is well-protected from empirical falsification, since it is not based on readily falsifiable assumptions. Nobody will contest that some L2 learning problems can be explained as interference phenomena, but this hypothesis lacks all predictive power and is, therefore, not very interesting from a scientific point of view: a description of the cause of a phenomenon X only has explanatory power if it has predictive power. A hypothesis without predictive power is, in fact, a contradiction in terms.

Two observations have been made which have raised doubts about the strong claim of CA:

(a) CAs predict L2 learning problems which do *not* occur;
(b) CAs turn out not to predict learning problems which *do* occur.

In other words: linguistic differences between L1 and L2 do not automatically lead to L2 learning problems, and not all L2 learning problems can be retraced to linguistic differences between L1 and L2.

The observation mentioned under (a) can be found for instance in Kielhöfer (1975:122); compare:

(7a) Gestern *bin ich* zum Bahnhof gegangen (L1 = German)
(7b) Hier *suis-je* à la gare *allé* (L2 = French)

Literal word order transfer as in (7b) is hardly ever found in L2 learning. Apparently, some linguistic differences are so striking that they will not give rise to L2 learning problems. Sharwood Smith (1979:352) notes the following example of non- (or rare) occurrence in French spoken by native speakers of English:

(8a) He is *giving* me the apple (L1 = English)
(8b) Il est *donning* moi la pomme (L2 = French)

/-ing/suffixes, like other instances of bound morphemes representing tense, aspect, number, etc. are typically treated as language-specific items by the L2 learner and tend not to be transferred from L1.

The observation mentioned under (b) relates to various phenomena. First of all, we have to distinguish between *interlingual* and *intralingual* L2 learning problems: in the first case, the learning problem is caused by the structure of L1; in the second case, it is caused by the structure of L2. Interlingual problems depend on linguistic differences between L1 and L2 and are traditionally interpreted as interference problems. Intralingual problems are by definition not predictable on the basis of CA: they cannot be traced back to differences between L1 and L2, but they relate to a specific interpretation of the target language and manifest themselves as universal phenomena, in any language learning process. We can find an early reference to intralingual L2 learning problems in Corder (1967:167):

(9) I seed him

Overgeneralizations such as *seed* (= saw) can be found in both L1 and L2 learning. Corder stresses that L1 *and* L2 learners have the cognitive capacity for making hypotheses about the language they are learning and that both use many similar procedures or strategies. 'Errors' in both cases are inevitable, necessary and systematic stages in the language learning process.

Apart from intralingual L2 learning problems there are more phenomena which cast doubt upon the strong claim of CA. The implicit assumptions of this claim have been mentioned earlier: linguistic differences lead to interference and absence of linguistic differences leads to facilitation. L2 learning problems, however, may also be the result of a *lack of contrast* between L1 and L2. Compare the following pairs of English and Dutch sentences (cf. also Kellerman 1979):

(10a) *Had I known these facts*, I wouldn't have come
(10b) *Had ik deze feiten geweten*, dan zou ik niet gekomen zijn
(11a) The cup *broke*
(11b) Het kopje *brak*
(12a) He murdered his grandmother *in cold blood*
(12b) Hij vermoordde z'n grootmoeder *in koelen bloede*

(13a) One could *cut the tension* in the room
(13b) Men kon *de spanning* in de kamer *snijden*

There is a one-to-one correspondence between L1 and L2 in the italicized parts. This lack of contrast will often lead L2 learners to avoid these constructions in L2 use, because they consider such a correspondence unlikely: they suspect the syntax of (10) and (11) (i.e. the parallelisms between word order and intransitivity respectively), and the idiomaticity of (12) and (13). It is difficult, by the way, to demonstrate such *avoidance phenomena* in a language corpus. We shall return to this matter at the end of 4.3.

Lastly, something should be said about the assumption that interference tends to increase proportionally to the linguistic differences between L1 and L2 (compare Weinreich 1953:1). The opposite seems to be the case from the learner's point of view: the less related L1 and L2 are, the fewer possibilities the learner has for literally transferring L1 structures, supposing them to be structures of the L2 as well. Interference phenomena are especially frequent between related languages: the amount of interference is determined, among other factors, by the degree of 'translatability' between L1 and L2 features. Notorious examples of such interference phenomena are the so-called *Schwere Wörter* in German for speakers of Dutch, or in Dutch for speakers of German (compare *scheinbar/schijnbaar, geistig/geestig, niedrig/nederig,* etc.).

Especially after 1970 there have been numerous attempts at classifying second language errors, i.e. at pointing out their cause. The best known publications can be found in readers edited by Nickel (1972a), Oller and Richards (1973), Svartvik (1973), Richards (1974) and Schumann and Stenson (1975). For bibliographical surveys, see Arabski (1973), Valdman and Walz (1975), Palmberg (1976, 1977) and Rattunde and Weller (1977).

In most publications errors have been classified in terms of the categories represented in fig. 4.6. A distinction between errors of competence and errors of performance was first suggested by Corder (1971):

- errors of competence are the result of the application of rules by the L2 learner which do not (yet) correspond to the L2 norm;
- errors of performance are the result of mistakes in language use and manifest themselves as repeats, false starts, corrections or slips of the tongue (see also 3.1.1.).

Errors of performance occur frequently in the speech of both native speakers and L2 learners. They are especially likely to occur when the speaker suffers from stress, indecision or fatigue. Corder has suggested the following operational criterion for differentiating between these two types of error: L2 learners can recognize and correct errors of performance, but not errors of competence.

However, identification of errors of competence will only be possible if we can establish a difference between actual and intended L2 utterances. According to Corder (1973:274) it will again preferably be the L2 learner himself who provides this information. Corder differentiates between:

- an *authoritative* interpretation: if the learner is available, we can ask him to

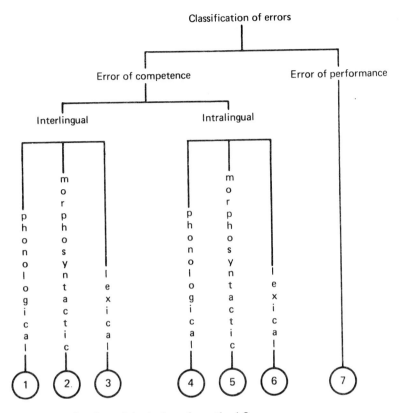

Fig. 4.6   Classification of deviations from the L2 norm

express his intentions in his mother tongue, and then translate his utterance into the target language, using whatever we can glean from his original attempt as a guide to the form he aimed at;

• a *plausible* interpretation: if the learner is absent, we have to do the best we can to infer what he intended to say from his utterance, its context and whatever we know about him and his knowledge of the world and the target language.

Later on we will come back to these distinctions.

We have already referred to the distinction between interlingual and intralingual deviations from the L2 norm. Both types of deviation are based on different operating principles. Intralingual operating principles occur in L2 learning as well as in L1 learning; in 3.2.3. we have discussed a number of these principles drawing on Slobin (1973) and Clark and Clark (1977). In addition, we can formulate the following interlingual operating principle:

> Assume that there is correspondence between L1 and L2

Transfer of prior linguistic knowledge is at play both in interlingual and intralingual operating principles. However, the latter occur in L1 learning as well as in L2 learning: they have a universal base. The interlingual operating principle mentioned above, on the other hand, is specific to L2 learning: in this case, 'prior linguistic knowledge' relates to an already existing L1 system.

We shall exemplify and discuss the categories which we have distinguished in fig. 4.6. Many of the examples are taken from Kielhöfer (1975) and Legenhausen (1975), which focus respectively on L2 French and L2 English of German learners.

(1) *Interlingual phonological errors*
    (14) This is a *na/ti/onal* newspaper (/tʃ/ instead of /ʃ/; German national)
    (15) A great *diver/s/ity* of arguments (/z/ instead of /s/; German Diversität)
    (16) Vous avez une très */j/olie* robe (/ʃ/ instead of /ʒ/; German schön)
    (17) C'est une spe/c/ialité du pays (/ts/ instead of /s/; German Spezialität)

(2) *Interlingual morphosyntactic errors*
    (18) Les roses sont *fleurs* (L1 Blumen = L2 des fleurs)
    (19) Il *demanda lui* (L1 fragte ihn = L2 lui demanda)
    (20) Can you give me some *informations* about this programme? (L1 Informationen = L2 information)
    (21) I *am back* in five minutes (L1 bin zurück = L2 will be back)

(3) *Interlingual lexical errors*
(a) *selection of wrong word when words are phonetically related in L1 and L2* (the so-called 'faux amis', or 'false friends')
    (22) He turned the last *side* (L1 Seite = L2 page)
    (23) Did you buy this in a *warehouse*? (L1 Warenhaus = L2 department store)
    (24) There are many *snakes* in the garden (L1 Schnecken = L2 snails)
    (25) He was astonished to find the following *notice* (L1 Notiz = L2 note)
    (26) Bradley went into the *floor* (L1 Flur = L2 hall)
    (27) Un *quartier pour la nuit* (L1 Nachtquartier = L2 lit)
    (28) Mon père est *académicien* (L1 Akademiker = L2 a fait des études universitaires)
    (29) Elle porte un *costume* (L1 Kostüm = L2 tailleur)
(b) *selection of wrong word in the case of divergence between L1 and L2* (see 4.2.)
    (30) A la récréation *prochaine*, tout le monde était sûr que . . . (L1 folgend = L2 prochaine/suivante)
    (31) Il alla au téléphone et *choisit* (L1 wählen = L2 voter/opter/élire/composer un numéro)
    (32) On *écoutait* seulement les plumes gratter le papier (L1 hören = L2 écouter/entendre)
    (33) He was a total *foreigner* to me (L1 Fremder = L2 stranger/foreigner)
(c) *word innovation as a result of literal translation from L1*
    (34) Le *friseur* (L1 Friseur = L2 coiffeur)

(35) Un *expériment* (Ll Experiment = L2 expérience)

(36) Le *policiste* (Ll Polizist = L2 policier)

(37) *Stabile* (Ll stabil = L2 stable)

(38) *Financiel* (Ll finanziell = L2 financier)

(39) La *maigresse* (Ll die Magerkeit = L2 la maigreur)

(40) *Unordinary* (Ll ungewöhnlich = L2 out of the ordinary)

(4) *Intralingual phonological errors*

    (41) *C/ou/ntry* and western music (/aʊ/ instead of /ʌ/, cf. county)

    (42) *G/oo/d* (/u/ instead of /ʊ/, cf. food)

    (43) They were having a *r/ow/* (/əʊ/ instead of /aʊ/, cf. rowboat)

(5) *Intralingual morphosyntactic errors*

(a) *innovation as a result of overgeneralization*

    (44) They *buyed* a new car (bought)

    (45) The *mouses* (mice)

    (46) Three *womans* (women)

    (47) A *librarist* (librarian)

    (48) L'ORTF a *émissioné* les informations (émis)

    (49) Une femme *instructionnée* (instruite)

    (50) On *n'entenda* plus rien (entendit)

    (51) *Faisez* un angle (faites)

    (52) Il a *offri* (offert)

(b) *deviation in word order*

    (53) Un *homme vieil* (vieil homme)

    (54) She saw *coming in a young girl* (a young girl coming in)

(6) *Intralingual lexical errors*

    selection of wrong word as a result of phonetic relatedness within L2

    (55) He let the pearls *dispose* in a drawer (disappear)

    (56) She was led out by a *niece* (nurse)

    (57) The price doesn't play an important *rule* (role)

    (58) The envelope *continued* the sealed document (contained)

    (59) I begged him to *retain* from gambling (refrain)

    (60) A large book *attached* his attention (attracted)

    (61) Avez-vous une chambre moins *chérie*? (chère)

    (62) Nous avons été à la coté cet hiver (la côte)

    (63) Il est le secrétaire *de la partie* (du parti)

(7) *Errors of performance*

    (64) They asked to keep *to keep* the bottle away (repeat)

    (65) They wanted *they said they wanted* to leave (correction + repeat)

    (66) On Wednesday he always *bruys* two loaves of bread (anticipation)

(1) *Errors in the production of verb groups*

be + verb stem for verb stem	*We are live in this hut*
be + verb stem + -ed for verb stem + -ed	*Farmers are went to their houses*
wrong form after *do*	*He did not found*
wrong form after modal verb	*She cannot goes*
be omitted before verb + stem + -ed	*He born in England*
-ed omitted after be + part. verb stem	*The sky is cover with clouds*
be omitted before verb + -ing	*They running very fast*
verb stem for stem + -s	*He come from India*

(2) *Errors in the distribution of verb groups*

be + verb + -ing for be + verb + -ed	*I am interesting in that*
be + verb + -ing for verb stem	*She is coming from Canada*
be + not + verb + -ing for do + not + verb	*I am not liking it*
be + verb + -ing for verb + -ed in narrative	*On Saturday we were going down town*
verb stem for verb + -ed in narrative	*One day they go into a wood*
have + verb + -ed for verb + -ed	*They had arrived just now*
have + be + verb + -ed for be + verb + -ed	*He has been married long ago*
verb (+ -ed) for have + verb + -ed	*We correspond with them up to now*
be + verb + -ed for verb stem	*This money is belonged to me*

(3) *Miscellaneous errors*

wrong verb form in adverb of time	*I shall meet him before the train will go*
object omitted or included unnecessarily	*We saw him play football and we admired*
errors in tense sequence	*He said that there is a boy in the garden*
confusion of *too/so/very*	*I am very lazy to stay at home*

(4) *Errors in the use of prepositions*

	Suffering with a cold
	At the evening
	I have been here for the 6th of June

(5) *Errors in the use of articles*

omission of *the*	*Sun is very hot*
the used instead of $\emptyset$	*After the breakfast*
a instead of *the*	*A best boy in the class*
a instead of $\emptyset$	*A bad news*
omission of *a*	*He was good boy*

(6) *Errors in the use of questions*

omission of inversion	*What was called the film?*
be omitted before verb + -ing	*What she doing?*
omission of *do*	*Where it happened?*
wrong form of/after auxiliary	*Do he go there? Did he went?*
inversion omitted in embedded sentences	*Please write down what is his name*

Fig. 4.7   Classification of errors in Richards 1971 (reduced survey)

From this illustration of the categories in fig. 4.6, we shall move on to a few much quoted publications on EA.

Richards (1971) is one of the first attempts at describing L2 learning problems on a non-contrastive basis. Using data collected by others (the oldest source is a long-neglected study by French 1949), Richards classifies errors in the English of L2 learners from various L1 backgrounds as in fig. 4.7. We do not adopt Richards's peculiar distinction between intralingual and developmental errors (1971:206) and conclude that in most cases we are dealing with morphosyntactic errors that would be classified under (5) in fig. 4.6. by Richards (see, however, James 1980:185–6).

Burt *et al.* (1973) have developed a method for measuring, via elicitation procedures, the degree of command of specific morphosyntactic structural elements: the so-called *Bilingual Syntax Measure*. The BSM was originally based on dual or 'unbiased' measuring procedures, because both L1 and L2 skills (Spanish and English, in this case) are taken into account. The elicitation procedures, although guided, are intended to elicit as natural language use as possible: subjects are expected to react spontaneously to 33 questions about 7 pictures. Using an adapted version of the BSM, Dulay and Burt (1974b) have studied deviations from the L2 norm in the English of 179 Spanish-speaking children between 5 and 8 years old. From the data thus obtained, 513 deviant utterances were selected which could 'without question' be classified as follows:

- developmental errors: those errors that are similar to L1 learning errors;
- interference errors: those errors that reflect Spanish structure;
- unique errors: those errors that are neither 'developmental' nor 'interference' errors.

Fig. 4.8. contains the results.

Age	N subjects	Developmental	Interference	Unique
5	33	98	5	2
6	51	113	6	16
7	52	123	7	13
8	43	113	6	11
Total	179	447	24	42

Fig. 4.8 Number and kind of errors (Dulay and Burt 1974b, 132)

Although one can wonder what the selection of the 513 errors is based on and whether or not there is an unequivocal developmental/ interference distinction (see also Abbott 1980), the data are a clear indication of the important role of intralingual deviations from the norm in L2 learning. These intralingual phenomena are strongly related to 'deviations' which have also been observed in L1 learning; see fig. 4.9..

It is not clear, however, why Dulay and Burt only consider intralingual deviations from the L2 norm to be evidence for a 'creative construction process', and explain away interlingual deviations as cases of 'habit formation'.

Syntactic structure		Realized	Intended
(1) NP-V-Pron		*Dog eat it*	*The dog ate it*
(2) Det-Adj-N		*Skinny man*	*The skinny man*
(3) Pron-(Aux)-(Neg)-VP		*He not eat*	*He doesn't eat*
(4) Det-N + Poss-N		*King food*	*The king's food*
(5) NP-*be*-Adj		*They hungry*	*They are hungry*
(6) (NP-Aux)-V + -*ing*-(Infin)-	{ NP-Prep-NP } { NP-NP }	{ *The mother give* { *food to birdie*	{ *The mother is giving* { *food to birdie*

Fig. 4.9   Elicited intralingual deviations from L2 norm (Dulay and Burt 1974b, 132–4)

We have pointed out earlier that interlingual as well as intralingual deviations from the L2 norm are indications of cognitive activities on the part of the L2 learner: in both cases the L2 learner uses specific operating principles to express structural characteristics in L2 (see also Sharwood Smith 1979:346–7).

Another often quoted attempt at describing and explaining errors in L2 use has been made by Taylor (1975). Taylor divided 20 adult Spanish speakers learning English into an elementary and an intermediate group on the basis of test scores and teacher judgments. He then presented 80 Spanish sentences for translation into English to both groups in two testing sessions; the sentences were presented twice, orally, in a different order, and the subjects had to write down their translations under time pressure (30 seconds). In this translation task, the focus was on syntactic problems in 8 different sentence types. Subsequently, the realizations of auxiliaries and verb phrases were subjected to an EA. When we limit ourselves to those errors which Taylor classified as intralingual ('overgeneralization') versus interlingual ('transfer'), we get the picture presented in fig. 4.10. Although interlingual errors are more frequent with elementary learners than with intermediate learners, both groups produce predominantly intralingual errors. The explanation Taylor suggests for the greater number of interlingual errors in the early stages of the L2 learning process is that L2 learners then have little other prior linguistic knowledge to fall back on besides their L1, while in later stages they make increasing use of prior L2 knowledge.

Lastly, we would like to point out a little-known case study by Bell (1973). Bell recorded the Asian immigrant English of one informant: an 18-year-old Punjabi-speaking Hindu who had been in Britain for about two months at the time of data-collecting. A 14-minute dialogue between researcher and informant yielded a transcribed record of approximately 1000 words. Using notions developed by Corder, Bell presents a careful and detailed analysis of the recorded data. Unfortunately, performance errors like false starts and repeats have been omitted from the transcription.

Whereas before 1970 it was generally supposed that deviations from the L2 norm in L2 learning were attributable to interference, after 1970 a number of empirical studies have provided data which show the role of interference in L2 learning to be considerably less prominent. The 'identity hypothesis' (L1 learning = L2 learning) of Dulay and Burt, however, has changed the traditional overexposure of interference phenomena into underexposure. A more interesting question than which percentage of errors in a certain body of data is

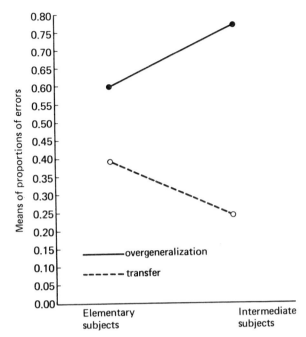

Fig. 4.10   Means of proportions of overgeneralization and transfer errors made by elementary and intermediate subjects (Taylor 1975, 85)

attributable to interference (see James 1980:146) is the question under what conditions interference is likely to occur in L2 learning. There are a number of factors whic influence the probability of occurrence of interference phenomena:

(a) *Amount and nature of L2 input*: interference is especially likely to occur when the L2 input is limited in quantity and scope. This situation occurs mainly where L2 is learned in an L1 environment (e.g. schools); most studies showing a limited role of interference focus on L2 learning in an L2 environment, where the L2 input is abundant and varied;

(b) *Level of linguistic analysis*: more L2 learning research has been done at the levels of morphology and syntax than at the phonological and lexical levels, (see 5.1.4. and 5.1.5.). It is especially with respect to the latter levels that interference phenomena are reported in the literature.

(c) *Linguistic distance between L1 and L2*: interference phenomena manifest themselves especially strongly between related linguistic systems: the degree of interference is partly determined by the degree of 'translatability' of L1 features into L2 features;

(d) *L2 learning stage*: there is some evidence (see e.g. Taylor 1975) that, for adult learners at least, interference phenomena are most frequent in the first stages of the L2 learning process;

(e) *Task focus*: if the focus of L2 use is on correct grammatical forms rather than on communicative effectiveness, interference is likely to occur: written translation tasks under time pressure constitute extremely favourable conditions for the occurrence of interference phenomena (see again Taylor 1975).

In so far as L1 interference occurs in L2 learning, CA plays, by definition, a complementary role. This fact has repeatedly been used in the defence of CA against the objections discussed in section 4.2. (see especially James 1971, Berman 1978). For the explanation of some phenomena in L2 learning CA is in fact indispensable. Furthermore, there are other phenomena besides interference which call for CA. One of these phenomena, which has attracted a lot of attention in the literature, is avoidance as a result of (lack of) correspondence between L1 and L2.

4.3.3 Limitations of error analysis

As we have remarked earlier, most error analyses result in a classification of deviations from the L2 norm in terms of fig. 4.6. However, any attempt to describe L2 learning phenomena in these terms will lead to some serious problems:

(1) The distinctions used in fig. 4.6. only have a limited use;
(2) Some L2 learning phenomena cannot be captured at all by EA;
(3) EA does not provide any insights into the course of the L2 learning process.

We shall discuss each of these problems below.

(1) The distinctions used in fig. 4.6. only have a limited use

In fig. 4.6. the first distinction is between errors of competence and errors of performance. It will be clear from the following examples that this distinction is by no means clear-cut:

(67) I felt very *revealed* when I found my keys again (intended: *relieved*)
(68) He *induced* me to Mr Bradley (intended: *introduced*)
(69) The dog *swimmed* against the stream (intended: *swam*)

In all cases, the verb forms used could be indicative of errors of performance (phonemic transposition, syllabic deletion and misderivation respectively) or of errors of competence (wrong choice of words in 67/68 because of phonetic similarity in L2, overgeneralization in 69).

Corder's operational criterion for distinguishing errors of performance (recognition and correction by the L2 learner himself) can of course only be used if the L2 learner is actually available. But even then, this criterion raises a number of questions:

• there is often a clear distinction between explicit knowledge of linguistic rules and the implicit application of rules in actual verbal performance (see Kielhöfer 1975:9); thus it is possible that an L2 learner can recognize and repair his errors on the basis of explicit L2 knowledge, but at the same time retains them in actual L2 use;
• also, a large number of errors of performance may indicate lack of auto-

maticity in using language skills, and therefore a lack of L2 competence on the part of the L2 learner (see Kielhöfer 1975:8);
- furthermore, the interpretation of those errors which are recognized but cannot be corrected by the L2 learner remains unclear (e.g. *swimmed* in 69, which the L2 learner may conceivably use as a 'makeshift form').

Corder's appeal to an 'authoritative interpretation' of errors of competence by the L2 learner himself is also problematic;
- Corder suggests a translation in two stages for this authoritative interpretation: the learner is asked to express his intentions in L1, which the researcher in turn translates correctly into L2. These stages, however, are often difficult to achieve in practice, because there need not be structurally equivalent possibilities in L1 and L2;
- furthermore, the learner will often no longer remember what he intended to say; this problem increases as the time between the original utterance and the reconstruction increases.

Lastly, there are some general problems in judgments about utterances by informants:
- judgments of language users about language presuppose that both researcher and informant can use a shared meta-language, at least to some extent; if such a meta-language is completely absent, the status of introspective judgments of informants becomes doubtful (see Bell 1974:46);
- judgments on language (behaviour) are not always constant and therefore not always reliable, let alone judgments of language learners; in addition, young children are even less capable than adults of giving useful or reliable judgments about their own language use.

It is also often far from easy to make a distinction between inter- and intralingual deviations from the L2 norm, because it often remains unclear which operating principle the L2 learner in fact uses. Compare the following utterances by L2 learners with a German L1 background:

(70) the *futural* design of the metro
(71) It was an *unordinary* event
(72) Il se heurte *à les* obstacles
(73) There are many *snakes* in the garden (intended: snails)

In all cases the operating principle applied may have been interlingual or intralingual, or even both:

Interlingual OP	Intralingual OP
(70) innovation analogous to *zukünftig*	innovation analogous to *structural*, etc.
(71) innovation analogous to *ungewöhnlich*	innovation analogous to *uncertain*, etc.
(72) no contraction analogous to *an den*	no contraction analogous to *à la*
(73) phonetic similarity to *Schnecken*	phonetic similarity to *snails*

Fig. 4.11   Alternative possibilities for classifying L2 utterances (L1 = German)

For a discussion of similar complications involved in the distinction between inter- and intralingual deviations from the L2 norm, see Knibbeler (1979) and Sheen (1980). Comparing Duskova (1969) and Dulay and Burt (1974b) we can see how differently deletions in L2 utterances can be classified:

- Duskova interprets article deletion in the English of adult Czechs as interference, 'because' Czech does not have an equivalent structure;
- Dulay and Burt interpret the same phenomenon in the English of Spanish children as an intralingual deviation from the norm, 'because' children learning English as L1 also omit articles.

Divergence phenomena are another notorious problem for classification (see section 4.2.). Earlier in this chapter, we have classified wrong lexical selection in the case of divergence between L1 and L2 as an intralingual deviation from the norm, e.g.:

(74) Il alla au téléphone et *choisit*

Kielhöfer (1975:143) points out lexical selection problems for L2 learners with German as L1 background:

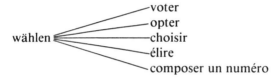

In some studies selection problems as a result of divergences between L1 and L2 are classified as intralingual errors, and in other studies as interlingual errors.

Lastly, the distinction proposed in fig. 4.6. between morphosyntactic and lexical errors is also problematic. Of course, here the classification is dependent upon a specific model of description, and can never be better than the model upon which it is dependent (see Legenhausen 1975:17). Compare the following utterances by L2 learners whose L1 is German:

(75) He *asked* a new book (see Legenhausen 1975:23)
(76) Il faut *user* la raison (see Kielhöfer 1976:61)

There are two plausible interpretations for (75):

(75a) He *asked* for a new book
(75b) He *requested* a new book

On the basis of interpretation (a), *asked* in (75) could be classified as a morphosyntactic deviation from the norm, and on the basis of interpretation (b) as a lexical deviation. In the case of (76), the plausible interpretation is:

(76a) Il faut *user de* la raison (Man muss den Verstand gebrauchen)

The use of *de* in (76a) is semantically motivated, and (76a) and (76) differ in meaning. It is not obvious whether (76) in the interpretation of (76a) should be taken to be a lexical or a morphosyntactic violation of the constraints on the French verb *user*.

(2) Some L2 learning phenomena cannot be captured at all by EA

The assumption which is not usually stated, but which underlies most discussions on EA, is that difficulty of learning is indicated by a greater frequency of errors in actual language behaviour. Nevertheless, the occurrence of error and the experiencing of difficulty by the learner need not coincide. Difficulty need not result in error, though the effort expended in producing a correct form may be considerable.

Some L2 learning problems are extremely elusive for EA because it seems that they cannot be captured at all in corpus-based research. One of these problems is *avoidance*. Avoidance does not lead to errors, but to under-representation of words or structures in L2 use. Learners may avoid L2 elements for various reasons. Levenston (1971) for instance points out the following preference: if formal and informal L2 structures are available, learners will prefer the more formal; compare:

(77a) *It is obvious* that they . . . .
(77b) *Obviously* they . . . .

The excessive use of some structures (e.g. 77a) and the exclusion of other structures (e.g. 77b) have been labelled 'over-indulgence' and 'under-representation' respectively by Levenston.

We shall restrict ourselves to avoidance phenomena as a result of linguistic differences, or the absence thereof, between L1 and L2. In this case, we have the following possible causes of avoidance:

(a) The learner thinks there is not enough difference between elements in L1 and L2;
(b) The learner thinks there is too much difference between elements in L1 and L2.

The first cause of avoidance has already been illustrated through examples 10–13. These are causes of linguistic (syntactic or idiomatic) disbelief. There is not only an increased chance of interference, but also of avoidance for fear of interference as the degree of difference between L1 and L2 decreases. Examples from written translations of Dutch learners of German are presented in fig. 4.12. (see also Jordens 1977:27–8, 33). On the basis of such avoidance phenomena we can establish the following operating principle for linguistically related languages:

> Assume that there is no correspondence between L1 and L2, and avoid structural similarity.

This immediately raises the question of when this operating principle replaces the operating principle formulated earlier:

> Assume that there is correspondence between L1 and L2

Dutch form	German equivalent	Avoidance phenomena
(78)Hij *heeft het tot minister gebracht*	Er *hat es zum Minister gebracht*	Er *hat sich zum M. empor gearbeitet*, Er *ist zum M. aufgerückt*, Er *ist bis zum Rang eines M. aufgestiegen*
(79)De dag *breekt aan*	Der Tag *bricht an*	*tritt ein, trifft ein, bricht ein, fängt an, kommt heran*
(80)*Voortaan*	*Fortan*	*in (der) Zukunft, ab jetzt, weiter(hin)*
(81)*Tastbare resultaten*	*Tastbare Resultate*	*spürbare, handfeste, (er)greifbare, fühlbare, fassbare, deutliche, konkrete, anschauliche Ergebnisse*
(82)*De aanzet*	*Der Ansatz*	*Der erste Versuch, der Anhieb*

Fig. 4.12   Avoidance phenomena of Dutch learners of German

Kellerman (1977:102 ff.) suggests the following list of items which will lead to non-transfer or transfer respectively:

(a) *language-specific items* (generally not transferred, even when it would be quite possible to do so and produce correct L2 forms):
proverbs, catchphrases, slang expressions, idioms;
inflectional morphology, except in very closely related languages (see sentence 8a);

(b) *language-neutral items* (often transferred):
internationalisms;
Latin expressions;
borrowings from other modern languages (see sentences 34–40);
conceptual differences as a result of divergence (see sentences 30–33);
count/non-count distinctions (see sentence 20);
writing/punctuation conventions.

Kellerman presented a list of idiomatic English or English-like sentences to Dutch university students learning English and asked them to judge them grammatically. There were four sentence types:

Code	Sentence type	Example
(1) + / +	correct L1 expr., correct L2 expr.	*the victory in the bag*
(2) + / −	correct L1 expr., incorrect L2 expr.	*to be the cigar*
(3) − / +	incorrect L1 expr., correct L2 expr.	*it's no use crying over spilt milk*
(4) − / −	incorrect L1 expr., incorrect L2 expr.	*he slept on both ears (from French)*

Fig. 4.13   Four types of idiomatic English or English-like sentences (Kellerman 1977)

The students were divided up into beginning, intermediate and advanced groups (N = 3 × 24). The results were as follows:

- beginning students rejected type -1/2 sentences more often than did advanced students;
- advanced students displayed 'knowledge' about the difference between type-l sentences and type-2 sentences.

The less advanced the students were, the more strongly they felt that there could be no correspondence between L1 and L2 for type-1/2 sentences. Jordens (1977) did a similar experiment with Dutch university students learning German. Contrary to what Kellerman found, Jordens concluded that beginners were more likely to accept type-1/2 sentences than advanced students. In other words: where Kellerman found a non-transfer strategy, Jordens found a transfer strategy. Kellerman attributes this difference to the fact that German and Dutch are linguistically more closely related than English and Dutch. Initial learners of an L2 which is closely related to their L1 tend to be less suspicious in the case of supposed or real correspondences between L1 and L2 than do advanced learners.

Kellerman (1978) reports on lexically oriented research into the notion of transferability. Kellerman's experiments on the polysemous verb *break* (Dutch *breken*) suggest that Dutch learners of English will transfer *breken* by *break* in proportion to the particular meaning of *breken* being related to a central or 'core' meaning. The nearer the meaning to this core, the more likely it is that *break* will be used in English. Conversely, the further the meaning from the core, the more likely it is that the learner will resort to synonyms or paraphrases.

Research on the second cause of avoidance mentioned has been done by Schachter (1974, 1979) and Kleinmann (1977). Schachter (1974) compared the structure of restrictive relative clauses (RRCs) in five unrelated languages (Persian, Arabic, Chinese, Japanese and English) on the following three points:

- left or right position of RRC with respect to head NP;
- type of subordination marking between RRC and head NP (arbitrary marker, pronominal particle, subordinate affix);
- + / − occurrence of a pronominal reflex in RRC.

On the basis of this structural comparison, Schachter predicted serious L2 learning problems especially for Chinese and Japanese learners of English, because in these two languages, unlike in English, Persian and Arabic, the RRC precedes the head NP (see Schachter 1974: 208–9 for more predictions on the basis of linguistic differences between L1 and L2). Schachter also analysed frequency and structure of RRCs in the English compositions of Persian, Arabic, Chinese, Japanese and American students (50 compositions per language group). The results are presented in fig. 4.14. It is not only striking that Chinese and Japanese learners make relatively few errors, but also that they produce relatively few RRCs. The first finding would seem to contradict the *a priori* claim mentioned above, but Schachter concludes from both these findings that Chinese and Japanese learners are aware of the difficulties

	Correct	Error	Total	Percentage of errors
Persian	131	43	174	25
Arab	123	31	154	20
Chinese	67	9	76	12
Japanese	58	5	63	8
American	173	0	173	—

Fig. 4.14   RRC production in five language groups (Schachter 1974, 209)

involved in RRCs and therefore avoid them. Their 'certainty' is reflected in a low number of errors, their 'uncertainty' is reflected in the low frequency of RRCs.

Comparable research has been done by Kleinmann (1977) and Schachter (1979). These studies show that CA should not be abandoned as a diagnostic tool for L2 learning problems, because of its potential for being able to account for at least some avoidance phenomena.

(3) Error analysis does not provide any insights into the course of the L2 learning process

After some critical remarks on various attempts at error classification we shall now discuss some more fundamental questions concerning EA.

In a number of ways, EA obscures our view of L2 learning behaviour:

• EA is restricted by definition to what the learner cannot do;
• EA traditionally gives no more than a static picture of L2 learning behaviour at some stage in the learning process.

The first step in nearly all EAs is compiling a corpus of L2 utterances (sentences in isolation or in context, produced spontaneously or in formal tests). The second stage is isolating the errors in such a corpus. After the second stage has been completed, the attention is usually entirely focused on what the learner cannot do, and no attention is paid to what he or she can do. Isolating relevant data in this way will obscure the overall view of the learning process (see also Svartvik 1973:8). This objection applies *a fortiori* to a restriction of EA to one or two static pictures of the learning process; such a restriction by definition obscures our view of the course of the L2 learning process. EA has too often remained a static, product-oriented type of research, whereas L2 learning processes require a dynamic approach focusing on the actual course of the process.

These limitations of EA clearly show in the notion of 'error'; such a notion does not consider the learner's point of view, but primarily the native speaker's point of view. This has led to errors being classified as 'substitutions', 'deletions', 'additions' and 'inversions' in those cases where L2 utterances do not yet correspond to the L2 norm. Such labels cannot be claimed to be process terms. A similar objection can be raised against the term 'simplification', e.g.:

(83) *Bus waiting* (intended: I am waiting for a bus)

The learner cannot simplify what he has not yet learned, and we can therefore not take the term 'simplification' to be descriptive of the learning process (see also Traugott 1977:153–4). The L2 learner does not have the same means available as the native speaker for the realization of his intended utterances. Basically, the process of language learning is one of elaboration or differentiation of linguistic structures used for expressing specific language functions. It is, however, possible to speak of simplification in the case of native speakers modifying their speech for learners (see 5.2.1.); in this case, the language user has more linguistic means available than he or she considers to be useful, in a given situation. In short, simplification presupposes choice.

Especially the limitations mentioned under (3) have been the cause of a shift of interest from EA to performance analysis.

5
Second language learning(2): performance analysis and discourse analysis

At the beginning of the preceding chapter (4.1.) we have outlined and motivated the structure of chapter 5 from a historical perspective. This chapter will be mainly devoted to performance analysis (5.1.). In 5.2. we shall discuss the role of discourse analysis within the field of L2 learning and L2 use.

5.1 Performance analysis

The problems concerned with error analysis which we have discussed in 4.3.3. have led to an increased interest in a procedural approach to L2 development: here the attention is no longer focused on deviations from the L2 norm ('errors') at a given point in time, but on the process of L2 learning as a whole. More and more researchers tend to be convinced that the language use of L2 learners in each stage of the learning process should be seen as an attempt to apply the structural principles of the target language in a systematic and coherent way.

Both L1 and L2 learning are based on the development of a hierarchically organized linguistic code (see 3.1.1. for a discussion of this hierarchy). In section 5.1. we shall pay attention to the development of various aspects of the L2 system. Not all of these aspects have received equal attention in the literature: much more research has been done into syntactic and morphological development than into lexical and phonological development. We shall, however, have to restrict ourselves in each of these fields, and for this reason refer the reader to the survey by McLaughlin (1978a, in this connection especially ch. 5) and the interesting readers by Hatch (1978) and Felix (1980). Some textual aspects of L2 use (more specifically, conversational aspects) will be discussed in 5.2.2.

Before discussing syntactic, morphological, lexical and phonological studies of L2 development (5.1.2.–5.1.5.), we shall briefly touch on some methodological aspects (5.1.1.).

5.1.1 Methodological aspects

One of the greatest problems in the description of actual language development in real time is that linguistics has not really developed the descriptive devices which could represent the dynamics of this process. Various attempts at describing L2 development in terms of a series of transitional or interim-grammars have been undertaken. Corder (1971:151) introduced the concept of 'transitional idiosyncratic dialect' for this purpose, and Nemser (1971:116) speaks of an 'approximative system'. Selinker's (1972:214) term 'interlanguage' has, however, become the most popular, in spite of the fact that there are some objections to this term (see also Corder 1978:74–5). What Selinker had in mind is that the interlanguage system is in a sense intermediate between L1 and L2; L2 development then consists of an increasing adaptation of L1 rules to L2 rules. However, as Corder has rightly pointed out, the concept of 'interlanguage' should be used in a noncommittal sense as to the nature of the continuum, and L2 development should be envisaged as a movement through a series of increasingly complex stages.

The basic idea is common to all proposals: the L2 learner constructs an internal grammar on the basis of the L2 input he receives; a grammar which in subsequent stages or 'varieties' keeps being reconstructed and will approximate a certain target variety of native speakers of that language more and more, although it will rarely be identical to it. This internal grammar is therefore characterized most importantly by instability in the sense of change. The learner acquires and drops specific varieties continuously.

Unfortunately, in most L2 studies there are hardly any concrete hints as to how these changing learning varieties might be described. One attempt to formally describe this development over time stems from the 'Heidelberger Forschungsprojekt' (see 5.4.2.) and has been inspired by quantitative studies of Labov, Bickerton, and others (see Hudson 1980:181 ff. for a survey of this earlier work.) Klein and Dittmar (1979:89) describe their basic idea of a developing grammar in the following 'variety space', where $t1$–4 are the time intervals (e.g. 6 months), Vt is the target variety, and Vf is the final variety of the L2 learner:

t_1	t_2	t_3	t_4	t_f	t_t
|	|	|	|	|	|
V_1	V_2	V_3	V_4	V_f	V_t

Fig. 5.1   Schema of learner varieties

This schema is simplified in several ways. There is in fact no real Vf (language development, especially lexical development, never stops), and there is no single Vt (the learner has to gain control over various registers). Furthermore, it can be shown that varieties do not only have a diachronic, but also a synchronic dimension. The quality of L2 use is not only determined by time, but also by circumstance. There are no single-style speakers. Every speaker shifts linguistic (phonological, morphosyntactic, lexical, pragmatic) variables, if the following factors change (see also Tarone 1979):

- social status of addresser-addressee
- language medium (spoken vs. written)
- topic of discourse
- linguistic task (naturalistic vs. experimental)
- physical surroundings (e.g. classroom, office, home, pub)
- amount of attention paid to speech (cf. monitored vs. unmonitored speech).

A further complication is that language change over time does not exclusively manifest itself in the form of progress. In addition to progress, one may also find 'levelling', or even regression ('back-sliding'). We speak of levelling if there is an impediment to further progress, while regression manifests itself in the shape of linguistic phenomena which are characteristic of an earlier stage of language development. Selinker (1972:215) uses the term 'fossilization' for both levelling and regression, and considers the chance of fossilization occurring especially high when the learner's attention is focused on other tasks than correct language use. Extreme tension or relaxation may also encourage fossilized speech. Selinker and Lamendella (1978) give the following possible causes of fossilization:

- low motivation for learning L2, as a consequence of lack of opportunity to communicate in L2 or psychological and/or social resistance against cultural identification with and acculturation within the L2 community;
- age: older L2 learners usually retain a clearly recognizable foreign accent (but see chapter 6.2.);
- limited range of L2 input: the L2 input may be severely restricted both quantitatively (period of time) and qualitatively (variation).

Selinker and Lamendella (1978:149–51) can be referred to for a number of interesting research questions about fossilization.

In addition to the methodological problems we have mentioned we can also conclude that in L2 performance studies considerable differences in research designs show up. These differences relate to choice of period of time, informants and data collection procedures (see also Burt and Dulay 1980:296–303).

Period of time

First of all a choice has to be made between longitudinal and cross-sectional research designs. In the first type of research, the language behaviour of one and the same informant or group of informants is registered for a certain period at specific intervals (e.g. one hour, twice a week, for 12 months.) In the second case, one single sample of the language behaviour of a group of informants is taken. From such a sample one may draw conclusions about which aspects of L2 have been mastered to what extent. In contrast with cross-sectional studies, where the time factor has in fact been eliminated, longitudinal studies give a picture of language development over time. Within both types of research design it is possible to make statements about sequences: a cross-sectional design allows statements on the order of accuracy (or order of difficulty) of a series of linguistic units, whereas only a longitudinal design allows statements on the order of acquisition. In many cross-sectional studies it is tacitly assumed that an observed order of accuracy reflects a non-observed order of acquisition (see e.g. Fathman 1977:30). In other words, synchronic data are interpreted diachronically. It should, however, be borne in mind that such an interpretation is based on assumptions only, the validity of which will have to be tested empirically.

A comparable methodological problem one finds in sociolinguistic research into language change. Labov (1972:160–5) gives the following assumption as a *uniformitarian doctrine*: 'the same mechanisms which operated to produce the large-scale changes of the past may be observed operating in the current changes taking place around us'. Assuming no distinction between real time and apparent time, diachronic statements (language change between generations) are made on the basis of synchronic observations (linguistic variation between age groups).

Although in longitudinal research there can always be discussion about choices made concerning the duration of the study and the intervals between each sampling, it will be clear that it has advantages over cross-sectional research. Nevertheless, a lot of research into language development is cross-sectional, which has to do with the fact that longitudinal research is by definition time-consuming (and therefore often expensive), and with the difficulty involved in applying it to large numbers of informants, a point that we shall deal with in the next section.

One way of avoiding some of the disadvantages of both a longitudinal and a cross-sectional design is to use the combined, so-called quasi-longitudinal design, in which cross-sectional samples of language behaviour of different groups of language learners, at earlier or later stages of development, are collected simultaneously and compared with each other (cf. Taylor 1975, which we have discussed in 4.3.2.).

Informants

Statements about language development can be based on observed behaviour of one, some, or many informants. Some well known and influential studies of L1 development have been based on single (Smith 1973) or multiple (R. Brown 1973) case studies. There are several disadvantages in case studies which one does not find in studies involving larger groups:

- it is impossible to generalize about language development on the basis of case studies;
- they do not, or only barely, allow for statements about individual variation in language development;
- they can easily lead to observer bias: the researcher may identify with the informant or informants to such an extent that he observes what he wishes to observe;
- frequent contact between researcher and informant which is aimed at collecting data on 'language' may influence the language development process in as yet unknown ways.

As we have indicated before, however, a preference for longitudinal research almost invariably involves resorting to case studies. There are hardly any examples of in-depth longitudinal studies over a considerable period of time involving larger groups of subjects (but see Perdue 1982).

Data collection procedures

Lastly, statements about language development may be based on data which may have been gathered in very diverse ways. There are many methods of data collection, ranging from observation of natural behaviour (or, at least, behaviour which is as natural as possible, since natural behaviour is hardly ever observed) to the most artificial experimental tasks.

There are arguments in favour of experimental tasks, and in favour of naturalistic observations (see also 3.1.2. for a discussion). We shall start with the latter:

- naturalistic observations yield data on how language is used under specific social conditions and with specific intentions; the informant's attention is not focused on language in isolation, as is often the case in experimental tasks, and there is the least possible risk of interference from skill in doing tests to linguistic skills;
- such observations are furthermore a rich source of expected and unexpected linguistic data.

By 'unexpected' we have indicated that naturalistic observations very often have the goal to generate hypotheses. This at the same time highlights one of the arguments in favour of experimental tasks:

- experimental research usually tests rather than generates hypotheses; on the basis of well defined hypothesis-oriented tasks it is easier to collect, order and interpret specific linguistic data;
- on the one hand, experimental research may prevent crucial gaps in the database (there are no 'accidental' data, as with naturalistic observations), while on the other hand, it prevents the emergence of a vast range of 'useless' data.

These difficult choices of period of time, informants and data collection procedures indicate that there is no such thing as a 'royal road' to insights into language development. Not surprisingly, the survey of Hatch (1978) gives us a very diverse approach to language learning research.

Nevertheless we can conclude that, at least as far as research into *second* language learning is concerned, the main divide is between 'cross-sectionalists' and 'longitudinalists'. Very often, one finds one of the following two research designs:

	Design A	Design B
Time period	longitudinal	cross-sectional
Informants	single/multiple case study	group(s) of subjects
Data collection	naturalistic	experimental

Fig. 5.2   Two common research designs in studies on L2 learning

Obviously, one also finds combinations of these two designs. The 'Heidelberger Forschungsprojekt', which we shall discuss in section 5.1.2., for instance, is mainly based on cross-sectional, naturalistic data of a sizeable group of subjects.

After 1970, the focus in studies on L2 learning was initially on type B designs (cf. especially the many morpheme studies following on the 1974 publications of

Dulay and Burt, see section 5.1.3.). One tends to encounter type A designs in more recent studies. We can point to McLaughlin (1978a:100–12) and Hatch (1978:91–271) for surveys of case studies on (successive) L2 learning. Wong-Fillmore (1976), Felix (1978), Pienemann (1981) and Wode (1981) are recent examples of longitudinal, multiple case studies on L2 learning by children. One of the very few longitudinal studies into L2 development of adults is Schumann's (1978c) single case study of Alberto. Recently, a comparative, longitudinal project on L2 learning by adults has been initiated by the European Science Foundation (see Perdue 1982).

5.1.2 Syntactic development

Rather than giving a rough outline of some projects concerned with syntactic development we shall take two examples and discuss them in detail. The examples will be the so-called 'Heidelberger Forschungsprojekt' (henceforth HDP), carried out by Wolfgang Klein *et al.*, which was aimed at the learning of L2 German by adult Italians and Spaniards, and a project directed by Courtney B. Cazden, which focused on the learning of L2 English by six speakers of Spanish (2 children, 2 adolescents and 2 adults.) Both studies focus on L2 learning in an L2 environment. Furthermore, the results of both projects are largely based on naturalistic data collection techniques. The design for the HDP, however, is cross-sectional, and involves a sizeable group of subjects $(n = 2 \times 24)$, while the Cazden project is longitudinal (duration 10 months) and restricts itself to a multiple case study $(n = 3 \times 2)$.

The 'Heidelberger Forschungsprojekt'

The HDP started in 1974 at the University of Heidelberg. Detailed information about the project in general is given in Heidelberger Forschungsprojekt (1975), especially with regard to data collection procedures, and in Dittmar *et al.* (1975). An outline of the design and results of the project are also given in Klein and Dittmar (1979). The informants were adult immigrant workers from the Heidelberg area. The composition of the sample is shown in figure 5.3.:

Duration of stay (years)	Italians		Spaniards		Σ
	men	women	men	women	
< 2.7	4	2	4	2	12
2.8–4.3	4	2	4	2	12
4.4–7.0	4	2	4	2	12
> 7.0	4	2	4	2	12
Σ	16	8	16	8	
	24		24		48

Fig. 5.3 Informant characteristics of the HDP

Data collection was based both on participant observation and non-standardized interviews. Participant observation was systematically done in factories (representing work contacts), in a pub (representing leisure contacts), and in an aliens registration office (representing contacts with authorities). The interviews took place in the informants' homes.

The corpus originally consisted of 15-minute transcripts of 60 interviews and was finally restricted to 100 sentences per informant (see Klein and Dittmar 1979:114–19 for a justification of sentence criteria and excluded speech fragments). In order to get some information about the 'target variety' of the L2 learners (i.e. the language of working-class people from the Heidelberg area), data based on interviews were also collected from 12 Heidelberg dialect speakers from the social contact domain of foreign workers.

Klein and Dittmar (1979) first of all introduce the concept of a variety grammar as a tool for the description of language variation and then apply this tool to the description of (second) language learning. The proposed variety grammar is probabilistic and context-free (see Klein and Dittmar 1979:38 for arguments in favour of a context-free grammar). There is probabilistic weighting of those rules which have the same symbol on the left-hand side of the arrow (say, for example, NP in fig. 5.4.). These rules can be grouped into 'rule blocks' (in this case an NP block). Each rule block gets a total probability of 1 (for each variety). This weighting technique allows for a precise modelling of L2 learning varieties. In fig. 5.4. six successive varieties are considered for NP development (see also Klein and Dittmar 1979:92–93):

	V_1	V_2	V_3	V_4	V_5	V_6	Example
(1) NP → N	0.9	0.6	0.3	0.2	0.2	0.2	*man*
(2) NP → Det N	0.1	0.3	0.3	0.3	0.3	0.3	*the man*
(3) NP → Det Adj N	0	0	0	0	0.4	0.4	*the old man*
(4) NP → Det N Adj	0	0.1	0.3	0.4	0	0	*the man old*
(5) NP → Det N Adv	0	0	0.1	0.1	0.1	0.1	*the man here*
Degree of variety	2	3	4	4	4	4	

Fig. 5.4   Six successive varieties for NP development (including degree of variety)

Fig. 5.4. gives a precise account of a whole series of developments. In V1, only simple NPs appear: mainly N and to some extent Det + N. More complex NPs do not occur. In V2 the first NPs with Adj appear, but in the 'wrong' position. This development continues in V3: the occurrence of simple NPs decreases, while Det + N + Adj constructions increase, and one more structure starts to appear: Det + N + Adv. While there is no great shift between V3 and V4, there is a dramatic change between V4 and V5: the learner has grasped the 'correct' rule for Adj placement, while Det + N + Adj has totally disappeared. In V6, nothing has changed: maybe the final variety has been reached, although the values may still differ from those of the target variety spoken by native speakers.

In this type of description, the notion 'error' plays no role. But the notion could be defined, if desired, within this framework as 'the occurrence of some rule which has probability value 0 in the target variety'.

Within the HDP the focus is on the development of specific syntactic categories (proposition, verbal/nominal/adverbial complex, subordinate clauses) and the development of word order characteristics (especially the position of verbs in affirmative main and subordinate clauses which have at least a subject). For the syntactic description of learner (and native) varieties, a context-free grammar as described in Klein and Dittmar (1979:115) was used. The proposed grammar contains 101 context-free rules grouped into 15 rule blocks. All applications of all 101 rules were counted per speaker, and on this basis the probabilistic weights of all rules within each rule block were calculated. The 101 values per informant give a sort of 'syntactic profile'. A special cumulative syntactic index was developed in order to be able to standardize the profile per informant (see Klein and Dittmar 1979:120–4 for a discussion of the procedures used). The combination of the following eight criteria determines the syntactic index per informant:

+/− Presence of subject
+/− Presence of verb
Complexity of VG with(out) Aux/Mod
Complexity of verb complements
Degree of pronominalization
Complexity of NP (+/− attributes)
Type of determiner
Type of adverbial complex

Fig. 5.5   Criteria for establishing the cumulative syntactic index per informant (adapted from Klein and Dittmar 1979, 122)

On the basis of this syntactic index, the 48 informants were divided up into four levels, with 12 subjects in each level, and this division into groups was taken as a basis for further syntactic description (see Klein and Dittmar 1979: 143–5 for an overview of the development of basic syntactic constituents).

Finally, the influence of various personal and environmental factors determining the success of L2 learning in the domain of syntax were studied. Of the factors analysed, the following six proved to be the most important ones (correlation between each of these factors and level of syntactic performance is given between brackets; see Klein and Dittmar 1979:208):

(a)   contacts with Germans in leisure time (0.64)
(b)   contacts with Germans at work place (0.53)
(c)   formal professional qualification, as acquired in native country (0.42)
(d)   age, at time of immigration (0.37)
(e)   attendance at school in the past (0.35)
(f)   duration of stay in Germany (0.28)

No significant relationship was found between the level of syntactic performance and sex or mother tongue. The most important factors are the two contact variables. Duration of stay seems to be important only for the first two years. The learning process then slows down, or even stops, and may start moving again when other environmental factors change.

There are many ways in which one can order and group speakers with regard to their use of syntactic rules; a device suggested earlier was the cumulative syntactic index. In this way, speakers are differentiated by the quantitative value of an index attached to them, and not by the 'presence' or 'absence' of a single rule. A better model for dealing with individual variability and systematicity in L2 learning may be implicational analysis (also known as scalogram analysis or Guttman scale analysis). Implicational analysis has been used in different areas of sociolinguistics (see Andersen 1978:223-4 for an overview). It has been applied to the analysis of L2 data by Hyltenstam (1977), Andersen (1978), Dittmar (1980), and others.

Implicational analysis is a technique for correlating specific linguistic units with informants (groups or individuals) of a given language in such a way that the presence of a unit X in the performance of informant Y *implies* the presence of certain other units in his or her performance. The correlation between presence or absence of linguistic items and the informants' use of them is usually displayed in an implicational table, as is shown in fig. 5.6.:

| | | Linguistic units | | | |
		A	B	C	D
(Groups of)	1	–	–	–	–
informants	2	+	–	–	–
	3	+	+	–	–
	4	+	+	+	–
	5	+	+	+	+

Fig. 5.6 Implicational table

The informants or groups of informants are listed in descending order; i.e. from the smallest to the largest number of linguistic units used by the informants. If there are implicational patterns in the data, i.e. if an item A is always used before an item B, and an item B before C, etc., then this fact is mirrored in the implicational table in such a way that in a certain row all the plusses are to the left of all the minuses. The display of the data can be based on indicating the use of a unit X by informant Y in binary terms (+ / –), or in exact quantitative terms.

Using the Heidelberg data, Dittmar (1980) proposes to rank speakers hierarchically by establishing implicational scales, as represented in fig. 5.7. The horizontal lines in each row separate five levels of learner varieties and the vertical lines mark the divisions between verb phrase rules which have or have not been used. Only two speakers (marked with –) do not fit the implicational pattern. On the basis of fig. 5.7., Dittmar (1980) distinguishes five varieties or stages in the acquisition of German verb phrase rules.

A number of concluding remarks on the HDP should be made:

Variety	Informant	Verb	Modal Verb + Verb	Copulative Verb	Auxiliary + Verb	Auxiliary + Modal Verb + Verb
V$_1$01	SP-35	15	—	—	—	—
02	IT-08	21	—	—	—	—
03	SP-15	31	—	—	—	—
04	SP-21	36	—	—	—	—
05	IT-09	40	—	—	—	—
06	SP-02	42	—	—	—	—
07	SP-22	49	—	—	—	—
08	SP-04	57	—	—	—	—
09	SP-12	65	—	—	—	—
10	SP-09	76	—	—	—	—
V$_2$11	SP-14	71	3	—	—	—
12	IT-23	24	2	—	—	—
13	IT-13	45	1	—	—	—
14	IT-12	42	9	—	—	—
15	IT-32	68	5	—	—	—
16	IT-26	70	8	—	—	—
V$_3$17	IT-24	51	—	3	—	—
18	SP-30	65	1	4	—	—
19	IT-29	66	1	2	—	—
20	SP-15	67	4	6	—	—
21	IT-28	60	2	4	—	—
22	SP-18	69	1	2	—	—
23	IT-18	55	10	1	—	—
24	IT-05	58	3	9	—	—
25	IT-25	48	2	23	—	—
26	IT-15	60	11	11	—	—
V$_4$27	SP-36	57	14	—	1	—
28	SP-01	40	13	11	1	—
29	IT-07	58	1	6	3	—
30	SP-08	52	1	7	1	—
31	SP-13	66	4	8	1	—
32	SP-17	50	2	31	2	—
33	SP-26	54	1	5	6	—
34	IT-16	65	2	5	3	—
35	SP-06	55	6	15	11	—
36	IT-20	69	9	5	8	—
37	IT-33	26	9	39	5	—
38	IT-06	47	4	21	24	—
39	IT-02	50	7	23	8	—
40	IT-22	55	2	23	14	—
41	IT-31	40	15	18	27	—
42	SP-31	44	2	28	18	—
43	IT-10	52	5	20	15	—
44	SP-24	52	11	11	24	—
45	SP-19	43	9	21	27	—
46	SP-29	34	7	24	23	—
V$_5$47	SP-11	11	3	24	59	3
48	IT-01	17	8	12	57	3

Fig. 5.7 Implicational scale-ordering of 48 adult learners, illustrated for five verb phrase rules (raw scores) (Dittmar 1980, 225)

(1) Implicational analysis offers a better method of dividing the 48 informants into 5 'natural' groups than does the arbitrary division into 4 groups of 12 informants as proposed in Klein and Dittmar (1979:124).

(2) Although intuitively the implicational pattern may serve as a model for distinguishing between developmental stages, it should nevertheless be noted that the Heidelberg data are based on cross-sectional performance at one particular moment in time, when the informants were each at a different level of L2 proficiency; the data were not culled from longitudinal studies of individual learners. Therefore, the use of the term 'acquisition order' should be avoided (see also Meisel *et al.* 1979).

(3) Furthermore, the HDP has a strongly descriptive orientation. Little attention is paid to attempting to explain the orders found. In reference to 3.2.3. one could wonder what sort of operating principles the L2 learner uses at various stages of L2 development. Wode (1979) contains an attempt at formulating such principles for some phonological aspects of L2 development.

(4) The corpus on which the syntactic description of L2 German is based has been 'normalized' (see Klein and Dittmar 1979:114–19). Apart from the fact that all sorts of aspects which are characteristic of spoken language will therefore remain inaccessible to analysis, the method and extent of 'normalization' are not precisely specified. This brings us to the last point:

(5) The entire corpus consists of only 100 sentences per informant. The limited size of the corpus and the relative paucity of L2 data actually presented contrast sharply with the detailed attention for the techniques of analysis used.

The L2 English project directed by C. Cazden

Although this project on the learning of English as L2 is much more limited in size than the HDP, and also less sophisticated from the point of view of linguistic description, it has a better presentation of actual L2 data. As we have indicated before, this project is also largely based on naturalistic data collection techniques. The data were collected in the following three ways (see Schumann 1978c:6–8):

• spontaneous conversations between experimenter and subject, about topics of mutual interest (major data source);

• elicited conversations (generated through games, pictures, and other elicitation instruments) as well as experimental elicitations (imitation of model utterances, transformation of affirmative into negative sentences, of active into passive sentences, and permutation of WH-words in elicited questions);

• pre-planned sociolinguistic interactions (based on taking the subjects to restaurants, museums, parties, etc.).

Each data collection session involved three people: the subject, the experimenter, and a bilingual (English/Spanish) transcriber. The sessions were held in the subjects' homes and generally lasted an hour.

In contrast to the HDP project, this project is longitudinal (duration 10 months, with data collection sessions once every two weeks) and it is limited to a multiple case study of six Spanish-speaking learners of English (2 children aged 5, 2 adolescents of 11 and 13, 2 adults of 25 and 33). All of the subjects had been in the US for less than four months at the outset of the project. The project started in 1973 and was carried out under the direction of Courtney B. Cazden by Herlinda Cancino, Ellen Rosansky, and John Schumann. Details of the project are given by Cancino *et al.* (1974, 1978), Schumann (1978a), and in a separate monograph by Schumann (1978c). Although the monograph by Schumann is, in fact, a single case study of one of the six subjects (a 33-year-old Costa Rican named Alberto), it also includes a lot of data on the other five subjects.

Cancino *et al.* (1978) discuss the acquisition of negatives and interrogatives by the six subjects. *Negatives* are acquired in four (sometimes overlapping) stages:

(1) *no + V*

Spanish speakers' first hypothesis is said to be that NEG in English is like NEG in Spanish, hence *no* is preposed to V, as in:

I no can see
You no walk on this
They no have water
I no understand

(2) *don't + V*:

The learners' next hypothesis appears to be that NEG in English is *don't*, again to be placed in pre-verbal position: *don't* is simply used as an allomorph of *no* and still seems to be essentially a Spanish-like negation, but slightly more anglicized, as in:

I don't hear
He don't like it
I don't can explain
I don't have a woman

(3) *Aux + NEG (where aux is primarily be/can)*

Now it has been learned that English NEG is formed by putting the NEG element (*n't/not*) after the first *aux* element, as in:

He can't see
It wasn't so big
It's no danger
He's not skinny

(4) *Appearance of 'analysed' forms of don't*:

In this final stage *no + V* utterances disappear and are replaced by 'analysed' forms of *don't: do not, doesn't, does not, didn't, did not*; as in:

I didn't even know
It doesn't make any difference
She didn't believe me
He doesn't laugh like us

Although Cancino *et al.* (1978) refer to interference from L1 Spanish structures in their explanation of the observed phenomena in stage (1) and stage (2), one has to bear in mind that both V-preposing and 'unanalysed' *don't* have been demonstrated to occur also with other subjects than Spanish-speaking learners of English, as in:

- L1 learning of English (Klima and Bellugi 1966);
- L2 learning of English, with L1 backgrounds other than Spanish (see e.g. Wode 1981 for similar phenomena in L2 English of German children).

Therefore, a 'universal' explanation of these developmental phenomena is preferable.

The relative frequencies of these four NEG devices in the speech of all six subjects have been compared. For example, the youngest (Marta, age 5) shows the following patterns:

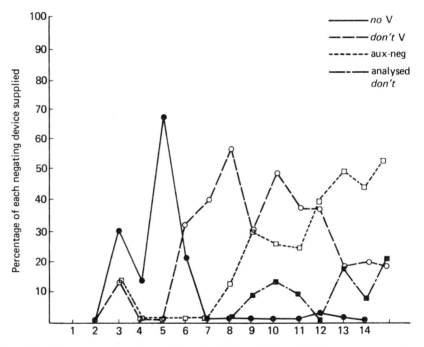

Fig. 5.8 Development of negation in Marta (during 14 taped sessions), showing proportion of each NEG device to total negatives in each sample (Hatch 1978, 212)

Marta has a clear *no* + *V* negation system until tape 6. The slight *don't* + *V* and *aux* + *NEG* peaks in tape 3 are the result of four utterances out of a relative small total sample of negatives (i.e. 14). On tape 6 *don't* + *V* becomes the dominant type of negation and *no* + *V* radically decreases. On tape 8, Marta begins to use *aux* + *NEG*, which by tape 9 reaches the same level as *don't* + *V*. Also on tape 9, analysed *don't* begins to appear, and, after some initial fluctuation, it seems to be on the increase by tape 15.

If early *do*-inversion is excluded (which can be considered as a simple question marker which can appear at the beginning of a declarative sentence: e.g. (*do*) *you go to school*?), two stages can be distinguished in the development of *yes/no questions*:

(1) *no inversion*, i.e. utterances are just given a rising intonation;
(2) *gradually increasing inversion*, but with variability.

The development of WH-questions seems to take place in the following stages (see Cancino *et al.* 1978:222):

(1) *undifferentiation*: the learner does not distinguish between simple and embedded WH-questions:
   (a) both simple and embedded WH-questions are uninverted, as in:
      What you study?
      What they are doing?
      That's what I do with my pillow
      I know what they are doing
   (b) variable inversion: simple WH-questions are sometimes inverted, sometimes not, whereas embeddings remain uninverted, as in:
      How can you say it?
      Where you get that?
   (c) generalization: increasing inversion in WH-questions with inversion extended to embedded questions, as in:
      I know where are you going

(2) *differentiation*: the learner distinguishes between simple and embedded WH-questions, as in:
   Where do you live?
   I don't know what he had

If we take another example, the development of *yes/no* questions and WH-questions as shown by Jorge (age 13), we get the picture presented in fig. 5.9. As far as WH-questions are concerned, Jorge passes through stages 1a/b/c/. Until tape 3 he remains in stage 1a. From tape 3 to tape 8 he is in stage 1b, whereas after tape 8 he is in stage 1c. With the subjects who showed evidence of a stage 1a (including Jorge), *yes-no* questions appear to be inverted at a time when WH-questions are not.

Alberto inverts only 11 times in *yes/no* questions and 12 times in WH-questions. He essentially remains in stage 1a for the whole period of study. Schumann's (1978c) case study of Alberto is aimed both at showing the structure/order of L2 development and at finding the possible causes for Alberto's low speed and rate of success in L2 development. With respect to the structure/order of L2 development, Schumann pays attention to syntactic aspects (development of negative and interrogative structures and of auxiliary) and morphological aspects (development of the possessive, past tense, plural and progressive morphemes). For Alberto's low speed and rate of success, Schumann considers the following possible causes: 'ability', social and psychological distance from English speakers, and age. Schumann takes the position that social and psychological distance are the primary factors impeding L2 development, and that Alberto's reduced and simplified English contains

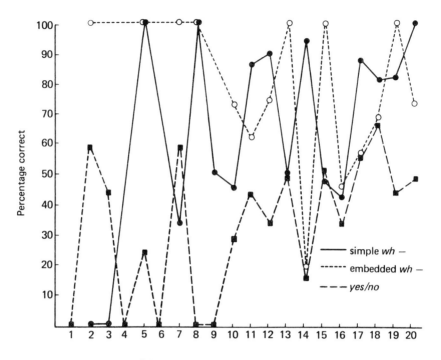

Fig. 5.9   Development of the interrogative in Jorge (during 20 taped sessions) with respect to inversion of Subject NP and Aux (Hatch 1978, 225)

features that are characteristic of pidgin languages. Several aspects of social and psychological distance affecting speed and success of L2 learning are discussed in detail (see Schumann 1978c:69–100; see also chapter 6 of the present book).

5.1.3 Morphological development

One study stands out as a source of inspiration for morphological research into L2 development: R. Brown's (1973) longitudinal multiple case study of L1 development. Brown's study aims to investigate the development of 14 'grammatical morphemes' in three children (named Adam, Eve, and Sarah), and it has led to the following main conclusions:

- the order of acquisition of these 14 morphemes is highly invariant for each of the children;
- this order is not determined by environmental factors such as morpheme frequencies in the parental language input to the children, but has to be explained on the basis of internal cognitive mechanisms, operating in the learner himself.

Brown's longitudinal findings were confirmed cross-sectionally in a larger replicative study with 21 children by De Villiers and De Villiers (1973). Following R. Brown (1973) and De Villiers and De Villiers (1973), researchers in the field of L2 learning started looking for answers to the following questions:

does L2 development also exhibit invariant orders?

in how far are those orders the same for L1 and L2 development?

in how far are L2 orders influenced by data/learner/input characteristics?

In addition to theoretical considerations, there were also practical considerations for this type of research: it was hoped that insight into orders of acquisition could contribute fundamentally to the discussion about principles of gradation in teaching programmes (see also 11.4.).

Many L2 order studies were, to use R. Brown's (1973) terminology, aimed at the development of 'grammatical morphemes' or 'functors', i.e. function words like prepositions, articles, and pronouns, on the one hand, and morphological word endings, like noun and verb inflections, on the other. Although from a semantic point of view such morphemes play only a minor role in verbal communication, there are several reasons for their popularity as a research subject:

they are extremely frequent in language use;

they can, also for this reason, be easily observed;

they can be relatively easily interpreted as correct or incorrect;

they are mostly acquired late in spite of their high frequency, and are therefore a good 'touchstone' for language proficiency.

A fair number of researchers have reported on morphological studies on L2 learning of English (in most cases in an L2 environment) in an extensive series of publications. Evaluative surveys of these studies can be found in Fathman (1979), Krashen (1981), and a very detailed one in Burt and Dulay (1980). The main studies are represented in fig. 5.10., with the 7 main research variables. From these studies we can conclude the following:

• most studies are based on a registration of oral-productive L2 skills;

• the data collection procedures used range from naturalistic to experimental, with lots of variants between both extremes;

• the design is usually cross-sectional (showing order of accuracy/difficulty) and hardly ever longitudinal (showing order of acquisition) (see also 5.1.1.);

• there is considerable variation with respect to number, L1 background, and age of the informants, with respect to type and amount of special ESL instruction, and with respect to the number of morphological functors studied.

In this chapter, we shall be especially concerned with two of the studies mentioned in figure 5.10.: Dulay and Burt (1974c) and Rosansky (1976). Dulay and Burt (1974c; see also their pilot study of 1973) signalled the start of this long series of L2 morpheme studies. In order to find out whether L2 learners from different L1 backgrounds exhibit similar L2 learning characteristics, they have used a modified version of the *Bilingual Syntax Measure* of Burt *et al.* (1973). We have already described this *Bilingual Syntax Measure* (BSM) in 4.3.2. Using this modified BSM, Dulay and Burt (1974c) investigated the order of accuracy of the 11 functors listed in fig. 5.11. in the spoken L2 English of 60 Spanish-speaking and 55 Chinese-speaking children between 6 and 8 years of age from New York.

Study	Type of data	Time period	N of informants	L1 background of informants	Age of informants	ESL instruction	N of functors studied
Dulay and Burt 1974	BSM[1]	cross-sectional	60+55	Spanish+Chinese	6-8	+	11
Bailey et al. 1974	BSM[1]	cross-sectional	33+40	Spanish+Various	17-55	+	8
Fathman 1975	SLOPE Test[2]	cross-sectional	60+60	Korean+Spanish	6-14	+ and -	20
Larsen-Freeman 1975	5 tasks[3]	cross-sectional	6+6+6+6	Arabic+Japanese Persian+Spanish	Adults	+	10
Hakuta 1976	spontaneous speech	longitudinal	1	Japanese	5	-	17
Krashen et al. 1976	SLOPE Test[2]	cross-sectional	66	Various	Adults	+ and -	20
Rosansky 1976	spontaneous speech elicited conversation	longitudinal	2	Spanish	11+13	?	11
Andersen 1977	writing	cross-sectional	89	Spanish	Adults	+	12
Krashen et al. 1977	casual conversation interviews	cross-sectional	22	Various	Adults	+	7
Wode 1981	classroom repetition spontaneous speech experimental data	longitudinal	4	German	3-8	-	3

Notes
[1] Bilingual Syntax Measure (described in 5.3.2)
[2] Second Language Oral Production English Test: 20 subtests each containing one specific morphosyntactic marker
[3] Reading, writing, listening, imitation, speaking

Fig. 5.10   Major morphological studies on L2 learning of English in an L2 environment

Functors	Structures	Examples
(1) Pronoun case	Pron-(Aux)-(Neg)-V-(Pron)	*He* doesn't like *him*
(2) Article	(Prep)-Det-(Adj)- $\left\{\begin{matrix} N \\ Pron \end{matrix}\right\}$ $\{\pm\}$ Poss $\}$ (N)in *the* fat guy's house
(3) Singular copula	$\left\{\begin{matrix} NP \\ Pron \end{matrix}\right\}$ -*(be)*- $\left\{\begin{matrix} Adj \\ NP \end{matrix}\right\}$	He*'s* fat
(4) *-ing*	($\left\{\begin{matrix} NP \\ Pron \end{matrix}\right\}$)-*(be)*-V $_{+\,-ing}$	(He's) mopp*ing*
(5) Plural	NP $_{+\,pl}$	window*s*
(6) Singular auxiliary	$\left\{\begin{matrix} NP \\ Pron \end{matrix}\right\}$ -*be*-V $_{+\,-ing}$	She*'s* dancing
(7) Past regular	$\left\{\begin{matrix} NP \\ Pron \end{matrix}\right\}$ -*(have)*-V $_{+\,pst}$ - $\left\{\begin{matrix} NP \\ Pron \end{matrix}\right\}$	He clos*ed* it.
(8) Past irregular	$\left\{\begin{matrix} NP \\ Pron \end{matrix}\right\}$ -V $_{+\,pst}$ -($\left\{\begin{matrix} NP \\ Pron \end{matrix}\right\}$)	He *stole* it
(9) Long plural	NP $_{+\,pl}$	hous*es*
(10) Possessive	Det-(Adj)-N $_{+\,poss}$ -(N)	the king*'s*
(11) 3rd person singular	$\left\{\begin{matrix} NP \\ Pron_{+\,sing} \end{matrix}\right\}$ -V $_{+\,tns}$ -(Adv)	he eat*s* too much

Fig. 5.11 Survey of functors studied (Dulay and Burt 1974c, 41)

The data-analysis is based on the procedure used by R. Brown (1973:225); what was established is in how far children use the functors listed correctly in obligatory linguistic contexts in their L2 speech. The following scoring system was used for each context:

0: no functor supplied (she's dance __)
1: misformed functor supplied (she's dance*s*)
2: correct functor supplied (she's danc*ing*)

Dulay and Burt used two methods to represent the results they obtained:

- the group score method: both the Spanish and Chinese group receive one single score for each functor;
- the group means method: to reduce the effect of variable performance (a functor is sometimes supplied by a child and sometimes not), the children who had fewer than three obligatory occasions for the functor in question were eliminated from the sample on which a score for that functor was computed.

For both groups of subjects, with their strongly different language backgrounds, Dulay and Burt observed an extremely high degree of similarity in the command of the 11 functors studied. As will be clear from fig. 5.12., this order of accuracy is hardly influenced by the method of analysis used. Dulay and Burt consider these results to support their hypothesis that in L2 learning in an L2 environment, L2 structures are acquired in an order which is much more determined by the structure of the target language than by the structure of the source language.

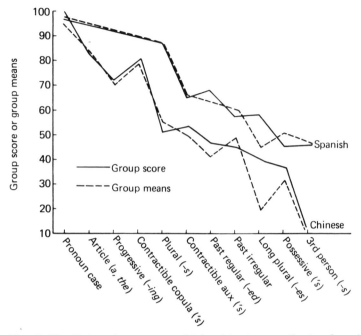

Fig. 5.12   Order of accuracy, obtained by two methods of analysis, for 11 functors in L2 performance of two groups of subjects (Dulay and Burt 1974c, 49)

While Dulay and Burt's (1974c) study was cross-sectional and involved large numbers of subjects, Rosansky (1976) used the longitudinal and spontaneous speech data gathered by Cancino *et al.* (1974, 1978) described in 5.1.2. (in this case, the data provided by the two adolescents, Jorge and Juan) to establish comparatively whether:

- spontaneous speech data yield the same orders as elicited BSM-based speech data;
- longitudinal data yield the same orders as cross-sectional data.

To start with the second question: the cross-sectionally obtained and longitudinally derived rank orders of the morphemes for one of the adolescents (Jorge) do *not* correlate.

In answer to the first question, Rosansky established the following rank correlations:

	Jorge (BSM)	Juan (Spontaneous)
Jorge (Spontaneous)	.088	− .50*
Juan (BSM)	.68*	.51

*p < .05

Fig. 5.13   Spearman rank correlations between the morpheme orders of Jorge and Juan for spontaneous speech and for the BSM (Rosansky 1976, 419)

There is a striking discrepancy between the boys on the BSM compared to their spontaneous speech: one order yields a positive and the other a negative correlation. Even more striking is the non-correlation of the BSM order and the spontaneous order for the same individual at the same point in time. Rosansky (1976:419) raises the question of whether the format of the BSM itself might not be somehow affecting the ordering of morphemes.

Nevertheless, the orders described in Dulay and Burt (1974c) have been confirmed to a high degree by a whole series of other morpheme studies. Krashen (1981:55 ff.) did a reanalysis of every morpheme study available, dealing with child L1 learners, child and adult L2 learners and adult agrammatics. He included both grouped and individual studies on the one hand, and longitudinal and cross-sectional studies on the other, but he did limit himself to morphemes with at least 10 obligatory occasions in a given study. In all studies in which language was used for communicative purposes and not for other linguistic tasks, an amazing degree of uniformity was found, resulting in the clustered order pattern shown in fig. 5.14.

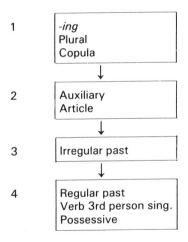

Fig. 5.14   Universal clustered order pattern for nine morphemes (Krashen 1981, 59)

The orders observed in most morpheme studies turn out to be invariant to a high degree, and therefore independent of the nature of the data collected (oral vs. written), independent of learner characteristics (L1 background, age), and independent of input characteristics (type/amount of ESL instruction).

Burt and Dulay (1980:288–96) observe that insofar as different orders in morpheme studies have been found, they have so far gone unexplained, or can be reduced to:

• variability in type of linguistic task:
  Larsen-Freeman's (1975) study shows that natural communication tasks yield a different type of data than 'linguistic manipulation' tasks do; in the latter case, the attention of the L2 learner is focused more on grammatical

form than on communication (see also Krashen 1981: 52);
- insufficient data for all subjects:
  when comparing the orders exhibited by subjects one must have enough examples of the structures whose order is being investigated for all subjects compared;
- level of proficiency of subjects:
  cross-sectional language data of learners with a very low or very high proficiency cannot provide a meaningful basis for making inferences about the development of, respectively, 'late', or 'early' structures;
- closeness of rank order scores:
  if the correct scores of structures are very close together (say, 82 and 84%, or 90 and 91%), these scores may not be ordered with respect to each other at all.

We wish to conclude our discussion of morpheme studies with the following five critical remarks:

(1) First of all, it has to be remarked that the list of orders presented in fig. 5.14. is very limited and out of proportion to the effort that has been put into this area of L2 research. To this we can add the observation that proposals for explaining the orders found are almost non-existent. Both Hatch (1974) and Larsen-Freeman (1976) have seriously occupied themselves with finding explanations for the order of acquisition and accuracy of morphemes. Factors that come to mind in this connection are formal complexity, perceptual saliency, or input frequency.

For the first factor, that of formal complexity, one has to bear in mind that the criteria for judging 'formal complexity' that we have at our disposal are extremely global, which confines us to drawing up global hypotheses about a development from 'simple' to 'complex'. In a discussion of possible explanations for acquisition orders in L1 development, Clark and Clark (1977:337–42) point to the vagueness of the underlying assumption: linguistic structures are formally complex when they exhibit irregularities as well as regularities. This criterion singles out, for instance, the past tense formation of English verbs as more complex than the possessive formation of nouns. The danger of a completely circular argumentation is, however, a very real one:
  (a) L2 learners acquire L2 structures in a certain order;
  (b) this order is a reflection of the relative formal complexity of these structures;
  (c) the formal complexity observed is then used to 'explain' L2 acquisition orders.
What is needed is, of course, an independent criterion for the notion of 'formal complexity', and what Clark and Clark (1977) show is that this is rather difficult to define.

As for the second factor, that of perceptual saliency, one could hypothesize, for instance, that syllabic morphemes are perceptually more salient to language learners than non-syllabic morphemes. From the order of accuracy observed by Dulay and Burt (1974c) we can conclude that the progressive /ing/ form is acquired quite early. On the other hand, we also find that non-syllabic plurals of nouns are acquired earlier than syllabic plurals.

Lastly, the third factor, that of input frequency. Although R. Brown (1973) observes no relation between L1 acquisition order of morphemes and their order of frequency in parental language input, Larsen-Freeman (1976) *does* find a certain similarity between the acquisition orders of the L2 learners she has observed (24 adults) and Brown's parental L1 order of frequency.

(2) None of these proposals for explanation is satisfactory. This raises the question of how useful it is to compare the morphemes which have been studied (see e.g. in R. Brown 1973: function words like *in* and *on* vs. bound /s/-morphemes). Dulay and Burt (1974c) separate out noun plurals into syllabic and non-syllabic (see fig. 5.12.), which R. Brown (1973) does not do, but, like R. Brown (1973), they treat definite and indefinite articles as constituting one category, that of 'article'. However, Andersen (1977:68-70) concludes that the articles *a* and *the* pose very different problems for learners. What we need, therefore, are more specific criteria for comparing morphemes in studies on language learning.

(3) In most morpheme studies with different groups of subjects more attention has been paid to the degree of similarity between groups than to the degree of similarity between individuals. The statistical procedures have tended to obscure the often considerable variation between individuals (see also Rosansky 1976:415-18, Andersen 1977).

(4) Also where morpheme studies are concerned it is the case that, in spite of the considerable variety of source languages involved, nearly all energy spent has gone into studying English as a target language. Claims about universal orders of acquisition will, however, have to be supported with data from morpheme studies involving other target languages. Extra (1978a), for instance, is a cross-sectional comparative study of order of accuracy of 10 morphemes (including articles, pronouns, final adjective marking, noun plurals and diminutives, and verb conjugation) for child learners of Dutch as L1, and Turkish adolescent learners of Dutch as L2. Not only was there a strong similarity in order of accuracy between the two groups, but also in the nature of the deviations from the target language norm.

(5) This brings us to our last point. The data-analysis in the morpheme studies available is primarily aimed at establishing the percentage of correct vs. incorrect realizations of various morphemes in obligatory contexts. Only very rarely does one find a discussion of the nature and causes of deviation from the L2 norm, or of the development of a specific morpheme, *before* it has been 'acquired' (but see Wode 1981:243-78). Through this bias towards the final result rather than towards the process of learning, morpheme order studies have tended to ignore those developments leading up to and preceding the final result (see also Wode 1981:64-5). Again, especially longitudinal studies can in these cases yield the required data.

5.1.4 Lexical development

Although the L2 speaker's lexicon determines to a large extent his possibilities of communication in the second language, research into lexical aspects of L2 learning is, in comparison with syntactic and morphological research, a severely neglected area. Also within contrastive analysis and error analysis the place reserved for lexical research has always been a modest one. One of the reasons which Levenston (1979:147–8) gives for this neglect is that the more interesting problems of lexical development do not emerge until relatively late in L2 development, whereas many studies on L2 learning have been concerned with the initial learner.

Levenston (1979:148 ff.) furthermore discusses a number of questions relating to L2 lexical development which need to be studied more seriously:

- to what extent are L1 and L2 vocabulary learning parallel processes?
- to what extent do personality characteristics affect the learning and use of vocabulary?
- by what stages, influenced by what factors, does the lexical stock of an L2 learner grow and expand?
- under what circumstances, and influenced by what factors, do (meanings of) words progress from being vaguely recognized to being accurately identified, and subsequently, from being sometimes produced to being fully utilized whenever required?
- do all words pass, and if so, how quickly, first from recognition into active production, or do some words enter directly into one's productive/receptive vocabulary, while others remain forever receptive?

Some of the relevant principles of learning L2 lexicon, as discussed by Levenston, may be formulated in the following ways:

(1) avoid two forms for what appears to be an identical meaning, given a referential situation (see also Ervin-Tripp 1974), e.g.:
L1 English *the* vs. L2 French $\begin{Bmatrix} la \\ le \end{Bmatrix}$ treated as synonymous

(2) try words which may be generalized to a large number of contexts, the result being overextension;

(3) avoid words which present semantic difficulty.

'Semantic difficulty' may be caused by the absence of a direct translation equivalent in L1, or by polysemy. Learners may avoid words in L2 with incompatible meanings, because they do not accept unreasonable polysemy, as in, for instance:

L1 Hebrew *levaqer* vs. L2 English $\begin{cases} to\ visit \\ to\ criticize: \text{avoided} \end{cases}$
L2 English *fast* $\begin{cases} \text{moving rapidly } (fast\ train) \\ \text{not moving at all } (hold\ fast): \text{avoided} \end{cases}$

The concept of 'avoidance' has been discussed earlier in 4.3.3. A problem with this concept is the obvious need to distinguish between the learner's conscious avoidance of L2 elements and his not yet having learned L2 elements. Avoidance presupposes choice: one cannot avoid what one has not learned. Certainly lexical avoidance is manifest in certain types of foreigner talk (see 5.2.1.), but in this case the language user will have more verbal means available than he considers appropriate for use in a given context. Similar remarks have been made in 4.3.3. in our discussion of the concept of 'simplification'.

Blum and Levenston (1978:401) attempt to get round this problem by distinguishing between 'apparent' avoidance (in L2 learner talk) and 'true' avoidance (e.g. in teacher talk). Largely on the basis of written translation tasks they describe 5 lexical principles according to which the L2 user 'makes do with few words'.

	Lexical principle	Realized	Expected*
(1)	usage of superordinate terms	*looked* *ran*	*gazed* *rushed*
(2)	approximation	*boy* *he hit*	*rebel* *he aimed a blow*
(3)	synonymy	*stayed* *chains*	*remained* *fetters*
(4)	transfer	see 4.3.2 sentences 22–40	
(5)	circumlocution or paraphrase	*didn't succeed* *failed* *she isn't married she is single*	

Fig. 5.15   Lexical principles in L2 use (*expected in written translation tasks)

The third principle may result in replacement of register-marked, infrequent words by unmarked, more frequent synonyms.

One of the very few longitudinal studies on L2 lexical development is Yoshida (1978). Yoshida studied the lexical development of a 3-year-old Japanese child learning English for a period of 7 months. In addition to observation of spontaneous L2 use, comprehension and production tests were administered in the 5th, 6th and 7th months, for which an adapted version of the Peabody Picture Vocabulary test was used. Not surprisingly, the subject's comprehension proved to be far superior to his production. As for production, he could use about 260 words after 7 months of exposure to English. The word-classes used most frequently after the 7-month period were (concrete) nouns (60.6 per cent), verbs (13 per cent), and modifiers like adjectives etc. (10.0 per cent). The other words were divided over many classes. In Japanese, there is a large collection of loan words from English, and generally these words are adapted to the Japanese phonological system. In as far as the child used such loan words in his English, some were pronounced in the 'English' way, and some in the 'Japanese' way. Finally, while the child was very explicit in choosing appropriate nouns, this was not the case for verbs. For expressing main verbs, the copulas *is/am/are* were used quite frequently, showing overextension of these forms, as in, for example:

realized	*intended*
Miki *is* long fish	Miki caught (saw?) a long fish
I *am* parade	I saw a parade
You *are* chocolate?	Do you have chocolate?

5.1.5 Phonological development

Within the tradition of contrastive analysis, phonology has received more attention than the lexicon. Evidence of phonological interference abounds in L2 use, and numerous reports of this phenomenon have appeared. Tarone (1978) offers a useful survey of this literature (showing transfer processes, but also other processes at work), and discusses physiological, psychological and socio-emotional explanations of phonological fossilization phenomena in adult L2 learning.

However, empirical *developmental* studies of phonology are as rare as empirical developmental studies of the lexicon. Tarone (1980) indicates four areas in which research on L2 phonology is necessary:

(1) developmental studies of segmental features (such as substitution of individual speech sounds for other speech sounds, or distortions of individual speech sounds) and suprasegmental features (such as stress, rhythm, intonation and syllabification);
(2) causes of phonological fossilization, especially with respect to advanced adult L2 learners;
(3) processes 'shaping' L2 phonology:
   which aspects of L2 phonology are most likely to be influenced by L1?
   to what extent are L1 and L2 learning of phonology similar and to what extent are they unique?
(4) variability in L2 phonology (pronunciation seems to be extremely sensitive to social situation) and instability of L2 phonology over time.

Garnica and Herbert (1979) have shown that phonological deviations from the L2 variety cannot always be looked upon as interference phenomena. They collected spontaneous and experimental data of American learners of Arabic, Polish and Russian in their first 10 weeks of L2 learning. Their study deals with approximately 100 non-interference deviations, which are categorized as follows:

- anticipation (labelled 'regressive sequential replacement');
  e.g. Russian / *paɲɛtnik* / (= cemetery monument) realized as /*paɲɪtnɪk*/;
- perseveration (labelled 'progressive sequential replacement');
  e.g. Polish / *kʃɛswo* /(= chair) realized as /*kʃɛʃwo*/;
- replacement;
  e.g. Polish / *robi* / (= to make) realized as /*rozi*/;
- metathesis;
  e.g. Russian / *raduga* / (= rainbow) realized as /*raguda*/.

Although Garnica and Herbert (1979) do not consider such a comparison appealing, these phenomena show considerable similarity to so-called 'slips of the tongue' in studies on the execution of speech plans by adult monolinguals (see Clark and Clark 1977:273–5 for a survey). With respect to anticipation, Garnica and Herbert (1979) found many more errors involving consonants than vowels. They hypothesize that this is due to vowels being the most prominent elements in the syllable, and therefore presumably the most salient elements perceived in language utterances. When he is under pressure to communicate, the learner seems to attend to utterances selectively, considering only certain phonetic features, and ignoring minor variations in the pronunciation of words or in the location of specific phonetic elements within the sequential arrangement of the word.

Tarone (1980) studied characteristics of English syllable structure in the L2 use of two Cantonese, two Portuguese and two Korean-speaking adults, on the basis of a picture description task. Whereas Portuguese and Cantonese are considered to be more or less 'open-syllable' languages (mostly of a /-CV/ type), Korean shows a much more complicated syllable structure, especially in its final consonant patterns. Although L1 transfer plays a dominant role in deviance from L2 syllable norms, at the same time an L1 independent universal preference for basic /-CV/ patterns is evidenced in two types of 'syllable simplification'; epenthesis (e.g. the addition of a final schwa in /blæŋkətə/), and deletion of final consonants, as, for instance, in /skuː/ (school).

In contrast to the two studies cited above, Wode (1981:207–42) gives a clearly defined developmental perspective on spontaneous phonological L2 phenomena. Wode describes the phonological development of four German-speaking children between 4 and 10 years old learning English as L2 in the US, and gives special attention to the development of /r/. While the development of other target phenomena may often be characterized as substitution of L2 phonemes by L1 phonemes, /r/ development (at least in initial or pre-vocalic position: /r-V/ or /Cr-V/) is rather more complex, and reflects the following stages for each of the four children:

substitution by uvular /R/;
e.g. *f/R/oggie,d/R/ink,/R/ight,*
substitution by /w/ (weak or no friction);
e.g. */w/eady,t/w/uck,T/w/inity,*
substitution by a central frictionless continuant /ɹ/;
e.g. *f/ɹ/ogs,/ɹ/ight,b/ɹ/oke,*
L2 target-like retroflex /r̠/;
e.g. *g/r̠/een,/r̠/ight,st/r̠/ike.*

Wode (1981:232 ff.) distinguishes two basic phonological processes in the learning of oral-productive L2 skills:

(1) if there is (enough) equivalence between L1 and L2 elements, it will be sufficient for L2 learners to substitute the familiar L1 elements in L2 speech;
(2) if there is non-equivalence between L1 elements and L2 elements, the

developmental process may mirror gradual L1 learning patterns to a considerable extent.

In both cases the L2 learner uses his mastery of L1 phonology as a basis. L2 phonological elements seem to be scanned by the L2 learner for equivalencies and non-equivalencies: L2 elements that are within the as yet unknown and crucial range of equivalence are matched and substituted by their respective L1 equivalents, whereas other L2 elements undergo developmental changes which are often parallel to changes in L1 learning. Wode furthermore shows, through comparison with older studies, that phonological processes in 'naturalistic' L2 learning (i.e. in an L2 environment) exhibit remarkable similarities to phonological processes in 'school' L2 learning (i.e. in an L1 environment). It seems that differences are mainly caused by knowledge of the orthographic system. However, in both types of L2 learning the 'typical' phonological errors differ systematically as a function of the phonological system of L1.

5.2 Discourse analysis

During the last few years, discourse analysis has assumed an increasingly important role within the study of language, mainly as a result of the growing need for linguistic analysis beyond the sentence level. A basic tenet of discourse analysis is that the study of language *in context* will offer a deeper insight into how meaning is attached to utterances than the study of language *in isolated sentences.*

The context of language may be considered both from a linguistic and from a social perspective:

- in most situations of language use, utterances will be preceded and followed by other utterances, resulting in a dialogic or monologic *text*;
- in all situations of language use, specific social relations between speaker and hearer will guide the structure of these utterances.

Hatch and Long (1980) and Brown (1980:189–207) give a survey of central research questions in discourse analysis and discuss such topics as a description of different (direct and indirect) speech acts in different communicative settings, and a description of conversational rules (e.g. in classrooms). Hatch and Long (1980:30) list several 'system constraints' for communication, such as back-channel feedback (informing that reception is occurring), turnover signals (indicating end of message, selection of next speaker), or norms à la Grice (1957, 1975: be relevant/informative/truthful/clear).

Although these constraints are universal, the way they are employed may vary between specific social, cultural, or linguistic groups (see James 1980:131–40 for a contrastive approach to some conversational rules).

Until now, the role of discourse analysis within the study of L2 learning and L2 use has been a modest one. Hatch (see especially Hatch 1978:401–35, Hatch and Long 1980) has been a poineer in this area. Larsen-Freeman (1980) is the first collection of discourse studies on L2 learning and use. Two journals have devoted special issues to this subject: *Applied Linguistics*, edited by Sinclair (1980), and *Jyväskylä Contrastive Studies*, edited by Sajaavara and Lehtonen

(1980). Furthermore, there is an analysis by Kasper (1981) of a number of conversational characteristics (initiating/responding speech acts, 'gambits', and opening/closing stages) of role play dialogues between native speakers of English and advanced German learners of English.

Until now, the attention has been focused mainly on the structure and function of native language input to non-native L2 learners. In 5.2.1., we shall consider the concept of 'foreigner talk'. This concept has been developed to describe the adjustments in the speech of a native speaker of a language who is in verbal contact with a non-native speaker or learner of that language. In 5.2.2., we shall discuss in a more eclectic way two conversational topics for which some evidence from L2 data exists: turn-taking and conversational correction.

5.2.1 Foreigner talk

The interest in the structure and function of 'foreigner talk' (henceforth FT) has developed subsequent to a similar interest in the linguistic input of adults to children learning L1 (see 3.2.3. for a survey of input characteristics).

Although the concept of FT goes back at least as far as Schuchardt (1909), the term itself was probably first used in Ferguson (1971a). The most common qualification of FT is 'simplification'. Here, simplification may be defined as adjustments intended to make utterances easier to understand. The term 'adjustments' draws our attention to two problems:

- in how far are these adjustments specific to the language use of native speakers (henceforth N) towards non-native (henceforth NN) speakers?
- in how far do these adjustments violate standard language rules?

As far as the first question is concerned, one would have to investigate whether such adjustments are restricted to N/NN conversations, or whether they could also be encountered in specific types of N/N conversation. This question can only be answered through controlled studies in which native speaker input to both Ns and NNs can be carefully compared. Such studies are extremely rare, however (but see Henzl 1973, and especially Arthur *et al.* 1980).

For the second question, Arthur *et al.* (1980:111–12) propose a distinction between FT and FR ('Foreigner Register'):

- FT may be characterized by rules either replacing or adding to rules which are characteristic of the structure of the standard language, while it is characteristic of FR that one finds modifications in the frequency or frequency range of various linguistic options available in the standard language;
- FT may be consciously used by the native speaker, whereas in the case of FR the degree of awareness and conscious control will be far lower.

As this distinction between FT and FR gives rise to a series of new questions (how can, for instance, the structure of spoken standard language be defined? How are degrees of consciousness to be defined?), and as in both cases we are still dealing with adjustments in the speech of Ns to NNs, we shall limit ourselves to giving a survey of such adjustments in various languages at various linguistic levels. Fig. 5.16. contains a classified account of observed FT strategies, based on Henzl (1973), Meisel (1975), Ferguson and DeBose (1977:100–7), Katz

Morphosyntactic strategies	Examples
(1) Avoid subordinate/embedded clauses, passive constructions, SV-inversion in interrogatives	Germ. *ich hören mehr geld für arbeit* Germ. *du verstehen was frau sagt?*
(2) Omit function words like art., prep., cop., aux., pers. pron.	Eng. *look on other side, listen me* Germ. *du schnell nach hause*

(3) Simplify category systems like:
  system of negation
  pronominal system
	
	Eng. *not/don't/didn't/won't > no(t)*
	Germ. *der/die/das > die*
	Germ. *sie/du > du**
	French *vous/tu > tu**
	Eng. *I/me > me*

inflectional noun/verb system:
  — use of inf. instead of conjug. V
  — deletion of final N/V marking
  — regularization of irregular N/V marking
  — avoidance of exceptional tenses (like future, conditional) or exceptional N/V marking
	
	Germ. *du auch blume essen?*

(4) Make discontinuous elements continuous	Germ. *wir gut aussehen*

(5) Produce well-formed utterances by avoiding:
  false starts
  unfinished sentences
  hesitation phenomena
  slips of the tongue	

(6) Produce short sentences by strategies mentioned under 1/2/4/5	

* Often as a result of 'talking down' to NN speakers who are felt to be socially inferior

Lexical strategies	Examples

(1) Restrict the diversity of vocabulary by avoiding:
  colloquial expressions, regionalisms, slang
  words with transferred meaning
  compound words
  idiomatic expressions
  or by overextended use of unmarked forms
	
	Eng. *have/be*, Germ. *haben/sein/tun/machen*

(2) Repeat words (or phrases)	

(3) Reformulate words by:
  using 'easier' synonyms
  circumlocutions or analytical paraphrases
	
	Eng. *aircraft > plane*
	Eng. *tomorrow > day after today*
	Germ. *ampel > rotes licht*

(4) Use confirmation-checking devices	Eng. *okay?, do-you-understand?*
(5) Use words which belong to the 'native stock' of the L2 learner	*amigo, capito?, compris?*

Phonological strategies	Examples
(1) Speak slowly* by: using many and/or long pauses between words/constituents avoiding reduced or contracted forms articulating separate words or even separate syllables/phonemes (see 3 below)	Eng. *he'll* > *he will* French *t'as compris?* > *tu as compris?*
(2) Speak loudly by: increasing the volume for key words	
(3) Speak with exaggerated pronunciation by: avoiding consonant cluster reduction inserting epenthetic vowels	Germ. *herbs* > *herbst* Eng. *I want (ɛ) this*
(4) Speak with exaggerated intonation	

* But see Arthur *et al.* 1980, 119

Fig. 5.16 Observed FT strategies at various linguistic levels

(1977:72-3), Clyne (1978:156), Hatch *et al.* (1978), Arthur *et al.* (1980), and Meisel (1980:18-24). In 1981 a special issue of the *International Journal of the Sociology of Language* (nr.28) was entirely devoted to FT. Henzl, Clyne, Hatch *et al.*, Arthur *et al.* and Meisel studied FT strategies in adult/adult conversations, while Katz's study is the only one which is based on child/child conversations. Henzl, and partially Hatch *et al.*, have selected a very specific kind of FT for their studies: teacher talk, i.e. the language input of teachers to L2 learners in classrooms. Henzl observed teacher talk strategies of adult native speakers of Czech addressing American NN learners of that language.

In a comparative study of NN learner talk of 35 migrant workers in Australia (L2 = English, 11 different L1s) and FT of 7 foremen speaking to them at work within 7 different industrial companies, Clyne (1978:156) demonstrates striking similarities between the two registers (see fig. 5.17.). Within both registers, the same 5 phenomena are predominant, albeit in different orders of frequency.

Hatch *et al.* (1978) also point out the similarities between the NN learner talk of Zoila (a Spanish-speaking learner of English) and FT of Rina (her American friend). A survey of the phenomena observed is presented in fig. 5.18. Furthermore, Hatch *et al.* (1978) found FT phenomena in the teacher talk of George, a teacher of English as L2 at a community adult school, which were very similar to Rita's FT and even more similar to Zoila's NN learner talk.

One question which keeps recurring in FT studies is that of who is adjusting his speech. Is FT an imitation of perceived NN learner talk or should NN learner talk be seen as a result of imitating FT? Meisel (1980:24-5) rejects both suggestions and stresses the fact that FT is not used in *all* N/NN contact situations: the language input of native speakers will show little (if any) traces of FT, if there is no clear hierarchical social order between native speaker and non-native speaker, and if the native speaker has met the non-native speaker before. Arthur

Observed phenomena	NN learner talk of migrant workers	FT of foremen
(1) Ellipsis	33 (8.75%)	13 (17.57%)
(2) Copula deletion	30 (8%)	11 (14.86%)
(3) Subject-pronoun deletion	76 (20.3%)	7 (9.46%)
(4) Incongruence, or generalizations of one verbal form	96 (25.6%)	17 (23.07%)
(5) Non-inversion of verb	2 (0.53%)	1 (1.35%)
(6) Aux-deletion	88 (23.5%)	14 (18.92%)
(7) Article deletion	25 (6.67%)	6 (8.11%)
(8) Object pronoun deletion	7 (1.87%)	2 (2.7%)
(9) *Me* for *I*	16 (4.27%)	—
For for *to*	1 (0.53%)	3 (4.05%)
	374	74

Fig. 5.17   Phenomena observed in NN learner talk and FT (Clyne 1978, 156)

Observed phenomena	Zoila NNLT	Rina FT	Examples
(1) Deletion of copula	+	−	*You jealous?*
(2) Deletion of *it*	+	+	*Is good for him*
(3) Lack of tense marking	+	+	*Everytime she come here*
(4) Deletion of progr. *-ing*	+	−	*So A. work now?*
(5) Deletion of *do*-marking	+	?	*She know about this?*
(6) Neg = *no* + V	+	+	*Is no old*
(7) Non-use of N poss. /s/	+	−	*The car de Carlo*

Fig. 5.18   Phenomena in NN learner talk and FT (based on Hatch *et al.* 1978)

et al. (1980:112) are of the opinion that in contemporary American society the persistent or public use of FT (at least FT violating standard language rules) among adults is extremely rare, because such use of FT would be considered to be condescending by native and non-native speakers alike.

The first longitudinal study (duration 11 months) of FT was carried out by Katz (1977). Katz registered, in biweekly sessions, the spontaneous verbal contacts between a five-year-old Hebrew child named Tamar, who was learning English as L2, and her American playmate and age-peer called Lisa. Katz notes the following interesting phenomena:

- the amount of FT across sessions is relatively low and fairly constant (between 2 and 19 per cent of all utterances of Lisa to Tamar);
- phonological FT features increase over time, while morphosyntactic FT features decrease (see Katz 1977:62–4 for possible explanations);
- on the other hand, the variety in morphosyntactic FT features increases over time;
- both NN learner talk and FT change over time but independently of each other.

Katz points out that Lisa's FT is not an exact reflection of how Tamar speaks, but rather of how she *thinks* that Tamar speaks. Several striking developmental phenomena in Tamar's speech do not show up at all in Lisa's FT (for example, the massive overextension of third person singular *she*).

5.2.2 Turn-taking and conversational correction

As we have already indicated in our introduction to section 5.2., we shall finally discuss in a more eclectic way two conversational topics for which some evidence from L2 data exists: turn-taking and conversational correction.

Turn-taking

Keller-Cohen (1979) studied turn-allocation (henceforth TA = turn-shifting in conversation between speakers) in verbal interaction between L1 English-speaking adults and three L2 English-speaking children of 4 and 5 years old (L1 = Japanese, Finnish and Swiss-German respectively). In all three cases, the adult/child interaction was videotaped, between 1–4 times a month, for eight months. The following pattern of TA devices of the L2-learning children emerged:

- TA devices were present in their speech from the beginning;
- the proportion of utterances containing TA devices nearly doubled or even tripled during the period of study;
- two general classes of TA devices were used: questions (WH-questions, and both inverted and non-inverted yes–no questions), and attention-directors (self-repetition, notice requests like *look/see/watch*, vocatives, imperatives, and markers of transfer/offering, such as *here*);
- the individual variation in the relative frequency of each of these devices over time was considerable.

For the L2 learner, the development of TA devices is of crucial importance, because such devices enable him to elicit information about the new code he is trying to learn. However, prior linguistic knowledge will facilitate the use of TA devices. On the basis of his knowledge of L1, an L2 learner will know that turns must be allocated in verbal interaction, and that there is a wide variety of TA techniques which may be used.

An analysis of turn-taking patterns in the classroom has been carried out by Allwright (1980). Allwright studied turn-taking behaviour in two groups of initial ESL-learning adults. His observations are based on audiotapes, collected in biweekly sessions, for a period of 10 weeks. Considerable attention is paid to the turn-taking patterns of one Russian learner of English, named Igor. The teacher called on him most, Igor did most of the discourse maintenance, and he requested turns most often. On the basis of a very detailed textual analysis, Allwright concludes that Igor's success in getting turns as frequently as he does depends more on an inability to make himself understood than on any ability to develop a topic. However, whether frequent turns in L2 learning behaviour indicate a lack rather than an abundance of communicative competence, must first be studied in different L2 learning situations, before any generalizations can be suggested.

Conversational correction

Verbal interaction involves all sorts of attempts at understanding and being understood. One important attempt is correction. In studying the role of correction in natural conversations, Schegloff *et al.* (1977) draw a distinction between self-correction and other-correction (henceforth SC and OC), depending on whether the correction is carried out by the speaker himself, or by someone else. While opportunities for SC occur more frequently than opportunities for OC, both phenomena are highly organized. Schegloff *et al.* discuss several characteristics of OC:

- OCs frequently occur after a pause; other speakers do not usually interrupt to make a correction;
- OCs are not generally emphatically asserted in a form like 'No + correction', but are frequently 'modulated' in such a way that they can be taken to display uncertainty (e.g. *I think . . ., Do you mean . . . .*);
- unmodulated OCs tend to occur in specific environments, for example after a rejection of a modulated OC, or after a statement or question to check understanding of utterances;
- OCs are frequently associated with disagreement: they often begin a sequence of conversation which has the effect of interrupting what was being said prior to the OC.

While the observations of Schegloff *et al.* are primarily based on native adult/adult conversations in English, Gaskill (1980) studied OC phenomena in conversations between an Iranian speaker of English and several native speakers of English, and obtained the following main results:

- OCs were relatively infrequent;
- OCs were modulated in that they displayed uncertainty;
- when OCs were unmodulated, they generally occurred after modulated OCs or understanding checks, or they occurred in the context of disagreement.

These results generally concur with those of Schegloff *et al.* for native speaker conversation.

Schwartz (1980) studied linguistic and extralinguistic characteristics of SC and OC in verbal interaction between non-native adult speakers of English from different L1 backgrounds. SC was announced by:

- lexical means, such as *I mean, you know*; e.g.:
  becuz I -I wanna take like you know I wanna take something to . . .
- nonlexical means, such as cutoffs (words which have not been fully articulated), pauses, uhs; e.g.:
  Hh yeah but you know what I always have a pro-some kind of problems. . . .
  Uh you uh could you uhh see uhh all the places?
- extralinguistic means, like changes in eye gaze, or hand movements.

The following observations about the structure of SCs and OCs were made:

self-correction:

- word replacement, e.g.:
  We talked about this school – university
- rearrangement, e.g.:
  Wha-what kind of English do they – what do they say?

other-correction:

- modified repetition:
  A: *Where did you buy your clothes?*
  B: *Where did I buyed it?*
- question words querying an entire proposition; e.g.:
  hmm? what? where? when?
- partial repetitions (sometimes plus additional question word), e.g.:
  About five hours? Too many whát?
- you mean + reformulation, e.g.:
  Yesterday? You mean after school?

5.3 Conclusion

In chapters 4 and 5 we have subsequently discussed contrastive analysis, error analysis, performance analysis, and discourse analysis. In the first section of chapter 4 we have introduced this historically motivated order, indicating that this order reflects the changes in our perspective on the L2 learner over time. In retrospect, we see that these changes in perspective have been accompanied by an explosive growth of the literature. Nevertheless, these changes should not be interpreted as providing the solution of problems signalled at the preceding levels of analysis.

Also at the beginning of chapter 4, we have made the following distinction between structural and temporal factors in L2 learning processes:

- the *structure/order* of L2 learning processes is determined to a large extent by general cognitive abilities and shows remarkable similarities under highly dissimilar L2 learning conditions: in all cases, L2 learners are faced with a similar task (i.e. to develop a hierarchically structured system of subskills), and seem to be using comparable operating principles (see 3.2.3. and 4.3.2.) to carry out that task;
- the *speed/success* of L2 learning processes, on the other hand, varies strongly between individuals, and is determined by social and psychological conditions of the L2 learner and his environment.

Although this distinction between structural and temporal factors is an important one, it is hardly ever made in the literature on L2 learning. This is, for example, illustrated by the discussion of the age-factor in L2 learning (see McLaughlin 1978a:47–71 for a survey): this discussion focuses on the question whether children learn *faster* than adults rather than on the at least equally important question whether and to what extent learning by children is a *different* process from learning by adults.

Chapters 4 and 5 have been mainly devoted to *structural* factors in L2 learning processes. We have to conclude that the attention paid to this particular aspect of L2 learning and use in the discourse studies carried out so far has been minimal.

In addition, we have paid some attention to *temporal* aspects of L2 learning. These temporal aspects have featured especially in 5.1.2. in our discussion of the Heidelberger Forschungsprojekt and in our discussion of Schumann's (1978c) case study of Alberto. It can easily be observed that there may be considerable variation in the degree of success with which people (learn to) use an L2. This leads to the question of what causes (lack of) success in L2 learning. Two types of factors come to mind in this connection: *learner* characteristics (such as attitude, motivation, age, personality) and *environmental* characteristics (such as the nature and degree of contact with native speakers, socio-economic status, the quality of L2 instruction).

The above factors usually do not operate independently of each other, and it is, therefore, impossible to study them in complete isolation. Furthermore, in so far as there have been studies of temporal factors (see e.g. Naiman *et al.* 1978, Schumann 1978c:69–100, Klein and Dittmar 1979:97–100, 198–209), such studies have hardly ever covered a period of more than 12 months. Consequently, as yet little is known about possible causes of retardation, stagnation or regression in L2 learning behaviour, phenomena which have been observed quite regularly, however.

In chapter 6 our focal point will be learner characteristics, which are often taken to be among the main causes of temporal differences in L2 learning.

6
Learner characteristics

6.1 Introduction

In the previous chapters we have attempted to outline the processes involved in L2 learning. We have concluded that the *structure* of the L2 learning processes under highly dissimilar learning conditions shows certain remarkable similarities. We have also concluded that, in spite of the similarities in the structure/order of the L2 learning processes, there may be considerable variation in the *speed* and *degree of success* with which a second language is learned. The two most important types of factors which influence speed/success in L2 learning probably are: *environmental* characteristics such as the ones mentioned in 5.3., and *learner* characteristics. On the basis of a series of studies of L2 learning Jakobovits (1970:98) suggests that the latter factors determine speed/success to a far greater degree than other factors. Learner characteristics, according to Jakobovits, play a dominant role in determining and predicting L2 learning speed/success.

There are two traditional conceptions about L2 learning which are relevant to a discussion of learner characteristics:

- children are better L2 learners than adults;
- there is such a thing as a special 'knack' or 'talent' for L2 learning – *aptitude* in the jargon – which not everybody possesses to the same degree.

It was apparently assumed on the basis of personal experience that differences in success in L2 learning could be explained to a large extent on the basis of differences in age and aptitude. When in the 1950s scientific research into the role of learner characteristics in L2 learning was started, it soon became clear that a whole host of learner characteristics is responsible for relative success or failure in L2 learning. See e.g. the taxonomies of Schumann (1976:15), Yorio (1976:61), Swain (1977:16), brought together in Brown (1980:247–9), and Schumann (1978b:164). In this chapter, we shall restrict ourselves to some of the better-researched and/or most relevant characteristics. Furthermore, we shall restrict ourselves to those characteristics which are particular to L2 learning. For this reason we shall, for instance, not devote any attention to intelligence. We shall deal, in that order, with the role of the age of the learner (6.2), the role of aptitude (6.3), the role of cognitive style (6.4), and the role of a number of affective characteristics (6.5), such as attitude, motivation and personality characteristics separately, although they are certainly related to a degree. For example, an integrative motivation to learn a second language presupposes a positive attitude towards speakers of that language, and a field dependent cognitive style is often found to co-occur with an empathic personality.

6.2 Age

It has been widely observed that children learn second languages more easily and more proficiently than do adults. After settling in another language community, children seem to be very efficient in picking up the new language, whereas their parents often seem to experience great difficulty in acquiring the same level of L2 proficiency as their children. This widely observed phenomenon has led to the hypothesis that there is such a thing as an *optimal age*, or a *critical period* (Lenneberg 1967), or a *sensitive period* (Oyama 1976) for L2 learning. In this section we will first review some of the main arguments – biological, cognitive, affective – that have been put forward as support for the notion of a critical period and then examine to what extent the critical period hypothesis is upheld by evidence from L2 learning studies (see also McLaughlin 1978a:47–59).

6.2.1 The critical period hypothesis

6.2.1.1 The biological argument

The first impetus for a discussion about the existence of a biologically based optimal age for language learning was given by the neurologists Penfield and Roberts. They argued that the child's greater ability to learn a language could be explained by the greater plasticity of its brains. This brain plasticity was found to decrease with age; Penfield and Roberts (1959) cited evidence that children have a remarkable capacity for re-learning language skills after injury or disease destroys the speech areas in the dominant cerebral hemisphere, usually the left hemisphere. Adults often do not recover normal speech. There are numerous cases of young children who, on incurring a lesion in the speech areas, transfer their language functions to the opposite hemisphere. Cases of adults doing this are rare. The reason for this, it is argued, is loss of brain plasticity. In their conclusion, Penfield and Roberts (1959:255) derive the following recommendation for FLT from these observations:

> The time to begin what might be called a general schooling in secondary languages, in accordance with the demands of brain psychology, is between the ages of 4 and 10.

The critical period hypothesis (CPH) is, however, usually associated with Lenneberg (1967). Lenneberg (1967:175–82) argued that natural language learning 'by mere exposure' can take place only during the 'critical period for language acquisition', roughly between age 2 and puberty. Before 2, language learning is impossible due to lack of maturation of the brain, while by the time of puberty lateralization of the language function to the dominant hemisphere is complete, resulting in the loss of cerebral plasticity needed for natural language learning. It is this biologically determined period that is responsible for the fact that after puberty languages 'have to be taught and learned through a conscious and laboured effort' and that 'foreign accents cannot be overcome easily after puberty' (Lenneberg 1967:176). Basing himself on Lenneberg's arguments for a critical period, Scovel (1969:252) takes the view that it is impossible for adults to master a language without a foreign accent, and suggests that it would be futile for teachers to try to rid students of their foreign accents.

Lenneberg (1967) cites two kinds of data in support of his argument that lateralization for language is complete by puberty: data from unilateral brain damage in children and adults, and data from hemispherectomies (surgical removal of an entire destroyed or diseased hemisphere). The data on unilateral brain damage suggest that right-sided lesions cause aphasia more often in children between ages 2 and 10 than in adults: of the 20 cases of speech disturbances in children reported by Basser (1962), 7 were from right-sided lesions, or 35 per cent. The percentage for adults is only 3 per cent, mainly accounted for by left-handed patients (Lenneberg 1967:151–2). From this it was concluded that lateralization is not complete until after age 10. The evidence from hemispherectomies, culled from Basser's (1962) survey of the literature, also suggests that children are less lateralized than adults. Left hemispherectomy of adults invariably caused aphasic symptoms, whereas in cases of right hemispherectomy no speech disturbance resulted. The picture is very different for children. Neither left nor right hemispherectomy for lesions incurred before teens, resulted in aphasia. This suggests that complete transfer of the language function from the diseased to the healthy hemisphere is only possible as long as lateralization is not complete. On completion of lateralization complete transfer is no longer possible (Lenneberg 1967:152–3).

Lenneberg's account of the process of lateralization has come under fire, however. Krashen (1973) reanalysed Basser's (1962) data on the effects of unilateral brain damage and hemispherectomy and concluded that all cases of right-sided lesions resulting in aphasia, and of left hemispherectomies with no resultant speech disorders, involved children younger than age 5. Krashen (1973) also reviewed the literature on dichotic listening research. In dichotic listening, subjects are presented with competing simultaneous auditory stimuli, one to each ear. Normally the right ear excels for verbal stimuli, reflecting left hemispheric specialization. The evidence from dichotic listening tests shows children of age 4 to have the same degree of right-ear superiority as children of age 9, which suggests that lateralization may even be complete by age 4 (Krashen 1973:66–7). If, as Lenneberg maintains, there is a direct link between the CPH and the development of lateralization, successful language learning should not be possible after age 4. Yet, L1 learning studies have shown language development to be far from complete by that age. More recently, the link between Lenneberg's critical period and lateralization has been shown to be even more tenuous: on the basis of experiments it has been suggested (see e.g. Molfese *et al.* 1975, Kinsbourne 1975) that the brain may be lateralized from birth. The CPH has also been put to a severe test by the case of Genie, an adolescent girl who endured $11\frac{1}{2}$ years of extreme social and experiential deprivation and who, on her emergence from isolation at the age of 13, began to acquire language *ex nihilo* (see Fromkin *et al.* 1974, Curtiss 1977).

As we have seen, according to Lenneberg (1967), the development of lateralization brings about specialization of function, with verbal functions located almost exclusively in the dominant hemisphere. On the completion of lateralization, the brain loses the plasticity required for efficient language learning. Recent research on age-dependent aphasia, however (see Seliger 1978 for a summary), has shown this view to be too simplistic. Lesions in the same area of the brain appeared to result in different aphasic symptoms, depending on the age of the patient. This would indicate that there is a continuing process of further specialization or localization of particular language functions in specific areas of the left hemisphere, continuing over most of one's lifetime. This has led Seliger (1978:16) to posit the existence of 'many critical periods, successive and perhaps overlapping, lasting probably throughout one's lifetime, each closing off different acquisition abilities'. Such a 'multiple critical periods hypothesis' could account for the alleged inability of adult L2 learners to master a native accent without a concomitant decrease in the ability to master L2 syntax and lexicon. Walsh and Diller (1981:18) argue that children may be superior in the area of pronunciation, because 'lower-order processes such as pronunciation are dependent on the early maturing and less adaptive macroneural circuits', whereas 'higher-order language functions, such as semantic relations, are more dependent on the late maturing neural circuits . . .'.

Theories on the neurophysiology of language learning reported so far have been almost exclusively based on evidence from experiments with monolinguals and from case studies of aphasic monolinguals. In a review of the literature pertaining to language lateralization in bilingualism, Albert and Obler (1978) presented evidence suggesting greater right lateralization, or less severe left lateralization, of language in the bilingual. Obler (1981), reporting the results of a study involving Hebrew-speaking schoolchildren at three different levels of proficiency in English, suggested that the right hemisphere may be more involved during the initial stages of L2 learning than in later stages. F. Carroll (1980), however, in a study of English-speaking adults enrolled in Spanish classes at three different levels of proficiency, reported no significant right hemisphere processing of the language being learned at any of the three levels, and in a recent review of experimental research on L2 processing Genesee (1982) concluded that there was little evidence of greater right hemisphere involvement during the early stages of L2 learning. Both F. Carroll (1980) and Galloway and Krashen (1980) hypothesize that the high degree of left hemisphere processing of the L2 in Carroll's subjects might be attributed to the formal classroom setting with its emphasis on conscious learning. Genesee's (1982) survey provides some support for this hypothesis. The studies reviewed by him show there to be greater right hemisphere involvement in L2 processing in bilinguals who learn the L2 in informal contexts. Other studies (for recent reviews see Vaid and Genesee 1980, Galloway 1981) have provided evidence suggesting that there may be modality effects on lateralization, reading and writing contributing to greater left lateralization. It is true, language lateralization in bilingualism is a relatively new field of research and many issues have not been decided, but it seems safe to conclude that the right hemisphere can make significant contributions to L2 learning and that the evidence for a biological barrier to successful language learning is lacking (see also Krashen 1981:81).

6.2.1.2 Other arguments

As the biological argument could not offer a satisfactory explanation for the alleged superiority of children over adults in L2 learning, other arguments, cognitive and affective, were advanced in support of the CPH. Rosansky (1975) and Krashen (1975) are exponents of the cognitive argumentation. It is argued that the onset of the stage of 'formal operations', in Piaget's sense, marks the beginning of the end of the critical period. At the onset of formal operations, the adolescent develops a capacity for abstract thought and is able to reflect on the (linguistic) rules he uses. He is able to step back, as it were, and look at his own linguistic behaviour from a distance. This meta-awareness allows the learner to create abstract theories of the language he is learning and thus blocks, it is suggested, the natural process of L2 learning. Taylor (1974) and Schumann (1975) link the notion of a critical period with the affective changes that occur in the learner at the onset of puberty. It is argued that children have a greater empathic capacity (the capacity to put oneself in someone else's shoes, see 6.5.2.) than adults, that children have not yet developed inhibitions about their self-identity, and are, therefore, not afraid to sound ridiculous and are prepared to take risks when experimenting with their as yet far from perfect L2 knowledge. Very young children are not yet hampered in their L2 learning by negative attitudes towards speakers of that language and children generally have a strong integrative motivation to learn the language (see 6.5.1.2.). This means that children characteristically approach the task of learning with a low 'socio-affective filter' (Dulay and Burt 1978).

On the other hand, it can be argued that adults have some cognitive and affective advantages over children, especially when languages are learned in classroom situations with much emphasis on formal correctness. Adults have a greater memory storage capacity, a greater capacity for analytic reasoning and can develop a strong instrumental motivation, qualities which can lead to very effective learning in such situations (see e.g. Stern 1963, Ausubel 1964).

Instead of speculating any further on the relative strengths of the arguments advanced, we will now examine whether there is any empirical evidence for the CPH.

6.2.1.3 Empirical evidence

In accordance with the CPH one would expect children to be faster L2 learners than adolescents and adults. The empirical evidence available, however, presents a rather different picture.

In a study of 140 children (ages 6–15) learning English in the US Fathman (1975b) found that the younger children (ages 6–10) were better at pronunciation, whereas the older children (ages 11–15) outperformed the younger children on a test of morphology and syntax. Ramirez and Politzer (1978) studied children learning English in kindergarten and grades 1, 3 and 5 of the elementary school, who had all entered school at kindergarten level as practically monolingual spea. s of Spanish, and two groups of junior and senior high-school students (ages 13–17), one group of which consisted of students who had newly arrived in the US (A1). The other group (A2) was made up of students who had been in the US for one year. A comprehension and production test, consisting of 14 grammatical categories, was administered to all groups. After six months the A1 group was nearly at the level of the third graders, who had started L2 English at kindergarten level. In a study of L2 learners of French from grades 1, 3 and 5 of the elementary school and grades 7 and 9 of the junior high-school, who did not know any French prior to the study, Politzer and Weiss (1969) found that pronunciation improved with the age of the subjects. In an experimental study comparing 20 elementary, 20 junior high, and 20 college students on a test of 33 German phonemes, Olson and Samuels (1973) found that the junior high and college groups did significantly better after two weeks of pronunciation instruction. In a laboratory study with 136 English-speaking subjects (ages 5–31) learning Dutch (Snow and Hoefnagel-Höhle 1977), the older learners also outperformed the younger learners on a pronunciation task. Snow and Hoefnagel-Höhle (1978a, 1978b) also studied 96 English-speaking subjects (age range 3–15, and adults) learning Dutch in the Netherlands in a natural setting. The measures included pronunciation, listening comprehension, morphology, vocabulary, sentence reproduction and translation tasks and were administered 3 times at 4, 5 month intervals. The 3 to 5-year-olds scored consistently worse than the older groups on all the tests and the 12 to 15-year-olds showed the fastest progress. Differences between the groups diminished, however, over time, especially for pronunciation. It is tentatively suggested that the superiority of the 12 to 15-year-olds over the adults in this study might be accounted for by environmental factors, favouring the former (Snow and Hoefnagel-Höhle 1978a:343).

The general picture that emerges from the studies reported so far (see also Krashen *et al.* 1979) is not in agreement with the predictions of the CPH: adolescents and adults are better L2 learners than children, especially in the areas of morphology, syntax and vocabulary. The picture is not entirely clear with reference to pronunciation: advantages of children over older learners have been found, but mostly in studies of L2 learning in an L2 environment, which suggests that other factors than the age factor as such may be involved. It should, however, be noted that the interpretation of the results of the studies mentioned so far as well as those discussed below, is somewhat hampered by the possibility that the tests employed may have favoured older learners over younger ones. Generally, the same tasks were administered to both young and older learners. The latter group's higher scores could conceivably be partly attributable to their greater 'testpertise' rather than to their superiority in language skills.

In a review of L2 learning studies Krashen *et al.* (1979) conclude that, although adolescents and adults have an initial advantage over children, it is the latter group that eventually attains the highest level of achievement. The material for this conclusion was provided by such studies as Asher and Garcia (1969) and Oyama (1976, 1978). Asher and Garcia (1969) studied 71 Cuban immigrants (ages 7–19), most of whom had been in the US for about 5 years, and found an inverted relationship between age of arrival in the US and pronunciation: those who had arrived between ages 1 and 6 were closest to native speaker level. Oyama (1976) arrived at similar conclusions in a study involving 60 Italian immigrants, who had arrived in the US between ages 6–20. Those who had arrived between ages 6–10 had better accents than the later arrivals. Virtually no effect for length of residence in the US was found. The group who had arrived in the US before age 10 was also superior on a listening comprehension test (Oyama 1978). It should, however, be noted that these studies all involve subjects learning English as L2 in an L2 environment. Our review of a number of FLES–experiments in different countries (see 9.2.4.2.) shows the picture to be quite different when the language is learned in an L1 environment.

The claim made by the CPH that it is impossible for adults to master a native-like accent in a new language has recently been tested by Neufeld (1977, 1978b, 1979). In a carefully controlled laboratory experiment Neufeld trained 20 Canadian students (ages 19–22) in the production of a number of Japanese, Chinese and Eskimo sound patterns via 18-hour individualized instruction pro-grammes for each language. Subjects' performance on a repetition task was judged by 3 native speakers each of Japanese or Chinese who had experience teaching their first language (no native judges of Eskimo were available). Nine subjects were judged to be native speakers of Japanese and eight native speakers of Chinese, which, in Neufeld's view, suggests that adults have not lost their original ability to achieve a perfect accent. The relevance of this study seems limited, however, in that subjects were given no clue as to the meaning or gram-matical structure of the sound patterns they were taught to produce. In fact, it could be argued that Neufeld's study has shown only that adults have not lost the ability to imitate sounds (see also Neufeld and Schneiderman 1980).

To conclude, the empirical evidence does not support the CPH. Those studies which showed children to be better learners of – some aspects of – an L2, have usually been directed at L2 learning in an L2 environment. This would suggest that not age as such, but the learning situation in combination with age-related affective and cognitive factors (see 6.2.1.2.) could account for some of the variation in success between child and adult L2 learning.

6.3 Aptitude

It is a fairly common assumption that there is such a thing as a special 'talent', 'knack', 'gift', or *aptitude* for L2 learning, which some learners possess to a greater extent than others and which is to a large extent responsible for indi-vidual differences in L2 learning success. A discussion of this learner charac-teristic as a variable in L2 learning is, however, severely hampered by a lack of consensus in the literature as to what constitutes this special talent for L2 learning, if, indeed, it exists at all.

Of course, as Neufeld (1978a:17) observes, 'linguistic aptitude as such most certainly exists, for without it language learning as we know it would be quite impossible'. All normal children are born with the ability to learn languages. More interesting, however, than the question whether there is such a thing as lin-guistic aptitude are the questions whether people vary in the degree to which they possess this ability and whether there exists a special L2 learning ability distinct from an L1 learning ability. Neufeld (*op. cit.*) argues, on the basis of the literature on early L1 learning, that the variation in L1 learning success among pre-school children is not such that it can only be accounted for by differences in linguistic aptitude. People do, however, seem to differ considerably as to the ultimate level of skill they reach in their native language. The fact that some people become highly competent L1 users whereas others do not, can perhaps only be accounted for by positing a special language learning ability, which some people have and others do not have. When compared with L1 learners, L2 learners do not only seem to differ considerably with respect to success in mastering high levels of skill in the target language, but also with respect to mastering more basic components of the target language.

How can one account for such considerable individual differences? Do some learners have a special *second* language learning ability which others do not have? Or can the individual differences be accounted for by other factors, such as the learning environment, method of teaching, course content, the learner's attitude and motivation, his personality and his cognitive style? Neufeld (1978a, 1979) – and we are inclined to go along with him – considers the second position to be the more plausible of the two. It is Neufeld's view that the ability to learn languages, whether first or second, is innate and does not differ significantly from individual to individual, that is to say, the ability to master the more basic components of language skill. Neufeld (1978a:21) is inclined to think that there is considerable variation in the innate ability to master the higher levels of skill in a language, first or second. In his view, factors like verbal and non-verbal intelligence are important here, which is another way of saying that a special talent for languages does not exist independently of the intelligence factor.

The position that learners differ in the degree to which they possess a special talent for L2 learning has traditionally been associated with the names of Carroll and Pimsleur. After five years of intensive research (see Carroll 1958, 1962), Carroll and Sapon (1959) published the *Modern Language Aptitude Test* (MLAT), which proved to be a successful predictor of L2 learning success in colleges and universities. Also after five years of research (see Pimsleur 1961, Pimsleur *et al.* 1962, Pimsleur *et al.* 1964), Pimsleur (1964) published another test of a similar predictive power, the *Language Aptitude Battery* (LAB). For a recent review of research on language aptitude see Carroll (1981). Before examining whether these tests provide any insight into the nature of L2 learning talent, it should be noted that the research had not been primarily concerned with identifying the components of this talent, but with attempting to predict success in foreign language courses. It is of course perfectly legitimate for tests aiming at predicting L2 learning success to contain subtests which do not measure L2 learning ability, as long as they contribute to the predictive validity of the test.

Carroll (1962:128–30) believed that he had identified four independent abilities constituting L2 learning talent:

(1) Phonetic coding ability – 'the ability to "code" auditory phonetic material in such a way that this can be recognized, identified, and remembered over something longer than a few seconds'.
(2) Grammatical sensitivity – the ability to recognize the grammatical function of words in sentence contexts.

(3) Inductive language learning ability – 'the ability to infer linguistic forms, rules and patterns from new linguistic content itself with a minimum of supervision or guidance'.

(4) Rote memorization ability – 'the ability to learn a large number of associations in a relatively short time'.

This last component is no longer mentioned in later publications (Carroll 1973, 1977), and will, therefore, not be considered here. The MLAT consists of five subtests: (1) number learning; (2) phonetic script; (3) spelling clues; (4) words in sentences; (5) paired associates. Phonetic coding ability is chiefly measured by the 'phonetic script' subtest, which involves the association of graphic symbols with speech sounds and is, in fact, a test of both sound–symbol association and auditory discrimination. Grammatical sensitivity is tapped by the 'words in sentences' subtest, which asks the testee to pick the word or phrase in one sentence that 'does the same thing' in that sentence as the capitalized word in another sentence, e.g.:

(1) He spoke VERY well of you
(2) *Suddenly the* music became *quite loud*
    1   2   3   4

Carroll (1962, 1977) suggested that this may be a learned trait and Gardner and Lambert (1965) found success on this test to be highly related to general academic achievement, which suggests that this subtest also tests reasoning skills in addition to, or, perhaps, rather than language aptitude. Inductive language learning ability is 'not measured to any appreciable degree' (Carroll 1962:130) by the MLAT, but it is suggested that this is the same kind of ability that is measured by tests of inductive reasoning, and is, therefore, closely associated with intelligence (Carroll 1977:8). All this suggests that phonetic coding ability may be the only specific component of linguistic aptitude incorporated in the MLAT.

Pimsleur (1966:182) distinguishes three components of language aptitude:

(1) Verbal intelligence, by which is meant both familiarity with words and the ability to reason analytically about verbal materials.
(2) Motivation.
(3) Auditory ability.

The LAB consists of six subtests: (1) Grade Point Average (GPA); (2) Interest; (3) Vocabulary; (4) Language Analysis; (5) Sound Discrimination; (6) Sound–Symbol. Verbal intelligence is measured by the third and fourth subtests. The vocabulary subtest measures knowledge of L1 vocabulary and can, therefore, hardly be said to tap L2 aptitude. The 'language analysis' subtest, in fact, makes heavy demands on the examinee's inductive reasoning ability and is, therefore, not a pure test of linguistic aptitude. The second component distinguished by Pimsleur, motivation, which is tapped by the 'interest' subtest, operates as an independent factor in L2 learning, as will be seen in 6.5. With the third component, auditory ability, which is measured by the last two subtests of the LAB, Pimsleur *et al.* (1964) believe to have identified the single factor which lies at the core of the 'talent' for L2 learning, operating independently of intelligence and motivation.

We are inclined to believe that the factor of auditory ability, which is also measured in the MLAT, is, indeed, a major component of linguistic aptitude, but it remains to be shown that this factor operates in L2 learning differently than in L1 learning. In other words, it has yet to be shown that there are two different linguistic aptitudes, one for L1 learning and one for L2 learning. To conclude this discussion, there is not much insight to be gained from existing aptitude tests into what constitutes a special L2 aptitude, if it exists at all. What these tests do is predict success in foreign language courses rather than measure language aptitude. In fact, these tests might better be termed prognostic tests rather than aptitude tests.

Both the MLAT and the LAB have been widely used. A short version of the former, intended for use in elementary schools, was published in 1967 – the EMLAT (Carroll and Sapon). A German adaptation of this version, the *Fremdsprachen-Eignungstest für die Unterstufe* (FTU 4–6), was prepared by Correll and Ingenkamp (1967). There is also an Italian version of the MLAT, prepared by Ferencich (1964), and a Japanese one (Murakami 1974). Carroll (1981) also mentions versions in French, Spanish, Turkish and Thai. Scores on these tests have tended to correlate highly with success in foreign language classes. Nevertheless, the predictive validity of these tests is not such that one could confidently conclude that an individual with high scores on an aptitude test will necessarily be a good language learner or one with low scores a poor one. L2 learning success also depends on a host of other factors, some of which are discussed in this chapter. Culhane (1970), Schütt (1974), Green (1974) and Scheibner-Herzig *et al.* (1977), who, among others, investigated the predictive validity of different versions of the MLAT, rightly concluded that it would be ill-advised to select pupils for or exclude them from foreign language study on the basis of aptitude test scores alone.

6.4 Cognitive styles

It was not until fairly recently (see H. Brown 1973) that L2 learning researchers began to look to the already extensive body of literature on cognitive styles, also termed learning styles, for possible explanations of individual differences in L2 learning success. Cognitive style has been defined by Ausubel (1968:170) as 'self-consistent and enduring individual differences in cognitive organization and functioning'. A fair number of different cognitive styles have been identified in the literature (see e.g. Ausubel 1968:171, Messick 1976:14–21, Kogan 1971), but so far fairly little research has been done on cognitive styles in L2 learning. In this paragraph we will, therefore, limit ourselves to discussing three major cognitive style dimensions which seem to be relevant to L2 learning: field independence/dependence, reflectivity/impulsivity and broad/narrow category width. For information on additional cognitive styles and their possible relevance to L2 learning see Naiman *et al.* (1978) and Brown (1980:89–99). Before discussing the three styles mentioned we would like to raise some general points on the issue of cognitive styles. First of all, although many different cognitive styles have been identified in the literature, there exists suspicion that in some cases researchers have used different tests and different labels for traits that seem largely identical (see e.g. McDonough 1981:130). Boekaerts (1979:158), in fact, argues that there are strong similarities between the first two cognitive style dimensions discussed below. Secondly, on the basis of their scores on cognitive style tests individuals are usually labelled *either* field independent *or* field dependent, or *either* reflective *or* impulsive, etc.. Such a discussion ignores the possibility that an individual may approach different learning tasks in different ways, adapting his cognitive style to the demands of the task (for an excellent discussion see Brown 1980:89 ff.) Thirdly, it can hardly be argued that cognitive style is strictly a matter of cognition only. It extends beyond the cognitive domain into other domains usually subsumed under 'personality' (see Witkin *et al.* 1977:10, Brown 1980:90).

Field independence and dependence

Among the cognitive styles identified so far, field independence/dependence has been the most extensively studied (for an overview see Witkin *et al.* 1962, Witkin *et al.* 1977). A field independent person tends to perceive analytically, that is, he tends to perceive particular relevant items in a 'field' as discrete from the surrounding field as a whole, rather than embedded in the field. A field dependent person tends to perceive globally; his perception tends to be dominated by the total field such that the parts embedded in the field are not easily perceived (Witkin *et al.* 1977:6-7). Field independence/dependence is usually measured by one of the various forms of the Embedded Figures Test (EFT; see Witkin *et al.* 1971). This test asks the testee to locate a simple figure within a larger complex figure (the 'field') in which it is embedded. Those testees who have little difficulty in locating the simple figure are labelled field independent and those who have great difficulty field dependent. Certain personality traits appear to covary with this cognitive style. It has been found that field dependent persons tend to show a strong 'social orientation' (Witkin *et al.* 1977:11); they are usually more empathic and more perceptive of feelings of others. Field independent persons, on the other hand, tend to show an 'impersonal orientation' (Witkin *et al.* 1977:13); they are generally individualistic and less aware of the things by which others are moved. As Brown (1980:91-2) observes, two conflicting hypotheses could be advanced with reference to L2 learning on the basis of these findings. First, it could be hypothesized that the field independent person is the better L2 learner, as he would be better able to focus on the relevant variables in a language lesson or a conversation than a field dependent person. This hypothesis was supported by the results of the Toronto study of the 'good language learner' (Naiman *et al.* 1978), in which field independence was found to correlate positively and significantly with L2 learning success in the classroom. In other studies, too (Tucker *et al.* 1976, Genesee and Hamayan 1980, Hansen and Stansfield 1981), field independence was found to correlate positively with L2 learning success in the classroom. It could also be hypothesized, however, that field dependent persons are, in virtue of their social orientation and greater empathy, superior L2 learners (see also 6.5.2.). Indeed, some pilot studies of field independence/dependence (see Brown 1977, 1980:92) indicated that field dependence correlated quite highly with a test of language proficiency in the case of adult English-learners in the US. Brown (1977, 1980) speculates that field independence may be more important in traditional classroom settings with a strong emphasis on analytical activities and that field dependence may be more important in the natural setting.

Reflectivity and impulsivity

Although this cognitive style has also been widely researched (for a review see Messer 1976), studies relating to L2 learning are hard to find. When confronted with a problem solving task with response uncertainty an impulsive person tends to make a quick, or gambling guess, whereas a reflective person tends to make a slower, more calculated decision (Brown 1980:93). Reflectivity/impulsivity is usually measured by the Matching Familiar Figures Test (MFFT; Kagan *et al.* 1964), which is available in different forms. The test format involves simultaneous presentation of a figure with a number of facsimiles differing in one or more details. On each of the test's items, the subject is asked to select from the alternatives the one that exactly matches the standard. Subjects whose response time is above average and whose number of errors is below average are called reflective, and subjects who are below average on response time and above average on errors are called impulsive. Affectively, reflectives tend to be more anxious about the quality of their performance than impulsives. They are also more capable of sustained attention. Some research findings seem to have implications for L2 learning and teaching. It has been found that impulsive children make more errors in L1 reading than reflective children (Messer 1976:1042-3). Brown (1980:94) mentions a study by Doron (1973), who found that adult ESL learners, who had been designated as reflective on the basis of their scores on the MFFT, were slower but more accurate readers than their fellow students who had been designated as impulsive. A high degree of impulsivity might hamper L2 learning. It is, in this connection, important to know that attempts to make impulsives more reflective have met with a fair degree of success (Messer 1976:1047-8). Another finding that may have some implications for teaching is reported by Kagan *et al.* (1966), who found inductive reasoning to be more effective with reflective persons, suggesting that reflective persons would benefit more from inductive learning situations.

Broad and narrow category width

A third type of cognitive style that may be relevant to L2 learning is the tendency that persons have to categorize items either broadly or narrowly. Broad categorizers tend to accept a wide range of items or instances as belonging to a category, thus risking the inclusion of items that do not really fit the category and narrow categorizers tend to accept a much more restricted range, thus risking the exclusion of items that do in fact fit the category. Category width is often measured by Pettigrew's Width Scale (Pettigrew 1958). This test involves questions of the following sort: 'It has been estimated that the average width of windows is 34 inches. What do you think is the width of the widest window..and of the narrowest window'? Those that give a wide range are considered broad categorizers and those that give a narrow range are considered narrow categorizers. It has been suggested (H. Brown 1973, 1980:96, Schumann 1978b:172) that L2 learners who are broad categorizers tend to produce lots of overgeneralization errors, in that they tend to subsume too many items under one linguistic rule, whereas narrow categorizers have difficulty in making the generalizations necessary for efficient L2 learning, in that they tend to create rules for every item. The relation of broad and narrow categorization to L2 learning has been researched by Naiman *et al.* (1978), who hypothesized that the best learners would be those who neither generalize too much nor too little. However, no statistical support for a relationship between category width and success in L2 French, as measured by a listening comprehension and an imitation test, was found.

From the above it can be concluded that research into the relationship between cognitive style factors and L2 learning success has been a fairly rare phenomenon and that research findings supporting the hypothesized relationship between cognitive style factors and success in L2 learning are even rarer.

6.5 Affective characteristics

In recent years there has been an increasing interest among researchers and teachers alike in the role of affective factors in L2 learning. Since in the late 1950s Lambert and Gardner initiated a large scale research project on the role of attitude and motivation in L2 learning, most research in this field has concentrated on these two factors, but many other affective learner characteristics, especially personality factors, have been researched as well. In these paragraphs we will limit ourselves to a discussion of attitude and motivation, and some of the most extensively researched personality characteristics. For discussion of additional factors see Schumann (1975) and especially Brown (1980:100–39).

6.5.1 Attitude and motivation

An interpretation of the respective roles of attitude and motivation in L2 learning is often severely hampered by the fact that these concepts are not always clearly distinguished in the literature. Thus Gardner and Lambert (1959) appear to treat attitude and motivation as one complex of factors related to L2 achievement. Spolsky (1969) concludes that subjects exhibit a particular type of motivation solely on the basis of their scores on a test measuring their attitudes towards speakers of the target language. The confusion is perhaps most clearly apparent in a recent statement by Gardner (1979:205): '. . . the motivation to learn a second language has been conceptualized as a combination of a *positive attitude (desire) to learn the language* and effort expended in that direction' (italics ours). In the following paragraphs we will, therefore, attempt a workable distinction between the concepts of attitude and motivation and discuss the relationship between the two notions before embarking on a discussion of some of the literature on attitude and motivation research.

6.5.1.1   The notion of attitude

Lemon (1973:1) calls attitude 'one of the most ubiquitous of all the terms used in social science'. In spite of its ubiquity, however, the notion has been defined in many different ways. Most theorists would, however, seem to agree that the term 'attitude' refers to some aspects of an individual's response to an object or class of objects (Lett 1977:269). Attitudes have often been considered in terms of the following components (see e.g. Krech *et al.* 1962, Lambert and Lambert 1964):

(1) a cognitive component, which refers to one's beliefs about the object;
(2) an affective component, which refers to the amount of positive or negative feeling one has towards the object;
(3) a conative component, which refers to one's behavioural intentions, or to one's actual behaviour towards the object.

There is also agreement that attitudes are learned (and are therefore, capable of modification by further learning) and that they are relatively stable or enduring (Fishbein and Ajzen 1975, Lemon 1973, Shaw and Wright 1967). A definition like the following can accommodate all that has been said so far: '. . . attitude can be described as a learned predisposition to respond in a consistently favorable or unfavorable manner with respect to a given object' (Fishbein and Ajzen 1975:6).

There is, however, some disagreement as to whether all of the three components mentioned above should be included under the rubric of attitude. Fishbein and Ajzen (1975) and Shaw and Wright (1967) suggest that the term 'attitude' should be applied to only the affective component. In fact, most attitude scales which have been used in research only measure the affective component. In the domain of L2 learning research, Cooper and Fishman (1977) is one of the very few exceptions in which all three components are measured. According to Rokeach (1972[2]) it does not really matter whether all or only one of the three components are measured: the relationship between the components is so close that sufficient information on an attitude can be obtained by measuring only one component, no matter which.

6.5.1.2   The notion of motivation

While, as Brown (1980:112) observes, 'motivation is probably the most often used catch-all term for explaining the success or failure of virtually any complex task', it is at the same time, according to Wall (1958:23), 'perhaps the most obscure and difficult of all theoretical issues in general and educational psychology'. Rather than go into the many controversies concerning this concept (for a recent discussion see Hilgard *et al.* 1979[7]:280–343), we will here limit ourselves to presenting some generally accepted views on and distinctions made with reference to the notion of motivation.

Most psychologists would agree that a theory of human motivation concerns itself with 'those factors that *energize* behaviour and give it *direction*' (Hilgard *et al.* 1979[7]:28). It is also generally accepted that human motives to engage in a particular activity are based on underlying needs. Many classifications of needs have been made in the past. Perhaps the most satisfactory classification available to date is the one devised by Maslow (1970[2]), who assumed a hierarchy of needs ascending from the basic physiological needs which are present at birth (need for food, warmth, etc.) to higher needs of approval, identity, self-esteem, achievement, knowledge, exploration, the fulfilment of which leads to self-actualization. Motives which are based on needs for food, etc. are called *biological motives* and are largely innate and motives which are based on the higher needs listed above are called *psychological motives* and are primarily influenced by learning and environmental factors (Hilgard *et al.* 1979[7]:315). Especially the latter motives are relevant to L2 learning research.

In educational psychology a distinction is also usually made between *intrinsic* and *extrinsic* motivation, the former of which is sometimes thought to relate to long-term success and the latter more to short-term success. Intrinsic motivation is usually defined as motivation which is guided by an interest in the task itself in which one is engaged, whereas extrinsic motivation is said to be guided by external stimuli, such as parental approval, offer of a reward, threat of punishment, a good grade, etc.

Of particular relevance to the study of L2 learning is the distinction between *instrumental* and *integrative* motivation, which was first suggested by Gardner and Lambert. A student is said to be instrumentally motivated 'if the purposes of language study reflect the more utilitarian value of linguistic achievement, such as getting ahead in one's occupation' and he is said to be integratively motivated if he 'wishes to learn more about the other cultural community because he is interested in it in an open-minded way, to the point of eventually being accepted as a member of that other group' (Gardner and Lambert 1972:3). The latter type of motivation was found to be particularly effective.

It is also important, in addition to knowing *why* a person desires to engage in a particular activity, to know how *strongly* he desires to do so. In motivation research, therefore, tests are usually administered which measure not only the direction of the motivation but also *motivational intensity*.

6.5.1.3 *The relation between attitude and motivation*

In the early literature on the role of attitude and motivation in L2 learning (see e.g. Gardner and Lambert 1959, 1972) attitudes and motivation have usually been lumped together into a cluster of factors which were held jointly responsible for relative success or failure in L2 learning. More recently, however, the distinctive roles of attitude and motivation have been redefined (see e.g. Oller 1977, Gardner 1979). It is now argued that attitudes are directly related to motivation, which in turn is directly related to L2 learning. In other words, attitudes should be viewed as motivational supports and not as factors which have a direct effect on L2 learning. Moreover, motivation to learn a language is not only determined by attitudes, but also by other 'motivational props' such as the desire to please teachers and parents, promise of a reward, or experience of success, etc. Also, the relation of attitude to motivation is dependent on the type of motivation. An integrative motivation, for example, presupposes a positive attitude of the learner towards target language speakers and their culture, but a learner who is instrumentally motivated does not necessarily have a positive attitude towards the target language group. Other attitudes which are relevant to L2 learning, such as attitudes towards the language, the teacher and the course, are probably related to both types of motivation.

6.5.1.4 Some research findings

Before embarking on a discussion of some research findings it should be pointed out that there are some weaknesses inherent in research on the relationship between attitudes and motivation (and, for that matter, other affective learner characteristics such as personality traits) and L2 proficiency. The problem with attitudes is that they are not directly observable but can only be inferred from behaviours or statements of the person in question. Of necessity, therefore, statements on the relationship between attitudes and proficiency have been largely based on self-reported attitude data. Oller and his colleagues (Oller and Perkins 1978a, 1978b, Oller 1979b, Oller *et al.* 1980, Oller 1981) have raised some serious questions regarding the validity of such measures. They have discussed some plausible sources of non-random but extraneous variance in measures of affective variables which 'may inflate estimates of reliability and validity of those measures substantially and produce spurious relationships with other variables – in particular language proficiency . . . and intelligence' (Oller and Perkins 1978b: 85–6). Three such sources are: *the approval motive, self-flattery* and *response set*. Respondents to attitude questionnaires tend to give answers which they view as acceptable in the eyes of others (approval motive) or which are acceptable in their own eyes (self-flattery). A third source is the tendency to be consistent in views expressed in responding to the various questions (response set). These weaknesses inherent in measures of affective variables should be borne in mind when reading the review of the literature in this and the next paragraph.

In the late 1950s Gardner and Lambert initiated a series of studies investigating the relation of attitudes and motivation to achievement in a second language. In their first study (Gardner and Lambert 1959) they administered a number of attitudinal and motivational variables to a group of 11 anglophone students studying French in Montreal. A factor analysis of the relationships among measures of aptitude, attitude and motivation, and proficiency in French showed two factors to be associated with French proficiency. One factor was defined by the indices of aptitude. The second factor received high loadings from measures of attitudes towards French Canadians, motivational intensity and an integrative orientation towards language study. The second factor was interpreted as providing evidence for a strong relationship between an *integrative motivation* for learning a second language and achievement in that language. A number of subsequent studies involving anglophone Canadians studying French, such as an early study by Gardner (1960), but also more recent studies (e.g. Gardner and Smythe 1975b, Gardner *et al.* 1976b, Clément *et al.* 1978, Gardner *et al.* 1979a) using a newly developed and validated attitude – motivation index (AMI), including measures of attitudes towards francophone communities, the French teacher and the French course, and motivational indices, showed integratively motivated students not only to be better achievers than instrumentally motivated students, but also to have greater persistence in studying French and to engage more actively in French class activities. Spolsky (1969), too, found a positive correlation between an integrative motivation and the English proficiency of foreign students at American universities. In Spolsky's study, subjects were concluded to be more or less integratively motivated on the basis of their scores on a questionnaire measuring their attitudes towards the target language group.

However, from other studies a more complicated pattern has emerged. Clément *et al.* (1977b) found that an integrative motivation was not strongly related to the L2 achievement of francophone Canadian students from Ontario learning English. Gardner and Lambert (1972:121–30) report on a study in the Philippines. They conclude that in the Philippines, where English is the major medium of instruction, 'students who approach the study of English with an instrumental outlook . . . are clearly more successful in developing proficiency in the language than are those who fail to adopt this orientation. . . . Apparently when there is a vital need to master a second language, the instrumental approach is very effective, perhaps more so than the integrative' (p. 130). Lukmani (1972) showed that among Marathi-speaking Indian students learning English in India an instrumental motivation was positively correlated with English proficiency, suggesting that in a post-colonial society an instrumental motivation is more effective than an integrative one. Cooper and Fishman (1977) conducted a study among a group of predominantly Hebrew-speaking Israeli high-school students. In Israel English is a required subject for all students from the fifth grade onwards. Knowledge of English is also indispensable for a university course or a prestigious occupation. In this learning context 'a basically instrumental view of English proved to be correlated to English proficiency . . .' (Cooper and Fishman 1977:272). From the above studies it would appear that the relative importance of an integrative or instrumental motivation depends to a large extent on the context in which a language is learned. An instrumental orientation seems to be particularly effective in situations where the target language is used as an intranational means of communication, as is the case with English in many third world countries, or target language skills are regarded as highly valued assets (as is, for instance, the case with English in such countries as Israel, the Netherlands, Sweden, Norway and Denmark, whose native languages are hardly used for the purposes of international communication).

Of those attitudes which have a special relevance for L2 learning, attitudes towards the target language and target language speakers have been most extensively researched. Most of the Canadian studies discussed above showed positive attitudes towards the target language group to lead to an integrative motivation to learn their language, which was in turn strongly related to L2 learning success in the Canadian bilingual cultural setting. There appeared to be a fairly strong, though indirect, relationship between positive attitudes and L2 proficiency. Other studies have shown the strength of the correlation between attitudes and proficiency to vary with age of the learner and learning context. Macnamara (1973:37) argued that 'a child suddenly transported from Toronto to Berlin will learn German no matter what he thinks of the Germans'. Indeed, in a recent study of 6-year-old anglophone Canadian children learning French in total immersion programmes, Genesee and Hamayan (1980) found no relationship between attitude factors and proficiency in French. Presumably, young children have not yet developed strong positive or negative feelings towards speakers of other languages. Oller and his colleagues conducted a series of studies on the relationship between attitudes and proficiency in English in different learning contexts. In a study of Chinese-speaking foreign students at American universities, attitudes towards the target language group were positively correlated with proficiency (Oller *et al*. 1977b). In another study (Oller *et al*. 1977a), of socioeconomically disadvantaged Mexican-American women learning English in New Mexico, attitudes were also correlated with proficiency, but this time negatively. Gardner (1980:266) suggests that 'perhaps the more successful women were striving to learn English to remove themselves from oppressive conditions brought about by their lack of English'. In a study of Japanese subjects learning English in Japan (Chihara and Oller 1978) only a weak relationship was found between attitudes and proficiency. Cooper and Fishman's (1977) results suggested 'that favorable attitudes towards English or native speakers of English are largely irrelevant with respect to Israelis learning and using English' (p. 272). These studies suggest that the correlation between attitude variables and attained proficiency tends to be stronger in bilingual contexts where there are many opportunities for learners to communicate with target language speakers than in monolingual contexts, where such opportunities are limited (see also Oller 1977).

As in many studies motivation to learn an L2 appeared to be supported by a positive attitude toward target language speakers, attempts were made to boost motivation through programmes aimed at creating positive attitudes towards target language speakers. It was suggested that bicultural exchanges and excursions and/or greater emphasis on cultural aspects in the regular language programmes might be particularly effective in fostering positive attitudes. Such programmes have, however, not always been very successful (see e.g. Savignon 1972, Gardner *et al*. 1976a, Clément *et al*. 1977a).

In most of the studies discussed so far it has been assumed that the direction of the relationship between attitudes and proficiency is one from attitudes to proficiency. This assumption has, however, been challenged in a number of studies. In a study of beginning college French students during their first semester at the University of Illinois, Savignon (1972) found no significant correlations between attitudinal factors measured at the beginning of the study and measures of final achievement. As the semester progressed, however, the correlations between these variables increased substantially, which suggests that positive attitudes are a function of L2 learning success rather than vice versa. In an evaluation of the British FLES-experiment (see ch. 9) Burstall *et al*. (1974:244) arrived at similar conclusions. More recently, it has been suggested that the relationship is one of dynamic interaction between attitudinal factors and achievement (Gardner 1979, also Oller and Perkins 1978a, 1978b).

Whereas numerous studies have investigated the relation of attitude and motivation to L2 achievement, relatively little research has been done on attitude changes occurring as a result of L2 study. Lambert *et al*. (1963) investigated students attending a six-week French summer school in Montreal. At the end of the programme students received higher scores on measures of *anomie*. The term *anomie* was originally coined by the sociologist Durkheim (1897) to refer to the feelings of social uncertainty or dissatisfaction which characterize the socially unattached person. Learning an L2 means partly losing one's cultural identity as expressed in the L1 while at the same time adopting features of the L2 culture. This can give rise to feelings of social insecurity which, in turn, can lead to negative feelings towards L2 use (see also Lambert 1967). Two other studies suggested that language training can make individuals less tolerant than before. In a study of high-school students registered in an intensive French programme (Gardner *et al.* 1977), it was found that over the course of the programme students tended to become more ethnocentric and in a study involving Canadian and American students registered in an intensive French programme in Northern Quebec (Gardner *et al.* 1979b), the American students developed less favourable attitudes towards French Canadians, in addition to less favourable attitudes towards bilingualism, as did the Canadian students.

As has been observed, most attitude research has tended to concentrate on attitudes towards target language and target language speakers. Much less research has been done on attitudes towards L2 learning, the L2 teacher and the L2 course, which are also important factors in L2 learning. It should be noted, however, that measures of these attitudes have been incorporated in the AMI developed by Gardner and his colleagues, which has been used in many of the post-1975 Canadian studies discussed. Specific studies of attitudes towards the L2 course have been conducted by, among others, Mueller and Miller (1970), Gardner *et al.* (1976a), and Bourgain (1978).

6.5.2 Personality

When compared with attitude and motivation, personality factors have received scant attention in the literature on the relationship between affective characteristics and L2 learning. Those personality traits that seem to have been most widely researched are *extroversion* (and its antithesis *introversion*) and *empathy*, and it is to these two factors that we will limit our discussion. Discussions of other relevant personality traits such as aggression, sensitivity to rejection, and self-esteem, are to be found in Schumann (1978b) and especially Brown (1980:100–12). Self-esteem is the subject of a study by Heyde (1979). The role of anxiety is discussed by Scovel (1978) and Kleinmann (1977), who found that subjects exhibiting debilitating anxiety typically resorted to avoidance behaviour with regard to certain target language structures (see also 5.3.3.). Although we devote separate paragraphs to personality traits, it should not be concluded from this that we believe personality traits to operate as factors independent of other learner characteristics. We have already argued in 6.4. that cognitive style factors and personality factors tend to operate in combination.

Extroversion

As Brown (1980:110) observes, 'the construct (of extroversion) is beyond adequate definition, but there is a general intuitive consensus on what is meant by extroversion'. When asked to describe a typically extrovert pupil a teacher would probably use labels such as outgoing, adventuresome, talkative, sociable. An introverted pupil would very likely be described as being reserved, shy and quiet. It is a popular belief that extroverts are better language learners than introverts, but the literature shows the relationship between extroversion and L2 achievement to be a very complex one.

In a study of university students learning French, German or Spanish in the US, Chastain (1975a) found that scores on the Marlowe – Crowne scale of reserved versus outgoing personality (Crowne and Marlowe 1974) were related to course grades, with the outgoing students receiving the higher grades, but in the Toronto study of the 'good language learner' (Naiman *et al.* 1978) no relationship was found between French proficiency and scores on Eysenck's Introversion – Extroversion scale (Eysenck and Eysenck 1963). In a study of Canadian anglophone grade seven students learning French in different programmes, Tucker *et al.* (1976), using the Jr – Sr High School Personality Questionnaire (HSPQ, Institute for Personality and Ability Testing 1969), reported that success in the interpersonal communication skills of listening comprehension and oral production among students in the Late Immersion Programme was associated with being adventuresome and attempting to use French in the community. In a follow-up study Hamayan *et al.* (1977) found a negative association between shyness and French reading proficiency among all students. Also proficiency in oral production and formal language skills was negatively associated with use of English with acquaintances. From this Hamayan *et al.* (1977:237) conclude: '. . . learning a second language is more effective when the language is practiced and, insofar as shy students may be less likely to practice it, they will attain less proficiency even when reading is concerned'. Solmecke and Boosch (1981), in a study of German university students of English and pupils of grades 9 and 10 of a *Gesamtschule*, report a positive correlation between extroversion and oral communicative ability in English. In a study of German *Realschule*–children learning English, aged about 15, reported by Thiele and Scheibner-Herzig (1978), positive correlations were found between extroversion and listening comprehension and between introversion and reading. Neither in this study nor in Suter's (1976) study of learners of English as L2 in the US did pronunciation accuracy seem to be related to the extroversion/introversion dimension. In Busch's study (1982) of Japanese learners of English in Japan a significant negative correlation was found between English pronunciation and extroversion. It is hard to reconcile these last findings with reports of positive correlations between success in interpersonal communication skills and extroversion. Perhaps the personality tests used do not adequately measure what they are supposed to measure. In fact, Naiman *et al.* (1978:67) are highly critical of the construct validity of the test used in their study. Suter (1976) and Busch (1982) used the same test.

Empathy

Like extroversion, empathy defies adequate definition. It is perhaps most simply described as 'the ability to put oneself in another's shoes' (Guiora *et al.* 1975:45). It refers to 'the projection of one's own personality into the personality of another in order to understand him better' (Brown 1980:107). It is often suggested that the superiority of children over adults in learning an L2, especially its pronunciation, is due to their greater empathic capacity, which is lost to a smaller or greater extent in the process of growing up. The relationship between empathy and L2 learning has been the subject of a series of studies conducted at the University of Michigan by Guiora and his associates. In a pilot study (Guiora *et al.* 1967) a positive correlation was found between the pronunciation accuracy of 14 teachers of French and their scores on the Micro – Momentary – Expression (MME) test, which was used as a measure of empathy. The MME consists of silent film clips of a woman in a psychiatric interview shown from shoulders upwards at varying speeds. Subjects are asked to indicate each observed change in the patient's facial expression. In subsequent studies, however, the hypothesis that empathy, as measured by the MME, is related to pronunciation accuracy, was not clearly supported. Taylor *et al.* (1971) report on an experiment in which 28 college students were given the MME as well as other measures of empathy, such as the Thematic Apperception Test (TAT)–Sensitivity to Feeling, and were then taught basic conversations in Japanese after which their pronunciation was evaluated. The MME scores were not related to the TAT-scores and correlated negatively with the pronunciation scores. In another study (Guiora *et al.* 1972b) with 411 students at the Defense Language Institute learning Japanese, Chinese-Mandarin, Thai, Russian or Spanish, subjects were given the MME as well as other empathy measures. The MME scores correlated with pronunciation scores for the several languages, but the correlation was positive for Spanish, Russian and Japanese, and negative for Thai and Chinese-Mandarin. Schumann (1975:222) concludes that the latter studies do not establish 'that the MME is a valid measure of empathy, and that neither study makes it unquestionably clear that the MME (and hence empathy) is positively related to authentic pronunciation in a second language'.

Then the Michigan research group decided to attack the problem of the proposed link between empathy and pronunciation through experimental manipulation. In one study (Guiora *et al.* 1972a) the effect of small amounts of alcohol on the ability of college students to pronounce words and phrases in a language totally unknown to them (Thai) was investigated. It was hypothesized that alcohol would temporarily lower inhibitions and heighten empathic capacity and thus have a beneficial effect on pronunciation. Students who had been given 1.5 ounces of alcohol obtained higher scores on a specially developed pronunciation test, the 'Standard Thai Procedure' (STP) than students who had been given no, less, or more alcohol. From this it was concluded that the hypothesized relationship between empathy and pronunciation ability indeed existed, but H. Brown (1973:234) offers a plausible alternative explanation: 'alcohol may lower inhibitions but alcohol also tends to affect muscular tension, and the latter may have been a more important factor than the former in the superior pronunciation performance of the alcohol-induced subjects'. In another study (Schumann *et al.* 1978) hypnosis was used as an experimental procedure, but no support was found for the hypothesis that hypnosis will improve pronunciation of a second language. Finally, in a recent study Guiora *et al.* (1980) investigated the effect of benzodiazepine (valium) on pronunciation ability. Contrary to expectation, no effects of valium on pronunciation scores were found. So neither the studies using the MME as a measure of empathy nor the alcohol, valium and hypnosis studies have proved beyond doubt that there is a relationship between empathy and pronunciation ability. Neither did Naiman *et al.* (1978), using Hogan's Empathy Scale (Hogan 1969) as an empathy measure, find a significant correlation between empathy and language success as measured by an imitation and a listening test. The authors observe, however, that there are serious methodological problems surrounding the use of Hogan's Empathy Scale with 'normal' subjects.

Although experimental verification is generally lacking, we are inclined to agree wtih Schumann's (1975:224) contention that the speculations concerning a relationship between empathy and L2 learning 'carry intuitive appeal'. Criticism on the validity of the empathy measures used is also voiced by Oller (1979b:114-16, 133-4). Unless the problems concerning the measurement of empathy are solved, experimental verification will, however, be very difficult to achieve.

6.6 Conclusion

Some learners are more successful in mastering second language skills than others. In this chapter we discussed some of the learner characteristics identified in the literature as factors contributing to individual variation in L2 learning success. First of all we reviewed the biological, cognitive and affective arguments which have been put forward in support of the hypothesis that there is an optimal age, or critical period for L2 learning, which ends around puberty. We saw that the hypothesis received scant support from the empirical evidence available. Next we discussed language aptitude as a relevant factor in L2 learning. We saw that most aptitude research was concerned with constructing tests that would accurately predict L2 learning success rather than with exploring the nature of language aptitude. Those few articles that have probed the nature of this special talent for L2 learning have shown the evidence for its existence to be meagre. Next we devoted a paragraph to cognitive styles, singling out field independence/dependence, reflectivity/impulsivity and broad/narrow category width for discussion. We also saw that research into the relationship between cognitive styles and L2 learning success is only a fairly recent phenomenon and that the evidence for the existence of such a relationship is far from abundant. Our last subsection was devoted to affective characteristics. We first considered the role of attitudes and motivation. We concluded that the relative importance of an integrative or an instrumental motivation depends to a large extent on the context in which the target language is learned. Whereas an integrative motivation appears to be particularly effective in the Canadian bilingual setting, an instrumental motivation can be very important in settings where the target language is used as an intra- or international means of communication, as is the case in e.g. the Philippines and Israel respectively. Of all attitudes relevant to L2 learning attitudes toward target language speakers appeared to be most extensively researched. We saw that the relationship between these attitudes and attained proficiency tended to be stronger in bilingual contexts where there are many opportunities for learners to communicate with target language speakers. We finally discussed the role of some personality characteristics, namely extroversion and empathy, and concluded the results of research in this area to be rather variable, which was seen to be, at least in part, due to lack of adequate measures of these characteristics.

Part III
Teaching Foreign Languages

7

The relevance of source disciplines

7.1 Introduction

In chapter 2 we argued, in our discussion of applied linguistic research, that in addition to linguistics there are other source disciplines to which the applied linguist turns when he is looking for answers to questions in the domain of FLT. In 2.2.2. we saw that many people recognize this fact, and that, besides to linguistics in the widest sense, one finds references to psychology, sociology, pedagogy and education as source disciplines which are used in FLT.

In the preceding chapters we have offered a detailed discussion of what language skills consist of and how these skills are learned. For this discussion, we have mainly drawn on linguistics, psychology and sociology. In this part of the book we shall deal with the main aspects of the question how L2 learners can be made to learn language skills in a teaching situation. For our discussion of this essentially pedagogical and didactic problem we shall of course have to draw upon data from two other source disciplines, pedagogy and education, quite regularly. Our knowledge of language, language use, language skill, and language learning will, however, also play an important role. In this chapter, which is in a sense pivotal, we want to address the question of how we can use our knowledge of the source disciplines, and what the domain of this knowledge is; in other words what we mean by 'applying' the source disciplines. We especially wish to discuss the principle of application as such; specific instances thereof will be given in subsequent chapters.

7.2 The source disciplines

The days that linguistics was considered to be the only suitable source discipline for FLT are over. Nowadays it is generally agreed that other source disciplines can also contribute to FLT, and that it is even incorrect in principle, and harmful in practice, to draw exclusively on linguistics. There is much less of a common opinion on the question of which other source disciplines should be used, and how important these are, relatively speaking. There are those who speak in vague terms about 'diverses autres sciences humaines' (Girard 1972b:9), those who explicitly mention psycholinguistics and/or psychology (Corder 1973:331, Matter 1976:26, Rivers 1964:6, Sharwood Smith n.d.:191), and those who explicitly add sociology to this list (Von Raffler Engel 1973:57, Roulet 1973:31).

We have ourselves just mentioned pedagogy and education as source disciplines in addition to linguistics, psychology and sociology. One finds the same in, for instance, Mair (1981:38), Schilder (1981:12) and Spolsky (1970:144). That we wish to include pedagogy and education as source disciplines in our discussion is a natural consequence of our approach which focuses on the whole didactic process of FL teaching and learning. The chapters of this part of the book are devoted to various aspects of the didactic cycle. Linguistics may reveal facts about language and language use, psychology and psycholinguistics may reveal facts about language skills and language learning, and sociolinguistics may reveal facts about language and language use as social phenomena, but these source disciplines yield insufficient information about guided language learning, especially in teaching situations.

We have already discussed the terminological problems inherent in the acceptance of other source disciplines than linguistics in chapter 2. The term 'applied linguistics' is incorrect for the discipline under discussion, if the second part of this term is taken literally. We shall discuss the relation between the source disciplines and their importance for FLT later, when we discuss what exactly it means to apply source disciplines. We do, however, first wish to make a few remarks on how the various source disciplines compare with each other.

First of all it should be clear that linguistics cannot be considered as the most important source discipline simply because the discipline discussed here is termed 'applied linguistics'. This will also have become clear from our discussion of the historical background of the terminological question in chapter 2. Apart from the etymological discussion there is also a lot of discussion about the question which of the source disciplines is the most important for FLT. Girard (1972b:14) says that linguistics 'may be' the most important of all; to James (1980:7) 'linguistics is the science it (i.e. applied linguistics) draws most heavily upon', but Mair (1981:38) claims that linguistics has, in comparison to pedagogy and psychology, 'nur einen geringen Einfluss auf die Neugestaltung der Methodologie ausgeübt'. It will not be useful to discuss this in any detail. One of the prerequisites for such a discussion would be to establish whether the term 'importance' is to be interpreted qualitatively or quantitatively. It seems appropriate to keep in mind that the contribution of the various source disciplines may vary depending on the area of applied linguistics involved. Linguistics, for instance, will play an important role in defining the object of FLT, i.e.

language, language use, and language skill, while pedagogy and education will have their main contribution in the shaping of the FL teaching and learning process (see e.g. Von Raffler Engel 1973:57). But it seems especially important to abandon the attitude that linguistics, and developments in linguistics, are the starting-point for the development of FLT. For a long time, developments in FLT were crucially dependent on developments in linguistics (see Mair 1981:38). Bausch (1979), like Bender (1979), argues in detail that one should use the actual situation in FLT as a starting-point for a search for useful insights that can be provided by the source disciplines, and that one should not proceed in the reverse order, by trying to find applications for interesting developments in the source disciplines.

7.3   Applying the source disciplines

The next question to ask is exactly what use can be made of the source disciplines which seem to have something to contribute to FLT. We shall first of all discuss this question in principle, and then illustrate it by means of some instances of more or less incorrect application.

7.3.1 Applications and implications

The history of FLT is full of instances of people expecting too much, for a long time, from the source disciplines; and in many cases, the wrong sort of thing. This is especially the case for linguistics, which, as we have seen, was quite regularly taken to be the only source discipline. Not only was FLT, in the words of Politzer (1967:4), 'the child of the linguist' for many years, but in many cases it was taken for granted that 'what is valid in linguistic theory must also be valid in language teaching', to quote Quinn's (1974:331) succinct wording of this view. For a long time people held the view, explicitly or implicitly, that the contributions of the source disciplines could be directly applied in FLT. Many have since pointed out that this position is incorrect and untenable. Roulet (1973:34) speaks of 'une conception unilaterale, simpliste et naïve de l'application de la linguistique à l'enseignement des langues'. Spolsky (1978b:3) says literally: 'The most primitive view of the relation between linguistics and second language pedagogy perceives that relationship as a direct application'. The idea that linguistics or any of the other source disciplines could be directly applied has come to be generally rejected. Compare, for instance, what Mackenzie (1979:25) says about TG, what Widdowson (1975:1) and Bender (1979) say about linguistics in general, and what Mair (1981:39), McDonough (1981:1) and Zonder (1978:12) say about all source disciplines, and especially about psychology. These doubts about the direct applicability of linguistics as a source discipline are not altogether new. One can also find them expressed in, for instance, Politzer (1960:2) and Mackey (1966:202). Quinn (1974:329 ff.) cites a number of linguists and FLT experts who have come to doubt the direct link between linguistics and FLT. In this connection, he speaks of 'a somewhat gloomy litany of reconsiderations', and a gradual process of 'decolonization' of FLT. This latter term suggests that the source disciplines, and especially linguistics, have for a long time colonized FLT, a sentiment also expressed in Mackey (1966:200): 'Much of the present state of applied linguistics in language teaching is due to the fact that some linguists have been more interested in finding an application for their science than in solving the problems of language teaching'. On the other hand, Bolinger (1968:31 ff.) points out that linguists, in spite of themselves, were often used as figureheads by foreign language teachers and pedagogues, so that FLT could be qualified as 'scientific' (see also ch. 2), and that it remains doubtful whether the so-called linguistic principles of the audio-lingual method (see ch. 8) would have been conceived and formulated in their present form by the structuralists, 'if they had had time and had really involved themselves in the movement instead of merely decorating it'. It is for instance unlikely that the structuralists would have come up with the list of 'principles' which Cárdenas (1961:179) presents as principles of which 'the conscious adherence to and application of' is claimed to be a direct result of the application of linguistics: (1) aural–oral approach; (2) systematization of materials presented on all levels; (3) emphasis on pattern practice by means of substitution and memorization to the point of overlearning; (4) postponement of syntactic and grammatical analysis until after memorization; (5) presentation of vocabulary in meaningful context; (6) translation from the target language to the native language reduced to a minimum.

If the relation between source disciplines and FLT is not one of direct application, what, then, is it? It seems to us that one important characteristic is that the source disciplines – to use Politzer's (1972:5) words, who in this case is talking only about linguistics – are 'the source of assumptions rather than the source of conclusions' for FLT. The relation between FLT and the source disciplines is indirect. This can hardly be called surprising, if we realize what it means that in FLT there are always simultaneous contributions from various source disciplines. Pedagogy, psychology, psycholinguistics and linguistics have something to say about guided L2 learning, but none of these has something to say about all aspects thereof, i.e. about language, language learning, and guiding the learning process. In FLT, insights from the various source disciplines will have to be coordinated and integrated, which will inevitably lead to a modification of the contribution of each of the source disciplines. Furthermore, as Zonder (1978:12) remarks correctly, the problems for which FLT seeks a contribution from the source disciplines have not in themselves been the object of research in the source disciplines. What Mackenzie (1981:36) says about one of the source disciplines: 'The goals and motivations of theoretical linguistic work are established independently of the interests of those who seek to benefit from the output of that work', in fact holds true for all source disciplines. What this actually means for research in this area is something we shall discuss in section 7.4.; suffice it to conclude here that it will be impossible to find ready-made answers to problems in FLT in any of the source disciplines.

The statement that the relation between the source disciplines and FLT is one of assumptions and implications rather than one of conclusions, needs some further qualification.

First of all, the relation between source disciplines and FLT may relate to different things. Let us take the 'application' of linguistics as an example. Linguistics may be relevant to the organization of FLT at at least three different levels (see Roulet 1978:43–4). Each linguistic theory expresses a view of language and, implicitly or explicitly, of language learning; this may be relevant to the organization of the teaching/learning process. The language descriptions produced by the linguist may furthermore, on the one hand, contribute 'à améliorer le contenu de l'enseignement', and, on the other hand, contain suggestions for grading course content on the basis of their structure and organization. Lastly, the analytical methods that linguists use have sometimes been taken to be suggestions for actual teaching procedures (see below). It will be clear that the degree to which 'applications' can be concretely and directly effectuated will differ for each of these three levels.

This is what Spolsky (1970:149 ff.) and Wilkins (1972b:220 ff.) point to when the former distinguishes between 'applications' and 'implications', and the latter between 'insights', 'implications', and 'applications'. Both see 'applications' as direct; Spolsky (1970:149) says that 'certain aspects of linguistics may be applied directly in teaching', and Wilkins (1972b:222) speaks of 'cases where notions and information drawn from linguistics act directly upon the process of language teaching'. What they are referring to in this case are 'the best possible descriptions of the language' (Spolsky), referred to by Wilkins as 'language descriptions'. What we would like to point out here is that although language descriptions are, of course, of more 'direct' use to FLT than some other linguistic data and insights, we cannot speak of direct application in the proper sense of the word even here. The language descriptions of linguists, too, will have to be adapted using didactic criteria, if we want them to be effective in the actual teaching process (see also 7.4.2.).

Lastly, we wish to point out that the question of '(direct) applications' vs. 'implications' is one that not only arises where the relation between the source disciplines on the one hand, and FLT on the other is concerned, but also quite frequently where relations *between* the source disciplines are concerned – a problem which very often does not receive sufficient attention. It is not uncommon among linguists, for instance, to presuppose that their view of language and language use has direct implications for a theory about language learning; 'communication strategies' are, for instance, often equated with 'learning strategies', as has also been pointed out by, e.g., Brown (1980:83). Quite regularly, researchers equate L1 learning with L2 learning, or assume that L2 learning in the classroom can be equated with L2 learning in a natural environment. If one considers applying insights and data from the source disciplines in FLT, the origins of these insights and data will, therefore, have to be traced. Some 'conclusive' insights about L2 learning are sometimes nothing more than 'assumptions' on the basis of L1 learning research.

7.3.2 Some examples of misapplication

Numerous examples of incorrect direct application of source disciplines can be found in the history of FLT and in present-day teaching practice. The critical reader will find many examples in general historical surveys such as Kelly (1969; see also ch. 8); publications such as Heindrichs *et al.* (1980), Helbig (1969), and

Taggart (1979) also contain many examples.

Misapplication could be discussed in three different ways. One could take the source disciplines and see what incorrect conclusions about the organization of FLT have been drawn from them. One could take the schools and methods of FLT and trace the origins and soundness of their principles. One could also take the various stages of the didactic cycle, which also determines the division of chapters within this part of the book, and critically examine the applications of the source disciplines for each of these stages. We have opted for the second approach. We shall discuss, by way of example, some instances of application of the main source disciplines in some of the most important schools of FLT, largely in a historical perspective. Instances of incorrect direct application of the source disciplines, or tendencies in that direction, will be discussed in various places in subsequent chapters. There we shall deal with the 'tendency in some quarters to allow terminal needs to *determine* teaching procedures', something Widdowson (1979c:251) points out in connection with the proposals to use predominantly authentic language materials in FLT. In the chapter about gradation we shall discuss the supposed relation between L2 acquisition orders and gradation of course content, which is, according to some 'a prime example of research findings whose pedagogical applications are obvious', to cite Rutherford (1980:65). Other examples can be found in the chapter on didactic procedures; for instance, the proposal to allow actual teaching procedures to be determined directly by the 'approximative systems of the learner's interlanguage', and by the ungrammaticality of interlanguage utterances, by consciously 'tampering with the well-formedness of sentences', which Rutherford (1980:67) calls 'pedagogical pidginization'.

Both form and content of FLT according to the *grammar–translation method* are to a large extent directly inspired by the linguistic tradition which was dominant in the nineteenth century. In linguistics, then comparatively and historically oriented, attention was focused especially on relations between languages and linguistic evolution and on discovering the laws relating to these. In order to discover systematic relations between languages and to distinguish between language families, linguists were mainly concerned with comparing languages in various stages of their development. The research data for linguistics necessarily consisted mainly of written texts. It will hardly come as a surprise, then, that the grammar–translation method limited the objectives of FLT to written language, and especially to reading skills; the more so since FLT in those days was heavily influenced by the teaching of Latin and Greek. Although in the teaching of these classical languages it was taken for granted that the main objective was to enable students to read the Classics, it was certainly strange, and also an incorrect conclusion from linguistic practice and the study of the classical languages, that reading, and especially reading the 'great authors', should also have been seen as the main objective of FLT.

Also with respect to the organization of FLT the grammar–translation method was strongly inspired by the nineteenth-century linguistic tradition, and by the teaching of Latin and Greek. The fascination of the linguists with laws implicitly led to a view of L2 learning in which 'l'hypothèse qu'on possède une langue quand on en connait les règles' (Roulet 1978:33) was central. The explicit learning of rules was therefore very important, and the rules in question were very often those which had been formulated in 'theoretical' (see below) grammars. This frequently meant that the learner was faced with rules which, for him, were incomprehensible or badly formulated, and that furthermore the entire rule system was presented, containing both those rules which are important to the learner, and those which are not. Moreover, modern languages were parsed into traditional grammatical categories developed for the classical languages (McDonough 1981:1), and the gradation of FLT material was based on 'la progression selon les parties du discours' (Matter 1976:26, also Roulet 1978:30).

These incorrect applications of insights from linguistics received some support from psychological and educational insights of those days. McDonough (1981:1) points out that in the educational theory of those days, with its emphasis on analysis and training, on 'the quickening of intellectual processes', a prominent place for 'grammar as a mental faculty' seemed justifiable. The problem here is, however, that both that particular psychological theory was not tested specifically for learning in classroom situations, and that data from linguistics was introduced without any adaptation; as if the form of the rules were not important once the correctness of the principle of rule-learning had been accepted. Girard (1972b:26) points out an analogous assumption, according to which the order in which linguistics frequently analyses the components of language, from the phonological to the textual level, should also be the order which should be used in FLT.

In our description of the *audiolingual method* (see 8.3.2.3.) we will show that this method especially contains applications of structural linguistics and behaviouristic learning theory. Here we limit ourselves to some aspects of applications of structuralism, but we do first of all wish to cite McDonough's (1981) remark that a number of these applications fitted marvellously in the views of behaviouristic theories of learning and the then dominant educational theory, with which, for instance, the emphasis on 'skill and the use of language for definite purposes' was in full agreement. But even in the latter case one can often speak of incorrect direct application.

We have already pointed out that audiolingualists often strove for the predicate 'scientific'. Appeals to structural linguistics, which was seen as the first type of truly scientific linguistics, were sometimes made without there being any real cause for them. In the opinion of Hanzeli (1968:44) this frequently led to structuralist linguistics being 'overstretched' and 'distorted'. The arguments in favour of exclusively focusing on oral language in the initial stages, inductive learning rather than deductive learning, and abandoning translation (see chapter 12), were 'psychological, pedagogical, pragmatic, commonsensical – but hardly linguistic', as some audiolingualists would have us believe (Hanzeli 1968:45).

First of all one can observe how the considerable emphasis which structuralism put on the analysis of spoken language naturally led to a number of conclusions about the objectives of FLT and the order in which language skills ought to be taught. Under the influence of linguistic field research, in which especially those languages which did not have a written tradition, such as the

American Indian languages, were the object of research, structuralists attributed such importance to spoken language that written language was in fact seen as no more than a derived form of spoken language. Audiolingualists adjusted their formulation of the objectives of FLT accordingly. As in L1 learning listening and speaking moreover precede reading and writing, the audiolingualists thought that the initial phase in FLT had to be one in which only listening and speaking were practised.

Even stronger was the influence of structuralism on ideas about how foreign languages should be taught. The main cause of this was the assumption that the discovery procedures of structuralist field research could be directly converted into didactic procedures and techniques. According to Roulet (1978:37) the influence of structuralism was so strong that fairly soon the thought within FLT became prevalent 'que la langue était la seule variable de la pédagogie des langues', which in turn led to the question of how people actually learn an L2 being virtually ignored, and that people were in general somewhat too easily satisfied with 'un modèle de comportement verbal aussi simpliste et inadéquat, Chomsky l'a démonstré clairement, que celui de Skinner'.

Politzer (1972) mentions a series of assumptions for FLT derived from structuralism. We shall not discuss these in detail, but only indicate a few in which the discovery procedures used in linguistic fieldwork can easily be recognized:

(1) by presenting minimal pairs learners should be taught to recognize and produce all L2 phonemic contrasts;
(2) grammatical morphemes should also be learned through exercises in which the use of a certain morpheme is contrasted with the use of other morphemes, including zero;
(3) words which are formed on the basis of the same derivational morphemes should be learned via drills in which these words are grouped together, and related to the basic structures from which they can be derived.

The link between the grammar–translation method and comparative historical linguistics on the one hand and between the audiolingual method and structuralist linguistics on the other is also characterized to a certain extent by the fact that linguists and language teachers were often the same people. Many eminent structuralists were originally foreign language teachers, and retained an interest in FLT as theoretical linguists.

Transformational generative grammar, on the other hand, has developed independently from FLT practice. Transformationalists have, for this reason, always been quite cautious about indicating applications of TG in FLT. Transformationalists have generally followed Chomsky's example, who assumes that 'principles of psychology and linguistics, and research in these disciplines, may supply insights useful to the language teacher', but explicitly states that 'there is very little in psychology or linguistics that he (i.e. the teacher) can accept on faith' (Chomsky 1966:45).

Some, however, have not been quite as circumspect as this in their attempts to improve FLT using insights from TG. In the first place we wish to mention those who thought they could draw conclusions about L2 learning, and the guiding thereof in the classroom, from the ideas about language learning inherent in

TG, most important of which is the hypothesized innate Language Acquisition Device or LAD (see 3.2.2.). The amazing thing is that the principles of TG can lead to two diametrically opposed teaching procedures. On the one hand, one finds the proposal to follow up Chomsky's (1968) idea 'to create a rich linguistic environment' for L2 learners. According to Ingram (1971:127–8) L2 learners will, like L1 learners, develop proficiency in a language through the LAD, which also operates in L2 learning. The only thing one has to do in the classroom is to create the proper conditions for the LAD to function; i.e. the learner literally has to be immersed in language, so that his LAD will enable him to pick up the L2 rule system inductively. This conviction can also be found in Newmark and Reibel (1968), Newmark (1970) and Strauch (1972). The latter only points out problems of a practical nature, such as dividing up the time available for teaching into hours or other units, but for the rest he is of the opinion that:

> Aus rein theoretischen Gründen müsste man für eine Methode totaler Immersion plädieren, weil damit linguistischer und kontextueller Input in idealem Masse gegeben wären . . . (Strauch 1972:29).

Whilst TG principles on the one hand lead some to propose a strongly inductively oriented FLT, they on the other hand lead others to plead for a largely deductive orientation (for a further discussion of the inductive/deductive controversy, see 12.2.4.). Why should one not assume, with equal justification, that the LAD is best addressed directly, by means of explicitly formulated rules? In Rutherford's (1968) language course one observes the attempts to find a place in FLT for linguistic rules as explicitly formulated in TG. Such attempts soon brought about the realization that the very formal and abstract set of TG rules could not possibly be incorporated in FLT without modifications (see e.g. Roulet 1978:40, Matter 1976:28).

Others felt strongly attracted by the ordering principles of the TG rule system, and for a time flirted with the thought of adapting the gradation of FLT material to it. But it became more and more clear that there is no direct correspondence 'entre l'ordre des règles de la description linguistique et la progression optimale d'un cours de grammaire' (Roulet 1978:40).

In fact, the impact of TG on FLT has been less direct than that of traditional linguistics and structuralism. Indirectly, however, TG has perhaps been of more importance to FLT than either of these linguistic theories: on the one hand, it led to a reassessment of the audiolingual principles, and on the other hand, it was quick to show up those who attempted to find analogous direct applications for the new contributions of TG. Especially these two facts have helped to bring about the realization that the relation between source disciplines and FLT needed fundamental reconsideration.

7.4 The contribution of the source disciplines

It will have become clear from the above paragraphs that the criteria for judging the applicability of the various source disciplines are not primarily to be found in the source disciplines themselves. In this section we shall argue that these criteria will first and foremost have to be provided by FLT itself, which should be studied in its own right. Prior to this, we shall discuss the question of whether there are certain aspects or versions of each of the source disciplines which are more applicable, in the sense of 7.3.1., than others. We shall illustrate this using linguistics as an example; we shall devote a separate discussion to the question of what an L2 grammar adapted for FLT purposes looks like.

7.4.1 The most applicable type of linguistics

We have already seen, in 7.2., that it is difficult to assess which of the source disciplines is most important for FLT. We have mentioned the fact that the relevance of the individual source disciplines may vary for each single aspect of the didactic cycle which we shall deal with in this part of the book. The same consideration emerges when one attempts to answer the question which theory or which model of each of the source disciplines can most fruitfully be used for FLT. We shall illustrate this briefly for linguistics.

Roulet (1978), who aims to give a systematic discussion of the importance for FLT of traditional linguistics, structuralism and TG respectively (see also Helbig 1969), shows that a discussion of which of these three linguistic theories contributes most to FLT is useless in the absence of a clear definition of 'application'. In 7.3.1. we have agreed with Roulet's point of view that the nature of application is indirect. Roulet furthermore distinguishes three levels of what exactly in linguistics can be applied, namely roughly these: a particular view on language learning, the actual linguistic description, and the linguistic discovery procedures. The contribution of the various linguistic models may, also for each of the three levels mentioned, differ for various aspects of the didactic cycle, for, for instance, the actual content of FLT as defined in the objectives (ch. 9), compared to the didactic approach to FLT as reflected in actual teaching (ch. 12).

Roulet (1973:38) points out that each of the three linguistic models mentioned provides insufficient insights for determining the actual content of teaching. All three are traditionally directed mainly toward the structural aspect of language, and neglect 'l'emploi de la langue comme instrument de communication dans une communauté linguistique', which in sociolinguistics would be one of the main objects of study. Mackenzie (1981:25), for instance, points out that many of the questions which are central to TG, such as complementation, pronominalization and NP movement, are totally irrelevant to determining the actual content of an FLT programme. Valency grammar, on the other hand, is much more concerned with problems which are central to FLT, such as the valency of the verb in the clause, and the occurrence of case-affixes and adpositions.

Bolinger (1968:34) argues correctly that when Chomsky is sceptical about the contribution that linguistics could make to FLT, he is mainly concerned with the insights which linguistics has to offer with regard to language learning, and fails to note the contributions to FLT provided by the linguistic descriptions which linguists have produced over the years. Roulet is indeed correct in pointing out the limitations of the activities of theoretical linguists in this field (Roulet

1973), but there is little doubt that there has been a definite and very substantial contribution from theoretical linguistics in determining what the object of FLT is. Scathing comments on contributions from theoretical linguistics should not obscure this fact.

If it is the case that the various linguistic models have qualitatively and quantitatively different contributions to make to the different aspects of the didactic cycle, especially with regard to the principal questions of what to teach and how to teach, then it follows that it will be impossible to single out one linguistic model which could be called the best for all aspects of FLT. It is likely that we will always have a situation in which one model is better for one aspect, while some other model is more suited to other aspects. FLT will therefore have to select contributions from linguistics, as from the other source disciplines, from those models which seem most suitable for the purpose in question. Furthermore, these contributions from linguistics will, as we have mentioned before, have to be coordinated with contributions from other source disciplines. And this in turn might mean, as Widdowson (1980:75 ff.) argues, that the model of theoretical linguistics or the linguistic description which linguists consider to be the best, does not necessarily provide the most important contributions to FLT, although one does sometimes encounter this opinion (see e.g. Stammerjohann 1975:36, Larsen-Freeman 1979:222). It might even be the case that the linguistic models which the linguistic analyst and the language user have in mind, are, to a certain extent, incompatible, 'in that they are related to two quite different ways of conceiving language' (Widdowson 1980:76). This, however, is a matter which we wish to reserve for subsequent paragraphs. In conclusion it can be said that, *insofar as the direct relation between FLT and the source disciplines is concerned*, it is hardly surprising to see it often referred to in the literature as 'eclectic' (see e.g. Corder 1973:136, Matter 1976:28). Quinn (1974:350) speaks of 'a healthy attitude of eclecticism vis-à-vis other fields', adding immediately that 'it is not an intellectually respectable posture', a sentiment expressed as follows by Bolinger (1968:41): 'This attitude is not likely to appeal to the intellectual esthete for whom eclecticism is a disgustingly uncommitted philosophy.' Eclecticism with regard to the contributions of the source disciplines need not, however, entail that applied linguistics as a discipline will necessarily be hopelessly incoherent, as we shall demonstrate below.

7.4.2 Pedagogical grammar

The realization that the products of linguistics cannot automatically be seen as teaching programmes for FLT is not a recent one, although the exact relation between linguistics and FLT was never very clear. For years now there has been a distinction between 'scientific' grammars on the one hand and 'pedagogical' grammars on the other. We shall briefly discuss here what is meant by pedagogical grammar, by way of introduction to the next subsection.

The first aim of theoretical linguistics is to describe and explain as fully as possible the phenomenon of language. The focus may be on the structural aspects of language, or it may be on the communicative aspects of language as a means of establishing interaction between people. Whatever the precise delineation of the object of study, in all cases theoretical linguistics is a 'self-contained discipline', 'an independent area of human intellectual inquiry', which is guided in its scientific concern with the phenomenon of language only by the aim to understand and describe this phenomenon as fully as possible (Berman 1979:281). The scientific grammars produced by theoretical linguists are by their very nature of a descriptive sort, and as such they aim at exhaustiveness.

For FLT purposes, scientific grammars offer too much on the one hand, and too little on the other. The objectives of FLT are only rarely to achieve a native or near-native level. FLT is therefore selective by nature, and needs only a subpart of what scientific grammars have to offer. On the other hand, scientific grammars do not contain everything which FLT needs. Scientific grammars are purely descriptive, but FLT will quite frequently need prescriptive statements, or at least advice about which linguistic elements are better or more efficient in language use, easier to learn, or easier to fit into the learning process. Furthermore, the ordering of a scientific grammar will take place on the basis of internal linguistic criteria, while the order in which linguistic elements are presented in teaching is also determined by didactic criteria. This other type of grammar, which is derived from scientific grammar, but is not an exact copy thereof, is commonly called 'pedagogical grammar'.

There are, roughly, two types of pedagogical grammar, to be distinguished by the interpretation given to the term 'pedagogical'. It may be only a label for the intended use of the grammar, FLT in this case. We are then dealing with something which is primarily a grammar, but a grammar which describes only that part of the L2 rule system which is relevant to FLT, or to a particular L2 syllabus. This is, in fact, a reduced version of a scientific grammar, and the qualification 'pedagogical' only indicates that it is intended for FLT. In the other type of pedagogical grammar, the term 'pedagogical' expresses an additional aspect, namely that its contents are not exclusively determined by scientific grammar, but also by psychological, pedagogical, didactic and educational considerations (see e.g. Engels 1979:15). 'Pedagogical grammar' in this sense of the word not only contains a reduced set of rules taken from scientific grammar, the selection having taken place on the basis of considerations of 'usefulness, frequency, conceptual familiarity, contrast with the source language' (Berman 1979:281) as well as on linguistic criteria, but it also contains 'tout matériel qui vise à développer dans l'élève la production de phrases grammaticalement acceptables' (Matter 1976:25). This means that in a pedagogical grammar of this sort, which 'aims to *impart* knowledge' and does not, as scientific grammar does, aim to 'first and foremost describe and thereby explain knowledge' (Berman 1979:281), the ordering of the material will be brought into line with the demands of teaching and learning; in this type of pedagogical grammar other aspects than just linguistic aspects, namely those which are relevant to the guiding of the teaching/learning process, will have a prominent place. Zimmermann (1979:97) appears to draw this distinction when he speaks of 'course-dependent' pedagogical grammars on the one hand, and 'course-independent' ones on the other.

7.4.3 Applied linguistics: a discipline in its own right

So far, we have stressed that within the discipline which is concerned with the teaching and learning of foreign languages, applied linguistics, contributions from more than one source discipline can be distinguished, and that those source disciplines are not directly applicable. Our intention is now to demonstrate that our earlier remark, in 7.4.1, about the eclectic attitude of applied linguistics towards the source disciplines does not entail that applied linguistics as a science is by definition hopelessly incoherent.

Several authors stress the fact that applied linguistics is an autonomous discipline. As an autonomous discipline, applied linguistics is not totally dependent on developments within the source disciplines, but determines which areas thereof are relevant to its own field of research (Mackey 1966:205). The problems of FLT are neither central to psychology nor to linguistics, but they are so to applied linguistics, which tries to solve them by means of, *inter alia*, a synthesis of the relevant findings in the appropriate fields. Applied linguistics is sometimes called interdisciplinary (Brown 1980:IX), because it does, in a sense, encompass a number of other disciplines. Girard (1972b:26) points out that there often is a conflict 'entre les nécessités linguistiques et les nécessités psychologiques, conflit qui ne peut pas se régler que par un compromis'. This compromise is achieved in applied linguistics, the autonomy of which is stressed by Quinn (1974:350), who points out the fact that, as a discipline concerned with the study of FLT, it can be seen as an 'autonomous art with its own conventional wisdom', accumulated over long periods.

The research questions which applied linguistics addresses originate primarily in FLT itself. These questions may be very diverse in nature, and in order to answer them applied linguistics will seek contributions from more than one source discipline. This is in fact what Schilder (1981:19) means when he points out that pedagogical grammar has come to be learner-centred. This attitude also shows in the enumeration of questions relevant to pedagogical grammars which Schilder then gives: Which foreign languages do L2 learners already know? When do they start learning a (new) L2? Which other languages are they learning simultaneously? Which other subjects are part of their curriculum? For what purpose do they learn the foreign language? Who should really learn languages? And who should teach them?

The contributions which the source disciplines can give to answering these questions are accomplished, as we have seen before, in an indirect manner. In fact, the source disciplines provide a set of hypotheses (called 'useful insights' in Chomsky (1966:45)) for FLT, but the important point to make is that these hypotheses have to be tested. It is especially this which makes applied linguistics an autonomous interdisciplinary science: the 'insights' from the source disciplines must 'be tested by empirical study of actual language teaching' (Spolsky 1970:153), 'must ultimately be evaluated by their ability to explain the facts of language teaching and to lead to improvement of instruction' (Politzer 1972:5), and the contributions from the source disciplines 'must be demonstrated, and cannot be presumed. It is the language teacher himself who must validate or refute any specific proposal' (Chomsky 1966:45).

Lastly, we wish to add the following. In the preceding paragraphs, we have only discussed the situation in which the source disciplines are turned to in order to find solutions for problems which have emerged in FLT. It can of course also happen that suggestions for changing and improving FLT are generated directly, i.e. 'spontaneously', by the source disciplines, especially when there are new developments in those source disciplines, e.g. an improved theory of L2 learning. There are of course no objections to this, provided that the new insights are not given any status above that of new hypotheses which have to be tested in FLT. As long as we keep this in mind, FLT will not be the child of fashion of any new development in the source disciplines. New insights in the source disciplines will, in this case, not automatically lead to different foreign language teaching procedures (Politzer 1972:5).

7.5 Conclusion

In this chapter we have discussed the question of what the various source disciplines have to offer towards solving problems which arise in FLT. The function of this chapter within the framework of the book is a pivotal one; it connects the preceding chapters, in which we have discussed language use and language learning, to the subsequent chapters, in which we shall discuss various aspects of guided language learning in a classroom setting.

First of all, we have mentioned the source disciplines for FLT: linguistics, psychology, sociology, pedagogy, and education. We had already pointed out earlier that in spite of the misleading name 'applied linguistics', linguistics is not the sole source discipline for FLT.

We have furthermore discussed the question of which of the source disciplines has most to offer for FLT. We have concluded that this will vary from source discipline to source discipline, for each of the stages, to be discussed in subsequent chapters, of the didactic cycle. Broadly speaking, linguistics will always remain quite important for FLT, and although it can be argued that linguistics may not be the most important source discipline for each of the different stages of the didactic cycle, we have, nevertheless, illustrated the points made in this chapter mainly by focusing on the relation between FLT and linguistics; we have, for instance, devoted a separate subsection to the phenomenon of 'pedagogical grammar'.

The most important subject of this chapter is what exactly the relation between the source disciplines and FLT is; what we understand by 'applying' the source disciplines. We have characterized this relation as one of 'implications' rather than 'applications'. Applied linguistics, the study of the teaching and learning of foreign languages, is an autonomous discipline. It is an interdisciplinary subject which takes its research questions from FLT itself and which in trying to answer them turns to the source disciplines in which it looks for hypotheses about possible solutions, which are then tested empirically.

8
Historical development

8.1 Introduction

When working on the development of a science, one will invariably have to incorporate an analysis of the present situation in one's considerations. One will also have to be informed about the past; otherwise one runs the risk of presenting as new what has already been tried, and of overestimating the importance of the proposed changes. Without a historical perspective theories will lack depth and continuity, and there is a risk of ending up in a vicious circle (Stern 1974:90). Where the proper historical foundation is lacking, dogmatism and persecution of 'dissidents' are not uncommon.

Only two independent publications have so far been devoted to the history of FLT as a whole, namely Titone (1968), who gives a chronological survey from classical times onward, and the detailed study by Kelly (1969), which is more thematically oriented. In addition, there are a number of publications that give a more or less limited survey of certain aspects of the history of FLT. The subject may be a certain period and/or a certain language, as in Harnisch *et al.* (1976), Von Walther (1980), and Weller (1980); or it may be a certain aspect of FLT as a whole (e.g. the monolingual principle in the presentation phase, as in Butzkamm 1973), or the role of linguistics in FLT, as in Szulc (1976); or a comparison of the place of empirical and rationalist theories of language learning in FLT, as in Diller (1971). There is a growing interest in the history of FLT; this will be clear from Schröder and Weller's bibliography (1980), and also from the fact that the West-German journal *Die Neueren Sprachen* devoted an entire issue to this theme in 1980.

Our focus for the historical description will be that of the 'method of FLT', which we hope will portray the development of FLT more or less as a whole. We will first of all give a general description of the development of FLT. We will then discuss a few specific FLT methods which have featured prominently in FLT and subsequently devote some attention to the present situation, to see what the result of this succession of methods has so far been. From what follows, it will be clear that lack of historical perspective in FLT circles has repeatedly impeded progress.

8.2 General description

Historical descriptions frequently have the unfortunate tendency to develop into broad abstractions (Schröder 1975b:XIX). Especially if the space available is limited, as is the case here, there is a danger that the historical reality will be distorted. In the case of the history of FLT this danger is especially acute, because much remains hidden. Certain periods, especially before the eighteenth and nineteenth centuries, have not yet been described for many countries, and even of the best-documented period, the last 150 years, many details are still unrecorded. Only a few of the historically relevant texts have been made generally accessible, as in for instance Hesse (1975), Hüllen (1979), and Schröder (1980). There is virtually no description and analysis of courses which have been used in the past: course materials, after all, are the concrete expression of theories and ideas. The first step towards such an analysis can be found in Schröder (1975b), although even in the opinion of the author himself the analysis is superficial. That Schröder is justified in his reservations about his own conclusions is shown by L. Jung (1980), who analyses 28 courses from the seventeenth and eighteenth centuries with regard to their didactic viewpoints as expressed by the authors in the prefaces; by comparing these with the way the ideas have been worked out in the courses themselves Jung demonstrates that theories and ideas are not always realized in practice.

Taking this into consideration, and also that developments did not take place in the same way and at the same rate in different countries, it still seems possible to characterize the general trend in the development of FLT, in very global terms, with the titles of the following sections: after centuries of development without progress it now seems as if FLT is on the way to a more scientific approach.

8.2.1 Development without progress

The best attempt so far at documenting FLT as a whole in a systematic fashion is Mackey (1965), a handbook of which the manuscript was finished as early as 1961. In it the necessary historical perspective is not lacking. Mackey's summary of his final conclusions about the developments of FLT has often been cited:

> While sciences have advanced by approximation in which each new stage results from an improvement, not a rejection, of what has gone before, language-teaching methods have followed the pendulum of fashion from one extreme to the other (Mackey 1965:138).

Kelly (1969), a publication which was written under Mackey's supervision, provides ample evidence for this position. Kelly comes to the same conclusions as Mackey: he shares the latter's opinion that much that is presented as new and revolutionary is in fact nothing more than thinking out once again and re-labelling old ideas and procedures (Kelly 1969:IX). Kelly's argumentation, which according to Krohn (1969) is not always very reliable, is as follows. He systematically traces the history of a number of ideas, methods and techniques which (could) play a role in FLT. He addresses the questions of what language is, what of a language should be learned, how a language can be taught and learned, and which techniques and aids are most useful.

We shall discuss a few examples that illustrate Mackey's (1965) conclusion, and then go into the causes of this characteristic lack of real progress. Two of the examples are taken from Kelly (1969).

8.2.1.1 Some examples

(1) Although the opposite is sometimes suggested, the question of what role rules should play in FLT does not date from the twentieth century. Nor does the conviction with which some scholars advocate an inductive approach on the one hand or a deductive one on the other date from this century. By induction we mean that the language learner acquires the command of the L2 rule system needed for proficiency in the language, directly from the language material presented. In the deductive approach the rules of the language are explicitly presented to the learner, so that the learner internalizes the rules on the basis of grammatical explanation and analysis. The starting-point in induction is the language material itself, and in deduction it is the rules which are given. In both cases the intention is to enable the learner to gain such a command of the rules of the language that he can use them; explicit knowledge of these rules is not a goal in itself. The discussion of induction versus deduction has been going on for centuries. And always there have been advocates of both approaches, although there have been periods where one or the other was dominant. The inductive approach, for instance, had much support in the late Renaissance and around 1900, while the deductive approach was dominant in the late Middle Ages, in the eighteenth century and in a major part of the nineteenth century (Kelly 1969:34).

(2) Practising sentence patterns in structural drills (see chapter 12) is not as new as its present-day advocates would have us believe. Hocking (1967:33), for instance, sees its development as a contemporary product of the progress made in linguistic analysis. New to our times, at least for the 1950s and 1960s, is only the prominent place that structural drills have occupied for some time. Kelly (1969:101) gives many examples of some types of this exercise from the days of Erasmus (1466–1536) onwards.

(3) Lastly, the opinions on the question of what the aims of FLT should be have been permanently subject to change, and it has always been the same objectives which have been vying for pole position. There has always been somebody who thought he was completely original in presenting the finding that language is a spoken phenomenon and that, for that reason, oral proficiency should be the aim of language teaching, and there have always been people who mainly want to see language as the medium of literature and for that reason are of the opinion that only reading skills are required (Banathy and Sawyer 1969:544). One should also realize that the importance recently attached to the aim of 'communicative competence' is not an entirely new discovery in the history of FLT. In it, we not only find important aspects of the structuroglobal method which we will deal with later on (see e.g. Guberina 1967), and of the ideas of the advocates of the Reform movement (see e.g. Jespersen 1904, 1967[13]:4), but we also find that in the seventeenth century 'communicative competence' was frequently taken to be the main aim of FLT (see L. Jung 1980:163).

8.2.1.2 Causes

(1) Taking the above into account, it is hardly surprising that Mackey (1965) should take ignorance about what has been done, said and thought in the past to be one of the causes of the fad-like changes in FLT. With respect to the main body of people concerned with FLT, i.e. the teachers, this ignorance must be attributed to a large extent to poor teacher-training programmes, the pedagogical component of teacher training in many countries having, until recently, been rather meagre. We do not need to elaborate on the need for good teacher-training programmes, and what teacher-training must consist of. Suffice it to say that a badly informed teacher will obstruct the progress of FLT. He will cling to his established methods and be averse to change. He will be suspicious of new, or rather, different ideas, basing himself on 'a pragmatism which is the result of a tradition of self-sufficiency' (Kelly 1969:387; see also Butzkamm 1973:21). It is equally difficult to convert those who have had some training, namely those who have had a training which is very specifically directed towards the use of certain courses, as was the case, for instance, with *Voix et Images de France* (see 8.3.2.4.). The danger of indoctrination here is very real: the course and the principles it is based on develop into timeless truths. New developments are sometimes severely obstructed by these 'vested interests' (Mackey 1965:139).

(2) The most important cause of the lack of progress in FLT through the years, which Mackey mentions first, is the state of our knowledge about language learning. In FLT language is the subject matter of the learning process. It will be obvious that a language teacher will let what is known about language and language development play a role in determining the form and content of his teaching. The developments in linguistics and (learning) psychology will therefore (have to) be reflected in FLT, and progress has been made in both disciplines. We shall not go into the question of what place we should allot to the achievements of these disciplines here, as this has been discussed in chapter 7 and will be returned to in the next section. We only wish to observe that changes within these fields will be reflected in FLT. That the swing of the pendulum in FLT has often been rather extreme can doubtlessly also be attributed to the developments within these fields.

8.2.2 Towards a more scientific approach

Butzkamm (1973:25) remarks about the title of Kelly (1969): *25 Centuries of Language Teaching* that on this apparently impressively long period of FLT the same judgment can be pronounced that also applies to other disciplines: 'a long past, but only a short history'. The real history of FLT did not start, according to Butzkamm, until, due to a more scientific approach in linguistics and the rise of experimental psychology, especially with regard to memory and learning, a more scientific approach in FLT became possible. This does not mean, however, that this new approach was immediately and fully realized in the nineteenth century. An example of this new approach is the following. For many years, there has been a controversy about methods in FLT (see 8.3.2.). In the history of FLT method after method has been propagated, but, in conformity with the characterization of 'development without progress', which we have referred to before, a subsequent method could never completely replace a previous one. Mackey (1965:51) points out that most methods which have ever been developed are still being applied, in some form or other, somewhere in the world, to this very day.

The controversy about methods would not have been so persistent, if there had been more insight into the entire range of factors which play a role in FLT. We shall not elaborate on just how wide this range of factors is; for this, we refer the reader to what has been said in chapter 1, where we introduce, *inter alia*, the distinction that Mackey (1965:156) draws between selection, gradation and presentation. It is not so much this particular division into three groups of factors which is of interest in this connection, but the fact that this division serves to underscore the diversity of factors involved in FLT. Although this lack of insight can be singled out as an important cause of the confusion that is evident from the controversy about method, it is certainly the case that, moreover, the confusion was augmented by a very careless use of the word 'method'. Schröder and Weller (1975:17) claim that the fact that the various methods are sometimes named after their 'inventor', sometimes after their objective, sometimes after their didactic principles, and sometimes after the aids employed, is characteristic of the absence of a well wrought didactic theory that could serve as a frame of reference for the various FLT methods.

Not only within FLT, but also outside it, is the word 'method' used for a variety of things. Different ways of organizing teaching, and different principles of gradation are often regarded as separate methods. Thus, different ways of organizing teaching, such as individualized versus group teaching, are labelled different methods; but this is also done with the different principles of gradation exhibited in differentiation and programmed instruction. Furthermore, we also find the term 'method' used for particular ways of grading course material, as, for instance, linear or cyclic gradation. In addition, different types of classroom methodology are raised to the status of method, so that we sometimes encounter terms like 'lecturing method' and 'self-instructional method'. Also, we find that the different types of exercise are sometimes termed 'methods', so that one may encounter 'pattern-drill method' in FLT. And lastly, it is not uncommon to use the word 'method' as synonymous with the course, or even the course book, in question.

What is meant here by the word 'method' is the total of considerations concerning the specification of objectives, the selection and gradation of course content, and the selection of didactic procedures. Put differently, what we mean by 'method' is the coherent whole of all considerations concerning what is taught and how it is taught. This is reflected in the way part III of this book is organized.

Considering the fact that in the past as well as in the present the word 'method' has been used to indicate such a variety of different things, it is hardly surprising that, in the quest for the one true method for FLT, entities have been contrasted as fundamentally different, even when the differences were few and sometimes only marginal. It is possible for one FLT 'method' to be different in the fields of selection, gradation, and classroom methodology, but a 'new method' could also be different in only one of these aspects. It is extremely confusing that in this way terms such as 'language laboratory method' or 'film method' came into being, where the emphasis is on one of the teaching aids and on nothing else. It has also happened that two methods are considered each other's polar opposites when they are not. This, for instance, happened to BASIC, which is characterized by a certain type of rigorous selection of lexical and structural items (see 10.4.3.1.), and the 'direct method', where it is mainly a specific way of teaching which is central. The contrast is incorrect, because the selection which is characteristic of the first method is compatible with a number of ways of teaching, including that of the second method.

Summarizing, one can say that one of the achievements of our time is that, due also to the analyses in a clear historical perspective by Mackey (1965) and Kelly (1969), a scientific approach has become possible such that in discussions about method we can distinguish between questions about the 'what', the 'when', and the 'how' of FLT.

A second achievement appears to be that we no longer have to engage in a quest for the 'best method' in FLT. From the empirical research that has been conducted so far into the learning effect of various methods we can only conclude that the entire controversy was in fact unfounded. It has turned out that there is no single method which is the best under all circumstances, and in general, the search for the one and only method has been abandoned:

> The search for *the* method has ended, not because we have found it, nor because we are a profession exhausted from an unproductive search, but because we have decided or discovered that we were searching for a myth (Jarvis 1972:202).

This movement away from the quest for the one true method, however, is not only attributable to the fact that the research data appear so provide so little support for the myth, but also to a different view of the applicability of the data from the disciplines which are basic to FLT; a view which we have discussed in chapter 7. Briefly, what this different view boils down to are the following two things: FLT is not made exclusively dependent on one of the source disciplines, and the relation between source disciplines and FLT is not a direct one. The latter entails that data, insights and achievements from the source disciplines cannot be applied directly; the slogan is: 'adapt, don't adopt'. In fact, Jespersen (1904, 1967[13]:4) already advocated this view when he claimed that the new Reform Method (see 8.3.2.2.) 'is not the whim of one man, but the sum of all the best linguistical and pedagogical ideas of our time, which, coming from many different sources, have found each other, and have made a beautiful alliance for the purpose of overturning the old routine'. Nevertheless it was not until recently that this view gradually came to be generally accepted.

8.3 Survey of FLT methods

8.3.1 Introduction

The need to learn languages has always existed in some form or other. It is only very recently, however, that the demand for FLT has become so great that there is a need for educational facilities for large groups of learners. In the days that only few sought to learn a second language, the most common procedure was to hire a private tutor. Many young Romans were in this way educated bilingually in Latin and Greek from a very early age. A different 'method', frequently used in the Renaissance, was to send people who wanted to learn a second language to the country in question, to acquire the necessary practical skills through direct contact with speakers of that language. In the Middle Ages Latin, which then still was a living language and served as the medium of communication among scholars, was taught to the non-initiated in an intensive and direct way: it was the medium of instruction for all subjects right from the very beginning.

FLT in classical times, in the Middle Ages and in the Renaissance shows of course in its approaches aspects which can also be found in later methods. But a real sense of method could only develop when, especially in the nineteenth century, the demand for FLT increased dramatically.

The changes in method through the ages have never affected the entire field in the same way and at the same speed. Many periods are characterized by a preference for a certain approach, but never does one single method gain a monopoly. One can say that generally the preference in the eighteenth century and a major part of the nineteenth century was for the grammar–translation method, and that the direct method became the most prevalent one round about 1900 and in the 1950s and 1960s. The change in methods, however, is so little time-bound that a chronological treatment will not be of interest. In this connection, we can refer, for our days, to Mackey's (1965:151) remark cited earlier, that most methods which have ever been developed still continue to exist in some form or other.

8.3.2 The methods

We shall not endeavour to discuss all methods, and certainly not all that has ever been referred to as 'a method'. Furthermore, the order in which we deal with the various methods is arbitrary. Not only is it not chronological, it is not based on any classification of methods either. There have been attempts at classification, but they have not led to very satisfactory results. This is hardly surprising, seeing that in all attempts so far one has tried to catalogue methods in pairs around polar opposites, when methods may differ from each other not only with respect to their objectives (the 'what' of FLT), but also with respect to the 'how' of FLT. This entails that if one employs a linear classification, only either the 'what' or the 'how' will receive attention. A classification using four points of comparison, which is the minimum number required if one wants to consider the 'what' and the 'how' simultaneously, has so far not been attempted.

Of the linear classifications those of Titone (1968:97 ff.) and Rivers

(1968:11 ff.) relate to FLT objectives. The former differentiates between 'formal' and 'functional' methods; the latter between 'formalists' and 'activists'. Titone uses a third category, that of the 'integrated' methods, but this last category is intended to indicate that not all methods by far represent either one or the other extreme where their objectives are concerned. Titone himself advocates the integrated method, a mixture of both perspectives. By no means everything from the past represents in a pure form one or the other of the two approaches, formal or functional, as will be clear from the example of Palmer's method (see 8.3.2.2.), which Palmer himself calls a 'multiple line of approach'. Titone (1968:98) gives as one of the main characteristics of a formal approach the fact that such an approach considers knowledge about the language to be more important than practical skill in that language. The functional approach, on the other hand, considers practical skills, especially oral skills, to be the main objective of FLT (Titone 1968:99). It is perhaps useful to point out that the word 'functional' here is not used in the specific sense of the 'functional-notional' approach to specifying objectives (see ch. 9.).

The linear pair that Bender (1979:12) discusses, 'analytic' versus 'synthetic', on the other hand, relates to the question of 'how' in FLT. In the 'analytic' method the learner is expected to achieve a command of the rules of the language directly from contact with samples of the language, while in the 'synthetic' method he attains such a command indirectly, namely via explicit instruction in the rules of the language to be learned. This pair corresponds to similar distinctions, a few of which we have already mentioned, such as the distinction between 'direct' and 'indirect', between 'mentalistic' and 'mechanistic', between 'inductive' and 'deductive', and between 'empiricist' and 'rationalist'.

8.3.2.1 The grammar–translation method

The grammar–translation method is also called the 'traditional method'. This does not mean that it is the oldest method. It has been, and still is, extensively used. The term 'traditional' probably relates to the fact that this method is a nearly perfect reflection of the way Latin and Greek have been taught for centuries. When they ceased to be the most commonly used languages among scholars, their continued study was motivated by the great educational value attached to reading the classics, and by the related argument that studying Greek and Latin helped to further a certain intellectual discipline: the mind being trained, it was asserted, by logical analysis of the language, extensive memorization of complicated rules and paradigms, and the application of these rules and paradigms in translation exercises (Rivers 1968:15). The reason why modern languages were taught in the same way as the classical languages was partly that in the competition between the two it had to be made clear that the educational value of the modern languages was at least equal to that of the classics.

This competition mainly took place in the nineteenth century, and it is therefore hardly surprising that the grammar–translation method was most pronounced and had its greatest advocates in that century. FLT in accordance with this method has as its objective to help learners acquire the L2 deductively, i.e. through the learning of explicitly formulated grammatical rules and paradigms. The most popular exercise is translation from L1 into L2 and *vice versa* (Strevens 1972:705). The emphasis is on form and the arrangement of exercises often reflects the grammatical ordering of word classes. There sometimes is an emphasis on the learning of rules to such an extent that the impression is created that rules have to be learned for their own sake. Words are initially not presented in context, but in bilingual lists which have to be learned by heart. The exercise sentences are very often (extremely) artificial. In this way knowledge and skills are taught which primarily benefit reading skills. Oral skills are clearly neglected, and little or no attention is paid to pronunciation practice. In addition, translation exercises are, as a rule, characterized by a predominant use of the L1 by teacher and pupils alike.

The grammar–translation method has no obvious theoreticians. The basic tenets have not been developed or formulated by one particular person. They are usually found in an applied form in the grammars and courses which were developed for teaching purposes. Someone who has been very influential through his courses in French in the nineteenth century is the German scholar Karl Plötz (1819–1881). He belongs to the group of people who are often associated with the grammar–translation method, although, according to Bender (1979:12), in his method he has attempted to align the synthetic and analytic approaches. It is a quirk of fate that the adherents of the Reform movement (see below) have selected him as the target of their most vehement criticism.

8.3.2.2 The direct method

The direct method is not one single method, but rather a collection of approaches and techniques. A number of these have a name of their own, but we shall not deal with these in detail here. We shall discuss the audiolingual and audiovisual methods separately in the following paragraphs, but like Segermann (1974:350) we wish to stress in advance that the differences between the various direct methods have never been fundamental, and usually boil down to different conclusions which are drawn for teaching from differences in emphasis on common principles.

For the major part, direct methods originated as reactions to the grammar–translation method. Again, it is important to recognize that we may either be dealing with a reaction against the 'what' of FLT, or against the 'how', or perhaps against both. The differences in origin of the various direct methods are reflected to a certain degree in the names one often finds, such as 'oral method' and 'natural method'. With respect to objectives, oral skills are generally much emphasized. With respect to classroom methodology, the reactions have as their important common characteristic that a learning process is advocated where L2 utterances are directly associated with the denoted objects and actions, since the use of L1 by teachers and/or learners is considered to be a detour which should be avoided. Listening is best learned through listening practice, speaking is best learned through speaking practice. Grammatical rules are not explicitly formulated, or at least not explicitly taught: the learner acquires 'knowledge' of grammatical structures inductively by practising with complete and meaningful utterances (Rivers 1968:18 ff.).

The direct method in the nineteenth century and thereafter was therefore clearly a reaction to the grammar-translation method. This does not mean, incidentally, that a number of its basic ideas have not been suggested or used before. A scholar who certainly deserves mention in this connection is the Czech Jan Amos Komenski, or Comenius. In the pedagogical work of this philosopher and theologian, FLT (in his case, mainly Latin) takes up an important place. In the days of Comenius, according to Bowen (see the introduction to his 1967 edition of Comenius, originally published in 1658), piety was the aim, Latin grammar the foundation, the Classics and the Church Fathers the content, and Quintilian the method of FLT. Quintilian stressed rote-learning and literal oral recitation of what had been learned. The ideas of Comenius, as expounded in a number of publications, can be summarized as follows (Titone 1968:14):

(1) The learner will acquire rules of grammar inductively. The best method is not to make the learner learn the rules themselves, but to provide direct practice in speaking and reading through imitation and repetition.
(2) The best method of teaching meaning is the one using sensory experience, generally visual perception.

It is, incidentally, incorrect to view Comenius in every respect as the forerunner of the direct method as we have described it above. Comenius clearly deviates from the direct method on one of the most important points. In his Latin courses he uses L1 as well as L2 (see Comenius 1658).

It is sometimes also asserted that the revolutionary work of Comenius has been poorly received until the nineteenth century. According to Bowen, the fact that the works of Comenius were frequently reprinted in a large number of languages in his own days, and continued to be reprinted until the nineteenth century, demonstrates that this is a gross oversimplification. But it remains true that ideas like those of Comenius were not drawn into the methodological controversy until the days of the competition between the direct method and the grammar-translation method.

This is for instance the case for the emphasis Comenius placed on learning through sensory perception. One of the innovators of the nineteenth century, François Gouin, gave on the basis of that idea a prominent place in his method to having learners act complete utterances in realistic contexts. This and all other elements of his new 'linguistic method' are explained in Gouin (1880). Gouin sets up a language course consisting of meaningful, coherent, short series of sentences relating to certain subjects. This 'series method' is extensively and enthusiastically discussed by Diller (1971:51 ff.). Whether the method itself deserves to be called highly original, as Diller does, remains doubtful, however.

Gouin himself calls his method 'direct', and also 'natural'. It has to be pointed out, however, that these terms are not completely correct, that is, if the avoidance of L1 is one of the most important characteristics of the direct method. Because for Gouin, L1 still functions as an intermediary. In his teaching procedure, for every new series the theme is indicated in L1, and the enumeration of the actions is also done in L1.

On close inspection, none of the designers of whatever variety of the direct method have ever as completely avoided the use of L1 as we have suggested in our earlier description. This lack of purity in method will also emerge in our discussion of Sweet and others below. Only the later followers of, amongst others, Gouin and Viëtor, have really taken this radical step. A nineteenth-century exception is Berlitz, a German who emigrated to America, who used the pure direct method in his schools – which still exist – right from the beginning and with great success. Right from the first lesson onwards, L2 is the only language used. By means of question-and-answer dialogues between teacher and learner, skills in L2 are gradually developed.

The reform method

We have said earlier that generally in the direct method there is a strong emphasis on the oral skills. One should not deduce from this that the written skills are neglected. It only means that the innovators wanted to make up for the neglect of the oral skills in the grammar–translation method. It is the case, incidentally, that especially with strongly linguistically oriented innovators such as Viëtor, Sweet and Jespersen, one is struck more by the constant demand for teaching language that the learner can use in order to communicate in day-to-day situations than by a pronounced preference for spoken language over written language. They do not question the teaching of written language as such, but they do address the question of what kind of written language should be taught. That this should not be primarily and exclusively literary language is one of the main points of the influential pamphlet of Wilhelm Viëtor (1850–1918), which was published under the pseudonym 'Quousque Tandem' (Viëtor 1882). It is one of the common issues of one of the groups that can be recognized especially within the direct method. Jespersen (1904, 1967[13]:3 ff.) is of the opinion that within this group one cannot clearly indicate the founders. In his opinion, it consists of a number of important linguists and a large number of pedagogues and teachers. The term most commonly used to refer to it is 'Reform Method'. That Jespersen himself feels great affinity for this method is demonstrated by the fact that in 1886 he, together with a number of other people, founded a society for the reformation of FLT under the name 'Quousque Tandem' (Jespersen 1904, 1967[13]:3 ff.).

A result of the demand for 'living' language is that considerable emphasis is placed on the teaching of pronunciation, and consequently, that phonetics occupies an important place. Great phoneticians have assisted in the improvement of FLT. The name of Henry Sweet (1845–1912) deserves to be mentioned in this connection. Besides a priority for phonetics Sweet repeatedly stresses the fact that every language has its own structure, and can therefore not be forced into the straitjacket of Latin grammar. Although Sweet can be seen as an advocate of the Reform movement, he was rather moderate, and much less controversial in his day than Viëtor (see e.g. Tanger 1888, in Hüllen 1979: 32–60). Where his didactic views are concerned we cannot straightforwardly group Sweet with those who are in principle against the use of translation and explicit rules of grammar. Sweet's great merit is that he has developed a theoretical framework for FLT which allows a distinction to be made between objectives, selection of course content, and gradation of course content.

Darian (1969:546) says of Otto Jespersen (1860-1943) that one finds a lot of attention for certain didactic principles in his work, such as the use of contextual learning material and pattern drills, that were to become very prominent later on. Jespersen cannot be lumped with those extreme behaviourists who in their fascination with pattern drills find little use for the incorporation of meaningful material. Jespersen (1904, 1967[13]:11 ff.) is strongly opposed to practising with disconnected sentences and with uninteresting and monotonous material.

The last person we can include in this group of innovators is Harold E. Palmer (1877-1949). Palmer saw himself primarily as a language teacher who was also interested in providing a scientific foundation for FLT. He thought it was high time that a start was made with scientific research into language learning (Palmer 1917, 1968[2]:3). He wanted to base the study of FLT on an integration of principles and data from linguistics, pedagogy and learning psychology (Titone 1968:60). Also in Palmer's approach one finds little of the prejudice against all traditional teaching which is so characteristic of a great number of other innovators. He for instance calls the exclusion of translation as a means to clarify meaning 'an uneconomical and unnatural principle' (Palmer 1917, 1968[2]:60). His conclusion with respect to the various methods of teaching meaning is that one can neither wholly reject nor wholly accept any one of them (Palmer 1917, 1968[2]:60 and 66).

The direct method has, as we have said before, been especially influential in its various forms in FLT around 1900. In a number of countries (e.g. France) it even at one time achieved the status of official language teaching method. After a sharp decline in the first few decades of this century it regained a lot of attention in the 1950s, as we shall see in the following paragraphs.

8.3.2.3 *The audiolingual method*

The audiolingual method can be seen as belonging to the group of direct methods, partly because of the didactic procedures advocated, and partly because of the emphasis on spoken language as the primary teaching objective. The didactics of this method are in part a reflection of the development and extensive availability of audio-technology during the 1950s (see ch. 13).

The learning principles on which a completely developed audiolingual method is based and their cognitive counterparts have been discussed extensively in part II. Some call the coalescence of structural views of language and behavioural views of language learning in the underlying theory a coincidence. Wächtler (1974:164) observes that the linguistic insights of the structuralists do not necessarily require a behaviourist model of language learning for their application.

Of course, a long period of development preceded what Stern (1974:63) calls the Golden Age of audiolingualism, the period between 1958 and 1964. Undoubtedly the rise of audiolingualism is partly attributable to the fact that in American FLT between the wars spoken language had been seriously neglected, eventually even as a result of a more or less official policy. The back-ground for this is as follows. The introduction of the direct method was problematic everywhere right from the start. Many teachers were not very fluent in the target language, nor did they possess the necessary didactic skills. An additional problem was that the time available in American schools for FLT was very limited. This led a number of people to conclude that teaching oral skills was not really feasible. In the period from 1924 to 1927 a thorough study of the FLT situation was undertaken in the US and Canada (The Modern Foreign Language Study). One of the recommendations of the committee responsible for the study was that considerably more attention should be devoted to reading skills within FLT. The committee argued that reading skills were generally considered to be the primary goal of FLT anyway (Coleman 1929:VI). In the report of the committee, we find further reflections on what a 'real reading method' should look like. The didactic recommendations, for instance, aim at direct comprehension of the texts presented, without recourse to L1. The texts in question contain a carefully selected and simple vocabulary. The 'reading method' for some time had absolute supremacy in FLT in the US.

The fact that, during World War II, the US all of a sudden faced the task of having to teach oral skills in a large variety of languages to a vast number of people in the military in a very short time, whereas oral skills had long been neglected at schools, contributed considerably to the rise of the audiolingual method. The Army sought the assistance of linguists to develop intensive language courses within the framework of the Army Specialized Training Program. The key to the success of these courses lay not only in the new methods of selection, gradation and presentation developed by these linguists, but also partly in the fact that they were intensive courses, taught to small groups of well motivated learners. It later turned out that the Army method, when used in an ordinary classroom situation, did not have the expected degree of success. The best-known linguist to work on the Army programme was Leonard Bloomfield. Bloomfield (1942) was the guideline for the organization, lay-out and execution of these intensive courses. This publication, although it could certainly not be called 'direct' in all respects, has affected the later development of the audiolingual method in important ways. From Bloomfield (1942:12) is the following statement, which captures an important didactic principle of the audiolingual method:

Language learning is overlearning: anything less is of no use.

In the development of the audiolingual method proper, which took place after 1945, the American linguists Charles C. Fries, Nelson Brooks and Robert Lado, who were all foreign language teachers themselves, played an important role. We shall discuss some important components of their method, such as the pattern drill, and the use of the most modern auditory aid, the language laboratory, later on in more detail. Another important component, contrastive analysis, has been discussed in chapter 4. It is very important to note that the audiolingual method bases itself on principles from a theory of linguistics (American structuralism) on the one hand, and on a learning theory (behaviourism) on the other. Characteristic of the method is the emphasis on spoken language as objective, and on a direct approach as teaching strategy.

The use of L1 was often avoided, although it was not made into an absolute principle (see e.g. Butzkamm 1973:94 ff.). An attempt was made to translate linguistic 'discovery procedures' into didactic procedures, which resulted in for instance practising, with pattern drills, sentence patterns which could be varied paradigmatically or syntagmatically. Rivers (1964) describes in considerable detail how the audiolingual method was based on the behaviourist learning theory which was current at the time. The basic assumption of the method is that L2 learning should be viewed as a mechanistic process of habit formation. From this assumption three conclusions are drawn:

(a) 'habits are strengthened by reinforcement';
(b) 'foreign language habits are formed most effectively by giving the right response, not by making mistakes';
(c) 'language is behaviour and behaviour can be learned only by inducing the student to behave'.

Although Fries (1945) had already established the basic principles of the new method, the name 'audiolingual' did not come into use until a later stage. Originally, the method was called the 'oral approach', or 'aural-oral method'. The term 'audiolingual' did not become popular until around 1960, and, as it turned out later, much to the regret of the man who was the first to use this term: Brooks (1975:236 ff.) says that his only reason for using the term 'audiolingual' was the avoidance of the rather unfortunate 'aural-oral' distinction to indicate oral skills, as opposed to 'visual-graphic' to indicate written skills; exclusively as an indication of the objectives of FLT therefore, and never as a name for a method. Brooks himself (1975:237) considers the combination 'audiolingual method' misleading and harmful, since it suggests that such a method intends to bypass written language completely.

The influence the audiolingual method has had in the US has also been clearly felt in Europe; it has, however, not been able to assume the position of monopoly that it has held for such a long period in the US (Strevens 1972:717).

8.3.2.4 *The audiovisual method*

To speak of *the* audiovisual method would be incorrect. Also in this case, we are again dealing with a conglomeration of approaches which differ one from the other, and which have as their most important common element that they all attach a great deal of importance to the use of visual elements. As far as the objectives of FLT are concerned, these approaches also have a common interest, namely the fact that they reserve first place for oral skills. The audiovisual methods as a group belong largely to the category of the direct methods; not only from the point of view of objectives, but also because of the view they take of teaching procedures. They have come to the foreground especially in the last few decades, mainly because of the improved facilities which the modern technology of producing and reproducing visual information has made available. Since the audiovisual methods were developed during the last 25 years, it will come as no surprise that their psychological and linguistic principles show considerable resemblance to those of other direct methods dating from this era, the most important of which is the audiolingual method. Rivers (1968:175) and Titone (1968:108) therefore see no reason to distinguish a separate group of audiovisual methods. To them, the visual component is no more than a collection of useful aids and techniques which can be used in various methods, and which by their application do not essentially change the method in question.

In chapter 13 we shall elaborate on the media, and, in connection with this, the role of the visual component in FLT. Visual elements could be objects or situations found in the classroom, but also – and this is what comes first to mind in connection with the audiolingual method – objects and situations which are introduced into the classroom by means of slides, pictures, films, etc. Not only real objects, but also actions and especially the situational context can be represented in this way. Visual aids, by the way, are not exclusively used for presentation. They can also be used in evoking objects and situations in the exercise phase of the learning process, as a stimulus for repetition and exploitation. An important principle of the audiovisual method is that the introduction of the visual element renders the use of L1 superfluous.

The structuroglobal audiovisual method

We wish to devote some attention separately to the most important representative of the audiovisual method, generally referred to as the 'structuroglobal method'. For this method one also finds the terms 'CREDIF-method' and 'Saint-Cloud method'; the method was developed first by the *Centre de Recherche et d'Etudes pour la Diffusion du Français* at Saint-Cloud, near Paris. In the last few years, the abbreviation SGAV has come to be current, and we shall use it henceforth. A fairly recent bibliography on this method can be found in Jimenez (1977). The development of *Le Français Fondamental* (FF) plays an important role in the history of the SGAV-method (for FF, see ch. 10). Building on the basic component of FF (premier degré, approx. 1475 words), which was completed in 1960, the well known audiovisual course *Voix et Images de France* (VIF) was developed.

The SGAV-method is a true direct method, both in its objectives (focus on spoken language) and in its didactic approach. The main characteristics of the method are the following:

(1) The method is 'structuroglobal'; i.e. it is linguistically oriented towards structuralism, but exhibits, in this orientation, marked differences with the audiolingual method, which is also oriented towards structuralism. American structuralism is, according to Van Vlasselaer (1972:26), a 'structuralisme désincarné'. Guberina (1972:10 ff.) says that he has added the word 'global' mainly because in his method it is not only the linguistic structures which are central. Every structure should be viewed as embedded in a situation of language use. Coste (1975:545) and Firges and Pelz (1976:6) point out that the SGAV has incorporated in its didactic procedures concepts which would later be elaborated in sociolinguistic and pragmalinguistic theories. In this respect, there are in fact some similarities between the SGAV and the more recently developed communicative approach to FLT.

(2) The second characteristic is closely related to the first: an integrated use of

the visual component. To Guberina (1967:75), language is 'un ensemble acoustico-visuel'. The linguistic expression may, as we have indicated before, not be separated from the situation in which it is used. The method assigns a double function to the visual component. The visual aspect, representing the situational context, becomes the starting-point for a verbal reaction, and furthermore helps the learner dissociate himself from his L1 situation. The visual component in this way forms an essential part of the SGAV-method.

(3) Lastly, the method is characterized by a great deal of early emphasis on correct pronunciation, not only of isolated sounds, but especially of those elements which should get most attention within a structuroglobal conception of language and teaching, namely suprasegmental or prosodic elements. The method of pronunciation correction which is characteristic of the SGAV method, is sometimes referred to as the 'méthode verbotonale'.

The SGAV has had considerable influence on FLT in many places. The VIF-course and later courses developed within the method have been, and still are, widely used. Not everyone, however, is convinced that the SGAV is something entirely new. Coste (1975:541) in his evaluation, for instance, concludes that it is somewhat surprising that the theoretical foundations of the audiovisual SGAV-method should have been so light. Ultimately, SGAV is more a technique than a method to him, and for this reason he does not find it surprising that SGAV has been applied in different ways by different people.

8.4 The present situation

In the introduction to this chapter we have already referred to the fact that changes in FLT do not take place at the same rate and to the same extent in all countries. This is still the case; even now we see that proposals for innovation are often prominent in one particular country, and are only later taken over in other countries, usually undergoing some changes in the process.

The desire for innovation has over the last few decades been especially prominent in a few specific countries. The US and the Netherlands are clear examples of countries which differ strongly with respect to their desire for change. In the history of FLT as we have described it so far, references to contributions from the Netherlands in the shape of new developments are absent. Dutch FLT has usually followed the developments in other countries, but always in such a way that new ideas were incorporated rather slowly, and in an adulterated form. Generally speaking, Dutch teachers, certainly until fairly recently, have used some modified form of the grammar–translation method. The discussions about the pros and cons of the direct method, which also in the Netherlands were quite heated, often had hardly any effect on the average teacher beyond causing him to incorporate some aspects of the method to a smaller or greater extent in his teaching. Dutch FLT has usually incorporated the new into the old, in spite of the fact that, in for instance the 1930s, such experts as the well known Dutch Anglicist Etsko Kruisinga, and the nationally well known pedagogue S. Rombouts (see Rombouts 1937) strongly and very coherently advocated innovation. Likewise, the Dutchman Herman Bongers, who was in close collaboration with Harold Palmer, did not have a decisive influence on Dutch teaching with his ideas on teaching through the direct method, although considerable attention was paid to his arguments for a more scientific approach to the selection of vocabulary (see Bongers 1947a).

Whence this difference? It seems to us that an explanation should mainly be sought in the two completely different sets of circumstances in which FLT finds itself in these two countries, and especially in the degree of importance that is attached to learning foreign languages in these countries. In the Netherlands, a command of one or more foreign languages has long been a necessity for nearly all inhabitants, and this necessity is generally recognized. As a result, the Dutch are accustomed to a considerable range of languages being offered in schools, and the place of FLT as such is not questioned. A result of this has also been that a strong tradition of FLT has had a chance to come into being, a tradition based on the experience of many teachers over many decades. In the Netherlands the schools themselves provide an extensive testing-ground for all sorts of innovations which one might wish to introduce. Consequently, proposals for innovation and change from outside the Dutch situation have always come up against a large body of collective experience, which cannot easily be induced to incorporate substantial changes, but cannot be easily taken by surprise by something untried and untested either. That the situation in the US with respect to the need for command of foreign languages is radically different, and that this has had consequences for FLT provisions, will not need detailed discussion here. The position of FLT in the US is not secure, and not very stable. Not only does this result in a lack of the kind of collective experience mentioned above, but also does FLT feel itself pushed into a position where it has to see to it that it is always attractive enough as a school option, so that enrollments and job opportunities will not suffer too much. It is therefore hardly surprising that within this particular set-up novelties are propagated which sometimes show a remarkable similarity to sales stunts in commerce. Nor will it come as a surprise that, if immediate success fails to materialize, disenchantment follows rapidly, and the search for a new eyecatcher starts again.

Taking all this into consideration, one has to observe nevertheless that, in general, the sensitivity to fads in FLT is diminishing all over the world. The contrasts between 'schools', and the changes from one innovation to the other tend to level off. More and more, as we have indicated before, do we find that people tend to relativize the search for the one true method. For two countries, the US and the Federal Republic of Germany, we can provide some more specific information. Warriner (1980) describes how the audiolingual method lost more and more ground in the US in the last 15 years. This loss of ground resulted in a general trend towards eclecticism, which in its turn was an excuse for many to 'slip back into the comfortable routine of teachers talking, students listening, texts occupying the constant attention of both, and little language proficiency developing' (Warriner 1980:82). Warriner wrongly suggests that if only the teachers had the necessary expertise, FLT could still become healthy, because the ingredients for good FLT are still present (*op.cit.*:86). She suggests, however, that these are largely the ingredients of the 'traditional' audiolingual method. This interpretation of the increased resistance against the audiolingual method of the last few years, however, does very little justice to the attempts by, for instance, Carroll (1966), who, on the basis of a new view on language learning, tried to arrive at a good method for FLT which could replace the inadequate audiolingual method. The Skinnerian idea that language consists of a set of habits formed through stimulus–response conditioning is one of the main principles of the audiolingual method. Carroll's view of language learning is that it is a creative process which uses cognitive principles to discover structures in language. Carroll's 'cognitive code-learning theory' could perhaps be called eclectic, as Carroll himself implicitly suggests when he speaks of 'a modified, up-to-date grammar–translation theory' (Carroll 1966:102), but it would be unfair to Carroll to attach negative connotations to this, as Warriner does.

For the Federal Republic of Germany, one can cite the proposals by Butzkamm (1973). On the basis of Dodson's (1967) 'bilingual method', he attempts to break the monopoly of unilingually based FLT in Germany by advocating a well considered place for L1 in the first stages of FLT. In spite of the fact that the charge of unprincipled theorizing was brought against him as well, his 'eclectic' position has found many followers in FLT.

If one looks at the number of more or less established methods which are still current, one first of all finds, as a relic of the past, the representatives of the direct method or grammar–translation method. In Benseler and Schulz's (1980) survey of the state of affairs in the US, these representatives are also still present.

There are, however, some new methods as well, also listed in Benseler and Schulz (1980). The most striking among these, which have also attracted most attention internationally, are the three methods described in considerable detail in Stevick (1980). These are: the 'Silent Way', developed by Gattegno, 'Community Language Learning', developed by Curran, and the 'Suggestopedia', developed by Lozanov. What these three methods have in common with each other and with other new approaches to FLT is their attempt to draw on more than just the cognitive learning capacity of human beings in the learning process. It is striking that these innovations are not linguistically inspired; they also have applications in the teaching of subjects other than foreign languages. The terms one encounters for these innovations are 'holistic' or 'humanistic' (see e.g. Titone 1977:310, Stevick 1980:31 ff.). A detailed discussion of these new developments would take us too far afield; we would therefore like to refer the reader to the publications we have cited earlier, and the literature referred to in these publications. Although these methods have all gone through their initial stages, it remains difficult to predict what impact they will eventually have on FLT in general. It seems extremely likely that a more prominent place will be given to other human capacities than the purely cognitive ones within FLT. The extent to which this will be the case, and whether the methods just mentioned, in their original form, stand any chance of being introduced into regular teaching still remains to be seen. Data from research are still far too scant, and the methods have been insufficiently tried. Furthermore, these methods have sprung from adult education, which is the only place where they have been truly applied so far.

9
Needs, educational policy, aims and objectives

9.1 Introduction

In an ideal situation, the share allotted to foreign languages in the total of available educational provisions in a community reflects the importance the community attaches to the knowledge of foreign languages of its members. In reality, however, the situation is only rarely ideal. It has often been observed in the past that the provisions for certain subject areas remained unchanged long after the arguments establishing the role of these areas had largely lost their relevance. Until fairly recently, for example, it was the case in a number of European countries that a considerable amount of time was invested, in some types of secondary education, in studying the classical languages, when the relevance of such an intensive study of these languages, for pupils of these types of schools, had long come to be considered doubtful. Also, it often takes a very long time for new subjects to establish themselves firmly in the educational system once their relevance has come to be generally recognized. The advocates of the status quo have, in the past, not met with much resistance, since the arguments for changes in the system were not usually backed by data obtained from detailed research into the desirability of the proposed changes.

It is the task of those who are responsible for an educational policy to see to it that foreign languages, in the total of educational provisions, are given the place that allows for the present and future needs for foreign languages to be met as much as possible. It is therefore of the greatest importance that it is recognized what these needs consist of. First of all, an answer needs to be found to questions like: 'Does the community consider it important that all its members know a foreign language, or is this considered necessary only for certain professional domains?', 'How many languages, and which languages, are felt to be necessary?', 'How great is the demand for each individual language?', 'Does everyone need the same skills, or the same level of command per skill?', 'Is there a stable needs pattern?'

Although the results of a needs analysis contribute the most important data for an FLT policy, there are also a number of other factors which need to be taken into consideration, such as the language policy advocated by neighbouring countries, the level of difficulty of the individual languages, and the availability of suitable teaching materials and adequately trained teachers. When all factors have been carefully considered, a responsible decision could be reached in matters like: 'Which language(s) do we incorporate into the school system, and for which languages do other provisions outside the school system suffice?',

'Do we make a start with FLT in primary education and, if we do, which foreign language do we teach?', 'How many lessons a week do we reserve for FLT in different types of schools, and how many lessons per individual language?'

In this chapter we shall not discuss policies regarding the teaching of languages having the status of official languages of administration in a given country. We shall, therefore, not discuss for example policies regarding the teaching of German to migrant workers in the Federal Republic of Germany or, to give another example, of English in third world countries where English is used as a *lingua franca*. For developments in the area of language policy which are not discussed here, we refer the reader to Rubin and Jernudd (1971), Rubin and Shuy (1973), Rubin *et al.* (1977) and the journals *Language Problems and Language Planning* and *Language Planning Newsletter*.

In the first part (9.2.) of this chapter we shall investigate a number of aspects which play a role in determining an FLT policy. Section 9.2.1. contains a detailed discussion of the role of the needs factor in an FLT policy. In 9.2.2. we pay attention to some other factors which also influence FLT policy. In 9.2.3. we discuss research into foreign language needs, paying special attention to what to our knowledge is the most comprehensive research project in this area: the analysis of foreign language needs in the Netherlands, carried out by the Institute of Applied Sociology (Instituut voor Toegepaste Sociologie, ITS) in Nijmegen (Claessen *et al.* 1978a, 1978b, 1978c). In 9.2.4. we shall discuss at length one aspect of FLT policy which has received considerable attention especially in the last few decades; namely the question whether an early start with FLT in primary education is desirable. We shall first of all discuss some arguments for and against such an early start (9.2.4.1.), and then summarize the experiences with foreign languages in the primary schools of a few countries (9.2.4.2.).

If a detailed needs analysis were to show that a certain group of people needs communicative skills in a certain foreign language, and if the bodies responsible were to conclude that these needs could best be satisfied by allotting an X number of hours of instruction in this foreign language in a certain type of school (also taking into account a number of the factors mentioned earlier), then a rough draft of the goal of instruction in this language and in this particular type of school has already implicitly been given. We could formulate this goal as follows:

The learner has at his disposal skills in a foreign language which enable him to communicate with users of that language.

Such a goal indicates *globally* what teachers and pupils should aim at, and functions as an indispensable point of orientation for both. On the other hand, such a *global* aim is of little help to the teacher in selecting course content and didactic procedures, and it will not make it sufficiently clear to the pupil what it is he should do to demonstrate if, and to what extent, he has satisfied the aims. It is therefore in the interest of education to make the global aims as concrete as possible. The second part (9.3.) of this chapter is devoted to FLT aims and objectives. We shall not devote any space to general teaching aims, such as training pupils to be independent, nor to the relations between general aims and FLT aims. We restrict ourselves to pointing out that FLT aims, like the aims of other school subjects, may never be incompatible with the general aims of education. In 9.3.1. we discuss the translation of global aims into concrete objectives. In 9.3.2. we examine the results of a few attempts at such a translation into concrete objectives. First, in 9.3.2.1. we examine in detail the achievements of a body of experts who, on an invitation from the Council for Cultural Cooperation of the Council of Europe, have attempted to develop a system for foreign language learning by adults in Europe. We have selected this project for discussion because it offers, to our knowledge, one of the most concrete descriptions of a level of language proficiency available today. The proficiency level under discussion is regarded as the minimal level needed for communication in a foreign language. This level has been called the *threshold level*. The English version, which appeared first, is discussed in detail, and versions which were developed later for other languages and different types of learners also receive some attention. We also briefly touch on some further developments within the project of the Council of Europe. In 9.3.2.2. we discuss the objectives as stated in the Foreign Language Certificates of the German *Volkshochschulverband* (i.e. the German organization of adult education institutes), the *VHS-Zertifikate*. We have chosen to discuss these because they represent an attempt, using the European Council approach as a starting-point, at formulating the objectives for the four skills as concretely as possible, and also because the *VHS-Zertifikate* are now to a certain extent internationally accepted, since they have also been adopted by the organizations of adult education institutes in Austria, Denmark, the Netherlands, Sweden and Switzerland.

9.2 Towards an FLT policy

In 1970 W.D. Halls presented a survey of the time reserved for the various modern languages in the curricula of English, German and French secondary schools. He concluded: 'Such figures seem to be as the result of mere chance rather than as flowing from deliberate acts of educational policy by the various governments concerned.' (Halls 1970:15). If he had examined the curricula of other Western European schools, he would have found little reason to change his conclusions. It is true that US government officials have shown considerable interest in teaching English to residents who speak little or no English, but until recently little attention was paid to teaching other languages than the 'national' language. An exception to this situation are the activities undertaken under the *National Defense Education Act* (NDEA), which had as a result that there emerged a keen, if short-lived, interest in foreign languages. For a short survey, see Chastain (1976[2], ch. 2).

Not only in government circles were people little concerned about the place of foreign languages in education; the same could be said of educational circles. At the end of the 1960s, however, developments leading to an increased interest in matters of FLT policy took place. In a number of European countries it was noted that, although there was an increased need for foreign language skills, there was less room available for them in school curricula, and in the US pupils' interest in foreign languages, after the boom mentioned earlier, was on the decrease again. Examining the situation in Western Europe, we can conclude that especially in the Federal Republic of Germany considerable effort is being put into setting up a well considered FLT policy, given the great number of publications on the subject, see Schröder (1972, 1973b, 1976, 1977a, 1977b, 1979a), Zapp (1975, 1976, 1977, 1978a, 1978b, 1979a, 1979b), Schröder and Zapp (1976), Christ and Liebe (1979, 1981), Christ *et al.* (1980) and especially Christ (1980). In 1976 an entire issue of *Die Neueren Sprachen*, edited by Schröder, was devoted to FLT policy. One can find indications of an increased interest in matters of policy, albeit to a lesser extent, in a few other countries as well; especially in Great Britain (Ingram 1976, Williams 1976, McNair 1977, Hawkins 1981) and the Netherlands (Van Els 1981, 1983). With respect to the American situation it is interesting to note that a few years ago an entire issue of *Foreign Language Annals* (11,1,1978) was devoted to 'Promoting Foreign Language Study' and that in that same year President Carter set up the *President's Commission on Foreign Language and International Studies*, which brought out a report (1979), which was subsequently widely discussed in FLT circles, often critically (see e.g. Putnam 1981a).

As we already indicated in section 9.1., those who are responsible for an FLT policy need to take a number of factors into account, most importantly the needs factor. The next two subsections will be devoted to these factors.

9.2.1 Needs as a policy-determining factor

Rivers (1968:8–9) mentions a number of frequently cited arguments in favour of teaching foreign languages; it is important for pupils to study foreign languages because:

- it aids their intellectual development;
- it aids their cultural development by bringing them into contact with the literature written in other languages;
- it enriches their personalities by bringing them into contact with other customs, norms and ways of thinking;
- it will deepen their understanding of the way in which language, also their native language, works;
- it enables them to communicate with speakers of a different language, either by means of the written word, or by means of the spoken word;
- it contributes to better international relations.

If one wants to convince educational authorities of the idea that learning a foreign language, no matter which language, should be an organic part of any education, all of these arguments could be used. This sort of situation is found the US and, to a lesser degree, in Great Britain, whose inhabitants can use their native language in large parts of the world. In most Western European countries, however, the question is not: 'Should we teach a foreign language?', but: 'Which languages, how many languages, and which skills should be taught to which levels?' The greater part of the above arguments are not very relevant to answering these questions. What is needed in such a context are not arguments that could be used for FLT in general, but arguments that favour one language over some other language; arguments for deciding to include one language in the curriculum but not another.

Arguments for teaching foreign languages can generally be related to needs. Needs are sometimes divided into 'personal' and 'social' needs. It seems to us that this division is hardly useful. First of all it is evident that social needs cannot be separated from personal needs: social needs are always reducible to the personal needs of (a number of) members of a social group, which means that in fact all needs are personal. On the other hand, not all personal needs are also social needs. Personal needs only take on a social dimension when society considers the needs of (groups of) individual citizens important enough to take them into account in formulating an educational policy.

Needs, whether they are termed personal or otherwise, may be very different in character. To estimate the importance that should be attached to the various arguments concerned with FLT policy it is important to gain insight into the relative importance of the different needs. It therefore seems useful to distinguish at least three categories of needs:

(1) needs for communicative skills;
(2) needs which are linked to the communicative skills in a foreign language, such as familiarity with the culture, way of life, and more specifically, the literature of another nation;
(3) needs which are not, or at best indirectly, linked to skills in the foreign language, such as learning to think logically and acquiring a certain intellectual discipline.

It will be evident that the relation between needs and skills in a foreign language becomes more indirect as we proceed down this list of categories. If the educational authorities decide to cater for the needs in the first category, they will have to make provision for the teaching of the language for which these needs are felt. It is possible to cater for some needs in the second category (such as a need for a better understanding of speakers of other languages in general) by providing teaching facilities for just one, no matter which, foreign language, and even by instruction through the mother tongue. In the third category the relation between needs and skills in a foreign language is very indirect indeed. It is presumably the case that FLT contributes to the development of a certain intellectual discipline, but this is certainly not something which only holds for FLT. As has been suggested before, arguments relating to needs in the first category will be more convincing than other arguments. This can be illustrated by means of the insecure position of FLT in the US. Turner (1974:195) writes that the lack of enthusiasm for foreign languages in that country should be mainly attributed to the fact that arguments in the first category do not obviously apply:

> Our society is essentially English-speaking and there is relatively little need to learn another language. From a practical standpoint, there is not enough justification for requiring everyone to study a foreign language when only a few of them will ever live or work outside the US. Those who travel abroad will meet any number of people who are anxious to improve their own use of English. The extrinsic argument [i.e. based on the practical uses of foreign

language skills] would be a strong one in our society if it had any significant basis in fact. It does not and students know it.

This has led to a greater emphasis on arguments based on the needs in the second and third categories (see e.g. Alatis 1976). In spite of considerable effort on the part of the American Council on the Teaching of Foreign Languages (see *Foreign Language Annals*, edited by the ACTFL), this did not result in an increased interest in learning foreign languages on the part of the students. Recently, the President's Commission on Foreign Language and International Studies brought out a report entitled *Strength through Wisdom: A Critique of U.S. Capability* (1979), in which it voiced its concern about 'Americans' scandalous incompetence in foreign languages' and in which it argued that the incompetence had become such that it posed 'threats to America's security and economic viability'.

If one is faced with the question if other languages should be added to supplement the languages already taught in schools, as is the case in for instance the Netherlands, where French, German and English are compulsory subjects in the curricula of most types of secondary education and claims are made for provisions for Russian and Spanish as well, arguments based on needs in the second and third categories will never carry much weight, since these needs are already to a large extent catered for by existing FLT provisions.

9.2.2 Other policy-determining factors

Factors the policy-maker should take into account besides the obviously important needs factor are numerous and diverse, and it therefore seems useful to divide them up into four categories: (1) language-policy factors, (2) psychological factors, (3) linguistic factors and (4) educational factors. We shall limit ourselves to a discussion of one or two illustrative examples of each of these factors, and we would like to point out that there is no strict separation between these four categories, that they overlap in places and that, furthermore, the needs factor plays a role within a number of these factors themselves.

Language-policy factors The political situation in a country has a number of consequences that will have to be taken into account. It will for instance often be desirable to make provision for the languages spoken in neighbouring countries, independent of the international status of those countries and their languages. The language policy pursued by the international organizations in which a country participates will also have to be taken into account. We shall illustrate the role played by the political contacts of a country by means of the situation in Europe, where many countries have united in organizations such as the Council of Europe and the European Community.

Although it might be possible that a majority of the citizens of the countries in question would be in favour of designating one language, presumably English, as the intra-European medium of communication (see for instance Macht and Schröder 1976:288–9), this will never happen. Considering that European political unity could best be furthered by stimulating the teaching of the national languages of the participant countries, the Council of Europe rejected the idea of favouring one language as the intra-European medium of communication as early as 1954 (see Christ and Liebe 1979:12–13). In 1969 it was decided in a resolution of the Council of Europe:

- that if full understanding is to be achieved among the countries of Europe, the language barriers between them must be removed;
- that linguistic diversity is part of the European cultural heritage and that it should, through the study of modern languages, provide a source of intellectual enrichment rather than an obstacle to unity;
- that only if the study of modern European languages becomes general will full mutual understanding and cooperation be possible in Europe (Council of Europe 1969:8).

In 1978, the European Parliament again confirmed these points of view (for a survey, see Zapp 1979a, Christ and Liebe 1979).

A European communication model which respects national feelings and at the same time could provide a workable solution for the linguistic problems within the European community has been worked out in the Federal Republic of Germany by Schröder (see Schröder 1973b, Schröder and Zapp 1976). Schematically, he proposes that every European should learn to understand, speak, read and perhaps write at least one foreign language, and also acquire receptive skills in at least two other languages. A conversation between two people would then far less frequently than now have to take place via a language which both have learned as a foreign language; a situation where conversations take place in which one or more people involved can use their native language would then become relatively normal. Such a situation obtains in Scandinavia, when Danes, Norwegians and Swedes converse with each other. Proposals along the lines suggested by Schröder have also been suggested by Davies (1976) and Ingram (1976). To adopt Schröder's model would mean radical changes in the tradition which exists in many European countries according to which the aims and programmes for the various languages offered are largely similar. In addition, it would mean developing an overall policy with respect to foreign languages, a policy in which countries would have to adjust closely to each other in selecting which languages to teach, and what aspects of these languages to teach. For outlines of such an overall European language policy, see Zapp (1979b) and Christ (1980). For a survey of the present FLT situation in the European Community, see Van Deth (1979).

Psychological factors   Two questions essentially belonging to the realm of learning psychology which confront one in the decision of whether to start with FLT in primary or in secondary education are:

(1) What is the optimal age for learning foreign languages?
(2) What consequences does making a start with more than one foreign language at the same time have?

Neither of these questions will concern us here. The first question has been discussed at length in chapter 6.2, and we shall return to the second question in 9.2.4.1.

Another important psychological factor is the level of difficulty of the various languages and skills. Experience has shown, for instance, that French is more difficult for Dutch pupils than English or German. Aiming at the same level of proficiency for these three languages will mean making more time available for French than for English or German. It is also a common assumption that pupils, and especially the weaker pupils, experience more difficulty in acquiring productive skills than in acquiring receptive skills (see Schröder 1975a:29, Littlewood 1978). The relevance of this factor becomes less obvious, however, when it is also observed that pupils, also the less gifted ones, tend on the whole to be more motivated for one of the productive skills, namely speaking (in addition to listening) (see e.g. Schröder 1977b:22, 1977c:165).

Linguistic factors An important linguistic factor, which, incidentally, is closely linked to the psychological factor mentioned earlier (level of difficulty of the various languages and various skills), is language distance. The smaller the distance between two languages is, the easier it will be, on the whole, for a speaker of one of these languages to learn the other language. This is a crucial factor in Schröder's European communication model. In his model, for the Federal Republic of Germany, an important place is reserved for French, on the assumption that a thorough knowledge of French will facilitate the acquisition of receptive skills in two related and important European languages, namely Spanish and Italian.

An altogether different linguistic factor has to do with the question as to how well needs can be translated into teaching programmes. If it turns out, for instance, that not everyone needs the same level of oral proficiency in German, then it remains to be seen to what extent such differences in levels of proficiency can be translated into concrete teaching programmes. We shall go into this matter in more detail in 9.2.3., in our discussion of the needs analysis carried out in the Netherlands.

Educational factors Perhaps the most important educational factor for the policy maker is the fact that there is only a limited amount of time available for FLT. It is unlikely, for instance, that in most secondary schools (which is where most FLT takes place) the available teaching time will increase. At the same time, there is an increased demand for foreign language skills, and new subjects claim a place in the school curriculum as well. It is therefore of the greatest importance that the limited time available is used optimally. This entails that a policy has to be developed in which all aspects of FLT receive attention, and not a policy in which just the languages which have been taught traditionally are considered. It should also be seriously considered whether languages which are not currently being taught could provide a contribution which would justify their place in a school curriculum. It is also important, when making plans for FLT in schools, to take into account the opportunities for FLT that are, or could be, offered by out-of-school education, for instance through courses provided by employers, correspondence courses, radio or television courses, and courses offered by adult education institutes. It is not always necessary to make provision for FLT exclusively in schools. Out-of-school education has a role to play in the overall educational system and offers specific opportunities catering for specific needs.

A last important educational factor we would like to mention is the availability of suitable teaching materials and adequately trained teachers. If these are not available, it is useless to decide to introduce a certain subject in schools. The disappointing results of a British experiment with French in primary schools (Burstall *et al*. 1974; see also 9.2.4.2.) can be attributed in part to the lack of suitable teaching materials and to the teaching methods adopted (Buckby 1976:345, Kunkle 1977:259-60).

From the preceding paragraphs it can be concluded that there are many aspects to the needs factor, aspects which need to be considered carefully, together with a number of other factors when a policy is set up. In the next paragraphs, we shall discuss research into what is the most important of all factors, namely the needs factor.

9.2.3 Research into foreign language needs

In the past, there has been research here and there into foreign language needs, but on the whole this has produced few useful results for an FLT policy. This is partly because the research concentrated on small and specific groups, and partly because the research itself was often badly designed. Exceptions to this rule are Dahllöf (1963), Emmans *et al*. (1974), and especially Claessen *et al*. (1978a, 1978b, 1978c; see also 1978d, which is a brief summary in English, and Claessen 1980). This last project, which is the most extensive of the three, will be discussed in detail. For summaries of research not mentioned here see Bausch *et al*. (1978:375-405) and Christ (1980:87-102).

The needs analysis of the ITS in Nijmegen

Between 1975 and 1978 Claessen and his colleagues, staff members of the ITS in Nijmegen, carried out research into foreign language needs in the Netherlands. This research was triggered by the sometimes heated debates that were the result of changes that had been taking place in FLT in secondary schools since 1968. Before 1968, most schools which were not directly occupation-oriented had final examinations in three foreign languages: German, English, and French. The new law on secondary education of 1968 gave students the freedom to select their own subjects for final examinations, albeit under certain restrictions. This had as a result that many students, after having been taught three foreign languages for only a few years, dropped one or two of these languages for the final examination. This had far-reaching consequences, especially for English and French. The share of English in the total number of hours set aside for FLT increased dramatically, while French experienced a considerable reduction in hours. Many people were of the opinion that this was an undesirable development. The resulting discussion finally led to the ITS receiving a commission to investigate foreign language needs in the Netherlands. It was assumed that the results of this research could contribute importantly to the setting up of future FLT policies.

Research design

The research question was approached from three different angles: research focusing on secondary education, general as well as vocational; research focusing on various social sectors (trade and industry, public administration, and tertiary education), and research in which data were gathered which could be considered indicative of foreign language needs—:

Fig. 9.1   Overall approach adopted in the ITS-needs analysis (Claessen *et al.* 1978a, 10)

The question the research project sought to answer, namely: 'What are the needs for foreign languages?' was interpreted in two ways; as a question concerning the *use* of foreign languages, and as a question concerning the *deficiencies* in foreign language skills as manifested in the use of foreign languages. In order to obtain an answer to these questions, the reseachers developed a list of 24 language use situations, attempting to provide as varied and complete a picture as possible of the situations in which a Dutchman can use his foreign language skills (see fig. 9.2.). This list is divided into three groups of eight items each; situations relating specifically to leisure, hobbies and holidays (1–8), situations connected with professional activities (9–16) and situations relating especially to education and study (17–24). Some situations focus exclusively on oral skills (e.g. 4, 22), other situations on written skills (e.g. 2, 19). In some situations, the focus is exclusively on receptive skills (e.g. listening in 5, 6 and reading in 1, 7), while in others both receptive and productive skills play a role (e.g. 4, 8). The topic is sometimes a specialist one (18), sometimes a non-specialist one (17). The number of participants in a conversation also varies (e.g. 4, 8) and the participants are sometimes business relations, and sometimes relatives or acquaintances (e.g. 2 vs. 3). This list was presented to ex-pupils of secondary schools, students and staff members of universities, employees of various firms and government personnel, and they were asked to indicate for German, English and French (by far the most widely taught foreign languages in the Netherlands) how often they were confronted with the situations listed (varying from never to several times a week), and also if their foreign language skills were such that they could handle these situations adequately, with difficulty or not at all. Secondary school pupils were asked how often they expected to find themselves in the situations specified and how well they expected to be able to deal with them. Moreover, additional data were gathered by means of questionnaires which were sent to administrative staff of schools, teachers, companies, government services and university staff.

(1) Light reading (illustrated periodicals, detective stories)
(2) Writing a short businesslike letter (in relation to e.g. holidays or a hobby)
(3) Writing a personal letter (to relatives or acquaintances)
(4) Giving, or asking for, simple information orally (asking the way, ordering a meal)
(5) Watching a film or TV programme without paying attention to the subtitles
(6) Listening to radio programmes in which understanding the spoken text plays a role
(7) Reading a novel, play, collection of short stories, etc.
(8) Having a conversation in a small group (2-5 people) on familiar topics such as travel, holidays, hobbies
(9) Reading a short piece of information, such as a conference announcement, or instructions
(10) Receiving French-speaking guest lecturers, students, or visitors
(11) Answering telephone calls and putting them through
(12) Conducting a business conversation on the telephone
(13) Writing a short business letter, asking for a report, registering at a congress
(14) Giving, or asking for, business information orally
(15) Participating in a meeting where French is spoken
(16) Giving or receiving oral instructions or advice specifically related to one's own work
(17) Reading a book or journal relating to one's own subject, or one's own work
(18) Reading a book or journal relating to a subject other than one's own
(19) Writing a report, article, summary or conference paper
(20) Reading a text aloud
(21) Attending a lecture
(22) Participating in a group discussion on one's own subject or related to one's own work
(23) Participating in a congress or course (not a language course) at which French is spoken
(24) Having a conversation with a colleague or fellow-student on one's own special subject

Fig. 9.2 List of language use situations used in the ITS-needs analysis, as used for French

In the research focusing on secondary schools, 3040 pupils and 1827 ex-pupils from 16 different types of schools and from 5 different sectors of secondary education, as well as 660 schools took part. In the research focusing on trade and industry, public administration and tertiary education, 740 companies, 312 government services, 485 university staff members and 1201 students participated.

Given the broad spectrum that was covered and the research instrument used, in which all the skills were represented, both in isolation and in combination, and in which also various levels of proficiency were distinguished, it was reasonable to expect that this research project would provide a clear picture of foreign language needs in the Netherlands. The project indeed produced a wealth of useful data, of which we will discuss only a part, after having pointed out the limitations of the project.

Range of research

Although the project has produced a wealth of facts concerning foreign language needs in the Netherlands, these facts should never be the sole guide in setting up an educational policy. It should for instance be pointed out that the ITS-research project has focused on only one of the three categories of needs which we have distinguished in 9.2.1., namely the needs for communicative skills. As we have argued earlier, other needs than the need for communicative skills, and other factors as well, will have to be taken into consideration. A second limitation resides in the definition of deficiency employed by the researchers, which was the following: We speak of a deficiency in the command of a language with respect to a certain situation if the person questioned indicates that (1.) the situation does occur from time to time in his or her experience and (2.) that he or she cannot deal with the situation at all or only with the greatest difficulty (Claessen *et al.* 1978a:34). In this project, therefore, deficiencies were only recorded for foreign language users. Deficiencies can also occur, of course, with people who do not use foreign languages. It is quite possible that people do not use a foreign language because, knowing their command of the language to be insufficient, they avoid situations in which they expect to have to use this language. In the third place, the data are data on foreign language needs within three different social sectors, namely education, trade and industry, and public administration. It will not be an easy task to arrive at a proper balance for the needs of these sectors. And lastly there is the question of how well the data can be translated into concrete teaching programmes. If we find that there is a need for different levels of proficiency (see below), will we then be able to indicate clearly what attaining a certain level in a certain skill stands for? With respect to this last issue, we are no longer completely at a loss; the attempts on the part of the Council of Europe at defining some levels of language proficiency are of some help. We shall return to this matter in 9.2.2.1.

Some results and their implications for an FLT policy

(1) From the data obtained in the research project it can be concluded that there exists a varied pattern of needs for French, German and English. Apart from the fact that not everyone needs the same skills, not everyone needs the same level of proficiency either. This is not reflected at all in the existing examination requirements: they are identical for French, German and English. The data provided by the ITS could be a reason for the educational authorities to review the examination requirements.

(2) From the investigation among pupils and ex-pupils of secondary schools it was concluded that French poses much more of a problem to them in actual (or expected) use than German or English does. That English poses few problems in comparison to French can be partly explained by the fact that almost everyone takes English as a final examination subject, while many pupils drop French two years before the final examination, and partly by the fact that most pupils find English easy and French difficult. German on the whole also poses relatively few problems, although the proportion of pupils that do not take German as a final examination subject is relatively high (although lower than for French). Apparently it is the case that the pupils who drop German have learned so much of this language that it is of real use to them later on, something which seems to be much less the case for French. This situation could be changed if the

educational authorities were to adopt a policy in which French is allotted more time in the period before the examination subjects are chosen, at the expense of either German and English or other school subjects. An alternative possibility would be to concentrate, within the time available for French, not on all four skills, but only on one or two, for instance receptive skills, so that a useful level of proficiency could be attained at least in some skills.

(3) It turned out that considerable differences exist in the ways in which the different types of schools cater for the foreign language needs of their students. It was shown, for instance, that especially pupils of some types of vocational schools will often need English and German later on in their careers, whereas in these schools little attention is paid to FLT. These results demonstrate clearly the need to make more room available for FLT in these schools.

(4) It also turned out that besides for German, French, and English, the central languages of the research project, there was a need, albeit a far less urgent one, for a number of other languages, mainly Russian, Spanish and Italian. Given that these needs are relatively minor, the educational authorities could perhaps conclude that these languages can be largely catered for by making provision for them outside the secondary school curricula.

What we hope to have demonstrated is that a needs analysis, if carried out properly, can contribute significantly to setting up an FLT policy. For some recent proposals, based on the ITS-needs analysis, see Van Els (1983).

9.2.4 An early start with FLT?

In the last few decades, the question whether it is desirable to start earlier with FLT in schools has become more and more prominent in the US and Europe. In the next two paragraphs, we shall discuss a number of arguments for and against this earlier start in schools, and review what has been done with respect to FLT to young children in a number of countries. We shall have to limit ourselves in this discussion. On the one hand, we shall not enter into a discussion on what the optimal age for FLT is, because this has already been discussed in detail in chapter 6. On the other hand, given the bias of the book towards foreign language learning in schools, we shall restrict ourselves to discussing a number of so-called FLES programmes (Foreign Languages in the Elementary School), programmes that relate to FLT in an environment where the language to be learned is generally not spoken outside the school and where the language is only used during foreign language classes.

9.2.4.1 Arguments for and against an early start

In the 1950s and 60s neurophysiological and psychological arguments were the most important ones in the discussion about FLES. As we have seen in chapter 6, arguments of this kind are not very strong, since research has not shown childhood to be a better age for learning foreign language skills than adolescence or adulthood, except perhaps in the area of pronunciation. In a survey article, Stern and Weinrib state (1977:19):

There may be no overpowering reason in the biology of child development in favour of teaching languages to younger children. But there are no overpowering reasons against it either.

They make similar remarks concerning the psychological argumentation. In other words: a decision for or against FLES is only a responsible decision if it is also based on other arguments. We shall examine some of these arguments in some more detail.

In 1963 Stern wrote a report on FLT to young children, in which the points of view of a group of experts who were together in Hamburg on an invitation from UNESCO are summarized. Stern notes in this report (Stern 1963, 1967[2]) that in the past primary education was marked by a one-sided emphasis on national history, language and culture, which resulted in pupils considering foreign speakers 'alien' or even 'inferior'. This is increasingly felt to be undesirable for both political and pedagogical reasons, and FLES is considered to be one of the most important ways in which this could be changed:

> The learning of a second language must be regarded as a necessary part of total personality formation in the modern world, since it should enable a person to live and move freely in more than one culture and free him from the limitations imposed by belonging to, and being educated within, a single cultural group and a single linguistic community. It is an essential not only from the point of view of society, but also for the individual himself and his personal education. Somehow, therefore, a second language must become part of the total educational process, not something reserved for the gifted, but a normal educational experience for the ordinary child. . . . The broad aim should be to give each child a new means of communication. If in the past reading and writing the native tongue have been regarded as the basic content of primary linguistic education it is now claimed that speaking another language must in the twentieth century be added to these requirements (Stern 1967[2]:8–9).

Internationally, Stern's report has drawn a lot of attention, and the arguments for FLES it contains have been taken over by advocates of FLES in many countries (see e.g. Van Willigen 1971, Doyé and Lüttge 1978[2]). An often heard counterargument is that the primary school curriculum is overloaded as it is, and that addition of a new subject would only reduce the rather limited time available for the subjects presently featuring in the curriculum. This is indeed a strong counterargument for countries where secondary education ensures ample exposure to one or more foreign languages, as is the case in countries such as the Netherlands and Belgium, but it loses much of its force in countries like the US and Great Britain, where such an exposure in secondary education is not ensured.

A second argument in favour of an earlier start concerns the total amount of time needed to attain the level of proficiency that is considered desirable. In a survey of the teaching of French as a foreign language in eight countries Carroll concluded (1975:276):

> The data of the present study suggest that the primary factor in the

attainment of proficiency in French (and presumably any foreign language) is the amount of instructional time provided. The study provides no clear evidence that there is any special advantage in starting the study of a foreign language very early other than the fact that this may provide the student more time to attain a desired performance level at a given age.

If this level of proficiency cannot be attained in secondary education, either because not enough time is made available or because the pupils drop the foreign language after a couple of years' teaching (see e.g. Andersson 1969:33 for a description of the situation in the US and Hawkins 1981:15 ff. for Great Britain), then introducing FLES seems to be the only solution.

A third argument which is often used is that if foreign languages are taught in primary schools, there will be more room for other foreign languages in secondary schools (see e.g. Hoy 1977:4).

An argument which is especially relevant for countries in which it is customary to teach more than one foreign language is advanced by Van Ek (1970:48-9):

> In order to reduce the disadvantages of parallel foreign language learning processes somewhat, one attempts not to start with more than one foreign language in any one year. In this way, the critical stage of the first steps in the second foreign language does not occur until the process of learning the first foreign language is well under way. However, the interval of one year only is considered very short; this is an added reason for making a start with the first foreign language in primary education.

Arguments which are frequently used against FLES are that, apart from the curriculum being too full as it is, introducing a foreign language would mean a drastic change in the character of the primary school, that FLT could have a negative influence on achievement in other subjects, especially the mother tongue, that FLES shows meagre results, and that therefore, the benefits do not outweigh the costs. These arguments can be countered to a large extent by introducing FLES according to a carefully considered plan. In the first place, it is a prerequisite that a curriculum is developed for the foreign language which can be considered to be a subpart of a coherent primary school curriculum. In other words, FLT in primary education will have different aims, content and didactic procedures from FLT in secondary education. In the second place, a lot of attention will have to be paid to longitudinal planning, so that there is a good link between FLT in primary and secondary education. Thirdly, a sufficient number of competent teachers will have to be available. It will appear from the discussion of a number of FLES experiments in 9.2.4.2. that, when competent teachers and suitable teaching materials are available, and when there is a good link between primary and secondary schools, the results of FLES can be satisfactory. It will also be shown that there are no grounds to fear a negative effect on the achievements in other subjects.

9.2.4.2 Experiences with FLES in a number of countries

In the middle of the 1950s, FLT in the US was about to enjoy an unusually favourable period. Long before that time foreign languages had been taught in primary schools, but not on a large scale, and neither the educational authorities nor the public showed much interest. For a well documented survey, see Kloss (1967) and Andersson (1969); the latter goes back in time as far as 1840. When World War I broke out, America increasingly isolated itself and the effects could also be felt in FLES. Especially German, which had until then been the most frequently taught language, became the victim. No fewer than 23 states even passed laws discouraging FLT. In 1939 only very few pupils in primary schools were taught a foreign language (McLaughlin 1978a:134). A total reversal of this situation occurred in the period after World War II. There are a number of reasons for this. In the first place, the US government became more and more convinced that it should abandon its isolationism. The US should establish lasting contacts with other countries, and an important obstacle to this was the lack of foreign language skills of the average American citizen. William Riley Parker, secretary of the *Modern Language Association of America*, wrote in 1954:

> Given an atmosphere of good will, an individual traveling abroad can, in a sense, 'get by' or 'get along' with English or, for that matter, with sign language. . . . But given an atmosphere of global tension, which is the atmosphere in which we live today, it would seem that no nation, particularly not a nation with frightening power and enviable wealth, can long 'get by' without even trying to talk the other fellow's language. One language makes a wall; it takes two to make a gate. That is why Americans, praying for peace and seeking an increase in international understanding, now often discuss foreign language study as a means to these ends (Parker 1961[3]:103).

The argument of international contacts convinced many American parents, who started to exercise pressure on the government and the school boards to include a foreign language in the curricula of primary schools (Pillet 1974:19). In that same period, an FLT method had been developed that seemed eminently suited to young children: the audiolingual method, because this was a method that did not require a high level of cognitive development and also appealed to the capacity of the child to imitate. Furthermore, neurophysiologists argued that it would be easier for children to learn foreign languages than for adolescents and adults because of the greater plasticity of the brain (see ch. 6). Lastly, the National Defense Education Act of 1958 provided an important impulse and made large sums of money available for FLT. This made the psychological and financial climate in the 1950s for introducing FLES programmes a favourable one, and it is therefore no surprise that the number of children who were taught a foreign language increased rapidly. In 1959, 1,227,000 children participated in FLES programmes. The language which was taught most frequently was Spanish, followed by French and German. At first, reports on the results of the FLES programmes were favourable (Dunkel and Pillet 1963, Donoghue 1969). However, the enthusiasm of the early years has waned, and in these last few years there is a clear decrease in the number of FLES programmes (Stern and Weinrib 1977:8, Donoghue and Kunkle 1979:29), because it turned out that they did not come up to the expectations. Oller and Nagato (1974:15) concluded about the effect of the programmes: 'Findings indicate moderate to insignificant results for most FLES programs in the US (notwithstanding the glowing but inaccurate reviews such as that by Donoghue, 1969).' In many publications (e.g. Pillet 1974, Stern and Weinrib 1977, McLaughlin 1978a, Donoghue and Kunkle 1979) the causes of these disappointing results are pointed out. Many FLES programmes were badly prepared, badly executed and badly evaluated. They were carried out by teachers who were insufficiently prepared for their task. In addition, the link with secondary education was in many cases inadequate or absent. Furthermore, the audiolingual method, of which the basic principles were often rigidly and dogmatically applied, did not bring the success that had been hoped for, and the neurophysiological arguments for FLT at an early age were largely shown to be inadequate (see ch. 6). Stern and Weinrib (1977:7) characterize the situation as follows:

> FLES is no longer seen, as it was by many American educators some 10 or 15 years ago, as the most important way of improving second-language proficiency. Improvements and innovations are looked for at the high-school level and in universities by catering more clearly to the individual interests and capabilities of students and by paying more attention to humanistic and affective aspects in foreign language education.

In England and Wales there existed little interest in FLES before 1960. This changed in 1963 when preparations were made for a project that became known as the *Pilot Scheme for the Teaching of French in Primary Schools*, instigated by the Ministry of Education. The project, which started in 1964, aimed to investigate 'whether it would be feasible and educationally desirable to extend the teaching of a foreign language to pupils who represented a wider range of age and ability than those to whom foreign languages had traditionally been taught' (Burstall *et al.* 1974:11). In September 1964 a beginning was made with teaching French to children from 8 years onwards. It was hoped that the introduction of French in primary schools would make room for other foreign languages, such as German, Russian and Spanish, in secondary schools (Schools Council 1966). The *National Foundation for Educational Research* (NFER) was asked to evaluate the project. The final report of this evaluation, which covered 10 years (1964–1974), appeared in 1974 (Burstall *et al.*). Approximately 125 schools from different parts of England and Wales participated in the project, which also attracted a growing interest from non-participants. In 1965 21 per cent of the primary schools included some French in their curricula and five years later the number of schoolchildren between 8 and 11 years of age who were taught French was estimated at 35 per cent (Hoy 1977:6). Many schools made use of the materials developed for the project. Three groups of pupils were considered in the evaluation of the project. Groups 1 and 3 (n = about 5300 and 6000 respectively) were under observation for five years (three years in primary education and two years in secondary education). Group 2 was under observation for eight years (three years in primary education and five years in secondary education). There was also a control group of pupils who started learning French at the age of 11, which is the usual age in Great Britain.

This extensive, carefully planned, longitudinal study produced a wealth of data, of which we can only mention a part here. The introduction of French had neither a negative nor a positive influence on the achievements in other primary school subjects. However, the expectation that because of the early start with French the other foreign languages would get a better chance in secondary education was not confirmed. On the contrary, the position of French as the most important foreign language in secondary education was strengthened. And also their experiences in primary schools had convinced many pupils that they could not learn a foreign language. It turned out that pupils reacted negatively to a number of aspects of the way in which they were taught, especially to the frequent use of tape recorders, which involved many repetition exercises, and reading aloud. Considerable problems were found to exist in the link between primary and secondary education. It proved impossible for many schools to give separate classes to those who had already had three years of French and those who had not had any French at all. But the most important and controversial result was that the experimental groups who had been taught French from the age of eight years onward were hardly any better in French than those who had started learning French at the age of eleven. The experimental groups proved to be slightly better only in understanding spoken language. The final report ends with a conclusion which can hardly be called encouraging:

> Now that the results of the evaluation are finally available, however, it is hard to resist the conclusion that the weight of the evidence has combined with the balance of opinion to tip the scales against a possible expansion of the teaching of French in primary schools (Burstall *et al.* 1974:246).

The report, and especially the final paragraph, led to a sharp controversy between advocates and opponents of FLT to young children. Especially the popular press pronounced in a number of commentaries a death sentence on French in primary schools. Others indicated their appreciation of the research project (although some aspects of the research design were criticized) and of the amount of valuable information that had been obtained, but they were of the opinion that the results of the project did not justify the conclusion contained in the final paragraph. The *National Association of Language Advisers* (NALA) accepted in 1975 a resolution in which FLES was supported for pedagogical reasons. Other publications (e.g. Bennett 1975, Buckby 1976, Kunkle 1977, Lee 1977, Hoy 1977) pointed out a number of positive results, such as the more positive attitudes of pupils who had been taught French from the age of eight onward to speaking the language, and attributed the poor results to the teaching materials, which relied heavily on audiolingual principles, the teaching methods used in the primary schools, and the inadequate link between primary and secondary education. The current opinion is that the NFER-report has not shown that the expansion of the teaching of French in primary schools is undesirable, but it has made it clear that a number of essential conditions have to be met if the teaching programme is to be successful. The enthusiasm of the 1960s for teaching French in primary schools, however, has cooled somewhat. Hoy (1977:35) estimated in 1977 that only about 20 per cent of the children between 8 and 11 were taught French. For a recent evaluation see Hawkins (1981:180–90).

In other European countries, too, many experiments have been and are still being carried out with FLT to young children. In the Federal Republic of Germany, for instance, a number of projects have been set up throughout the country since 1970. Most projects focus on English, but a few taking place in the areas adjoining France (Baden-Württemberg, Saarland and Rheinland-Pfalz) are concerned with French. Annotated bibliographical surveys of the German FLES experiments have been provided by Sauer (1975, 1979). Hilgendorf and his colleagues (1970) and Doyé and Lüttge (1978[2]) are examples of well designed experimental research. Hilgendorf and his colleagues compared the results in English as obtained by children in primary schools in Berlin who had started with English in the third form (8 years old) with the results of those who had started with English in the fifth form. At the end of the sixth form the oral proficiency of the first group was at a higher level than that of the second group, whereas there was no difference in their written proficiency. Although the introduction of English classes reduced the teaching time available for other subjects, such as German and arithmetic, this had no negative influence on the achievements in these subjects. Doyé and Lüttge observed a large number of primary school pupils in Braunschweig (initially 1170) from their third year at school, which was when they were first taught English, to their seventh year at school, i.e. into secondary education. In this project, care was taken to establish a proper link in secondary education with what had already been taught in primary education. Doyé and Lüttge, too, drew conclusions favouring an early start. At the end of their seventh year in school those pupils who had started early had a higher score on nearly all the tests used in the experiment than the control group, which consisted of pupils who had started with English in their fifth year. Also in this experiment a negative influence (of an early start with a foreign language) on either the mother tongue or arithmetic could not be demonstrated to exist. Useful documentation on experiments carried out in the Federal Republic of Germany as well as in other European countries is also provided by Gompf (1975).

After Luxemburg and Malta, Sweden is the third European country that has made a foreign language obligatory in primary education. Since 1972, children are taught English from their third year in school (9 years old) onwards. At the same time, experiments with FLT to even younger children are being carried out. The best-known project is the EPÅL-project, started in 1969. The background to this project is provided in Holmstrand (1975). In a subproject, reported on in Holmstrand (1979), research was carried out into the effect on results in other subjects of teaching English from the second semester in the first year at school onwards (7–8 years of age). Both pupils who had started with English in their first year and pupils who had started with English in their third year were given tests in arithmetic in several forms (at the end of years 1, 2, 3, and 6), and tests of proficiency in Swedish (at the end of years 1, 2, 3, 4 and, in some cases, 6). The pupils who had made an early start did not obtain poorer results for arithmetic and Swedish than those who had started later with English. Some test results even pointed to a slight advantage for the early starters where Swedish was concerned. For a summary of the results of the EPÅL-project see Holmstrand (1982).

Also in a number of cantons in Switzerland experiments have been carried out with lowering the age for FLT. An example of good experimental research is provided by Bühler (1972), who compared the results of teaching French to German-speaking pupils from the fourth form (10 years) and fifth form (11 years) of primary school onwards with each other. After three quarters of a year, there were no significant differences in level of proficiency between the two groups, but after a year and a half the results of the latter group were significantly better than those of the former. Bühler seeks to explain this by referring to the learning conditions, which were less favourable for fourth-form pupils.

The last two projects which need mentioning are an Austrian project, reported on in Doyé and Lüttge (1978[2]:120–1), and a Dutch project, discussed in detail in Carpay and Bol (1974). The Austrian project was an investigation of the effects of starting with English in the third year in school, English normally being taught from the fifth year onwards. The research was carried out among pupils who attended the *Gesamtschule* from the fifth year at school onwards. The experimental group consisted of pupils who had been taught English from their third year in school and the control group was formed by pupils who started with English in their fifth year in school. At the end of the sixth school year (the second year at the *Gesamtschule*) there no longer existed a significant difference in level of proficiency between pupils who had started with English in their third year and pupils who had started in their fifth year. The disappointing results of the first group are mainly attributed to the poor link between the teaching of English in primary school and in the *Gesamtschule*.

In Utrecht in the Netherlands a project called the EIBO-project was started in 1968, with the aim to obtain the necessary scientific and practical experience to make the introduction of English in primary schools from the fifth year onwards (*c.* 10 years of age) possible on a national scale. In this project, teaching materials for primary school pupils and a model for training teachers were developed and tested. After 1972 virtually no work was done on the project until in 1978 it was handed over to the Foundation for Curriculum Development (SLO) in Enschede. The SLO was asked by the Ministry of Education to:

- develop a model curriculum for English in primary schools, with a clear relation to other primary school subjects and also to the curriculum for English in secondary education;
- develop a model teaching programme for English in primary schools;
- develop a model for training teachers in primary schools to teach English;
- take into account, in the execution of the above, the experiences and materials obtained in the Utrecht phase of the project (SLO 1979).

The SLO started the project in 1979 by initiating a teacher-training programme. Meanwhile much work has been done on each of the aspects mentioned. From 1985 English will gradually be incorporated as a compulsory subject in the curricula of all Dutch primary schools.

To sum up our discussion, we can observe that especially since 1960 experiments have been carried out with FLT to young children in many countries and that these experiments have shown clearly that FLES can only be useful when at least the following three conditions are met:

(1) a sufficient number of adequately trained teachers must be available;
(2) teaching materials suited to young children must be available;
(3) there must be an adequate link between primary and secondary education.

9.3 Aims

9.3.1 From aims to objectives

In 9.1. we have described a possible goal of FLT as follows:

> The learner has at his disposal skills in a foreign language which enable him to communicate with users of that language.

The term *aim* is often used for such a global description (Huhse 1968, Roberts 1972), and one also finds the terms *goal* and *purpose* (Valette and Disick 1972, Steiner 1975). The term *Richtziel*, introduced by Möller (1969), is usually preferred in the German literature. Such a general description has an important function as a frame of reference for FLT. An important drawback of such a description is that because of its generality it does not provide an unequivocal basis and guideline for the development of curricula and instruments of evaluation: neither the pupil nor the teacher are given a clear insight into what is expected of them. It is therefore important to make such a description more concrete by specifying as exactly as possible what the learner must be able to do in the foreign language. Referring to what has just been said, it will cause no great surprise that in many countries no serious attempts to develop such behavioural specifications of FLT aims were made, until the need for developing new language proficiency tests arose. The following guidelines, inspired by Mager (1962), could be used in making aims more concrete:

(1) Indicate which observable activity or task the pupil can carry out when he has achieved the aims.
(2) Indicate the subject matter (learning content) with respect to which the pupil can carry out the task described.
(3) Indicate the conditions under which the pupil can carry out the tasks described.
(4) Indicate the criteria for acceptable performance.

When aims have been described according to such guidelines, one usually no longer speaks of *aims* but of *objectives* (Huhse 1968, Roberts 1972), often further specified as *instructional objectives* (e.g. Mager 1962), *behavioural objectives* (e.g. Gage and Berliner 1975) or *performance objectives* (e.g. Valette and Disick 1972, Steiner 1975). In the German literature the term *Feinziel* (Möller 1969) is often used.

Defining FLT objectives is no easy matter; it entails at least:

• specifying what pupils can do in the target language (behavioural specification), e.g.: 'The pupil can read novels in the original, non-adapted editions',

or 'The pupil can call the railway station for information about departure times';
- specifying the linguistic elements (or language forms) necessary to carry out the tasks specified (linguistic specification). This could for instance include:
providing phonetic/phonological information about the target language;
compiling a vocabulary list;
compiling a list of structures;
specifying the level of proficiency in listening, speaking, reading and writing.

In 9.3.2. we discuss some examples of objectives that have been developed, and we shall see that the last aspect, specifying the level of proficiency, has received the least adequate treatment.

Although we can posit in general that it is important for an aim to be made more concrete, we should also remark that the extent to which it should be made concrete depends on the function the aim has within the educational structure of a given country. In the Netherlands, for instance, curricula are developed which serve as guidelines to all schools, while in the Federal Republic of Germany the individual states have their own curricula. A 'national' aim for FLT could for this reason be further specified in the Netherlands than it could be in the FRG. The highest degree of specification of an aim will be found at the level of each individual school, since it is at this level that objectives will have to be formulated that obtain for the school in question, of course within the framework provided by the aims and objectives agreed on nationally or in the state or district in which the school is situated.

For a treatment of some other aspects of the aims issue and for a detailed bibliography see Gage and Berliner (1975), De Corte *et al.* (1976[4]), and for a treatment specifically concerned with FLT see Valette and Disick (1972) and Steiner (1975).

9.3.2 Some attempts at specifying objectives

9.3.2.1 *The European unit/credit system for modern language learning by adults*

In 9.2.2. we have already seen that the Council of Europe takes great pains to stimulate FLT in the affiliated countries in order to advance European unity. In 1971 one of the main bodies within the Council of Europe, namely the Council for Cultural Cooperation, organized a symposium in Rüschlikon (Switzerland) for delegates of the member states in order to determine what could be done in order to improve and/or stimulate FLT, and specifically FLT to adults. From the discussions at the symposium it could be concluded that FLT for adults was in a situation of chaos in most of these countries. A number of possibilities to improve this situation were discussed and, more specifically, it was suggested to develop a general European system for FLT to adults in the shape of a so-called *unit–credit* system, defined as follows on this occasion by Kingsbury (1971:11):

> an educational system in which the syllabus, curriculum or body of material (knowledge and skills) to be studied, learned or acquired, is broken down into

a number of quantum units of work, each with its own precise definition of the terminal behaviour to be achieved by the learner, all of the units being accompanied by a carefully constructed system of credit ratings.

It is proposed that, after a *unit* has been successfully completed, a *credit* is given, i.e. a certificate stating that the unit has been successfully completed. The system is flexible in so far that the student can set up his own programme by choosing certain combinations of *units*. Such a system, especially when introduced on a large scale, can only be made to work if the objectives are defined so unequivocally as to limit differences in interpretation between users to an acceptable minimum. After the Rüschlikon Symposium a committee was formed which was asked to investigate in how far a European *unit-credit* system was feasible. The committee originally consisted of Trim (Chairman), Van Ek, Richterich and Wilkins. The first important result of the activities of this committee was the publication in 1975 of a report by Van Ek, with an appendix by Alexander, in which a level of linguistic proficiency was described which was termed *threshold level* (or *T-level*):

> The lowest level of general foreign language ability to be recognized in the unit-credit system (Van Ek and Alexander 1975:7)

The *T-level* functions as a keystone in a wider *unit–credit* system covering the entire area of foreign language learning. On the basis of the *T-level* a number of more advanced levels of linguistic proficiency can be defined from which learners can make a choice, depending on their needs (Van Ek and Alexander 1975:ii–iii). We shall see below that eventually a level below the *T-level* was also defined, but this should not be seen as an independent unit in the system: it merely has the function of a halfway stage for the *T-level*.

The first task the committee had to carry out was drawing up a profile of the target group for which the *T-level* would be defined. This target group would have to contain as many potential adult foreign language learners as possible. In the end, the following description, based on Richterich (1972) was decided on: the target group consists of adults:

(1) who will be temporary visitors to the foreign country (especially tourists);
(2) who will have temporary contacts with foreigners in their own country;
(3) whose contacts with foreign language speakers will, on the whole, be of a superficial, non-professional type;
(4) who will primarily need only a basic level of command of the foreign language (Van Ek and Alexander 1975:9).

The *T-level* described in Van Ek and Alexander is proposed as a *variant* of the *T-level*, namely the variant which is relevant to the target group under discussion. This means that one could define other variants for other target groups. It is pointed out that the different variants of *T-level* should not differ too much; this could endanger the *unit-credit* system, since the system can only function if the different units are properly integrated.

After the profile of the target group had been outlined the *T-level* was filled in on the basis of a model for specifying foreign language learning objectives in which the studies of Richterich (1972) and Wilkins (1972a) play an important part. This model specifies the following components (Van Ek and Alexander 1975:5):

(1) The *situations* in which the foreign language will be used, including the *topics* that may occur in these situations (such as *personal identification; house and home; trade, profession, occupation; leisure time, entertainment*). In addition to the topics, the following situational components are distinguished: the *settings* (such as *apartment, hotel, camp site, railway station*), the *social roles* the learner will fulfil (for instance *friend/friend* and *stranger/stranger*) and the *psychological roles* he will fulfil (*neutrality, equality, sympathy* and *antipathy*).

(2) The *language activities* the learner will engage in and the *skills* which he will have at his command. The level of proficiency in listening and speaking is such that the learner can participate in conversations about the topics specified. In this context, more is demanded of the skill of listening than of the speaking skill. In the catalogue of *language forms* (see point 7), the distinction is made between items for productive and items for receptive use. For reading and writing only a very low level of proficiency is aimed at.

(3) The *language functions* the learner will be able to fulfil, such as giving factual information, turning down an offer, expressing dislike. From the list in Van Ek and Alexander (1975) it can be concluded that what they call language functions corresponds to a large extent to what is usually called *speech acts* in linguistics.

(4) Specifications in terms of behaviour; i.e. what the learner will be able to do with respect to each of the topics specified. With respect to the topic '*trade, profession, occupation*' he will be able to supply and obtain information about the nature of certain professions, place of work, working conditions, income and prospects.

(5) The *general notions* the learner will be able to handle. This includes notions such as time, space, quality, quantity, goal, cause, effect.

(6) The *specific notions* the learner will be able to handle. These are the notions related to the topics specified. The learner will for instance be able to use the notions related to the topic '*personal identification*' such as first name, family name, and initials. So far the model is not language-specific and can be used for the description of *T-levels* in any language.

(7) The *language forms* (lexical and (morpho-) syntactic elements) the learner will be able to use with respect to the specified language functions and general and specific notions. This component is of course language-specific, and in Van Ek and Alexander (1975) it has been filled in for English. The lexicon contains approximately 1050 items for productive and receptive use (P-items) and another 450 words for receptive use only (R-items). An inventory of syntactic structures has also been drawn up and added to the report as *Appendix 2*.

(8) An indication of the degree of skill with which the learner will be able to do what has been specified in 1–7. The most important criterion for acceptable performance at *T-level* is the criterion that communication should be achieved by means of the foreign language. In addition, the communication

achieved should meet certain criteria for efficiency. For the oral skills which, as we have seen earlier, are central in the *T-level*, these criteria are:

(i)   that as a speaker the learner can make himself easily understood by a listener with native or near-native command of the language;

(ii) that as a listener the learner can understand the essence of what is said to him by a speaker with native or near-native command of the language without obliging the speaker to exert himself unduly (Van Ek and Alexander 1975:113).

As to the first criterion Van Ek and Alexander consider a speaker to be 'easily understood' if he can express himself at a reasonable pace, with sufficient precision and reasonably correctly. In a comment on the second criterion it is posited that a learner will have to be able to understand a speaker who expresses himself without many repetitions, with an accent which is similar to or closely resembles the standard accent, and with a speed which is not 'below the lower range of what is "normal"'. These are of course characterizations which are, as is admitted in the report, 'still far from explicit' (Van Ek and Alexander 1975:114), and which certainly would have to be made more precise.

Finally, we would like to point out that the variant of *T-level* discussed in the report is not intended to be considered as the ultimate specification, or the only specification possible, for English for the target group under discussion. In various places in the report (see e.g. Van Ek and Alexander 1975:33) it is stated that the method used in specifying the various *T-level* components was of necessity often a subjective one, based on introspection, intuition and experience. In the version which was developed later specifically for schools it is stated with regard to the words and structures listed that they are intended 'as no more than *recommended* language forms' (Van Ek 1976:19).

It is evident from our description of the *T-level* that a clear choice has been made for an approach to syllabus design in which the choice of language forms is subsequent to an explicit description of the intended communicative language behaviour of the target group. Such an approach, which in selecting and grading language material always takes the intended communicative language behaviour as a basis, has received increasing attention in the past ten years. The approach is often referred to in the literature as 'communicative', 'functional', 'notional' or 'functional–notional' (see e.g. Wilkins 1975, 1976a, Peck 1976, Shaw 1977, Munby 1978, Alexander 1979). The traditional approach, usually referred to as 'structural', 'formal' or 'grammatical', takes as a starting-point structural or formal characteristics of the language. In this book, we will use the terms 'functional–notional' and 'grammatical'. From the above it will be clear that the new approach has great advantages where formulating objectives is concerned. We shall discuss the consequences of this new approach for selection and gradation of course content in chapters 10 and 11.

The publication of Van Ek and Alexander (1975) called forth a host of positive as well as negative reactions in many European journals. Before we discuss these, however, we shall devote some attention to some of the developments that have taken place since the report first appeared, so that we can include these in our evaluation.

Since 1975 work has been done on filling in the *T-level* for languages other than English. A version for French, compiled by staff members of CREDIF under Coste, was published in 1976 with the title *Un niveau-seuil.* In a number of places, it deviates considerably from the original English version. The two most important differences, in our opinion, relate to the definition of the target group and the definition of what Van Ek and Alexander (1975) call *language functions* and Coste *et al.* (1976) *actes de parole. Un niveau-seuil* is not intended for one target group, as the *T-Level* is, but for five target groups, described as follows (Coste *et al.* 1976:47):

- des touristes, voyageurs;
- les travailleurs migrants et leurs familles;
- des spécialistes et professionels ayant besoin d'une language étrangère mais restant dans leur pays d'origine;
- des adolescents en système scolaire;
- de grands adolescents et de jeunes adultes en situation scolaire ou universitaire.

In *Un niveau-seuil* the various stages that are distinguished in the specification of the objective are not dealt with separately for each individual target group. The lists of *actes de parole* (Van Ek's *language functions*), for instance, the *notions* and their translation into French words and structures are always given for the five target groups together. It is left to the user to make those choices which are relevant to the target group he is aiming at. This gives *Un niveau-seuil* a more open character than the *T-Level*. A second important difference relates to the category of *actes de parole*, in which the language functions of the *T-Level* are further specified. The *actes de parole* are classified in the following manner (Coste *et al.* 1976:88–90):

- *intentions énonciatives*, the speech intentions on which utterances are based;
- *actes d'ordre (1)*: utterances which are not a response to other utterances;
- *actes d'ordre (2)*: responses to utterances under (1);
- *actes sociaux*, such as *saluer, prendre congé.* These could also have been included under *actes d'ordre (1)* or (2), but have been separated out because the translation into language forms allows little variation;
- *opérations discursives*: language functions relating to the discourse itself, such as *préciser, comparer, faire une digression.*

Furthermore, the distinctions drawn within these five sections are much more refined than in the *T-Level*. As Van Ek says in Coste *et al.* (1976:v): 'Bien que considérablement plus complexe que le système de catégories employé dans le *Threshold Level*, la classification qui en résulte permet bien davantage de rendre compte de toute la richesse de l'interaction linguistique.'

In addition to the French version, versions for Spanish (*Un nivel umbral*, Slagter 1979), for German (*Kontaktschwelle*, Baldegger *et al.* 1980) and for Italian (*Livello soglia*, Galli de' Paratesi 1981) have recently been published, and versions for Danish and Swedish have also been developed (Trim 1981:XIII).

Since 1975, a start has also been made with the specification of levels other than the *T-level*. An 'intermediary objective, roughly halfway between zero and the *Threshold Level*', from which it has directly been derived (Van Ek *et al.* 1977:2), called *Waystage*, was published in 1977. Furthermore, work based on the principles underlying the *T-Level*, but at a more advanced level is in progress (Van Ek 1978:37–8).

In the meantime, the influence of the ideas developed in the Council of Europe on FLT to adults has become clearly noticeable. In the revision of the specification of objectives of the 3-year certificate courses of the *Deutscher Volkshochschulverband* (see 9.3.2.2.), which have been adopted by the organizations of adult education institutes in five countries, these ideas have been used as a frame of reference. In the definition of a lower level – a *Grundbaustein* – which can be achieved after 1.5 to 2 years, the cooperation of the group of experts of the Council of Europe was sought in order to bring the descriptions of *T-level* and *Grundbaustein* into line with one another.

The *T-Level* has also become known in regular education. In 1976 Van Ek published a version for secondary education called *The Threshold Level for Modern Language Learning in Schools*, which deviates in only a few respects from the original model. Listening and speaking remain the most important skills, but for reading and writing a somewhat higher level is aimed at. The most important changes were made in the lists of topics: there is less emphasis on subjects which typically appeal to adults, and less attention is paid to tourism. On the other hand, topics concerned with education and schooling receive more attention. These changes are reflected in the lists of specific notions and the language forms needed to express these notions. The lists of language functions and general notions have remained virtually unchanged, since they are much less dependent on the choice of topics because of their general character. In other words, the language functions and general notions form the *common core* of every *T-level* variant. The difference between the version for adults and the one for schools is marginal: '. . . they are not really two different objectives but two versions of one and the same objective. We may consequently regard the threshold level as a master-objective for oral communication designed for the overall target-population of general beginners, with versions for various subgroups' (Van Ek 1976:19–20). In addition to the school version of the *T-Level* an adaptation of *Un niveau-seuil* for use in schools has also been made available (Porcher *et al.* 1980). A number of countries are considering incorporating the *T-level* objectives, with adaptations if necessary, into the official curricula. This has already been done in a few places, for instance in the state of Hessen in the Federal Republic of Germany, where they play a part in the *Rahmenrichtlinien* for the *Sekundarstufe I* (see Van Ek 1978:27; Raasch 1978b:466; Lauerbach 1979b:149). They are also the basis of a memorandum which was published and discussed widely in the Netherlands in 1977, in which proposals were made for the development of a national curriculum for foreign languages (Van Ek and Groot 1977).

Within the project of the Council of Europe work is not only being done on the specification of objectives for different proficiency levels, although this receives most attention. P. Groot and A. Harrison have developed a specimen test for the English version of the *Threshold Level*, and have tried them out in various countries for some years (see Groot 1977), and L. Alexander has published a report in which he discusses some methodological implications of *Waystage* and *T-Level* (Alexander 1977).

Lastly, we would like to mention a report by the chairman of the committee, in which suggestions are made for a further development of the European *unit-credit* system for modern language learning by adults (Trim 1977), and a report on the activities of the committee during 1971–1981 (Trim 1981).

The work of the group of experts of the Council of Europe has, as we have seen, received ample attention in the various journals. Apart from great appreciation for the model for defining objectives, a lot of criticism was also voiced, which was justified in some cases, but which in other cases can be attributed to a wrong interpretation of the model presented. In their discussion of Van Ek and Alexander (1975), Ickenroth and Nas (1977:17) conclude: 'the approach developed by the Council of Europe group does not succeed in showing us what it promised to do: how a definition of situations in terms of settings, roles, topics and notions will define lists that the system should ultimately "generate", i.e. the lists of words and structures.' This, however, was not promised in the *T-Level*. What is offered there is a number of steps which have to be taken consecutively in specifying foreign language learning objectives. The model prescribes that at every stage that which has been specified in the previous stage should be taken into account; in other words, the choice made with respect to for instance the language forms may not clash with what is contained in the list of specific notions. At every stage, therefore, a choice is made. At no point is it stated, as Ickenroth and Nas seem to suggest, that decisions taken at an earlier stage completely determine those at a later stage in advance (see also Van Els 1977). Van Ek (1978:38) states clearly, much more so than Van Ek and Alexander (1975), that the model 'enables the user to adapt the specifications by revising choices at any stage of the decision procedure'.

The bulk of the criticism of the work done by the Council of Europe group relates to the choices made at the various stages, and specifically to the choice of language forms (see e.g. Hoffmann 1976, Quetz 1977, Ickenroth and Nas 1977, Hill 1977). The arbitrary character of the choices, of which, as we have said before, the authors were very well aware, has repeatedly been pointed out, and the list of language forms has been shown to need revision in many places. Hill (1977) and Lauerbach (1979b), for instance, point out that, although the *T-Level* focuses mainly on oral skills, and more specifically on successful participation in conversations, the language forms which normally play an important role in conversation, for instance 'fillers' such as 'you know', 'I see', 'Well, I mean', and 'question tags', hardly occur in the lists of language forms. Groot (1977) encountered a different sort of problem when drawing up a specimen test for the English version of the *T-Level*. He concluded that the inventory of language forms is not adequate for doing what has been specified in other components of the model. In other words, more was promised in the behavioural specifications than could be realized through the language forms specified. Other problems are pointed out by Raasch (1978a), De Vriendt (1977), Zapp (1979a) and Lauerbach (1979b). Raasch regrets that a phonetic/phonological description of the language forms is lacking. De Vriendt criticizes the emphasis on tourism in the *T-Level*, which allegedly makes for a bias towards certain social groups. De Vriendt also questions the emphasis on oral skills, and Zapp does the same with respect to the version intended for use in schools. Lauerbach has another objection to this latter version: it is directed too much towards the *lingua franca* type of English that is used internationally. She adds (p. 153): 'Es besteht die Gefahr, dass eine solche Interpretation . . . zu Lehrmaterialien führen wird, die fremdsprachliche Kommunikation als steriles, weil von sozio-kulturellen Bezügen losgelöstes, kommunikatives Verhalten modellieren.' A last point of criticism has already been advanced in our discussion of the last component of the model: the indication of the degree of skill with which the learner will be able to do what has been specified in previous components. The characterization given is open to many interpretations and will have to be made more specific.

The many critical discussions which have been devoted to the project of the Council of Europe have indicated a number of areas in which the specifications that have appeared so far could be improved. On the whole, however, the model underlying these specifications has been favourably received; it has a number of clear advantages. In the first place, it is quite flexible, and can in principle be applied to any target group. Secondly, the model yields objectives with a high degree of explicitness. It gives the learner a clear indication of what he will be able to do and which language forms he will need to do it. In the third place, the model yields comparable objectives for different target groups, since it will always be possible to find out if, and to what extent, different choices have been made by comparing the specifications of the various components.

As we have said before, the definition of the objectives of a threshold level developed on the basis of this model has had some influence on European FLT, both in regular school teaching and outside it. Whether the original goal of the project of the Council of Europe, developing a European *unit–credit* system for FLT to adults, will ever be realized is still an open question, since for such a system to function properly the various units must be closely integrated. Because of the open character of the various stages in the definition of the objectives, especially in *Un niveau-seuil*, such an integration is bound to meet with many problems.

9.3.2.2 The Volkshochschulzertifikate

In the middle of the 1960s the *Deutscher Volkshochschulverband* (DVV) started with the development of certificates (the *VHS-Zertifikate*) in order to systematize and harmonize FLT in the adult education institutes united in the DVV. First of all, a certificate for English was developed, and introduced in 1968. The certificate for English was followed by certificates for French (1969), German (1971), Russian (1971), Spanish (1971) and Italian (1973). An *Aufbau-zertifikat Englisch Wirtschaft* was developed in 1972 (PAS-DVV 1977[5]:6). By now, the *VHS-Zertifikate* are no longer an exclusively German affair. In 1970, the organizations of adult education institutes in Austria and Switzerland joined the programme and recently Denmark, the Netherlands and Sweden have also joined, so that the *VHS-Zertifikate* have now been introduced in six countries, which are united in the *Internationale Zertifikatskonferenz* (IZK). Participants in the certificate courses can, if they wish, sit for the certificate exam, which is held simultaneously in the six countries. The exam papers are drawn up by the *Pädagogische Arbeitsstelle* (PAS), the DVV institute which is responsible for the evaluation of the project, and which also prepares new developments in collaboration with delegates from the six countries.

In 1967 the aims of the *VHS-Zertifikate* were described as follows (Nowacek 1973[3]:5):

> Mit der Prüfung zum VHS-Zertifikat . . . erbringt ein Teilnehmer den Nachweis, dass er den Grad an Fertigkeit im mündlichen und schriftlichen Gebrauch der . . . Umgangssprache erreicht hat, der es ihm ermöglicht, sich bei einem Auslandsaufenthalt in allen wichtigen Situationen sprachlich zu behaupten. Er soll in der Lage sein, ein in natürlichem Sprachtempo geführtes Gespräch über Themen des täglichen Lebens zu verstehen and sich daran zu beteiligen. Er soll ferner eigene Gedanken im Rahmen des vorgegebenen Sprachmaterials mündlich und schriftlich so formulieren können, dass die Verständigung nicht beeinträchtigt wird.

These global aims were then made somewhat more concrete by means of an added vocabulary list, containing between 1600 and 2200 entries, depending on the target language, a list of syntactic structures, and some sample tests.

In 1973 a beginning was made with an extensive evaluation of the *VHS-Zertifikate* for the various languages. This evaluation demonstrated that there were considerable differences between the *Zertifikate*, in spite of the fact that they were based on the same aims. There was also some unease about the emphasis on tourism in the *VHS-Zertifikate*, since it is not the case that one only uses the foreign language 'bei einem Auslandsaufenthalt', but also, and perhaps even mainly, in one's own country; when listening to the radio or reading books or periodicals for instance. On the basis of the results from the evaluation it was decided to harmonize the certificates for the various languages. This need became all the more pressing because of the growing number of people signing up for the certificate courses. In 1976 approximately 10,000 people took part in the certificate examinations, while an even larger number attended the courses without taking the exam (Bianchi 1977a:158). It was decided that this harmonization could best be brought about by having a common interpretation of the global aims, based on a model for specifying objectives which was largely not language-specific, and by developing a testing model which could be used for all certificate examinations. The first step taken was to specify the degree of skill with which the learner can understand, speak, read and write the foreign language at the end of the certificate course. We shall give an abridged version of the definitions per skill, in Bianchi's translation (Bianchi 1977b:31–2). For the complete specifications in German see PAS-DVV (1977[5]:14–17).

> *Listening Comprehension*: At the end of the course the student should be able to understand the gist and detail of everyday utterances made at normal speed by native speakers using a standard variety of English with only slight variations in accent.

Speaking: At the end of the course the student should be able to express himself adequately in terms of content and expression, using generally comprehensible intonation and pronunciation and predominantly correct grammar
- in spontaneous, brief reaction in everyday situations;
- in expressing opinions, giving information or descriptions within the framework of everyday conversational exchange.

Intelligibility and linguistic appropriateness are more important than correct grammar.

Reading: At the end of the course the student should be able to read hitherto unseen texts and to understand both the gist and the detail.

Writing: At the end of the course the student should be able to write personal and semi-formal letters, expressing himself adequately in terms of content and expression, using predominantly correct grammar and spelling. Intelligibility and linguistic appropriateness are more important than correct grammar or spelling.

Each of these definitions is given an extensive gloss. 'Normal speed' in the definition of listening comprehension, for instance, means that the rate of speech has not been slowed down for teaching purposes, and that it has not been affected by strong emotions on the part of the speaker. There is also some elaboration on what is meant by 'standard variety', and 'utterances' are further specified. It is also recognized that these descriptions do not provide a clear indication of the degree of skill reached at the end of the course; this is why the reader is also referred to a chapter in which the final tests are described, as well as the grading system to be used (PAS-DVV 1977[5], ch. 4). What strikes one in the definitions cited here is that the emphasis placed on 'Auslandsaufenthalt' in the description of the global aims has disappeared, and that there is now a separate heading for reading. The grading system also shows that the reading skill has gained in importance in the new certificates, and that listening comprehension has also become more important.

After specifying the degree of proficiency, the next step was to indicate more precisely how phrases such as 'in allen wichtigen Situationen' and 'Themen des täglichen Lebens' in the descriptions of the aims should be interpreted. Four lists were drawn up (PAS-DVV 1977[5]:25–35):

(1) a list of language functions the learner will have at his command. The terms used for language functions are *Intentionen* and *Sprachabsichten*;
(2) a list of topics with respect to which the learner will be able to use the foreign language. The term *Themen* is used for topics;
(3) a list of settings, called *Situationen*, in which the learner will be able to use the foreign language. In this list the roles the learner will be able to fulfil are also indicated;
(4) a list of types of texts the learner will be able to understand or produce.

For the first three lists, Van Ek and Alexander's *Threshold Level* (1975) served as a frame of reference.

Thus far, the certificate model is not language-specific. The lists of words and structures, which constitute the third part of the new certificate model, are of course language-specific. They have been taken over from the 'old' certificates for the different languages. It did not seem necessary to change the content of these lists since the objectives described above 'can be reached using the linguistic material contained in [these] lists' (Bianchi 1977b:32). As we have said before, the learner is given information about what he will have to do to obtain the certificate in addition to the information contained in the objectives described above. He is also given extensive information about the way in which the final examination and the grading system have been set up. Furthermore, a sample test of each part of the examination is provided. The first certificate examination new style was held in the six affiliated countries in the spring of 1978.

Although it is not difficult to criticize the new *VHS-Zertifikate* on a number of points, we agree with Gutschow's (1978:2) opinion: 'Es kann kein Zweifel daran bestehen, dass die vorliegende Überarbeitung einen wesentlichen Fortschritt innerhalb einer seit Jahren bewährten Konzeption darstellt.' For a number of critical remarks see also Gutschow (1978).

To conclude, we shall discuss some recent developments very briefly. We have already mentioned in 9.3.2.1. that the DVV sought the cooperation of the Council of Europe group in the development of a *Grundbaustein*, a level that can be reached in 50–60 per cent of the time needed to obtain a *Zertifikat*. The aim was to gear the *Grundbaustein* as closely as possible to the *T-Level*. By the end of 1981 *Grundbausteine* were available for English, French, German, Russian and Spanish and an Italian version was in preparation (PAS-DVV 1981). There is also a proposal under consideration to split up the *Grundbaustein* into two levels, *Grundbaustein* part I and II. Furthermore, there is a proposal to develop other options, such as English and French for the technical professions and for trade and commerce, alongside with the present *Zertifikate* and as a continuation of the *Grundbaustein*. Finally, there are plans to extend the system upwards by offering other options beside the already existing *Aufbauzertifikat Englisch Wirtschaft* which continue from the certificate level. An extension of the system to two more languages, Danish and Dutch, is also envisaged (Bogenschneider 1982). The journals *Zielsprache Deutsch, Zielsprache Englisch, Zielsprache Französisch* and *Zielsprache Spanisch*, edited under the auspices of DVV and the Austrian and Swiss organizations of adult education institutes, will keep the reader informed of these and future developments.

9.4 Conclusion

In the first part of this chapter we argued that there has been a considerable growth of interest in FLT on the part of governments and educational circles in a number of countries. More and more people have begun to ask themselves whether foreign language needs were optimally catered for, and in a number of countries research has been done into the nature and extent of these needs. Our discussion of the Dutch needs analysis demonstrated that such research can contribute significantly to the determination of an FLT policy, but we have also seen that it is not easy to translate research data into a policy and that other factors than just the needs factor will have to be taken into account. We have also devoted some attention to a special aspect of FLT policy, namely the desirability of FLT to young children, and we have discussed the experiences gained with FLES in a number of countries. The second part of this chapter was devoted to a discussion of aims and objectives, and the desirability of translating the former into the latter. We have paid considerable attention to the *T-level* and the *VHS-Zertifikate*, exponents of the functional–notional approach to curriculum development. We have seen that there are considerable advantages to such an approach, since it yields objectives that explicitly describe what a learner can do at the end of the teaching programme. What this new approach has not (yet) provided is a more explicit description of the *degree* of skill the learner will achieve in the target language than has been provided in the past. The *T-Level*, too, contains formulations such as 'reasonable speed', 'sufficient precision', 'reasonable correctness', and 'normal speech rate'. In the next two chapters we shall discuss the implications for selection and gradation of course content of the new approach.

10
Selection of course content

10.1 Introduction

It is impossible to teach or learn everything of a foreign language, even if there were no limits to the time available: there is no native speaker who has a complete command of all the aspects of his native tongue. In education we shall always have to make do with a limited number of hours that can be spent on (a) foreign language(s). This makes it all the more imperative that a well founded choice is made. In doing this we should be guided in the first place by the objectives that have been formulated, since it is necessary that the course content is selected in such a way that it enables the pupil to do what is specified in the objectives. In selecting course content we shall also have to pay attention to a number of other factors, such as the specific level for which the selection is made, and the amount of teaching time available. We discuss the relation between each of these three factors and the selection of course content separately in 10.2., although these factors are in fact closely related. For instance, in the formulation of the objectives the time factor will already have been taken into account of course. We shall call these factors 'external', because they do not belong to the domain of language itself, they are not linguistic; this in contrast with factors which also play a role in the selection of course content, such as the size of linguistic classes; factors, in other words, which are 'internal' to the language.

Following Halliday *et al.* (1964:202–7) and Corder (1973:205) we shall distinguish two parts in the selection process. In 10.3. we shall pay attention to the first part of the process, which relates to the demarcation of the *type* of language material. From the total of language material we first of all select the type of dialect, register, style, and medium to be taught. In making this choice we will be guided by the objectives and other external factors. After the *type* of language material has been delineated, we shall have to make a decision about *how many* and *which items* (or *language forms*) should be selected. We shall discuss this second part in the selection process in detail in 10.4. In the selection of the *language forms* as well as in the selection of the *type* of language material the external factors mentioned above play an important role. The selection of the language forms, however, is also dependent on characteristics of the language itself. At the phonological level one can hardly even speak of a selection. The phonemes constitute a very small class of highly frequent items, which can, therefore, hardly be dispensed with. On the other hand, the possibilities for selection at the lexical level are abundant, as the lexicon constitutes a very extensive open class (see 10.4.1.). Where selection is possible it is obvious that one should try to develop criteria for selection. In 10.4.2. we shall discuss a number of criteria for selection, namely frequency, range, availability, coverage, and psychological and didactic criteria. Finally, in 10.4.3., we shall discuss the process of selection at the linguistic levels at which such a choice is possible and/or meaningful. We shall discuss the process of selection of words, structures and texts in the order indicated here, whereby we shall mainly focus on the selection of words.

10.2　The role of external factors

Before making a selection it should be known for which objectives and level the selection is made, and how much teaching time is available. Objectives, level and available time are external factors which are of considerable importance to the selection process. They delineate the framework within which the selection of type of language material, amount of language material, and individual language forms should take place. These factors will be dealt with separately, although, as has been remarked earlier in 10.1., they are in fact closely related.

Objectives　Of the external factors influencing selection the objectives are the most important, since the selection must be such that· it will enable the learners to carry out the tasks described in the objectives. It makes an important difference whether the selection is made within the framework of FLT for general purposes or of FLT for special purposes. When selecting for 'general' courses one usually bases oneself on a large number of different types of language material, and when selecting for 'special' courses one bases oneself on special types of language material. This does not mean that the material selected in special courses is totally different from the material one encounters in general courses. Both types of course will have a certain amount of language material in common, a *common core* which is at the basis of any form of language use. A course which has as its objective: 'The learner has skills at his disposal in the foreign language enabling him to get along as a tourist in those countries in which the language in question is spoken' will have, apart from the *common core*, not much in common with a course which is based on the following objective: 'The learner can read scientific texts in the foreign language relating to his profession.' On the other hand, different courses which are aimed at different scientific areas will have more teaching material in common than just the *common core* which can be found in *all* courses. Within the language of science we can again distinguish a core of elements which are common to the individual scientific areas (see e.g. Erk 1972:2).

Not only the distinction between FLT for general purposes and FLT for special purposes plays a role in the selection of course content, but also the distinction between aims and objectives. Aims only give us limited insight into the type of language material that should be incorporated into the course, and only roughly determine the area within which the selection of language forms (words, structures, etc.) should take place. When objectives are available, as is for instance the case in the *T-level* or *Un Niveau-seuil* (which are both exponents of a functional–notional approach, see 9.3.2.1.), including, among other things, a specification of the *settings* in which the learner will be able to use the foreign language, the *topics* he will be able to discuss, the *notions* he will be able to use, and the *language functions* he will be able to fulfil in the foreign language, then there is also a precise delineation of the areas within which the selection of language forms should take place. Because much more attention is paid to the precise description of target language behaviour in a functional–notional approach than in a grammatical approach, it can supply the framework within which the selection of language material should take place much more clearly and readily than the grammatical approach. For the importance of objectives for the selection of course content, see also Corder (1973:223), Raasch (1977), Schumacher (1978:50–5) and Kühn (1979:59–69).

Level   The level aimed at is a second external factor influencing selection. A course for beginners will not contain the same type and the same amount of language material as a course for advanced learners. There are other ways in which the level influences selection. The higher the level for which one selects, the more important it is to have concrete objectives at one's disposal. At the very lowest level this is less important because of the fact that any language contains a certain number of elements – the *common core* – which any language learner will have to master, irrespective of the use he will put the language to.

Time   The last external factor which is of importance in carrying out a well founded selection is the number of hours available for FLT, and how they are spread through the curriculum. It stands to reason that more material can be incorporated into a two-year course of three contact-hours a week than in a two-year course of two contact-hours a week, but it also matters whether the course in question is an *intensive* one (for instance, 120 contact-hours spread out over six weeks) or a *non-intensive* one (for instance 120 contact-hours spread out over two years and divided up into two periods of 30 weeks with two contact-hours per week). DeFrancis (1971:291), for instance, concludes on the basis of experience that in a *non-intensive* course more material can usually be worked through than in an *intensive* course of comparable length, something he mainly ascribes to the more ample opportunity of assigning homework inherent in *non-intensive* courses. A good insight into the optimum amount of material to be learned over the entire course period as well as over individual parts thereof would be very useful in selecting course content. However, little research has been done in this area, and the research that has been done (see e.g. Fiks and Corbino 1967) is full of flaws, so that few generalizations can be made on the basis of the results obtained.

Some other factors   We have already seen that the amount of material which can be dealt with in a certain period may depend on the type of course that is provided (*intensive* or *non-intensive*) and on the level of proficiency already attained by the learner. We wish to mention two more factors which should play a role in determining the optimal quantity of learning material for a course or parts thereof:

(1)   the type of school attended by the learner. As a type of school like the British grammar school is attended by learners who on the whole experience less difficulty in foreign language learning than pupils from a type of school

like the secondary modern school, more material can be dealt with in the first type of school than in the second type;

(2) the language background of the learner. In one hour of Spanish for native speakers of Italian, for instance, it will be possible to deal with more material than could be dealt with in an hour of Spanish for native speakers of Swedish.

Not only the L1 background is an important factor, but also the L2 background may play a role. A speaker of German who has learned French will in general have less trouble attaining a certain level of proficiency in Spanish or Italian than a German who does not know French (9.2.2.).

10.3 Selection of type of language material

The selection of the type of language material is guided by the objectives and other external factors, as indicated in the previous paragraphs. Selection of the type of language entails selection in the area of linguistic variation: dialect, register, style and medium (Mackey 1965:163).

10.3.1 Dialect

Any language encompasses a large number of socially and geographically determined varieties (regional and social dialects), from which a choice should be made for FLT purposes. In general this choice will not be a difficult one, especially where FLT to beginners is concerned, since the foreign language learner will in general find most use for the standard language, by which we mean proficiency in the variety which is recognized as the norm by the native speakers of that language. It is the variety mostly used in the media (books, newspapers, radio, TV) and in education (Criper and Widdowson 1975:170, Bell 1976:153). There are languages, however, that exhibit a number of regional varieties which have themselves attained standard language status. We could mention Spanish, incorporating for example Castilian and a number of South-American varieties, and English, incorporating for example British English and American English. These varieties differ not only in accent but also in grammatical form (for instance, American English *I have gotten* vs. British English *I have got*) and lexically (for instance American English *hood* vs. British English *bonnet*). Another regional variety of English which has attained the status of standard language is Australian English, which increasingly serves as a model for the teaching of English as a foreign language in parts of Southeast Asia. The variety spoken in India, even though this variety is spoken as a native language only by a limited number of people, appears to have gained in status as a norm for Indian speakers of English (Halliday *et al.* 1964:173-4, 293-6). The choice of one of the varieties mentioned above largely depends on geographical and/or political considerations. Most European countries have in the past chosen for British English, but more and more teachers have begun to wonder about the desirability of exclusively opting for this variety of English (see e.g. Atkinson 1975, Gutknecht 1975, Dahlmann-Resing 1978).

If a standard variety of a language has been selected, then this does not yet mean that a certain accent has also been selected, since there may be considerable differences between speakers of the standard language with respect to their accent. The selection of a certain accent is not always an easy matter, since it is not always possible to single out an accent which clearly has a higher status than other accents. For American English and British English the choice is not a very difficult one, since in the US no other accent has more prestige than General American, and in Great Britain the accent usually referred to as RP (received pronunciation) has the highest status (Windsor Lewis 1971).

When making a choice from a number of dialects and/or accents it is finally of importance to know for which level and which skills the selection is made. For a basic level and for productive skills one will in general opt for the standard language and a prestigious accent, while a selection for receptive skills, especially for an advanced level, would probably also include different dialects and almost certainly different accents.

10.3.2 Register

We have seen in 10.2. that it is important for the selection of course content to know whether the selection is made within the framework of FLT for general purposes, i.e. teaching directed at language use that is not restricted to certain situations or subject areas, or of FLT for special purposes, i.e. teaching directed at certain specific situations or subject areas. Language use which is characteristic for certain situations or subject areas is usually referred to as *register* in the literature (Halliday *et al*. 1964). A term also encountered is *jargon*. One can for instance distinguish between a register used at Union meetings and a register used in scientific articles, which can again be split up into different registers for different subject areas. Registers are usually primarily distinguished at the lexical level; it is usually the terminology belonging to a certain situation or a certain subject area that distinguishes one register from another. It is, however, also possible to distinguish between registers on a syntactic basis. Passive sentences, for instance, will occur more frequently in scientific articles than in football reports. A selection of course content based on objectives therefore entails a selection among registers.

10.3.3 Style

Selection of course content may also mean a selection regarding style. Joos (1961) distinguishes five styles: *frozen, formal, consultative, casual* and *intimate*, ranked in a hierarchy of decreasing formality. Most linguists (e.g. Crystal and Davy 1969, Turner 1973, Trudgill 1974) consider such a division premature and prefer to speak of a style continuum, ranging from formal to informal, because the only thing that can be demonstrated is that one style contains more linguistic characteristics indicative of (in)formal language use than some other style; in other words, one can only indicate relative differences between styles. The use of a more or less formal style depends on a large number of closely interrelated factors, such as the social status of the various participants in linguistic interaction, the nature of the subject matter, and of the setting, and the medium used. It is therefore hardly surprising that for most forms of FLT no specific choice is made between either a formal or an informal style, but in some cases such a choice can be useful. In the selection of material for a course which has the specific objective to teach skills in reading books and articles in a certain professional area, the obvious choice will be a formal style.

10.3.4 Medium

Selection of medium relates to the distinction between spoken and written language. Until a few decades ago, courses were almost exclusively constructed on the basis of written material. This had to do with the fact that linguistic research had been mainly concerned with written language. Systematic research into spoken language did not become possible until the human voice could be properly recorded. Research has shown that considerable differences exist between spoken and written language. Sciarone (1979b:75-7) found such differences on the basis of a comparison between the frequency lists of French words of Juilland *et al.* (1970), which is based on written language, and Gougenheim *et al.* (1967²), which is based on spoken language. Schonell *et al.* (1956) also concluded, on the basis of research into the oral productive vocabulary of adult native speakers of English, that there are significant differences between written and spoken language. In 9.3.2.1. we have already pointed to the use of 'fillers' such as 'you know' and 'I see', which is characteristic of spoken language, as are a number of stereotyped phrases which help the speaker plan his utterances. They enable him to collect his thoughts and to concentrate; for instance:

(1) *First of all I would like to say that. . . . . . .*
(2) *Zunächst einmal möchte ich Folgendes sagen. . .*

Rath (1975) points out the fact that anacoluthon and correction frequently occur, often in combination, in spoken language, something which hardly ever happens in written language, because one can correct oneself in the course of writing without the corrections showing up in the final text; for example:

(3) *(. . .) die extrem flache Form. Mit dem mit der kann man natürlich(. . . .) (Van Os 1974:220)*
(4) *und das ist also eine wirklich ein ein ein weites Feld für Wissenschaftler (op. cit.:227)*
(5) *das Merkwürdige ist dass ja doch jetzt eigentlich die Boulette oder, nehmen wir an, die besteht aus Hackfleisch (op. cit.:229)*

Granted that many differences exist between written and spoken language, it still remains the question in how far these differences will affect the selection of course content. For a course which is primarily aimed at developing oral skills, it will be useful to incorporate a number of elements which are typical of spoken language, such as certain lexical items, the 'fillers' discussed above, and certain stereotyped phrases. It will be less useful, except perhaps for developing listening comprehension, to select language containing many anacolutha, corrections, etc. In the first place it should be noted that texts containing many of these elements are very hard to follow when written out in full, and in the second place there is no urgent need to train learners in using anacolutha and corrections.

These ways of sustaining language production are, unlike 'fillers' and stereo-typed phrases, universal characteristics of language production processes. When we correct ourselves during foreign language production, we do this in essentially the same way as we do in our native language (see also 3.1.1.).

In previous paragraphs we have discussed selection with regard to dialect, register, style and medium separately. This should not lead to the conclusion, however, that the choices can be made independently, since a choice in one area can determine the choice in another area to a considerable extent. For example, selecting the register that is characteristic of scientific articles, means also selecting standard language and formal style.

10.4 Selection of language forms: which and how many?

The selection of the *type* of language material having been made, the next ques-tion that presents itself is *how many* and *which* language forms ought to be selected. The selection of language forms will be guided by the type of material selected and by external factors, the most important of which we consider to be the objectives. In this connection it is especially important to know if the objec-tives only include the receptive skills, or the productive skills as well. In the latter case, it will be useful to differentiate in the selection between items which only have to be used receptively, and items which also have to be available produc-tively. Here we again wish to point out the importance of well specified objec-tives, since the better the objectives are specified, the easier it will be to make a well motivated choice of the type of language material and the language forms; in other words, the better the objectives are specified, the more limited the options open to us. Our options, however, are not solely dependent on external factors, but also on the properties of the language itself. The selection is partly determined by the linguistic level to which the selection relates.

10.4.1 Options at the linguistic levels

The options at the various linguistic levels are largely dependent on the size of the linguistic classes at these levels and on the frequency of the elements within these classes. The smaller the classes, and the higher the frequency of the elements within these classes, the more limited the options are. The larger the classes, and the lower the frequency of the elements in these classes, the more possibilities for choice there are. This explains why the options are most limited at the phonological level, and least limited at the text level. Just how limited the possibilities at the phonological level are is clearly shown by the fact that the phonological systems of most languages encompass fewer than 50 distinctive units. British English (RP) has only 44 phonemes, if we follow Gimson's (1980[3]) classification.

The options are limited at the morphological level as well; the grammatical morphemes, for example, constitute a closed system of a limited number of rules which in general have a high frequency. There may, incidentally, be con-siderable differences in the possibilities for selection in different languages. A Dutch course which pays no attention to diminutive formation rules is virtually unthinkable, but an English course without such rules could get one quite a long way.

It is not until one gets to the syntactic level that one can realistically speak of a possibility and a need for selection. It is possible to indicate certain patterns within the total number of sentence patterns occurring in a language without which efficient language use would be impossible. The following structures will occur in any basic English course:

(1) *John is coming* (SV)
(2) *He is a crook* (SVC)
(3) *Mary is in the house* (SVA)
(4) *He caught the ball* (SVO)
(5) *I put it on the table* (SVOA)

On the other hand, the following structures, which are not very frequent and can furthermore be replaced by other structures, will probably not even occur in a course for advanced learners:

(6) *Naked as/that I was,* I braved the storm
(7) *Miraculous though their survival seemed,* it was nothing to what lay ahead
(8) *Be he friend or enemy,* the law regards him as a criminal
                    (examples taken from Quirk *et al.* 1972:748–52).

That selection at the syntactic level is considered possible and useful is evidenced by the existence of 'basic structure lists' alongside 'basic vocabulary lists' (see 10.4.3.1. and 10.4.3.2.). By a 'basic structure list' we mean a list of structures (or, in the case of a basic vocabulary list, words) which is the minimum that a learner needs to be able to communicate in the foreign language at the level indicated in the objectives. In comparison to the possibilities for selection at the lexical level, however, the options are still rather limited.

The possibilities for selection at the lexical level are extensive for two reasons: on the one hand, the lexicon of a language contains many items, and on the other hand, many of these items occur only very infrequently. One of the oldest and best-known word counts (Kaeding 1898), which is based on a corpus of written German of nearly 11,000,000 words, yielded a total of 258,173 lexical forms, of which approximately half occurred only once. It will be clear that only a very small proportion of the total number of words in a language can be selected. It should be added here, however, that the possibilities for selection, or rather, reduction of the total number of words to a number that can be managed in teaching, differ from category to category. Figure 10.1, which indicates the ratio between the relative sizes of different word classes and the frequency with which they are used, gives a clear picture of the possibilities for selection per word class. The figure comes from Mackey (1965:169), who based himself on figures obtained for French, provided by Guiraud (1960:36). It clearly shows that the possibilities for selection are the most abundant within the class of nouns and the most limited for function words, also called structure words. In comparison with most word classes, the latter are very few in number: less than one per cent of the total number of words, but they have a relative frequency of

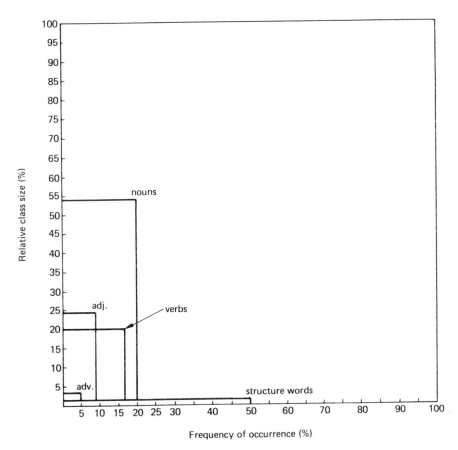

Fig. 10.1   Relation between class size and frequency (Mackey 1965, 169)

approximately 50 per cent. In other words, half of the words we use are function words. When the relative sizes of the word classes at the various frequency levels are examined (e.g. 1–100, 101–200, 201–300, 301–400), a picture emerges as in fig. 10.2. From these figures it can be concluded that a large number of function words belongs to the group of most frequent words. This fact has led to function words no longer being taken into consideration in some counts carried out for FLT purposes, but being unconditionally incorporated into the basic vocabulary lists.

We have seen that the possibilities for selection at the phonological, morphological, syntactic and lexical levels are largely determined by the size of the various linguistic classes and by the frequency of the elements within these classes. The criteria for selection discussed below are all based on the presupposition that it is possible and useful to reduce the number of language forms to be learned to manageable proportions. In other words, the selection criteria discussed below all presuppose countability. It will be clear, therefore, that such

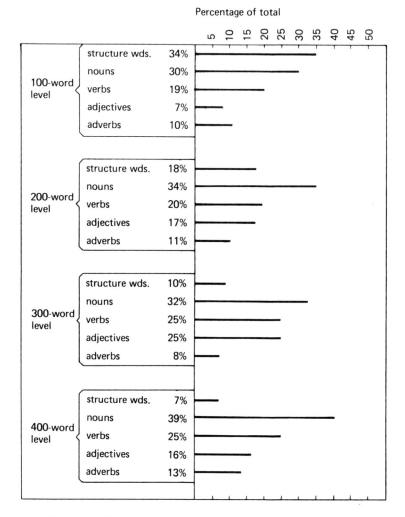

Fig. 10.2 Relation between size of word classes and level of frequency
(Mackey 1965, 171)

criteria are not, or at most indirectly, applicable to the choice of texts for use in FLT.

10.4.2 Some criteria for selection

At those levels at which a choice has to be made, one will try to select those language forms which will enable the learner, within the amount of teaching time available, to carry out the tasks described in the objectives as efficiently as possible. In other words, selection of course content entails a conscious selection of those forms which are considered most 'useful', 'suitable', or 'important', given the objectives. In making such a choice one could be guided by one's own intuitions and experience. There is, however, a not inconsiderable chance that the results of such a selection will not be the best possible, and that someone else would arrive at a rather different selection on the basis of his own experience and intuitions. For this reason, one will usually not want to base oneself solely on one's own intuitions and experience, but also on those of one's colleagues, for instance by asking them to comment on the material selected, or by forming a group of colleagues who each draw up their own lists. In the latter case the selection is eventually achieved by compiling a new list based on the lists obtained in this manner. This is usually referred to as intersubjective selection.

In general, however, one will feel the need for a firmer basis, and one will therefore start looking for more objective criteria that could be used as guidelines in making a selection. In the course of time some criteria for selection have been developed, of which we will discuss the most important ones in this and subsequent paragraphs. We shall limit ourselves in this paragraph to a brief characterization. In the later paragraphs we shall discuss the assumptions on which these criteria are based in more detail, and we shall furthermore discuss the role that these criteria play at the various linguistic levels. We shall see that most criteria under discussion have been developed first of all for, and have been mainly applied in, lexical selection. For this reason we have included a more detailed discussion of these criteria, their background, applications and limitations in the paragraph on lexical selection (10.4.3.1.). Some of these criteria were later also used for syntactic selection. We shall discuss the criteria separately, but in reality one does not usually use one criterion, but a combination of criteria, as will be demonstrated in the following paragraphs.

Frequency One of the best-known criteria is the criterion of how frequently words and structures occur in a sample of texts which are representative of the language use described in the objectives. Words and structures which occur most frequently in the sample are preferred to less frequent words and structures.

Range By range (also called *distribution, dispersion* or *repartition*) is meant the way in which words and structures are distributed over the various parts of which the sample consists. In applying the criterion of range, words and structures which are evenly distributed over the various parts of the sample will be preferred to words and structures which are very frequent in some parts but occur very infrequently or not at all in other parts.

Availability The criterion of availability (a translation of the original French term *disponibilité*) relates to the readiness with which a word is remembered and used in relation to a specific situation or theme (Mackey 1965:183). Michéa (1953:340), who developed this criterion as a participant in the *Français Fondamental* (FF) project, gives us the following global definition: 'Un mot disponible est un mot qui, sans être particulièrement fréquent, est cependant toujours prêt à être employé, et se présente immédiatement à l'esprit au moment où l'on en a besoin. C'est un mot qui, faisant partie d'associations d'idées usuelles, existe en puissance chez le sujet parlant, dès que ces associations entrent en jeu.' Michéa found that such concrete words as *fourchette, coude, dent* and *jupe*, which are readily available to even very young children for use in situations in which these words are indispensable, were not very frequent in the corpus of spoken French compiled for FF. In order to determine the availability of such words, it was decided to ask a large number of subjects to write down the most useful words relating to a number of themes (*centres d'intérêt*). The results were used as a basis for correcting the frequencies in the oral records of the FF project (see 10.4.3.1.).

Coverage   The criterion of coverage relates to the extent to which a word can replace other words or, in other words, the extent to which a word can do the work of other words. Mackey (1965:184–6) and Savard (1970:19–30) in more detail, discuss a number of criteria that can be used to determine the coverage of a word:

(1) *Definition*. The coverage of a word is related to the extent to which it can be used to define other words. Verbs like *get* and *take*, nouns like *person* and *part*, adjectives like *old* and *young* are words which can replace quite a number of other words. By combining for instance *young* with *sheep, cow, dog* and *cat* we can avoid the words *foal, calf, puppy* and *kitten*.

(2) *Inclusion*. Hyperonyms rate highly because they include the meanings of a number of other words and can therefore be used instead of these words, while this is not the case the other way around. The word *siège*, for instance, can replace the words *fauteuil, chaise, divan* and *sofa*.

(3) *Combination*. Words which can be combined into compounds which can replace other words rate more highly than words which cannot be combined in this manner. Mackey (1965:185) gives the following examples: the combination of *news + paper + man* makes the word *journalist* redundant, as do the words *hand + book* for *manual*.

(4) *Extension*. Words with many meanings rate more highly than words with few meanings. On the basis of this criterion one would prefer selecting a word like *head*, for which the *Longman Dictionary of Contemporary English* (1978) lists a few dozen meanings, to selecting a word like *spine*, for which only three meanings are listed.

We shall see in 10.4.3.1. that the criterion of coverage underlies the composition of BASIC.

Psychological and didactic criteria   In the selection of language material the degree of difficulty or *learnability* of words and structures, which may be determined by factors such as the language distance between L1 and L2 and the regularity/irregularity of items, is often taken into account. The selection may also be affected by the age, motivation and attitudes of the learner. And finally, the selection may be affected by considerations about the *teachability* of words and structures. For example, textbooks based on the direct method, which advocates avoidance of the L1 in L2 instruction, often incorporated mainly concrete words in the initial stages of teaching. These words were considered eminently teachable, because the meaning of such words could be illustrated quite easily through pictures, whereby use of L1 could be avoided. The role of such psychological and didactic factors will be gone into more deeply in 10.4.3.1.

10.4.3 The process of selection at the linguistic levels

In the previous paragraph we have seen that in the selection of language forms one can be guided by one's own intuitions and experience, or intersubjective intuitions and experience, but that a number of more objective criteria for selection have also been developed. We have seen in 10.4.1. that one can hardly speak of selection at the phonological and morphological levels, and that the options at the syntactic level are limited in comparison with the possibilities that are available at the lexical level. Not only the selection of words and structures, but also the selection of texts is an important aspect of the construction of teaching materials. We shall therefore limit ourselves in the following paragraphs to a discussion of the selection process at the last three levels mentioned. We shall investigate which methods are being used in practice to arrive at a selection, and we shall pay considerable attention to a number of selection criteria, their background, applications and limitations. We shall first of all discuss lexical selection, because most research has been done in this area. We shall then pay some attention to the selection of structures, since a number of the criteria that have been developed for lexical selection have also been used for selection at the syntactic level. We shall conclude by discussing the selection of texts; on the one hand because little research has been done into this area, and on the other hand because one encounters an altogether different type of problem in text selection than in lexical or syntactic selection.

10.4.3.1 Selection of words

In the drawing up of word lists for FLT experience has traditionally been the most important guideline. A recent example of a word list based on: 'introspection, intuition, experience' is the *Lexicon for T-level English*, to be found in Van Ek and Alexander's *Threshold Level* (1975) (see 9.3.2.1.). In order to reduce the subjective element in his selection Van Ek compared his list with a number of existing lists, most notably the various *Mindestwortschätze* of the German *Volkshochschulverband*. As we have already seen in 9.3.2.1., this list has been the subject of criticism from many quarters. In this connection, we could also mention Sciarone (1979b:37), who wonders why Van Ek has incorporated *small* but not *great*, and why *eye* and *face* are missing when *arm, leg, foot* and *tooth* have been selected. As Van Ek himself admits, basing oneself solely on one's own intuition and experience is risky, and he indicates that he would also have preferred a 'more scientific approach' – without indicating what this should consist of – had he had the necessary 'huge resources' at his disposal (Van Ek and Alexander 1975:33). The word list of the *Threshold Level* clearly shows that experience, even if we can fall back on very concrete objectives, is not the best of guides to rely on. It is therefore preferable, even if one has objectives which provide clear descriptions of the language use envisaged (see below), to use criteria for the selection of words which have especially been developed for the purpose (see also Raasch 1979:30).

Frequency and range

The frequency of words in language use and the distribution of words over various kinds of language use are criteria which have been used, usually in combination, in the selection of words for FLT purposes. An assumption of this approach is that the most frequent words with the widest range are the most useful ones. It is theoretically as well as practically impossible to use all the utterances of a language as data in the calculation of the frequency and range of words. It is therefore necessary to limit oneself to drawing a *sample* from the body of available language data. The collection of language utterances obtained in this manner, which can be used for quantitative analyses, is called a (*language*) *corpus*. Since the results of the quantitative analyses are dependent on the content of the corpus, it is very important to compile a corpus as conscientiously as possible. Any corpus, of whatever nature, is compiled with a certain goal in mind. If one therefore compiles a corpus for FLT purposes, this should ideally be done in terms of the FLT objectives. This means that the texts constituting the corpus should be as exact a reflection as possible of the language use described in the objectives; in other words, the corpus must be representative of the language use which is defined in the objectives. Raasch (1972:239) and Kaufmann (1977:64-5) respectively mention the necessity of a 'lernzieladäquates' or a 'lernzielorientiertes' corpus in this connection. It will be clear that it is extremely useful to have concretely formulated objectives at one's disposal in the compilation of a corpus: the more concretely the language use aimed at has been defined, the stricter are the guidelines for the incorporation of texts into a corpus.

A corpus should be representative, but it is also important to see to it that the corpus is adequate in size, i.e. that the number of running words in the corpus is sufficiently large. When words are selected on the basis of their frequency of occurrence in a corpus, one wants to be sure that the order of frequency found for these words corresponds to the relative importance of these words in the language use described in the objectives. This means that one should be sure that the frequencies obtained cannot be attributed to chance to a great extent: in other words, the reliability (stability) of these frequencies will have to meet certain requirements. The higher the frequency, the better the chance that the order of frequency obtained is reliable. What this means in practice for the size of the corpus we shall discuss later on in this subsection.

After the decisions about content and size of the corpus have been taken, a start can be made with the quantitative analysis of the corpus, that is, when the corpus consists only of written texts. Spoken texts will have to be transcribed first. This is not only a time-consuming, but also a difficult operation, especially for spontaneous speech. It frequently happens, even to experienced transcribers, that they misunderstand or even fail to understand parts of a text. A transcript, incidentally, is always a reduced representation of a spoken text, since for instance pronunciation and intonation will be lost. Another difficulty with spoken texts is that they contain many ungrammatical sentences (see 10.3.4.), which create problems in the definition of the counting unit, especially at the syntactic level. Such sentences are sometimes not incorporated into the corpus.

When all the texts in a corpus are available in written form, a start can be made with the calculation of the frequency and range of the words in the corpus. This means that first of all a decision will have to be taken about the counting unit. In most frequency counts the *word form* is the counting unit. This means, for instance, that verb forms like *sein, bin, bist, ist, sind, seid, war, warst, waren, wart, sei, seien, wäre, wären*, and *gewesen* are all counted separately and get their separate places in the frequency list (see for instance Kaeding 1898). In a number of word counts which have been carried out for FLT it is not the word form but the *lemma* (dictionary entry) which has been used as the counting unit. This means that only the lemma appears in the frequency list and that the frequency indicated for a certain lemma relates to the frequencies of all the forms in which the lemma appears. The frequencies of the various verb forms *bin, bist, ist*, etc. will be added up together and the total frequency will appear in the list for the lemma *sein*. In the rest of this subsection, in which we shall discuss the notions of frequency and range in more detail, we shall assume that the counting unit is the lemma.

A corpus consists of n running words, called *tokens* in language statistics. All identical tokens together form a class, called *type*. Which tokens should be considered to be identical depends on the counting unit used: word form or lemma. In the latter case, we mean by 'identical tokens' all occurrences of a lemma. The number of times that a lemma (referred to as a *word* for ease of exposition in the rest of this chapter) occurs in a corpus is called its *absolute frequency*. When the absolute frequency is related to the total number of tokens in a corpus, we obtain the *relative frequency*. If, in a corpus of Dutch texts consisting of 100,000 tokens, the article *de* occurs 8312 times, then the absolute frequency of that article is 8312 and the relative frequency is 8312/100,000 = 8.312 per cent, or 0.08312. When we rank the words in a corpus according to their absolute frequencies, we obtain a so-called *frequency list*. A frequency list is a list in which the word with the highest frequency is assigned rank number 1, the word with the highest but one frequency rank number 2, and so on. Of course the words can also be listed alphabetically, as they usually are in frequency dictionaries, but then for each word its number in the frequency list and sometimes the frequency itself are indicated. The relative frequency of a word becomes more stable or, in other words, less sensitive to accidental factors and therefore more reliable, as the size of the corpus increases. The more stable the frequency, the more likely it will be that the frequency found in the corpus will correspond to the frequency in another corpus consisting of the same number of tokens and comparable texts, or in other words, the more reliable the prediction is that can be made with respect to the relative frequency of words in comparable language use. When using frequency as a criterion for word selection it is important to select words with a sufficiently stable frequency. Sciarone (1979b:50) refers to the tradition introduced by Frumkina (1963), to select only those words of which we can assume with 95 per cent certainty that their frequency corresponds within a 30 per cent margin to their frequency in any other corpus of equal size and consisting of similar texts. This means that only words with a frequency of ⩾ 40 are considered as candidates for selection. Sciarone (1979b:53) also investigated what this means in terms of desirable size of corpora. He found that corpora consisting of 500,000 tokens yielded approximately 1150 words with a frequency of ⩾ 40. For a list of 2000 words a corpus of approximately 1,000,000 tokens is required, and from a corpus of approximately 2,000,000 tokens some

3000 words can be selected, according to Sciarone.

In this connection, the question presents itself of how many words one should minimally select to have the guarantee that learners will understand any written or spoken text. It appears that a relatively small number of words will make up a large percentage of any text. Mackey (1965:170) gives some figures which are based on various frequency counts of written English texts:

Number of different words	Percentage of text covered
4,500	99
3,000	97.5
1,000	90
732	75
50	50
9	25

Fig. 10.3   Text coverage (after Mackey 1965, 170)

Schonell *et al.*'s (1956:73) conclusions regarding spoken English are even more striking: the 1000 most frequent words cover 94 per cent of the text, the 100 most frequent words cover 72 per cent. And in Jones and Wepman's (1966) spoken word count the 33 most frequent words account for more than 50 per cent of all words uttered. In considering these figures it should be kept in mind, however, that text coverage is not the same as comprehension of a text, even though the two are connected. A text coverage of 90 per cent, for instance, still means that in every line of written text there is one word which is not covered, and quite frequently it may be exactly that one word which conveys most information. Furthermore, text comprehension is not just a function of the proportion of familiar words, but depends on a number of other factors as well, such as the subject matter of the text, the way in which the writer approaches the subject, and the extent to which the reader is already familiar with the subject.

Not only word frequencies are important data, but also the distribution of a word over the entire corpus or a subpart thereof, in other words its *range*. The wider the range of a word, the more likely it is that the word will regularly occur in the language use of which the corpus is representative. Range is therefore also a factor in the stability of a word, with the restriction that the absolute frequency of the word should always be greater than the number of parts of the corpus over which one wishes to calculate the range. It is hardly useful to calculate range at very low frequencies. A word with a frequency of one can only occur in one part of the corpus: in this case, the range coefficient cannot predict the likelihood of occurrence. For very high frequencies range is not very relevant either. If the corpus consists of 20 parts and the frequency of a word is 10,000, then it is not very likely that the word will not occur, or only occasionally occur, in one of the parts of the corpus. Range, therefore, is especially important for words which have neither a very low nor a very high frequency. To determine range with some precision one should not only take the number of parts of the corpus in which the word occurs into account, but also the absolute frequency of the word within each of these parts, because this will provide considerable insight into the stability of the word. This will be clear from fig. 10.4:

Parts of the corpus	Absolute frequency of word x	Absolute frequency of word y
A	2	4
B	1	4
C	18	4
D	1	5
E	3	4
F	0	4
	frequency = 25	frequency = 25

Fig. 10.4   Range of absolute frequencies

The range of words in a corpus can therefore be considered a yardstick of the homogeneity of the language use represented in the corpus. In word selection for FLT purposes the criterion of range is often used to make corrections in the frequency list, for instance by eliminating frequent words with a very uneven distribution. For further particulars about various ways of calculating range see Juilland and Chang-Rodriguez (1964) and Carroll *et al.* (1971).

What follows will be a short historical survey of the development of frequency research, presented in the framework of a discussion of some frequency lists which, incidentally, were not all developed primarily for educational purposes. They exhibit a number of striking aspects:

(1) Most frequency lists are based on corpora consisting only of written texts.
(2) The lemma is not always used as the counting unit.
(3) Often only the frequency and not the range has been calculated.
(4) The corpora tend to vary considerably in size.
(5) Many corpora are supposed to represent a cross-section of the language, which often appears not to be the case.

In this survey we have incorporated the most important corpora for English, French, German, Spanish, Italian and Russian, plus information concerning the five points mentioned above; this can be found in fig. 10.5. Where relevant, we shall indicate whether or not the lists in the survey have been made use of in FLT.

In 1921 Thorndike published a frequency dictionary based on an extensive corpus of written English texts. It contains a list of 10,000 word forms, which was extended to 20,000 in 1932. In 1944 Thorndike and Lorge published a list of 30,000 words (lemmata) which was based on four corpora of approximately 4,500,000 tokens each, namely the 1921 corpus, the 'Lorge magazine count', the 'Thorndike–Lorge semantic count' and the 'Thorndike juvenile count'. Although not intended for such use, this list has been taken as a basis for word

Author and date of first edition	Language	Number of tokens	Number of entries in list	Counting unit	Range indicated ?	Spoken language/ written language	Content of corpus
Aristizabal 1938	French	460,727	12,038	lemma	no	written	letters from adults and texts written spontaneously by children
Bortolini et al. 1971	Italian	500,000	5,356	lemma	yes	written	novels, magazines, newspapers, school books
Buchanan 1927	Spanish	1,200,000	—	lemma	yes	written	mainly literary texts from 17th-20th centuries
Carroll et al. 1971	English	5,088,721	86,741	word form	yes	written	school books from grades 3-9
Gougenheim et al. 1956	French	312,135	1,063	lemma	yes	spoken	interviews
Henmon 1924	French	400,000	3,905	lemma	no	written	literary texts from 19th century
Hofland and Johansson 1982	English	c. 1,000,000	c. 50,000	word form	no	written	informative and literary prose published in 1961
Garcia Hoz 1953	Spanish	400,000	12,402	lemma	yes	written	letters, newspapers, documents, books
Josselson 1953	Russian	1,000,000	5,230	lemma	yes	written	plays, magazines, literary and scientific texts etc. from 1830-post 1918
Juilland and Chang-Rodriguez 1964	Spanish	500,000	5,024	lemma	yes	written	plays, novels, scientific and technical texts, newspapers etc. from 1920 40
Juilland et al. 1970	French	500,000	5,083	lemma	yes	written	plays, novels, scientific and technical texts, newspapers etc. from 1920 40
Juilland et al. 1973	Italian	500,000	5,014	lemma	yes	written	essays, novels, magazines, newspapers etc. from 1920-40
Kaeding 1898	German	10,910,777	258,173	word form	no	written	great variety of prose texts

Reference	Language						
Kučera and Francis 1967	English	1,014,232	50,406	word form	yes	written	informative and literary prose published in 1961
Pfeffer 1964	German	595,000	25,000	lemma	yes	spoken	interviews
Rodriguez-Bou 1952	Spanish	7,066,637	10,000	lemma	no	spoken/written	great variety of texts
Sciarone 1977	Italian	1,500,000	2,726	lemma	no	written	Bortolini et al. (1971), Juilland et al. (1973), newspapers, magazines, novels etc.
Steinfeldt n.d. (1962?)	Russian	400,000	2,500	lemma	—	spoken/written	literary texts, radio texts, newspapers etc.
Thorndike 1921	English	4,500,000	10,000	word form	no	written	mainly literary and scientific prose from different periods
Thorndike and Lorge 1944	English	18,00,000	30,000	lemma	no	written	Thorndike 1921, Lorge magazine count, Thorndike-Lorge semantic count, Thorndike juvenile count
Vander Beke 1929	French	1,147,748	6,067	lemma	yes	written	literary and scientific texts and newspapers from 19th and 20th centuries

Fig. 10.5 Frequency lists

lists to be used in the teaching of English as a foreign language. The list was consulted, for instance, for West's *General Service List* (1953), which has been used in many countries, and Bongers's *Three Thousand-Word English* (1947b), well known especially in the Netherlands. West's list was in turn the basis for, amongst others, the *Mindestwortschatz* of the *Zertifikat Englisch* of the DVV (West and Hoffmann 1974). A discussion of Thorndike's work and a short history of the English vocabulary control movement is found in McArthur (1978). The more recent counts of Kučera and Francis (1967), which was based on the Brown corpus, of Hofland and Johansson (1982), which was based on the Lancaster-Oslo/Bergen (LOB) corpus, and of Carroll *et al.* (1971) are all based on written texts, have not been adapted for use in FLT, and have the word form as a counting unit. Lemmatized lists are, however, in preparation for both the Brown corpus and the LOB corpus. More information on these corpora is given in 10.4.3.2.

Henmon (1924) was the first person to use the lemma as a counting unit for his frequency list based on a corpus of French literary texts. Vander Beke (1929) used a part of Henmon's corpus and added a large number of texts. He excluded the words with a very high frequency in Henmon (function words, some adjectives, nouns and verbs) and also proper names, a procedure which some later counts have followed. He also excluded some words with a high frequency but a small range from the count. In Europe as well as in the US a whole series of lists appeared, based on Henmon and Vander Beke, such as Tharp (1939), Schlyter (1951) and Verlée (1954). Aristizabal (1938) based himself on a corpus of letters from adults and texts written by children. This count was carried out with a view to improving first language teaching, and has been used mainly in teaching spelling. The list of Gougenheim *et al.* (1956) is based on a corpus of spoken language. We shall return to the latter in our discussion of *Français Fondamental*. Finally, Juilland *et al.* (1970) is based on a corpus of written, mainly literary French from the period between 1920 and 1940. This corpus, of approximately 500,000 tokens, was not compiled for word selection purposes; in fact, none of the other corpora in which Juilland was involved were (see below).

The oldest frequency dictionary is that of Kaeding (1898), a word-form count based on a corpus of written German consisting of nearly 11 million tokens. The aim of this count was to aid the improvement of a system of abbreviations for stenography. Only later was the usefulness of this material for FLT realized. Morgan (1928), which forms the basis of the basic vocabulary list of Wadepuhl and Morgan (1934), partly recounted the material with the lemma as counting unit, and Meier (1964) further reanalysed Kaeding's material. Pfeffer (1964) based his word count on a corpus of spoken German of nearly 600,000 tokens, which he used for his Basic German word lists (Pfeffer 1964, 1970), lists which also contain words selected on the basis of other criteria, most importantly availability. For a survey, see Pfeffer (1975). Lastly we would like to mention the frequency dictionary of Rosengren (1972, 1977), not intended for use in FLT, which is based on an extensive corpus which consists solely of German newspapers.

The Spanish frequency dictionary of Buchanan (1927) is based on a corpus of written, mostly literary texts from the seventeenth to the twentieth century.

Rodriguez-Bou (1952) incorporated Buchanan's material in his corpus, which he extended to over 7 million tokens. He also incorporated spoken language. Garcia Hoz (1953) again based himself on a corpus which consisted exclusively of written texts, just like Juilland and Chang-Rodriguez (1964), whose corpus consists of mainly literary texts, taken exclusively from the period between 1920 and 1940, comprising 500,000 tokens. The latter frequency dictionary was used for the *Mindestwortschatz* of the *Zertifikat Spanisch* of the DVV (Halm and Barrera-Vidal 1973).

For Italian, three counts ought to be mentioned, based exclusively on written texts. The count of Bortolini *et al.* (1971) was carried out for the teaching of Italian and is based on a corpus of 500,000 tokens from texts written between 1947 and 1968. The corpus of Juilland *et al.* (1973) also comprises 500,000 tokens and is composed of texts from between 1920 and 1940. Like Bortolini *et al.*, Sciarone (1977) has a pedagogical purpose. Sciarone's count is based on the corpora of his two predecessors and a corpus of his own of 500,000 tokens. The only criterion for incorporation into Sciarone's list was frequency; words with a frequency $f \leqslant 40$ were not incorporated into the list.

Lastly, we would like to mention two frequency counts of Russian. Josselson (1953) is based on a corpus of written texts, mostly literary, from three periods: 1830–1900, 1900–1918, and post-1918. The corpus contained one million tokens. Steinfeldt (n.d.) is based on 400,000 tokens, and comprises literary texts for 7 to 15-year-old children, literary texts for adults, journalistic texts, and radio programmes for adolescents (25 per cent of the texts). For further bibliographical information on frequency counts and word lists based on frequency counts see CILT (1973[2]), and especially for German, Fink (1977).

Many objections can be raised against the use of frequency and range of words in a corpus as the only criteria for word selection for FLT. Such objections have been known for a long time and therefore few word lists are currently being used in FLT which have been exclusively compiled by taking the first 1000, 2000, 3000, etc. words of a frequency list. In those cases where frequency lists were the only basis, words were usually deleted from the list, and words were added on the basis of intuition and experience. Most lists, however, are the result of the application of a combination of criteria. The objections against using frequency and range as criteria for selection can partly be related to objections against the composition of the corpora that the frequency lists are based on. Most corpora were not composed with a view to improving FLT. Moreover, they usually consist exclusively of written texts, and literary texts constitute a very important part indeed of many corpora. Furthermore, a number of corpora contain a not inconsiderable amount of dated language material. In addition, one could object to the small size of a number of corpora; we have already pointed out that the size of a corpus determines the stability of the frequency of the words in the corpus to a large extent. Both these objections could be met by composing a corpus which is representative of the language use specified in the objectives, and which is sufficiently large. It should be added, however, that composing a corpus and analysing it quantitatively is an expensive and time-consuming affair, which in practice means that it will be impossible to make a 'lernzielorientiertes' corpus for every target group.

Other objections concern the counting unit used in making the counts. We have already mentioned that counts carried out with educational aims in mind usually use the lemma rather than the word form as a counting unit. In many counts, however, the problem of homographs has not yet been solved. The frequency indicated for *can*, for instance, often relates to the verb *can* as well as the noun *can*. The frequency of a lemma is indeed an important piece of information, but it is at least equally important to know how many meanings a lemma has and what the relative frequency of each of these meanings is. In many cases, it will be impossible and useless to teach all the meanings of the words selected. The verb *take*, for instance, has more than 40 meanings (leaving out the considerable number of meanings that the verb may have in combination with particles or prepositions, or in idiomatic expressions) according to the *Longman Dictionary of Contemporary English*, which is aimed especially at learners of English as a foreign language. Information on the relative frequency of the various meanings of a lemma would be very useful when selecting for teaching purposes (see also Barrera-Vidal and Kühlwein 1975:83-4). Lastly, we would like to point out that a strict use of the frequency criterion may cut straight across lexical connections. The following figure gives the absolute frequency and the rank number of a number of lexical opposites from the frequency list of Meier (1964):

Word form	Frequency	Rank number
schnell	1757	573
langsam	953	1073
hart	404	2466
sanft	305	3255
warm	251	3859
kalt	502	2009
gross	1568	636
klein	640	1589
teuer	345	2892
billig	318	3122
gesund	519	1950
krank	407	2450

Fig. 10.6   Frequency of a number of lexical opposites in the list of Meier (1964)

If one selects the 1000 most frequent words, then *schnell* and *gross* will be on the list, but not *langsam* and *klein*. If one selects the 2000 most frequent words, one will incorporate *gesund* but not *krank*, and if one does not select words beyond rank number 3000 one will incorporate *hart, kalt* and *teuer*, but not *sanft, warm* and *billig*. Strict use of the frequency criterion may also lead to selection of certain items from a closed class, but not others. For days of the week, for instance, *Dienstag, Mittwoch, Freitag* and *Samstag* are not listed among the first 5000 words in Meier's list, and *Mittwoch* and *Samstag* not even in the first 7000 words. For a further discussion of these and other objections which can be raised against the criteria discussed here see Kühn (1979:40–59).

We can conclude that using the criteria of range and frequency alone will not guarantee the selection of the most useful words, even when an adequate corpus is available. This fact, as has been pointed out before, was recognized at an early stage by foreign language teachers, which is why research was undertaken with a view to supplementing or replacing these criteria with others.

Availability

The criterion of availability was first used by Gougenheim, Michéa, Rivenc and Sauvageot, who compiled a basic vocabulary list for learners of French as a foreign language, originally called *Français élémentaire* (Gougenheim *et al.* 1956), a name which soon changed to *Français Fondamental* (Gougenheim *et al.* 1959, 1967²). The number of words incorporated into the list solely on the basis of the availability criterion, incidentally, is relatively limited. The list of *Français Fondamental 1er degré* (FF1) that was eventually drawn up contains some 1475 words, of which 712 (48 per cent) were selected on the basis of their frequency, 240 (16 per cent) on the basis of the availability criterion, and 520 (36 per cent) on the basis of other considerations of the FF committee (Rivenc 1979:18).

The first step taken in the FF project was that of compiling a list of the most frequent words of spoken French. Existing frequency counts could not be used, since they were all based on corpora of written French. Therefore, a new corpus was compiled, consisting mostly of interviews with 275 native speakers of French of different age, sex, geographical background and profession. The corpus comprised 312,135 tokens, divided over 7995 types. The corpus was divided, according to subject, into 163 different groups of texts, and the range of the words over these groups was calculated. At first, all words with a frequency of $f > 20$ (1063 in all) were incorporated into the list (Gougenheim *et al.* 1967²:61–89).

An analysis of the list obtained in this manner led to the conclusion that many words which the committee considered useful, especially concrete words, were lacking. This was, according to the committee (*op. cit.* 137–9), because concrete words, in contrast with function words, adjectives, verbs and nouns 'de caractère général', such as *chose, homme, personne, enfant*, which can occur in all sorts of situations, are used only in certain contexts. Nevertheless, it is important that these words are available to a language user when a situation arises in which they are required. Examples of such concrete words are *soap* and *toothpaste*, which are available to the native speaker, but which he hardly uses. For this reason, Gougenheim *et al.* decided to incorporate not only the most frequent words, but also the most available words into the FF vocabulary list. A list of 16 themes (*centres d'intérêt*) was drawn up, such as clothing, body parts, means of transport, food and drink, school, home, village, town, animals, and professions. To determine the availability of the words within these themes, over 900 pupils of the highest forms of primary schools in four districts were asked to write down the 20 words that they considered the most useful for each theme. It was then calculated how many different words per theme had been written down. The words were also ranked per theme according to the number of times that they had been written down by pupils (Gougenheim *et al.*

1967[2]:146 ff.). From the availability lists obtained in this manner a total of 240 words were selected for FF1.

After that, a number of operations were carried out on the above mentioned frequency list of 1063 words. First of all, the number of words was greatly reduced by only incorporating words with a frequency of f > 29. Then, it was decided, for various reasons, to exclude a number of other words, such as 'les mots à la mode', including e.g. *formidable* and *sympathique*, 'les mots familiers et vulgaires', including e.g. *bougain, copain, se foutre, gars, gosse, machin, truc, type*, and words which were, it was claimed, clearly a function of the collection of corpus texts, such as *micro* and *enregistrer* (Gougenheim *et al.* 1967[2]:197–202), leaving 712 words of the original frequency list.

Next, 520 words were added to the list for various reasons; a number of words were added, for instance, because they made it possible 'd'exprimer des notions morales, civiques et culturelles', which meant, in this case, words like *art, artiste, effort, courage, liberté, poésie, sculpteur, tableau* (Gougenheim *et al.* 1967[2]:203). Eventually, all these operations resulted in a list containing some 1475 words.

The compilers of FF1 have received much praise for the conscientious way in which they have carried out their task. Nevertheless, one can raise well founded objections against important parts of the work. In the first place, the committee has assumed, somewhat hastily, that concrete words are insufficiently represented in frequency lists. Sciarone (1979b:32–5) shows this assumption to be incorrect for a number of frequency lists, which immediately leads to the question of the quality of the frequency research carried out by the committee. Presumably, a partial solution to the problem of underrepresentation of concrete words relating to certain situations and themes would have been to see to it that texts concerned with these situations and themes were better represented in the sample. One can also wonder how important it is for a foreign learner to have words at his disposal which native speakers seldom use, even though they know these words. Secondly, one could criticize the way in which the availability list was drawn up. The list consists only of nouns as a result of the choice of themes and the instructions given to the pupils. When one asks pupils to write down the most useful words relating to the theme 'body parts', one will of course get a list of nouns indicating body parts. We are informed, for instance, that the five most available words relating to this theme are *oeil, oreille, nez, bras, jambes*, but we are not given important information also relating to this theme, for instance on the availability of verbs indicating what can be done with the body parts mentioned (Rivenc 1979:19, Sciarone 1979a:327). But the most important point of criticism that can be raised relates to the way in which the authors have deleted words from the frequency list, and added other words. The decision not to incorporate 'les mots familiers et vulgaires', for instance, can only be called highly unfortunate, even though it is perhaps understandable in the historical context of FF1 (Besse 1979). Likewise it was unfortunate to exclude words with a very high frequency such as *impression, cas, sujet, général*, and *normal*, because they were not considered useful 'à ce degré', while non-frequent 'mots permittant d'exprimer des notions morales, civiques et culturelles' were added to the list. One of the compilers, of FF1, Rivenc, writes in a recent retrospective article 'que parmi les 520 mots introduits par la Commission du français fondamental, beaucoup l'ont été d'une manière très arbitraire' (Rivenc 1979:22). FF1 has had a considerable influence on the teaching of French as a foreign language. In many textbooks, throughout the world, the influence of FF1 can be recognized. The method used by Gougenheim and his colleagues for selecting vocabulary has also been used in projects for languages other than French, and notably in the well known work of Pfeffer for German (see Pfeffer 1975).

Coverage

The criterion of coverage has found its best-known application in BASIC. In the literature, one often finds the term *basic English* (for BASIC), which strictly speaking is not correct, since it suggests that BASIC is a list of English words and structures through which a basic skill in English can be attained, which could then subsequently be expanded by learning additional words and structures. BASIC stands for *British American Scientific International Commercial*, and is neither basic, since it claims to be a complete linguistic system, nor English, even if it is based on English. The development of BASIC, like that of Esperanto, fits into the age-old tradition of the search for a universal language which would solve communication problems between nations. BASIC, which has its roots in Ogden and Richards (1923), and was developed by Ogden in subsequent years (see Ogden 1968, which is a collection of the relevant literature), is a closed linguistic system which consists of 850 words and a limited number of morphological and syntactic rules. The vocabulary list of BASIC consists of 600 nouns and 100 adjectives plus the semantic opposites of 50 of these adjectives (*hard-soft; old-new*). The semantic opposites of the other 50 adjectives are formed by means of the prefix *un*, which yields English words like *unable* and *uncommon*, but also un-English words like *unnormal, unresponsible* and *unregular*. BASIC has only 18 verbs, including verbs like *put, take, get* ('operation words') which, in combination with prepositions, can replace nearly all other verbs. The 'operation words' and prepositions form together with pronouns and other function words the class of operators, which comprises 100 words. We will provide some examples and their equivalents in BASIC, derived from Bongers (1947a:132):

English	BASIC
to ask	to make a request, to put a question
to count	to get the number of
to eat	to take food
enemy	one who is not a friend, nation at war
God	Father of All, First Cause
heavy	of great weight
to like	to be pleased with, to have a taste for
to listen	to give ear, attention
many	a number
to stand	to get on feet, be upright

BASIC has been taught throughout the world, but often not as BASIC but as *basic English*, for which it is not suited, because it contains many words and expressions which are not part of the English language. For a critical discussion of BASIC see Bongers (1947a:119–34), who points out that a user of BASIC will be able to make himself understood to English speakers, but will not be able to understand them, because they will use many words which do not occur in BASIC. Incidentally, it will be very difficult for a native speaker of English to learn BASIC, precisely because many frequently used English words do not occur in BASIC, but are replaced by, or paraphrased by means of, other words. Bongers also observes that, in practice, BASIC had expanded to 1993 words. Little is left of the original enthusiasm for BASIC in the 1930s and 1940s, an enthusiasm shared by politicians such as Churchill and Roosevelt.

In 10.4.2. we have seen that Mackey (1965) distinguished four aspects of coverage: *definition, inclusion, combination* and *extension*. In the development of BASIC especially the first aspect has served as a basis. Savard (1970) has made an attempt at calculating the coverage value of the words in Gougenheim's *Dictionnaire fondamental de la langue française* (1958), which contains the words of FF *1er degré* and *2ième degré*. To do this, he calculated for every word the extent to which it can be used to define other words (*la puissance de définition*), the extent to which it can include the meanings of other words (*la puissance d'inclusion*), the extent to which it can be combined into compounds with other words (*la puissance de combination*) and the number of meanings it can have (*la puissance d'extension*). The average of these values yields the coverage value of a word. Savard and Richards (1970) calculated the utility value of these same words by adding together the frequency value, range value, availability value and coverage value of each word. The 10 words with the highest coverage values are in descending order: *prendre, homme, passer, mourir, aller, faire, mettre, tête, tirer, petit*, and the 10 words with the highest utility values are *faire, maison, parler, passer, vouloir, aller, prendre, mettre, petit, tête*. For a critical discussion of the method of calculation used by Savard and Richards, see Quémada (1974).

In word selection for basic vocabulary lists for use in FLT the coverage criterion is not very fashionable anymore. Especially the value of the *puissance d'extension* is the subject of considerable doubt, since it does not matter so much how many meanings a word has, but which meanings one wants to see incorporated into the list (see also Kühn 1979:27–28).

Psychological and didactic criteria

The criteria for selection discussed so far do not take into consideration whether or not words are easy to learn and/or teach. In other words, psychological and didactic criteria have not yet been dealt with. In this subsection we shall first of all discuss some psychological criteria in detail, and then briefly deal with an example of a didactic criterion.

The learnability of L2 words partly depends on the language distance between the L2 on the one hand and the L1 of the language learner and other languages he might know on the other hand. If the L2 is closely related to the L1, many words will be the same or very similar in both languages where spelling and meaning are concerned. These words are called *cognates*. Although in general it is not correct to equate 'same' with 'easy' (see 5.3.3.), it cannot be denied that cognates may facilitate the development of skills in another language. Because of spelling similarities, it is easy to recognize cognates in written texts. In spoken texts cognates are of course harder to recognize, but recognition may be facilitated by some phonetic and phonological instruction about the target language. As cognates are in the first place words which can easily be recognized, it would be wise to take advantage of their existence especially in the selection of words for the development of receptive skills.

Hammer (1979) carried out research in Canada into the extent to which speakers of English could make use of English–French cognates in learning French. In order to determine the number of English–French cognates, Hammer and Monod (1976) analysed the Larousse *Dictionnaire Moderne Français-Anglais* (1960), which yielded a list of 10,993 English–French cognates. For their operationalization of the term *cognate* see Hammer (1979:62–3). A comparison of Hammer and Monod (1976) with Gougenheim *et al.* (1967²), Savard and Richards (1970) and Mackey *et al.* (1971) led to the conclusion that 1837 of these cognates '[were] of high frequency and utility in French' (Hammer 1979:69). Hammer tried to determine whether it was possible to speed up the development of receptive skills (especially reading) by pointing out English–French cognates to learners. To be able to profit from a 'cognate approach' learners should be able to recognize cognates as such and also know the English meaning of these words. Hammer assumed that high-school and university students would know the meaning of the 1837 cognates referred to above and would also, considering their age and stage of cognitive development, be able to recognize cognates as such (Hammer 1979:80–2). She subsequently developed an *English–French Cognate Unit* (Hammer 1979:160–244), a mini-course consisting of seven lessons aimed at improving cognate recognition. She finally tested the effect that this Unit had by comparing the results on written cognate recognition tests and French reading tests of students who had worked with this Unit with those of students who had not worked with it. The most important conclusion was that high-school (grade 10) and university students using the Cognate Unit scored significantly higher than the control groups (Hammer 1979:96–7). This demonstrates that cognates, given a certain degree of cognitive development of the learner, are eminently learnable and teachable words. Adding cognates to a vocabulary list for receptive use will therefore add little to the learning load.

Heuer (1973b) and Lauerbach (1979a) suggest taking word associations into account in word selection. They carried out word association experiments with German secondary school pupils and German university students of English. They either asked their subjects, within a time limit, to write down or to mention one word as a reaction to English stimulus words from a list of 100 words first used by Kent and Rosanoff (1910) in word association research. Then, the primary associations (words mentioned most often per stimulus word) were compared to those of American pupils and college students, as set out in the norm tables of Palermo and Jenkins (1964). Lauerbach also compared the primary associations of her subjects with those of native speakers of German for

German translations of the original English stimulus words, listed in Russell and Meseck (1959). In both experiments differences (which the authors partly ascribe to L1 influence and to teaching) as well as parallels between the English associations of German subjects and those of American college students were observed. The authors, however, draw different (if very tentative) conclusions for word selection. Heuer (1973b:82) suggests two possibilities, without opting for either:

(1) where stimulus words evoke the same associations from native speakers of both the first language and the target language, we make use of these associations;
(2) we make use of the associations of foreign language learners, even if they deviate from those of the native speakers of the target language.

Lauerbach (1979a:388) suggests that we should concentrate in the first place on the associations of native speakers of the target language. As yet, word association research has not yielded much more for word selection than a few tentative suggestions.

Whether a word is difficult to learn or teach also depends on the age of the learners. Abstract words pose more difficulties for young children than for adults and are therefore usually avoided as much as possible in FLT to young children.

Also, irregular words are in general harder to learn than regular words, which is why they are sometimes not incorporated into elementary courses. Past tenses of irregular verbs, for instance, are lacking in the course that was developed during the first phase of the Dutch FLES-project (the EIBO-project) which we discussed earlier (see 9.2.4.2.).

Lastly, we would like to give an example of a pedagogical criterion that has often been used in the various forms of the direct method. As we have already seen in chapter 8, the advocates of the direct method have generally supported exclusive use of the L2 in FLT. Use of the L1 should be avoided as much as possible. A popular technique for this purpose is illustrating the meaning of words by using pictures, pointing out objects, or making gestures (see also 12.2.2.1.). As it is much easier to illustrate the meaning of concrete words in this manner than the meaning of abstract words, it is not surprising that one should find mainly concrete words in textbooks that are strictly based on the direct method, especially in the early stages. It should be noted that the selection of these words is primarily motivated pedagogically rather than psychologically; that is to say, teachability was used as criterion for selection rather than learnability. Except for young children, abstract words are definitely not always difficult to learn; that is, if one does not adhere to the principle that the L1 should be avoided at all costs in FLT. Cognates are a case in point. As demonstrated by Hammer (1979), cognates, whether concrete or abstract, are words that are easy to learn, given a certain level of cognitive development of the learner.

To conclude this section on word selection, it should be pointed out that, to be suitable for FLT purposes, vocabulary lists purely based on criteria such as frequency, range and availability, should always first be 'edited', using psychological and pedagogical criteria.

10.4.3.2 Selection of structures

Although the possibilities for selection are much more limited at the syntactic level than they are at the lexical level, the number of syntactic structures is sufficiently large to warrant selection, given the limited teaching time. That one is aware of this is evidenced by the fact that alongside basic vocabulary lists, many basic structure lists have been drawn up for FLT; we only have to mention the well known publications of Palmer (1934), Jespersen (1937), Fries (1952) and Hornby (1954) for English, the FF list for French, and the more recent lists of the *Deutsche Volkshochschulverband* and of the *Threshold Level* project of the Council of Europe for various languages.

In the selection of structures a traditional starting-point has often been the notions one had as to what are simple and central structures in a language and what are complex and peripheral ones. Such notions were based to a considerable extent on an acquaintance with available syntactic descriptions of the target language. The starting-point was, in other words, what we have called a grammatical approach. Recently the functional–notional approach, in which the selection of structures is made dependent on the communicative acts specified in the objectives, has attracted a lot of attention. One may wonder in how far the final results of both approaches differ with respect to the selection of structures. We shall attempt to answer this question on the basis of an example. Wilkins (1976a:59–61), one of the co-designers of the *T-level*, gives a list of structures that could be used for asking permission. This list, which 'cannot possibly be said to be exhaustive' (Wilkins 1976a:59), is too long to print in full, which is why we shall cite a few examples:

(1)   Can ⎫
         ⎬ I use your telephone, (please)?
      May ⎭
(2)   Please let me use your telephone?
(3)   Is it all right to use your telephone?
(4)   If it's all right with you, I'll use your telephone?
(5)   Am I allowed to use your telephone?
(6)   Do you mind if I use your telephone?
(7)   Do you mind me using your telephone?
(8)   Would you mind if I used your telephone?
(9)   You don't mind, if I use your telephone (, do you)?
(10) I wonder if you have any objection to me using your telephone?
(11) Would you permit me to use your telephone?
(12) Would you be so kind as to allow me to use your telephone?
(13) Would it be possible (for me) to use your telephone?
(14) Do you think you could let me use your telephone?
(15) I should be most grateful if you would permit me to use your telephone.

If we now look at the specification of language forms in the *T-Level*, we find that the compilers have selected the following structures on the basis of intuition, introspection and experience for what they call the *language function 'seeking permission'* (Van Ek and Alexander 1975:39):

May I + VP
Can I + VP
Let me + VP
Do you mind + *if*-clause

Only the first two of these are intended for productive use. It seems unlikely that in a grammatical approach a different selection would have been made. As yet it seems that as far as selection of structures is concerned, it does not make all that much difference whether one opts for a grammatical or a functional–notional approach, especially where basic courses are concerned.

In the selection of structures much less use has been made of criteria like frequency and range than in the selection of words. One of the few lists which are (partly) based on a frequency count of structures is the one found in FF (see Gougenheim *et al.* 1967[2]:211–30). There has also been much less research into the frequency and range of structures in a language corpus than into the frequency and range of words. On the one hand, this is because there exist considerable differences of opinion about the analysis and classification of sentence structures, depending on which particular linguistic approach one adheres to; in other words, the definition of the counting unit is much more problematic for structure counts than it is for word counts. On the other hand, coding corpora for computerized structure counts is very problematic, especially for corpora of spoken language.

As far as we are aware, there are no frequency lists of all structures in a corpus available to date. There is a legitimate hope that we may have such lists available in the future, especially given the considerable developments in the last few years in setting up syntactic coding systems (see e.g. Johansson 1979, 1982), and given the fact that for a number of languages corpora are available which have been coded syntactically and either have been put on computer tape, or are being put on computer tape. We shall mention the most important of these corpora briefly.

The best-known British English corpus is the corpus of the *Survey of English Usage* from University College, London, comprising both written and spoken language. The corpus is stored on paper slips in filing cabinets at University College. The spoken part of the corpus has been transferred to computer tape in Lund. This part is known as the London–Lund corpus. For both corpora see Quirk and Svartvik (1979). The collaboration has already had two important results: the London–Lund corpus, which consists of 87 spoken texts, each of 5000 words, is now available, in its entirety, on magnetic tape for computer use and 34 of the texts have also appeared in print (Svartvik and Quirk 1980). For recent information on this corpus see Svartvik *et al.* (1982). The best-known American English corpus is the Brown corpus, compiled by staff of Brown University. This corpus, on which the frequency dictionary of Kučera and Francis (1967) is based, consists of approximately 1,000,000 words from texts printed in 1961 (see Kučera and Francis 1967 and also Francis 1979, 1980). A frequency analysis of part of the grammatical structures in the Brown corpus will soon be available in print (Francis and Kučera, in press). Lastly, the Lancaster–Oslo/Bergen (LOB) corpus was set up as a British English counterpart of the Brown corpus, and is strictly comparable with it in size and composition (see Johansson 1982). The Brown corpus, the London–Lund corpus and the LOB corpus are all distributed through the International Computer Archive of Modern English (ICAME), which is located at the University of Bergen, Norway.

The most important German corpus is the *Freiburger Korpus gesprochener deutscher Standardsprache*, compiled by members of the *Institut für deutsche Sprache* (IdS), *Forschungsstelle Freiburg*. This corpus, comprising approximately 600,000 words, selected from a bank of 820 tapes totalling 580 hours of speech, and especially compiled with the improvement of the teaching of German as a foreign language in mind, is reported on in Engel and Vogel (1973), and more recently in Berens (1979). For French, the Orléans corpus should be mentioned; this is a corpus consisting of spoken French compiled by a team consisting mainly of English researchers especially for the teaching of French as a foreign language. Blanc and Biggs (1971) report on this corpus, which consists of approximately 4,500,000 words, but is only partly available in transcribed form. Much syntactic research, including some research into the frequency of (a number of) syntactic structures, has been done on these corpora, especially on those of *The Survey of English Usage* and the *IdS*, which has already led to improvements in FLT materials.

Lastly we would like to point out that, as in lexical selection, whether a grammatical or a functional–notional approach is adopted, and whether or not use is made of the results of frequency research, the final choice will also have to depend on a number of other matters such as the relationship between L1 and L2, the age of the learners, the teachability of syntactic structures, etc. One should therefore, in selecting structures, always take considerations of a psychological and didactic nature into account as well.

10.4.3.3 Selection of texts

As we have seen in 10.4.1. and 10.4.2., selection criteria presupposing countability do not play a direct role in text selection. They do, of course, play an indirect role. In the selection and/or construction of texts for use in FLT one will take the words and structures into account that have been selected and this choice will often be partly determined by selection criteria such as frequency and range. The selection (and construction) of texts will, therefore, generally be based primarily on other criteria than the ones discussed above.

In the selection of texts one of course has to take the level of L2 proficiency the learners have already attained into account. A frequently made error of the past, however, is that the choice of texts was exclusively determined by the words and structures discussed in a lesson and that not much attention was paid to the contents of the texts *per se*. This often resulted in typical textbook texts which only served to introduce or illustrate the words and structures dealt with in the lesson concerned and the contents of which were marked by a considerable measure of uniformity and triviality. This lack of respect for the contents of texts, frequent in, but not particular to, the audiolingual method, has recently been pointed out by many authors (e.g. Freese 1977, Butzkamm 1978 and

Walter 1979:117–29). Today, such aspects receive more attention, which is reflected in the desire to select texts which will interest the learners. More attention is also being paid to whether the texts provide reliable information about the people whose language is being taught and the society they live in.

In the selection of texts one should not only pay attention to the degree of L2 proficiency the learners have already attained, and their interests, but also to the degree of difficulty of texts. We have already pointed out, in a different connection (see 10.4.3.1.), that the degree of difficulty of a text is not only determined by the number of words and structures known, but also by things such as the subject matter of the text, the way in which the writer approaches the subject, and the knowledge the learners already have about the subject.

A question which is closely related to the matters discussed above is the question whether we should select authentic, non-edited texts, or texts especially written or edited for FLT. Authentic texts are, in general, difficult, not only because they do not take the degree of L2 proficiency of the learner into account, but also because native-speaker knowledge of a subject is assumed in the discussion of that subject. Authentic texts are therefore often hardly usable in elementary courses, and even for teaching advanced learners it will often be necessary to provide additional information in advance about the subject under discussion. At an advanced level it will be necessary to use authentic written and spoken texts if the objective is for learners to be able to understand the foreign language as it is used by native speakers, since understanding of texts especially edited for FLT does not guarantee that authentic language materials will be understood.

Lastly, the possibilities for exploitation of a text need to be taken into account. If one for instance selects original spoken texts, one should realize that such texts can usually only be used for training listening comprehension, and perhaps as a starting-point for discussion. They have few other possibilities, since such texts, when written out, are often very hard to follow (see 10.3.4.).

10.5 Conclusion

After the formulation and specification of objectives the next step in the process of designing a course is the selection of course content which will enable the learner to achieve the objectives as efficiently as possible. We have discussed a number of aspects of course content selection in considerable detail in this chapter, and concluded that two parts can be distinguished in the selection process. The first relates to the choice of the type of language material, and the second to the choice of language forms. The first part entails choices about dialect, register, style and medium, and the second choices about words, structures, etc. which have to be incorporated into a course. We have argued that the selection of the type of language material is guided by a number of external factors, most importantly the objectives. These factors also play a role in the selection of language forms. As we have seen, the more concrete the objectives are, the easier it will be to make a well motivated choice of the language material to be taught. We have also concluded that a functional–notional approach to syllabus design is preferable to a grammatical approach, since the former can give a more explicit description of the language use aimed at than the latter. Furthermore, we have shown that the selection of language forms is not only dependent on external factors, but also on the properties of the language itself. These properties are for instance responsible for a wealth of options at the lexical level, whereas there is no real possibility of choice at the phonological level. We then argued that where a selection is possible and meaningful, it would be wise not to rely solely on one's own intuition and experience, but to use criteria for selection developed especially for the purpose. We then briefly mentioned a number of criteria which we discussed in detail with respect to their applications in the selection process at the lexical and syntactic levels. Finally, we discussed some considerations which play a role in the selection of texts. We devoted most attention to word selection, because most research has been done in this area, and the selection criteria discussed have largely been developed in the first place for word selection.

11
Gradation of course content

11.1 Introduction

In the preceding two chapters, we have dealt with a number of aspects of the formulation of objectives and the selection of course content. In this chapter we shall focus on the third step in syllabus design, namely the problem of how the material that has been selected can be ordered in such a way that the objectives are attained in the most efficient manner possible. Frequently used terms for ordering language material for teaching purposes are *gradation, grading*, and *sequencing*. We prefer the term *gradation* because the term *grading* is also used for the marking of tests and examination papers (see also Mackey 1965:205), and because the term *sequencing* could suggest that the ordering of the material to be learned only consists of arranging items in a certain sequential order, whereas the grouping together of items which belong together is also an important aspect of the ordering of language material for teaching purposes.

Gradation of course content is necessary, not only because it is obviously impossible to present the total body of selected language material at once, but also because foreign languages are strongly sequential. They are more sequential – that is, future learning depends more on previous learning – than most other subjects taught in schools, according to Pimsleur *et al.* (1964) and Sauer (1971). It can be observed that learners continue to be affected by gaps in their knowledge of such subjects, and that insufficient results keep recurring. In order to avoid this, one will have to see to it that the material to be learned is presented in a systematic fashion, and that there is sufficient opportunity to repeat parts of it. Foreign languages typically are subjects which require a 'coordinated program to ensure orderly progress through successive stages of learning' (Pimsleur *et al.* 1964:135). These insights, by the way, are by no means new; consider the following proposals by the seventeenth-century scholar Comenius, as summarized by Mackey (1965:205):

> The beginning should be slow and accurate, rightly understood and immediately tested. Unless the first layer is firm, nothing should be built on it; for the whole structure will be developed from the foundations. All parts should be bound together so that one flows out of the other, and later units include earlier ones. Whatever precedes forms a step to what follows and the last step should be traceable to the first by a clear chain of connection.

The importance of a well considered gradation of course content was stressed again around the turn of the century by such well known experts in the field of

FLT as Sweet (1899, 1964[2]), Jespersen (1904, 1967[13]) and Palmer (1922, 1964[2]). The latter even devoted an entire chapter to 'gradation'.

Assuming systematic gradation to be necessary, we can now limit ourselves to the question of *how* the language material could best be ordered. In the preceding chapter (10.2.) we have seen that a number of 'external' factors play an important role in the selection of course content; primarily the objectives, the level and the teaching time available. These same factors can also play a role in choosing a specific type of gradation. This we shall briefly discuss in 11.2.

Before we can address the question, in designing a course, of which place is best for each individual item in the course, we shall first have to answer two other questions, relating to gradation in general on the one hand, and specifically to gradation of language material for FLT purposes on the other:

(1) Should we prefer cyclic or linear gradation?
(2) Should we order the material selected according to grammatical, situational, or functional–notional principles, or should we use other principles still, e.g. lexical categories?

We shall discuss these two questions in detail in 11.3. With regard to the second question we shall confine ourselves to discussing the three approaches to gradation mentioned first under (2), since these are the approaches which have received most attention in the literature.

Lastly, each item should be given the place in the course where it is learned most effectively. There are a number of criteria which could lead to the decision to present an item early or late in a course, and to have it preceded or followed by other items; criteria which have already been partly discussed in the previous chapter on selection. We shall briefly discuss the role of some of these criteria in gradation in 11.4.

So far, we have tacitly assumed in our discussion that we will have a teaching situation in which the learners form a more or less homogeneous group. In practice, however, the teacher will usually be confronted with a fairly heterogeneous group of pupils. When the teacher organizes his teaching in such a way that he can cater for the differences in initial skills, aptitude and motivation among his pupils, he is said to *differentiate*. Individual differences between pupils can for instance be catered for by ordering the material to be learned in such a fashion that it becomes possible to select different routes through the material.

We have also assumed so far that there will be a teacher who acts as a mediator between the learner and the material to be learned. This need not necessarily be the case. Attempts have been made at ordering course content in such a fashion that a learner could learn a foreign language effectively without the intervention of a teacher. *Programmed instruction* (PI) comes to mind in this connection; a form of instruction which allows the learner to operate independently, assisted only by some learning aid (often of a mechanical nature). We have opted for a separate discussion of these matters in this chapter because PI is essentially a special form of gradation, and because differentiation contains aspects specifically related to gradation. A discussion of the problems involved in differentiation, however, cannot restrict itself to aspects of gradation. We shall therefore extend our discussion to aspects which are related to objectives, selection and didactic procedures.

11.2 The role of external factors

As in selection, external factors such as objectives, proficiency level and available teaching time will have to be taken into consideration in gradation. The relation between objectives and gradation can be described as follows: the material should be ordered in such a way that the students attain the level specified in the objectives in the most effective manner possible. What precisely the most effective way of ordering is, however, is still a controversial issue. Does a functional–notional approach to specifying objectives for instance entail that the material should be ordered according to functional–notional categories? We shall discuss this question in 11.3.2., and limit ourselves in this paragraph to observing that in general gradation along strictly functional–notional lines is not considered adequate for courses for general purposes, especially where basic courses are concerned. Choosing a certain type of gradation may also depend on the total number of hours available for FLT, and on whether these hours are allotted over longer or shorter periods. The question whether one teaches beginning or advanced students may also matter to our choice. Both of these questions will be discussed in 11.3.2.3.

The need for systematic gradation, incidentally, decreases as the level of L2 proficiency of the learners increases. Lack of gradation will especially be felt in the early stages, when the basis for further development is established. Once a firm basis has been established, the importance of strict gradation decreases.

11.3 Some types of gradation

In the previous paragraph we have discussed the possible influence of a number of external factors on the selection of a particular type of gradation. In the paragraphs that follow, we shall devote a separate discussion to these types. Since options between linear and cyclic gradation on the one hand and grammatical, situational and functional–notional gradation on the other can be made independently of each other, we shall discuss these options separately.

11.3.1 Linear and cyclic gradation

Anyone who designs a course, be it a foreign language, history or biology course, will be confronted with a choice basically between two types of gradation, often called *linear* and *cyclic* in the literature. In the rest of this chapter, we shall use these two terms, although one can also find the terms *successive* for *linear*, and *spiral* and *concentric* for *cyclic*. Linear gradation has been used most frequently in the past, also in FLT, but the last 10 or 15 years have witnessed a growing interest in cyclic gradation. We shall discuss both types of gradation in relation to their application in FLT. We shall devote separate paragraphs to each, although in reality they are not so strictly separated.

11.3.1.1 Linear gradation

In a typically linearly ordered course the items are presented one by one in a strictly linear sequence which is maintained throughout the course. Each item is discussed in detail, and the aim is to attain complete command of the item before proceeding to the next item (Bosco and DiPietro 1970:15, Corder 1973:296-7, Howatt 1974b:19-20, Marton 1974:20-1).

In the literature, one will sometimes find linear gradation equated with grammatical gradation. Schäpers (1972:23), for instance, speaks of 'die früher übliche "lineare" Progression, die Anordnung des Sprachmaterials nach grammatischen Kategorien'; Schäfer (1972:35) says that linear gradation 'seiner Anlage nach formal ausgerichtet [ist]', while Alexander (1976:91) devotes a passage to 'structural, or linear grading, as it is often called . . .' It is not only incorrect to equate the two; it is also misleading. It is incorrect because it creates the impression that grammatical gradation cannot be combined with cyclic gradation and that functional–notional gradation cannot co-occur with linear gradation, and it is misleading because a rejection of linear gradation in this case will imply a rejection of grammatical gradation.

A survey of the literature of the last 10 years will lead to the conclusion that nowadays linear gradation is generally not considered to be very suitable for foreign language courses. The following are the main objections against linear gradation:

- in a strictly linearly ordered course an item is presented only once, practised intensively, and subsequently largely ignored, although most courses contain a number of 'revision' units, in which the course material is reviewed briefly and usually in the original context. Studies of retention have shown, however, that an item will be better remembered if it keeps recurring in different contexts (see e.g. Martin 1978 and the literature cited therein);
- progress will be very slow at first, because each item is discussed in great detail. It will take considerable time, especially in grammatically ordered courses, before the learners can use what they have learned in communicative situations. This may have a negative effect on the motivation of the learners, or it may lead them to question the use of what they have learned.

In addition one can observe that, although a distinction between material for productive use and material for receptive use is certainly not incompatible with the principles of linear gradation, many linearly ordered courses do not make this distinction (Marton 1974:26-7). This severely limits the amount of material that can be offered and will therefore present grave difficulties to anyone who wants to provide exercises in the shape of spoken or written texts. These problems can be overcome more easily in cyclically ordered courses.

11.3.1.2 Cyclic gradation

Bosco and DiPietro (1970:15) give a short definition of cyclic gradation which clearly illustrates its essential characteristics:

The feature cyclic refers to the presentation of a point in a way leading to gradual familiarization by returning to it at different intervals in the course of instruction. . . . In the cyclic approach mastery is achieved by successive approximation to a given standard.

In a course in which the material is ordered cyclically the individual items are not presented and discussed exhaustively, as in strictly linear gradation, but only essential aspects of the item in question are presented initially. These items then keep recurring in the course, and every time new aspects will be introduced which will be related to and integrated with what has already been learned. Cyclic gradation means, according to Corder (1973:297):

> . . . returning to some more general area of syntax or semantics, for example, or some domain of language use, developing a deeper or more extensive or more abstract understanding of the items, processes or symbols involved, relating them and integrating them with the other material already presented and learned.

Corder (1973:296) advocates cyclic gradation because it is much more strongly related to the way in which language is structured than linear gradation:

> A simple linear sequence would of course be appropriate if the items or groups of items were, linguistically speaking, in some sort of logical relation of dependence to each other, or, alternatively, were all logically independent (in which case any sequence would be equally effective). But . . . neither is the case. The structure of a language is a 'system of systems', or a 'network' of interrelated categories, no part of which is wholly independent or wholly dependent upon another.

Howatt (1974b:20) advocates cyclic gradation because it resembles the natural process of language learning more closely:

> Whereas the natural process of learning a language is 'spiral', i.e. the same things keep turning up in different combinations with different meanings, the language teaching process is usually linear, i.e. new points are strung along in a line and each one is, so to speak, sucked dry before moving to the next.

Cyclic gradation has a number of clear advantages:

- constantly recurring revision in different contexts of the material which has already been presented is catered for; we have already indicated the relevance of this in 11.3.1.1.;
- progress in the early stages is relatively quick. As the initial presentation of the material is limited to a small number of essential aspects, the learner will very soon find that he has command of a coherent system which he can use to communicate in the foreign language, albeit in a limited way. This will encourage the learner to make a greater effort in learning the language (see also Marton 1974:23);
- Marton (1974:26–8) points out the wider range of possibilities offered by cyclic gradation in distinguishing between material for productive and material for receptive use. It is, for instance, possible to present an amount of material for productive use together with a (larger) amount of material for

receptive use at each presentation of an item. This makes it easier to make the course material more interesting. It will also be possible, because the same items keep recurring, to present material which has already been learned for receptive use later on as material to be learned for productive use (see also Valdman 1978:575-6). Cyclic gradation also offers more scope for differentiation (see 11.5.). One could, for example, give the better learners the opportunity to learn the material for receptive use for productive use as well.

We shall now illustrate the application of cyclic gradation by means of an example from Corder (1973:303). The item concerned is a syntactic category, *simple present*. The numbers 1, 8, etc. indicate the sections where the various aspects of the item *simple present* are presented in the course discussed by Corder:

1	Present state	This is John
8	Habitual action	I come to school every day
104	'Timeless' truths	Cows give milk
118	Verbs of perception	This mango looks good
194	Timeless conditional sentences	I eat if I'm hungry
222	Future reference	When I go to Dacca, I shall see my father

We have already mentioned that nowadays cyclic gradation is generally considered more suitable for foreign language courses than linear gradation. The discussion about the pros and cons of linear and cyclic gradation in the literature has largely been replaced by a discussion about the desirability of ordering the material along either grammatical or functional–notional lines.

11.3.2 Grammatical, situational, and functional–notional gradation

In compiling a foreign language course one will not only be confronted with the question whether the language material selected should be ordered linearly or cyclically, but also with the question which linguistic categories provide the best criteria for ordering the material. In FLT, course content was traditionally primarily ordered in morpho-syntactic categories. A course in which the language material has been ordered in this way is usually referred to in the literature as exhibiting *grammatical* gradation (which is the term we shall use in the rest of this chapter). One also finds the term *structural* gradation. More recently, proposals have been developed for ordering material in situational and functional–notional categories. Which (combination) of these three types of gradation will lead to the most effective attainment of the objectives? The following paragraphs are devoted to a discussion of each of these three types, and we shall attempt to answer the question asked above.

11.3.2.1 Grammatical gradation

Traditionally, it was generally assumed that the process of foreign language learning could best be advanced by ordering the language material selected primarily on the basis of its structural characteristics. The assumption was that a fair command of the morpho-syntactic rule system of the foreign language is a prerequisite for effective communication.

In a typically grammatically ordered course the units centre around one or more syntactic or morphological structures. In such a course, the units are often named after the structures discussed, e.g. *present tense* or *possessive singular*. For a very detailed proposal for a course based on morpho-syntactic structures, see Ritchie (1967). In the course of years, a number of criteria have been developed that can help one find the most effective gradation of the grammatical content of a course. Although these criteria sometimes appear to clash with each other, there is a certain degree of consensus between course designers with respect to the most effective gradation; something which need not surprise us all that much, given the long history of grammatical gradation (Alexander 1976:91–2). Later on in this chapter, we shall see that we do not yet have much insight into the most effective gradation of situational or functional–notional units.

A number of objections have been raised over the years against a primarily grammatical gradation of course content. In this paragraph, we shall discuss two objections which have received a lot of attention in the literature, and it will be seen that these two objections are really more objections against certain characteristics of a large number of grammatically ordered courses than against the principles of grammatical gradation. The objection which one encounters most frequently is that because of the emphasis on a command of the morpho-syntactic rule system, it is frequently forgotten that 'linguistic forms provide a means to an end and that the end is communication' (Wilkins 1974b:120–1). More than just a command of morpho-syntactic rules is needed for verbal communication; it is also necessary to be able to use language appropriately in context. Therefore the rules of language use have to be learned as well as the rules of grammar. In other words, FLT should not only focus on the development of *linguistic competence*, but also, and in the first place, on the development of *communicative competence* (Corder 1973:197, Candlin 1973:58, Canale and Swain 1980).

Those who object against grammatical gradation sometimes forget that using a grammatically ordered course does not necessarily entail learning 'in a kind of communicative vacuum in which structures are learned like mathematical formulae' (Brumfit and Johnson 1979:2). What is needed is that in such courses great care should be taken to present and practice the structures which are the focus of a particular lesson in realistic communicative contexts (see also Freudenstein 1981a:61, Johnson 1982:109). In the following paragraphs we shall see, however, that proposals have been developed for reordering the language material on the basis of situational or functional–notional categories, on the assumption that gradation along such lines will provide a better guarantee that communicative competence is attained than grammatical gradation will. But it is sometimes forgotten that communicative competence not only includes a command of rules of language use, but also a command of morpho-syntactic rules, and that in the absence of some form of grammatical gradation there is no guarantee that the latter will be attained (Jung 1979:90–2, Partington 1980:25). Canale and Swain (1980:11) point to the danger of 'fossilization' of certain grammatical inaccuracies, if grammatical accuracy is not emphasized from the start.

A second frequently heard objection is that many grammatically ordered courses suffer from a poverty in lexical items. Palmer's (1922, 1964[2]:68) recommendation to limit the presentation of lexical material in the very first stages of foreign language learning so as to be able to pay as much attention as possible to the basic structures was accepted also for later stages in many courses. The result was that the learners had a fair command of the rule system, but did not know enough words to function adequately in communicative situations.

Although this objection can certainly be raised against certain grammatically ordered courses, it really is more an objection concerning selection of course content than concerning gradation. If the objectives match the needs of the future language user and the selection of course content is based on these objectives, then the course is certain to contain sufficient language material.

11.3.2.2 Situational gradation

The experience that learners who had been taught from grammatically ordered courses were often unable to apply what they had learned in actual communicative situations has, amongst other things, led to the proposal to replace grammatical gradation by situational gradation. This means that the situations in which the learners will have to be able to use the language constitute the most important consideration in gradation, whereby situation is interpreted as the physical environment in which language use takes place. For this reason, units in situational courses are often given names such as: 'In the post office', 'In the restaurant' and 'Doing the shopping' (Wilkins 1976a:15–18).

Situational gradation should not be confused with what Widdowson (1968:139) has called a 'contextually aided structural approach'. When, in the past, the audiolingual method turned out not to yield the expected results, this was often ascribed to the abundance of meaningless, mechanical exercises that marked most of the courses based on this method. People often sought to remedy this by providing 'realistic contexts or situations' (Candlin 1972:37). Situational or contextualized pattern drills, for instance, were developed in addition to the mechanical pattern drill. Gradation, however, was as before based on the morpho-syntactic structures of the language. It was only in the practice sections that a situational aspect was incorporated, and even then it was often no more than mere decoration. Widdowson (*loc. cit.*) correctly considers this to be a variant of the grammatical approach to syllabus design.

As we have observed before, the situational approach to gradation is one in which the most important factor is the physical environment in which utterances are produced. The underlying assumption of course is that the physical environment of language use predetermines, to a large extent, what language material will be used. Wilkins (1976a:17) however correctly remarks that 'it would be naive to think that the speaker is somehow linguistically at the mercy of the physical situation in which he finds himself'. The content of an utterance is determined by a number of underlying, related factors, of which the physical environment is only one. Other factors are, for instance, the social and psychological roles the various participants in a conversation play, and the most important factor is surely the goal which one wants to achieve by means of the utterance. One of the main objections against a strictly situational gradation therefore relates to the excessive emphasis on the relation between the linguistic content of utterances and the physical environment in which they take place; it will be difficult for the learner to apply what he has learned in situations which have not been dealt with in the course. Only in those rare cases in which one could precisely predict in which situations the future language user will need the foreign language, would it be advisable to consider situational gradation (Wilkins 1974a:256-7, 1976a:18). It is also not at all clear how the various situations could best be ordered with respect to each other; situations do not show the kind of internal ordering which is characteristic of the grammatical structure of language.

11.3.2.3   Functional-notional gradation

In the last 10 years a new approach to syllabus design, which we have called the functional–notional approach in 9.3.2.1., has received considerable attention. The most important ideas were provided by Wilkins (1972a, 1974a, 1974b, 1975, 1976b, and especially 1976a), who uses the term *notional*. Van Ek and Alexander (1975) have formulated concrete objectives, including inventories of language functions, notions and language forms. These contents are set out as unordered lists. Van Ek and Alexander make no proposals for gradation of this material, but proposals for gradation on the basis of functional–notional categories constitute an important part of the publications by Wilkins cited above. Before discussing this, it will be useful to look at some of the differences in terminology between Van Ek and Alexander (1975) and Wilkins. Wilkins (1976a:21-54) differentiates between three different types of functional–notional category:

(1) *Semantico-grammatical categories*, relating to 'our perceptions of events, processes, states and abstractions' (Wilkins 1976a:21). These correspond to Van Ek and Alexander's *general notions*.
(2) *Categories of modal meaning*, relating to the way in which a language user 'expresses his own attitude towards what he is saying (or writing)' (Wilkins 1976a:22).
(3) *Categories of communicative function*, used to indicate 'what to *do* through language', as opposed to 'what we report by means of language' (Wilkins 1976a:41).

Van Ek and Alexander subsume the last two categories under *language functions*. Wilkins (1976a:23) considers his work on the third category 'the more original part' of his contribution, which is something one can also conclude from his description of the starting-point of his research: 'what people want to do through language is more important than mastery of language as an unapplied system' (Wilkins 1972a:12).

Wilkins (1976a:19) motivates his preference for a functional–notional approach as follows:

The advantage of the notional syllabus is that it takes the communicative facts of language into account from the beginning without losing sight of grammatical and situational factors. It is potentially superior to the grammatical syllabus because it will produce a communicative competence and because its evident concern with the use of language will sustain the motivation of the learners. It is superior to the situational syllabus because it can ensure that the most important grammatical forms are included and because it can cover all kinds of language functions, not only those that typically occur in certain situations.

Although situational factors certainly do have a certain influence on the selection of language forms for the realization of a functional–notional category (the category *suasion* in a meeting, for instance, will be differently realized linguistically in situations in the home), it is certainly correct to observe that a certain realization of such a category can be used in many different situations. A functional–notional category is, therefore, 'a more powerful category for generalization than the situation' (Shaw 1977:223). Wilkins (1976a:66) recognizes that 'a notional syllabus no less than a grammatical syllabus must seek to ensure that the grammatical system is properly assimilated by the learner'. To attain this, Wilkins (1976a:55, 64–6) proposes to order the language material cyclically. The first cycle, then, will have to contain the simplest or most productive realizations of each of the functional–notional categories the course contains. In the next cycle, these categories are taken up again, but this time the language material is structurally more complex. In such an approach, therefore, we have grammatical gradation *between* the various cycles, but *within* the cycles the language material is ordered on a purely functional–notional basis. In this connection it has to be noted, however, that we have as yet very little insight into the most effective gradation of functional–notional categories. Wilkins (1976b:9), for i stance, writes: '. . . . while recognizing the importance of the individual semai.tic categories that we have established, some higher organizing principle – a kind of hierarchy – is needed that groups such categories together in useful ways.' Wilkins has repeatedly warned against replacing grammatical gradation by strictly functional–notional gradation; given the very superficial knowledge that we have of the linguistic realizations of the various functional–notional categories, and our lack of insight into the most effective gradation of these categories, it would be 'decidedly premature' to abandon 'the partly negotiable currency of the grammatical approach for the crock of gold at the end of the functional rainbow' (Wilkins 1974b:120).

Wilkins's ideas have received considerable attention, and have rekindled the discussion about the objectives and content of FLT, especially in Europe. Advocates of the new approach, however, have sometimes completely identified the end with the means to the end. Piepho (1974, 1979) and Harlow (1978), for instance, apparently assume that if one formulates one's objectives in functional–notional terms, one has to order the material to be learned on a functional–notional basis. In 11.1. we have pointed out the absolute need for systematic gradation, especially in basic courses. Given our knowledge of the morpho-syntactic rule system, and the availability of usable criteria for gradation, we can order course content in a reasonably systematic way. Wilkins (*op. cit.*) mentions, and Brumfit (1978a:39) stresses, the fact that we have no 'comparable understanding of the system of communicative functions'. In the absence of criteria which can be used to impose a systematic gradation on functional–notional categories, a number of the objections raised against situational gradation (see 11.3.2.2.) can also be raised against functional–notional gradation. These objections have led many people to abandon a primarily functional–notional gradation – given the present state of our knowledge – especially where it concerns FLT to beginners in general courses. Brumfit (1978a, 1978b, 1979), Johnson (1979b, 1982), Jung (1979) and Knapp-Potthoff (1979:48–52) advise to order the language material on a grammatical basis for the time being, but at the same time, in order to make learners communicatively competent as well as linguistically competent, to pay much more attention than formerly to the communicative use that can be made of language material. The long-term aim for gradation is to integrate communicative and structural aspects of language:

> Mit dem Ausbau der Pragmalinguistik – insbesondere der wünschenswerten eindeutigen Relationierung von Redeabsichten und Sprachmitteln – ist als langfristiges Ziel eine Umorganisierung zugunsten einer pragmalinguistischen Progression anzustreben, die – von den noch in ihren Lernschwierigkeiten zu gewichtenden Typen von Kommunikationssituationen und Formen von Redeabsichten ausgehend – die entsprechenden fremdsprachlichen Mittel aneignen hilft und deren kommunikative Funktion sichtbar macht (Jung 1979:94).

Similar views are expressed in Canale and Swain (1980). Proposals for integrating communicative and structural aspects can be found in for instance Van Ek (1976:27) and Alexander (1976, 1981).

Although in general a strictly functional–notional gradation is considered to be unsuitable for elementary general courses, its possibilities for application in advanced and remedial courses are recognized (see Wilkins 1974b:121–2, 1976a:69–75, Leech and Svartvik 1975:11, Johnson 1977:670–1, 1979b:27, Stratton 1977). In both cases, one can speak of a 'fresh departure' for material which has already been dealt with repeatedly. In this way, one can attempt to motivate the learners anew, and liberate them from what Leech and Svartvik (1975:11) call 'grammar fatigue'. Wilkins (1976a:69–75) points out the possibilities for application in special purpose courses, and in limited duration courses, in which the aim is to make the learner communicatively competent in a number of language use situations in a very short period of time.

To conclude our discussion of the functional–notional approach we shall devote some attention to some points of criticism raised by Widdowson (1979b, 1979c). Widdowson recognizes that the new approach has shifted the focal point in FLT to the communicative characteristics of language, but does not recognize Wilkins's (1976a:19) claim that the functional–notional approach 'takes the communicative facts of the language into account'. He objects that what has come out of the approach is little more than an inventory of functional–notional categories, and that such an inventory 'does not, and cannot of its nature, take into account . . . that communication does not take place through the linguistic exponence of concepts and functions as self-contained units of meaning. It takes place as discourse, whereby meanings are negotiated through interaction' (Widdowson 1979c:253). He then proceeds to point out that 'this interaction creates hierarchical structures whereby the combination of propositions and illocutions builds up to larger units of communication', and suggests basing gradation on these hierarchical structures (Widdowson 1979c:257). It seems to us, however, that such an approach disregards the fact that a foreign language learner, being a competent speaker of his native tongue, will already have a thorough implicit knowledge of the rules that govern the use of language in an interaction process, and that he will not again have to be taught these rules from scratch; certainly not where the language in question is the language of a culturally related nation (see also Canale and Swain 1980:12, Ross 1981:237–8).

11.3.3 Evaluation

In 11.1. we have seen that foreign languages are among those subjects which are strongly sequential in character. It has been shown that learners have great difficulty in filling up any gaps in their knowledge or skills. In order to avoid such gaps as much as possible it is necessary first of all to present the material in a systematic way, and secondly, to provide opportunities for constant revision of material already presented. The main reason to prefer cyclic gradation to linear gradation is that this can be incorporated into the former much more easily than into the latter. The first requirement, which is to order the material systematically, can best be met by grammatical gradation. A disadvantage of many grammatically ordered courses, however, is that the command of the morphosyntactic rules is the focal point to such an extent that pupils who were taught from such courses could indeed produce grammatically correct sentences, but were not sufficiently capable of applying what they had learned in actual communicative situations. To overcome this difficulty, proposals to order the language material on a situational or a functional–notional basis were formulated. One objection against the former type of gradation is that it stresses the relation between language use and physical context overmuch. An objection which relates to both types of gradation is that there is insufficient insight into the system of situational and functional–notional categories, and that there are hardly any criteria which could be used in establishing the optimal order of presentation of such categories. For the time being, the best policy seems to be to start with a primarily grammatical approach, especially in elementary courses for general purposes, and at the same time pay attention to the use of the language material presented as a vehicle of communication where possible. This will also aid the learner's motivation, since he will recognize the aims he has in mind more readily if the material is presented in this way. A long-term goal should be the integration of aspects of language use and language structure in gradation (which is what Alexander 1976:95 calls 'functional/structural' gradation).

11.4 Some criteria for gradation

After having devoted the previous paragraphs to an argument that a primarily grammatical gradation seems to be the best option for the time being, we shall devote a paragraph to a discussion of a number of criteria that could be used in establishing the optimal gradation of morpho-syntactic structures. It should not be concluded from this, however, that we consider ordering at the lexical and textual levels to be unimportant. But for reasons of space, and because the criteria for *selection* discussed in the previous chapter can also be used for *gradation*, we shall restrict ourselves to mentioning the relevant passages (10.4.2., 10.4.3.1., 10.4.3.3.). For further information, see Palmer (1922, 1964[2]:ch. 10) and Mackey (1965:ch. 7).

Traditionally, criteria for ordering morpho-syntactic structures have often been derived from descriptive grammars of the target language. It was thought that structures could best be ordered hierarchically, ranging from structurally simple to structurally complex, and it was assumed that the linguistic complexity of a structure gave a fair indication of the degree of difficulty of that structure. Psycholinguistic research, however, has shown that on the whole this assumption tends not to be correct (see 3.1.1.). Furthermore, the different linguistic theories do not always adhere to the same notion of linguistic complexity. Other criteria derived from the description of the target language are *frequency of occurrence* (see Hoffmann 1970, Larsen 1975) and *functional load*, defined by Dubin and Olshtain (1977:40) as 'the productivity of a particular structure, its utility in constructing a large variety of sentences and its function as a basis for other structures'. However, we have seen in 10.4.3.2. that we have little objective data on the frequency of structures, and we have even less objective data on the 'functional load' of structures.

Criteria for gradation have also often been based on contrastive analyses of L1 and L2 grammars (see James 1980:153-4). Following the assumption that 'Those elements that are similar to his [i.e. the learner's] native language will be simple for him and those elements that are different will be difficult' (Lado 1957:2), an assumption which is fraught with problems, as we have seen in chapter 4, it was often concluded that isomorphic structures should be taught first. However, there is also an inherent psychological danger in presenting isomorphic structures first: the learner may be led to expect continuing positive transfer from his L1, also in those cases where there is no isomorphism between L1 and L2. Politzer (1968), therefore, conducted a number of experiments to investigate which of the two approaches to gradation results in more effective learning: presenting parallel structures before contrasting ones (p–c) or vice versa (c–p). In four out of five experiments with first-year English-speaking learners of French or Spanish, the latter approach resulted in more successful learning than the former. Although only very low levels of significance were registered, it can be concluded that the p–c sequence does not necessarily provide an optimal gradation of structures.

So far, we have only examined the grammars of the L2 (and of the L1) for ways of ordering morpho-syntactic structures as efficiently as possible. A plausible alternative to this approach would be to derive ordering principles, where possible, not from what we know of the *structure of language* but from what we know of the *structure of the learning process*. It might, therefore, be worthwhile to consider what insights can be obtained from available studies of L2 learning that could be usefully applied to the ordering of morpho-syntactic structures. First of all, it has to be pointed out that, although the 1970s have witnessed a spectacular increase in research into L2 development, most of this research has been concerned with the (informal) learning of L2 English and, moreover, with only a very small area of morphology and syntax. In fact, L2 learning research has focused to date mainly on a limited number of morphemes (see 5.1.3.), on negation, yes/no questions and WH-questions (see e.g. Hatch 1978, Wode 1981, Felix 1982, 6.1.2. and the studies cited there), relative clauses (see Schumann 1980) and on some structures which C. Chomsky (1969, 1972) has shown to appear late in L1 learning (see d'Anglejan and Tucker 1975, Cooper *et al.* 1979, Bongaerts 1983). Secondly, serious questions can be raised about the applicability of the results of such studies as have been made in the ordering of structures for teaching purposes. Let us take the morpheme studies and the studies on the development of negation as examples.

In the morpheme studies discussed in 5.1.3. the following universal pattern was observed. The first cluster of morphemes to be used correctly are *-ing, plural* and *copula*; the second cluster consists of *auxiliary* and *article; irregular past* is the next morpheme to be used correctly; and *regular past, verb third person singular*, and *possessive* make up the last cluster. Krashen *et al.* (1975:46) concluded from the observed invariant order found: 'it is plausible that using a sequence identical to that difficulty order will be more comfortable and efficient, that is, learning might proceed more rapidly and with less frustration on the part of the student and teacher', and put the observed order forward as 'a candidate for the optimal teaching sequence' (*op. cit.* 52).

In 5.1.2. it was observed that four steps could be distinguished in the development of negation in L2 English: (1) *no + V*, (2) 'unanalysed' *don't + V*, (3) *Aux + NEG* (where aux is mainly *is/can*), (4) 'analysed' *don't*. Suggestions have been made to base the order of presentation of structures on such developmental sequences, cf. Corder (1975:213), who mentions Nickel's (1973) suggestion that 'language materials should reflect the sequence of approximative systems of the learner to the point of actually teaching "incorrect forms"'.

It seems to us that such proposals are decidedly premature. First of all, although quite a bit is known about the order in which certain L2 structures develop in the learner, researchers have so far been largely unable to determine *why* the structures are learned in the observed orders (see our discussion of the morpheme studies in 5.1.3.) and without such insights a rationale for sequencing structures according to these orders is lacking. Secondly, the practical consequences of such proposals should be seriously considered. Following Krashen *et al.*'s and Nickel's suggestions to the letter would mean, e.g., that the functor *-ing* would have to be introduced before the auxiliary needed to present the progressive, which would yield ungrammatical sentences like **I reading a book,* and that we would have to actually teach forms like *I no can see, *He don't like it, *I don't can explain it, *It's not danger*, before introducing the learners to the correct target language forms. This is, to quote Rutherford (1980:66) 'a very short step to suggesting that . . . . one should actually teach a pidginized form of English and over a stretch of learning time gradually bring it into alignment with standard English'. Such an approach would also seem to build on the assumption that learners would be willing to be taught 'incorrect' English over a considerable period of time and that teachers would not only be willing but also be able to use in the classroom the developmental forms which are characteristic of the learners' current variety of English. Thirdly, although it has been suggested to base the ordering of structures on the sequences which have been observed in L2 learning, such gradation has hardly been tried out in practice, so that we are largely uninformed about the effect of such gradation. Valdman (1975) is, in fact, a rare exception. He studied the learning of the following interrogative structures by American learners of L2 French:

(1) Inversion
    Où va Jean?
(2) Est-ce que
    Où est-ce que Jean va?
(3) WH-fronting
    Où Jean va?
(4) Pronominalization
    Jean va où?

Type (3) and (4) constructions are considered 'colloquial or downright vulgar' by educated native speakers of French, '. . . despite the fact that they use them extensively in unmonitored daily speech' (Valdman (1975:110)). These constructions did not occur in the course materials used by the students. Nevertheless, in an oral test the students produced a considerable number of WH-fronted interrogative structures. Valdman (1975:114) concluded that questions of this type 'were generalized by some sort of restructuring process'. Valdman then reorganized the course materials: type 3 interrogative structures were incorporated and presented first. The remarkable result was that students who had worked with the revised course materials, produced, in a final oral test, far fewer type 3 interrogative structures than students who had worked with the old course materials, and also produced a high percentage of type 2 sentences. By taking the way in which learners restructure the language input into account in ordering course content, better results could be obtained.

From the above it can be concluded that, although in the ideal situation criteria for gradation should be based on knowledge of learning processes, our knowledge of such processes is still very scanty and can as yet hardly provide a solid basis for ordering.

In order to illustrate how complex the problem of arriving at an optimal teaching sequence is, we would finally like to mention Knapp (1980), who tried to determine the effects of five different ways of ordering English restrictive relative clauses on 11 to 12-year-old German pupils. The five orders of presentation were arrived at by combining criteria based on existing L2 descriptions of relative clauses, on a contrastive analysis of such clauses in German and English, and on data from L2 learning research in different ways. The pattern that emerged was very complex. None of the orders guaranteed that all aspects of restrictive relative clause structure were learned optimally. An order which proved most effective for learning one aspect often proved to have negative effects on the learning of another aspect of this structure. Some other results:

- aspects which were presented early were generally learned better than aspects which were presented late, a position halfway through the presentation sequence proving least effective;
- contrasting structures generally proved more difficult than parallel ones, but the order in which such structures were presented (p–c or c–p) appeared to make little difference;
- a special effect was found for relative clauses with deleted relative pronouns, a structure typically acquired late in L1 and L2 learning: early presentation of this structure appeared to have harmful effects on other aspects of restrictive relative clause structure.

11.5 Differentiation

By differentiation we mean those didactic measures which are aimed at gearing teaching as much as possible to the needs and capabilities of individual learners. In the literature, we find the following three main types of differentiation: *institutional differentiation*, *external differentiation* and *internal differentiation* (De Corte 1976[4]:293–5). We shall discuss the first two briefly, but the last in some more detail; firstly because it has been receiving a lot of attention of late, and secondly because with this type of differentiation there are more aspects which are specific for FLT.

(1) *Institutional differentiation* ('inter-school' grouping, 'Differenzierung im Schulsystem'). In contrast with the US, secondary education in most Western European countries is characterized by the existence of various types of schools, differing in level and character. Until after 1960, as a rule a type of school was selected for pupils at the age of 11 or 12, after a uniform period of primary education. The choice was mainly determined by such factors as the achievements in primary school, socio-economic background, and the preferences of parents and pupils. In this manner, the various types of schools received a relatively homogeneous selection of pupils. However, it gradually became more and more evident that it was not possible to make a well founded choice at such an early age, and steps were taken in many countries which were aimed at keeping pupils together as long as possible, thereby postponing the moment of choice as long as possible. This was the origin of the Swedish *Grundskolan*, the British *Comprehensive School*, and the German *Gesamtschule*, and it led to the introduction of common introductory periods of one or more years for some or all types of schools in other countries. The result was, of course, that the population of pupils became rather heterogeneous. This led to the important question of how to deal most adequately with the differences between pupils: by forming homogeneous groups with respect to aptitude, achievement, etc., or by adapting

the teaching to the different abilities of individual pupils within the same heterogeneous class?

(2) *External differentiation* ('inter-class grouping', 'äussere Differenzierung'). Here, we can distinguish between two types:

- *streaming*, i.e. forming homogeneous groups on the basis of average achievement in all subjects, or on the basis of intelligence tests;
- *setting*, or *differentiation per subject*; i.e. forming homogeneous groups of pupils per subject on the basis of their achievements in that subject, or their aptitude for it (as established by means of aptitude tests).

Both types of external differentiation, but especially *streaming*, turned out to be rather disadvantageous for the weaker pupils in a number of respects. The main drawback was that pupils once assigned to the lower achievement groups could hardly move into the higher groups, so that usually the initial division turned out to be the final division, so that in fact a pre-selection to institutional differentiation emerged. For a more detailed discussion, see Gutschow (1974) and Berg (1976:27 ff.).

(3) *Internal differentiation* ('individualization'; 'innere Differenzierung', 'Binnendifferenzierung'). In this approach, which is currently receiving most attention, the heterogeneous group is maintained, and it is attempted to adapt teaching in such a way that every individual pupil benefits maximally. Internal differentiation is considered to be pedagogically the most preferable type of differentiation, because it has the advantage that the pupil remains in his own class, which reduces estrangement, prevents the pupil from being assigned to a particular level too early, allows the weaker pupils to benefit from the better ones, and forces the teacher, much more than in other types of differentiation, to take differences between pupils into account in his teaching. For these reasons, incidentally, we prefer the term *internal differentiation* to the term *individualization*, frequently encountered especially in the English literature on the subject; the former implies much less that catering for the abilities and interests of individual pupils is effected by purely individual teaching, although internal differentiation by no means excludes the possibility that the teacher allows pupils to do parts of the programme individually, with or without the aid of completely programmed materials (see 11.6.).

Although the interest in internal differentiation as a way of organizing teaching is by no means a recent phenomenon – widely publicized differentiation plans of more than 50 years ago come to mind, such as Helen Pankhurst's Dalton Plan and Carleton Washburne's Winnetka Plan (see Grittner 1975) – the interest in differentiation specifically for FLT is fairly recent. Internally differentiated FLT found itself in the centre of attention fairly suddenly in the US at the end of the 1960s. This can be accounted for by the fact that many American universities dropped their *foreign language requirement*, so that there was no longer a need for many high-school pupils to learn a foreign language. This meant that foreign languages had to be made attractive for pupils, and this was attempted by adapting the programmes as much as possible to the needs and interests of individual pupils. A series of monographs and collections of papers about internal differentiation in FLT were published: for instance, Lange (1970), Altman and Politzer (1971), Altman (1972), Gougher (1972), Logan (1973), Grittner and Laleike (1973), Disick (1975), the May 1977 issue of *System*, a special issue on differentiation edited by Howard B. Altman, and the April 1980 issue of *Bulletin de l'ACLA*, which is also entirely devoted to differentiation. Disick (1975:4) even goes so far as to characterize the 1970s as the era of internal differentiation, in the same way as the 1960s have been characterized as the era of audiolingualism. In most Western European countries, where foreign languages are important and obligatory subjects in the curricula of secondary schools, we can observe a growing interest in internal differentiation. Here it is not the need to attract pupils, but the heterogeneity of the pupils which necessitates differentiated teaching. The possibilities for internal differentiation are far more limited in Western Europe than in the US. Most Western European countries have uniform objectives for FLT in each type of school, specifying the level that has to be attained by all pupils of a particular school type at the end of their school career. These objectives are set so high that the room to cater for individual abilities, needs or interests is very limited. In the US such objectives are generally not used; instead, minimal objectives are usually specified for all pupils to attain, which are consciously kept limited. This leaves plenty of time to cater for the demands of each individual pupil.

In the rest of this section we shall discuss a few models of internal differentiation, using the following definition by Disick (1975:5) as our starting-point:

> Briefly, individualized instruction is an approach to teaching and learning that offers choices in four areas: objectives of learning, rate of learning, method (or style) of learning, and content of learning. The extent to which choices are offered determines the degree of individualization in a particular program.

Two frequently used models of internal differentiation offer choices in objectives, rate of learning, and learning content. De Corte *et al.* (1976[4]:296) calls them *linear* and *branching* respectively, but we shall call them *self-pacing* (Grittner and Laleike 1973:9) and *flexible pacing* (Disick 1975:62), in order to avoid terminological confusion between these two types of differentiation and two types of programmed instruction (see 11.6.) that go by the same name. In internal differentiation it is first of all necessary to establish the *minimal* or *basic* objectives that have to be attained by all pupils, and the *differential* objectives which pupils can attain in addition to the basic objectives. On the basis of these objectives the learning material is divided into basic material (called *Fundamentum* or *Pensum* in the German literature; see Schröder 1979b:130) and the additional material (*Additum* in the German literature; see Schröder, *loc. cit.*). It is characteristic of the self-pacing model that pupils first of all go through all the basic material at their own pace, and then go through the additional material. However, this method has some considerable drawbacks; there will be considerable difference in the rate of progress, which makes group teaching virtually impossible and forces the pupils to work on their own most of the time, which is contrary to their natural desire for interaction with classmates and also makes exercises in communicative use of language virtually impossible (see De Corte *et al.* 1976[4]:296, Disick 1975:61). There is also a considerable danger that pupils who have fallen behind will fail to catch up again. It is characteristic of flexible pacing that the programme is divided into a number of units, each consisting of an amount of basic material and an amount of additional material. The pupils first of all go through the basic material collectively, and this is followed by a diagnostic test. Those pupils who have not (yet) learned all the basic material, are given remedial material related to the part of the basic material they have not yet mastered. The other pupils can start working on the additional material, and they can make their own choice of this material to a certain extent. The additional material should be selected in such a way that it is a useful extension of the basic material, without anticipating future basic material, in order to prevent the collective treatment of the basic material from being disrupted. After a unit has been completed, all pupils start simultaneously on the basic material of the next unit. De Corte *et al.* (1976[4]:296) mention as the most important advantages that class instruction remains possible, that pupils will not remain fixed at their level of achievement, and that they will not be discouraged. In practice, however, it proves to be difficult to find additional material which is both useful and does not include future basic material. Pupils who time and again go through the additional material, which could for instance consist of extra reading matter with a greater variety of words and structures, will have an advantage over the other pupils which increases with each new unit. Schröder's (1974, 1979b) proposal to focus on the receptive skills in the *Fundamentum*, and, in the *Additum*, to focus on the productive command of the material presented for receptive use only in the *Fundamentum*, in addition to providing extra exercises in writing and speaking seems only to provide a partial solution to this problem, since a better command of one skill will certainly have a beneficial influence on the command of other skills. Eventually, there will be such differences in progress between pupils that they will have to be re-grouped, for instance by means of *setting*.

We have not yet discussed differentiation according to *style of learning* (see the above quotation from Disick 1975), but this is because systematic variation of didactic procedures aimed at catering for variations in learner characteristics has hardly been practised yet, in spite of the fact that this is widely recognized to be an important condition for achieving maximally effective teaching (see e.g. Müller 1973, Chastain 1975b, Dubin and Olshtain 1977:141–4). Although there has been an increase in research into learning styles or *cognitive styles* (see chapter 6.4.) in recent years, and into the interaction between learner characteristics and methods of instruction in so-called *Aptitude–Treatment–Interaction* (ATI) research (see Cronbach and Snow 1977), we unfortunately have to conclude that the findings from this research are still hardly applicable to school-teaching.

Applying internal differentiation will mean that pupils are often not doing the same things in class. This has certain consequences for the classroom procedures to be used. Formal teaching, which is often used in undifferentiated class instruction, is not a very suitable procedure for internal differentiation, but individual assignments and work in small groups are eminently suitable. Lastly, we would like to point out that internal differentiation will not make the teacher's task any easier. In homogeneous groups, the teacher can pitch his teaching at the 'average pupil', but in heterogeneous classes he will have to be able to deal with the sometimes considerable differences in interests and abilities between pupils. It is hardly surprising, therefore, that Grittner and Laleike (1973:98) and Disick (1975:71) should be of the opinion that it will be virtually impossible for the teacher to apply internal differentiation in groups of 25 pupils or more.

11.6 Programmed instruction (PI)

The essential characteristic of PI is that the pupil deals with the material to be learned all on his own, assisted only by a learning aid, which may be a book, but also a teaching machine or a computer. PI furthermore has the following characteristics:

- there is a precise description of the target behaviour;
- the course content is divided into small, closely linked units, called *frames*;
- the learner is informed of his achievements immediately after the completion of each unit;
- the learner goes through the programme at his own speed.

In all types of PI, the programme consists of a number of consecutive links. The best-known PI models are the *linear* model, associated with Skinner's name, and the *branching* model, associated with the American psychologist N.A. Crowder. In the linear model the units are very small, in order to reduce the risk of errors to a minimum. Each unit provides immediate reinforcement of the learner's response elicited by the programme. The units are strictly linearly ordered, so that all learners go through the programme in exactly the same way (see fig. 11.1.).

Fig. 11.1   Diagram of the linear model

In the branching model, the units are usually somewhat larger, and an assumption is that learners can learn from their own errors, provided that these errors are dealt with in an appropriate fashion by the programme. Each unit is usually concluded by a multiple-choice test. If the learner selects the correct answer, he can immediately proceed to the next unit, but if he selects the wrong answer, he is referred to an additional link containing remedial material (see fig. 11.2.). For a further discussion of some general aspects of PI see the introductions by Hayes *et al.* (1962), Carroll (1963), and Howatt (1969, 1974a).

Much was expected of PI for FLT. In the early 1960s, especially in the US, a lot of time, money and effort was invested in it. Projects were set up which were aimed at providing complete and fully programmed courses. In the US, PI was seen as the panacea for the strongly increasing demand for FLT. At the same time, Skinner's theory of language learning appeared to have given the

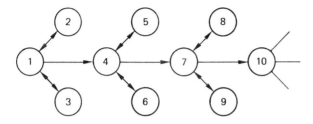

Fig. 11.2   Diagram of the branching model

definitive answer to the question of how exactly languages are learned, and this model predicted language to be eminently suited to programming. Educational technology also made rapid progress. It all fitted so beautifully that one simply could not but have great expectations. The first programmes, naturally, were of Skinner's linear type (see Hayes *et al.* 1962:22, Spolsky 1966:120, Chastain 1970:225). These expectations, however, were disappointed: 'the magic breakthroughs which had been so breathlessly awaited' failed to materialize, and 'the inevitable post-honeymoon period of disillusionment and stocktaking' began (Ornstein 1970:215).

When the results that had been hoped for failed to materialize, researchers started looking for explanations eagerly. Spolsky (1966) and Valdman (1968) argued that the fact that the behaviouristic theory of language learning that PI was based on proved to be untenable partly accounted for its lack of success. PI based on such a theory will only produce imitative language behaviour in the learner, according to Valdman (1968:50). Chastain (1970:228–30), however, demonstrates that there need not be such a direct link between PI and behaviourism as has often been suggested, and he gives some examples of PI based on cognitive learning principles. The branching PI model which we have already discussed is such an example of PI which is not purely based on behaviourism. PI is nowadays seen as 'a vehicle capable of accommodating and serving the most diverse psychological and linguistic theories' (Ornstein 1970:220, see also Carroll 1968:72–3).

There has also been much discussion about whether a language is fully programmable or not. Ornstein (1970:215) says that 'The cold, hard fact is that the applicability of PI is in direct proportion to the concreteness and specificity of a subject.' The more abstract or varied a subject is, the more difficult it will be to program: it is hardly surprising, therefore, that programmers consider FLT to be one of the 'elusive' subjects. Language presupposes communication and in a truly communicative situation the reactions of participants are often hardly predictable. On the basis of such considerations Valdman (1969:50–1) concludes that natural communication is not programmable by definition, but immediately adds to this statement that this does not necessarily exclude PI from FLT (see also Littlewood 1974:14, Wolff 1976:109). On the contrary, he has no doubts that PI can be very useful for certain subskills of the skills to be acquired. This sentiment is common nowadays. Programmed lesson units, e.g. on certain aspects of phonetics and syntax, can help the learner acquire tools which, with practice in the use of language in real situations, could enable him to attain fluency in a relatively short time (Carroll 1968:65). Most writers (e.g. Valdman 1968:59, 1969:53, Mueller 1968b:49, Ornstein 1970:217) conclude that a combination of PI and practice in a natural situation in which interaction between learners, and between learners and teacher is possible, would be the best solution. Ornstein therefore prefers the term *program-assisted instruction* (PAI).

The degree to which PI can be applied in FLT also depends on the skills which are taught. PI for the teaching of oral productive skills, for instance, will always encounter the problem that if immediate reinforcement is to have any effect, the learner will have to be able to discriminate between sounds. The learner will have to be able to distinguish between the sounds of the target language in such a way that he will be able to assess the degree of correctness of his own rendering by comparing it with the correct form which is given. It is a fact that many people are not proficient in discriminating between foreign language sounds in this fashion. This problem has not yet been solved, although the situation could be improved by providing separate exercises in sound discrimination prior to the study of the language as such.

In the early stages of PI, books or teaching machines were practically the only aids used. Nowadays, there is a growing interest in PI in which computers are used; in these cases, one speaks of CAI (*computer-assisted instruction*), or CALI (*computer-assisted language instruction*) where FLT is concerned (see also 13.4.). Although the possibilities of CALI have as yet not been fully researched, it is clear that CALI has some considerable advantages over PI using other media of instruction. A major advantage is that the computer has many more possibilities for interaction with the learner. CALI programs have been developed, for instance, which make it possible to take the specific problems of individual learners into account by using analyses, made by the computer, of errors which have been made by the learner (see also 13.4.). Nelson *et al.* (1976) give a number of examples of this. A recent survey of the use of CALI in foreign language departments of American universities and colleges (Olsen 1980) showed that CALI was used mainly in the basic language courses and that most CALI programs dealt with grammar and vocabulary, although programs for improving listening comprehension, reading comprehension and translation skills were also in use. Olsen (1980) and Holmes and Kidd (1982) also mention attempts to use the computer to promote oral proficiency. It is, however, in the area of oral productive skills that CALI has least to offer. The computer is baffled by speech to a large extent. It cannot analyse sounds except within strictly defined limits. It can synthesize speech in a crude way and thereby act as a transmitter of language, but 'there is little evidence to suggest that in the near future the computer will ever be a useful receiver' (Holmes and Kidd 1982:514). As long as the computer cannot understand speech, it will hardly be able to promote the development of oral proficiency. In considering using computers in FLT, one will have to ask oneself if the advantages of CALI over other types of PI justify the considerable extra costs of such programs.

11.7 Conclusion

The present chapter has focused on a number of aspects of the gradation of course content. More specifically, the first part of the chapter was devoted to a discussion of various types of gradation of language materials and of a number of criteria that could help one arrive at an optimal gradation, and the second part dealt with differentiation in FLT and with (the role of) programmed instruction in FLT. Our discussion of various types of gradation has shown that cyclic gradation, which allows for a gradual familiarization with the items in a language course by continually returning to them in various ways and by introducing new items in such a way that learners are helped to relate them to and integrate them with items that have already been taught, is to be preferred to linear gradation, in which items are typically strung along in a line and each item is taught extensively before the next one is introduced. In our discussion of the pros and cons of the grammatical, situational and functional–notional approaches to the gradation of course content we have argued that it is decidedly premature to abandon the traditional, grammatical approach completely and sequence language materials exclusively along situational or functional–notional lines, that is, especially in elementary courses for general purposes. An integration of grammatical and functional–notional aspects of language use should be the long-term goal, but for the time being the best policy seems to be to start with a primarily grammatical approach and at the same time pay attention, where possible, to the communicative uses to which the language can be put. In our discussion of criteria for gradation, criteria derived from target language grammars and from contrastive analyses were briefly touched on and criteria based on data from studies of L2 learning were more extensively dealt with. The conclusion was that, although decisions on gradation should ideally be largely based on knowledge of L2 learning processes, our knowledge of such processes is still very incomplete and hardly provides a solid basis for gradation. In the second part of the chapter we briefly discussed some types of differentiation, focusing mainly on the type currently receiving most attention, that is, on internal differentiation, and finally we devoted some attention to programmed instruction, ending the chapter with a brief discussion of computer-assisted language instruction and its possible uses in FLT.

12

Didactic procedures

12.1 Introduction

Now that in previous chapters the questions of whom to teach, what to teach, and when to teach have been dealt with, we can address the question of how the language material, which has been selected and ordered on the basis of clearly formulated objectives, should be taught to the target group. We have earlier referred to the fact that the logical order of this procedure often corresponds to a chronological order. It is not the case, however, that one exclusively proceeds from objectives through selection and gradation of course content to didactic procedures: for example, when formulating one's objectives, one should keep an eye on how far it will be possible to attain them in the last phase of the didactic cycle, i.e. the phase during which the actual teaching takes place, as we have already seen in our discussion of some of the factors which determine FLT policy (see 9.2.2.).

Not everybody has the same ideas about what belongs to the domain of didactic procedures and what does not. Given the fact that formulating objectives, selection and gradation of course content, and choice of didactic procedures are extremely closely related, it will be evident that a clear distinction cannot always be drawn, and that for instance the domain of didactic procedures will sometimes overlap with the domain of gradation of course content. We intend to discuss, under the heading of didactic procedures, only those aspects which relate directly to the teaching/learning processes in the classroom. We shall not discuss the various FLT methods referred to in chapter 8 (see 8.3.) in any detail here.

We shall not attempt to advocate any one (set of) didactic procedures as the best for all purposes. The language learning process differs from situation to situation, because there may be much variation in the factors which may influence it, for instance objectives (which skills, and to which level of proficiency), learners (age, cognitive style, motivation, language background), teachers (level of proficiency, didactic skills), and media (tape recorder, language laboratory). Small wonder, therefore, that with so many variables it is impossible to single out any one set of didactic procedures which will yield the best results under all circumstances. Our discussion of didactic procedures will be general in the sense that it will not be specifically related to or directed towards any particular 'established' FLT methods. In those cases where we do pay attention to a few new methods, we do this not to propagate them, but to draw the attention to some new general tendencies.

We have mentioned earlier that we wish to discuss especially those aspects which relate to the teaching/learning processes which take place *in the classroom*. This means that we first of all wish to exclude procedures which are specific to self-instructional, individualized programmes. Furthermore, as elsewhere in this book, our main interest is in FLT in regular education. This means that we shall concentrate on FLT to children and adolescents as an obligatory subject in the curricula of schools offering general education. We shall not discuss adult education separately, and we shall devote little or no attention to special types of education, such as FLT for special or specific purposes, or FLT in the shape of intensive courses.

In addition to the limits we have set ourselves with respect to the subject of our discussion, there are two further points relating to the *way* in which we shall discuss didactic procedures. First of all, we shall not pay any specific attention to the general pedagogical framework in which problems concerning the selection and use of didactic procedures in FLT are of course encompassed.

Secondly, one could use various angles of approach to a discussion of didactic procedures. We could have opted for a systematic discussion of teaching/learning processes specific to each of the four skills, or to each level of linguistic functioning, from the phonological to the textual level, or to the different levels of language proficiency, e.g. elementary, intermediate and advanced. We have selected an angle of approach which we think will enable us to discuss adequately the whole complex issue of the choice and use of didactic procedures in FLT. There are two aspects to our approach. We shall first discuss some general matters relating to didactic procedures, and then discuss the three phases that can be distinguished in the teaching/learning process separately, viz. presentation, repetition and exploitation. We shall conclude by discussing a number of recent developments in the area of FLT methodology which have a specific bearing on didactic procedures.

12.2 Some general aspects

Four of the general aspects that are dealt with here have featured prominently in discussions about the optimal arrangement of L2 teaching/learning processes. These aspects are the use of L1 in FLT, use of the printed word, rule-learning, and correction procedures. Before going into these aspects, however, we will first of all devote a short paragraph to the stimulation of motivation in FLT.

12.2.1 Stimulation of motivation

In our discussion of learner characteristics and the role they play in L2 learning, we have concluded that motivation is one of the most important factors influencing learning success (see 6.5.1.). Its importance relative to other factors has not yet been empirically established. It seems doubtful whether it can ever be established with any degree of precision. It is, for instance, common experience that motivation does not only increase success, but that success in turn may increase motivation.

Knowing that motivation is an important factor in determining success, and that motivation is subject to change and can therefore be influenced and guided, educationalists have incessantly looked for ways in which the motivation of learners may be improved. In earlier chapters we have already occasionally indicated how, in determining the objectives of FLT (see e.g. 9.2.2.) and in the selection and gradation of course content, the effect on motivation of certain choices may be taken into account. However, it is especially at the level of didactic procedures that there is ample opportunity to improve the motivation of the learners. The teacher in the classroom in particular is in a position to generate, increase and maintain the motivation of his pupils through his teaching. Much has been written about this; see, for instance, Burstall (1975), Gardner and Smythe (1975a) and Hancock (1972), and nearly all handbooks on FLT also contain a chapter on motivation. One will not, however, find much in the line of specific information on guiding motivation. Much of the information is of a general pedagogical-didactic nature, advising one to use a varied and lively way of teaching, having the learner recognize the objectives underlying the what and how of teaching, and to demonstrate as a teacher, at all times, that one is inspired by the subject one teaches and that one cares.

Looking in the literature for possibilities to enhance motivation specifically in FLT, one finds very little. Walmsley (1979:110), who compares several existing teaching programmes with respect to the didactic procedures used, finds first of all that there are very few programmes which have, in addition to a presentation phase and an exploitation phase (see below), a separate (introductory) motivation phase. As general advice with respect to stimulating motivation we find in Hancock (1972:149) that learners in class should explicitly be given the opportunity 'to experience the pleasure of being able to communicate through a language other than their own'. Furthermore, it will hardly come as a surprise that, if the desire for identification with native speakers of the L2 has, indeed, a beneficial effect on L2 learning success (see 6.5.1.4.), it is advisable to incorporate some introduction to the culture of the target language speakers in order to increase the so-called integrative motivation. And lastly, one finds in nearly all pleas for communicatively oriented FLT as one of the arguments in favour of this approach that communicative exercises stimulate motivation, not only because they actively involve all learners, but also because of 'most learners' prior conception of language as a means of communication' (Littlewood 1981:17).

12.2.2 Use of L1

In the struggle against the grammar–translation method, in which, as we have seen in chapter 8, the bilingual word list was the most important means of teaching new L2 vocabulary, and translation from and into L2 the most important exercises, the advocates of the direct method made the principle of unilingualism in the teaching/learning process, i.e. using only L2, a central issue. Learning had to take place 'in the foreign language, with the foreign language, and by means of the foreign language', as Mihm (1972:281) puts it. This principle was declared to be applicable to all phases of the teaching/learning process: to the presentation of new material, the manipulation thereof in practice sessions, and to the exploitation of the newly acquired material (see 12.3.), and also to the actual didactic instruction surrounding it, such as, for instance, the explanation of grammatical rules (see 12.2.4.). The unilingual principle does, of course, also play an important role in the developments within FLT after World War II, developments which are characterized by a revival of the direct method. In the 1960s, according to Butzkamm (1979:173), FLT specialists in the Federal Republic of Germany were far more strict and dogmatic about avoiding L1 in FLT than the proponents of the direct method of around 1900. On the other hand Butzkamm (1973:97 ff.) remarks, referring to such great advocates of the audiolingual method as Wilga Rivers and Robert Politzer, that it would be incorrect to say that this American variant of the direct method prescribes, as a principle, that FLT be strictly unilingual.

We shall discuss the use of L1 in the context of vocabulary learning and of translation as an exercise. Concerning the use of L1 in the rest of the teaching/learning process we would like to remark the following: it is generally assumed that a skill will only be truly mastered if it is practised in the function in which it will eventually have to be used (Butzkamm 1973:128; Wilkins 1974c:60 ff.). If, therefore, one of the objectives of FLT is that learners should be able to use L2 productively, then it is only natural that learners practise in and with L2. In this connection anyone, even the most fervent advocate of a mainly bilingual FLT, will approve if standard expressions that regularly recur in the teaching/learning process, are phrased exclusively in L2 from the very beginning. Learning a few of these phrases takes little time, and gradually the range can be extended quite considerably. Neither need there be much disagreement on the question of whether L1 may be used in explaining the L2 rule system; for reasons of efficiency – and efficiency is one aspect which will have to be considered given the limitations on, for example, time and manpower – L1 can be used for this limited purpose in certain situations.

12.2.2.1   The learning of L2 vocabulary

There are two sides to the problem of vocabulary learning in FLT. Every new word should be presented in such a way that its meaning becomes clear to the learner (= semantization), and secondly the word, with its meaning, should be stored in the memory in such a way that the learner can use it effectively in language use situations (= internalization). This second aspect is closely linked to, and to a large extent dependent on, the way in which a word is semanticized. If semantization has been achieved, the first and most important condition for internalization has been fulfilled. It is, however, not sufficient. Semantization forms part of the first phase, the presentation phase, of a cycle which is constituted of two more phases (for further discussions, see 12.3.). If we wish to obtain the desired learning effect, which is the actual use of the word in communicative situations, repetition of the word in question will in most cases be essential. Internalization is not achieved until the subsequent two phases, repetition and exploitation, have been completed. The focus of our discussion of the learning of L2 vocabulary will be on the first phase, that of semantization.

Semantization in L2 learning is not the same as in L1 learning, as we have already pointed out in 5.1.4. In L1 learning, knowledge of a word is acquired simultaneously with the meaning or concept associated with the word. The conceptual development in L1 of the L2 learner has usually been such that he already possesses the concepts which the L2 words refer to, so that all he really has to do is learn the words as a second set of labels for concepts or meanings already available. In this sense, vocabulary learning in L2 is essentially different from vocabulary learning in L1.

No hasty conclusions about the presentation of new L2 words should be drawn from this fact, however. It will be clear that, conceptually, words from L1 and L2 will often correspond to a considerable extent, but hardly on a truly one-to-one basis, not only because different languages categorize reality in different ways, but also because the underlying reality is not always entirely identical. The meaning of words is not determined solely by what they denote, but also by their connotations, and these differ between language communities and between cultures. We shall discuss some of the implications of this later on in this chapter.

There are essentially three ways of presenting new L2 words:

(1) non-verbal presentation: the meaning or concept associated with an L2 word is demonstrated through concrete objects, visual aids, or through mime and acting;
(2) verbal presentation, using L2: the concept in question is described or defined by means of L2 words which have already been learned, or alternatively it is presented in an L2 context. A third possibility is clarifying the meaning of the L2 word by exploiting certain systematic semantic relations, such as synonymy (*Samstag-Sonnabend*), hyponymy (*flower-rose*) or antonymy (*male-female*);
(3) verbal presentation, using L1: the L2 word to be learned is linked directly with a word in L1 which has the same or nearly the same meaning.

The first two ways presuppose an exclusively unilingual presentation of new L2 words. We shall now discuss the advantages and disadvantages of bilingual and unilingual presentation.

The main objection that can be raised against the use of L1 in semanticizing new words is the danger that learners too easily assume that there is a one-to-one correspondence between L1 words and L2 words. The type of presentation we have in mind here involves working with lists of L1 words and their L2 equivalents; the so-called bilingual word lists. There are, of course, also other methods of presentation where L1 is used in the semantization of L2 words, but bilingual word lists are perhaps the most extreme, and certainly the most frequent, method of presentation in which L1 is used. One should, on the other hand, not exaggerate the objection concerning the absence of a one-to-one correspondence between L1 words and L2 words. The concepts underlying, for instance, the English word *house* and the Dutch word *huis*, are not so divergent that objections could be raised against learners equating these two words. Furthermore, also a paraphrase of the meaning of a word exclusively in L2, an alternative which is frequently suggested, in many cases only gives incomplete information about the meaning of a word (see Hüllen 1971:164). And lastly, why should full understanding of the meaning of an L2 word be achieved at once, and not develop gradually, as in L1 development?

A second objection against bilingual word lists is that they present new L2 words completely independently of the context which determines their full meaning. The subtle differences in meaning which one finds in most words are usually specific to certain contexts and situations. This objection to bilingual word lists will of course become particularly acute if the context in which a word is used is ignored both in the phase of semantization and in the phase of internalization. We could, furthermore, point out that, if words are presented only out of context, in bilingual word lists, there will be a very real danger that they will be known only within the context of the lists.

Another important objection against bilingual word lists which is raised quite frequently is that they could encourage interference from L1. Interference in the sense that, in attempts at L2 use, L2 words are repressed by their L1 equivalents in the word lists, or in the sense that the L1 words present themselves first, after which the L2 words are retrieved through them, will, at the least, slow down L2 production. This, however, leaves open the question whether, in FLT, all reference to the L1 system should under any circumstances and in all cases be avoided, and, more specifically, whether bilingual word lists should be avoided because of the danger of interference which they represent. We will return to these matters below.

A more general objection from the angle of learning psychology, lastly, is that learning new words in bilingual word lists will generally fail to stimulate the learner, and thus have a negative influence on his motivation. Learning such word lists is also said to require a considerable amount of time and effort. These, however, are matters concerning which there is much variation between individual learners, a question we will also return to later on in this chapter.

There is, on the other hand, one very general objection which can be raised against entirely unilingual vocabulary learning, and that is that the means and procedures employed are often circuitous and ineffective. It is very difficult, for instance, to illustrate abstract terms, synonyms which differ only slightly in meaning, idiomatic expressions and collocations, if only the L2 is used for this purpose.

The main objection, however, is not so much an objection against exclusively employing L2 in the semantization of L2 words, as a query about the assumption that if one only employs L2, interference from L1 will not occur. It is rather naïve to assume that the L2 learner may be brought to bypass his L1 knowledge, when L1 is avoided in the semantization of L2 words; actual teaching practice shows that this is simply not the case. L2 learners think and feel largely in L1 (Butzkamm 1973:177), and L1 cannot be completely avoided, no matter how hard one tries (Butzkamm 1976:230).

As we have already implied in the preceding few paragraphs, there are a number of variables to be taken into account in selecting the most effective procedures for learning L2 vocabulary. It is impossible to single out any one procedure for vocabulary learning which will be optimal in all teaching situations. Some of the obvious factors which will have to be considered are the motivation of the learners; aspects of the actual teaching situation, such as the presence or absence of certain media; and characteristics of the teacher, such as his expressive skills. In a more specific sense, some characteristics of the material to be learned and some learner characteristics are interesting in the context of L2 vocabulary learning.

We have already pointed out some of the relevant aspects of the material to be learned. In connection with learner characteristics, Celce-Murcia and Rosensweig (1979:242), among others, point out that different learners employ different strategies for learning vocabulary, depending on their level of L2 proficiency and on their age. It is a well known fact that adults have a different attitude than children towards certain instructional materials. Younger learners with learning difficulties often have special problems with respect to the visual representation of certain concepts and objects (Schiffler 1974:234). In the framework of the Swedish GUME-project (see also 12.2.4.) the effects of unilingual vs. bilingual vocabulary learning by adults have been studied. Not only do adults prefer to learn vocabulary bilingually (see e.g. Von Elek 1978:362), but they also learn vocabulary more effectively in this manner (see e.g. Oskarsson 1975:29). Lastly, in relation to the role which the level of L2 proficiency plays, it will be obvious that certain procedures, such as paraphrase, for instance, will be easier to use with learners of a relatively high level of L2 proficiency, and it stands to reason that the longer learners have been exposed to L2, the more susceptible they will be to unilingual presentation of new L2 words.

At present, neither in FLT theory, nor in FLT practice are extremist points of view held with regard to the use of L1 in the semantization of new L2 words or in language teaching in general. Larsen-Freeman (1979:219) assumes that a considered use of L1 in FLT will increase the efficiency of instruction, but only if all the learners in a class share the same L1. The view that L1 should be avoided at all costs has disappeared. There do remain, however, two different approaches to the issue of L1 use in FLT.

On the one hand, there is a strong tendency to compromise: L1 is avoided where possible, but it will be used in those situations where it is considered to be inevitable. A representative of this approach is, for instance, the Dutch psychologist C.P. van Parreren, whose views were very influential in the Federal Republic of Germany in the 1970s. A summary of his views can be found in Van Parreren (1972). On the one hand, Van Parreren is adamant in his rejection of bilingual word lists, but on the other hand, he suggests certain modifications of the unilingual approach to semantization. In his approach, new L2 words are presented in a meaningful context and repeated a number of times in various sentences of the same text in which they are introduced. If it is feared that the new word will not be properly understood, the L1 equivalent is also given, preferably in the margin of the text in question. As little attention as possible is paid to the L1 equivalent, in order to prevent the learner from associating it too strongly with the L2 word to be learned.

The approach adopted by the West German didactician Wolfgang Butzkamm, who has elaborated his ideas on 'Aufgeklärte Einsprachigkeit', which were partly based on Dodson (1967), in a number of publications, is fundamentally different. His conviction is that L1 should not be seen as a

'Störfaktor', but as a 'Lernhilfe' (Butzkamm 1979:175). In another publication, Butzkamm puts it as follows:

> die Muttersprache . . . wird nicht nur hier und da geduldet, sondern übernimmt eine Reihe unverzichtbarer Funktionen auch und gerade da, wo ihr Einwirken bisher als lernhemmend betrachtet wurde (Butzkamm 1976:228).

In Butzkamm's approach, L1 will be consciously used in the initial stages of learning; semantization is achieved through L1 equivalents. Butzkamm is aware of the danger of learners too readily assuming a one-to-one correspondence between L1 words and L2 words, but he does not consider this to be an argument for avoiding L1 altogether, since learners will look for such correspondences whether L1 is used or not. Teachers will, however, have to impress upon the learners that some caution is essential in drawing conclusions about the possible semantic range of L2 words on the basis of L1 equivalence (Butzkamm 1973:125). The essence of Butzkamm's proposal for the learning of L2 vocabulary is that L1 be used for semantization, but that the internalization of the new words be achieved through a sequence of exercises in which L2 comes to play an increasingly important role. His hypothesis is that those L2 to L1 translations which play a role in the semantization of the L2 words, will not necessarily lead to interference, because the L1 word, in his approach, does not function so much as an independent entity, but only serves to evoke the concept underlying the L2 word, so that a direct link may be made between concept and (new) L2 word, without there first of all being a link between L1 words and L2 words (Butzkamm 1973:141). In the later stages of the learning process, Butzkamm gradually moves towards a completely unilingual application of the language material which has been learned without, incidentally, preventing on principle the spontaneous use of L1 in free communication (Butzkamm 1980a:15).

There are no experimental data to support either Butzkamm's or Van Parreren's views and proposals. Insofar as any experiments have been carried out, they only demonstrate that the intended learning effects have indeed been achieved with the procedures proposed, but they do not establish whether the same, or even better, learning effects could not have been achieved through different procedures. Intuitively, Butzkamm's suggestions seem well-considered and balanced, but no certainty about the question of whether and how L1 should play a role in the semantization of L2 words will be forthcoming until experimental research reveals some relevant facts about the organization of the bilingual mental lexicon, and about how the lexical organization may be affected by variations in didactic procedures. As yet, very little is known about how L2 words are learned (see 5.1.4., and also Celce-Murcia and Rosensweig 1979:242), and there is also very little experimental evidence for the relationship between L1 and L2 (or, for that matter, any additional L) in the bilingual brain. Once a number of aspects of the organization of the bilingual mental lexicon have been revealed, the question of whether L1 should be used in the semantization of L2 words will be somewhat easier to answer.

12.2.2.2 Translation

Translation may play many roles in FLT (see e.g. Besse 1975, I and II). In this section, we shall not discuss translation as an objective of FLT, nor shall we discuss the use of translation as a test of language proficiency. We shall only discuss the functions which translation from L1 into L2, and vice versa, may fulfil in the teaching/learning process as a means to achieve semantization and internalization of new L2 words.

Translation has lost a lot of ground as a didactic procedure and this is of course quite understandable in those cases where avoidance of L1 has been made into a basic principle of the teaching/learning process; there is no place for translation in such approaches. In the case of approaches which do not strictly reject L1 use, translation has also been pushed into the background, which, although it is not a self-evident development, can be accounted for on historical grounds. In the days when translation used to have a near-monopoly as a testing procedure, it very often assumed both the position of didactic procedure and of teaching objective. This caused a disproportionate amount of attention to be paid to translation in FLT, which had a disastrous influence on all language skills but receptive written skills. When the productive skills, and especially the oral skills, regained an important place in FLT, translation, being strongly associated with the older type of FLT and its objectives, was jettisoned, also as didactic procedure.

We have already seen that in more recent approaches, such as Butzkamm's, translation from L2 to L1 has regained a position within FLT as a procedure for the semantization of new L2 words. One also finds, in proposals specifically oriented towards reading skills, the suggestion that new L2 words should be directly translated into L1, either with the translation of the new L2 word being printed in between the lines, directly above the new word in question, or with L2 text and L1 translation being printed in parallel columns, side by side.

If one is in favour of bilingual semantization procedures, this does not automatically mean that one is also in favour of translation as a means of practising L2 skills; Butzkamm (1973:98), for instance, does not profess to be an advocate of translation for this purpose. Translation practice, from L1 to L2 and vice versa, need not only be a means of internalizing new L2 words. Translation may also be used as a means of improving skill in the combined use of lexical, syntactic and textual levels. Translation is a more precise method of practising this combination than most other didactic procedures; L1 stimuli, for instance, can be used to single out precisely those words and syntactic structures which need to be practised. Open assignments and questions often allow learners to use alternative solutions. Translation has as a disadvantage, of course, that it underrates one essential aspect of language production, namely truly creative language use. In conclusion one might say that there is a real use for translation in FLT, in combination with other didactic procedures, but not as a replacement of them.

12.2.3 Use of the written word

Writing is a fairly recent development in the history of mankind. Even now there are languages which have not been committed to writing. Many structuralist linguists, working within a tradition which focused mainly on spoken language, were involved in describing American Indian languages for which no spelling system had been developed as yet. It is hardly surprising, therefore, that in the audiolingual method, which is partly based on structuralist linguistics (see chapter 8), one tends to find some reservation with respect to the use of written language:

> language materials must be presented in spoken form before they are introduced in written form. In the initial phase of language instruction, the audiolingual skills must be dominant over reading and writing (Politzer 1972:37 ff.).

With other advocates of the audiolingual method, this recommendation very frequently tends to hold that the language in written form should not be presented to the learner for at least some lessons, and sometimes even for months. The argument in defence of this practice is that L2 learners who have already learned to write in their L1, will exhibit a strong tendency to associate letters which are used both for L1 and L2 with their pronunciation in L1. It is suggested that early introduction of L2 in written form before the sound system of L2 has been fully presented and internalized, might lead to strong interference from L1 (see e.g. Ferguson 1972:30 ff. and 206). 'The harmful influence of reading on the pronunciation of the foreign language learner [was] an article of faith', as U. Jung (1980:253) puts it, to quite a few people, although there was little agreement on just how long the written language should be avoided in the initial stages.

There are also objections of a more practical nature; it may, for instance, be difficult to differentiate between possible meanings of such ambiguous sequences as 'a name/an aim' or 'that's tough/that stuff', if one cannot resort to their written forms (U. Jung 1980:253). Furthermore, without written texts it is hardly possible to practise on one's own outside the classroom, and it will become very difficult to test progress effectively. Also, learners who, for some reason or other, lag behind, will find it very difficult to catch up: they cannot refer to a book if they wish to look up what has been taught; nor can they trace newly introduced words in a vocabulary list. Especially in connection with this latter objection, learners have sometimes been referred to as 'prisoners of the method'.

In order to solve the problems noted above in connection with total avoidance of written language on the one hand, and to prevent the occurrence of interference from spelling on the other, the use of some type of phonetic script in the initial stages of FLT has been proposed, especially by such advocates of the Reform movement as Sweet (see chapter 8). It turns out that in practice many of the learners who initially acquire a native accent in this manner tend to run into problems caused by their L1 background again as soon as the actual spelling system is introduced, leaving us with the question whether the considerable amount of time invested in learning a phonetic script is justified.

What we can conclude from this discussion is that the spoken and written forms of language should not be presented strictly separately, and most certainly one can have serious doubts about an initial period in which only the spoken form is presented. The written form should be used right from the start as an important teaching and learning aid. It should also be kept in mind that the objectives of FLT usually encompass more than just a certain level of correctness in pronunciation, and to attempt to achieve a high level of correctness in pronunciation is a dubious undertaking, if this level can only be achieved by obstructing the attainment of other teaching objectives. Especially vocabulary learning will suffer from the absence of spelling. To limit the problem of grapho-phonemic interference in learning the pronunciation of L2 as much as possible, Rivers (1964:160) advises teachers to see to it that especially in the initial stages learners do not read any material which they have not previously been taught to pronounce, unless such material is read out to them while they are reading it (see also Hüllen 1971, Wilkins 1974c). It may, incidentally, be pointed out that Rivers made this recommendation when the audiolingual method was in its heyday.

12.2.4 The learning of rules

The expression 'knowledge of the L2 rule system' can be used to refer to two things. It can refer to the metalinguistic ability to make explicit statements about the structure of language: sometimes this knowledge of L2 rules is a teaching objective in FLT, but it is not the type of knowledge of rules which one usually has in mind in FLT. This second type of knowledge of rules has to do with mastery of the rule system as an essential component of language proficiency, and it is this type of knowledge which we shall discuss in this paragraph. The rules we will be referring to are not only morphological and syntactic rules, but also rules relating to the phonological, lexical and textual levels of language use, as well as to rules governing communicative interaction as such.

Three questions keep turning up in the discussion about rule learning and its didactic implications:

(1) the question whether learners should learn L2 rules inductively or deductively;
(2) the question whether, and in how far, the rules in question may or must be

those of descriptive and/or theoretical linguistics;
(3) the question which school of descriptive and/or theoretical linguistics pro-
     vides the most adequate description of the L2 rule system for FLT purposes.

The last question may be answered very briefly; we have already referred to this
question in chapter 7. The main consideration is that it will be impossible to give
a definitive answer to this question as long as there is no agreement on what, in
itself, is the most adequate description of the L2 rule system.

The first question is the most important one in connection with this paragraph: should learners consciously learn explicitly formulated L2 rules in order
to achieve an improved command of the rule system, i.e. a higher level of L2
proficiency? Whatever the organization of FLT in this particular respect, the
aim will always be to increase the learner's command of the L2 rule system in
such a way that he can actually use these rules in L2 perception and production.
This aim does not entail explicit knowledge of L2 rules; most people have a very
good command of their L1 without being able to formulate its rules explicitly.
There is no disagreement about whether explicit knowledge of L2 rules is a prerequisite for L2 *use*. On the contrary, there seems to be general agreement that
explicit reference to L2 rules during perception and production of language is a
hindrance to efficient communication. This, however, does not entail that such
explicitly formulated rules could not be a useful or even an essential aid in L2
learning, or at least in a certain stage of the learning process. Should the learner
be allowed to assimilate inductively the rule system which he eventually will have
to use automatically and subconsciously, on the basis of the language material
presented to him, or should he be given explicitly formulated rules, in the hope
that he will thus be able to achieve the internalization which is necessary for
efficient and fluent language use. It will be clear that the inductive procedure
will involve the use of many language samples that are representative of the rules
to be learned, and that practice with such samples has an important place in this
procedure. In the deductive procedure, on the other hand, explicitly formulated
rules feature prominently in the presentation of learning material, together with
examples illustrating the rules. Practice with relevant language material only
takes place after that. The two procedures are, of course, not always applied
strictly separately. One may find an essentially inductive procedure, in which
the teaching/learning process is concluded with an explicit formulation, in some
form or other, of the rules in question, and essentially deductive procedures may
differ in the amount of time and attention devoted to explicit rules and rule practice. Berman (1979:294) sums up the inductive vs. deductive contrast as follows:
examples → practice → (rules) versus rules → examples → (practice). Lastly, it is
important to keep in mind that both inductive and deductive procedures presuppose gradation of course content. For in inductive procedures non-explicitly
formulated rules do, of course, determine the nature of the language samples
presented.

There has, generally speaking, as yet been no solution to the deductive vs.
inductive controversy; see e.g. Fisher (1979), who presents a brief historical survey of the controversy. We do not yet know enough about the L2 learning process and how it may be influenced by teaching. We do know, from classroom

experience and from the research which has been carried out, that, in any case, an exclusively inductively oriented procedure, as proposed by quite a few advocates of the direct method, is not the right approach (see also Carroll 1974:138). At present, a less extreme approach is generally adopted, one which integrates deductive and inductive procedures. There is general agreement on Newmark's (1970:226) observation that learning explicitly formulated rules is not sufficient to achieve a command of those rules, but there are reservations about the second part of Newmark's observation that learning such rules is unnecessary. Furthermore, in this connection it is often observed that all L2 learners have a natural tendency to integrate all new linguistic data which they are confronted with into the rule system they already have at their disposal, whether this be an interlanguage system or their own L1 system, and will as a result of this often come to wrong conclusions unless they are guided (see Meys 1981:121). Canale and Swain (1980:11) point out that adult L2 learners do not like to offend against the L2 rule system, and, therefore, want to know exactly what the rules in question are. Another practical factor which Mihm (1972:300) points out is that limitations on the time and means available may necessitate the somewhat less circuitous route of explicit formulation of L2 rules.

It will have become clear that the answer to the question whether inductive or deductive procedures should be adopted, and how the demonstration of rules through language samples, or the explanation of the L2 rule system through explicitly formulated rules should be implemented, will depend to a considerable extent on factors which may vary from situation to situation. Age, cognitive development, experience and L2 proficiency level suggest themselves as obviously relevant factors in this connection. Differences in susceptibility to deductive or inductive procedures in relation to age were one of the research questions in a series of experiments which have come to be known as the GUME-project (*Göteborg Undervisningsmetoder i Engelska*). This project is an ambitious attempt at comparing the effects which the audiolingual and the so-called 'cognitive' teaching methods have on the learning of English by Swedish adults. This project is described in Levin (1972), Von Elek and Oskarsson (1972a, 1972b, 1973a, 1973b, 1975), Oskarsson (1973), and Von Elek (1976).

In the first experiment, which is described in Von Elek and Oskarsson (1972a, 1972b), three groups of adults received implicit (= inductive, IM) instruction in the rule system for 15 weeks, and three groups of adults received explicit (= deductive, EX) instruction for the same period. The IM-classes involved intensive pattern practice without any explanation of the rule system, which in the EX-classes was replaced by explanation of the rule system, contrastive presentation of L1 and L2 rules and translation exercises. All other aspects concerning design and implementation of the experiment were carefully controlled, although Freedman (1979:193) is somewhat critical of the fact that the teacher variable was not sufficiently controlled. It turned out that all groups had made progress, but that the groups which had received deductive instruction had progressed significantly more than the groups which had received inductive instruction. One of the experiments attempting to replicate these results was carried out with 12-year-olds (see Von Elek and Oskarsson 1973a). Some striking conclusions from this experiment were that the EX-groups no longer obtained significantly better results than the IM-groups, and that there was an interaction between the procedure used and language aptitude for these young learners: the IM-procedure yielded better results with learners with a lower aptitude than the EX-procedure.

It is partly because of the results of the GUME-project that an exclusively inductively oriented approach to the teaching of the L2 rule system is no longer strongly advocated in FLT.

The answer to the question in how far the L2 rules to be learned can or should be the rules of theoretical and descriptive linguistics has already been given in a general sense in chapter 7. There we have seen that linguistic rule descriptions cannot be directly applied in FLT. They will have to be adapted for teaching, thus yielding a 'pedagogical' grammar, which is based on a 'scientific' grammar. In a pedagogical grammar, linguistic information should be presented in such a way that the L2 learner can internalize it and so improve his L2 proficiency. The aims of a pedagogical grammar have been sufficiently discussed in 7.4.2. What we wish to discuss in this paragraph is the content and form of the rules in a pedagogical grammar.

First of all, one uses different criteria for pedagogical grammars and scientific grammars. One of the most important criteria for the latter is that its description must be complete, whereas some modification of this criterion of completeness seems obvious for a pedagogical grammar, given the fact that in FLT complete mastery of the entire L2 rule system is hardly ever aimed for. The organization of a scientific grammar, furthermore, will be dictated by linguistic criteria, whereas in a pedagogical grammar, the organization may also be partly determined by what is known about acquisition orders (Rutherford 1980:65). Lastly, it has also been suggested that the content of the L2 rules which are presented to the learner could be adapted to 'the approximative systems of the learner's interlanguage', which may mean that one 'tampers with the well-formedness of sentences'. Rutherford (1980:67) calls this 'pedagogical pidginization', and has clear reservations about it (see also 11.4. for a discussion of such criteria for gradation).

The form of the rules in a pedagogical grammar should be such that they are comprehensible to the learner, but the simplifications which may be necessary to achieve this should not clash with the contents of scientific grammars. This means that the rules of a pedagogical grammar are not only presented through (simplified) verbal formulations, but sometimes visually as well. Palmer's (1917, 1968[2]) substitution tables are such a simplified presentation of L2 rules. Each substitution table presents one sentence pattern, together with its linguistic structure, and it allows the learner to practise this sentence pattern by paradigmatically and syntagmatically varying its components. The substitution table in fig. 12.1. allows 1024 sentences to be formed:

he	puts is putting will put put	my your his her	pen pencil book key	on in over under	the	box basket bag desk

Fig. 12.1   Substitution table

Engels (1970) is of the opinion that substitution tables are very useful for training short-term memory. He does not consider them to be suitable, however, to be retained by the learner in his memory, and to be applied in actual language use. He wants a pedagogical grammar to present rules which 'enable students to make a direct transition (without detours) from a functional grammatical insight to its application in language production' (Engels 1970:17). Engels sees visual, iconic signs and symbols as the means by which L2 rules can be presented clearly and applied 'without any supplementary decoding by means of pronounced or verbalized expressions (e.g. verbal rules)' (Engels 1970:19). He calls these abstract representations of L2 rules 'mediators'. They are a 'rational and easily communicable code', which functions much better than verbal rules (Beheydt 1974:54). Such simple symbols as arrows, circles, plusses and minuses are frequently employed.

12.2.5 Correction

Correction can be defined as 'feedback on errors'. In this paragraph, we shall limit ourselves almost exclusively to correction, because it is this type of feedback which one encounters most frequently in teaching. There should, of course, also be a place in teaching for feedback on what was done correctly, or rather, *that* something was done correctly, but the why and how of this type of feedback seem to be rather less problematic than of correction. It is worth noticing that the reinforcement phase in pattern drills (see 12.3.2.) is intended, *inter alia*, to provide this type of 'positive feedback'.

We shall single out only a few aspects of correction for a brief discussion, and devote some special attention only to the correction of pronunciation. A few important aspects of correction are of a general pedagogical-didactic nature. For this reason, we shall not include such matters as the following in our discussion:

(1) the positive and negative effects of correction on the motivation of the learner, and especially of the way in which correction is implemented; more specifically, of correction which is coupled to the giving of marks;
(2) the question whether correction should be provided explicitly or implicitly;
(3) the question whether correction should be provided immediately or after some delay;
(4) the question whether correction of errors should be provided only by the teacher, or whether peers should be called upon to provide correction as well. There are indications that 'peer evaluation' and 'self-evaluation' are useful supplementary techniques in FLT (Hendrickson 1978:393; see also Bailey and Celce-Murcia 1979:325).

The answer to questions connected with correction in FLT is determined to a large extent by two factors. First of all by the objectives of the teaching programme in question; a factor which sometimes tends to be forgotten (see also Hendrickson 1980b:217). It is possible, for instance, that in free conversation a number of errors are ignored because these errors are not at variance with the level of communicative skills which the teaching programme aims to achieve.

Secondly, the answer is strongly determined by the views one has on the teaching/learning process. A clear example of this is provided by the attitude of many audiolingualists towards correction. This attitude, which should be seen in the light of the behaviouristic orientation of this teaching method, will be clear from the following quotations:

> Language behaviour is created most efficiently by exercises in which correct responses by the student are elicited and reinforced (Politzer 1972:38).

> Like sin, error is to be avoided and its influence overcome, but its presence is to be expected (Brooks 1964:58).

Extremists in audiolingual FLT have drawn the conclusion from statements like these that only correct answers should be made possible in the teaching/learning process, thus eliminating the need for correction altogether. The view of L2 learning held by Newmark and Reibel (1968), who propose to have a completely inductively oriented FLT in order to replicate L1 learning processes as much as possible, also excludes correction by the teacher, because they assume that learners will learn from their own errors without any help from outside. In their opinion, the learner himself is capable of making 'increasingly complex and increasingly correct hypotheses' about the L2 rule system (see Politzer 1972:51 ff.). The contrast with the view that especially adults generally like to be corrected in their attempts to use L2 will be obvious (Canale and Swain 1980:11, Hendrickson 1980b:216).

In section 4.3.1., we have already paid considerable attention to the more positive approach to errors which was developed in the framework of ideas about 'interlanguage'. In this view, deviations from the L2 norm are necessary steps in the L2 learning process. According to Hendrickson (1978:389–90), 'an obsessive concern with error avoidance [is] counter-productive to learning a foreign language'. The teacher should take a constructive view of learner errors, and as a rule permit rather than correct errors.

But as soon as a decision not to correct all errors is taken, the question immediately arises which errors should be corrected, and which errors should not be. Two types of errors are singled out in the literature as errors which should be corrected:

- errors that impede the intelligibility of a message (Hendrickson 1978:390, 1980b:217, Magnan 1979:343, Bailey and Celce-Murcia 1979:325).
- errors that stigmatize the learner from the native speaker's perspective (Hendrickson 1978:391, 1980b:217, Magnan 1979:343).

One of the problems with both types of errors is that it will be difficult to establish exactly when intelligibility is impeded, or the learner stigmatized. Olsson (1972) is a serious attempt at determining experimentally which deviations from well-formedness most frequently lead to unintelligibility. One of her hypotheses was that grammatical errors are less detrimental to intelligibility than lexical errors (Olsson 1972:47), a hypothesis which was confirmed in her study. Hendrickson (1978:391) proposes to develop the notions of 'local' and 'global' errors, introduced by Burt and Kiparsky (1975). Global errors should be the subject of error correction, according to Hendrickson, who defines a global error as 'a communicative error that causes a proficient speaker of a foreign language to either misinterpret an oral or written message or to consider the message incomprehensible with the textual content of the error'. Such errors usually are, in Hendrickson's opinion, due to 'inadequate lexical knowledge, misuse of prepositions and pronouns, and seriously misspelled lexical items'.

In addition to these types of errors, which are distinguished on qualitative grounds, Hendrickson (1978:392, 1980b:217) also mentions especially frequent errors as candidates for correction.

Pronunciation correction

FLT which puts special emphasis on oral productive language skills will naturally pay attention to the correction of pronunciation errors. Our discussion will not focus on which standards should be set for pronunciation, and which errors should therefore be corrected (see e.g. Bowen 1979 and Johansson 1980 for a discussion), but on the way in which correction should be implemented. For a detailed discussion of pronunciation correction in FLT, see Kelz (1976). Ferguson (1972:71 ff.) distinguishes two main types of pronunciation correction, the second of which can again be subdivided. First of all, there is the *articulatory* approach, in which it is attempted to teach the learner to pronounce L2 sounds correctly mainly by explaining to him how the speech organs are involved in the production of the sounds in question. Quite apart from the question whether explanation will lead to learning (see 12.2.4.), objections which could be raised against this approach are that it is sometimes far from easy to explain how sounds are articulated (the articulatory positions for consonants, for instance, are easier to explain than those for vowels), and that it tends to ignore such factors as intonation and rhythm. The other approach, called the *auditory* approach, can be divided into three subtypes. First of all, we have the global auditory approach, which assumes that the learner will arrive at a correct pronunciation by repeatedly listening to L2 material and by repeating it. Experience has shown, however, that many learners are insufficiently capable of discriminating between sounds, and because of this tend to acquire an incorrect pronunciation especially with the global approach. The second subtype of the auditory approach is less global. It is characterized by the use of minimal pairs, i.e. pairs of words which differ with respect to only one phonological element (e.g. *peer, beer*). This approach does not, however, entirely eliminate the risk of learners who cannot discriminate sufficiently between sounds acquiring an incorrect pronunciation. The third subtype of the auditory approach, which Ferguson himself advocates, attempts to present only the characteristic elements of the sounds to be acquired to the learner, either by filtering out redundant components of the speech stream before it reaches the learner's ear, or by manipulating the production of the sounds. Elements which might hinder the learner in his learning are avoided in the one case by filtering out the less optimal frequencies, and in the other case by presenting sounds to be acquired in an environment in which they can be optimally perceived. To illustrate the latter approach, Ferguson gives the example of the /i:/ which is presented in the environment of consonants such as /f/ and /s/ in order to highlight the high frequency of this vowel. It should be observed, by the way, that in practice one usually finds a combination of articulatory and auditory approaches in pronunciation teaching.

The use of various visual media for pronunciation correction should also be mentioned. Simple anatomical sketches of the vocal tract have long been used to facilitate articulatory explanation. There are also a number of notational systems which are used to provide simple visual information on stress and intonation, while one can also use gestures to indicate intonation contours. A far more advanced technique seeks to visualize sounds, combinations of sounds, stress and intonation patterns instrumentally; especially the visualization of intonation contours with the aim of providing feedback has been the subject of a considerable amount of recent experimental research. We would like to mention the research reported on in Léon and Martin (1971), and research carried out in the Netherlands. The latter has demonstrated that learners who receive visual feedback on their imitations of certain intonation contours achieve better results than those learners who only receive auditory feedback (see e.g. De Bot 1981, De Bot and Mailfert 1982).

12.3 The cycle of teaching/learning activities

Via teaching the learner will have to be made to master language forms which he has not yet mastered. Command of a language is a hierarchically structured skill which is largely automatic (see ch. 4). It is not unusual to distinguish three steps in the process of learning hierarchically ordered skills: the learning of the individual components, the integration of newly learned components into other components, and, lastly, the automatic use of the new components. This cycle applies, in principle, to the learning of each new chunk of material in FLT: the learner will first have to be acquainted with the new material, will subsequently have to relate it to what he already knows, and will finally have to make it function automatically. This cycle, which we will term 'cycle of teaching/learning activities', is called 'teaching unit' by Walmsley (1979); it relates to any part of the learning material which a textbook presents as one coherent unit. Such a unit may cover one lesson, or it may cover a series of lessons.

In practice, the cycle of teaching/learning activities varies with regard to number and nature of the phases which are distinguished by the authors of textbooks (for a good survey, see Walmsley 1979:106–9). In all textbooks, whatever the teaching method on which they are based, one will find the following three phases which correspond closely to the above mentioned three steps in the learning of hierarchically ordered skills:

(1) *presentation*: the teacher presents the material and explains it;
(2) *repetition*: the teacher has the learner repeat the material and relates it to what the learner has already acquired;
(3) *exploitation*: the teacher gives the learner the opportunity to use the newly acquired knowledge productively and creatively.

There are some differences in the terms one finds used in the literature. Peck (1979:128), for example, uses the terms *presentation, manipulation*, and *transfer* and Ferguson (1972:179 ff.) speaks of *presentation, repetition*, and *comprehension and development*.

The order of these three phases is usually the one in which we have presented them above, but Walmsley (1979:110 ff.) proposes to reverse the order of *repetition* and *exploitation*, thus advocating a form of 'discovery learning'. In this way, the learner will be put in a communicative situation in which the new material must be used immediately after it has first been presented to him. The role of repetition would then be restricted to providing remedial work to correct errors made in the exploitation phase. This avoids the problem of unnecessarily subjecting learners to practice sessions on aspects which do not harbour any problems for them. One drawback of this procedure which, in our opinion, outweighs its advantages, is that teachers will have, time and again, to make a diagnosis of the deficiencies in each individual learner's performance, and design a remedial programme on the basis of it. It is incorrect to argue, in support of this procedure, that application is something that in L1 learning also takes place at a very early stage. And it is naïve to want to rediscover, again and again, the accumulated experience of many years of FLT to beginners of widely varying aptitudes. Most beginners cannot apply all they have just been presented with without errors, unless they first have some practice, and we are sufficiently familiar with the problems which beginners encounter most frequently. We shall discuss other objections which could be raised against having learners communicate (too) early in the L2 later on this chapter (12.4.2.).

In our discussion of the three phases of the cycle of teaching/learning activities we shall concentrate on classroom activities; for each of the phases we shall discuss those activities which are the most suitable. There is no sharp dividing line between the three phases (presentation, for instance, presupposes at least a modicum of repetition), and some of the classroom activities may be encountered across the phases. Dialogue, for instance, is a procedure which is often applied in the presentation phase, but in memorized form it also plays a role in the second phase, and in the third phase as well, viz. in some forms of role-playing. It will, therefore, hardly come as a surprise that different authors discuss the same classroom activities under different headings, and have drawn up different typologies. A further complicating factor in many publications on this subject is that not all authors set themselves the aim of discussing the classroom activities for each of the three phases of the cycle of teaching/learning activities; if this is the case, then the resulting typology cannot be seen as aiming to chart the whole range of activities. In Littlewood (1981:50) one finds a division into five types (memorized dialogues, contextualized drills, cued dialogues, role-playing, and improvisation), but these refer only to activities which are used in the repetition and exploitation phases, because Littlewood aims to show how learners can effectively be brought from 'control' to 'creativity'.

Our discussion of classroom activities will be selective rather than exhaustive, and will not go into any great detail; exhaustive and detailed discussions of classroom activities belong in didactic handbooks with a practical orientation. There are a large number of publications of this type; we refer the reader to such handbooks as Dubin and Olshtain (1977), Haycraft (1978), Paulston and Bruder (1976), and the practical guides which Wilga Rivers, partly in cooperation with others, has written for teachers of French, of German, and of Spanish (see

Rivers 1975, Rivers *et al*. 1975, Rivers *et al*. 1976). Celce-Murcia and McIntosh (1979) contains separate chapters with practical suggestions for exercises for the four skills, as well as for grammar and vocabulary. We furthermore wish to mention such publications as Leeson (1975), Littlewood (1981), Grewer *et al*. (1978), and Neuner *et al*. (1981).

12.3.1 Presentation

New material is presented as much as possible within passages of natural language; new material is presented in context. The actual form of these passages of natural language may vary: it may be spoken language, in monologues, dialogues, or news broadcasts, or written language, in letters, fiction, or diaries (see e.g. Paulston and Bruder 1976:34).

Especially in elementary courses dialogues have acquired a prominent place as a means of presentation. Dialogues allow the teacher to present new language material functionally, in a communicative situation, which makes it easier for learners to grasp the new material. The language material which is specific to dialogues is difficult to present in any other form, and it is important for learners to be able to use their language skills effectively in dialogues. Other didactic arguments in favour of dialogues as a means of presentation are that they are realistic, which makes learners curious and captures their attention; that the language material contained in dialogues can easily be used for analogous dialogic situations in class, and that it will tend to stimulate learners, because they find themselves able to participate in a conversation relatively early.

Within the audiolingual method, which accords them such a prominent place, the presentation of dialogues consists of two phases: the actual presentation, and explanation. In presentation the dialogue is given without further comment: if the presentation is audiovisual, then the visual stimuli will be presented just before the verbal material. Explanation, which is usually given after presentation has been repeated without modifications, takes place according to a fixed pattern, certainly in the initial stages. Each separate sentence is repeated, its meaning is explained first of all within the context in which it occurs, the sentence is then analysed, its individual elements discussed, and lastly, the whole sentence is repeated one or more times.

As a form of presentation, however, dialogues harbour some problems. A decent presentation of a dialogue, and certainly the explanation of it, places some considerable demands on the didactic skills of the teacher; especially if a unilingual approach is adopted. The frequent repetition of the dialogue in presentation and explanation will mean that teachers have considerable problems in keeping the pupils interested. These problems are aggravated, because the contents of dialogues have usually been kept as simple as possible for the sake of clarity: the number of participants and topics in a dialogue will usually be quite limited. It is, therefore, hardly surprising that the dialogue should no longer be strongly propagated as the only means of presentation, and that the rather strict pattern of presentation and explanation of dialogues which we have described above, should no longer be universally followed.

12.3.2 Repetition

As we have seen before, a good command of a language involves a certain degree of automaticity: language skills, whether they be productive or receptive, cannot be learned exclusively through perception of language material, even when this material is explained. For this reason, part of a language lesson will have to be devoted to practice in the shape of repetition. This is especially the case for the learning of oral skills, because these involve a greater degree of automaticity. Oral language use leaves participants little time for reflection (see also ch. 3.1.1.). This does not necessarily mean that the learning of skills can be seen exclusively as essentially a mechanical process of habit formation. The typical aspects of repetition, and the discussion about repetition, are best illustrated by examining one particular rather well known classroom activity, the pattern drill, in some detail.

Structural characteristics of pattern drills

The terms 'pattern drills', 'pattern practice', as well as the French term 'exercises structuraux', indicate quite clearly that these activities are used to practise structural characteristics of L2. These characteristics are usually syntactic and morphological, but they may also be of a phonological nature.

Pattern drills had a central position in the audiolingual method. They embody the form into which audiolingualists have moulded their behaviourist notions about L2 learning. As we have seen earlier (see ch. 8.3.2.3.), their theoretical position was that in the teaching/learning process habit formation should be achieved and that learning-by-analogy is a far more effective means of achieving this than learning-through-analysis. Brooks (1964:153) has called analogy 'the secret and guiding principle of pattern practice'. Substitution tables, based on structuralist linguistic theory, provide the basis for practice with sentence patterns, which can be varied paradigmatically or syntagmatically. By minimally varying a basic structure and making a learner practise that structure until he could respond instantly to the stimulus presented, it was hoped that automatic habits would be formed. Pattern practice had to lead to an 'imprinting' of structures, so that the language learner could then automatically use them in communicative situations.

Two conclusions ('corrollaries') which Rivers (1964:51 ff.) draws from behaviouristic learning principles have had a strong influence on the shape of pattern drills; she formulates them as follows:

(1) Foreign language habits are formed most effectively by giving the right response, not by making mistakes.
(2) Habits are strengthened by reinforcement.

A well designed pattern drill will allow learning to proceed only little by little, thus leaving the learner very little room to make errors. A pattern drill always consists of a number of more or less identical items which all deal with the same structure and which usually gradually become more difficult.

Secondly, each item is structured in such a way that reinforcement plays an important role. Items usually consist of three, four, or five phases. A three-phase item consists of the following elements:

(1)　The learner hears a stimulus utterance: S1.
(2)　The learner responds to the stimulus by changing it in a given way: R1.
(3)　The learner hears the correct response offered to him by way of reinforcement: S2.

If the drill contains four or five phases, the following phases are added:

(4)　The learner repeats the correct response: R2.
(5)　The learner once again hears the correct response offered to him, by way of additional reinforcement: S3.

The immediate feedback provided by S2 (and S3) informs the learner about the correctness of his R1 (and R2). The stimuli need not be verbal. The teacher can also use non-verbal stimuli, such as drawings of objects or actions, or the objects or actions themselves (see e.g. Mackey 1965:421 ff., Rivers 1968:109). Nor need the use of pattern drills be restricted to language laboratories (see ch. 13.2.3.2.); they may also be used in class (see e.g. Rivers 1968:105 ff.). Lastly, pattern drills need not always be unilingual; stimuli as well as responses may also be in L1. Butzkamm (1973:94 ff.) gives some examples of 'translation pattern practice', and of 'oral translation drills'.

There are many types of pattern drills. Politzer and Politzer (1972:36 ff.) divide them into three types on the basis of the type of R1 the learner is expected to produce: *substitution*, *expansion*, and *transformation*. It is characteristic of substitution that the structure itself is not changed, but that the individual elements making up the structure can be substituted (e.g. *many/foreign/ students/study/engineering.*) Expansion also leaves the basic structure unchanged, but it adds elements, for instance to the subject or the predicate. Transformation, lastly, involves a syntactic operation on a sentence such that its basic structure is changed.

Paulston and Bruder (1975) classify pattern drills not on the basis of the type of operation which the learner has to carry out, but on the basis of expected terminal behaviour. They arrive at the following tripartition:

(1)　*mechanical drills*, where there is complete control of the response, and the expected terminal behaviour is the automatic use of manipulative patterns;
(2)　*meaningful drills*, where there is still control of the response, but the learner may express himself in more than one way;
(3)　*communicative drills*, where the expected terminal behaviour is normal speech for communication, 'or, if one prefers, the free transfer of learned language patterns to appropriate situations' (Paulston and Bruder 1975:15).

In the discussion about pattern drills one comes across two misunderstandings about the relation between drills and the audiolingual method. One misunderstanding is that in the audiolingual method pattern drills were not only developed to perfection, but also that pattern drills were not regularly used until the rise of this method. Practice with L2 sentence patterns is, however, found as early as Erasmus (1466–1536), as Kelly (1969:101) has shown, and we have already referred to the substitution procedures developed by Palmer (1917, 1968[2]). A second misunderstanding is that advocates of the audiolingual method based their teaching solely on meaningless and context-free pattern drills. But it is quite clear from many publications by audiolingualists, and from audiolingual teaching practice, that all pretence of communication was only abandoned where (certain types of) pattern drills were concerned. In addition to pattern drills, they also quite frequently used dialogues or conversation practice on the basis of real or simulated situations.

The effect of pattern drills

Pattern drills have been strongly criticized from various quarters, and they certainly no longer occupy the central position in FLT which they occupied in the heyday of the audiolingual method. Quite rightly, greater importance has come to be attached to the exploitation phase within the cycle of teaching/learning activities, and, consequently, other types of classroom activities have gained a more prominent position. Quite rightly, too, arguments have been advanced in favour of banning some types of pattern drill from FLT altogether. The emphasis put on practising the 'mechanics of grammar' by certain groups of audiolingualists has resulted in the use of pattern drills of the following type:

S1 John is going to be a teacher	R1 John is going to be a teacher
S1 (Mary)	R1 Mary is going to be a teacher
S1 (Father)	R1 Father is going to be a teacher
S1 (Granny)	R1 Granny is going to be a teacher

Not only has all 'pretence of communication' been abandoned in this type of pattern drill but it is also possible to do this type of drill without making any mistakes whatsoever, and still be totally unaware of the meaning of the utterance and the learning problem involved.

More objections could be raised against pattern drills. They may have a negative effect on the learners' motivation, especially in those cases where the language material to be practised is not truly meaningful. There are also serious doubts about the ability of learners to correct an initially incorrect R1 in the fourth (R2) phase. This doubt has certainly not been mitigated by observations of learning behaviour during pattern drills: many learners do not execute the R2 as intended, either because they do not understand what the intention is, or because they are not motivated to do so, or because the preceding phase has not had the intended corrective effect. In this connection, we can refer to observations of learners of L2 Dutch, who were required to do a large number of pattern drills in a fully individualized language laboratory setting (see Extra 1974, 1978b). One could also argue for a re-examination of the emphasis on intensive, concentrated repetition which is characteristic of pattern drills, since psychological research has indicated that repetition when it is spread out at different intervals over the entire period of learning, is generally more effective. Lastly, it can be pointed out that pattern drills, and especially substitution drills, very often have quite unnatural stress and intonation patterns, because learners have a tendency to give special prominence to the word which is substituted.

These objections have changed the position of pattern drills in FLT considerably. Two tendencies can be observed: one is to drop pattern drills altogether without replacing them by other types of exercise, and the other is to put more emphasis on explicit knowledge of rules, especially in intermediate and advanced classes (see Mockridge-Fong 1979:92). However important one may find explicit rule knowledge, it would be incorrect to conclude that practice should be jettisoned altogether. Bolinger (1968:40) observed in this connection: 'To imagine that drills are to be displaced by rule-giving is to imagine that digestion can be displaced by swallowing.'

We shall devote some further attention to the second tendency in our discussion of the recent development of the 'communicative approach' (see 12.4.2.), and the next paragraph will also touch upon it. The importance placed upon the communicative aspect of language use in practice sessions, implying 'meaningful practice' whenever possible, has in some cases not only led to a complete rejection of pattern drills, but also resulted in no attention being paid at all to the L2 rule system or to practice with that system; an approach which has, in turn, generated a lot of opposition. Rivers (1972:74) and Butzkamm (1980b:244) point out that it is indeed necessary for didactic materials, pattern drills included, to be interesting to the learner, but that the 'real-life' materials used for this purpose, which often amount to 'the colorless, socially correct actions of Dick and Jane, or of Maria and Pedro', are often much less attractive for the learner than, for instance, absurd or nonsensical material. At the stage of 'skill getting', learners are prepared to accept the artificiality of drills and exercises which force them to lie. At this stage, when the learner 'must learn to articulate acceptably and construct comprehensible foreign language sequences by rapid association of learned elements' (Rivers 1972:73), there is no real objection to practice with 'pseudo-communication'. Butzkamm (1980b:242) strongly rejects the emphasis on communication which has led some people to abandon pattern drills altogether. He has the following arguments for his position:

- sticking to one structure for a certain time is a facilitating device;
- the student performing a pattern drill is saved the trouble of finding the correct expression of his ideas;
- students do in fact need a number of imitative and manipulative contacts with new language material before they can safely venture into what approaches 'normal' communication.

Although not many people will wish to go as far as Paulston and Bruder (1975:iii), who see 'grammar, the systematic learning of rules, and the structural pattern drills, the practising and internalizing of language rules in language context' as 'the heart of the language lesson', it will be clear that pattern drills, provided they are not too mechanistic in character, offer many opportunities for effective use in FLT.

12.3.3 Exploitation

In the exploitation phase, the teacher creates opportunities for learners to use the knowledge and skills which they have just acquired, productively and creatively. If we put it this way, we are referring to the productive skills only, and especially to speaking. There are, of course, also moments in the exploitation phase when opportunities are created to practise receptive skills. In the exploitation phase the learner is guided towards 'skill using', 'performance in interaction' (Rivers 1972:73). The learner should be presented with *real* communicative exercises, in which he first of all 'is on his own . . ., not supported or directed by the teacher', and in which he 'will learn . . . to fight to put his meaning across . . ., to try to meet any situation by putting what he knows to maximum use'. Summarizing, Rivers (1972:76) says that the exploitation phase should give learners opportunities for *autonomous expression*, and for developing an *adventurous spirit*. Such terminology is also found in subsequent publications. The intention of the exploitation phase is to integrate language forms which have been introduced earlier and which have been repeated and practised, into fluent verbal behaviour, into real language use which is 'not a purely linguistic exchange, but is influenced by a host of factors, cognitive, attitudinal and purposive, which impinge on the participants and modify their behaviour accordingly' (Leeson 1975:148). Verbal behaviour is a 'complex multi-faceted phenomenon' (Leeson 1975:150), with which the learner must be confronted in some phase in the cycle of teaching/learning activities. Leeson's remarks relate to 'fluent' verbal behaviour. Exploitation in the sense in which we have used it, is, however, not just a phase which only occurs in FLT programmes which aim to achieve (near-)native L2 competence; it is, as Rivers (1972) stresses, a phase in which the learner learns to use in free performance what he has acquired, whatever the level of L2 competence involved.

There is a great variety of activities that can be used in the exploitation phase. Not only is there a lot of variation with regard to type of activity (contextualized pattern drills on the one hand, or free conversation exercises on the other), but also within these types and within each of these types there is variation with regard to degree of 'control' versus 'creativity' (see Littlewood 1981:50). There is also variation in the number of learners who can participate in a given activity. Hendrickson (1980a) divides the 40 classroom activities he discusses into tête-à-tête conversations, small group interactions and whole class activities. The enumeration which Rivers (1972:76) gives of 'activities for natural use of language in interaction' will make it clear that it will be impossible to discuss all of these activities within the framework of this chapter. The following is a selection from her enumeration: establishing and maintaining social relations, seeking and giving information, hiding one's intentions, talking one's way out of trouble, sharing leisure activities, entertaining. We refer the reader to the publications cited for further information on such activities; the only two types we shall discuss here are conversation and drama.

In the audiolingual method, and especially within the audiovisual SGAV method (see 8.3.2.3. and 8.3.2.4.), conversation as a way of actively and creatively applying newly learned language material features prominently. In the use of conversation in the exploitation phase three types can be distinguished: elementary, guided, and supervised conversation, depending on how advanced the learners are. Elementary conversation may involve asking questions about the dialogue used for presentation, giving a summary of this dialogue or acting it out, and using the newly learned material in a situation which is analogous to that of the dialogue. In guided conversation, the teacher will continue to monitor the practice session, especially by asking specific questions, but the conversation will be further removed from the original dialogue used for presentation; a lot of visual materials are used, for instance drawings, or films, and not only the verbal and visual materials of the presentation dialogue. In supervised conversation, finally, the conversation is much freer still, and is usually based on a specially selected text, interview, poem, or scene from a movie or play. The teacher will often not participate directly in the conversation, but supervise it as a participant observer.

Drama also occupies a special place in the exploitation phase. One important aspect of drama, including role-playing, is that the learner gets the opportunity to use his own personality 'in creating the material on which *part* of the language class is to be based' (Maley and Duff 1978:1). It relies on 'the natural ability of every person to imitate, mimic and express himself through gesture'. In Maley and Duff (1978) one will find a wealth of information on various drama techniques. Drama can be used at any level, and, contrary to what is sometimes argued, for any age group, including adults and adolescents. Games are closely related to drama. Wright *et al.* (1979) give a survey of various types of games and their applications in FLT, and classify them according to degree of guidance needed, level of L2 proficiency required, and according to whether they are intended for use by classes, groups, pairs, or individuals. Because drama and games create contexts in which 'language is useful and meaningful' (Wright *et al.* 1979:1), they are more likely than pattern drills to cause learners to feel that they are doing something useful.

12.4 Recent pedagogical developments

What is loosely called the 'communicative approach' is undoubtedly the most interesting and most frequently discussed development of the last few decades. It is this approach which will be central to this section. We shall examine in some detail to what extent the 'communicative approach' is a completely new approach in FLT and what its relevance is especially in relation to a discussion of didactic procedures.

Although today one tends to be generally cautious in the search for *the* best method, one can still find proposals for innovation which are advertised as FLT 'methods' which can solve all FLT problems. We have devoted some attention to this matter in 8.4. There we did not discuss such 'methods' in full detail, and we shall refrain from doing so here. We shall restrict ourselves to a discussion of some of the main points, especially in relation to didactic procedures.

We shall first of all devote a separate discussion to the fairly widespread proposal to focus, for didactic reasons, on reception in the initial stages of learning.

12.4.1 Reception before production

We first of all wish to state quite clearly that the present discussion does not concern FLT objectives. The question we are discussing here is whether, if the learning of one or more productive skills is the aim of FLT, early and frequent practice in those skills is the best way to achieve that aim. In the heyday of the audiolingual method this question, which is a quite legitimate one, as we have argued in chapter 7, was sometimes lost sight of. At present this question is asked quite explicitly, and also answered in a way which differs from the (implicit) answer of the audiolingualists.

Doubts about the audiolingualist answer are not exclusively of a recent date. Law (1973:236), for instance, advocates being careful not to ask learners to actively produce L2 utterances, either spoken or written, too early, basing himself on Palmer (1917, 1968[2]). He is of the opinion that learners should have an initial stage in which to assimilate the new language material; learners should have a chance to acquaint themselves receptively with the new material. Similar views are expressed in Wilkins (1974c:66 ff.). He stresses that, if one has learners practise only the productive skills, the new material offered will necessarily be rather limited, which causes the process of getting acquainted with the new language to be very slow indeed, whereas there are many indications that, for language learning, 'the context of presentation should be as rich and varied as possible' (Wilkins 1974c:80). Furthermore, Dietrich (1973:350) has pointed out that activities which aim at early practice exclusively in the productive skills, and especially oral skills, paradoxically constitute an impediment to communication in the classroom. As there are strong limitations on what the learner can express, his participation in the communicative process and his self-activity will of necessity be minimal for a considerable period of time. Especially in foreign language classes learners will not be able to express themselves in the same way, and to the same extent, as in other classes.

Until fairly recently there was only incidental criticism of early exclusively productive practice, but nowadays one could speak of a 'movement', whose proponents argue strongly in favour of emphasizing the receptive skills especially in the initial stages of the teaching/learning process. Nord (1980:4) argues that FLT has depended too much on 'a response-oriented production-focused methodology'. A result of this is that learners are expected too quickly to use language productively. Nord (1980:7) questions whether production as such is a 'necessary prerequisite' for learning. He is of the opinion that to expect production before the learning process is well under way, may do more harm than good. He refers to Postovsky (1976) and Winitz and Reeds (1975) for the view that speaking will not be possible until a fair degree of receptive skill has been attained. Both these publications attribute a crucial role to processing of auditory input and to internalizing the L2 rule system through problem solving. Davies (1978) contains the results of a survey of the literature on the value of 'putting receptive skills first' in the teaching/learning process. He discusses a number of 'methods' and projects in which this is the guiding principle, such as the 'Total Physical Response Method' (TPR), developed and tested by the psychologist James Asher (see e.g. Asher *et al.* 1974). One of the main characteristics of this method is that learners physically carry out orders which they are given, without adding any verbal reactions in the initial stages. Davies (1978:15–16) states quite clearly that in his opinion 'listening is the place to start, and the listening-skill the first to be developed'. The learner, however, should be taught to listen very carefully, as in for instance TPR: he should learn to distinguish between correct and incorrect for himself. Like Winitz and Reeds (1975:67), Davies (1978:23) remarks that the preference for reception before production in the teaching/learning process is as yet only based on the disappointing results of production practice from the very beginning, and that it has not yet been experimentally demonstrated to be more effective.

12.4.2 Communicative approach

There are few subjects in applied linguistics nowadays which attract as much attention as 'communicative FLT' does. Germain (1981) is an annotated bibliography of over 100 titles which appeared between 1975 and 1980, and yet it does not claim to be exhaustive. There seems to be an almost daily flow of monographs and readers on the subject; see e.g. Brumfit and Johnson (1979), Johnson (1982), Littlewood (1981), and Piepho (1979), to mention but a few. So much has been written on this subject in such a short time, that misunderstandings and terminological confusions are inevitable.

The first source of confusion is that authors often fail to indicate what exactly they mean by 'going communicative'. Are they referring to one particular phase in the didactic cycle, or to the whole process of formulating objectives, selecting and ordering course content, and selecting didactic procedures? The terminological confusion which has muddled the discussion on methods for such a long time (see 8.2.2.), can also be found in discussions about the communicative approach.

What is more serious is that, with respect to communicative FLT, it is often supposed, be it usually implicitly, that the objectives and the characterization of language and language use which they contain, allow direct conclusions to be drawn regarding the best method of achieving these objectives. We have discussed the question of 'direct applications' in a general sense in chapter 7. The following quotation from Canale and Swain (1980:33) serves to make clear that frequently such direct applications are indeed what people have in mind:

> With respect to teaching methodology, it is crucial that classroom activities reflect, in the most optimally direct manner, those communicative activities that the learner is most likely to engage in.

We quote from this in many respects excellent publication to demonstrate how widespread and persistent this view is. Our opinion that, also in communicative FLT, objectives cannot be directly converted into didactic procedures is shared by, for instance, Peck (1979:127), who states categorically that it is wrong to think that 'language objectives defined by categories of communicative competence require *any* special method', and that 'there should be any methodological swing of the pendulum away from the best established practice of the present time'. Also Widdowson (1979c:251–2) strongly disapproves of 'the tendency in some quarters to allow terminal needs to determine teaching procedures'. How language should be learned and taught 'has to be established by reference to pedagogical criteria', and learner needs, however well defined they may be, leave 'the responsibility for devising a methodology' unaffected: 'an uncritical belief in the direct route, an undue compliance with need specification' are to be avoided.

Piepho (1979:80) concludes that the discussion on communicative FLT has led many to assume wrongly that a new didactic school had arisen which would revolutionarize FLT. Piepho's concern is with a didactic approach in which the familiar and necessary practice with individual components of language skills is not jettisoned, but in which such matters as situational context and communicative activities are equally central.

If didactic procedures in communicative FLT cannot be directly derived from communicative objectives, would it then perhaps be possible to designate some didactic procedures as being specific for communicative FLT, and if so, what are they?

It can be observed that serious advocates of communicative FLT are not after developing the one (communicative) didactic procedure which will be valid for all time and for all people. Littlewood (1981:95) concludes that 'nobody will ever produce a definite teaching methodology', not least because two of the most important factors which have to be taken into account (the communicative situation outside the classroom, and the learner himself and the way he functions both inside and outside the classroom) are extremely complex and poorly understood. To Pérez (1981:51) 'flexibility and diversification' are 'two of the key words of this new movement', especially because each new learner or group of learners will have specific characteristics.

Using language for communicative purposes means more than just using language forms correctly, as we have seen in chapter 4. Sociolinguistics and ethnolinguistics have made it clear that the context in which language is used is extremely relevant to linguistic interaction between groups and individuals, and that this context, too, is structured and has a rule system, so that the competent language user will have to apply this rule system as well in order to be able to communicate adequately. It will be evident that these 'other' aspects of language are emphasized especially in the objectives of the communicative approach. FLT objectives have, therefore, become more comprehensive. In Littlewood's (1981:VIII) words, the learners must 'develop strategies for relating these (linguistic) structures to their communicative functions in real situations and real time'.

Littlewood (*loc. cit.*) concludes from this that 'we must provide learners with ample opportunities to use the language themselves for communicative purposes'. To Johnson (1979a:199–200, 1982:149–50) this means that two aspects of communicative language use should be clearly incorporated into the teaching/learning process. In the first place, 'task-oriented' activities have to be included, i.e. the learner has to be set 'tasks to be mediated through language'; 'actual meaning' should be central to these tasks, which should be of the type 'where success or failure is seen to be judged in terms of whether or not these tasks are performed'. The emphasis should be on the ability to understand and convey information; Johnson (1979a:199) refers to this aspect as the 'instrumentality of language teaching'.

The second aspect of communicative language use which Littlewood considers to be of clear importance to FLT is the 'information gap principle'. For the teaching/learning process to be successful, the language material used should be as realistic as possible, and this precludes making learners converse about matters with which both the learners and their conversation partners are already fully informed. FLT will become non-communicative as soon as the learner knows exactly what is going to happen in the communicative process in which he has been asked to participate, as soon as there is no 'information gap', no 'element of doubt' in the communicative process.

These starting-points for communicative FLT are reiterated, in more or less the same words, by a number of authors. One can find a wealth of classroom activities, especially in Littlewood (1981), in which these two principles are put into practice. We shall now discuss how tenable these principles are.

First of all it will have struck the reader that in our references to Littlewood (1981) and Johnson (1979a, 1982) we have called these two principles 'the most important' principles, which should be given special emphasis. These two authors share this view: they do not lose sight of the fact that the *structural* elements of language and language skill must also be taught and practised. Littlewood (1981:IX) posits that in addition to 'ample opportunities to use the language for communicative purposes', 'a perfect mastery of individual structures' is also important to the learner as 'a useful step towards the broader goal'. Johnson (1982:200) is doubtful whether the 'deep end strategy in communicative language teaching', in which the learner is confronted with communicative problems which he has to solve without first having been given the linguistic means to do so, can be used for all types of learners under all circumstances and at all L2 proficiency levels. Such suggestions should, in our opinion, indeed be rejected; structural elements will always have to be practised. The correct ratio of 'functional' elements and 'structural' elements may, however, differ from situation to situation.

There are more observations to be made about Johnson's (1979a, 1982) two principles. First of all, there is the risk that the role of the context of language use, and of being able to understand and handle functional and situational aspects of the communicative process, will be exaggerated in FLT. One often tends to forget, as we have mentioned before (see 11.3.2.3.), that the learner will already be familiar with many of these aspects through his L1; he will certainly be familiar with the essence thereof, and, depending on the distance between L1 and L2, also with the actual form they take. This familiarity with situational and functional aspects of L2 is also recognized by Littlewood (1981:4, 43), who remarks in connection with the social acceptability of L2 utterances by learners that 'learners will automatically attempt to conform to an appropriate role in the way they speak'. This fact is, however, not always sufficiently recognized by Littlewood, when he gives didactic advice in other places in his book. Sinclair (1980:258) remarks that the recent interest in the functional aspects of communicative language use – with which he is in agreement – should not degenerate into the explicit teaching of discourse rules as such, and also that it is not necessary, for the sake of making the teaching/learning process more 'real', to maintain the authenticity of texts by means of retaining all the original features of recorded speech, including hesitations, slips of the tongue, and repeats (see also 10.3.4.). Swan's (1979:5) characterization of functional teaching is to the point, if somewhat charged:

> The learner is seen as a sort of linguistically gifted idiot, who does not possess normal communicative strategies, or has surprising difficulty in transferring them from his mother tongue.

According to Swan, one can generally assume that learners can transfer their L1 communicative strategies, but that they are not linguistically gifted, and that they will therefore have to be provided with linguistic knowledge to which they can transfer their L1 communicative strategies.

One can have similar reservations about the second principle: again there seems to be a tendency to underestimate the learner. One could wonder if learners, i.e. all learners, of all ages, and all levels of L2 proficiency, always need materials which have all the characteristics of real communication, such as the 'element of doubt' referred to earlier. Learners are not so naïve that they do not realize that their situation is a teaching/learning situation. Many learners will be prepared to accept at least the unnaturalness and lack of authenticity characteristic of a lot of teaching materials, and there will be situations in which they will prefer efficiency in the teaching/learning process to authenticity.

For these reasons, the two principles of communicative FLT should, in our opinion, never be pushed to their extremes, that is they should never be allowed to completely determine teaching. There is a place for practice with 'real communication' in FLT, namely where transfer has to be brought about between the teaching/learning situation and real communication. And the two principles discussed will play a role in the selection and construction of materials needed for this transfer to be achieved.

In the preceding discussion, we have raised some objections against organizing the teaching/learning process in such a way that FLT always reflects communicative reality, as if the learner were totally uninitiated to the secrets of verbal communication. An argument in favour of introducing communicatively realistic components in the teaching/learning process is that the learner has to be taught to make the best possible use of his limited L2 means in real communication. Perhaps learners have to develop certain special strategies to function adequately in communicative situations in spite of their linguistic shortcomings. Littlewood (1981:4) also points this out (without devoting any further attention to it) when he says that L2 learners should be confronted with situations in which 'the emphasis is on using their available resources for communicating meanings as efficiently and economically as possible'.

12.4.3 Didactic procedures and new methods

At the end of chapter 8, we have made a few brief remarks on what Hawkins (1981) calls 'recent panaceas'. In this section, we wish to discuss especially those new methods which contain new proposals about the organization of teaching/learning activities. It should, incidentally, be observed that Hawkins' (1981:195 ff.) treatment of two of such methods is less negative than the term 'panaceas' suggests.

Madsen (1979) contains a good description of a dozen of what he calls 'innovative methodologies', and Westphal (1979) discusses most of them in addition to the familiar and established methods. Of the new methods which are particularly relevant to a discussion of didactic procedures, Westphal (1979:141) says that 'psychological approaches are the common thread that runs through them'. We have already pointed out that they are sometimes grouped together as 'humanistic' or 'holistic' approaches. A synonymous term seems to be 'affective' approaches, and such concepts as 'awareness', 'self-actualization', and 'self-esteem' are also associated with these approaches (see Moskowitz 1978:1-2). Assuming 'the understanding and acceptance of other cultures' to be the main objective of FLT, Moskowitz (1980:45) concludes that especially 'humanistic techniques' will be of great relevance to FLT, since 'spreading acceptance of different cultures may best begin right in the foreign-language class by spreading acceptance among those who meet there daily'. Curran's Community Language Learning, also called Counseling-Learning (see 8.4.), devotes a lot of attention to this aspect of 'humanistic' learning. The idea is that learners feel responsible as a group for the learning tasks they have been set ('caring and sharing'). The teacher acts as a 'counseler', who may be referred to for information, but for the rest is 'considered to be non-existent in the communicating circle of clients' (Madsen 1979:34). This 'method' relies heavily on learning activities in which group communication is essential.

Suggestopedia and Silent Way embody other attempts at appealing to other abilities than just the cognitive learning abilities of human beings. Suggestopedia is primarily an attempt at giving full scope to all cognitive learning abilities by eliminating all affective impediments. A pleasant learning environment is thought to be essential to this. The learner gets a comfortable chair, is from time to time given relaxation exercises, and part of the presentation of learning material is accompanied by soothing music. A completely different approach is the Silent Way, which has as its main characteristic that the learner himself solves the problems he is confronted with: the teacher remains silent. The most important beneficial effect of the Silent Way, as of other problem-solving procedures, might well be that solving the problems in itself gives satisfaction to the learner and in this way functions as an incentive to learn.

Madsen (1979:30-6), in his discussion of the results of these three new approaches, stresses the fact that they affect different learners in different ways. This is, in a way, true for all approaches, but it will come as no great surprise that approaches which rely so heavily on affective characteristics of individuals show considerable differences in this respect. This is why we wish to reiterate that it is far from certain that such 'methods' will ever be introduced on a large scale in regular, general education. On the other hand, some familiarity with the principles and techniques of these methods may have a favourable effect on the didactic behaviour of FLT teachers in general. A similar conclusion, be it more negatively worded, is drawn by Howatt (1979:13) with respect to the so-called 'natural methods'. These methods do, in his opinion, often amount to nothing less than 'processes of frustration if not outright failure' for most adolescents and adults. They invariably fail in the classroom because L2 learning 'requires deliberate analytic action', and because, for adults at least, 'instructional intervention is necessary' (Howatt 1979:10). Howatt (1979:13) concludes:

> Perhaps the alarming labels indicating imminent and agonizing death which sometimes describe these methods ('sunburn', 'exposure', 'total immersion') should be taken seriously.

12.5 Conclusion

In this chapter we have approached the question of *how* language material should be taught in FLT from three different angles. We have seen that in the teaching/learning process, however differently it is conceived by different textbook writers, there usually are three phases which together form a sort of cycle of teaching/learning activities. The discussion of this cycle is central to this chapter and is separated out for the three different phases: presentation, repetition and exploitation. We have seen that pattern drills, as a learning activity in the second phase, have lost a great deal of ground since the heyday of the audiolingual method.

We have prefaced our discussion of the cycle of teaching/learning activities by a discussion of some aspects which are relevant to the whole of this cycle. In particular, we have discussed the use of exclusively unilingual procedures in the teaching/learning process with special reference to the teaching of L2 vocabulary, and how the L2 learner should be made to master the L2 rule system. We have seen that two important principles of the direct method, namely that only L2 should be used in the classroom and that the L2 rule system may only be taught inductively, are not tenable.

The third angle, which concludes this chapter, has led to a discussion of some recent didactic developments, namely the 'reception-before-production' movement, the implications of the 'communicative approach' for the selection and use of didactic procedures, and finally some aspects of the so-called 'holistic' or 'humanistic' methods.

13
Media

13.1 Introduction

By media we mean all aids which may be used by teachers and learners to attain certain educational objectives. We shall restrict ourselves in some respects in our treatment of the media which may be used in FLT. Only those media which have a direct contribution to make to the teaching/learning process will be discussed. We shall also restrict ourselves to the use of media in the classroom; we shall not discuss the use of media in the various forms of distance study such as language courses on radio or television. For this we refer the reader to a very detailed and excellent survey in *The British Journal of Language Teaching* 28, 2/3, 1980, 59–226, to Hill (1981), Buttjes (1980), and the special issue of *Le Français dans le Monde* 157, 1980. We shall furthermore only give the technical details of the media discussed when absolutely necessary.

Various considerations have traditionally led people to advocate the use of media in FLT. As Schilder (1977) points out in his study of the history of media use, there was and still is a consensus as to the usefulness of media. The developments that have taken place have changed little in this respect. These developments can be attributed on the one hand to the technological innovations which continued to expand the range of reliable and accessible media, and on the other hand to changes in linguistic, psychological and didactic insights. Another important factor is constituted by the changes in education itself, e.g. with respect to objectives and curricula and the role played by FLT in them.

Given the above definition, media can be specified in different ways. Erdmenger (1979:24) lists a number of points of view from which media can be considered:

(1) the nature of the information conveyed by the media (i.e. linguistic and non-linguistic information);
(2) the channel of information (auditory, visual, or audiovisual media);
(3) the phases in the process of teaching and testing (are they used for the presentation, repetition, and exploitation of learning material, or for testing?);
(4) the didactic function (are they used to motivate learners, to convey information, or to stimulate free language use?).

To these four we could add:

(5) the degree of accessibility and adaptability (Mindt 1978, Macht and Schlossbauer 1978, Heaton 1979:39);

(6) the possibilities for supporting, supplementing, or replacing the teacher (Ahrens 1980);
(7) the use of media by individuals or in groups.

In this chapter our main point of reference will be the channel of information. We shall subsequently discuss auditory media (13.2.), visual and audiovisual media (13.3.), and some of the so-called teaching machines (13.4.). In each of these sections other aspects referred to above will also be considered. In 13.5. we shall discuss a few studies on the effectiveness of media use.

13.2 Auditory media

There is considerable agreement on the positive role of auditory media in FLT, and it can also be observed that hardly any new points of view have been advanced in the last few years. There is a great variety of auditory media available today, whose technical qualities are excellent.

At a time when oral skills feature prominently in FLT objectives, it is hardly surprising that such media as radios, tape recorders, gramophones, televisions and video recorders receive considerable attention. The use of such media requires a specific type of course material. Although especially in the early days of the use of technological media in education a lot of materials were developed by the teachers themselves, it is a fact that the construction of high-quality course materials requires such an extensive investment of time and such a degree of expertise that this will often have to be done by experts, in collaboration with teachers. And however ideal the situation with respect to the provision of such materials may be, they will always have to be adapted to specific needs as much as ordinary textbooks do (see 14.3.). The use of media also often meets with organizational and financial problems. Because of the expenses involved equipment and software are often not bought and one often finds that the available media are not used, or used inadequately, either because the equipment is lacking in flexibility or because of lack of maintenance, or because suitable software is not sufficiently available. One of the clearest examples of a wrong policy of media use in schools is the language laboratory (Macht 1979:56, Freudenstein 1981b; see also 13.2.3.2.). In spite of these problems it can be concluded that there are parts of the teaching programme which benefit from the use of auditory media, and that other parts could not be done at all without them. We shall give a brief summary of the advantages:

(a) auditory media offer learners the opportunity to practise with spoken materials without the teacher or some other 'informant' being present; this can even be done outside the classroom, at home;
(b) the voices of many native speakers can be presented in class, with any desired variation with respect to age, rate of speech, clarity of diction, situational context and type of language use;
(c) they can present an invariable model for tasks involving frequent repetition, in for instance pronunciation correction, resolving difficulties in understanding spoken texts, and providing feedback in pattern drills. The model may be presented as frequently as necessary without any change in quality;

(d) media which can record sound make it possible to check learners' utterances, which allows a certain degree of objectiveness in testing and evaluation to be achieved. The recorded utterances are then also available for later use, for instance for subsequent evaluation by external judges.

Summarizing, we can say that generally in FLT the auditory media are of inestimable value. They can present spoken texts and provide opportunities for practising with them. They supplement the teacher with regard to his oral proficiency and may also make his physical presence superfluous at certain moments. This makes it possible for the learner to practise at his own speed and as long as he wants to. That these factors do not apply to all media in the same way will become clear in the following paragraphs, where we will deal with each of the auditory media separately.

13.2.1 Radio

The radio is an important source of high-quality materials. Interviews, news broadcasts, quizzes, etc. make an enormous variety of language material available which is very useful in teaching, in spite of the fact that it has not been specifically designed for teaching. The disadvantage of such material is that very often it has to be edited for classroom use, while the advantage is that because it is topical and authentic, learners generally find it motivating. The amount and variety of topical and authentic material the teacher may record from radio broadcasts could never be equalled in commercial publishing.

The flexibility of the radio as a teaching aid may be increased significantly, and a considerable degree of editing and preparation by the teacher becomes possible, if radio programmes are not presented directly as they are broadcast, but recorded on tape. The great advantage of tape-recorded material is that especially repetition and exploitation can be arranged more flexibly.

The main function of radio programmes in FLT is that they can be used in training listening proficiency, as a basis for conversational activities, and as a means to improve cultural background knowledge.

13.2.2 Tape recorder

As we have already seen, tape recorders and, increasingly, cassette recorders, play a supporting role in the use of radio programmes. The tape recorder is the most widely usable auditory medium. It can be used in all phases of the cycle of teaching/learning activities, can both reproduce and record spoken language, can be used for individual as well as for group work, it is flexible, and it is not very expensive. Furthermore, a large quantity of course materials suitable for the tape recorder is available, and it is relatively easy to develop one's own materials for it. The technical qualities of most tape recorders are such that high quality recording and reproduction, which are indispensable in FLT, are guaranteed. Although speech contains a lot of redundant information which a trained listener does not need to be able to understand what is being said, in FLT most learners are not trained listeners. Language learners, and especially initial learners, will have to be able to receive all of the information as fully as possible.

The same demands of technical excellence also apply to microphones, headphones, speakers and tapes, and it goes without saying that tape recorders should be so easy to operate that they disrupt the teaching/learning process as little as possible.

13.2.3 Language laboratory

The heated discussions about language laboratories are over. Nevertheless, a look at language laboratories is very informative for anyone who wishes to be informed about the role of media in general. This is especially useful at a time when new media appear on the market, as is the case with computers today (see 13.4.).

Today language laboratories occupy a position within the whole range of audiovisual media which is rather different from what it was a few decades ago. After the boom of the 1960s, and a subsequent relatively general rejection of this medium, language laboratories were again discussed in a strikingly large number of readers and monographs in the 1970s. In the literature of the last few years, we find predictions of a 'resurrection' (see Epting and Bowen 1979) of language laboratories, albeit in a somewhat different form and under somewhat different circumstances.

We shall first of all give a brief description of the different language laboratory types, then a survey of the history of this medium, and lastly a discussion and summary of the possibilities of language laboratory use in present-day FLT. For a discussion of research into the effectiveness of language laboratories in FLT the reader is referred to 13.5.2.

13.2.3.1 Language laboratory types

By language laboratories we mean mechanical and electronic equipment which makes it possible for spoken language to be presented in such a way that learners can react to it individually, all at the same time. They can usually also be monitored individually by the teacher (see Freudenstein 1971:43). We shall pay some attention to the main language laboratory types that can be distinguished. For a brief survey of the main characteristics of these types, see fig. 13.1. The differences between the types reside mainly in the possibilities for the learner to record his own voice independently of the group and for the teacher to monitor the learners' utterances.

(1) *Audio-passive (AP)* The teacher has at his disposal one or more tape recorders and a switchboard; the learners each have a headphone, but no microphone. The teacher can broadcast lessons to all learners or to groups of learners. The learners practise in essentially the same way as they do in the classroom, but there is a difference: because of the headphone they cannot hear their classmates, and they can only hear a distorted version of their own speech utterances. Learner activity is restricted to listening in isolation during the presentation phase, and to non-interactive production or reproduction during the exploitation phase.

(2) *Audio-active (AA)* In this type of language laboratory learners have

Types	Technical facilities		Didactic possibilities	
	Teacher	Learner	Teacher	Learner
AP	tape recorder(s); (possibly) groupwiring	headphone (listening only)	broadcasting programmes, (possibly) different programmes simultaneously to different groups	listening and speaking in isolation
AA	same as AP; (usually) 'intercom' with learners; (usually) recording of learner utterances	headphone + microphone (listening + speaking)	same as AP; usually listening in to learner; (usually) discussion of recorded learner utterances	same as AP; hearing own voice through headphone; (possibly) working in groups
AAC	same as AA	same as AA; one tape recorder for each learner	same as AA; providing assistance to individual learners or groups of learners	same as AA; working individually with programme; asking for individual assistance from teacher
AAD	(usually) central control of learner recorders	same as AA; one tape recorder for each group of learners	same as AA; providing assistance to groups of learners	same as AA; working with a programme in a group, with or without assistance from teacher

Fig. 13.1　Language laboratory types

headphones with a microphone, which means that they can hear their own voices undistorted. This also makes it possible for the teacher to play back the voices of each individual learner. This type of language laboratory supplements the possibilities for the recording of the utterances of individual learners with some facilities for self-correction on the part of the learners, and for correction of the utterances produced by individual learners by the teacher.

(3) *Audio-active-comparative (AAC)*   All booths have a double-track tape recorder with a teacher track (master track) and a learner track (practice track). The master track can only be operated by the teacher. The learner can listen to the master track, but he cannot erase it, and he can compare his own speech to the stimulus presented on the master track (comparative). He can then erase the practice track, and make a new recording. A four-phase pattern drill (see 12.3.2.) can be represented schematically as in fig. 13.2. (in which S = stimulus, and R = response).

Master track (non-erasable)	S1	(pause)	S2	(pause)
Learner track (erasable)		R1		R2

Fig. 13.2   Schematic representation of four-phase pattern drill on learner recorder

AAC laboratories, then, allow learners to use a programme completely individually. With some more advanced types, the teacher can also broadcast several programmes simultaneously, form several groups of learners, control some or all of the functions of the recorders of the learners, and record the utterances of individual learners on the master track.

(4) *Other types*   In addition to the audio-active-distributive (AAD) language laboratory, in which there is one tape recorder available for a small group of learners but which in other respects has all the characteristics of the AAC laboratory, there are such laboratories as the open access and dial-access laboratories. The latter type allows the learner to gain access to a learning programme in a central storage system by dialling a number, thus allowing individual use of language laboratory facilities to be extended. This type of language laboratory, however, is not only very expensive, but also requires a type of software which for ordinary FLT in schools is still hardly available (see Harding-Esch 1982:25). In many places language laboratories have been installed of which the basic equipment has been supplemented with a number of visual and audiovisual aids. We shall return to this in 13.3.

13.2.3.2 Historical development

The development of the language laboratory is closely related to the development of the tape recorder, which is the central piece of equipment in language laboratories. Around 1950, tape recorder technology introduced multi-track recorders, which were essential for the development of the AAC laboratory with its possibilities of individual use. Before, each learner working on his own needed two tape recorders. As early as 1924, Ohio State University had already developed such equipment, which they called *language laboratory*. In the US, the development of the language laboratory was stimulated by the *National Defense Education Act* (NDEA) of 1958, which made large sums of money available for FLT. A substantial number of influential publications appeared, which also attracted attention outside the US, such as Stack (1960) and Holton *et al.* (1961), which were especially directed towards the practical problems of language laboratory work. Psychological support for the language laboratory came from Skinner's behaviourism (see 3.2.1.) and linguistic support from structuralist linguistics. The rise of the audiolingual method, and the publication of a great number of courses based on this method, account for the initial popularity of language laboratories. Brooks, one of the strongest advocates of audiolingualism, wrote:

> The language laboratory can be effective in learning (. . .) in terms of the repetition and overlearning of behaviour patterns that are to become habitual. The advantage of the machine over the living person for purposes of sustained repetition is obvious: the machine can repeat in identical fashion what was said before, and it can do so without fatigue or irritation (Brooks 1964:189).

Characteristic of the audiolingual method are pattern practice and pattern drills, aimed at habitualization of linguistic structures. Language laboratories are the ideal media for this type of practice, because they make overlearning and reinforcement easily attainable. It is hardly surprising, therefore, to find the term *language laboratory method* used for this method (see also 8.2.2.).

In the US, objections against the audiolingual method and language laboratory work soon arose. These objections were both of a psychological and of a practical nature (see Rivers 1964). The situation in Europe was different. Although many language laboratories were installed in many countries, this was not always attended by acceptance of the audiolingual method. This can be partly accounted for by the European education systems and traditions, which tend to react slowly to such innovations. A second factor is that at the same time a different method of language learning, the so-called audiovisual structuroglobal method, was being developed in Europe (see 8.3.2.4.), which came to be quite popular. In this method language laboratories are used in quite a different way than in the audiolingual method.

The unchecked growth in the number of language laboratories in the 1960s has ended. There is even a marked decrease in the popularity of this medium, as appears from titles such as: 'Eine Diagnose des Scheiterns' (Hooper 1975) and 'Fehlinvestition Sprachlabor?' (Jung and Haase 1975). The language laboratory, however, has had, and will continue to have, its uses: it certainly has not been written off, as is also demonstrated by the remarkable fact that the second printing of Jung and Haase (1975), which appeared in 1978, bears the much more neutral title of 'Das Sprachlabor'. But there is no longer a tendency to overestimate the contribution of language laboratories to FLT (see Dakin 1973).

13.2.4 Some general aspects of the use of auditory media in the classroom

Auditory media can only be used successfully and efficiently, if certain conditions are fulfilled. These first of all concern the equipment itself (such technical aspects as ease of operation and reliability), organizational aspects (such as accessibility and maintenance) and financial aspects. Secondly, teachers are needed who know how to use media efficiently. Thirdly, adequate language learning materials which are geared to the objectives in general and to specific teaching- and learning tasks in particular, must be sufficiently available. These conditions, which also apply to other media, are frequently emphasized in the literature. Many disappointing experiences with auditory media, and especially with language laboratories, can be attributed to a failure to fulfil the conditions mentioned above. Failure to do so will lead to misuse of media. The role of the teacher is central in this connection:

> There is no empirical proof of the fact that media use *per se* accounts for more motivation, interesting teaching, or better learning results, nor will there ever be. Machines can always only be as good and helpful as the individual teacher thinks they are (Freudenstein 1981b:270).

Teachers must first of all be familiar with the possibilities and limitations of the media which are used in FLT; an awareness of the possibilities and impossibilities may prevent some disappointments. Such awareness enables teachers to judge the relevance of the main functions of auditory media (objectification, individualization, intensification and enrichment) for his own teaching.

Auditory media can be used for presentation, repetition and exploitation, for training listening and speaking skills, but also for dictation, spelling exercises and various other aspects of writing, as well as for the testing of these skills. Whether they are used or not will depend, as we have argued earlier, on the objectives of the teaching programme. An auditory medium like the tape recorder is not maximally useful for the teaching of meaning, if it is not supported by visual media, but it is eminently suited for the presentation of spoken texts, for repetition exercises, for pattern drills, and for guiding oral productive language use.

Compilers of materials for FLT in which media use plays an important role have no easy task. They have to strike a balance between what has been laid down in the objectives and the possibilities and limitations of auditory media. Dakin (1973), Macht and Schlossbauer (1978) and Beile (1979) contain surveys of suitable exercises. Dakin gives innumerable examples of the uses language laboratories can be put to, including free conversation practice.

Many authors (e.g. Ahrens 1980) express the opinion that especially in the later stages of the teaching/learning process the media should be 'in the hands of the learners'. The possibilities of the language laboratory, for example, with regard to recording and reproduction, monitoring and correction, and of evaluation and assessment will then become more transparent for the learners, take over tasks from the teacher, and provide a first step towards real communication. It is hardly surprising, given its history, that the language laboratory should often be associated with what Dakin (1973) calls 'tum-te-te-tum drills'.

Language laboratory work need not, however, be limited to practising by means of structural or contextualized drills. In the last few years many other suggestions for the use of language laboratories have been put forward. The suggestion of using the language laboratory for a variety of learning tasks simultaneously is an especially interesting one, which for instance prevents the learners from automatically associating language laboratory work with a particular type of learning task. Tasks which can be carried out simultaneously by individual learners or by groups of learners with the aid of a language laboratory are, for instance, dictation exercises, grammar- and vocabulary exercises, listening comprehension exercises, pronunciation exercises, and oral proficiency tests. Comprehension exercises can also be based on written texts, in which case the language laboratory can serve as a means to allow learners to work in groups more easily during the exploitation phase. They can communicate through the headphones and record both their discussions about the text and the outcome thereof, and evaluate them later, either together with the teacher or the entire class.

Although this type of language laboratory work is only relevant for a part of the curriculum, and although there are learning tasks for which the language laboratory cannot be usefully employed, the language laboratory can be a very useful medium, especially for those learning tasks which can be carried out individually or in small groups. In this connection it is useful to divide learning tasks up into modules which can be presented as independent units.

Most proposals for learning activities incorporate some visual support for the auditory media, as will be seen below.

13.3 Visual and audiovisual media

There is no strict separation between visual and audiovisual media with respect to their use in FLT. Nevertheless, television, video and film are usually regarded as the audiovisual media proper, because of the combination of sound and image in these media. All visual media, however, can in principle be combined with all auditory media.

In the next paragraphs we shall first discuss visual media (13.3.1.), then audiovisual media (13.3.2.), and, finally, their use in the classroom (13.3.3).

13.3.1 Visual media

The visual element has long played an important role in FLT. Schilder (1977:14) has shown that as long as a century ago a surprising number of visual media, such as prints, drawings, and maps of cities and countries was used in FLT: in fact, long before such auditory media as we have discussed in the preceding paragraphs came to be used.

The difference in approach to the use of visual media in FLT that the last few decades have witnessed, cannot exclusively be attributed to the fact that modern technology has enabled us to produce a rich variety of such media; a development which has taken us into an age in which 'the visual component is an increasingly important dimension of communication' (Griffin 1981:7, Wipf 1978:111–12). An even more important factor has been the extension of the functions of visual media. They are no longer just a means of making FLT more lively, to intensify it, and add some frills to it (mainly to motivate the learners), but they have now also acquired the function of 'didactic intermediary' in the sense that they can be used to provide prestructured guidance of the learner's use of an L2 structure through a visual representation of that structure.

There is considerable agreement in the literature on the positive effect which the use of visual media has on FLT. But it is also generally agreed that a number of conditions must be met if the use of visual media is to be effective (see Weiand 1978:22, and also our remarks on auditory media in 13.2.). Some of these conditions will be mentioned in our enumeration of visual media below.

A number of visual media could be grouped together as 'non-technical teaching aids' (Celce-Murcia 1979). These include aids such as blackboards, magnetic boards and pegboards, pictures, charts, scrolls, flashcards, word-and-picture pocket books, photographs, and cartoons. They are all easily available and adaptable (cf. 13.1.). That is to say, a great variety of such aids can be bought because they are relatively inexpensive, which in turn makes them more flexible for use in FLT. Schilder (1980:344) emphasizes that the use of media should be structured in such a way that learners can choose from a rich selection of aids for a considerable number of learning tasks, initially, with the teacher's help, and later, independently. This also creates possibilities for differentiation, in that learners can work individually or in small groups. Another important aspect of visual aids of this kind is that they do not date very quickly, which makes them rather more usable than other types. Many of such aids can be made by the teacher himself. A considerable number of guides to the production of such and other aids have appeared: Ayton and Morgan (1981), Hinz (1979), Gutschow (1980), and Hunziker (1977).

The second group mentioned by Celce-Murcia (1979) are the 'technical projected aids'. The difference with the first group is that some technical device is needed. This group includes slides, transparencies, films, filmstrips, videotapes and the technical equipment needed for projecting them. Non-technical aids may also be projected with the help of, for instance, a video camera and a monitor. The most flexible device is the overhead projector: it is very easy to produce transparencies for it, which can be easily adapted to all sorts of learning tasks. Slides are much less flexible, while films, TV and video are least flexible, and are very difficult to adapt.

13.3.2 Audiovisual media

The combination of sound and image and the use of rather expensive equipment characterize audiovisual media in the narrow sense of the word, namely films, TV and video. The presentation of moving pictures is one of the most important differences between these and other media. This makes it possible to achieve a considerable degree of contextualization, i.e. presentation of authentic language use in real situations. One of the main disadvantages of this type of material is, however, that it dates very quickly as a result of technical, political and cultural developments.

In FLT, films are losing ground to TV and video. This can be largely accounted for by problems inherent in the use of films: they are difficult to operate, the equipment is usually rather noisy, the sound quality is often poor, and the classroom has to be darkened. Films, furthermore, often contain too much language material to be usefully exploited in the classroom. There are only very few films especially designed for FLT, and it is hardly possible to produce such films oneself. TV and video suffer much less from these disadvantages. There is, however, one important barrier to an optimal use of the possibilities offered by video: the existence of many different video systems which are not interchangeable.

In so-called multi-media systems a great number of media are employed. Characteristic of multi-media packages is the functional division of the various media over the various parts of the course and the different phases of the teaching/learning process. Sometimes the media are used separately, sometimes in combination with each other. In many cases, for instance in the FEoLL-project in the Federal Republic of Germany (see FEoLL 1975), use is made of radio and TV broadcasts, which play an important role especially in the presentation phase. For the repetition and exploitation phases, as well as for additional activities (e.g. for the teaching of cultural background), auditory and visual material is made available, such as slides, tapes for use in groups and individual use, flashcards, transparencies, readers, workbooks and wall charts. In the multi-media approach, however, textbooks retain their central function of setting out the structure of the course, and of providing the link between the media. This role is especially important in view of the not inconsiderable danger that the media will dominate the teaching programme. In this context, a lesson can be drawn from the Berlin multi-media instruction room, intended as an experiment and equipped with an abundance of auditory and visual media, which could be used at any given moment. Freudenstein (1981b:274) voiced the following criticism: 'Fortunately, this concept has not become common practice. If it had, it would have been a perfect example of the dehumanizing effect of media use without consideration for actual instructional needs.'

13.3.3 Some general aspects of the use of visual and audiovisual media in the classroom

In the preceding paragraphs we have put much emphasis on usability, flexibility and adaptability of audiovisual media in order to make it clear that the use of such media can only be effective if they are in all respects 'user-friendly'. If they are not, media use is bound to meet with irritation on the part of both learners and teachers.

Media are generally said to have two main functions: they serve to make FLT more lively, and they are an integral part of the teaching/learning process. These two functions may be reflected in a large number of practical measures, some of which will be reported on in this paragraph. There is a considerable literature on the use of audiovisual media in the classroom: we only mention Macht and Schlossbauer (1978), Geddes and Sturtridge (1982), Ayton and Morgan (1981), Maley and Duff (1976) and Weiand (1978). The last book contains useful suggestions for further reading.

With respect to the first function mentioned, visual and audiovisual media mostly provide additional information. This includes, for instance, furnishing the classroom with wall charts, notice boards, posters, maps, pictures, etc., or providing visual or audiovisual support for parts of the teaching programme, for instance, the cultural background part. Especially useful for this purpose are series of slides with an accompanying prerecorded commentary, films, TV and video. It is usually quite easy to obtain up-to-date material from TV programmes. This material does, however, nearly always require adaptation, which necessitates the use of a video recorder. Adaptation is very time-consuming, especially if one wants to keep one's stock of materials up to date. Some of the main problems in using films and TV for FLT are that the non-linguistic information generally far exceeds the linguistic information, that the linguistic information is usually pitched far above the level of proficiency of the learners, and that, as a consequence, these media are used less for actually teaching the learners than for entertaining them.

With respect to the second function it should be observed that the actual use of media largely depends on the particular phase in the cycle of teaching/learning activities in which they are used. This will be demonstrated for each of the three phases of the cycle of teaching/learning activities which we have distinguished in 12.3.

Downes (1980:130–31) gives an example of a multi-media approach in which the use of a particular medium is always linked to a particular aspect of the teaching/learning process:

'flashcards to present main lexical items;
filmstrip and tape recording bring lexical items into context;
cassette recordings of conversations printed in pupil's book give listening practice with good quality sound;
pupil's book exercises and workbook exercises give explanation and practice of structures used;
language laboratory gives intensive practice through contextualized drills;
television brings together the above into visual, living contexts;
colour slides give high quality photographs for detailed study.'

In the presentation phase, visual media (flashcards and filmstrips) provide the visual support for the acoustic memory (Schiffler 1973:22) and aid the semantization of the language material which has been presented auditorily. The next step in the above example is bringing the language material into context. Linguistic communication is not exclusively verbal behaviour. Such elements as paralinguistic signals (gestures and facial expressions) are also relevant. Furthermore, the meaning of language is also determined by the situation in which it is used, which is constituted by a number of factors, including the speaker, the behaviour of the conversation partner before, during and after the linguistic exchange, and the environment. We use our eyes and our ears to register different aspects of the language use situation. It is, therefore, often advisable to make use of visual media, certainly where aspects of the language use situation are concerned which are strongly culturally determined. It is very important to adapt the visual material for use in the presentation phase. Drawings, presented through textbooks, slide projectors, flashcards, and overhead projectors are eminently suitable. Pictures, films and television are less suitable, especially in the initial stages of the teaching/learning process. A teacher with even the most rudimentary drawing skills can easily adapt the materials to suit the needs of the learners.

In the repetition phase, visual media may be used to aid the internalization of rules and to correct pronunciation (see 12.2.4. and 12.2.5.). In situational exercises they may serve to initiate and guide practice. They make it possible to work quickly and efficiently, without resorting to L1 (Borel 1970:54). Especially conversational practice can be initiated quite easily by means of visual aids. For this purpose not only the simple visual media are useful, but also the more complex audiovisual media such as TV. In the above example, both auditory (language laboratory) and visual (TV and colour slides) media are used in the repetition phase.

In the exploitation phase media are especially important because they can provide stimuli for free conversation. Both auditory, visual and audiovisual media are relevant in this connection, as discussion may be prompted by verbal, visual, and situational stimuli. Spontaneous language use on the part of the learner ceases, however, at the point where knowledge and skills are no longer adequate to react to such stimuli. This means that the material which is intended to provide the stimuli must be adapted to the level of the learners. In the example of Downes (1980), there is a gradual build-up towards free conversation, which may exploit all audiovisual media or any combination thereof. This building-up phase, which is aimed at helping learners who tend to adhere too closely to the learning materials to work independently of them, can also be implemented by the learners themselves in small groups. They should be given the opportunity to listen to and/or watch the stimuli carefully and to take notes. Written instructions, to set up a question-and-answer game for example, would be very helpful in this connection. The last step towards free conversation is in this way introduced through a form of guided conversation.

13.4 Teaching machines

By teaching machines we mean equipment which is capable of storing and presenting learning materials, and of automatically processing learner responses. Equipment with these characteristics can be used for those parts of a language course which can be programmed, i.e. which can be divided up into a number of more or less predictable and ordered steps (see 11.6.).

The history of teaching machines has shown that they are ill-equipped to handle adequately all parts of a language learning programme. Teaching machines are, in fact, often designed specifically for particular learning tasks.

Examples of such teaching machines are the *Suvag Lingua*, a device for pro-nunciation correction (Guberina 1973), the *Speech Visualizer*, which can be used for intonation correction by means of visual information (Léon and Martin 1972, De Bot 1980), and the *Language Master*, which can be used for simple learning tasks in a stimulus–response framework (Howatt 1969:228). Unlike these devices, computers seem to be capable of guiding or supervising a whole range of learning tasks.

Generally speaking, the development of teaching machines was motivated by a desire to individualize and intensify the teaching/learning process. It therefore comes as a bit of a surprise to find that computers are generally found to be most useful as a medium of instruction when they are incorporated into the normal classroom schedule: '. . . although "computer-tutors" were (the) initial goal, it is now clear that the computer is most likely to be useful as a supplement to class-room instruction' (Putnam 1981b:67; see also Marty 1981, Leidy *et al.* 1980:13). These authors emphasize that computers should be regarded as one medium of instruction among many others.

We have reasons to expect that the computer will become more common as a medium of instruction in FLT than other machines such as the *Suvag Lingua* and the *Language Master*, not only because computers can do what these and other machines can do, but also because they can carry out other tasks, such as administering and evaluating learner performance. For this reason we shall dis-cuss CALI (Computer Assisted Language Instruction) in some more detail.

The best account of the present situation and some well founded views on future developments, can be found in Marty (1981, 1982). Marty is associated with PLATO (= Programmed Logic for Automatic Teaching Operations), a CAI system of Control Data Corporation, which has been in operation for some 20 years. PLATO is a macro-system, in which a central computer controls a large number of terminals. Among the advantages of this system are its large memory capacity, the wide selection of learning programs and exercises it offers, its ease of operation, and its special computer language TUTOR, which is suitable for programming language lessons. One major disadvantage is that the costs involved for the user are very high. The installation of mini- or micro-computers could perhaps solve this problem in the foreseeable future. The necessary software, however – computer languages and learning programs – is not yet optimally available (Roberts 1981).

Developments in computer technology suggest that the range of possibilities for CALI can be extended. While most existing CALI programs deal with grammar and vocabulary, and programs for improving listening comprehen-sion, reading comprehension and translation skills are also in use (see 11.6.), certain aspects of pronunciation, intonation and guided conversation could also be taught by means of a CALI system, so that 'the teacher can devote a greater proportion of the class time to something which is beyond the capability of any present or future computer: the development of creative free expression' (Marty 1981:88).

The main advantages of CALI are that it can individualize the learning pro-cess by taking into consideration the initial skills and the learning rate of each individual learner, and by offering choices with respect to type and amount of instruction and practice. It can also intensify the learning process and reduce learning time, it can provide immediate feedback, give random access to programs and exercises, and, lastly, it can increase motivation precisely because programs can be tailored to the needs of the individual, and also because of the intrinsic attraction of the machine; most studies agree on the enthusiasm which learners display in working with computers. CALI still leaves a lot to be desired, however; cf. Marty (1982:5–7), who mentions some areas for improvement:

(1) the computer can only provide partial error analyses of the language produced by learners, since the lists of errors fed into the computer cannot be exhaustive: one has to make do with a list of predictable errors. Nevertheless, the present lists could be improved in a number of ways;
(2) the possibilities for review must be improved in order to prevent, for instance, learners repeating too long, too short, or incorrectly;
(3) there is a need for improvement of computer languages and computer programs in order to make it possible, for instance, for some of the exercises to be generated automatically.

Furthermore, CALI can be improved by adding a visual component to the computer. Visual support of computerized instruction by means of slides and microfiche is possible at the moment. More advanced equipment, such as videodiscs which can both record and reproduce sound, is still being developed.

The computer does not seem to have much to offer in the area of creative writing. Quite apart from the considerable problems involved in the automatic linguistic analysis that this would require, the computer cannot monitor the actual content of what the learners produce.

Another area in which substantial improvement seems unlikely is oral interaction with the computer. Marty (1982:17) writes: 'it is pure fantasy to believe that one day we will have devices which can understand the types of badly formed sentences FL learners are apt to produce and that those devices will provide the students with a correction.'

To sum up, the computer has most to offer in the area of written skills, with the exception of creative writing, and least in the area of oral productive skills. Although some progress has been made also in this area, it is likely that, in the near feature, the computer will continue to be baffled by speech to a large extent (see also 11.6.). It seems realistic to aim for a rather modest role for CALI for the time being. This modesty is motivated not only by present expectations with regard to technological developments, but also by previous experiences with media, the costs involved, and the as yet limited expertise in designing and using computerized learning materials. This latter problem may also cause a widening of the gap between the technical and the didactic aspects of CALI, which may be difficult to bridge.

13.5 Evaluation of media use

Visual and auditory media have a long history in FLT, but their didactic functions did not become the subject of scientific discussion until the rise of the language laboratory. The close connections between behaviourist learning psychology and structuralist linguistics on the one hand and the language laboratory as a means of realizing psychological and linguistic insights about language learning in FLT on the other hand, as well as the subsequent examination of the learning effects of using this medium, have led to critical questions concerning the use of media in FLT in general.

We shall first discuss research into the effectiveness of language laboratories, as this medium has been studied most extensively, and subsequently devote some attention to studies of the effectiveness of multi-media systems. For a survey of research into the effectiveness of these and other media, see Macht (1979:62–7).

13.5.1 Research into the effectiveness of language laboratories

The language laboratory is the medium which has been most widely researched. In the 1970s a great number of reports were published, e.g. Olechowski (1970:52), Schödel and Stille (1973:78 ff.), Jung and Haase (1975), Macht (1979), and Beile (1979:49 ff.).

In language laboratory research one can distinguish between:

(a) research projects which compare entire teaching methods, the use of the language laboratory being one particular aspect within the method;
(b) research in which the language laboratory is the main variable. In this type of research 'normal classroom teaching' is compared with 'normal classroom teaching plus use of language laboratory';
(c) research in which the effectiveness of certain – usually specially constructed – learning materials, which are used both by the experimental group in the language laboratory and by the control group in the classroom, is examined;
(d) research into the effectiveness of a number of technical variables, such as different language laboratory types.

In experiments of types (a) and (b) the number of variables is so large that they cannot be adequately controlled. The results of a number of these research projects have, for this reason, been called in question. The first major research project (Keating 1963) attempted to reveal the effect of the language laboratory as used in actual practice on the learning of listening, speaking and reading skills. In 21 schools the results of pupils who had not practised in a laboratory were compared with the results of pupils who had. It was concluded that it made no difference whether or not a language laboratory was used. This was the first time that research into the effectiveness of language laboratories produced such a clearly negative result. The results of Lorge's (1964) experiments, on the other hand, were positive. The language laboratory groups were generally better in oral skills, and turned out not to be inferior to the groups who had not received language laboratory instruction, in such 'conventional' areas as knowledge of grammar and vocabulary.

The *Pennsylvania Foreign Language Project* (Smith 1970) was set up to prove that the negative results reported in Keating (1963) were attributable to a faulty research design. Careful plans were made for a large-scale project which would have to provide answers to the following questions:

(1) Which of the following three teaching methods leads to the best results for the four skills: the grammar–translation method, the audiolingual method, or a combination of the two?
(2) Which type of language laboratory is the most suitable for teaching pronunciation and grammar, both from a didactic and an economic point of view?
(3) Which combination of method and language laboratory is optimal?

The dependent variables in this project were the learning effect, measured by means of standardized tests, and the interest in and attitude towards studying a foreign language. Over 100 teachers of German and French, distributed over some 60 schools, participated in the project, which ran from 1965/1966 to 1968/1969. The results greatly disappointed the researchers. Their expectations regarding the methods and the use of the language laboratory were not confirmed at all: the audiolingual method turned out not to be better than the other methods, and the language laboratory equipment, as used in the experiment, turned out not to have led to better learning. These results have led to heated discussions about the project.

It is striking that precisely those experiments which seemed to be the most reliable in view of the design, size of sample, period covered, and statistical analyses of the data, turned out not to demonstrate significantly better learning effects for the language laboratory. This is especially true of the studies of Scherer and Wertheimer (1964), and Smith (1970). Beile (1979) demonstrates that even in experiments which have been planned very carefully, not all variables can be controlled equally well. One of the variables in language laboratory research is the learning materials which are used by the experimental and the control groups. Beile analysed the materials used in the best-known experiments, paying special attention to the exercises. He concluded that in most experiments a careful description of the exercises is lacking. Such analyses as 'well written' and 'well presented' are hopelessly insufficient to control this variable. He also criticizes the sheer size of these experiments and draws the following conclusions with respect to future research (Beile 1979:59):

(1) in the research design a clear distinction should be made between the effectiveness of the medium and the effectiveness of the teaching method or the learning materials;
(2) the teaching objectives should be attainable with the help of the medium and the contents of the learning materials;
(3) the materials should be suitable for the medium; i.e. they should fully exploit the specific characteristics of the language laboratory;
(4) the materials used should be systematically described in full detail;
(5) the same holds true for the materials used by the control groups.

These requirements point clearly towards carefully planned small-scale projects, in which the control variables can be better controlled, and in which the research variables are less complex than in many of the large-scale experiments.

Freedman (1982) is an example of such research. Macht (1979), in his analysis of language laboratory research, also concludes that small-scale research is to be preferred. He emphasizes that one cannot expect one medium, e.g. the language laboratory or television, to have a decisive positive influence on overall achievement; inconclusive findings with respect to effects on overall achievement do not warrant a total rejection of the medium in question.

13.5.2 Research into the effectiveness of multi-media systems

The effectiveness of multi-media use has hardly been studied, and only in non-experimental situations. Macht (1979:58) reports that studies of multi-media use in other school subjects are numerous and have generally shown multi-media use not to yield significantly better results than 'normal' teaching without multi-media use. From this he concludes that in FLT, too, multi-media use is not likely to substantially improve learning results.

The results of the rather limited quantity of non-experimental research hardly allow useful generalizations to be made. Erdmenger (1979) reports on a study in which a multi-media based course was evaluated. The media involved were: a television programme, a school radio programme, a language laboratory tape, printed materials for learners, exercises on special worksheets, and for the teacher, transparencies for overhead projector use, and a teachers' manual. The extremely large and heterogeneous population, and the secondary role of media as a variable in the study, which Erdmenger himself refers to as 'quasi-experimental', do not allow any clear conclusions to be drawn about the learning effects of a multi-media approach in FLT. Neither can any clear conclusions be drawn with respect to its effects on the attitudes and motivation of the learners.

Too few small-scale studies have been carried out to date to allow more than tentative conclusions to be made. One cannot but conclude with Macht (1979) and Beile (1979), that a whole series of new studies should be started, if only to create the conditions in which well controlled large-scale studies can be effectuated.

13.6 Conclusion

The use of media, in some form or other, is generally considered useful and important for all types of FLT. We have argued that in FLT a specific use of media is both possible and desirable. If media are intended to support, supplement, or replace the teacher with respect to a number of tasks, then one should first of all ask the question whether and in how far media should be used, for which task, and at which particular stage in the teaching/learning process.

Media do not necessarily become more effective as they become technically more advanced. The results of complex media systems also depend on the quality of the learning materials used. It would be wrong to attribute didactic value *a priori* to any one medium. Flashcards may, under certain circumstances, be more effective than computers or television.

14

Textbook selection

14.1 Introduction

The dominant role that a textbook plays in FLT makes the selection of that textbook an important decision. Individual teachers have, in general, little influence on such important matters as educational policy, objectives, duration of the course, curriculum, etc., but the textbook, which, being a focal point for both learner and teacher and determining the daily activities in the classroom to a considerable extent, forms within the framework of the didactic cycle a component with respect to which teachers and learners can make their own decisions. The textbook plays an important role because it dictates to a considerable extent the content and form of teaching: the textbook is structured, ideally, in such a way that it reflects the available insights, ideas, traditions, experience, and research data.

We will use the term *textbook* for a coherent body of teaching materials which may consist of either just the course book(s), but also of a learning package consisting of several parts. We will use the term *method*, which some authors (e.g. Mackey 1965) use to refer to a 'textbook', to describe a coherent body of considerations about the 'what' and 'how' of teaching (see 8.2.2.).

In this chapter we will present a survey of the means which are available to enable the teacher to arrive at a well motivated selection of textbooks. Information about textbooks can be obtained from two sources: the textbook itself and the users of the textbook. We shall use the term *textbook description* for the collection and description of data on the form and content of the textbook itself, and the term *textbook evaluation* will be used for the collection and description of data on the effects textbooks have on their users. Judgments on *possible* effects of textbooks are not included in our definition of textbook evaluation; they are often part of textbook descriptions and will, for that reason, be discussed in the latter context. Textbook description and evaluation can apply to single items as well as to sets of materials.

Textbook description and evaluation have gradually gained in importance over the last few decades, both from a practical (teaching) point of view, and from a research point of view. Neuner (1979:9) gives the most important reasons for this ever-increasing interest. The number of textbooks, mostly very diverse in content and in methodological and didactic approach, has increased dramatically. Furthermore, textbooks have become more comprehensive in the sense that such aspects as texts, exercises, tests, and also hints for both teachers and learners often receive considerable and detailed attention.

It is striking that, relatively speaking, a lot of attention is paid to textbook description and evaluation in the Federal Republic of Germany and in the Netherlands. In the German literature one even encounters the terms *textbook research* (*Lehrwerkforschung*) and *textbook theory* (*Lehrwerktheorie*, see Heuer *et al.* 1970:9). The factors mentioned above, as well as certain factors of educational policy, are doubtlessly the cause of this attention. In the FRG, the fact that only those textbooks which have been approved by a team of experts are officially accepted, relates directly to the existence of relatively detailed curricula which are subject to government control. Neuner (1979:35), however, is of the opinion that the fact that the ratification committees operate behind closed doors is harmful to the development of textbook description and evaluation. In his opinion, making the criteria for approval public would be extremely beneficial. This hypothesis is certainly not borne out by textbook description as it takes place in the Netherlands, where there are no official guidelines for textbooks. Neuner assumes that publications such as the *Mannheimer Gutachten* (Engel *et al.* 1977, 1979), which analyses and judges textbooks of L2 German, could start a development towards a systematic approach to textbook description and evaluation. Attempts at arriving at such an approach have indeed been undertaken, but the conditions are still far from ideal, not even in those countries where many textbook descriptions and also textbook evaluations have been carried out and published. We shall discuss this in some more detail in the next few paragraphs.

Most teachers are not in a position to collect, order, and edit in a form which is suitable for teaching the necessary materials to construct their own textbooks. This means that they will have to rely largely on commercially produced textbooks, or other materials not collected by themselves. Fixed points of reference for the selection of any textbook are the objectives, the curriculum, the teaching situation in question, and the way in which the school is organized. This is the framework within which teachers will have to operate in making their choice.

There are sources of information available which enable teachers to arrive at a well motivated choice. We shall discuss information made available by authors and publishers of textbooks (14.2.1.), textbook reviews (14.2.2.), checklists of points relevant to description and evaluation (14.2.3.), while in 14.2.4. we shall discuss both textbook descriptions and the development of descriptive tools. We shall deal with users' judgments in 14.3.1., and discuss experimental textbook research briefly in section 14.3.2.

It seems useful to distinguish between the following two stages in the selection of a textbook:

(1) Global selection. This is a first selection of textbooks which have sufficient superficial appeal. The information needed to make such a choice can be obtained from textbook reviews, users' judgments, information from authors and publishers, and the teacher's own global analysis (based, for instance, on a textbook typology).
(2) Analysis of the textbooks remaining after first selection. For this purpose checklists, comparative textbook descriptions, detailed comments from

users, and, where available, reports on empirical research into the effects of the textbooks in question can be very useful.

One can, it will be clear, either collect the necessary information oneself, or get it from elsewhere. If one has to collect the information oneself, the sources are limited: checklists and information provided by authors and publishers. In this case, a considerable part of the information needed is lacking and it will be necessary to seek professional assistance. In the next few paragraphs we shall discuss to what extent this help can be given, and what the relative importance of the different sources of information is.

14.2   Textbook description

In section 14.1. we defined textbook description as the collection and description of data on the content and form of the textbook itself. Ideally, the description should be objective. Although evaluations by authors of reviews and textbook descriptions not based on experience or experimental research, but on insight into and experience with textbooks in general are not strictly objective, and as such should not be called textbook descriptions proper, we will deal with them briefly, because they can also serve a very useful purpose for textbook selection.

14.2.1   Authors' and publishers' information

The information provided by authors and publishers of textbooks usually leaves much to be desired. Boot (1976) defines giving information as 'the provision of pertinent and verifiable details about a textbook', and concludes that authors and publishers can hardly be said to give such information.

Textbooks are usually commercial products. Neuner (1979:34) points out that commercial considerations are involved in the information provided by publishers. Leaflets from publishers are hardly useful in textbook selection, because they are intended as advertisements. They are not independent or unbiased, and for that reason do not meet the standards to be set for textbook descriptions.

Swallow (1981) and Ewer and Boys (1981) report on research which they have carried out into the recommendations and claims made by textbook authors. Swallow investigated the *Longman Audio-Visual French Course*, which the authors claim to be 'a complete and integrated course for secondary schools, covering four or five years' work to O-Level or CSE standard'. The course comprises stages A1–A5 intended for O-level, and stages A1, A2, B3, B4 intended for the Certificate of Secondary Education, the final exams for 16- and 15-year-olds respectively in the British educational system. Swallow concludes that this recommendation by the authors has led many teachers to adapt their teaching to suit it, but that the division into two levels is based on nothing but vague impressions of level of difficulty and the amount of language material required. He does so on the basis of a comparison of vocabulary and grammar in textbooks A1–A5 and A1–B4 to a number of O-level exam papers from between 1976 and

1978. Swallow's conclusion is that A1–B4 provided sufficient preparation for O-level where dictation, essay, letter-writing, composition, translation, and reading comprehension are concerned. He did not investigate the contents of the course for the Oral Examination, but, according to Swallow, experience strongly suggested that the vocabulary contained in A1–B4 would be more than adequate for the purpose of the O-level oral examination.

Although this study has not provided unequivocal support for the hypothesis that A1–B4 are sufficient preparation for all components of the O-level examination, it does demonstrate that the differences between the two textbook levels are more marginal than the authors would have us believe. This, in Swallow's opinion, suggests that they rather overestimate the exam requirements.

Ewer and Boys (1981) investigated 10 EST (English of Science and Technology) textbooks. The main claim of the textbooks concerned is that they teach the language of science and technology. Ewer and Boys conclude that there is little in the textbooks themselves to suggest that the authors have taken the trouble to find out what exactly EST is. Also, the selection of course content is judged to be haphazard and limited, and the didactic approach used gives rise to serious objections. This severe criticism is supplemented with an observation worth citing. It turns out that previous reviewers of the textbooks in question base themselves on the same claims as the authors of the book, without having investigated the claims themselves. What Ewer and Boys put their finger on is the fact that in the area of special purpose courses course design has made less progress than in the area of general purpose courses.

If we take the giving of information to be the provision of pertinent and veri-fiable data, what sort of data are we then talking about? It seems to us that it can only be those aspects of a textbook about which one can make precise and veri-fiable statements. These statements will often be of a quantitative nature, for instance about lexical items and sentence structures, the way in which these are interspersed in the textbook, about types of exercise material, and the way these are divided over the textbook. In Bung's (1977:233–4) opinion, the provision of such information is primarily the task of the author, who has this information at his disposal. The author should also give a motivation for the objectives and design of the textbook, in spite of the fact that the concomitant claims can often only be checked by means of detailed analyses.

14.2.2 Textbook reviews

Reviews could be called the most general and widely used type of textbook description. The most important merit of reviews is that they provide prompt information, if, of course, the editors of journals publish quickly enough. Reviews are, however, severely limited in comparison to the textbook descriptions discussed in section 14.2.4. They often contain only summary and superficial information and may be very subjective. They are written and published by different authors, who will not judge by comparable standards. Attempts have been made at making reviews more objective, but so far it has been impossible to standardize criteria and coordinate frames of reference.

Especially the lack of a common frame of reference requires a lot of reinter-
pretation of the data provided by the reviewer.

The limited usefulness of reviews as an instrument for textbook selection has
been repeatedly pointed out in the literature. Pfister and Rada (1974:144) have
investigated the information content of a number of reviews of the same textbooks, and conclude that descriptions vary enormously and that shared
opinions are hard to find. The main reason for this is the fact that reviewers
usually do not limit themselves to giving a description, but often also give a
value judgment, for which the frame of reference is often rather vague. It would
however be wrong to conclude from this that reviews as a source of information
are always unreliable. If the review meets the requirements that it (a) provides all
pertinent information and (b) has an explicit frame of reference, so that value
judgments can be interpreted accordingly, the reviews can play a more important role in textbook selection than has been the case so far. To meet these
requirements, reviewers would have to work along more or less parallel lines
(cf. also Neuner 1979:31, Murdoch 1978:87). A standardization of this type
could be implemented in the shape of a checklist; something we shall discuss
in 14.2.3.

One important question that remains is whether the information provided by
the reviews in fact reaches the teacher who is looking for a suitable textbook.
Bartel (1974:326) is relatively pessimistic about this, simply because most
teachers do not have the time or the opportunity to read all textbook reviews in
the journals. But this problem is not limited to reviews. Many other sources of
information are not accessible enough for the individual teacher when he needs
them.

14.2.3 Checklists

Both textbook description and evaluation can be carried out on the basis of
checklists. We shall limit ourselves to checklists aimed at textbook description.
Many such lists have been published, and in some cases textbooks have been
analysed and described with the aid of these checklists. Textbooks can be
described at different levels and with different aims in mind, which is one of the
reasons why one finds lists differing in size, composition and detail. The more
limited official influence (government, boards of education, educational
institutions) on the selection of course content and on the planning and execution of the teaching programme is, and the greater the scope for different interpretations of the objectives, the greater the need will be for an aid in textbook
selection. If this aid is a checklist, its components should meet the following
requirements:

(1) they should be unequivocal;
(2) they should allow differentiation;
(3) they should yield only descriptions;
(4) they should be directed at clearly delimited and identifiable parts of the
    textbook;
(5) they should be immediately usable.

The main requirements are that the items in a checklist should be descriptive in character and immediately usable. By the latter requirement we mean that the items in a checklist should enable the teacher to collect the data he is looking for himself. For an adequate textbook description, Ewer and Boys (1981) think that a detailed analysis, which is difficult to carry out even for experienced teachers, is necessary. Seen in this light, it is hardly useful to include points in a checklist which would need such analyses. Checklists should also be descriptive; i.e. its components, and especially the way in which they are phrased, should not invite value judgments, especially not if the frame of reference is not given together with the description. In general, one can say that these two points are the main areas in which existing checklists are inadequate. We shall illustrate this by discussing the *Mannheimer Gutachten* (Engel *et al.* 1977, 1979).

The checklist designed for the *Mannheimer Gutachten* (see Engel *et al.* 1979:36–40) is not essentially different in nature and size from many other checklists. It is an attempt to summarize all relevant aspects of textbooks as exhaustively as possible. The compilers of the list stress the point that in spite of the fact that it has gone through a whole series of operations, it is still inadequate in places. These inadequacies relate especially to requirements 1, 2 and 4 which we have mentioned earlier in this paragraph. The main categories of the checklist are:

   objectives and methodology
   structure of the textbook
   organization of teaching
   didactic conception
   exercises
   motivation and activation of learners
   texts
   grammar
   phonetics
   morphosyntax
   vocabulary
   communicative categories, speech acts
   contrastivity
   thematic goals
   communicative, social, situational context
   culture, intercultural communication

Although the many reactions to the *Mannheimer Gutachten* demonstrate that it has made a valuable contribution to a critical discussion of textbooks, they also reveal the limitations of textbook description on the basis of checklists. If one does not limit oneself to description – it has to be mentioned that the checklist has been designed in such a way as not to immediately invite value judgments – one will tend to voice opinions which will depend on one's own point of view, which may or may not correspond with the point of view of those who will use the data yielded by the description. As the linguistic and didactic convictions of the authors of the *Mannheimer Gutachten* are relatively modern, this checklist does suggest a preference for more recent textbooks. This automatically places textbooks of a slightly less recent date at a disadvantage (see Heindrichs *et al*. 1980:150–1).

14.2.4 Textbook descriptions and the development of new descriptive tools

Textbook description has traditionally been mainly concerned with single text-books or aspects of a single textbook, although comparative descriptions of a number of (aspects of) textbooks have also been published. We shall discuss a number of textbook descriptions, mainly because of the descriptive tools which are used, or are being developed and tested. The development of new descriptive tools mainly concerns – leaving aside, for the moment, the compiling of check-lists, which are usually intended for the description of entire textbooks and which we have discussed in 14.2.3. – certain aspects of textbooks such as syntax, vocabulary, exercises, and audiovisual materials.

We have investigated a large number of titles, a survey of which is presented in fig. 14.1. This survey appears to point to a certain preference for specific aspects of textbooks. In 20 of the titles investigated the development of descriptive tools was the primary aim rather than the description of a textbook for a specific language (see the non-specific column).

	French	German	English	Dutch	Spanish	Non-specific	Totals
Vocabulary	9	–	3	1	–	2	15
Grammar/ syntax	12	2	3	2	1	3	23
Pronunciation	–	–	1	–	–	–	1
Exercises	–	2	3	1	–	–	6
Texts	2	3	4	–	1	5	15
Audio-visual materials	–	1	2	–	–	–	3
Culture	9	7	13	–	1	10	40
	32	15	29	4	3	20	103

Fig. 14.1 Survey of descriptions of aspects of textbooks

Although this survey certainly does not claim to be representative, some of the figures are striking. The relatively large number of descriptions of vocabulary in French textbooks is doubtlessly due to the discussion engendered by *Français Fondamental* (see 10.4.3.1.). Another striking figure is the one relating to descriptions of cultural, social and ideological contents of textbooks, grouped under the heading of culture in fig. 14.1. In many cases both aspects which are easily quantifiable, such as lexical items, and aspects which are at first sight less easy to quantify, are given a quantitative description. Quantitative textbook descriptions comprise the major part of all textbook descriptions published. A large number of aspects of textbooks have been quantitatively described, such as lexical items (Frechette 1969, Willée 1976), grammatical structures (Willée 1976), phonology (Nübold 1977), cultural content (Kirkwood 1973, Kressel 1974, Joiner 1974, Moreau and Pfister 1978), texts (Eppert 1972, Köhler 1977, Mann 1981). A comprehensive comparative study of language laboratory textbooks can be found in Wulf (1978). Knapp-Potthoff (1979) has developed a typology of exercises, and an instrument for describing exercises in textbooks.

Bung (1977) is an attempt at describing in quantitative terms aspects of textbooks which have usually been looked upon as being of a primarily qualitative nature. Bung investigates the value of *content analysis* as a descriptive tool. Content analysis is an empirical method of text analysis originally developed for the media. It has three characteristics: it is objective in the sense that results can be compared intersubjectively, which means that they can be verified; it is systematic in that aspects of textbooks are described within a theoretical framework of categories; and it is quantifiable. Quantifiability is the main characteristic of content analysis. According to Bung, content analysis can only supplement a subjective investigation of the material in question; it cannot replace it (Bung 1977:69). By this he indicates that quantitative analysis is not an adequate tool to fully investigate all aspects of the contents of texts. This approach to textbook description one can find exemplified in the following empirical investigations by Bung:

(1) a frequency analysis of situational language use (everyday communicative situations, in which a realistic type of English is spoken) in a number of English textbooks for secondary schools;
(2) a frequency analysis of the treatment of social and cultural aspects in a number of English textbooks published in the Federal Republic of Germany and the German Democratic Republic;
(3) an analysis of English textbooks within the framework of an actual textbook selection procedure for a particular secondary school.

The last is an attempt at carrying out a textbook description directly for the purpose of textbook selection. It includes an analysis of the readability of texts and a frequency analysis of speech acts (Bung 1977:146–224). The readability of texts was investigated to obtain a standard for the relative degree of difficulty of the textbooks of which one would eventually have to be selected. Taylor's (1953) cloze procedure was used to determine readability. The frequency of speech acts was expected to provide a quantitative answer to the question what aspects of communicative competence could be attained with the textbooks under investigation. By 'communicative competence' is meant the learner's ability to communicate by, *inter alia*, fulfilling a number of language functions (see 9.3. 2.1.). The five textbooks under investigation had been specifically written for the type of school in question, or were considered suitable for it.

Readability

The texts of all units in the five textbooks were analysed by means of a cloze procedure. Four subjects (German near-native speakers of English) were asked to complete the texts from which each fifth or sixth word had been deleted. Then the readability values, expressed in percentages of words correctly filled in, were determined for each subject, each textbook and each unit, and rank-ordered according to readability value. After significance had been computed it could be concluded that the textbooks ranking 1 and 2 were clearly above average, and that there was agreement between the subjects on this ranking. The textbooks ranked 4 and 5 were clearly below average with respect to readability value, and there was clearly less agreement between subjects. Textbook 1 could therefore be considered the easiest. A comparison of the readability values of all the units within each textbook showed that the expected increase in the degree of difficulty did not materialize. There was no increase in the degree of difficulty in textbook 1, and hardly any in 2. Bung considers the research strategy used valid, and the results of the cloze analysis satisfactory. He does stress, however, that the empirical value of the results will have to be established through further research.

Frequency analysis of speech acts

A system of categories for speech acts was used, based on Searle's classification: representatives, directives, declarations, commissives and expressives (see Clark and Clark 1977:88). On the basis of this system of categories, in the project the speech acts in the textbooks were counted by four subjects. The frequency counts showed all the textbooks to suffer from an imbalance in the occurrence of the various categories of speech acts. It is not surprising that the language functions of 'concluding' and 'informing' (representatives) should be the most frequent ones in all textbooks. The data, however, do not provide an answer to the question which textbook could best be used to attain the objective of communicative competence. A methodological conclusion was that content analysis is a suitable instrument for determining frequency of occurrence of speech acts, but also that the available categories of speech acts are not clearly enough defined for the results of a content analysis to be very satisfactory; i.e. it is difficult to arrive at precisely defined counting units.

In Bung's advice to the school, available descriptions and users' judgments of the textbooks in question were also taken into consideration. A review of the literature yielded extremely disappointing results. Bung concludes that some aspects of some textbooks have been described, but that comparative textbook descriptions were totally nonexistent. In his conclusion, Bung says that the content analysis carried out for the school in question was only one of the factors involved in the process of textbook selection, but also that the recommendations made were not all completely accepted. One of the objections against content analysis is that it is very time-consuming. A second problem is establishing a system of categories; a problem which is particularly acute in the case of linguistic aspects of textbooks about which there is little agreement among linguists. The fact that Bung is apparently forced to introduce a category of *ambiguous speech acts* is a good illustration. Möhle and Raupach's (1979) comparative work encounters similar problems.

Not only is the quantification of the linguistic content of textbooks sometimes problematic, it is especially problematic with respect to pedagogical, sociocultural and socioeconomic aspects. Such aspects, incidentally, are not only to be found in listening and reading texts, but are also hidden in e.g. exercise sentences.

A topical issue in textbook research is the role of women. Freudenstein (1978b) is a collection of essays written on this subject for the International Women's Year of the United Nations (1975), and numerous publications on the subject can be found elsewhere. Most of these studies aim at providing evidence for the attitudes towards the role of women as expressed in, for instance, exercise materials. Freudenstein's collection is a good introduction to textbook description which is not purely quantitative.

14.3 Textbook evaluation

Research into the use of textbooks in schools and their effects on teaching and learning can play a very important role in textbook selection. Such research, in which the textbook is an important variable, may have as a result that it is not a strong belief in certain teaching methods and materials but objective data which determines the criteria for textbook selection. Extending our knowledge of the effects of textbooks on learning will bring about new, or improved, criteria for textbook selection. The number of wrong choices made as a result of speculations about expected or hoped-for effects of textbooks could, in this way, be somewhat reduced.

In textbook evaluation, we distinguish between users' judgments (14.3.1.), and experimental research into the effects of textbooks (14.3.2.). We will give a rough outline of the possibilities and problems of textbook evaluation, and a description of a few projects.

Textbook evaluation in the form of users' judgments has its roots in daily teaching practice. Such evaluation usually leads to adaptation of the textbook which is currently used. There is a fairly extensive literature on this subject (e.g. Stevick 1971, Madsen and Bowen 1978). The connection between evaluation and adaptation is explicitly dealt with in Candlin and Breen (1979) and Breen and Candlin (1981). They present a set of questions which could serve as a guide for textbook evaluation by the teacher, and a number of proposals which could serve as a basis for both adaptation of the textbook in question and the construction of a new textbook.

The adaptability of a textbook is an important factor in textbook selection. It depends not only on the structure of the textbook itself, but, perhaps even to an equal degree, on the nature of the shortcomings that emerge when the textbook is being used. Usually, necessary adaptations that affect the structure of the textbook will lead to a decision to look for a different textbook. Nevertheless, one generally finds considerable adaptation and supplementation to be possible. They usually relate to such components as classroom activities, tests, and supplementary texts. More recent activities such as role playing and language games, and tests such as the cloze test, can often easily replace or supplement the activities and tests in the textbook. Textbook adaptation and supplementation are preferable to introducing a new textbook, if the general structure of the textbook is still adequate. Shortcomings of a textbook in these areas will attract a lot of attention, because one is frequently confronted with them in daily teaching practice, but because of their high degree of adaptability they do not immediately necessitate choosing a new textbook. This puts a certain emphasis on the way the teacher functions, and therefore on teacher training. Just as Bung would like teacher training colleges to carry out textbook descriptions (see 14.2.4.), Morley (1978:18–22), amongst others, advocates a greater emphasis on textbooks and textbook adaptation in teacher training.

14.3.1 Users' judgments

For the users of textbooks, teachers and learners, negative experiences with a textbook may have two effects: either the textbook is adapted in the places where it is found to be lacking (see 14.3.), or a search for a new textbook is started. Users' judgments may play an important role in textbook selection, but more often than not they are very hard to come by. Most textbooks, in fact, have been on the market for years before the opinions that have been formed of them become in any way generally known. In principle, however, this information could be compiled rather easily and made available to other users. A prerequisite is that the terminology of the evaluative descriptions is standardized. In contrast to what we have said about textbook descriptions (see 14.2.4.), we cannot say that the literature on users' judgments is very extensive. Apart from one or two projects which were set up to develop an evaluation procedure, only reports of individual teachers and schools or institutes on current textbooks are available (e.g. Cole 1968). Sometimes these reports are necessarily global and impressionistic ('I find it impossible to work with this textbook') and as such will be of little practical use to prospective users when it comes to weighing the pros and cons of a new textbook. There have been attempts at making users' judgments more objective and collecting them in so-called standardized descriptions which could be of use to those who are looking for a new textbook or otherwise wish to make use of the experiences of others.

The study by Van Meerem and Tordoir (1977) is part of an extensive long-term project at the University of Amsterdam aiming to develop descriptive tools for textbooks. The researchers distinguish various types of descriptive categories in the description of textbooks:

(1) characteristics which require no detailed analysis, such as title, author, price, etc.;
(2) characteristics of textbook content which can be reliably described by experienced teachers;
(3) characteristics which are closely related to actual classroom use and which can therefore only be described and evaluated on the basis of users' judgments.

The study attempts to establish which (types of) characteristics should be evaluated on the basis of users' judgments, which of these characteristics are judged consistently by teachers and learners, and lastly, whether the instruments used, such as interviews and questionnaires, are adequate for all textbook characteristics evaluated. The interviews and questionnaires were conducted among groups of teachers and pupils to obtain information on methodological and didactic characteristics of the textbooks, and the appreciation of them by learners. The results are summarized in a so-called standardized description per textbook, in such a way that the opinions of teachers about what a textbook should be are listed alongside their opinions of the textbooks used; i.e. a frame of reference is given alongside the actual evaluation.

Especially this last aspect is very important in our opinion, because it prevents users' judgments from being interpreted as absolutes. Furthermore, this study confirms what we have observed in 14.2.4.: where possible, there should be a distinction between the description of textbook characteristics and the evaluation thereof. Also, the assumption of the study that information about some aspects of textbooks is best obtained through users' judgments has been confirmed. One of these aspects occurs in the checklist drawn up by Heindrichs *et al.* (1980:160), which poses the question whether the target group can identify with the communicative situations presented in the textbook. It is indeed advisable to ask the users such a question, because the appreciation of a textbook or parts thereof by learners is mostly very hard to predict. This is also shown by the research carried out by Heuer (1973a) into the preferences of 11- and 12-year-old pupils, who could choose between five textbooks, one of which they used in class. Preference was in this study equated with the degree of motivation of the pupils. One of the most striking results was that the two textbooks which scored highest in preference differed considerably in content and organization and that the textbook which the pupils used got a very low score. In addition, pupils using the same textbook were interviewed. They were asked which lessons they had liked best and which they had liked least. There was much variation in preference. The highest degree of preference was scored by a lesson in which an extremely idyllic picture is given of a textbook family and the environment in which it lived: a very surprising result to the researcher (compare also Düwell 1979 and Radden 1980). Therefore, it seems wise to incorporate such users' judgments into experimental research into the effects of textbooks.

14.3.2 Experimental research into the effects of textbooks

Experimental research into the effects of textbooks is high on the list of desiderata of many authors (Heuer and Müller 1973:7, Bung 1977:233, Heindrichs *et al.* 1980:153, Hatfield 1968:386), but it is only rarely carried out, especially where entire textbooks are concerned. The research which has been carried out is almost exclusively directed towards certain aspects of textbooks, often in a comparative framework, in which the aspects of the textbooks are the independent variables and the degree of learning success the dependent variable. They are usually small-scale experiments within a normal classroom context. They are more limited in size than such extensive projects in which global comparisons of the effects of different teaching methods are made, such as the Pennsylvania Foreign Language Project (see 13.5.1.) and the GUME-project (see 12.2.4.). They were concerned more with teaching methods than with textbooks as such. Neither project gave clear answers to the questions whether the audiolingual method should be preferred to a cognitive code-learning one, or implicit grammar-teaching to explicit grammar-teaching. Knapp (1980) is one of those who criticize these projects. As learning success is doubtlessly a function of many variables, statements on the effect of manipulating one of these variables are not straightforwardly applicable or generalizable, unless, as a minimum requirement, the most important other variables have been kept constant. In his opinion such research is not hampered primarily by the fundamental weaknesses of the existing empirical methods, but by organizational problems. This is why he considers small-scale experiments within a normal teaching context the most suitable form of research into the effects of textbooks. In his comparative study of different ways of ordering restrictive relative clauses as taught to German pupils in their second year of English, Knapp (1980) limits himself to an experiment lasting two weeks, in which the structures in question were taught for a total of six hours to five groups of subjects (for more information see 11.4.). This study shows that even with such a small experiment it is extremely difficult to control all the crucial variables, which is one of the reasons why Knapp regards his project as preliminary to research into the influence of certain types of teaching material on L2 learning.

Erdmenger (1979) is rather more positive in his recommendation of the textbook *Speak Out*, which he has investigated. His study comprises various aspects of the textbook. *Speak Out*'s effectivity in comparison with other, 'conventional' textbooks was investigated, and the possibilities which this textbook offers for differentiation, as well as the effectivity of the use of some media. A number of language proficiency tests, a test for measuring the effectivity of the media used, and questionnaires presented to teachers and learners were used in this study. In all three respects the results were mildly positive, but the favourable opinions of teachers and learners did not always correspond to the test results. From a methodological point of view, this study once more confirms that conclusions about generalizability and applicability of research results are very often drawn on the basis of inadequate empirical evidence.

Empirical research into the effects of textbooks has as yet failed to play a significant role in textbook selection. This is hardly surprising, since this type of research has only just been started. But in spite of these somewhat discouraging facts, empirical research is the only method of obtaining reliable information about the role of textbooks in education.

14.4 Conclusion

Some critical remarks have to be made about textbook description and textbook evaluation as they take place now. Although there are some publications devoted to the development of reliable and usable descriptive and evaluative tools, and although qualitative as well as quantitative analyses of (parts of) textbooks have been carried out, it would be premature to conclude that they have, as yet, produced a wealth of applicable results for textbook selection. Neuner (1979:32), among many others, points this out and attributes it to the fact that most contributions are of an occasional and ill-coordinated nature, originating from the personal fields of interest of the authors rather than from a more general theoretical concern. We do not share this opinion, although we do wish to point out that an early initiative at coordinating research (Heuer and Müller

1973, 1975) accomplished little, and that other attempts have not been developed to a stage where they yield results which could be used in teaching practice. In our opinion textbook description and evaluation, which are intended as aids in textbook selection, should primarily be practically oriented, and provide descriptive and evaluative tools which can be used in teaching practice. We also share the frequently voiced desire to make recently published textbooks more systematically accessible to teachers by means of comparative textbook descriptions. In addition to this, professional researchers or institutes, such as educational research institutes, departments of applied linguistics and teachers' organizations, could carry out experimental research into textbooks which are currently being used, or evaluate them by means of users' judgments. If teachers are to profit from the often valuable work of which we have given only a few examples in this chapter, considerable attention should be paid to the organizational aspects mentioned earlier.

15
Language testing

15.1 Introduction

Language testing is a complex matter. It involves elements from linguistics, from psychometrics, and from language didactics (Klein-Braley 1981). Several factors have to be taken into account in developing and applying tests. The purposes of testing are not always the same. The what of testing can be quite complex and diverse. Tests may be compiled by individual teachers, or by professional institutions. Testees exhibit different characteristics. And, last but not least, decisions about individuals taken on the basis of test results may be trivial or extremely important. Why a test is set, what is tested, who is tested, and when a test is set are questions which determine the actual testing procedure, and which may lead to different requirements with respect to the quality of a test. A test, for instance, which yields reliable data for decisions based on aggregated group data need not yield reliable data for decisions focused on individuals (Popham 1978:146). Spolsky remarked in this context: 'testers as a profession should continue to speak out about the dangers of the misuse of their tests' (Spolsky 1981:29). This is especially relevant if one's test subjects are of different cultural backgrounds. Tests bear the characteristics of the social and cultural context in which they originated. Whether they like it or not, test constructors have certain presuppositions which their testees are supposed to share. A number of authors, for instance Condon (1975), Mohan (1979), and Spolsky (1981) have pointed out the occurrence of cultural bias in tests. The phenomenon of tests is, in fact, in itself culturally determined. Not all parts of the world have as much test experience as the US has, for instance. People from cultures which do not attach such paramount importance to individual achievement or to working under time pressure will react differently to tests. This may entail that using tests, or taking the results of one test population as a basis for comparing those of some other test population, can be unjustified in some cases.

In other words, there are plenty of reasons for being cautious in using tests and in interpreting test results, but there are no reasons at all for mystification; testing procedures should be as transparent as possible, which is why testees should be aware of what is expected of them right from the start (Rohrer 1981). They should know what content is tested, how it is tested, and what criteria will be used in rating. For this purpose the testees could be given a number of specimen tests.

We shall limit ourselves in this chapter to a general discussion of the main aspects of language testing. We refer the reader to Allen and Davies (1977), Canale (1981), B. Carroll (1980), Clark (1972), Cohen (1980), Davies (1978), Harris (1969), Heaton (1975), Ingram (1974), Lado (1961), Oller (1979b) and Valette (1977) for more detailed information on language testing.

15.2   Purposes of language testing

Language tests may be used for different purposes, and in the literature on testing one therefore finds a variety of frameworks within which tests may be characterized. In this chapter we shall not deal with the role and nature of tests used in empirical research into language and language learning. We do wish to point out, however, that these tests, too, will have to meet the standards set for tests used in a different context. The context in which language testing takes place is usually language teaching. In the context of teaching, tests do not only have the purpose of measuring the language behaviour of individuals, but they are also useful instruments for evaluating programmes by means of an analysis of the results of an entire group of learners. If this evaluation takes place at the end of a programme, and has the purpose of evaluating that programme as a whole, we speak of *summative evaluation. Formative evaluation* takes place during the programme and is intended to adjust or guide the programme. The terms 'summative evaluation' and 'formative evaluation' are used to refer not only to the evaluation of an entire programme but also to the evaluation of individual achievement. In the latter case the term 'summative evaluation' is used to refer to a final test which measures what an individual has learned in the entire programme; and the term 'formative evaluation' is used to refer to testing in the course of the programme, in order to determine what the learner has and has not learned, so that the programme can be adapted to the specific needs of the individual learner.

Not only can one test during or at the end of a teaching programme, but also before the start of the programme. Tests which are used to determine the initial level of proficiency of learners who have enrolled for a particular course in order to be able to assign them to elementary, intermediate or advanced level groups, are called *placement* tests.

Tests which do not assume initial foreign language skills on the part of the learners, but which are intended to provide information on the likelihood of success or failure in language learning, are called *aptitude* tests. These tests have a predictive function; they predict language learning success in an FLT context. A different type of predictive test, which seeks to predict language behaviour in a real-life situation (*proficiency* tests), will be discussed later in this section. We refer the reader to 6.3. for a brief discussion of aptitude tests.

If one wishes to establish what exactly a learner has learned in a given teaching context, we speak of *achievement* tests. Achievement tests are closely related to a curriculum: they only test what has been taught. Achievement tests may be used to measure progress in smaller units within a curriculum – Valette (1977) calls this type of test a progress test – or they may be used as final tests after course completion. What exactly is tested (mastery of linguistic components, or application in actual communicative context) will of course be determined by the objectives of the curriculum.

Diagnostic tests are also closely linked to a particular curriculum. Unlike achievement tests, diagnostic tests do not only provide an impression of the level of proficiency that has been attained, but they should furthermore establish exactly what a learner has or has not mastered, and, ideally speaking, should help to discover the causes of failure. Diagnostic tests should not be used in isolation, but always have a follow-up, in the sense that materials for revision should be provided. Diagnostic tests should provide data which can be used to adapt a teaching programme. This may be done for an entire group, but is usually done for individual learners. This is why diagnostic tests play an important role in differentiated teaching. It will be clear that diagnostic tests provide much more specific information than achievement tests do. Achievement tests answer the question *how much* the learner knows, while diagnostic tests answer the question *what* he knows, and should also help to answer the question *why* he knows or does not know something (Ingram 1968:73). Spolsky (1981:9) summarizes the difference as follows: 'achievement tests . . . are tests with a past orientation, tests that ask, "Has such and such been learned or taught?", and diagnostic tests [are tests] with a future orientation, tests that ask, "Do we need to teach this or is it already known"?' It has often been pointed out, for instance by B. Carroll (1980:81), that global language proficiency tests are of little diagnostic value: diagnostic tests are generally used to test skills or knowledge in isolation, although Oller (1979b) is of the opposite opinion.

A type of test which is not related to any particular curriculum and which one also encounters outside FLT is the *general proficiency* test. Harris (1969:3) describes this type of test as follows: 'a general proficiency test indicates what an individual is capable of doing now (as a result of his cumulative learning experiences), though it may also serve as a basis for predicting future attainment.' We have already seen that proficiency tests are sometimes used for placement. They are also frequently used as an instrument for measuring 'skill for real-life purposes' (Cohen 1979:332). They are then for instance used to predict if someone is sufficiently proficient in a foreign language to pursue a certain profession, or to attend classes in which the target language of the test is also the language of instruction. Cases in point would be for instance language tests for prospective diplomats, or foreign students registering for a university course. Proficiency tests may be direct or indirect assessments of the target skill or skills. Upshur (1979) is of the opinion that proficiency tests can be very good predictors; i.e. that they can give a very good idea of *who is proficient*, but that they provide little explanation of *what proficiency is*. This last fact might well explain why the proficiency test should be the most frequently discussed type of test.

It is hardly surprising that the question of what language proficiency is should be so central especially in proficiency tests. Tests are always operationalizations of objectives; indeed, the operationalization of objectives is often mentioned as one of the functions of tests. In the case of tests which are closely related to a certain curriculum, such as achievement tests, or diagnostic tests, the answer to the question what the objectives of testing are will be largely determined by the nature of the objectives of the curriculum. If there is no such relation between tests and curriculum, selection procedures for testing will have to involve a far larger sample, and decisions on which criteria will be relevant for evaluation will have to be taken. Given our present knowledge of language behaviour and language learning, this is a nearly impossible task. The degree of precision in specification of objectives in terms of content and behaviour is of direct importance for the interpretation of test results.

15.3 Norm-referenced and criterion-referenced measurement

In *norm-referenced* measurement, the *test score* is interpreted in relation to other scores. In *criterion-referenced* measurement, one attempts to produce a clear description of what a testee's performance on a test actually means: in other words, a description of what an individual can or cannot do. Popham (1978:90) says: 'The most fundamental distinction between norm- and criterion-referenced measures hinges on the quality of the descriptions yielded by the two kinds of tests. Traditional [i.e. norm-referenced] measurement people tend to be preoccupied with the creation and refinement of measures that do a dandy job in spreading examinees out so that we can tell who is better or worse than whom.' Norm-referenced measurement is useful if the aim of the test is to make comparisons between individuals. It is, for instance, necessary in a situation where a fixed quota of the best achievers has to be selected. Criterion-referenced measurement is not intended to rank-order testees, i.e. to ascertain a testee's relative status. Criterion-referenced tests want to measure what an individual's status is with respect to a well defined behavioural domain (Popham 1978:94). The items of such tests measure whether or not a learner has mastered a set of specific objectives. It is, therefore, hardly surprising that the demand for criterion-referenced measurement should have developed especially in response to the rise of mastery learning and the emphasis on the use of behavioural objectives in teaching.

Descriptions of what learners will be able to do after instruction that they could not do before, demand a detailed operationalization of objectives. The psychometric descriptions of norm-referenced testing take classical test theory as their starting-point, which is based on a normal distribution of test scores; i.e. a few high scores, a few low scores, and most scores around the mean. This view, however, is not always compatible with pedagogical intentions (Kleber 1979, Popham 1978). The ideal item in a norm-referenced test is one that is scored correct by 50% of the learners. An item which 90% of the learners get right is a bad item in this view, because it hardly differentiates between good and poor learners. If, however, one is interested in the question whether or not a learner has mastered something, such an item might very well be a good item; and the same holds for items which are too difficult. In norm-referenced tests items which are either too easy or too difficult are excluded; a result of this procedure may be that parts of the domain to be tested are excluded from testing.

There is no unanimous agreement in the literature on the desirability or usefulness of criterion-referenced testing. The general tendency is one for caution in dismissing norm-referenced testing, since the statistical framework for criterion-referenced testing is still being developed and has not yet reached the degree of maturity that classical testing theory for norm-referenced measurement has attained. One conclusion which can be drawn in any case is that the better it has been described in advance what mastery of an item means, the better the test scores can be interpreted.

We do, however, have to keep in mind that in both cases the question what exactly the desired level of proficiency is remains unanswered. The outcome of using a norm-referenced test will be a score which can be compared with the scores of a norm group. The outcome of a criterion-referenced test will be a series of statements about the skills or subskills which a learner has or has not mastered. The pass–fail cut-off point will still have to be determined.

15.4 Some general requirements for tests

Tests are means of gathering information. They are constructed according to certain criteria which are intended to safeguard the quality of this information (Kleber 1979). The most important criteria are *reliability* and *validity*.

Before discussing the concepts of reliability and validity we shall make a few brief remarks on the difference between standardized tests and teacher-made tests, as well as on the objectivity of tests, since objectivity is the necessary prerequisite for reliability and validity (see Klein-Braley and Lück 1980).

We cannot make all tests subject to the same stringent demands on quality which, for instance, we subject standardized tests to. 'Standardized tests are designed to make it possible to compare the performance of a particular pupil to the performance of large numbers of other pupils' (Biehler 1978:630). In order to be able to compare the performances of individual learners with each other, the tests that are used have to be objective in a number of respects. Test-conditions and tasks have to be the same for all participants (i.e. they have to be standardized). Objectivity of evaluation is a second very important prerequisite. The instructions for the judges have to be such that different judges, marking a test independently of each other, come up with the same evaluation. Lastly, the test results should not leave room for different interpretations (Kleber 1979). Standardized tests are usually developed by professional teams, consisting of people from different disciplines, and take a lot of time to construct.

Generally, tests produced by classroom teachers do not meet the sometimes perhaps excessively high level of sophistication required for professional tests. This need not be an objection, provided that this limitation is taken into account in decisions taken on the basis of results obtained from such tests. This is also an argument for frequent and varied testing in the classroom. Our description of the requirements for standardized tests is not intended to suggest that these are the only acceptable types of tests. Our main intention is to point out the relevance of these criteria in dealing with standardized tests. All professional tests should include a manual in which the user of the test is informed about the methods used in designing it, the sample on which the norms are calibrated, psychometric aspects, etc. Secondly, these criteria are also important for the classroom teacher to take into account when he constructs and analyses his own tests, and especially when he interprets the results.

15.4.1 Reliability

The extent to which a test is internally consistent and consistent over time is referred to as its reliability. The less reliable a test is the less perfect a reflection it will be of the true level of attainment: 'A test is unreliable if it provides very different results when administered to two different groups of equal ability' (Leemann 1981:119). One way of estimating reliability is to administer the same test twice to the same subjects (*test–retest method*). This method provides an indication of the stability of the test score. The higher the correlation between the two administrations, the higher is the reliability of the test. Another method of estimating reliability is to administer parallel or equivalent forms of a test (*parallel-forms method*). The correlation between the two forms of the test is a measure of their equivalence. In many situations it is not convenient or impossible to administer a test twice or to construct parallel, equivalent tests. Another aspect of the reliability of a test is internal consistency. A fairly simple procedure to estimate internal consistency is the *split-half method*. The test is divided into two halves, usually into odd and even items. Scores are obtained on the two halves and these are correlated. A more sophisticated internal consistency method is the Kuder-Richardson formula 20 (KR20). This formula can be shown to equal the average of all possible split-half reliability coefficients. It is used when the scores are dichotomous (i.e. correct–incorrect). For these ways to estimate reliability see also Hatch and Farhady (1982:243–9).

Another useful indicator for the interpretation of test scores is the standard error of measurement. This statistic provides an estimate of the fluctuation which one might expect in any one individual's performance if he were to do the test several times, which, as we have mentioned before, is an indication of the stability of the test. A test score hardly ever exactly represents the true performance of the testee; it may underestimate or overestimate his performance. In order to prevent wrong conclusions with respect to the performance of a subject, one could, for instance, calculate the standard confidence limits, which is the score plus or minus the standard error of measurement, and conclude that two scores are only then different when the two confidence intervals do not overlap.

There are a number of factors which contribute to a greater degree of reliability and which can be taken into account in the construction or revision of tests. We have already mentioned objectivity. A further factor is the length of a test. A larger number of items will increase the amount of information about the proficiency of the testee. The fact that a wide range in scores increases reliability in traditional reliability analyses, is the reason why one has to be careful in estimating the reliability of criterion-referenced tests on the basis of correlational approaches. Criterion-referenced tests do not automatically produce a set of scores with little or no variance, but scores *can* be uniformly high or low (Popham 1978:143 ff.). The quality of individual test items is, of course, very important. One of the indices for items is the p-value, which indicates degree of difficulty. This index is obtained by dividing the number of items scored correctly by the total number of testees. In norm-referenced tests one aims at p-values between 0.50 and 0.75. In criterion-referenced tests p-values may be higher or lower. In this way one can also calculate the degree of difficulty for each of the distractors in a multiple-choice test; this is called the a-value. An index for the degree to which learners who score correctly on one individual item also do well on the test as a whole is called item–test correlation (r_{it}). This index is used only for dichotomously scored items. As calculating r_{it} is a rather complicated procedure, in practice the d-value, or discrimination value, which is in fact an estimate of r_{it}, is often used instead. The d-value is calculated as follows: testees are rank-ordered and divided into three equal groups (top, middle and bottom), and the following formula is then applied:

$$ d = \frac{\left(\begin{array}{c} \text{Number of correct} \\ \text{answers for top group} \end{array} \right) - \left(\begin{array}{c} \text{Number of correct} \\ \text{answers for bottom group} \end{array} \right)}{1/3 \times \text{total number of testees}} $$

One shold be cautious in applying rules of thumb; a usual target d-value for items is >0.30. In criterion-referenced tests a discrimination-index can be obtained by calculating Dpp (i.e. discrimination post-test (after instruction) – pre-test (before instruction)).

A reliable test, however, is still of little value if it does not measure what it purports to measure. Reliability is a prerequisite for validity: a valid test must be reliable, but a reliable test is not always valid.

15.4.2 Validity

Validity is the most important notion in test evaluation. A general definition is that a test is valid if it measures what it is supposed to measure. Validity, however, is not a property of the test itself: a test will not be valid for all purposes and for all groups. It is essential for test users to define precisely what information they wish to obtain from a test before they can decide whether or not it is valid (see Leemann 1981:116). If we see a test not only as the instrument of measurement itself, but also as including such factors as are mentioned in 15.5, then 'the general purpose of the validation procedure is . . . to investigate the extent to which inferences can properly be drawn from performance' (Palmer and Groot 1981:2).

A validation procedure which is incorporated into the process of test construction itself, and therefore takes place before the test is used, is *content validation*. For content validity it has to be demonstrated that the test measures a representative sample of the behaviour or content domain which one wishes to measure. Content validation, in contrast with other types of validation, is usually based on human judgment. One can also consult experts and use the homogeneity of these judgments as a criterion. In curriculum-related tests the criterion will be the contents of the teaching programme. The content validity of proficiency tests is more difficult to demonstrate because of the fact that language proficiency is difficult to describe adequately.

When test scores are related to some independent – that is external – criterion, a *criterion-related validation* procedure is employed. There are two forms of criterion-related validity. If a test – say an aptitude test – is used to predict future performance – say the scores on a language test after one year of instruction – we are dealing with *predictive validity*. If, however, the scores on one test are compared with the scores on another test administered without any intervening time, we are checking *concurrent validity*. The latter procedure is for example particularly relevant if we wish to replace one test by another test for practical reasons. Criterion-related validation is not a valid procedure for demonstrating what a test actually measures. In that case the validity of the criterion measure will have to be established; in other words, it must be known what it is that the criterion test measures. This is the aim of construct validation (Palmer and Groot 1981:4).

In *construct validation* a test is validated against a theory of the construct to be tested, for instance grammar or speaking ability. Such a theory will have to define what traits are central to the construct in question. The definitions are then operationalized by means of a test, hypotheses are formulated about the relationships between subjects' scores on the various tests, the tests are administered and scored, and finally the obtained results are compared with the hypothesized results. Palmer and Groot (1981:5) give construct validation of communicative competence as an example. Taking Canale and Swain (1980), who consider the construct of communicative competence to consist of linguistic, sociolinguistic and strategic components, as a starting-point, one should be able to make predictions about the degree to which tests measuring each of the individual components separately will correlate with a global communicative competence test.

Canale (1981) points to the relation between test content and test method, and the influence which method factors may have on test scores. In order to determine whether a construct which one intends to test is indeed distinct from any other construct, irrespective of the test method, one uses the multitrait-multimethod convergent–divergent validation procedure. An example of such a procedure is the construct validation of the FSI (Foreign Service Institute) Oral Interview by Bachman and Palmer (1981a, 1981b). In their study, two different constructs (traits), speaking ability and reading ability, were measured in three different ways (methods): interview, translation and self-rating. The hypotheses were, *inter alia*:

(1) The correlation between tests which use different methods to measure the same constructs should be significantly higher than zero and sufficiently large to encourage further examination of validity. High correlations between different methods for measuring the same construct are seen as evidence for convergent validity.
(2) Convergent validity coefficients should be higher than the correlations between tests which measure different constructs by means of the same method.
(3) Convergent validity coefficients should of course be higher than correlations between tests which use different methods to measure different constructs.

Bachman and Palmer (1981b) claim to have engaged in their research because the FSI interview is frequently used as a criterion in criterion-related validation of other oral tests, which makes the need for evidence demonstrating its validity more pressing. Many oral tests are incorrectly claimed to be valid on the basis of their *face validity* (Stevenson 1981). Face validity could be described as the layman's impression of what a test measures. A test must have a certain degree of face validity for the user. If a test does not appear to be measuring what it purports to measure, this could for instance be detrimental to the motivation of the testees, and in this manner influence their test performance. This however, does not mean that a test can be said to be valid only because it has face validity.

15.5 Some relevant factors in language testing

In our discussion of validity we have already argued that a test is more than just the testing instrument itself, and that it includes the whole range of factors which play a role in testing. Canale (1981:84) gives a useful survey of important method factors. In addition to content and purpose of the test, its mode, i.e. whether it is oral or written, receptive or productive, also plays a role. And within these distinctions we can then further differentiate between stimulus and response; orally presented information could for instance be transmitted in written form. The response types may be in discrete point form, or they may be integrative, and they may be intended to measure behaviour directly or indirectly. There may or may not be a time limit on the administration of a test; if the time in which a certain task can be executed is a relevant factor, we speak of speed tests; a test in which time is not a relevant factor is sometimes called a power test (Valette 1977). Test instructions are also relevant. Not only should these be clear to all concerned, but, if the aim is to test objectively, they should also be the same for everybody. Situational factors may play a role: the setting in which a test takes place, and the person administering the test, for instance. One last extremely important factor is scoring; scoring can be done in an objective way or in a more subjective way. In the latter case, not only the type and number of judges play a role, but also especially the criteria which are applied.

The precise role of each of these factors is difficult to determine, because they interact. Which of the variants mentioned should be applied depends entirely on the type of behaviour one wishes to measure, who the testees are, what the purpose of the test is, and what the practical limitations are. If one is of the opinion, for instance, that an oral interview with a person having the same ethnic background, judged by more than one person is the best test, then it will still not be possible to administer this test in a situation in which language skills of hundreds of learners have to be assessed within a short period of time. We shall discuss some of these aspects in the following sections, and more specifically in relation to some types of tests in section 15.6.4., where we shall review a number of test types.

15.5.1 Discrete point and integrative skill testing

As we have seen in the preceding few sections, a discrete point test is analytical in character, and aimed at measuring only one point at a time. A typical discrete point test would for instance be phoneme discrimination as a component of listening proficiency:

(1) bed–bad
(2) man–men
(3) bad–bad

The learner will in each case have to indicate whether the words are the same or different.

An integrative test, on the other hand, measures global skills. In integrative tests all components of language are integrated and tested in combination in a meaningful context. An integrative test may test listening, reading, writing and speaking separately, but need not do so. Oral interviews are a typical example of an integrative test involving more than one skill. This suggests that the difference between the two types of test resides only in the tasks that are set, but the rating procedure also plays a role. If an interview, for instance, is rated exclusively with respect to certain aspects such as pronunciation or morphology and syntax, such a task will tend to be discrete point rather than integrative in character (McCollum and Day 1981). In actual practice a test will hardly ever be purely discrete point or integrative. Rather, these labels are the extremes of a continuum within which all kinds of gradation are possible. Cohen (1980:65) draws a further distinction, namely between direct and indirect tests. This distinction concerns the degree to which a task resembles a normal language use situation. A test may be direct-discrete point (e.g. interview rated on one characteristic only), indirect-discrete point (phoneme recognition), direct-integrative (globally assessed interview), or indirect-integrative (cloze test).

Whether one prefers discrete point tests or integrative tests depends to a large extent on the what and why of testing. In general, discrete point tests are considered suitable for testing linguistic competence especially in the initial stages of the learning process. Especially the diagnostic value of discrete point tests is usually stressed. Cornell (1981) points out the usefulness of discrete point tests in those cases where a high level of accuracy is required, as for instance in teacher training. The most frequently cited arguments against discrete point tests are:

- language proficiency is more than just the sum of discrete elements;
- it is impossible to compile a representative sample from all the elements of a language;
- it is impossible to assess the contribution of the individual elements to the whole;
- there is no sense in isolating elements from their context.

Farhady (1979) concludes from the high correlations between integrative and discrete point tests and from the fact that both types show high loadings on a general factor, that there are no statistical reasons for assuming there to be a difference between the two types. Integrative tests may enjoy a theoretical, but not a statistical superiority over discrete point tests. He then argues for the administration of both types, because different individuals with different backgrounds and characteristics may perform differently on certain kinds of tests. Administering a single type of test may create an artificial bias.

15.5.2 Test format

We shall restrict ourselves to a general discussion of possible formats. For specific information we would like to refer the reader to the publications mentioned in the introduction. Both stimulus and response may be verbal or non-verbal, with pictures being a frequently used type of non-verbal stimulus. A problem with pictures may be that they cannot always be unequivocally interpreted, either because they are simply ambiguous, or because they presuppose a certain cultural background, educational level, socioeconomic status, or age (Cohen 1980:75). A typical example of non-verbal response is physically carrying out tasks. Response types can be divided into the following three main categories: closed-ended, restricted, and open-ended.

Closed-ended tests   It is characteristic of closed-ended tests that the testees themselves do not have to formulate answers. The most frequent types are:

- true/false: a condition for this type of question is that the statement has to be absolutely true or false within the given context;
- matching: here the correct combinations have to be selected from two columns of options;
- multiple-choice: the learner has to select the correct answer from three or more alternatives.

Multiple-choice tests are objective, easy to score and take little time to administer, but they take much time to construct and it is difficult to find good distractors (= 'plausible' wrong answers). One method of finding good distractors is collecting frequent learner errors from open-ended tests. Another drawback is that testees can take a gamble on the correct answer, which Valette (1977:49) sees as a serious problem especially in speed tests, but much less in power tests. Hopkins (1980) remarks that somebody who has only partly mastered the material can still obtain a high score by eliminating the incorrect answers. The remedy he suggests is to make testees indicate for each alternative whether it is correct or not: this he claims to have the advantage that it will discourage guesswork, and it is furthermore quite suitable for language tests, because these allow many correct alternatives. B. Carroll (1980:35) is of the opinion that closed-ended tests should only be used on a limited scale, not only because they do not measure directly, but also because of the possibility that they can have a negative effect on teaching (back-wash). Research has shown that in the Netherlands, where multiple-choice reading comprehension tests form part of the national final examinations, teaching is certainly not completely dominated by these tests. A relatively small amount of teaching time is devoted to training with multiple-choice tests. Only in the final year does one find an increase of such training (Zijlmans and Wesdorp 1979).

Restricted-response tests   In a restricted-response test the answers are formulated by the testees themselves. As the answers are short and predictable, this type of test can be scored objectively. With this type of test it is, however, essential that, before the test is administered, a scoring system is developed which is based on agreements on which responses, which spellings or which pronunciation will be considered acceptable. Restricted-response tests are easy to construct and are frequently used in the classroom. A restricted-response test may require a testee to give a short answer or to fill in a blank, as in for instance:

How much is eight times seven?
Response: (Eight times seven is) fifty-six.
Edinburgh is a large town but London is even ....
Response: larger.

With respect to blank-filling tests Klein-Braley (1981:25) remarks that they are more reliable, more valid and are preferred by teachers. They also yield more diagnostic information than multiple-choice tests do; an opinion shared by Clark (1978).

Open-ended tests In general, open-ended tests are considered to be the most valid type of language test, especially from a communicative point of view. They may be oral or written. One problem in these types of tests is of course comparability: responses may vary quite considerably. Open-ended tests may be made more reliable by standardizing tasks, and by using explicit criteria in rating.

15.5.3 Rating

Closed-ended tests are easy and restricted-response tests are fairly easy to rate, but rating open-ended tests is fraught with problems. Answers are much less predictable, and may vary greatly. Therefore the criteria to be used in rating will have to be agreed on before rating takes place. This may not be easy to achieve: what is, for instance, the relative importance of pronunciation errors and grammatical errors? How does one compare a long answer with many errors to a short answer with few errors? How appropriate is an answer within a given context? In order to make the test more objective, it is often rated by more than one person; this is necessary anyway if one wants to establish the reliability of a rating system. The reliability of the rating of oral and written open-ended tests can be established in two ways. The inter-rater reliability coefficient indicates the degree of agreement between judges. Intra-rater reliability is an indication of the consistency in the rating of one and the same judge rating a test more than once.

There are many ways of assessing subjects' performance on a language test; Valette (1977:44 ff.) contains a survey of various rating procedures. Some rating scales are based on separate ratings of different aspects. A much-used system is the FSI Oral Interview rating technique. In this procedure, accent, grammar, vocabulary, fluency and comprehension are rated separately. This produces an essentially discrete point scale. Other criteria which are used are, for instance, the amount of information given, the effort to communicate, and situational appropriateness. And finally, another common procedure is global assessment, in which there are no subscales for different aspects. A number of researchers have found high correlations between global rating procedures and more analytically oriented ones. Knibbeler (1980) concludes that global assessment produces the same results as an analytic procedure. Mullen (1980) recommends an overall scale as a measurement of oral proficiency on the basis of the fact that the subscales contribute significantly and in equal measure to the overall score. In the same study, she also concludes that it is better to have more than one judge, because individual differences between judges often occur. Callaway (1980:111), too, found that 'all the raters tended to make holistic unidimensional evaluations'. He also found that the ratings of naïve judges were nearly as reliable as those of teachers. Francis (1981) also concludes that there is hardly any difference between impressionistic and analytic methods, and furthermore reports to have found some support for earlier findings that rating live is more reliable than rating from tapes afterwards. Oller (1979b:392) mentions that studies of the FSI Oral Interview have always reported a high degree of reliability; one of the reasons for this is that the interviews are always rated by well trained examiners. Summarizing, we can say that subjective rating may also be reliable, and that, for the purpose of rank-ordering testees, it is not always necessary to score the different aspects separately. This does, of course, not mean that in global assessment it is not necessary to indicate the criteria which will have to be taken into account. It is useful to have more than one judge. Training the examiners will increase reliability, but also teachers and even naïve judges appear to be capable of differentiating between levels of proficiency in a reliable manner.

15.6 Approaches in language testing

We have already pointed out the multidisciplinary character of language testing in the introduction. Insights from linguistics, psychometrics and language pedagogy affect ideas about language testing and its implementation. For this reason, it does not seem useful to use a particular typology of language tests originating from any one of these disciplines as a basis for our discussion. Spolsky (1978c, 1981) distinguishes three main trends in the area of language testing: the pre-scientific or traditional approach, the psychometric-structuralist or modern approach, and the psycholinguistic-sociolinguistic or post-modern approach. He points out that this is an overgeneralization, and that trends overlap both with respect to time and approach. His description does, however, present a clear picture of the developments in this field, and the relative importance of the various disciplines. In this section, we shall devote some further attention to the trends which Spolsky describes, and then discuss some types of tests. In this we shall restrict ourselves to a few types of tests which belong to the most recent approach, the psycholinguistic-sociolinguistic approach. For more detailed information on aspects of tests and test construction, we refer the reader to the literature mentioned in the introduction.

15.6.1 The traditional approach

Spolsky (1978c:217 ff., 1981:14) calls the traditional approach pre-scientific, because it devotes no attention to such matters as reliability and objectivity and does not use statistical methods. It is, therefore, better to call them methods of examining rather than tests. Spolsky characterizes this approach as belonging within the traditional way of thinking: elitist and authoritarian. A justification for the selection of a particular test does not have to be provided and the testees' performance is judged by one person, usually the teacher. Spolsky, incidentally, is far from suggesting that this is done in an irresponsible way. On the contrary, he regards the acknowledgement of personal responsibility as a major advantage of this approach. The most frequently used types of test within the traditional approach are translation, essay-writing, testing knowledge of grammar, and sometimes oral tests. Klein-Braley (1981) points out that the high face validity of these types of test still does not prove them to be truly valid. The subjective character of the assessment makes it difficult to compare results. This raises doubts about the reliability, and, consequently, about the validity of these tests.

15.6.2 The psychometric-structuralist approach

In the traditional approach, measuring language proficiency is not seen as a specific area of scientific interest: it is the concern of teachers. The assumption is that whoever teaches language can also test language. Spolsky (1978c:218 ff.) sees the moment when measurement experts started to become interested in language testing by attacking the reliability of traditional examinations as the start of the modern approach. This approach is mainly characterized by the conviction that 'testing can be objective, precise, reliable, scientific' (Spolsky 1978c:218). This led, on the one hand, to the development of techniques to make traditional tests more reliable, and, on the other hand, to the development of tests with multiple-choice questions. In the initial stages, linguistics had hardly any influence. The link between psychometrics and linguistics is mainly due to Robert Lado. Two of the points which he stressed have become very important: that tests should test language usage and not knowledge about language, and that the structures to be tested should be valid structures in colloquial language use (Klein-Braley:1981). The structuralist sentence-based view of language fitted in quite well with the psychometric quest for samples of individual elements to be tested. This resulted in standardized tests, further divided into subtests, with an emphasis on discrete point items. Klein-Braley (1981) observes in these modern tests a move away from smaller to larger units, and later also a change in the criteria for assessment: student responses should not only be linguistically correct, but also situationally appropriate.

15.6.3 The psycholinguistic-sociolinguistic approach

Whereas in the modern approach psychometrics is the driving force, in the postmodern approach the driving force is linguistics, especially psycholinguistics and sociolinguistics. Spolsky (1978c:225) points out that John B. Carroll emphasized early as 1961 that, in addition to discrete point tests, integrative tests should be used, tests which are not so much aimed at testing separate elements but at measuring 'the total communicative effect of an utterance' (Carroll 1972:318). Directly related to psycholinguistics is the question which plays a central role at this stage, namely: 'what is language competence?'. There exist, roughly speaking, two conflicting views of language competence, namely the divisible competence hypothesis and the unitary competence hypothesis (Vollmer 1981). The first hypothesis presupposes that within language competence, a number of linguistic and non-linguistic competences can be distinguished. The second hypothesis assumes that there is such a thing as overall language proficiency, and that this is based on an underlying linguistic competence. On the basis of the fact that integrative tests correlate more highly with various discrete point tests than discrete point tests do with each other, and because various studies have demonstrated that loadings on a general factor of tests which aim to measure different aspects are higher than loadings on any other factor, Oller (see Oller 1979a, 1979b:424 ff., Oller and Perkins 1980) concludes in favour of unitary competence. His explanation for this is the operation of a pragmatic expectancy grammar (Oller 1978, 1979b):

> The term expectancy grammar calls attention to the peculiarly sequential organization of language in actual use. . . . The term pragmatic expectancy grammar further calls attention to the fact that the sequences of classes of elements, and hierarchies of them which constitute a language are available to the language user in real-life situations because they are somehow indexed with reference to their appropriateness to extralinguistic contexts (Oller 1979b:24).

Vollmer and Sang (1980) criticize the rather rash way in which Oller draws his conclusions, which in their opinion, are neither theoretically nor statistically wholly justified. They claim it is still too early for any clear conclusions to be drawn. The assumption of the existence of some overall language proficiency has led to the development of tests measuring overall proficiency, the most well known ones being cloze tests and dictation tasks.

Related to sociolinguistics is the interest in communicative competence. Research into variation in language use has led to the addition of a functional dimension to language testing. Fishman and Cooper (1978) illustrate with a few examples of contextualized tests that it is necessary to specify the communicative contexts in which the behaviour to be measured occurs. In addition to a specification of the various language use situations which may be relevant to the behaviour to be measured, the appropriateness of an utterance within a certain situational context must be part of the assessment.

In this approach, which is strongly concerned with the validity of tests, the attention is focused on integrative tests, also on the types of tests used in the traditional approach, but this time special care is taken with respect to the psychometric quality of the measuring instruments.

15.6.4 Some recent types of test

In the following few paragraphs we shall discuss a number of direct and indirect tests which have received quite a bit of attention in the recent literature. Indirect tests include, for instance, cloze tests, dictation tests, and editing tests. Unlike direct tests, indirect tests comprise tasks which are far removed from real-life language situations. The value of indirect tests does not reside in their face validity or content validity, but in the degree to which the test scores correlate with more direct measures of language proficiency (Clark 1978:27). Because of the ease with which indirect tests can be constructed, administered and scored, they can, under certain circumstances, be used to obtain an indication of possible performance on direct tests.

15.6.4.1 Cloze procedures

A standard cloze test is a text in which every nth word has been deleted. The testee has to try to restore the text by filling in as many of the deleted words as he can. In doing so, he will use 'linguistic knowledge, textual knowledge and knowledge of the world' (Cohen 1980:97). Initially, cloze tests, which were introduced by Taylor (1953), were used only to determine the readability of texts in the reader's native language and to test the reading skills of native speakers. Later they also came to be used in L2 testing. Initially, the results with cloze tests were not encouraging (Carroll *et al.* 1959). In the 1970s, when cloze tests became very popular, this changed. At present, a lot of the research involving cloze tests is aimed at determining the concurrent validity of the cloze test. In general, cloze tests tend to correlate moderately to highly with standardized tests or parts thereof, although not to the same degree with all types of subtests. Oller (1973) reports high correlations especially with respect to listening comprehension. Mullen (1979b) reports that cloze scores are better predictors of performance on a composition task than of scores on an oral interview. Cohen (1980), on the other hand, mentions a study by Shohamy (1978), in which the correlation between cloze scores and FSI Oral ratings turns out to be between 0.81 and 0.84. Hinofotis (1980) observed the highest correlations between cloze tests and reading subtests of two different test batteries. These findings point to a relation with global skills. Alderson (1979b) found cloze tests to relate more to tests of grammar and vocabulary than to tests of reading comprehension and not to relate more to dictation than to a standardized test consisting of several subtests. His conclusion is that it appears that cloze procedures measure lower-order skills rather than higher-order skills. Klein-Braley (1981) came to similar conclusions when she found the p-values for cloze tests to correlate with the proportions of structure and content words deleted in the various cloze tests. She did an in-depth study of the validity of cloze tests for German university students of English, who form a relatively homogeneous group with the same L1 background. She concluded that cloze tests are not reliable enough for this group and for this purpose, and for this reason advises not to use cloze tests to replace test batteries, but at best to use them as subtests of such batteries. Brière and Hinofotis (1979a) also voice this opinion, though less emphatically, on account of the fact that there exists no clearly preferable procedure to determine cut-off points for decisions about placement, and on account of the lack of face validity of cloze tests. With heterogeneous groups they do, however, find significant correlations with placement exams.

We might conclude that there certainly is a relation between scores on cloze tests and scores on tests measuring different kinds of language proficiency, but that it is not possible to establish exactly what a cloze test does measure.

We have, in the preceding paragraphs, discussed cloze procedures in general. Various researchers have remarked that not all cloze tests are automatically equally reliable and valid, but that these virtues have to be demonstrated for each individual cloze test (Alderson 1979b, Porter 1978, Klein-Braley 1981). The nature and the degree of difficulty of the text in question can have a certain effect. The distance between deleted words can play a role, and especially the scoring procedure is an important factor. Oller (1979b) states that nearly any type of text is suitable, and that the degree of difficulty does not greatly affect the range of scores that will be produced.

There are two methods for deleting words: the *fixed ratio method*, in which every nth word in a passage is deleted, and the *variable ratio method*, in which the words to be omitted are selected on the basis of certain characteristics (e.g. only content words are deleted). Unless a test is intended to measure specific aspects, the fixed ratio method seems preferable.

Cloze tests may be scored in many different ways; one could, for example, give more weight to grammaticality or to appropriateness in context. We shall here only discuss the most current methods. The strictest type of scoring is the *exact word method*, which only counts those words as correct which occurred in the original text. A second method is the *acceptable word method*, which counts every word which is appropriate in the context as correct. It will be clear that the first method is more objective than the second. A comparison of the two scoring methods used for the same test will as a rule yield extremely high correlations, which could lead to the conclusion that it is preferable to use the exact word method. It does, however, have some disadvantages. Many test users do not consider it to be a fair method, and studies involving L2 learners have generally shown it to yield slightly lower correlations with criterion tests than the acceptable word method (Mullen 1979b, Alderson 1979a, Hinofotis 1980). A third, somewhat laborious method, is *clozentropy*, introduced by Darnell (1968), which uses native speakers' responses on a test as the norm: a response becomes more highly valued as it is more frequently given by native speakers. Alderson (1980) calls this method misleading, because there may be a lot of variation in the language proficiency of native speakers: therefore, it cannot be a good criterion.

A variant of the open-ended cloze test discussed above is the multiple-choice cloze test. Hinofotis and Snow (1980) call the results with this test promising, but open-ended tests discriminated better, and correlated slightly more highly with a standard criterion test. A cloze test can also be admininstered in oral form, the oral cloze. Streiff (1978) used this technique with bilingual children and observed that on the basis of the correlation between oral and written cloze procedures, the former could be replaced by the latter for this specific population.

15.6.4.2 Dictation

Traditionally, dictation was seen exclusively as a spelling test, but since Valette (1964) reported high correlations with reading, writing and listening, it has been gaining ground as a general language proficiency test, as will be clear from the following quotation from Oller and Streiff (1975:78): 'Since dictation activates the learner's internalized grammar of expectancy, which we assume is the central component of his language competence, it is not surprising that a dictation test yields substantial information concerning his overall proficiency in the language – indeed, more information than some other tests that have been blessed with greater approval by the "experts".' The psycholinguistic explanation for this is that a learner, in carrying out a dictation task, as in filling in a cloze test, is actively involved in analysis-by-synthesis. A standard dictation task is one in which a learner has to write out in full an orally presented text. The text should not consist of isolated sentences, but should be a piece of discourse. Pauses in presentation should occur at natural boundaries, and they should be spaced so as to 'challenge the limits of the short-term memory of the learners and to force a deeper level of processing than mere phonetic echoing' (Oller 1979b:273). Texts are presented at normal speech rate, usually once as a whole, and then with pauses. Oller (1979b:269) refers to dictation as 'a promising way of investigating how well learners can handle a variety of school-related discourse processing tasks', when texts are selected from the material which is presented to the learners in the normal course of teaching. The scoring procedure usually adopted is to count each correct word and to ignore spelling errors. The reason for this is that spelling has turned out to be practically unrelated to other language skills (Oller 1979b:280 ff., Bacheller 1980:71). It is, of course, not always easy to determine whether an error is a spelling error, or some other type of error. Bacheller (1980) used a Scale of Communicative Effectiveness in scoring dictations and found a correlation of 0.94 with the correct word score.

A variant of dictation is the noise test (Spolsky *et al.* 1968), in which redundancy is reduced by adding white noise; a communicative situation not dissimilar to a bad telephone line. The idea behind this is that the better a person is at understanding such speech, the higher his level of proficiency is. Spolsky *et al.*'s (1968) data point to a relation between scores obtained on noise tests and scores on the usual test batteries. Caulfield and Smith (1981) confirm these findings. Gradman and Gaies (1978), using different white noise levels, found that the noise level did not greatly affect the results. An analysis of the sentences indicated that syntactic and lexical complexity had more influence.

Johansson (1973) reports poor results with noise tests. He found that partial dictations correlated better with other tests measuring language proficiency than noise tests. With partial dictation the entire text is presented in oral form and part of it also in written form. The learner then has to fill in the missing fragments. The whole test is presented orally only once. The length of the pauses is approximately twice the time needed to spell the missing parts. The scoring procedure is again to count each correct word and to ignore spelling errors.

A variant of this procedure, which is sometimes used with children who are not yet fully literate, is elicited imitation, that is to say, children are requested to reproduce orally, not in written form, a text which is presented orally. The scoring procedure can be focused on some aspects, on verbatim repetition, or on content, depending on the purpose of the test. Oller (1979b) assumes there will be a high correlation between verbatim repetition and scores based on content.

15.6.4.3   Editing tasks

In a cloze test the testee has to fill in blanks. In an editing test he has to delete what is alien. An editing test is constructed by randomly inserting new words into an existing test. These words are systematically taken from some other text; e.g. by selecting the second word from the third line on each fourth page. This test was originally developed by Davies as a speeded reading test and formed part of the English Proficiency Test Battery. Bowen (1978) incorporated this test into a proficiency battery and called it neither an overwhelming success nor a hopeless failure. Like Davies (1975), Bowen found the test to be reliable, and to yield correlation coefficients of between 0.46 and 0.74. Mullen (1979a) showed considerably more enthusiasm. She compared an editing test, in this case without time pressure, with cloze test, composition and interview. She also studied scoring procedures. Editing tests may involve two types of error. Either a randomly inserted word is not recognized as such (non-identification), or a word which has not been inserted is crossed out (misidentification). This gives three scoring procedures: the non-identification measure, the misidentification measure, and a combination of the two. The non-identification measure appeared to be superior. Similar conclusions were reached by Migchielsen (1982), who administered an editing test to 350 L2 learners of Dutch aged between 12 and 16. Mullen (1979a) concludes that in her study the editing test was superior to the acceptable-word cloze test because it correlated more highly with composition and interview, and because of the better psychometric quality of the items.

Of each of the three types of test we have discussed it can be said that they are usually reliable measures of language proficiency for groups which are not very homogeneous, that criterion-related research has, in most cases, demonstrated a clear relation to other proficiency tests, but that the interpretation of the scores remains difficult. The scores can only be interpreted in relation to the scores of others on the same test. It is difficult to say what an individual score means.

15.6.4.4   Communicative testing

As we have already seen, the rise of sociolinguistics has brought about a shift of interest from linguistic competence (knowledge of the rules of a language) to communicative competence (knowledge of the rules of language use). This shift can also be observed in FLT, where more and more emphasis is put on actual performance in ordinary situations. Communicative teaching asks for communicative testing. Developments in communicative testing can, therefore, be viewed as attempts to come to terms with the communicative language teaching movement. Testing, on the other hand, requires an explicitation of the theory of language, of languge use, and of language learning (Alderson 1981), and in this way affects the teaching approach. Communicative testing, like communicative teaching, is a relatively recent development. One of the very few publications which contains concrete information about how communicative tests should be designed, administered, and rated is B. Carroll's (1980) 'Testing Communicative Performance', which is cautiously subtitled 'An Interim Study'. Both this publication and Canale and Swain (1980) contain a long list of matters which need further research. One of the characteristics of the communicative approach is a strong emphasis on actual use of language in real-life settings which have to be based on the communicative needs of the learners. A result of this for testing is that there is no need for one overall test of language proficiency, but rather for a collection of tasks at different levels, which have to resemble authentic situations as closely as possible. These tests should answer the question of what a candidate can do, which in turn implies that they are performance tests (Morrow 1979).

This gives rise, as Morrow (1979) also indicates, to a number of problems. In the first place there is the problem of sampling and extrapolation. Which tasks should be selected, how representative are they, and what predictions can be made on the basis of performance on one task about performance on other tasks? Secondly, one might wonder in how far conditions for actual real-life communication are replicable in a test situation (Weir 1980). Lastly, there is the problem of assessment. As performance tests are necessarily integrative tests, quantitative assessment procedures are unsuitable, and what is needed is qualitative assessment (Morrow 1979:151). This type of assessment is less objective, which in turn will affect reliability. One sometimes finds 'banded' mark schemes used for assessment of levels of proficiency. Such schemes consist of a set of descriptions of what a candidate can or cannot do, and which strategies he uses at different levels. Such descriptions are based on criteria such as accuracy, appropriateness, flexibility, etc. (B. Carroll 1980). The examiner scores the test impressionistically, and assigns the band of the mark scheme which is most appropriate to the candidate's performance.

The literature on communicative testing contains more information about testing productive skills than about testing receptive skills. In testing receptive skills one can apply criteria for what should be understood in terms of size, complexity etc., but it is much more difficult to discover what strategies and skills the learners use. Morrow (1979) therefore suggests focusing the questions on so-called enabling skills. These are skills which are used to execute global tasks. Enabling skills in globally understanding a reading text are, for instance, understanding text relations through grammatical cohesion devices, or deducing meaning of unfamiliar lexis (cf. Munby 1978). As with linguistic discrete point items, one might wonder what the contribution of an enabling skill is to the whole of language proficiency. It is furthermore not at all clear which enabling skills do play a role, or whether they are enabling skills in the first place (Alderson 1981).

Concluding, one might say that communicative testing is still in its infancy. Far too little is known about the grammar of language in use to systematically base tests on it. There are as yet no clear results of empirical research into communicative testing. In general, however, the idea of testing the effects of communicative teaching by means of communicative tests is met with approval. It has some clear advantages; the behaviour-oriented character, the specification of language use, and the close relation to learner needs. But one should exercise caution in exclusively using communicative tests.

15.7 Conclusion

Not all tests can be used in all situations. A number of questions have to be answered before we can establish whether a test is suitable or not. In this chapter, we have first of all discussed the purpose and function of tests, and we have shown that in many cases the purpose of a test affects the nature of the test. We then argued that the purpose of a test can also affect the nature of measurement. If the purpose of the test is a selective one, norm-referenced measurement is appropriate. If the purpose is diagnostic, criterion-referenced measurement is an obvious choice. Two criteria are extremely important for the quality of a test, namely reliability and validity. As we have seen in various places in this chapter, there exists a certain tension between these two criteria. In tests where there is a strong emphasis on reliability, one could often question the validity, and vice versa. We then observed that in a discussion of testing, all factors affecting tests should play a role, to stress the fact that each of these factors should be taken into account in using or constructing tests. In our discussion we have gone a bit more deeply into the difference between discrete point tests and integrative tests, into test formats, and into the rating of oral and written utterances. Lastly, we have used Spolsky's (1978a, 1981) division into different trends in order to present a general picture of developments in the area of language testing and to be able to account for these developments. In doing so, we have not discussed all possible types of tests, but we have restricted ourselves to discussing cloze tests, dictation tests and editing tests, which are representative of indirect overall language proficiency tests, and communicative tests, which can be characterized as direct tests.

At the end of our discussion of communicative tests we observed that one generally warns against only using such tests. This could be reiterated for all types of tests. We have repeatedly stressed the importance of using more than one type of test. It is advisable to use more than one measurement procedure for two reasons. First of all, there is a considerable risk that a test of a certain type will systematically fail to do justice to particular testees. Secondly, there is a serious risk that learners will adapt their learning behaviour to the test, and this might lead to the neglect of certain skills which are not tested. This so-called 'back-wash' effect will be aggravated if a certain skill is tested exclusively by means of a certain method: the curriculum might then be determined by the test.

Bibliography

Aaronson, D., R. Rieber (eds.) (1975), *Developmental psycholinguistics and communication disorders*, New York 1975.

Abbott, G. (1980), Towards a more rigorous analysis of foreign language errors, *International Review of Applied Linguistics in Language Teaching* 18, 1980, 121-34.

Agard, F., R. DiPietro (1965a), *The grammatical structures of English and Italian*, Chicago 1965.

Agard, F., R. DiPietro (1965b), *The sounds of English and Italian*, Chicago 1965.

Agnew, N., S. Pyke (1978), *The science game: an introduction to research in the behavioral sciences*, Englewood Cliffs, NJ 1978, 2nd ed.

Ahrens, R. (1980), Visuelle Medien und Unterrichtsphasen im fremdsprachlichen Anfangsunterricht, *Die Neueren Sprachen* 79, 1980, 361-77.

Alatis, J. (ed.) (1968), *Contrastive linguistics and its pedagogical implications*, Washington, DC 1968.

Alatis, J. (ed.) (1970), *Linguistics and the teaching of standard English to speakers of other languages*, Washington, DC 1970.

Alatis, J. (1976), Teaching foreign languages – why? A new look at an old question, *Foreign Language Annals* 9, 1976, 447-58.

Alatis, J., H. Altman, P. Alatis (eds.) (1981), *The second language classroom: directions for the 1980s*, Oxford 1981.

Albert, M., L. Obler (1978), *The bilingual brain. Neurolinguistic aspects of bilingualism*, New York 1978.

Alderson, J. (1979a), Scoring procedures for use on cloze tests, in: Yorio *et al.* (1979), 193-205.

Alderson, J. (1979b), The cloze procedure and proficiency in English as a foreign language, *TESOL Quarterly* 13, 1979, 219-27.

Alderson, J. (1980), Native and nonnative speaker performance on cloze tests, *Language Learning* 30, 1980, 59-76.

Alderson, J. (1981), Reaction to the Morrow paper (3), in: Alderson and Hughes (1981), 45-54.

Alderson, J., A. Hughes (eds.) (1981), *Issues in language testing*, London 1981.

Alexander, L. (1976), Where do we go from here? A reconsideration of some basic assumptions affecting course design, *English Language Teaching Journal* 30, 1976, 89-103.

Alexander, L. (1977), *Some methodological implications of Waystage and Threshold Level*, Strasbourg 1977.

Alexander, L. (1979), A functional/notional approach to course design, *Audio-Visual Language Journal* 17, 1979, 109-13.

Alexander, L. (1981), Materials design: issues for the 1980s. A European point of view, in: Alatis *et al.* (1981), 245-65.

Allen, H., R. Campbell (eds.) (1972), *Teaching English as a second language: a book of readings*, New York 1972. 2nd ed.

Allen, J., S. Corder (eds.) (1973), *Readings for applied linguistics*, The Edinburgh

Course in Applied Linguistics, vol. 1, London 1973.

Allen, J., S. Corder (eds.) (1974), *Techniques in applied linguistics*, The Edinburgh Course in Applied Linguistics, vol. 3, London 1974.

Allen, J., S. Corder (eds.) (1975), *Papers in applied linguistics*, The Edinburgh Course in Applied Linguistics, vol. 2, London 1975.

Allen, J., A. Davies (eds.) (1977), *Testing and experimental methods*, The Edinburgh Course in Applied Linguistics, vol. 4, London 1977.

Allwright, R. (1980), Turns, topics, and tasks: patterns of participation in language learning and teaching, in: Larsen-Freeman (1980), 165–87.

Altman, H. (ed.) (1972), *Individualizing the foreign language classroom. Perspectives for teachers*, Rowley, Mass. 1972.

Altman, H., R. Politzer (eds.) (1971), *Individualizing foreign language instruction*, Rowley, Mass. 1971.

Andersen, R. (1977), The impoverished state of cross-sectional morpheme acquisition/accuracy methodology (or: the leftovers are more nourishing than the main course), *Working Papers on Bilingualism* 14, 1977, 47–82.

Andersen, R. (1978), An implicational model for second language research, *Language Learning* 28, 1978, 221–82.

Andersson, T. (1969), *Foreign languages in the elementary school. A struggle against mediocrity*, Austin 1969.

d'Anglejan, A., G. Tucker (1975), The acquisition of complex English structures by adult learners, *Language Learning* 25, 1975, 281–96.

Arabski, J. (1973), Selected bibliography on error analysis and related areas, in: Svartvik (1973), 161–71.

Aristizabal, G. (1938), *Détermination expérimentale du vocabulaire écrit pour servir à l'enregistrement de l'orthographe à l'école primaire*, Louvain 1938.

Arthur, B., R. Weiner, M. Culver, Y. Lee (1980), The register of imperial discourse to foreigners: verbal adjustments to foreign accent, in: Larsen-Freeman (1980), 111–24.

Asher, J., R. Garcia (1969), The optimal age to learn a foreign language, *The Modern Language Journal* 53, 1969, 334–41.

Asher, J., J. Kusudo, R. De la Torre (1974), Learning a second language through commands: the second field test, *The Modern Language Journal* 58, 1974, 24–32.

Atkinson, R. (1975), RP and English as a world language, *International Review of Applied Linguistics in Language Teaching* 13, 1975, 69–72.

Ausubel, D. (1964), Adults versus children in second-language learning: psychological considerations, *The Modern Language Journal* 48, 1964, 420–4.

Ausubel, D. (1968), *Educational psychology. A cognitive view*, New York 1968.

Ayton, A., M. Morgan (1981), *Photographic slides in language teaching. Practical language teaching No. 6*, London 1981.

Bacheller, F. (1980), Communicative effectiveness as predicted by judgement of the severity of learner errors in dictations, in: Oller and Perkins (1980), 66–71.

Bachman, L., A. Palmer (1981a), A multitrait-multimethod investigation into the construct validity of six tests of speaking and reading, in: Palmer *et al.* (1981), 149–65.

Bachman, L., A. Palmer (1981b), The construct validity of the FSI Oral Interview, *Language Learning* 31, 1981, 67–86.

Back, O. (1970), Was bedeutet und was bezeichnet der Ausdruck 'angewandte Sprachwissenschaft'?, *Die Sprache* 16, 1970, 21–53.

Bailey, K., M. Celce-Murcia (1979), Classroom skills for ESL teachers, in: Celce-Murcia and McIntosh (1979), 315–31.

Bailey, N., C. Madden, S. Krashen (1974), Is there a 'natural sequence' in adult second language learning?, *Language Learning* 24, 1974, 235–43.

Baldegger, M., M. Müller, G. Schneider, A. Näf (1980), *Kontaktschwelle Deutsch als Fremdsprache*, Strasbourg 1980.

Banathy, B., J. Sawyer (1969), The primacy of speech: an historical sketch, *The Modern Language Journal* 53, 1969, 537–44.

Barrera-Vidal, A., W. Kühlwein (1975), *Angewandte Linguistik für den fremdsprachlichen Unterricht*, Dortmund 1975.

Barrera-Vidal, A., W. Kühlwein (eds.) (1977), *Kritische Bibliographie zur Angewandten Linguistik, Fachbereich Französisch*, Dortmund 1977.

Bartel, K. (1974), Selecting the foreign language textbook, *The Modern Language Journal* 58, 1974, 326–9.

Basser, L. (1962), Hemiplegia of early onset and the faculty of speech with special reference to the effects of hemispherectomy, *Brain* 85, 1962, 427–60.

Bausch, K. (1974), Vorwort, *Zeitschrift für Literaturwissenschaft und Linguistik* 13, 1974, 7–12.

Bausch, K. (1977), Kontrastive Linguistik und Fehleranalyse, in: Kühlwein and Barrera-Vidal (1977), Lfrg. 7.

Bausch, K. (ed.) (1979), *Beiträge zur Didaktischen Grammatik. Probleme, Konzepte, Beispiele*, Königstein/Ts 1979.

Bausch, K., U. Bliesener, H. Christ, K. Schröder, U. Weisbrod (eds.) (1978), *Beiträge zum Verhältnis von Fachsprache und Gemeinsprache im Fremdsprachenunterricht der Sekundarstufe II*, Bochum 1978.

Beheydt, L. (1974), Foreign language teaching methodology. A critical discussion, *ITL Review of Applied Linguistics* 23, 1974, 39–57.

Beile, W. (1979), *Typologie von Übungen im Sprachlabor. Zur Entmythologisierung eines umstrittenen Sachfelds*, Frankfurt/M. 1979.

Bell, R. (1973), The English of an Indian immigrant: an essay in error analysis, *ITL Review of Applied Linguistics* 22, 1973, 11–61.

Bell, R. (1974), Error analysis: a recent pseudoprocedure in applied linguistics, *ITL Review of Applied Linguistics* 25/26, 1974, 35–51.

Bell, R. (1976), *Sociolinguistics*, London 1976.

Bender, J. (1979), *Zum gegenwärtigen Stand der Diskussion um Sprachwissenschaft und Sprachunterricht*, Frankfurt/M. 1979.

Bennett, S. (1975), Weighing the evidence: a review of Primary French in the balance, *British Journal of Educational Psychology* 45, 1975, 337–40.

Benseler, D., R. Schulz (1980), Methodological trends in college foreign language instruction, *The Modern Language Journal* 64, 1980, 88–96.

Berens, F. (1979), Das Freiburger Korpus gesprochener deutscher Standardsprache: Möglichkeiten seiner Auswertung am Beispiel der Untersuchung der Lexeme Freude und freuen und ihrer Ableitungen, in: Bergenholtz and Schaeder (1979), 268–80.

Berg, D. (1976), *Differenzierung im Englischanfangsunterricht. Eine empirische Studie*, Stuttgart 1976.

Bergenholtz, H., B. Schaeder (eds.) (1979), *Empirische Textwissenschaft. Aufbau und Auswertung von Text-Corpora*, Königstein/Ts 1979.

Berman, R. (1978), Contrastive analysis revisited; obligatory, systematic, and incidental differences between languages, *Interlanguage Studies Bulletin* 3, 2, 1978, 212–33.

Berman, R. (1979), Rule of grammar or rule of thumb?, *International Review of Applied Linguistics in Language Teaching* 17, 1979, 279–302.

Besse, H. (1975), Traduction et didactique des langues, I and II, *Die Neueren Sprachen*, 74, 3, 1975, 238–48, and 74, 4, 1975, 339–53.

Besse, H. (1979), Contribution à l'histoire du français fondamental, *Le Français dans le monde* 148, 1979, 23–30.

Bianchi, M. (1977a), Lernzielorientierte Fremdsprachenprüfungen in der Erwachsenenbildung, in: Kühlwein, W., A. Raasch (eds.), *Kongressberichte der 7. Jahrestagung der Gesellschaft für Angewandte Linguistik GAL*, vol. 2, Stuttgart 1977, 151–66.

Bianchi, M. (1977b), The 'new' Volkshochschul-Certificate in English, *Zielsprache Englisch* 7, 3, 1977, 30–3.

Biehler, R. (1978), *Psychology applied to teaching*, Boston 1978.

Bilodeau, E. (ed.) (1966), *Acquisition of skill*, New York/London 1966.

Blanc, M., P. Biggs (1971), L'enquête socio-linguistique sur le français parlé à Orleans, *Le Français dans le monde* 85, 1971, 16-25.

Bloomfield, L. (1933), *Language*, New York 1933.

Bloomfield, L. (1942), *Outline guide for the practical study of foreign languages*, Baltimore 1942.

Blum, S., E. Levenston (1978), Universals of lexical simplification, *Language Learning* 28, 1978, 399-415.

Blumenthal, A. (1970), *Language and psychology: historical aspects of psycholinguistics*, New York 1970.

Boekaerts, M. (1979), *Towards a theory of learning based on individual differences*, Ghent 1979.

Bogenschneider, K. (1982), Die Entwicklung der VHS-Sprachenzertifikate beobachtet und miterlebt, *Zielsprache Englisch* 14, 1, 1982, 26-31.

Bolinger, D. (1968), The theorist and the language teacher, *Foreign Language Annals* 2, 1968, 30-41.

Bongaerts, T. (1983), The comprehension of three complex English structures by Dutch learners, *Language Learning* 33, 1983, 159-82.

Bongers, H. (1947a), *The history and principles of vocabulary control*, Woerden 1947.

Bongers, H. (1947b), *Three Thousand-Word English*, Amsterdam 1947.

Boot, M. (1976), Auteur en informant, *Levende Talen* 316, 1976, 71-85.

Borel, J. (1970), L'emploi de l'image dans l'enseignement des langues, *Bulletin CILA* 11, 1970, 51-6.

Bortolini, U., C. Tagliavini, A. Zampolli (1971), *Lessico di frequenza della lingua italiana contemporanea*, IBM Italia 1971. Also Milano 1972.

Bosco, F., R. DiPietro (1970), Instructional strategies: their psychological and linguistic bases, *International Review of Applied Linguistics in Language Teaching* 8, 1970, 1-19.

Bourgain, D. (1978), Attitudes et apprentissage, in: Ferenczi, V. (ed.), *Psychologie, langage et apprentissage*, Paris 1978, 67-84.

Bouton, C. (1978), *La linguistique appliquée*, Paris 1978.

Bouton, L. (1976), The problem of equivalence in contrastive analysis, *International Review of Applied Linguistics in Language Teaching* 14, 1976, 143-63.

Bowen, J. (1978), The identification of irrelevant lexical distraction: an editing task, *TESL Reporter* 12, 1978, 1-3 and 14-16.

Bowen, J. (1979), Contextualizing pronunciation practice in the ESOL classroom, in: Celce-Murcia and McIntosh (1979), 101-10.

Breen, M., C. Candlin (1981), *The communicative curriculum in language teaching*, London 1981.

Brière, E., F. Hinofotis (1979a), Cloze test cutoff points for placing students in ESL classes, in: Brière and Hinofotis (1979b), 12-20.

Brière, E., F. Hinofotis (eds.) (1979b), *Concepts in language testing*, Washington, DC 1979.

Brooks, N. (1964), *Language and language learning. Theory and practice*, New York 1964.

Brooks, N. (1975), The meaning of audiolingual, *The Modern Language Journal* 54, 1975, 234-40.

Broughton, G., C. Brumfit, R. Flavell, P. Hill, A. Pincas (1980), *Teaching English as a foreign language*, London 1980.

Brown, H. (1973), Affective variables in second language acquisition, *Language Learning* 23, 1973, 231-44.

Brown, H. (1977), Cognitive and affective characteristics of good language learners, in: Henning (1977), 349-54.

Brown, H. (1980), *Principles of language learning and teaching*, Englewood Cliffs, NJ 1980.

Brown, R. (1973), *A first language. The early stages*, London 1973.

Brown, R., U. Bellugi (1964), Three processes in the child's acquisition of syntax, *Harvard Educational Review* 34, 1964, 133–51.

Brown, R., C. Cazden, U. Bellugi (1968), The child's grammar from 1 to 3, in: Hill, J. (ed.), *The 1967 Minnesota symposium on child psychology*, Minneapolis 1968, 28–73.

Brumfit, C. (1978a), 'Communicative' language teaching: an assessment, in: Strevens, P. (ed.), *In honour of A.S. Hornby*, London 1978, 33–44.

Brumfit, C. (1978b), Review of D. Wilkins, 'Notional syllabuses', *English Language Teaching Journal* 33, 1978, 79–82.

Brumfit, C. (1979), Notional syllabuses – a reassessment, *System* 7, 1, 1979, 111–16.

Brumfit, C. (1980), Being interdisciplinary – some problems facing applied linguistics, *Applied Linguistics* 1, 2, 1980, 158–64.

Brumfit, C., K. Johnson (eds.) (1979), *The communicative approach to language teaching*, London 1979.

Buchanan, M. (1927), *A graded Spanish word book*, Toronto 1927.

Buckby, M. (1976), Is Primary French really in the balance?, *The Modern Language Journal* 60, 1976, 340–6.

Bühler, U. (1972), *Empirische und lernpsychologische Beiträge zur Wahl des Zeitpunktes für den Fremdsprachunterrichtsbeginn*, Zürich 1972.

Bung, P. (1977), *Systematische Lehrwerkanalyse*, Kastellaun 1977.

Burstall, C. (1975), Factors affecting foreign language learning: a consideration of some recent research findings, *Language Teaching & Linguistics: Abstracts* 8, 1, 1975, 5–25.

Burstall, C., M. Jamieson, S. Cohen, M. Hargreaves (1974), *Primary French in the balance*, Windsor 1974.

Burt, M., H. Dulay (eds.) (1975), *New directions in second language learning, teaching and bilingual education*, Washington, DC 1975.

Burt, M., H. Dulay (1980), On acquisition orders, in: Felix (1980), 265–327.

Burt, M., H. Dulay, M. Finocchiaro (eds.) (1977), *Viewpoints on English as a second language*, New York 1977.

Burt, M., H. Dulay, E. Hernández (1973), *Bilingual Syntax Measure*, New York 1973.

Burt, M., C. Kiparsky (1975), Global and local mistakes, in: Schumann and Stenson (1975), 71–80.

Busch, D. (1982), Introversion-extraversion and the EFL proficiency of Japanese students, *Language Learning* 32, 1982, 109–32.

Buttjes, D. (1980), Schulfernsehen im Englischunterricht: fach- und medienspezifische Leistungen am Beispiel des Westdeutschen Schulfernsehens, *Die Neueren Sprachen* 79, 1980, 378–95.

Butzkamm, W. (1973), *Aufgeklärte Einsprachigkeit. Zur Entdogmatisierung der Methode im Fremdsprachenunterricht*, Heidelberg 1973.

Butzkamm, W. (1976), Methodenstreit und kein Ende – 10 Thesen zur Konzeption und Rezeption der aufgeklärten Einsprachigkeit, *Praxis des neusprachlichen Unterrichts* 23, 1976, 227–35.

Butzkamm, W. (1978), Zur Frage der Textinhalte im fremdsprachlichen Anfangsunterricht, *Praxis des neusprachlichen Unterrichts* 25, 1978, 148–52.

Butzkamm, W. (1979), Zur Rolle der Muttersprache im Fremdsprachenunterricht – die Entwicklung in den siebziger Jahren, in: Kleine (1979), 172–8.

Butzkamm, W. (1980a), *Praxis und Theorie der bilingualen Methode*, Heidelberg 1980.

Butzkamm, W. (1980b), Verbal play and pattern practice. The comparison of a L1 learning strategy and a L2 teaching technique, in: Felix (1980), 233–48.

Callaway, D. (1980), Accent and the evaluation of ESL oral proficiency, in: Oller and

Perkins (1980), 102-11.

Canale, M. (1981), Communication: how to evaluate it?, *Bulletin de l'ACLA* 3, 2, 1981, 77-94.

Canale, M., M. Swain (1980), Theoretical bases of communicative approaches to second language teaching and testing, *Applied Linguistics* 1, 1980, 1-47.

Cancino, H., E. Rosansky, J. Schumann (1974), Testing hypotheses about second language acquisition: the copula and negative in three subjects, *Working Papers on Bilingualism* 3, 1974, 80-96.

Cancino, H., E. Rosansky, J. Schumann (1978), The acquisition of English negatives and interrogatives by native Spanish speakers, in: Hatch (1978), 207-30.

Candlin, C. (1972), Sociolinguistics and communicative language teaching, *ITL Review of Applied Linguistics* 16, 1972, 37-44.

Candlin, C. (1973), The status of pedagogical grammars, in: Corder, S., E. Roulet (eds.), *Theoretical linguistic models in applied linguistics*, Brussels/Paris 1973, 55-64.

Candlin, C., M. Breen (1979), Evaluating and designing language teaching materials, *Practical Papers in English Language Education* 2, 1979, 172-216.

Cárdenas, D. (1961), The application of linguistics in the teaching of Spanish, in: Belasco, S. (ed.), *Anthology for use with A Guide for Teachers in NDEA Language Institutes*, Boston 1961, 175-80. Reprinted from: *Hispania* 40, 1957, 455-60.

Carpay, J., E. Bol (1974), *Engels in het basisonderwijs. Een studie op het gebied van de leerplanontwikkeling*, Den Bosch 1974.

Carroll, B. (1980), *Testing communicative performance. An interim study*, Oxford 1980.

Carroll, F. (1980), Neurological processing of a second language: experimental evidence, in: Scarcella and Krashen (1980), 81-6.

Carroll, J. (1958), A factor analysis of two foreign language aptitude batteries, *Journal of General Psychology* 59, 1958, 3-19.

Carroll, J. (1962), The prediction of success in intensive foreign language training, in: Glaser, R. (ed.), *Training research and education*, Pittsburgh 1962, 87-136.

Carroll, J. (1963), A primer of programmed instruction in foreign language teaching, *International Review of Applied Linguistics in Language Teaching* 1, 1963, 115-41.

Carroll, J. (1966), The contributions of psychological theory and educational research to the teaching of foreign languages, in: Valdman (1966), 93-106.

Carroll, J. (1968), Psychological aspects of programmed learning in foreign languages, In: Mueller (1968a), 63-73.

Carroll, J. (1972), Fundamental considerations in testing for English language proficiency of foreign students, in: Allen and Campbell (1972), 313-21.

Carroll, J. (1973), Implications of aptitude test research and psycholinguistic theory for foreign-language teaching, *International Journal of Psycholinguistics* 2, 1973, 5-13.

Carroll, J. (1974), Learning theory for the classroom teacher, in: Jarvis (1974), 113-49.

Carroll, J. (1975), *The teaching of French as a foreign language in eight countries*, New York 1975.

Carroll, J. (1977), Characteristics of successful second language learners, in: Burt *et al.* (1977), 1-7.

Carroll, J. (1981), Twenty-five years of research on foreign language aptitude, in: Diller (1981), 83-118.

Carroll, J., A. Carton, C. Wilds (1959), *An investigation of cloze items in the measurement of achievement in foreign languages*, Cambridge, Mass. 1959.

Carroll, J., P. Davies, B. Richman (1971), *The American Heritage word frequency book*, New York 1971.

Carroll, J., S. Sapon (1959), *Modern language aptitude test*, New York 1959.

Carroll, J., S. Sapon (1967), *Modern language aptitude test - elementary*, New York 1967.

Caulfield, J., W. Smith (1981), The reduced redundancy test and the cloze procedure as measures of global language proficiency, *The Modern Language Journal* 65, 1981, 54-8.

Celce-Murcia, M. (1979), Language teaching aids, in: Celce-Murcia and McIntosh (1979), 307-15.

Celce-Murcia, M., L. McIntosh (eds.) (1979), *Teaching English as a second or foreign language*, Rowley, Mass. 1979.

Celce-Murcia, M., F. Rosensweig (1979), Teaching vocabulary in the ESL classroom, in: Celce-Murcia and McIntosh (1979), 241-57.

Chastain, K. (1970), Behavioristic and cognitive approaches in programmed instruction, *Language Learning* 20, 1970, 223-35.

Chastain, K. (1975a), Affective and ability factors in second-language acquisition, *Language Learning* 25, 1975, 153-61.

Chastain, K. (1975b), An examination of the basic assumptions of 'individualized' instruction, *The Modern Language Journal* 59, 1975, 334-44.

Chastain, K. (1976), *Developing second-language skills: theory to practice*, Chicago 1976. 2nd ed.

Chihara, T., J. Oller (1978), Attitudes and attained proficiency in EFL: a sociolinguistic study of adult Japanese speakers, *Language Learning* 28, 1978, 55-68.

Chomsky, C. (1969), *The acquisition of syntax in children from 5 to 10*, Cambridge, Mass. 1969.

Chomsky, C. (1972), Stages in language development and reading exposure, *Harvard Educational Review* 42, 1972, 1-33.

Chomsky, N. (1959), Review of: B. F. Skinner, Verbal Behavior 1957, *Language* 35, 1959, 26-58.

Chomsky, N. (1965), *Aspects of the theory of syntax*, Cambridge, Mass. 1965.

Chomsky, N. (1966), Linguistic theory, in: Mead, R. (ed.), *Language teaching: broader contexts*, New York 1966, 43-9.

Chomsky, N. (1968), BBC-interview, *The Listener* 79, 1968, 685-91.

Christ, H. (1980), *Fremdsprachenunterricht und Sprachenpolitik*, Stuttgart 1980.

Christ, H., E. Liebe (eds.) (1979), *Dokumente zur Schulsprachenpolitik in der Bundesrepublik Deutschland*, Augsburg 1979.

Christ, H., E. Liebe (eds.) (1981), *Fremdsprachenunterricht in amtlichen Verlautbarungen*, Augsburg 1981.

Christ, H., K. Schröder, H. Weinrich, F. Zapp (1980), *Fremdsprachenpolitik in Europa. Homburger Empfehlungen für eine sprachenteilige Gesellschaft*, Augsburg 1980.

CILT (1973), *Word-lists based on frequency studies*, select list 5, London 1973. 2nd ed.

Claessen, J. (1980), *Moderne vreemde talen uit balans. Een onderzoek naar behoeften aan moderne vreemde talen in relatie tot het vreemde-talenonderwijs*, The Hague 1980.

Claessen, J., A. van Galen, M. Oud-de Glas (1978a), *De behoeften aan moderne vreemde talen. Een onderzoek onder leerlingen, oud-leerlingen en scholen*, studies over het onderwijs in de moderne vreemde talen IV, ITS, Nijmegen 1978.

Claessen, J., A. van Galen, M. Oud-de Glas (1978b), *De behoeften aan moderne vreemde talen. Een onderzoek onder stafleden en studenten van universiteiten en hogescholen*, studies over het onderwijs in de moderne vreemde talen V, ITS, Nijmegen 1978.

Claessen, J., A. van Galen, M. Oud-de Glas (1978c), *De behoeften aan moderne vreemde talen. Een onderzoek onder bedrijven en overheidsdiensten*, studies over het onderwijs in de moderne vreemde talen VI, ITS, Nijmegen 1978.

Claessen, J., A. van Galen, M. Oud-de Glas (1978d), Foreign language needs in the Netherlands: an educational research project, paper, AILA congress, Montréal 1978.

Clark, H., E. Clark (1977), *Psychology and language. An introduction to psycholinguistics*, New York 1977.

Clark, J. (1972), *Foreign language testing. Theory and practice*, Philadelphia 1972.

Clark, J. (1978), Psychometric considerations in language testing, in: Spolsky (1978a), 15–30.

Clément, R., R. Gardner, P. Smythe (1977a), Interethnic contact: attitudinal consequences, *Canadian Journal of Behavioural Science* 9, 1977, 205–15.

Clément, R., L. Major, R. Gardner, P. Smythe (1977b), Attitudes and motivation in second-language acquisition: an investigation of Ontario francophones, *Working Papers on Bilingualism* 12, 1977, 1–20.

Clément, R., P. Smythe, R. Gardner (1978), Persistence in second-language study: motivational considerations, *The Canadian Modern Language Review* 34, 1978, 688–94.

Clyne, M. (1978), Some remarks on foreigner talk, in: Dittmar, N. (ed.), *Papers from the first Scandinavian-German symposium on the language of immigrant workers and their children*, Roskilde 1978, 155–69.

Cohen, A. (1979), Second language testing, in: Celce-Murcia and McIntosh (1979), 331–60.

Cohen, A. (1980), *Testing language ability in the classroom*, Rowley, Mass. 1980.

Cole, L. (1968), Entender y hablar: a user's report, *Audio-Visual Language Journal* 5, 1968, 137–42.

Coleman, A. (1929), *The teaching of modern foreign languages in the United States*, New York 1929.

Comenius, J. (1967), *Orbis sensualium pictus*, Sydney 1967. Facsimile of the 3rd London ed. 1672.

Condon, E. (1975), The cultural context of language testing, in: Palmer, A., B. Spolsky (eds.), *Papers on language testing 1967–1974*, Washington, DC 1975, 205–17.

Cooper, R., J. Fishman (1977), A study of language attitudes, in: Fishman, J., R. Cooper, A. Conrad (eds.), *The spread of English. The sociology of English as an additional language*, Rowley, Mass. 1977, 239–76.

Cooper, R., E. Olshtain, G. Tucker, M. Waterbury (1979), The acquisition of complex English structures by adult native speakers of Arabic and Hebrew, *Language Learning* 29, 1979, 255–75.

Corder, S. (1967), The significance of learner's errors, *International Review of Applied Linguistics in Language Teaching* 5, 1967, 161–70.

Corder, S. (1971), Idiosyncratic dialects and error analysis, *International Review of Applied Linguistics in Language Teaching* 9, 1971, 147–60.

Corder, S. (1972), La linguistique appliquée: interprétations et pratiques diverses, *Bulletin CILA* 16, 1972, 6–28.

Corder, S. (1973), *Introducing applied linguistics*, Harmondsworth 1973.

Corder, S. (1974), Problems and solutions in applied linguistics, in: Qvistgaard *et al.* (1974), 3–23.

Corder, S. (1975), Error analysis, interlanguage and second language acquisition, *Language Teaching & Linguistics: Abstracts* 8, 1975, 201–18.

Corder, S. (1978), Language-learner language, in: Richards (1978), 71–93.

Corder, S., E. Roulet (eds.) (1977), *The notions of simplification, interlanguages and pidgins and their relations to second language pedagogy*, Neuchâtel 1977.

Cornell, A. (1981), Identifying learning problems at advanced level: the uses of bad items in language tests, *Praxis des neusprachlichen Unterrichts* 28, 1981, 14–21.

Correll, W., K. Ingenkamp (1967), *Fremdsprachen-Eignungstest für die Unterstufe FTU 4–6*, Berlin 1967.

Coseriu, E. (1972), Über Leistung und Grenzen der kontrastiven Grammatik, in: Nickel (1972b), 39–58.

Coste, D. (1975), Remarques sur les avatars de l'enseignement audio-visuel des langues, *Die Neueren Sprachen* 74, 1975, 539–48.

Coste, D., J. Courtillon, V. Ferenczi, M. Martins-Baltar, E. Papo (1976), *Un niveau-seuil*, Strasbourg 1976.

Council of Europe (1969), *The work of the Council of Europe in the field of modern languages*, Strasbourg 1969.

Criper, C., H. Widdowson (1975), Sociolinguistics and language teaching, in: Allen and Corder (1975), 155–217.

Cronbach, L., R. Snow (1977), *Aptitudes and instructional methods*, New York 1977.

Crowne, D., P. Marlowe (1964), *The approval motive*, New York 1964.

Crystal, D., D. Davy (1969), *Investigating English style*, London 1969.

Culhane, P. (1970), The predictive validity of MLAT, in: Culhane, P. (ed.), *University of Essex Language Centre. Occasional Papers No. 7*, Colchester 1970, 22–8.

Curtiss, S. (1977), *Genie: a psycholinguistic study of a modern-day 'wild child'*, New York 1977.

Dahllöf, U. (1963), *Kraven på gymnasiet. Undersökningar vid universitet och högskolor, i förvaltning och näringsliv*, Stockholm 1963.

Dahlmann-Resing, G. (1978), Die Besonderheiten der Aussprache des Amerikanischen Englisch und ihre Vermittlung in Lehrwerken, *Zielsprache Englisch* 8, 1, 1978, 13–8.

Dakin, J. (1973), *The language laboratory and language learning*, London 1973.

Dale, P. (1976), *Language development, structure and function*, New York 1976. 2nd rev. ed.

Darian, S. (1969), Backgrounds of modern language teaching: Sweet, Jespersen, and Palmer, *The Modern Language Journal* 53, 1969, 545–50.

Darnell, D. (1968), *The development of an English language proficiency test of foreign students, using a clozentropy procedure*. Final Report, Boulder 1968.

Davies, A. (1975), Two tests of speeded reading, in: Jones and Spolsky (1975), 119–30.

Davies, A. (1978), Language testing, *Language Teaching & Linguistics: Abstracts* 11, 1978, 145–59 and 215–31.

Davies, N. (1976), Receptive versus productive skills in foreign language learning, *The Modern Language Journal* 60, 1976, 440–3.

Davies, N. (1978), *Putting receptive skills first*. An investigation into sequencing in modern language learning. Report, University of Linköping, Sweden, Linköping 1978.

De Bot, K. (1980), The role of feedback and feedforward in the teaching of pronunciation – an overview, *System* 8, 1980, 35–45.

De Bot, K. (1981), Visual feedback of English intonation, *Proceedings of the Institute of Phonetics*, University of Nijmegen 5, 1981, 24–40

De Bot, K., K. Mailfert (1982), The teaching of intonation. Fundamental research and classroom applications, *TESOL Quarterly* 16, 1982, 71–7.

De Corte, E., C. Geerlings, N. Lagerwey, J. Peters, R. Vandenberghe (1976), *Beknopte didaxologie*, Groningen 1976. 4th ed.

De Saussure, F. (1916), *Cours de linguistique générale*, Paris 1916.

De Vriendt, M. (1977), Le Threshold Level ou le niveau seuil en langue anglaise, *Revue de Phonétique Appliquée* 41, 1977, 9–12.

DeFrancis, J. (1971), The time factor in language learning, *Foreign Language Annals* 4, 1971, 287–92.

De Villiers, J., P. De Villiers (1973), A cross-sectional study of the acquisition of grammatical morphemes in child speech, *Journal of Psycholinguistic Research* 2, 1973, 267–78.

De Villiers, J., P. De Villiers (1978), *Language acquisition*, Cambridge, Mass. 1978.

Dietrich, I. (1973), Pädagogische Implikationen der Einsprachigkeit im Fremdsprachenunterricht, *Praxis des neusprachlichen Unterrichts* 20, 1973, 349–58.

Diller, K. (1971), *Generative grammar, structural linguistics, and language teaching*, Rowley, Mass. 1971.

Diller, K. (ed.) (1981), *Individual differences and universals in language learning aptitude*, Rowley, Mass. 1981.

DiPietro, R. (1971), *Language structures in contrast*, Rowley, Mass. 1971.

Disick, R. (1975), *Individualizing language instruction. Strategies and methods*, New York 1975.

Dittmar, N. (1976), *Sociolinguistics: a critical survey of theory and application*, London 1976.

Dittmar, N. (1980), Ordering adult learners according to language abilities, in: Felix (1980), 205-31.

Dittmar, N. *et al.* (1975), Untersuchungen zum Pidgin-Deutsch spanischer und italienischer Arbeiter in der Bundesrepublik. Ein Arbeitsbericht, in: Wierlacher, A. *et al.* (eds.), – *Jahrbuch Deutsch als Fremdsprache*, vol. 1, Heidelberg 1975, 170-94.

Dodson, C. (1967), *Language teaching and the bilingual method*, London 1967.

Donoghue, M. (1969), *Foreign languages in the elementary school: effects and instructional arrangements according to research*, New York 1969.

Donoghue, M., J. Kunkle (1979), *Second languages in primary education*, Rowley, Mass. 1979.

Doron, S. (1973), Reflectivity–impulsivity and their influence on reading for inference for adult students of ESL, unpubl. report, University of Michigan, Ann Arbor, Mich. 1973.

Downes, P. (1980), A multi-media approach to language teaching. 'Variations on a theme', *The British Journal of Language Teaching* 18, 1980, 129-31.

Doyé, P., D. Lüttge (1978), *Untersuchungen zum Englischunterricht in der Grundschule. Bericht über das Braunschweiger Forschungsprojekt 'Frühbeginn des Englischunterrichts'*, Braunschweig 1978. 2nd ed.

Dubin, F., E. Olshtain (1977), *Facilitating language learning*, New York 1977.

Dulay, H., M. Burt (1973), Should we teach children syntax?, *Language Learning* 23, 1973, 245-58.

Dulay, H., M. Burt (1974a), A new perspective on the creative construction process in child second language acquisition, *Language Learning* 24, 1974, 253-78.

Dulay, H., M. Burt (1974b), Errors and strategies in child second language acquisition, *TESOL Quarterly* 8, 1974, 129-36.

Dulay, H., M. Burt (1974c), Natural sequences in child second language acquisition, *Language Learning* 24, 1974, 37-53.

Dulay, H., M. Burt (1974d), You can't learn without goofing, in: Richards (1974), 95-123.

Dulay, H., M. Burt (1978), Some remarks on creativity in language acquisition, in: Ritchie (1978), 65-89.

Dunkel, H., R. Pillet (1963), *French in the elementary school. Five years' experience*, Chicago 1963.

Durkheim, E. (1897), *Le suicide*, Paris 1897.

Duskova, L. (1969), On sources of errors in foreign language learning, *International Review of Applied Linguistics in Language Teaching* 7, 1969, 11-37.

Düwell, H. (1979), *Fremdsprachenunterricht im Schülerurteil. Untersuchungen zu Motivation, Einstellungen und Interessen von Schülern im Fremdsprachenunterricht, Schwerpunkt Französisch*, Tübingen 1979.

Ebneter, T. (1976), *Angewandte Linguistik I, II*, München 1976.

Edwards, J. (1979), *Language and disadvantage*, London 1979.

Emmans, K., E. Hawkins, A. Westoby (1974), *The use of foreign languages in the private sector of industry and commerce*, Language Teaching Centre, University of York, York 1974.

Engel, U., H. Krumm, A. Wierlacher (1979), *Mannheimer Gutachten zu ausgewählten Lehrwerken Deutsch als Fremdsprache, Band 2*, Heidelberg 1979.

Engel, U., I. Vogel (eds.) (1973), *Gesprochene Sprache. Bericht der Forschungsstelle Freiburg*, Tübingen 1973. 2nd ed.

Engel, U. *et al.* (1977), *Mannheimer Gutachten zu ausgewählten Lehrwerken Deutsch als Fremdsprache*, Heidelberg 1977.

Engels, L. (1968), Applied linguistics, *ITL Review of Applied Linguistics* 1, 1968, 5–11.

Engels, L. (1979), Pedagogical grammars, *Glottodidactica* 12, 1979, 13–33.

Eppert, F. (1972), Grammatikalität, Akzeptabilität und Üblichkeit. Ein Lehrbuch-Dialog – kritisch gesehen, *Die Unterrichtspraxis* 5, 1, 1972, 27–30.

Epting, R., J. Bowen (1979), Resurrecting the language lab for teaching listening comprehension, in: Celce-Murcia and McIntosh (1979), 74–9.

Erdmenger, M. (1979), *Englischunterricht im Medienverbund*, Weinheim/Basel 1979.

Erickson, J., D. Omark (1981), *Communication assessment of the bilingual, bicultural child: issues and guidelines*, Baltimore 1981.

Erk, H. (1972), *Zur Lexik wissenschaftlicher Fachtexte*, München 1972.

Ervin, S. (1964), Imitation and structural change in children's language, in: Lenneberg, E. (ed.), *New directions in the study of language*, Cambridge, Mass. 1964, 163–89.

Ervin-Tripp, S. (1974), Is second language learning like the first, *TESOL Quarterly* 8, 1974, 111–27.

Ewer, J., O. Boys (1981), The EST textbook situation: an enquiry, *ESP Journal* 1, 1981, 87–105.

Extra, G. (1974), Fremdsprachenerwerb in einer individualisierten Lernsituation. Eine Beschreibung von Lernverhalten, *ITL Review of Applied Linguistics* 25/26, 1974, 198–223.

Extra, G. (1978a), *Eerste- en tweede-taalverwerving: de ontwikkeling van morfologische vaardigheden*, Muiderberg 1978.

Extra, G. (1978b), Nederlands van buitenlanders. Psycholinguïstische aspekten van vreemde-taalverwerving, unpubl. doctoral dissertation, Katholieke Universiteit, Nijmegen 1978.

Eysenck, H., S. Eysenck (1963), *Manual for the Eysenck Personality Inventory*, San Diego 1963.

Farhady, H. (1979), The disjunctive fallacy between discrete-point and integrative tests, *TESOL Quarterly* 13, 1979, 347–58.

Fathman, A. (1975a), Language background, age and the order of acquisition of English structures, in: Burt and Dulay (1975), 33–43.

Fathman, A. (1975b), The relationship between age and second language productive ability, *Language Learning* 25, 1975, 245–53.

Fathman, A. (1977), Similarities and simplification in the interlanguage of second language learners, in: Corder and Roulet (1977), 30–8.

Fathman, A. (1979), The value of morpheme order studies for second language learning, *Working Papers on Bilingualism* 18, 1979, 179–99.

Felix, S. (1978), *Linguistische Untersuchungen zum natürlichen Zweitsprachenerwerb*, München 1978.

Felix, S. (ed.) (1980), *Second language development. Trends and issues*, Tübingen 1980.

Felix, S. (1981), The effect of formal instruction on second language acquisition, *Language Learning* 31, 1981, 87–112.

Felix, S. (1982), *Psycholinguistische Aspekte des Zweitsprachenerwerbs*, Tübingen 1982.

FEoLL (1975), *Schulfernsehen und Schulfunk im fremdsprachlichen Medienverbund*, Paderborn 1975.

Ferencich, M. (1964), *Reattivo di attitudine linguistica: adattamento italiano e taratura*, Firenze 1964.

Ferguson, C. (1971a), Absence of copula and the notion of simplicity, in: Hymes, D. (ed.), *Pidginization and creolization of language*, Cambridge, Mass. 1971, 141–50.

Ferguson, C. (1971b), Linguistic theory and language learning, in: Dil, A. (ed.), *Language structure and language use. Essays by Charles A. Ferguson*, Stanford 1971, 97–111.

Ferguson, C., C. DeBose (1977), Simplified registers, broken language, and pidginization, in: Valdman, A. (ed.), *Pidgin and creole linguistics*, Bloomington/London 1977, 99-125.

Ferguson, C., D. Slobin (1973), *Studies of child language development*, New York 1973.

Ferguson, G. (1981), *Statistical analysis in psychology and education*, New York 1981. 5th ed.

Ferguson, N. (1972), *Teaching English as a foreign language: theory and practice*, Lausanne 1972.

Fiks, A., J. Corbino (1967), Course density and student perception, *Language Learning* 17, 1967, 3-8.

Fink, K. (1977), Selected bibliography of literature in German special register courses and word frequency counts for German, in: Cowan, J. (ed.), *Studies in language learning 2*, 1977, 172-4.

Firges, J., M. Pelz (eds.) (1976), *Innovationen des audio-visuellen Fremdsprachenunterrichts*, Frankfurt/M. 1976.

Fishbein, M., I. Ajzen (1975), *Belief, attitude, intention, and behavior: an introduction to theory and research*, Reading, Mass. 1975.

Fisher, R. (1979), The inductive–deductive controversy revisited, *The Modern Language Journal* 63, 1979, 98-105.

Fishman, J., R. Cooper (1978), The sociolinguistic foundation of language testing, in: Spolsky (1978a), 31-8.

Fisiak, J., M. Lipinska-Grzegorik, T. Zabrocki (1978), *An introductory English–Polish contrastive grammar*, Warszawa 1978.

Flechsig, K. (ed.) (1965), *Neusprachlicher Unterricht I*, Weinheim 1965.

Foss, D., D. Hakes (1978), *Psycholinguistics: an introduction to the psychology of language*, Englewood Cliffs, NJ 1978.

Francis, J. (1981), The reliability of two methods of marking oral tests in modern language examinations, *The British Journal of Language Teaching* 19, 1981, 15-23.

Francis, W. (1979), Problems of assembling and computerizing large corpora, in: Bergenholtz and Schaeder (1979), 110-23.

Francis, W. (1980), A tagged corpus – problems and prospects, in: Greenbaum, S., G. Leech, J. Svartvik (eds.), *Studies in English linguistics for Randolph Quirk*, London 1980, 192-209.

Francis, W., H. Kučera (in press), *Frequency analysis of English usage: lexicon and grammar*, Boston.

Frechette, E. (1969), *A critical evaluation of the vocabulary of 10 French textbooks*, Ann Arbor, Mich. 1969.

Freedman, E. (1979), Valid research into foreign language teaching – two recent projects, *System* 7, 1979, 187-99.

Freedman, E. (1982), Experimentation into foreign language teaching methodology: the research findings, *System* 10, 1982, 119-33.

Freese, P. (1977), Zur Auswahl von Texten für den fortgeschrittenen Englischunterricht, in: Hunfeld (1977), 146-56.

French, F. (1949), *Common errors in English: their cause, prevention and cure*, London 1949.

Freudenstein, R. (1971), *Unterrichtsmittel Sprachlabor*, Bochum 1971.

Freudenstein, R. (ed.) (1978a), *Language learning: individual needs, interdisciplinary co-operation, bi- and multilingualism*, Brussels 1978.

Freudenstein, R. (ed.) (1978b), *The role of women in foreign-language textbooks*, Brussels 1978.

Freudenstein, R. (1981a), Grammatische Progression und 'kommunikative Kompetenz'. Überlegungen zum Stellenwert einer pragmatischen Progression im englischen Anfangsunterricht, *Englisch* 16, 1981, 58-62.

Freudenstein, R. (1981b), Media in the second language program: form and uses for the eighties, in: Alatis *et al.* (1981), 269–80.

Fries, C. (1945), *Teaching and learning English as a foreign language*, Ann Arbor, Mich. 1945.

Fries, C. (1952), *The structure of English*, New York 1952.

Fromkin, V., S. Krashen, S. Curtiss, D. Rigler, M. Rigler (1974), The development of language in Genie: a case of language acquisition beyond the critical period, *Brain and Language* 1, 1974, 81–107.

Frumkina, R. (1963), The application of statistical methods in linguistic research, in: Akhmanova, O., I. Mel'chuk, R. Frumkina, E. Paducheva (eds.), *Exact methods in linguistic research*, Berkeley/Los Angeles 1963, 80–118.

Gage, N., D. Berliner (1975), *Educational psychology*, Chicago 1975.

Galisson, R., D. Coste (1976), *Dictionnaire de didactique des langues*, Paris 1976.

Galli de' Paratesi, N. (1981), *Livello soglia per l'insegnamento dell'italiano come lingua straniera*, Strasbourg 1981.

Galloway, L. (1981), The convolutions of second language: a theoretical article with a critical review and some new hypotheses towards a neuropsychological model of bilingualism and second language performance, *Language Learning* 31, 1981, 439–64.

Galloway, L., S. Krashen (1980), Cerebral organization in bilingualism and second language, in: Scarcella and Krashen (1980), 74–80.

Garcia Hoz, V. (1953), *Vocabulario usual, vocabulario comun y vocabulario fundamental*, Madrid 1953.

Gardner, R. (1960), Motivational variables in second-language acquisition, unpubl. doctoral dissertation, McGill University, Montreal 1960. Summarized in: Gardner and Lambert (1972), 199–216.

Gardner, R. (1979), Social psychological aspects of second language acquisition, in: Giles, H., R. St. Clair (eds.), *Language and social psychology*, Oxford 1979, 193–220.

Gardner, R. (1980), On the validity of affective variables in second language acquisition: conceptual, contextual, and statistical considerations, *Language Learning* 30, 1980, 225–70.

Gardner, R., R. Clément, P. Smythe, C. Smythe (1979a), *Attitudes and motivation test battery – revised manual*, Research Bulletin No. 15, Language Research Group, Dept. of Psychology, University of Western Ontario, London, Ont. 1979.

Gardner, R., R. Ginsberg, P. Smythe (1976a), Attitudes and motivation in second language learning: course related changes, *The Canadian Modern Language Review* 32, 1976, 243–66.

Gardner, R., W. Lambert (1959), Motivational variables in second language acquisition, *Canadian Journal of Psychology* 13, 1959, 266–72. Reprinted in: Gardner and Lambert (1972), 191–7.

Gardner, R., W. Lambert (1965), Language aptitude, intelligence and second language achievement, *Journal of Educational Psychology* 56, 1965, 191–9. Reprinted in: Gardner and Lambert (1972), 282–92.

Gardner, R., W. Lambert (1972), *Attitudes and motivation in second-language learning*, Rowley, Mass. 1972.

Gardner, R., P. Smythe (1975a), Motivation and second-language acquisition, *The Canadian Modern Language Review* 31, 1975, 218–30.

Gardner, R., P. Smythe (1975b), *Second-language acquisition: a social psychological approach*, Research Bulletin No. 332, Dept. of Psychology, University of Western Ontario, London, Ont. 1975.

Gardner, R., P. Smythe, G. Brunet (1977), Intensive second language study: effects on attitudes, motivation and French achievement, *Language Learning* 27, 1977, 243–61.

Gardner, R., P. Smythe, R. Clément (1979b), Intensive second language study in a bicultural milieu: an investigation of attitudes, motivation and language proficiency, *Language Learning* 29, 1979, 305-20.

Gardner, R., P. Smythe, R. Clément, L. Gliksman (1976b), Second-language learning: a social psychological perspective, *The Canadian Modern Language Review* 32, 1976, 198-213.

Garnica, O., R. Herbert (1979), Some phonological errors in second language learning: interference doesn't tell it all, *International Journal of Psycholinguistics* 14, 1979, 5-19.

Gaskill, W. (1980), Correction in native speaker–nonnative speaker conversation, in: Larsen and Freeman (1980), 125-37.

Gass, S. (1979), Language transfer and universal grammatical relations, *Language Learning* 29, 1979, 327-44.

Geddes, M., G. Sturtridge (eds.) (1982), *Video in the language classroom. Practical language teaching no. 7*, London 1982.

Genesee, F. (1982), Experimental research on second language processing, *TESOL Quarterly* 16, 1982, 315-21.

Genesee, F., E. Hamayan (1980), Individual differences in second language learning, *Applied Psycholinguistics* 1, 1980, 95-110.

Germain, C. (1981), L'approche communicative: bibliographie descriptive (1975-1980), *Bulletin de l'ACLA* 3, 1, 1981, 61-108.

Gimson, A. (1980), *An introduction to the pronunciation of English*, London 1980. 3rd ed.

Girard, D. (1972a), *Linguistics and foreign language teaching*, London 1972.

Girard, D. (1972b), *Linguistique appliquée et didactique des langues*, Paris 1972. 3rd ed.

Gompf, G. (1975), *Englischunterricht auf der Primarstufe*, Frankfurt/M. 1975.

Gougenheim, G. (1958), *Dictionnaire fondamental de la langue française*, Paris 1958.

Gougenheim, G., R. Michéa, P. Rivenc, A. Sauvageot (1956), *L'élaboration du français élémentaire*, Paris 1956.

Gougenheim, G., R. Michéa, P. Rivenc, A. Sauvageot (1967), *L'élaboration du français fondamental (1er degré)*, Paris 1967. 2nd ed. First published 1959.

Gougher, R. (ed.) (1972), *Individualization of instruction in foreign languages: a practical guide*, Philadelphia 1972.

Gouin, F. (1880), *L'art d'enseigner et d'étudier les langues*, Paris 1880.

Gradman, H., S. Gaies (1978), Reduced redundancy and error analysis: a study of selected performance on the 'noise test', in: Nickel (1978), 73-84.

Green, P. (1974), Aptitude testing – an on-going experiment, *Audio-Visual Language Journal* 12, 1974, 205-10.

Grewer, U., T. Moston, M. Sexton (1978), Übungstypologie zum Lernziel kommunikative Kompetenz, in: Edelhoff, C. (ed.), *Kommunikativer Englischunterricht. Prinzipien und Übungstypologie*, München 1978, 69-192.

Grice, H. (1957), Meaning, *Philosophical Review* 66, 1957, 377-88.

Grice, H. (1975), Logic and conversation, in: Cole, P., J. Morgan (eds.), *Syntax and semantics 3*, New York 1975, 41-58.

Griffin, S. (1981), Video studios: the language labs for the 1980s, *NALLD Journal* 15, 1981, 5-15.

Grittner, F. (1975), Individualized instruction: an historical perspective, *The Modern Language Journal* 59, 1975, 323-33.

Grittner, F., F. Laleike (1973), *Individualized foreign language instruction*, Skokie, Ill. 1973.

Groot, P. (1977), *Présentation des travaux en cours sur un 'Specimen de test au niveau seuil'*, Strasbourg 1977.

Grotjahn, R., E. Hopkins (eds.) (1980), *Empirical research on language teaching and language acquisition*. Quantitative Linguistics 6, Bochum 1980.

Guberina, P. (1967), La méthode audio-visuelle structuro-globale, in: Jansen, W., K. Simons (eds.), *Audio-visuele media en taalonderricht*, Antwerpen 1967, 72-83.

Guberina, P. (1972), Sur la notion de 'structuro-global' (citations), *Revue de Phonétique Appliquée* 21, 1972, 9-13.

Guberina, P. (1973), Les appareils Suvag et Suvag Lingua, *Revue de Phonétique Appliquée* 27/28, 1973, 7-16.

Guiora, A., W. Acton, R. Erard, F. Strickland (1980), The effects of Benzodiazepine (Valium) on permeability of language ego boundaries, *Language Learning* 30, 1980, 351-63.

Guiora, A., B. Beit-Hallahmi, R. Brannon, C. Dull, T. Scovel (1972a), The effects of experimentally induced changes in ego states on pronunciation ability in a second language: an exploratory study, *Comprehensive Psychiatry* 13, 1972, 421-8.

Guiora, A., R. Brannon, C. Dull (1972b), Empathy and second-language learning, *Language Learning* 22, 1972, 111-30.

Guiora, A., H. Lane, L. Bosworth (1967), An exploration of some personality variables in authentic pronunciation of a second language, in: Lane, H., E. Zale (eds.), *Studies in language and language behavior 4*, 1967, 261-6.

Guiora, A., M. Paluszny, B. Beit-Hallahmi, J. Catford, R. Cooley, C. Dull (1975), Language and person: studies in language behavior, *Language Learning* 25, 1975, 43-61.

Guiraud, P. (1960), *Les caractères statistiques du vocabulaire*, Paris 1960.

Gutfleisch, I., B. Rieck, N. Dittmar (1979), Interimsprachen- und Fehleranalyse. Teilkommentierte Bibliographie zur Zweitsprachenerwerbsforschung 1967-1978 (Teil 1), *Linguistische Berichte* 64, 1979, 105-42.

Gutfleisch, I., B. Rieck, N. Dittmar (1980), Interimsprachen- und Fehleranalyse. Teilkommentierte Bibliographie zur Zweitsprachenerwerbsforschung 1967-1978 (Teil 2), *Linguistische Berichte* 65, 1980, 51-81.

Gutknecht, C. (ed.) (1975a), *Contributions to applied linguistics 1*, Frankfurt/M. 1975.

Gutknecht, C. (1975b), Some critical remarks about the teaching of English pronunciation in German universities and schools, in: Gutknecht (1975a), 189-202.

Gutschow, H. (1974), Leistungsdifferenzierter Unterricht, in: Gutschow, H. (ed.), *Englisch. Didaktik Methodik Sprache Landeskunde*, Berlin 1974, 345-63.

Gutschow, H. (1978), Die Neufassung des VHS-Zertifikats Englisch, *Zielsprache Englisch* 8, 4, 1978, 1-6.

Gutschow, H. (1980), *Englisch an der Tafel. Anregungen zum Tafelzeichnen*, Berlin 1980.

Haas, M. (1953), The application of linguistics to language teaching, in: Kroeber, A. (ed.), *Anthropology today*, Chicago 1953, 807-18.

Hakuta, K. (1976), A case study of a Japanese child learning English as a second language, *Language Learning* 26, 1976, 321-51.

Hakuta, K., H. Cancino (1977), Trends in second-language acquisition research, *Harvard Educational Review* 47, 1977, 294-316.

Halliday, M., A. McIntosh, P. Strevens (1964), *The linguistic sciences and language teaching*, London 1964.

Halls, W. (1970), *Foreign languages and education in Western Europe*, London 1970.

Halm, W., A. Barrera-Vidal (1973), *Spanischer Mindestwortschatz*, München 1973.

Hamayan, E., F. Genesee, G. Tucker (1977), Affective factors and language exposure in second language learning, *Language Learning* 27, 1977, 225-41.

Hammer, J., F. Rice (1965), *A bibliography of contrastive linguistics*, Washington, DC 1965.

Hammer, P. (1979), *What's the use of cognates?*, Edmonton 1979.

Hammer, P., M. Monod (1976), *English-French cognate dictionary*, Edmonton 1976.

Hancock, C. (1972), Student aptitude, attitude, and motivation, in: Lange, D., C. James (eds.), *Foreign language education: a reappraisal*, Skokie, Ill. 1972, 127-55.

Hansen, J., C. Stansfield (1981), The relationship of field dependent-independent cognitive styles to foreign language achievement, *Language Learning* 31, 1981, 349–67.

Hanzeli, V. (1968), Linguistics and the language teacher, *Foreign Language Annals* 2, 1968, 42–50.

Harding-Esch, E. (1982), The open access sound and video library of the University of Cambridge: progress report and development, *System* 10, 1982, 13–28.

Harlow, L. (1978), An alternative to structurally oriented textbooks, *Foreign Language Annals* 11, 1978, 559–78.

Harnisch, J., V. Kilian, K. Wickert (1976), Der Fremdsprachenunterricht seit 1945 – Geschichte und Ideologie, in: Kramer, J. (ed.), *Bestandsaufnahme Fremdsprachenunterricht*, Stuttgart 1976, 3–45.

Harris, D. (1969), *Testing English as a second language*, New York 1969.

Hatch, E. (1974), Second language learning – universals?, *Working Papers on Bilingualism* 3, 1974, 1–17.

Hatch, E. (ed.) (1978), *Second language acquisition. A book of readings*, Rowley, Mass. 1978.

Hatch, E., H. Farhady (1982), *Research design and statistics for applied linguistics*, Rowley, Mass. 1982.

Hatch, E., M. Long (1980), Discourse analysis, what's that?, in: Larsen-Freeman (1980), 1–40.

Hatch, E., R. Shapira, J. Gough (1978), 'Foreigner-talk' discourse, *ITL Review of Applied Linguistics* 39 and 40, 1978, 39–60.

Hatfield, W. (1968), Foreign language program evaluation, in: Birkmaier, E. (ed.), *Britannica review of foreign language education*, vol. 1, Chicago 1968, 375–88.

Hawkins, E. (1981), *Modern languages in the curriculum*, Cambridge 1981.

Haycraft, J. (1978), *An introduction to English language teaching*, London 1978.

Hayes, A., H. Lane, T. Mueller, W. Sweet, W. Starr (1962), A new look at learning, in: Bottiglia, W. (ed.), *Current issues in language teaching. Reports of the working committees. Northeast Conference*, New York 1962, 18–60.

Heaton, J. (1975), *Writing English language tests*, London 1975.

Heaton, J. (1979), An audiovisual method for ESL, in: Celce-Murcia and McIntosh (1979), 38–48.

Heidelberger Forschungsprojekt (1975), *Sprache und Kommunikation ausländischer Arbeiter*, Kronberg/Ts 1975.

Heindrichs, W., F. Gester, H. Kelz (1980), *Sprachlehrforschung. Angewandte Linguistik und Fremdsprachenunterricht*, Stuttgart 1980.

Helbig, G. (1969), Zur Anwendbarkeit moderner linguistischer Theorien im Fremdsprachenunterricht und zu den Beziehungen zwischen Sprach- und Lerntheorien, *Sprache im technischen Zeitalter* 32, 1969, 287–305. Reprinted in: Hüllen (1979), 315–39.

Hendrickson, J. (1978), Error correction in FLT: recent theory, research and practice, *The Modern Language Journal* 62, 1978, 387–98.

Hendrickson, J. (1980a), Listening and speaking activation for FL learners, *The Canadian Modern Language Review* 36, 1980, 735–48.

Hendrickson, J. (1980b), The treatment of error in written work, *The Modern Language Journal* 64, 1980, 216–21.

Henmon, V. (1924), *A French word book based on a count of 400,000 running words*, Madison, Wisc. 1924.

Henning, C. (ed.) (1977), *Proceedings of the Los Angeles second language research forum*, Los Angeles 1977.

Henzl, V. (1973), Linguistic register of foreign language instruction, *Language Learning* 23, 1973, 207–22.

Hesse, M. (ed.) (1975), *Approaches to teaching foreign languages*, Amsterdam 1975.

Heuer, H. (1973a), Psychologische Aspekte der Lehrwerkkritik, in: Heuer and Müller (1973), 15-30.

Heuer, H. (1973b), Wortassoziationen in der Fremdsprachendidaktik, in: Hüllen (1973), 66-83.

Heuer, H., R. Müller (eds.) (1973), *Lehrwerkkritik - ein Neuansatz*, Dortmund 1973.

Heuer, H., R. Müller (eds.) (1975), *Lehrwerkkritik 2. Landeskunde - Illustrationen - Grammatik*, Dortmund 1975.

Heuer, H., R. Müller, H. Schrey (1970), Möglichkeiten der Lehrwerkforschung und Lehrwerkkritik, *Praxis des neusprachlichen Unterrichts* 17, 1970, 1-6.

Heyde, A. (1979), The relationship between self-esteem and the oral production of a second language, unpubl. doctoral dissertation, University of Michigan, Ann Arbor, Mich. 1979.

Hilgard, E., R. Atkinson, R. Atkinson (1979), *Introduction to psychology*, New York 1979. 7th ed.

Hilgendorf, E., C. Holzkamp, I. Münzberg (1970), *Frühbeginn des Englischunterrichts. Probleme und Ergebnisse einer Effektivitätsuntersuchung*, Weinheim 1970.

Hill, B. (1981), Some applications of media technology to the teaching and learning of languages, *Language Teaching & Linguistics: Abstracts* 14, 1981, 147-61.

Hill, C. (1977), Review of the Threshold Level, *English Language Teaching* 31, 1977, 334-5.

Hinofotis, F. (1980), Cloze as an alternative method of ESL-placement and proficiency testing, in: Oller and Perkins (1980), 121-8.

Hinofotis, F., B. Snow (1980), An alternative cloze testing procedure: multiple choice format, in: Oller and Perkins (1980), 129-33.

Hinz, K. (1979), *Der Overheadprojektor im Englischunterricht. Didaktisch-methodische Handreichungen*, Düsseldorf 1979.

Hocking, E. (1967), *Language laboratory and language learning*, Washington, DC 1967.

Hoffmann, H. (1976), Cabbage at the cabaret, *Zielsprache Englisch* 6, 2, 1976, 17.

Hoffmann, L. (1970), Die Bedeutung statistischer Untersuchungen für den Fremdsprachenunterricht, *Glottodidactica* 3/4, 1970, 47-81.

Hofland, K., S. Johansson (1982), *Word frequencies in British and American English*, Bergen 1982.

Hogan, R. (1969), Development of an empathy scale, *Journal of Consulting and Clinical Psychology* 33, 1969, 307-16.

Holmes, G., M. Kidd (1982), Second-language learning and computers, *The Canadian Modern Language Review* 38, 1982, 503-16.

Holmstrand, L. (1975), *An introduction to the EPAL project. Background, problems and design*, Pedagogiska Institutionen, Uppsala 1975.

Holmstrand, L. (1979), *The effects on general school achievement of early commencement of English instruction*, Uppsala reports on education no. 4, Uppsala 1979.

Holmstrand, L. (1982), *English in the elementary school. Theoretical and empirical aspects of the early teaching of English as a foreign language*, Stockholm 1982.

Holton, J., P. King, G. Mathieu, K. Pond (1961), *Sound language teaching. The state of the art today*, New York 1961.

Hooper, R. (1975), Eine Diagnose des Scheiterns, in: Dichanz, H., G. Kolb (eds.), *Quellentexte zur Unterrichtstechnologie I*, Stuttgart 1975, 61-83.

Hopkins, P. (1980), More than one choice in objective testing, *English Language Teaching* 34, 1980, 221-3.

Hörmann, H. (1981), *Einführung in die Psycholinguistik*, Darmstadt 1981.

Hornby, A. (1954), *Guide to patterns and usage in English*, London 1954. 2nd ed. 1975.

Howatt, A. (1969), *Programmed learning and the language teacher*, London 1969.

Howatt, A. (1974a), Programmed instruction, in: Allen and Corder (1974), 232-54.

Howatt, A. (1974b), The background to course design, in: Allen and Corder (1974), 1-23.

Howatt, A. (1979), Deliberate semantics - an 'interventionist' approach to second language teaching methodology, *Bulletin CILA* 29, 1979, 5-22.

Hoy, P. (1977), *The early teaching of modern languages*, London 1977.

Hudson, R. (1980), *Sociolinguistics*, Cambridge 1980.

Huhse, K. (1968), *Theorie und Praxis der Curriculum-Entwicklung*, Berlin 1968.

Hüllen, W. (1971), *Linguistik und Englischunterricht*, Heidelberg 1971.

Hüllen, W. (ed.) (1973), *Neusser Vorträge zur Fremdsprachendidaktik*, Berlin 1973.

Hüllen, W. (1974), Zur Anwendung der Linguistik innerhalb der Sprachlehrforschung, *Zeitschrift für Literaturwissenschaft und Linguistik* 13, 1974, 13-30.

Hüllen, W. (ed.) (1979), *Didaktik des Englischunterrichts*, Darmstadt 1979.

Hüllen, W., A. Raasch, F. Zapp (eds.) (1975), *Lernzielbestimmung und Leistungsmessung im modernen Fremdsprachenunterricht*, Frankfurt/M. 1975.

Hüllen, W., A. Raasch, F. Zapp (eds.) (1977), *Sprachminima und Abschlussprofile*, Frankfurt/M. 1977.

Hunfeld, H. (ed.) (1977), *Neue Perspektiven der Fremdsprachendidaktik*, Kronberg/Ts 1977.

Hunfeld, H., K. Schröder (eds.) (1979), *Grundkurs Didaktik Englisch*, Königstein/Ts 1979.

Hunziker, H. (1977), *Bild und Ton im Unterricht. Handbuch der Lerntechnologie 1978/79*, Zürich 1977.

Hyltenstam, K. (1977), Implicational patterns in interlanguage syntax variation, *Language Learning* 27, 1977, 383-411.

Ickenroth, J., G. Nas (1977), A critical examination of a new way to define language learning objectives, *Interlanguage Studies Bulletin* 2, 1, 1977, 7-32.

Ingram, D. (1971), Implications of the theory of innate ideas for the foreign language teacher, *Audio-Visual Language Journal* 9, 1971, 127-31.

Ingram, E. (n.d.), Applied linguistics, linguistic research and the empirical model, *Studies in Second Language Acquisition* 1, 2, n.d., 37-53.

Ingram, E. (1968), Attainment and diagnostic testing, in: Davies, A. (ed.), *Language testing symposium. A psycholinguistic approach*, London 1968, 70-97.

Ingram, E. (1974), Language testing, in: Allen and Corder (1974), 313-43.

Ingram, S. (1976), *Teaching foreign languages in Great-Britain – Why?*, London 1976.

Institute for Personality and Ability Testing (1969), *The Jr.-Sr. High School Personality Questionnaire*, Champaign, Ill. 1969.

Jakobovits, L. (1969), Second language learning and transfer theory: a theoretical assessment, *Language Learning* 19, 1969, 55-87.

Jakobovits, L. (1970), *Foreign language learning. A psycholinguistic analysis of the issues*, Rowley, Mass. 1970.

James, A., P. Westney (eds.) (1981), *New linguistic impulses in foreign language teaching*, Tübingen 1981.

James, C. (1971), The exculpation of contrastive linguistics, in: Nickel (1971), 53-68.

James, C. (1980), *Contrastive analysis*, Harlow 1980.

Jarvis, G. (1972), Teacher education goals: they're tearing up the street where I was born, *Foreign Language Annals* 6, 1972, 198-205.

Jarvis, G. (ed.) (1974), *Responding to new realities*, Skokie, Ill. 1974.

Jespersen, O. (1904), *How to teach a foreign language?*, London 1904. 13th ed. 1967.

Jespersen, O. (1937), *Analytic syntax*, Copenhagen 1937.

Jiménez, P. (1977), Contribution à une bibliographie sur la méthodologie SGAV et le système verbo-tonal, *Revue de Phonétique Appliquée* 41, 1977, 81-93.

Johansson, S. (1973), *Dictation techniques in the testing of foreign language proficiency*, Hasselt 1973.

Johansson, S. (ed.) (1979), *ICAME News. Newsletter of the International Computer Archive of Modern English (ICAME)*, no. 3, University of Bergen, Bergen 1979.

Johansson, S. (1980), Another look at foreign accent and speech distortion, *Revue de*

Phonétique Appliquée 53, 1980, 35–48.

Johansson, S. (ed.) (1982), *Computer corpora in English language research*, Bergen 1982.

Johnson, F. (1969), The failure of the discipline of linguistics in language teaching, *Language Learning* 19, 1969, 235–44.

Johnson, K. (1977), The adoption of functional syllabuses for general language teaching courses, *The Canadian Modern Language Review* 33, 1977, 667–80.

Johnson, K. (1979a), Communicative approaches and communicative processes, in: Brumfit and Johnson (1979), 192–205.

Johnson, K. (1979b), Progression nach Strukturen und Progression nach Sprechakten – ein Widerspruch, *Praxis des neusprachlichen Unterrichts* 26, 1979, 24–30.

Johnson, K. (1982), *Communicative syllabus design and methodology*, Oxford 1982.

Joiner, E. (1974), Evaluating the cultural content of foreign-language texts, *The Modern Language Journal* 58, 1974, 242–4.

Jones, L., J. Wepman (1966), *A spoken word count. Adults*, Chicago 1966.

Jones, R., B. Spolsky (eds.) (1975), *Testing language proficiency*, Arlington, VA 1975.

Joos, M. (1961), *The five clocks*, New York 1961.

Jordens, P. (1977), Rules, grammatical intuitions and strategies in foreign language learning, *Interlanguage Studies Bulletin* 2, 2, 1977, 5–76.

Josselson, H. (1953), *The Russian word count and frequency analysis of grammatical categories of standard literary Russian*, Detroit 1953.

Juilland, A., D. Brodin, C. Davidovitch (1970), *Frequency dictionary of French words*, The Hague 1970.

Juilland, A., E. Chang-Rodriguez (1964), *Frequency dictionary of Spanish words*, The Hague 1964.

Juilland, A., V. Traversa, A. Beltramo, S. Di Blasi (1973), *Frequency dictionary of Italian words*, The Hague 1973.

Jung, L. (1979), Pragma- versus systemlinguistische Progression im Fremdsprachenunterricht, in: Neuner (1979), 84–94.

Jung, L. (1980), Sprachdidaktische Erwägungen in Lehrmaterialien zum Englischunterricht des 17. und 18. Jahrhunderts, *Die Neueren Sprachen* 79, 1980, 161–74.

Jung, U. (1980), Reading, writing, and phonology in modern foreign-language teaching, in: Felix (1980), 249–63.

Jung, U., M. Haase (eds.) (1975), *Fehlinvestition Sprachlabor? Beiträge zu einem konstruktiven Sprachunterricht mit technischen Medien*, Kiel 1975.

Kaeding, J. (1898), *Häufigkeitswörterbuch der deutschen Sprache*, Steglitz 1898.

Kagan, J., L. Pearson, L. Welch (1966), Conceptual impulsivity and inductive reasoning, *Child Development* 37, 1966, 583–94.

Kagan, J., B. Rosman, D. Day, J. Albert, W. Phillips (1964), Information processing in the child: significance of analytic and reflective attitudes, *Psychological Monographs* 78, 1964, whole no. 578.

Kandler, G. (1952), Angewandte Sprachwissenschaft, Name und Wesen eines kommenden Wissenszweiges, *Wirkendes Wort* 3, 1952, 257–71.

Kaplan, R. (ed.) (1980), *On the scope of applied linguistics*, Rowley, Mass. 1980.

Kasper, G. (1981), *Pragmatische Aspekte in der Interimsprache. Eine Untersuchung des Englischen fortgeschrittener deutscher Lerner*, Tübingen 1981.

Katz, J. (1977), Foreigner talk input in child second language acquisition: its form and function over time, in: Henning (1977), 61–75.

Kaufmann, G. (1977), Die Gewinnung lexikalischer und grammatischer Minima als linguistisches und didaktisches Problem, in: Hüllen *et al.* (1977), 48–70.

Keating, R. (1963), *A study of the effectiveness of language laboratories*, New York 1963.

Keller-Cohen, D. (1979), Systematicity and variation in the non-native child's acquisition of conversational skills, *Language Learning* 29, 1979, 27–44.

Kellerman, E. (1977), Towards a characterization of the strategy of transfer in second language learning, *Interlanguage Studies Bulletin* 2, 1, 1977, 58–145.

Kellerman, E. (1978), Giving the learners a break: native language intuitions as a source of predictions about transferability, *Working Papers on Bilingualism* 15, 1978, 59–72.

Kellerman, E. (1979), The problem with difficulty, *Interlanguage Studies Bulletin* 4, 1979, 27–48.

Kelly, L. (1969), *25 Centuries of language teaching*, Rowley, Mass. 1969.

Kelz, H. (1976), *Phonetische Probleme im Fremdsprachenunterricht*, Hamburg 1976.

Kent, G., A. Rosanoff (1910), A study of association in insanity, *American Journal of Insanity* 67, 1910, 37–96 and 317–90.

Kielhöfer, B. (1975), *Fehlerlinguistik des Fremdsprachenerwerbs*, Kronberg/Ts 1975.

Kielhöfer, B. (1976), Möglichkeiten und Grenzen einer Fehlertypologie, in: Börner, W., B. Kielhöfer, K. Vogel (eds.), *Französisch lehren und lernen. Aspekte der Sprachlehrforschung*, Kronberg/Ts 1976, 59–81.

Kingsbury, R. (1971), A proposed model for critical discussion and study of a possible Unit/Credit System in modern language learning and teaching for adults in Europe, in: Council of Europe (ed.), *Linguistic content, means of evaluation and their interaction in the teaching and learning of modern languages in adult education. Symposium organized at Rüschlikon 3–7 May 1971*, Strasbourg 1971, 10–16.

Kinsbourne, M. (1975), The ontogeny of cerebral dominance, in: Aaronson and Rieber (1975), 244–50.

Kirkwood, J. (1973), Analysing the linguistic and cultural content of foreign language text-books – An application of variety theory, *International Review of Applied Linguistics in Language Teaching* 11, 1973, 369–85.

Kleber, A. (1979), *Tests in der Schule. Instrumente zur Gewinnung diagnostischer Information zur Lernsteuerung und Lernkontrolle*, München/Basel 1979.

Klein, W., N. Dittmar (1979), *Developing grammars*, Berlin/Heidelberg/New York 1979.

Klein-Braley, C. (1981), Empirical investigations of cloze tests. An examination of the validity of cloze tests as tests of general language proficiency in English for German University students, unpubl. doctoral dissertation, Duisburg 1981.

Klein-Braley, C., H. Lück (1980), The development of the Duisburg English language test for advanced students (DELTA), in: Grotjahn and Hopkins (1980), 85–126.

Klein-Braley, C., D. Stevenson (eds.) (1981), *Practice and problems in language testing*, Frankfurt/M./Bern 1981.

Kleine, W. (ed.) (1979), *Perspektiven des Fremdsprachenunterrichts in der Bundesrepublik Deutschland*, Frankfurt/M. 1979.

Kleinmann, H. (1977), Avoidance behavior in adult second language acquisition, *Language Learning* 27, 1977, 93–107.

Klima, E., U. Bellugi (1966), Syntactic regularities in the speech of children, in: Lyons, J., R. Wales (eds.), *Psycholinguistic papers. The proceedings of the 1966 Edinburgh Conference*, Edinburgh 1966, 183–208.

Kloss, H. (1967), *Zum Problem des Fremdsprachenunterrichts an Grundschulen Amerikas und Europas*, Bad Godesberg 1967.

Knapp, K. (1980), *Lehrsequenzen für den Zweitsprachenerwerb. Ein komparatives Experiment*, Braunschweig/Wiesbaden 1980.

Knapp-Potthoff, A. (1979), *Fremdsprachliche Aufgaben. Ein Instrument zur Lernmaterialanalyse*, Tübingen 1979.

Knibbeler, W. (1979), The elusiveness of interlanguage revisited, *Interlanguage Studies Bulletin* 4, 1, 1979, 84–94.

Knibbeler, W. (1980), Measurement or global assessment of oral foreign language proficiency?, in: Grotjahn and Hopkins (1980), 127–44.

Kogan, N. (1971), Educational implications of cognitive styles, in: Lesser, G. (ed.),

Psychology and educational practice, Glenview, Ill. 1971, 242–92.

Köhler, F. (1977), Lehrbuchtexte – Beispiele zwischenmenschlicher Kommunikation?, *Linguistische Berichte* 52, 1977, 74–82.

König, E. (1970), *Transformational grammar and contrastive analysis*, Stuttgart 1970.

Krashen, S. (1973), Lateralization, language learning and the critical period: some new evidence, *Language Learning* 23, 1973, 63–74.

Krashen, S. (1975), The critical period for language acquisition and its possible bases, in: Aaronson and Rieber (1975), 211–24.

Krashen, S. (1977), The monitor model for adult second language performance, in: Burt *et al.* (1977), 152–61.

Krashen, S. (1979), A response to McLaughlin, *Language Learning* 29, 1979, 151–67.

Krashen, S. (1981), *Second language acquisition and second language learning*, Oxford 1981.

Krashen, S., N. Houck, P. Giunchi, S. Bode, R. Birnbaum, G. Strei (1977), Difficulty order for grammatical morphemes for adult second language performers using free speech, *TESOL Quarterly* 11, 1977, 338–41.

Krashen, S., M. Long, R. Scarcella (1979), Age, rate and eventual attainment in second language acquisition, *TESOL Quarterly* 13, 1979, 573–82.

Krashen, S., C. Madden, N. Bailey (1975), Theoretical aspects of grammatical sequencing, in: Burt and Dulay (1975), 44–54.

Krashen, S., V. Sferlazza, L. Feldman, A. Fathman (1976), Adult performance on the slope test: more evidence for a natural sequence in adult second language acquisition, *Language Learning* 26, 1976, 145–51.

Krech, D., R. Crutchfield, E. Ballachey (1962), *The individual in society*, New York 1962.

Kressel, R. (1974), The textbook family and the culturally deprived pupil, *English Language Teaching* 28, 1974, 312–15.

Krohn, R. (1969), Review of: '25 Centuries of language teaching' (1969) by Louis G. Kelly, *Language Learning* 19, 1969, 307–10.

Krzeszowski, T. (1971), Equivalence, congruence and deep structure, in: Nickel (1971), 37–48.

Krzeszowski, T. (1972), Kontrastive generative Grammatik, in: Nickel (1972b), 75–84.

Krzeszowski, T. (1979), *Contrastive generative grammar: theoretical foundations*, Tübingen 1979.

Kučera, H., W. Francis (1967), *Computational analysis of present-day American English*, Providence, RI 1967.

Kufner, H. (1962), *The grammatical structures of English and German. A contrastive sketch*, Chicago 1962.

Kühlwein, W. (1979), Angewandte Linguistik, *Anglistik & Englischunterricht* 7, 1979, 155–67.

Kühlwein, W., A. Barrera-Vidal (eds.) (1977), *Kritische Bibliographie zur Angewandten Linguistik, Fachbereich Englisch*, Dortmund 1977.

Kühn, P. (1979), *Der Grundwortschatz. Bestimmung und Systematisierung*, Tübingen 1979.

Kunkle, J. (1977), Conclusions from the British FLES experiment, *Foreign Language Annals* 10, 1977, 253–60.

Labov, W. (1972), *Sociolinguistic patterns*, Philadelphia 1972.

Labov, W. (1975), *What is a linguistic fact?*, Lisse 1975.

Lado, R. (1957), *Linguistics across cultures*, Ann Arbor, Mich. 1957.

Lado, R. (1961), *Language testing. The construction and use of foreign language tests. A teacher's book*, London 1961.

Lambert, W. (1967), A social psychology of bilingualism, *The Journal of Social Issues* 23, 1967, 91–109.

Lambert, W., R. Gardner, H. Barik, K. Tunstall (1963), Attitudinal and cognitive aspects of intensive study of a second language, *Journal of Abnormal and Social Psychology* 66, 1963, 358–68. Reprinted in: Gardner and Lambert (1972), 228–45.

Lambert, W., W. Lambert (1964), *Social psychology*, Englewood Cliffs, NJ 1964.

Lange, D. (ed.) (1970), *Britannica review of foreign language education*, vol. 2, Chicago 1970.

Larsen, D. (1975), A re-evaluation of grammatical structure sequencing, in: Crymes, R., W. Norris (eds.), *ON TESOL 1974*, Washington, DC 1975, 151–61.

Larsen-Freeman, D. (1975), The acquisition of grammatical morphemes by adult ESL students, *TESOL Quarterly* 9, 1975, 409–19.

Larsen-Freeman, D. (1976), An explanation for the morpheme acquisition order of second language learners, *Language Learning* 26, 1976, 125–34.

Larsen-Freeman, D. (1979), Issues in the teaching of grammar, in: Celce-Murcia and McIntosh (1979), 217–28.

Larsen-Freeman, D. (ed.) (1980), *Discourse analysis in second language research*, Rowley, Mass. 1980.

Lauerbach, G. (1979a), Das Wortassoziationsexperiment als Forschungsinstrument der Fremdsprachendidaktik, *Die Neueren Sprachen* 78, 1979, 379–91.

Lauerbach, G. (1979b), The Threshold Level – for schools? Kritische Anmerkungen zum Verständnis von 'Kommunikationsfähigkeit in der Fremdsprache', *Neusprachliche Mitteilungen* 32, 1979, 149–56.

Law, M. (1973), Assumptions in linguistics and the psychology of learning made in current modern language courses, *Praxis des neusprachlichen Unterrichts* 20, 1973, 231–8.

Lee, W. (1977), For and against an early start, *Foreign Language Annals* 10, 1977, 263–70.

Leech, G., J. Svartvik (1975), *A communicative grammar of English*, London 1975.

Leemann, E. (1981), Evaluating language assessment tests. Some practical considerations, in: Erickson and Omark (1981), 115–28.

Leeson, R. (1975), *Fluency and language teaching*, London 1975.

Legenhausen, L. (1975), *Fehleranalyse und Fehlerbewertung. Untersuchungen an englischen Reifeprüfungsnacherzählungen*, Berlin 1975.

Lehiste, I. (1971), Grammatical variability and the difference between native and non-native speakers, in: Nickel (1971), 69–74.

Leidy, J., A. Burke, A. Merkel, M. Howard (1980), Using computer assisted instruction in an ESL language program, *NALLD Journal* 15, 1, 1980, 13–24.

Lemon, N. (1973), *Attitudes and their measurement*, London 1973.

Lenneberg, E. (1967), *Biological foundations of language*, New York 1967.

Léon, P., P. Martin (1971), Linguistique appliquée et enseignement de l'intonation, *Etudes de Linguistique Appliquée* 3, 1971, 36–45.

Léon, P., P. Martin (1972), Machines and measurements, in: Bolinger, D. (ed.), *Intonation*, Hardmondsworth 1972, 30–47.

Leopold, W. (1939–1949), *Speech development of a bilingual child, Vols I–IV*, Evanston, Ill. 1939–1949.

Lester, M. (ed.) (1970), *Readings in applied transformational grammar*, New York 1970.

Lett, J. (1977), Assessing attitudinal outcomes, in: Phillips, J. (ed.), *The language connection: from the classroom to the world*, Skokie, Ill. 1977, 267–302.

Levelt, W. (1974), *Formal grammars in linguistics and psycholinguistics. Vol. 3: Psycholinguistic applications*, The Hague 1974.

Levelt, W., G. Kempen (1979), Language, in: Michon, J., E. Eijkman, L. de Klerk (eds.), *Handbook of psychonomics, vol. 2*, Amsterdam 1979, 347–407.

Levenston, E. (1971), Over-indulgence and under-representation, aspects of mother-tongue interference, in: Nickel (1971), 115–21.

Levenston, E. (1979), Second language acquisition: issues and problems, *Interlanguage Studies Bulletin* 4, 1979, 147–60.

Levin, L. (1972), *Comparative studies in foreign-language teaching*, Stockholm 1972.

Littlewood, W. (1974), Programmed instruction and language teaching, *Modern Languages* 55, 1974, 12–16.

Littlewood, W. (1978), Receptive skills as an objective for slow learners, *Der fremdsprachliche Unterricht* 12, 1978, 11–20.

Littlewood, W. (1981), *Communicative language teaching. An introduction*, Cambridge 1981.

Lockhart, L. (1931), *Word economy: an essay in applied linguistics*, London 1931.

Logan, G. (1973), *Individualized foreign language learning: an organic process*, Rowley, Mass. 1973.

Lorge, S. (1964), Language laboratory. Research studies in New York City High Schools. A discussion of the program and the findings, *The Modern Language Journal* 48, 1964, 409–19.

Lukmani, Y. (1972), Motivation to learn and language proficiency, *Language Learning* 22, 1972, 261–74.

Macht, K. (1979), Medieneinsatz und Unterrichtserfolg, in: Walter and Schröder (1979), 56–67.

Macht, K., R. Schlossbauer (1978), *Englischunterricht audiovisuell*. Reihe Exempla Band 10, Donauwörth 1978.

Macht, K., K. Schröder (1976), Moderne Fremdsprachen aus der Sicht von Studienanfängern. Ergebnisse einer Umfrage, *Die Neueren Sprachen* 75, 1976, 274–92.

Mackenzie, J. (1981), Pedagogically relevant aspects of case grammar, in: James and Westney (1981), 23–37.

Mackey, W. (1965), *Language teaching analysis*, London 1965.

Mackey, W. (1966), Applied linguistics: its meaning and use, *English Language Teaching* 20, 1966, 197–206.

Mackey, W. (1973), Language didactics and applied linguistics, in: Oller and Richards (1973), 4–15.

Mackey, W., J. Savard, P. Ardouin (1971), *Le vocabulaire disponible du français*, Montréal 1971.

Macnamara, M. (1973), Attitudes and learning a second language, in: Shuy, R., R. Fasold (eds.), *Language attitudes: current trends and prospects*, Washington, DC 1973, 36–40.

Madsen, H. (1979), Innovative methodologies applicable to TESL, in: Celce-Murcia and McIntosh (1979), 26–38.

Madsen, H., J. Bowen (1978), *Adaptation in language teaching*, Rowley, Mass. 1978.

Mager, R. (1962), *Preparing instructional objectives*, Belmont, Cal. 1962.

Magnan, S. (1979), Reduction and error correction for communicative language use: the focus approach, *The Modern Language Journal* 63, 1979, 342–9.

Mair, W. (1981), Der Methodenwechsel im Fremdsprachenunterricht: eine sozialgeschichtliche Skizze, in: Mair, W., H. Meter (eds.), *Fremdsprachenunterricht – wozu? Historische und methodologische Überlegungen zur Situation der Sprachdidaktik*, Tübingen 1981, 11–90.

Maley, A., A. Duff (1976), The use of pictures in language teaching, *Bulletin Pédagogique IUT* 42, 1976, 32–51.

Maley, A., A. Duff (1978), *Drama techniques in language teaching*, Cambridge 1978.

Mann, R. (1981), Bestandsaufnahme Lehrbuchtext. Bewertungskriterien für den kommunikativen Wert von Lehrbuchtexten für den Englischunterricht, *Praxis des neusprachlichen Unterrichts* 28, 1981, 21–9.

Martin, M. (1978), The application of spiralling to the teaching of grammar, *TESOL Quarterly* 12, 1978, 151–60.

Marton, W. (1972), Some methodological assumptions for transformational contrastive studies, in: Filipovic, R. (ed.), *Active methods and modern aids in the teaching of foreign languages*, Oxford 1972, 198–205.

Marton, W. (1974), Syllabus design and the cognitive approach to foreign language learning, *ITL Review of Applied Linguistics* 25/26, 1974, 19–34.

Marty, F. (1981), Reflections on the use of computers in second language acquisition (I), *System* 9, 1981, 85–98.

Marty, F. (1982), Reflections on the use of computers in second language acquisition (II), *System* 10, 1982, 1–11.

Maslow, A. (1970), *Motivation and personality*, New York 1970. 2nd ed.

Mathesius, V. (1936), On some problems of the systematic analysis of grammar, *Travaux du cercle linguistique de Prague* 6, 1936, 95–107.

Matter, J. (1976), Grammaire pédagogique et grammaire théorique, *Toegepaste Taalwetenschap in Artikelen* 1, 1976, 23–36.

McArthur, T. (1978), The vocabulary-control movement in the English language, 1844–1953, *Indian Journal of Applied Linguistics* 4, 1, 1978, 47–68.

McCollum, P., E. Day (1981), Quasi-integrative approaches. Competence. Discrete point scoring of expressive language samples, in: Erickson and Omark (1981), 163–77.

McDonough, S. (1981), *Psychology in foreign language teaching*, London 1981.

McLaughlin, B. (1978a), *Second-language acquisition in childhood*, Hillsdale, NJ 1978.

McLaughlin, B. (1978b), The monitor-model: some methodological considerations, *Language Learning* 28, 1978, 309–32.

McNair, J. (1977), Modern languages in today's curriculum, *Modern Languages* 58, 1977, 167–74.

Meier, H. (1964), *Deutsche Sprachstatistik*, Hildesheim 1964.

Meisel, J. (1975), Ausländerdeutsch und Deutsch ausländischer Arbeiter. Zur möglichen Entstehung eines Pidgin in der BRD, *Zeitschrift für Literaturwissenschaft und Linguistik* 18, 1975, 9–53.

Meisel, J. (1980), Linguistic simplification, in: Felix (1980), 13–40.

Meisel, J., H. Clahsen, M. Pienemann (1979), On determining developmental stages in natural second language acquisition, *Wuppertaler Arbeitspapiere zur Sprachwissenschaft* 2, 1979, 1–53.

Messer, S. (1976), Reflection–impulsivity: a review, *Psychological Bulletin* 83, 1976, 1026–52.

Messick, S. (1976), *Individuality in learning*, San Francisco 1976.

Meyers, L., N. Grossen (1978), *Behavioral research: theory, procedure, and design*, San Francisco 1978. 2nd ed.

Meys, W. (1981), Morphology and second language teaching, in: James and Westney (1981), 121–46.

Michéa, R. (1953), Mots fréquents et mots disponibles. Un aspect nouveau de la statistique de langage, *Les Langues Modernes* 47, 1953, 338–44.

Migchielsen, M. (1982), Een editing test als indicator van niveau van taalvaardigheid, unpubl. report, Nijmegen 1982.

Mihm, E. (1972), *Die Krise der neusprachlichen Didaktik*, Frankfurt/M. 1972.

Mindt, D. (1978), *Medien im Fremdsprachenunterricht: eine Klassifizierung unter didaktischem Aspekt*, Trier 1978.

Mockridge-Fong, S. (1979), Teaching and speaking skill, in: Celce-Murcia and McIntosh (1979), 90–101.

Mohan, B. (1979), Cultural bias in reading comprehension tests, in: Yorio *et al.* (1979), 171–7.

Möhle, D., M. Raupach (1979), Pragmalinguistische Analyse von Lehrwerken für den Französischunterricht, in: Neuner (1979), 167–241.

Molfese, D., R. Freeman, D. Palermo (1975), The ontogeny of brain lateralization for speech and nonspeech stimuli, *Brain and Language* 2, 1975, 356–68.

Möller, C. (1969), *Technik der Lernplanung. Methoden und Probleme der Lernzielerstellung*, Weinheim 1969.

Moreau, P., G. Pfister (1978), An analysis of the deep cultural aspects in second-year college French textbooks published from 1972 to 1974, *Foreign Language Annals* 11, 1978, 165-71.

Morgan, B. (1928), *A German frequency word book. Based on Kaeding's Häufigkeitswörterbuch der deutschen Sprache*, New York 1928.

Morley, G. (1978), Selecting course material, *Audio-Visual Language Journal* 16, 1978, 175-7.

Morrow, K. (1979), Communicative language testing: revolution or evolution?, in: Brumfit and Johnson (1979), 143-58.

Moskowitz, G. (1978), *Caring and sharing in the foreign language class. A sourcebook on humanistic techniques*, Rowley, Mass. 1978.

Moskowitz, G. (1980), Out of limbo into humanistic heaven, *The Canadian Modern Language Review* 37, 1980, 36-45.

Moulton, W. (1962), *The sounds of English and German*, Chicago 1962.

Moulton, W. (1965), Applied linguistics in the classroom, in: Allen, H. (ed.), *Teaching English as a second language*, New York 1965, 74-83.

Mueller, T. (ed.) (1968a), *Proceedings of the seminar on programmed learning*, New York 1968.

Mueller, T. (1968b), Programmed language instruction six years later, in: Mueller (1968a), 38-49.

Mueller, T., R. Miller (1970), A study of student attitudes and motivation in a collegiate French course using programmed language instruction, *International Review of Applied Linguistics in Language Teaching* 8, 1970, 297-320.

Mullen, K. (1979a), An alternative to the cloze test, in: Yorio *et al.* (1979), 187-92.

Mullen, K. (1979b), More on cloze tests as tests of proficiency in English as a second language, in: Brière and Hinofotis (1979b), 21-32.

Mullen, K. (1980), Rater reliability and oral proficiency evaluations, in: Oller and Perkins (1980), 91-101.

Müller, K. (1973), Methodische Differenzierung im Englischunterricht als Weg zur Individualisierung von Lehr- und Lernprozessen, in: Keutsch, W. (ed.), *Fachdidaktik Englisch. Beiträge zur Theorie und Praxis an Schule und Hochschule*, Bebenhausen 1973, 83-93.

Müller, R. (1975), Fremdsprachendidaktik als Wissenschaft und Studienfach, *Praxis des neusprachlichen Unterrichts* 22, 1975, 141-7.

Munby, J. (1978), *Communicative syllabus design*, London 1978.

Murakami, K. (1974), A language aptitude test for the Japanese (GTT), *System* 2, 3, 1974, 31-47.

Murdoch, B. (1978), Secondhand scholarship? The value of the review, *Die Unterrichtspraxis* 11, 2, 1978, 85-9.

Naiman, A., M. Fröhlich, H. Stern, A. Todesco (1978), *The good language learner*, Toronto 1978.

Nelson, G., J. Ward, S. Desch, R. Kaplow (1976), Two new strategies for computer-assisted language instruction (CALI), *Foreign Language Annals* 9, 1976, 28-37.

Nemser, W. (1971), Approximative systems of foreign language learners, *International Review of Applied Linguistics in Language Teaching* 9, 1971, 115-23.

Neufeld, G. (1977), Language learning ability in adults: a study on the acquisition of prosodic and articulatory features, *Working Papers on Bilingualism* 12, 1977, 46-60.

Neufeld, G. (1978a), A theoretical perspective on the nature of linguistic aptitude, *International Review of Applied Linguistics in Language Teaching* 16, 1978, 15-25.

Neufeld, G. (1978b), On the acquisition of prosodic and articulatory features in adult language learning, *The Canadian Modern Language Review* 34, 1978, 163-74.

Neufeld, G. (1979), Towards a theory of language learning ability, *Language Learning* 29, 1979, 227-41.

Neufeld, G., E. Schneiderman (1980), Prosodic and articulatory features in adult language learning, in: Scarcella and Krashen (1980), 105-9.

Neuner, G. (ed.) (1979), *Zur Analyse fremdsprachlicher Lehrwerke*, Frankfurt/M. 1979.

Neuner, G., M. Krüger, U. Grewer (1981), *Übungstypologie zum kommunikativen Deutschunterricht*, Berlin 1981.

Newmark, L. (1970), How not to interfere with language learning, in: Lester (1970), 219-27.

Newmark, L., D. Reibel (1968), Necessity and sufficiency in language learning, *International Review of Applied Linguistics in Language Teaching* 6, 1968, 145-64. Reprinted in: Lester (1970), 220-44.

Nickel, G. (ed.) (1971), *Papers in contrastive linguistics*, Cambridge 1971.

Nickel, G. (ed.) (1972a), *Fehlerkunde. Beiträge zur Fehleranalyse, Fehlerbewertung und Fehlertherapie*, Berlin 1972.

Nickel, G. (ed.) (1972b), *Reader zur kontrastiven Linguistik*, Frankfurt/M. 1972.

Nickel, G. (1973), Aspects of error evaluation and grading, in: Svartvik (1973), 24-8.

Nickel, G. (ed.) (1976), *Proceedings of the Fourth International Congress of Applied Linguistics, Vol. 3*, Stuttgart 1976.

Nickel, G. (ed.) (1978), *Language testing*, Stuttgart 1978.

Nord, J. (1980), Developing listening fluency before speaking: an alternative paradigm, *System* 8, 1980, 1-22.

Nowacek, R. (1973), *Das VHS-Zertifikat Englisch*, Bonn 1973. 3rd ed. First published 1967.

Nübold, P. (1977), Distinktive Merkmale und phonologische Progression in deutschen Lehrwerken des Englischen, unpubl. doctoral dissertation, Technische Universität Braunschweig, Braunschweig 1977.

Obler, L. (1981), Right hemisphere participation in second language acquisition, in: Diller (1981), 53-64.

Ogden, C. (1968), *Basic English: international second language*, New York 1968.

Ogden, C., I. Richards (1923), *The meaning of meaning*, London 1923.

Oksaar, E. (1972), Zum Passiv im Deutschen und Schwedischen, in: Nickel (1972b), 85-105.

Olechowski, R. (1970), Experimenteller Vergleich der Effektivität verschiedener Sprachlabor-Typen bei Kindern und Erwachsenen, *Das Sprachlabor* 4, 1970, 98-103.

Oller, J. (1973), Cloze tests of second language proficiency and what they measure, *Language Learning* 23, 1973, 105-18.

Oller, J. (1977), Attitude variables in second language learning, in: Burt *et al.* (1977), 172-84.

Oller, J. (1978), Pragmatics and language testing, in: Spolsky (1978a), 39-57.

Oller, J. (1979a), Explaining the reliable variance in tests: the validation problem, in: Brière and Hinofotis (1979b), 61-74.

Oller, J. (1979b), *Language tests at school. A pragmatic approach*, London 1979.

Oller, J. (1979c), The psychology of language and contrastive linguistics: the research and the debate, *Foreign Language Annals* 12, 1979, 299-310.

Oller, J. (1981), Research on the measurement of affective variables: some remaining questions, in: Andersen, R. (ed.), *New dimensions in second language acquisition research*, Rowley, Mass. 1981, 14-27.

Oller, J., L. Baca, F. Vigil (1977a), Attitudes and attained proficiency in ESL: a sociolinguistic study of Mexican Americans in the Southwest, *TESOL Quarterly* 11, 1977, 173-83.

Oller, J., A. Hudson, P. Liu (1977b), Attitudes and attained proficiency in ESL: a sociolinguistic study of native speakers of Chinese in the United States, *Language Learning* 27, 1977, 1-27.

Oller, J., N. Nagato (1974), The long-term effect of FLES: an experiment, *The Modern Language Journal* 58, 1974, 15-19.

Oller, J., K. Perkins (1978a), A further comment on language proficiency as a source of variance in certain affective measures, *Language Learning* 28, 1978, 417–23.

Oller, J., K. Perkins (1978b), Intelligence and language proficiency as sources of variance in self-reported affective variables, *Language Learning* 28, 1978, 85–97.

Oller, J., K. Perkins (eds.) (1980), *Research in language testing*, Rowley, Mass. 1980.

Oller, J., K. Perkins, M. Murakami (1980), Seven types of learner variables in relation to ESL learning, in: Oller and Perkins (1980), 223–40.

Oller, J., J. Richards (eds.) (1973), *Focus on the learner: pragmatic perspectives for the language teacher*, Rowley, Mass. 1973.

Oller, J., V. Streiff (1975), Dictation: a test of grammar based expectancies, in: Jones and Spolsky (1975), 71–8.

Olsen, S. (1980), Foreign language departments and computer assisted instruction: a survey, *The Modern Language Journal* 64, 1980, 341–9.

Olson, L., S. Samuels (1973), The relationship between age and accuracy of foreign language pronunciation, *The Journal of Educational Research* 66, 1973, 263–8.

Olsson, M. (1972), *Intelligibility. An evaluation of some features of English produced by Swedish 14-year-olds*, Gothenburg 1972.

Ornstein, J. (1970), Once more: programmed instruction in the language field: the state of the art, *Language Learning* 20, 1970, 213–22.

Oskarsson, M. (1973), Assessing the relative effectiveness of two methods of teaching English to adults: a replication experiment, *International Review of Applied Linguistics in Language Teaching* 11, 1973, 251–61.

Oskarsson, M. (1975), On the role of the mother tongue in learning foreign language vocabulary: an empirical investigation, *ITL Review of Applied Linguistics* 27, 1975, 19–32.

Oyama, S. (1976), The sensitive period for the acquisition of a nonnative phonological system, *Journal of Psycholinguistic Research* 5, 1976, 261–83.

Oyama, S. (1978), The sensitive period and comprehension of speech, *Working Papers on Bilingualism* 16, 1978, 1–17.

Palermo, D. (1978), *Psychology of language*, Glenview, Ill. 1978.

Palermo, D., J. Jenkins (1964), *Word association norms. Grade school through college*, Minneapolis 1964.

Palmberg, R. (1976), A select bibliography of error analysis and related topics, *Interlanguage Studies Bulletin* 1, 2–3, 1976, 340–89.

Palmberg, R. (1977), Bibliography additions, *Interlanguage Studies Bulletin* 2, 3, 1977, 91–9.

Palmer, A., P. Groot (1981), An introduction, in: Palmer *et al.* (1981), 1–11.

Palmer, A., P. Groot, G. Trosper (eds.) (1981), *The construct validation of tests of communicative competence*, Washington, DC 1981.

Palmer, H. (1917), *The scientific study and teaching of languages*, London 1917. 2nd ed. 1968.

Palmer, H. (1922), *The principle of language-study*, London 1922. 2nd. ed. 1964.

Palmer, H. (1934), *Specimens of English construction patterns*, Tokyo 1934.

Parker, W. (1954), *The national interest and foreign languages*, Washington, DC 1954. 3rd ed. 1961.

Partington, J. (1980), My cup of Co Co runneth over, *The British Journal of Language Teaching* 18, 1980, 23–7.

PAS-DVV (1977), *Das VHS-Zertifikat Englisch*, Bonn 1977. 5th ed.

PAS-DVV (1981), *Der Grundbaustein zum VHS-Zertifikat*, Bonn 1981.

Paulston, C., M. Bruder (1975), *From substitution to substance. A handbook of structural pattern drills*, Rowley, Mass. 1975.

Paulston, C., M. Bruder (1976), *Teaching English as a second language. Techniques and procedures*, Cambridge, Mass. 1976.

Peck, A. (1976), Functional-notional syllabuses and their importance for defining levels of linguistic proficiency, *Audio-Visual Language Journal* 14, 1976, 95-105.

Peck, A. (1979), Communicative methodology and its implications for teaching strategy, *Modern Languages* 60, 1979, 127-36.

Penfield, W., L. Roberts (1959), *Speech and brain-mechanisms*, Princeton 1959.

Perdue, C. (1982), *Second language acquisition by adult immigrants. A field manual*, Strasbourg 1982.

Perez, M. (1981), L'approche communicative: quelques difficultés de mise en application, *Bulletin de l'ACLA* 3, 1, 1981, 7-59.

Pettigrew, T. (1958), The measurement and correlates of category width as a cognitive variable, *Journal of Personality* 26, 1958, 532-44.

Pfeffer, J. (1964), *Basic spoken German word list, Grundstufe*, Englewood Cliffs, NJ 1964.

Pfeffer, J. (1970), *Basic spoken German word list, Mittelstufe*, Pittsburgh 1970.

Pfeffer, J. (1975), *Grunddeutsch. Erarbeitung und Wertung dreier deutscher Korpora*, Tübingen 1975.

Pfister, G., H. Rada (1974), The dilemma of textbook selection: an objective evaluation as an alternative to book reviews, *Die Unterrichtspraxis* 7, 2, 1974, 143-8.

Pienemann, M. (1981), *Der Zweitsprachenerwerb ausländischer Arbeiterkinder*, Bonn 1981.

Piepho, H. (1974), *Kommunikative Kompetenz als übergeordnetes Lernziel im Englischunterricht*, Dornburg/Frickhofen 1974.

Piepho, H. (1979), *Kommunikative Didaktik des Englischunterrichts*, Limburg 1979.

Pillet, R. (1974), *Foreign language study: perspective and prospect*, Chicago 1974.

Pimsleur, P. (1961), A study of foreign language learning ability: parts I and II, in: Zarechnak, M. (ed.), *Monograph series on languages and linguistics 14*, Washington, DC 1961, 57-72.

Pimsleur, P. (1964), *Language aptitude battery*, New York 1964.

Pimsleur, P. (1966), Testing foreign language learning, in: Valdman (1966), 175-214.

Pimsleur, P., R. Stockwell, A. Comrey (1962), Foreign language learning ability, *Journal of Educational Psychology* 53, 1962, 15-26.

Pimsleur, P., D. Sundland, R. McIntire (1964), Under-achievement in foreign language learning, *International Review of Applied Linguistics in Language Teaching* 2, 1964, 113-50.

Politzer, R. (1960), *Teaching French: an introduction to applied linguistics*, Boston 1960.

Politzer, R. (1967), Preface, in: Léon, P. (ed.), *Applied linguistics and the teaching of French*, Montreal 1967, 3-5.

Politzer, R. (1968), An experiment in the presentation of parallel and contrasting structures, *Language Learning* 18, 1968, 35-43.

Politzer, R. (1972), *Linguistics and applied linguistics: aims and methods*, Philadelphia 1972.

Politzer, R., F. Politzer (1972), *Teaching English as a second language*, Lexington, Mass. 1972.

Politzer, R., L. Weiss (1969), Developmental aspects of auditory discrimination, echo response, and recall, *The Modern Language Journal* 53, 1969, 75-85.

Popham, W. (1978), *Criterion-referenced measurement*, Englewood Cliffs, NJ 1978.

Porcher, L., M. Huart, F. Mariet (1980), *Adaptation de 'Un niveau seuil' pour des contextes scolaires*, Strasbourg 1980.

Porter, D. (1978), Cloze procedure and equivalence, *Language Learning* 28, 1978, 333-41.

Postovsky, V. (1976), The priority of aural comprehension in the language acquisition process, in: Nickel, G. (ed.), *Proceedings of the Fourth International Congress of Applied Linguistics, Vol. 3*, Stuttgart 1976, 457-67.

President's Commission on Foreign Language and International Studies (1979),

Strength through wisdom: a critique of U.S. capability, Washington, DC 1979. Also published in *The Modern Language Journal* 64, 1980, 9–57.

Putnam, C. (1981a), Assessing the assessment: a review of the President's Commission report, *Foreign Language Annals* 14, 1981, 11–15.

Putnam, C. (1981b), Technology and foreign language teaching, *The British Journal of Language Teaching* 19, 1981, 63–8.

Quémada, B. (1974), Remarques de méthode sur une recherche d'indices d'utilité du vocabulaire, *Le Français dans le monde* 103, 1974, 18–24.

Quetz, J. (1977), Anmerkungen zur Wortschatzliste des Threshold Level, *Zielsprache Englisch* 7, 3, 1977, 29–30.

Quinn, T. (1974), Theoretical foundations in linguistics and related fields, in: Jarvis (1974), 329–53.

Quirk, R., S. Greenbaum, G. Leech, J. Svartvik (1972), *A grammar of contemporary English*, London 1972.

Quirk, R., J. Svartvik (1979), A corpus of modern English, in: Bergenholtz and Schaeder (1979), 204–18.

Qvistgaard, J. *et al.* (eds.) (1974), *Applied linguistics. Problems and solutions*, Heidelberg 1974.

Raabe, H. (1972), Zum Verhältnis von kontrastiver Grammatik und Übersetzung, in: Nickel (1972b), 59–74.

Raasch, A. (1972), Neue Wege zu einem Grundwortschatz, *Praxis des neusprachlichen Unterrichts* 19, 1972, 235–44.

Raasch, A. (1977), Lernzielorientierte Sprachinventare im Französischen, in: Hüllen *et al.* (1977), 71–80.

Raasch, A. (1978a), Ein europäisches Projekt zur Förderung des Fremdsprachenerwerbs – Zwischenbilanz –, in: Detering, K., R. Högel (eds.), *Englisch auf der Sekundarstufe 1*, Hannover 1978, 216–29.

Raasch, A. (1978b), Kolloquium zum Thema 'Un niveau seuil und Französischunterricht in der Bundesrepublik', *Die Neueren Sprachen* 77, 1978, 465–7.

Raasch, A. (1979), Lernziele und Sprachinventare, in: Kleine (1979), 16–31.

Radden, G. (1980), *Schülermeinungen zu ihrem Englischlehrwerk*, Trier 1980.

Ramirez, A., R. Politzer (1978), Comprehension and production in English as a second language by elementary school children and adolescents, in: Hatch (1978), 313–32.

Rath, R. (1975), Gesprochenes Deutsch – unter besonderer Berücksichtigung der Frage: Anakoluth und Korrektur, in: Funke, H. (ed.), *Grundfragen der Methodik des Deutschunterrichts und ihre praktischen Verfahren*, München 1975, 98–108.

Rattunde, E. (1977), Transfer-Interferenz? Probleme der Begriffsdefinition bei der Fehleranalyse, *Die Neueren Sprachen* 76, 1977, 4–14.

Rattunde, E., F. Weller (1977), Auswahlbibliographie zur Fehlerkunde (Veröffentlichungen 1967–1976), *Die Neueren Sprachen* 76, 1977, 102–13.

Richards, D. (1975), In search of relevant foundations – towards a more integrated 'Applied Linguistics'?, *ITL Review of Applied Linguistics* 29, 1975, 1–18.

Richards, J. (1971), A non-contrastive approach to error analysis, *English Language Teaching* 25, 1971, 204–19.

Richards, J. (ed.) (1974), *Error analysis. Perspectives on second language acquisition*, London 1974.

Richards, J. (ed.) (1978), *Understanding second and foreign language learning: issues and approaches*, Rowley, Mass. 1978.

Richterich, R. (1972), *A model for the definition of language needs of adults learning a modern language*, Strasbourg 1972.

Ritchie, W. (1967), Some implications of generative grammar for the construction of courses in English as a foreign language, *Language Learning* 17, 1967, 45–69 and 111–31.

Ritchie, W. (ed.) (1978), *Second language acquisition research. Issues and implications*,

New York 1978.

Rivenc, P. (1979), Le français fondamental vingt-cinq ans après, *Le Français dans le monde* 148, 1979, 15-22.

Rivers, W. (1964), *The psychologist and the foreign-language teacher*, Chicago 1964.

Rivers, W. (1968), *Teaching foreign language skills*, Chicago 1968.

Rivers, W. (1972), Talking off the top of their heads, *TESOL Quarterly* 6, 1972, 71-81.

Rivers, W. (1975), *A practical guide to the teaching of French*, New York 1975.

Rivers, W., M. Azevedo, W. Heflin, R. Hyman-Opler (1976), *A practical guide to the teaching of Spanish*, New York 1976.

Rivers, W., K. Dell-Orto, V. Dell-Orto (1976), *A practical guide to the teaching of German*, New York 1976.

Roberts, G. (1981), The use of microcomputers for the teaching of modern languages, *The British Journal of Language Teaching* 19, 3, 1981, 125-9.

Roberts, R. (1972), Aims and objectives in language teaching, *English Language Teaching* 26, 1972, 224-9.

Rodriguez-Bou, L. (1952), *Recuento de vocabulario espanol*, Puerto Rico 1952.

Rohrer, J. (1981), Problems and practice in language testing: a view from the Bundessprachenamt, in: Klein-Braley and Stevenson (1981), 31-4.

Rokeach, M. (1972), *Attitudes and values*, San Francisco 1972. 2nd ed.

Rombouts, S. (1937), *Waarheen met ons vreemde-talenonderwijs?*, Tilburg 1937.

Rosansky, E. (1975), The critical period for the acquisition of language: some cognitive developmental considerations, *Working Papers on Bilingualism* 6, 1975, 93-100.

Rosansky, E. (1976), Methods and morphemes in second language acquisition research, *Language Learning* 26, 1976, 409-25.

Rosengren, I. (ed.) (1972), *Ein Frequenzwörterbuch der deutschen Zeitungssprache: Die Welt. Süddeutsche Zeitung* vol. 1, Copenhagen/Lund 1972.

Rosengren, I. (ed.) (1977), *Ein Frequenzwörterbuch der deutschen Zeitungssprache: Die Welt, Süddeutsche Zeitung* vol. 2, Copenhagen/Lund 1977.

Ross, D. (1981), From theory to practice: some critical comments on the communicative approach to language teaching, *Language Learning* 31, 1981, 223-42.

Roulet, E. (1973), L'élaboration de matériel didactique pour l'enseignement des langues maternelle et secondes: leçons de la linguistique appliquée, *Bulletin CILA* 18, 1973, 31-46.

Roulet, E. (1978), Les modèles de grammaire et leurs applications à l'enseignement des langues vivantes, in: Bouacha, A. (ed.), *La pédagogie du français langue étrangère*, Paris 1978, 29-48.

Rubin, J., B. Jernudd (eds.) (1971), *Can language be planned?*, Honolulu 1971.

Rubin, J., B. Jernudd, J. Das Gupta, J. Fishman, C. Ferguson (eds.) (1977), *Language planning processes*, The Hague 1977.

Rubin, J., R. Shuy (eds.) (1973), *Language planning: current issues and research*, Washington, DC 1973.

Rusiecki, J. (1976), The development of contrastive linguistics, *Interlanguage Studies Bulletin* 1, 1, 1976, 12-44.

Russell, W., O. Meseck (1959), Der Einfluss der Assoziation auf das Erinnern von Wörtern in der deutschen, französischen und englischen Sprache, *Zeitschrift für Experimentelle und Angewandte Psychologie* 6, 1959, 191-211.

Rutherford, W. (1968), *Modern English: a textbook for foreign students*, New York 1968.

Rutherford, W. (1980), Aspects of pedagogical grammar, *Applied Linguistics* 1, 1980, 60-73.

Sajavaara, K., J. Lehtonen (eds.) (1980), *Papers in discourse and contrastive discourse analysis. Jyväskylä Contrastive Studies 5*, Jyväskylä 1980.

Sauer, H. (1971), Sequentialität als Ursache für Minderleistungen im Fremdsprachenunterricht, *Neusprachliche Mitteilungen* 24, 1971, 133-43.

Sauer, H. (1975), Annotierte Auswahlbibliographie zum Fremdsprachenunterricht auf der Primarstufe, in: Sauer, H. (ed.), *Englisch auf der Primarstufe. Texte und Informationen zum Frühbeginn des Fremdsprachenunterrichts*, Paderborn 1975, 217–32.

Sauer, H. (1979), Frühbeginn des Zweitsprachenunterrichts als Problem in Schule und Hochschule. Eine Bestandsaufnahme, in: Walter and Schröder (1979), 82–93.

Savard, J. (1970), *La valence lexicale*, Paris 1970.

Savard, J., J. Richards (1970), *Les indices d'utilité du vocabulaire fondamental français*, Québec 1970.

Savignon, S. (1972), *Communicative competence: an experiment in foreign language teaching*, Philadelphia 1972.

Scarcella, R., S. Krashen (eds.) (1980), *Research in second language acquisition*, Rowley, Mass. 1980.

Schachter, J. (1959), Contrastive analysis of English and Paganesian, unpubl. doctoral dissertation, University of California, Los Angeles 1959.

Schachter, J. (1974), An error in error analysis, *Language Learning* 24, 1974, 205–15.

Schachter, J. (1979), Reflections on error production, *Interlanguage Studies Bulletin* 4, 1, 1979, 15–26.

Schäfer, H. (1972), Skizze zu einer Progressionstypologie. Reihende und umkreiserweiternde Lehrfortschritte, *Zielsprache Deutsch* 3, 1, 1972, 29–36.

Schäpers, R. (1972), Lineare Progression und konzentrischer Aufbau, *Zielsprache Deutsch* 3, 1, 1972, 22–8.

Schegloff, E., G. Jefferson, H. Sacks (1977), The preference for self-correction in the organization of repair in conversation, *Language* 53, 1977, 361–82.

Scheibner-Herzig, G., R. Grosse-Oetringhaus, A. Pieper (1977), Prediction of nine-year-old children's language learning aptitude, *International Review of Applied Linguistics in Language Teaching* 15, 1977, 197–208.

Scherer, G., M. Wertheimer (1964), *A psycholinguistic experiment in foreign-language teaching*, New York 1964.

Schiffler, L. (1973), *Einführung in den audiovisuellen Fremdsprachenunterricht*, Heidelberg 1973.

Schiffler, L. (1974), Diskussionsthema: Einsprachigkeit. Die Untersuchungen Dodsons, *Praxis des neusprachlichen Unterrichts* 21, 1974, 227–38.

Schilder, H. (1977), *Medien im neusprachlichen Unterricht seit 1880*, Kronberg/Ts 1977.

Schilder, H. (1980), Stationen der neusprachlichen Mediendidaktik seit 1945. Versuch einer Ortsbestimmung, *Die Neueren Sprachen* 79, 1980, 330–48.

Schilder, H. (1981), Das Verhältnis von Sprachtheorie und Sprachdidaktik, *System* 9, 1981, 11–22.

Schlyter, B. (1951), *Centrala ordförrådet i franskan*, Uppsala 1951.

Schödel, A., O. Stille (1973), *Tonträger und Sprachlabor im Englischunterricht*, Frankfurt/M. 1973.

Schonell, F., I. Meddleton, B. Shaw et al. (1956), *A study of the oral vocabulary of adults*, London/Brisbane 1956.

Schools Council (1966), *French in the primary school*, London 1966.

Schröder, K. (1972), Sprachenpolitik aus der Sicht einer erweiterten EWG, Gastarbeit und gegenwärtiger Fremdsprachenunterricht an unseren Schulen, *Die Neueren Sprachen* 71, 1972, 520–30.

Schröder, K. (1973a), Fremdsprachendidaktische Studiengänge in der Universität. Legitimation–Ziele–Gewichtungen, in: Schröder, K., G. Walter (eds.), *Fremdsprachendidaktisches Studium in der Universität*, München 1973, 9–25.

Schröder, K. (1973b), Sprachenunterricht, Sprachenpolitik und internationale Kommunikation, in: Hüllen (1973), 138–51.

Schröder, K. (1974), Differenzierter oder nicht-differenzierter Fremdsprachenunterricht, *Die Neueren Sprachen* 23, 1974, 393–409.

Schröder, K. (1975a), Differenzierter oder nicht-differenzierter Fremdsprachenunterricht?, in: Hüllen *et al.* (1975), 16–34.

Schröder, K. (1975b), *Lehrwerke für den Englischunterricht im deutschsprachigen Raum 1665–1900*, Darmstadt 1975.

Schröder, K. (1976), Fremdsprachenpolitik und Fremdsprachendidaktik, *Die Neueren Sprachen* 75, 1976, 238–44.

Schröder, K. (1977a), Französisch am Ausgang seiner Epoche?, *Neusprachliche Mitteilungen* 30, 1977, 194–201.

Schröder, K. (1977b), Hörverständnis und Fremdsprachenplanung, in: Dirven, R. (ed.), *Hörverständnis im Fremdsprachenunterricht: listening comprehension in foreign language teaching*, Kronberg/Ts 1977, 14–26.

Schröder, K. (1977c), 'Tertiärsprachen' im Urteil von Studienanfängern, *Neusprachliche Mitteilungen* 30, 1977, 162–5.

Schröder, K. (1979a), Italiano come lingua straniere. Status quo, Bedarf und Bedürfnis, *Neusprachliche Mitteilungen* 32, 1979, 162–7.

Schröder, K. (1979b), Zur Frage der Differenzierung und Individualisierung im Fremdsprachenunterricht, in: Walter and Schröder (1979), 129–37.

Schröder, K. (1980), Kleine Chronik zur Frühzeit des Fremdsprachenlernens und des Fremdsprachenunterrichts im deutschsprachigen Raum, unter besonderer Berücksichtigung des 16. Jahrhunderts, *Die Neueren Sprachen* 79, 1980, 114–35.

Schröder, K., F. Weller (1975), Erwägungen zum Begriffsfeld Methodik aus fremdsprachendidaktischer Sicht, *Die Neueren Sprachen* 24, 1975, 210–33.

Schröder, K., F. Weller (1980), Bibliographie zur Geschichtsschreibung im Bereich des Fremdsprachenunterrichts und der fremdsprachlichen Philologien, *Die Neueren Sprachen* 79, 1980, 221–32.

Schröder, K., F. Zapp (1976), Protokoll des Werkstatt-Gesprächs Fremdsprachenplanung – Fremdsprachenpolitik im Rahmen des XII. FIPLV-Kongresses in Washington vom 25. und 26.11.1975, *Die Neueren Sprachen* 75, 1976, 306–19.

Schuchardt, H. (1909), Die lingua franca, *Zeitschrift für Romanische Philologie* 33, 1909, 441–61.

Schumacher, H. (1978), Grundwortschatzsammlungen des Deutschen. Zu Hilfsmitteln der Didaktik des Deutschen als Fremdsprache, in: Wierlacher, A. *et al.* (eds.), *Jahrbuch Deutsch als Fremdsprache*, vol. 4, Heidelberg 1978, 41–55.

Schumann, J. (1975), Affective factors and the problem of age in second language acquisition, *Language Learning* 25, 1975, 209–25.

Schumann, J. (1976), Second language acquisition research: getting a more global look at the learner, *Language Learning*, special issue no. 4, 1976, 15–28.

Schumann, J. (1978a), Second language acquisition: the pidginization hypothesis, in: Hatch (1978), 256–71.

Schumann, J. (1978b), Social and psychological factors in second language acquisition, in: Richards (1978), 163–78.

Schumann, J. (1978c), *The pidginization process*, Rowley, Mass. 1978.

Schumann, J. (1980), The acquisition of English relative clauses by second language learners, in: Scarcella and Krashen (1980), 118–31.

Schumann, J., J. Holroyd, R. Campbell (1978), Improvement of foreign language pronunciation under hypnosis: a preliminary study, *Language Learning* 28, 1978, 143–8.

Schumann, J., N. Stenson (eds.) (1975), *New frontiers in second language learning*, Rowley, Mass. 1975.

Schütt, H. (1974), *Fremdsprachenbegabung und Fremdsprachenleistung. Ein Beitrag zum Problem der prognostischen Gültigkeit von Fremdsprachenbegabungstests*, Frankfurt/M. 1974.

Schwartz, J. (1980), The negotiation for meaning: repair in conversations between second language learners of English, in: Larsen-Freeman (1980), 138–53.

Schwarze, C. (ed.) (1978), *Kasusgrammatik und Sprachvergleich*, Tübingen 1978.

Sciarone, A. (1977), *Vocabulario fondamentale delle lingua italiana*, Bergamo 1977.

Sciarone, A. (1979a), Fréquence et disponibilité, *Die Neueren Sprachen* 78, 1979, 324-31.

Sciarone, A. (1979b), *Woordjes leren in het vreemdetalenonderwijs*, Muiderberg 1979.

Scovel, T. (1969), Foreign accents, language acquisition, and cerebral dominance, *Language Learning* 19, 1969, 245-54.

Scovel, T. (1978), The effect of affect on foreign language learning: a review of the anxiety research, *Language Learning* 28, 1978, 129-42.

Segermann, K. (1974), Zur Überwindung des Methodenstreits in der fachdidaktischen Diskussion, *Praxis des neusprachlichen Unterrichts* 21, 1974, 339-53.

Seliger, H. (1978), Implications of a multiple critical periods hypothesis for second language learning, in: Ritchie (1978), 11-19.

Selinker, L. (1972), Interlanguage, *International Review of Applied Linguistics in Language Teaching* 10, 1972, 209-31.

Selinker, L., J. Lamendella (1978), Two perspectives on fossilization in interlanguage learning, *Interlanguage Studies Bulletin* 3, 1978, 143-91.

Selinker, L., P. Selinker (1972), An annotated bibliography of US PhD dissertations in contrastive linguistics, in: Filipovic, R. (ed.), *Reports. The Yugoslav Serbo-Croatian-English Contrastive Project*, Zagreb 1972, 1-40.

Sharwood Smith, M. (n.d.), Applied linguistics and the psychology of instruction - a case for transfusion?, *Studies in Second Language Acquisition* 1, 2, n.d., 91-115.

Sharwood Smith, M. (1979), Strategies, language transfer and the simulation of the second language learner's mental operations, *Language Learning* 29, 1979, 345-62.

Shaw, A. (1977), Foreign-language syllabus development: some recent approaches, *Language Teaching & Linguistics: Abstracts* 10, 1977, 217-33.

Shaw, M., J. Wright (1967), *Scales for the measurement of attitudes*, New York 1967.

Sheen, R. (1980), The importance of negative transfer in the speech of near-bilinguals, *International Review of Applied Linguistics in Language Teaching* 18, 1980, 105-21.

Shohamy, E. (1978), Investigation of the concurrent validity of the oral interview with cloze procedure for measuring proficiency in Hebrew as a second language, unpubl. doctoral dissertation, University of Minnesota 1978.

Siegrist, L. (1977), *Bibliographie zur kontrastiven Linguistik Deutsch/andere Sprachen (1965-1976)*, Trier 1977.

Sinclair, J. (1980), Some implications of discourse analysis for ESP methodology, *Applied Linguistics* 1, 1980, 253-61.

Skinner, B. (1957), *Verbal behavior*, New York 1957.

Slagter, P. (1979), *Un nivel umbral*, Strasbourg 1979.

Slama-Cazacu, T. (1976), Kontrastive Analyse 'in abstracto', oder die Funktion des Zusammentreffens sprachlicher Systeme im Lerner? Kontrastive Analyse im Licht der Psycholinguistik, in: Raabe, H. (ed.), *Trends in kontrastiver Linguistik*, Bd. 2, Tübingen 1976, 189-207.

SLO (1979), *Projectplan Engels in het basisonderwijs*, Enschede 1979.

Slobin, D. (1973), Cognitive prerequisites for the development of grammar, in: Ferguson and Slobin (1973), 175-208.

Slobin, D. (1979), *Psycholinguistics*, Glenview, Ill. 1979. 2nd ed.

Smith, N. (1973), *The acquisition of phonology: a case study*, Cambridge 1973.

Smith, P. (1970), *A comparison of the cognitive and audiolingual approaches to foreign language instruction*, Philadelphia 1970.

Snow, C., M. Hoefnagel-Höhle (1977), Age differences in the pronunciation of foreign sounds, *Language and Speech* 20, 1977, 357-65.

Snow, C., M. Hoefnagel-Höhle (1978a), Age differences in second language acquisition, in: Hatch (1978), 333-44.

Snow, C., M. Hoefnagel-Höhle (1978b), The critical period for language acquisition: evidence from second language acquisition, *Child Development* 49, 1978, 1114-28.

Solmecke, G., A. Boosch (1981), *Affektive Komponenten der Lernerpersönlichkeit und Fremdsprachenerwerb*, Tübingen 1981.

Spencer, N. (1973), Differences between linguists and non-linguists in intuitions of grammaticality-acceptability, *Journal of Psycholinguistic Research* 2, 1973, 83-98.

Spillner, B. (1977), On the theoretical foundations of applied linguistics, *International Review of Applied Linguistics in Language Teaching* 15, 1977, 154-7.

Spolsky, B. (1966), A psycholinguistic critique of programmed foreign language instruction, *International Review of Applied Linguistics in Language Teaching* 4, 1966, 119-29.

Spolsky, B. (1969), Attitudinal aspects of second language learning, *Language Learning* 29, 1969, 271-83.

Spolsky, B. (1970), Linguistics and language pedagogy – applications or implications?, in: Alatis (1970), 143-55.

Spolsky, B. (ed.) (1978a), *Approaches in language testing. Advances in language testing 2*, Arlington, VA 1978.

Spolsky, B. (1978b), *Educational linguistics. An introduction*, Rowley, Mass. 1978.

Spolsky, B. (1978c), Language testing: art or science, in: Nickel (1978), 215-34.

Spolsky, B. (1981), Some ethical questions about language testing, in: Klein-Braley and Stevenson (1981), 5-30.

Spolsky, B., B. Sigurd, M. Sato, E. Walker, C. Arterburn (1968), Preliminary studies in the development of techniques for testing overall second language proficiency, *Language Learning*, special issue, number 3, 1968, 79-101.

Stack, E. (1960), *The language laboratory and modern language teaching*, New York 1960.

Stammerjohann, H. (ed.) (1975), *Handbuch der Linguistik. Allgemeine und angewandte Sprachwissenschaft*, Darmstadt 1975.

Stegeman, J. (1979), *Aspekte der kontrastiven Syntax am Beispiel des Niederländischen und Deutschen*, Berlin/New York 1979.

Steiner, F. (1975), *Performing with objectives*, Rowley, Mass. 1975.

Steinfeldt, E. (n.d.), *Russian word count: 2500 words most commonly used in modern literary Russian*, Moscow n.d.

Stern, C., W. Stern (1907), *Die Kindersprache: eine psychologische und sprachtheoretische Untersuchung*, Leipzig 1907.

Stern, H. (1963), *Foreign languages in primary education*, London 1963. 2nd ed. 1967.

Stern, H. (1974), Directions in language teaching theory and research, in: Qvistgaard *et al.* (1974), 61-108.

Stern, H. (1980), Review of B. Spolsky, Educational Linguistics, *Applied Linguistics* 1, 1, 1980, 85-7.

Stern, H., A. Weinrib (1977), Foreign languages for younger children: trends and assessment, *Language Teaching & Linguistics: Abstracts* 10, 1977, 5-25.

Stevenson, D. (1981), Beyond faith and face validity: the multitrait-multimethod matrix and the convergent and discriminant validity of oral proficiency tests, in: Palmer *et al.* (1981), 37-61.

Stevick, E. (1971), *Adapting and writing language lessons*, Washington, DC 1971.

Stevick, E. (1980), *Teaching languages. A way and ways*, Rowley, Mass. 1980.

Stockwell, R. (1957), *Contrastive analysis of English and Tagalog*, Los Angeles 1957.

Stockwell, R., J. Bowen (1965), *The sounds of English and Spanish*, Chicago 1965.

Stockwell, R., J. Bowen, J. Martin (1965), *The grammatical structure of English and Spanish*, Chicago 1965.

Stratton, F. (1977), Putting the communicative syllabus in its place, *TESOL Quarterly* 11, 1977, 131-41.

Strauch, R. (1972), Bemerkungen zum Verhältnis von theoretischer Linguistik und Fremdsprachendidaktik, *Linguistik und Didaktik* 3, 1972, 20-32.

Streiff, V. (1978), Relationship among oral and written cloze scores and achievement test scores in a bilingual setting, in; Oller, J., K. Perkins (eds.), *Language in education: testing the tests*, Rowley, Mass. 1978, 65–103.

Strevens, P. (1966), Announcement. International Association of Applied Linguistics, *International Review of Applied Linguistics in Language Teaching* 4, 1966, 63–5.

Strevens, P. (1972), Language teaching, in: Sebeok, T. (ed.), *Current trends in linguistics, vol. 9: Linguistics in Western Europe*, The Hague 1972, 702–32.

Suter, R. (1976), Predictors of pronunciation accuracy in second language learning, *Language Learning* 26, 1976, 233–53.

Svartvik, J. (ed.) (1973), *Errata. Papers in error analysis*, Lund 1973.

Svartvik, J., M. Eeg-Olofsson, O. Forsheden, B. Oreström, C. Thavenius (1982), *Survey of spoken English. Report on research 1975–81*, Lund 1982.

Svartvik, J., R. Quirk (eds.) (1980), *A corpus of English conversation*, Lund 1980.

Swain, M. (1977), Future directions in second language research, in: Henning (1977), 15–28.

Swallow, T. (1981), Courses for the horses. An examination of Longman Audio-Visual French Course in relation to preparation for O level, *The British Journal of Language Teaching* 19, 1981, 27–33.

Swan, M. (1979), Language teaching is teaching language, *EFL Bulletin* 3, 1979, 5–6.

Sweet, H. (1899), *The practical study of languages*, London 1899. 2nd ed. 1964.

Szulc, A. (1976), *Die Fremdsprachendidaktik. Konzeptionen–Methoden–Theorien*, Warszawa 1976.

Taggart, G. (1979), L'enseignement d'une langue seconde: problèmes de théorie et de méthodologie, in: Rondeau, G., G. Bibeau, G. Gagné, G. Taggart (eds.), *Vingt-cinq ans de linguistique au Canada. Hommage à Jean-Paul Vinay*, Montréal 1979, 459–74.

Tanger, G. (1888), Muss der Sprachunterricht umkehren?, in: Hüllen (1979), 32–60.

Tarone, E. (1978), The phonology of interlanguage, in: Richards (1978), 15–33.

Tarone, E. (1979), Interlanguage as chameleon, *Language Learning* 29, 1979, 181–91.

Tarone, E. (1980), Some influences on the syllable structure of interlanguage phonology, *International Review of Applied Linguistics in Language Teaching* 18, 1980, 139–52.

Taylor, B. (1974), Toward a theory of language acquisition, *Language Learning* 24, 1974, 23–35.

Taylor, B. (1975), The use of overgeneralization and transfer learning strategies by elementary and intermediate students in ESL, *Language Learning* 25, 1975, 73–108.

Taylor, L., J. Catford, A. Guiora, H. Lane (1971), Psychological variables and ability to pronounce a second language, *Language and Speech* 14, 1971, 146–57.

Taylor, W. (1953), Cloze procedure: a new tool for measuring readability, *Journalism Quarterly* 30, 1953, 415–33.

Tharp, J. (1939), *The basic French vocabulary*, New York 1939.

Thiele, A., G. Scheibner-Herzig (1978), Untersuchungen zu Fremdsprachenleistung und Schülerpersönlichkeit, in: Melenizek, A. (ed.), *Technische Medien im Sprachenunterricht*, Konstanz 1978, 23–32.

Thiem, R. (1969), Bibliography of contrastive linguistics, *PAKS-Arbeitsbericht* 2, 3, 4, 1969, 79–86 and 93–120.

Thorndike, E. (1921), *The teacher's word book*, New York 1921.

Thorndike, E. (1932), *A teacher's word book of the 20,000 words found most frequently and widely in general reading for children and young people*, New York 1932.

Thorndike, E., I. Lorge (1944), *The teacher's word book of 30,000 words*, New York 1944.

Titone, R. (1968), *Teaching foreign languages: an historical sketch*, Washington, DC 1968.

Titone, R. (1977), A humanistic approach to language behavior and language learning,

The Canadian Modern Language Review 32, 1977, 309-17.

Traugott, E. (1977), Natural semantax: its role in the study of second language acquisition, in: Corder and Roulet (1977), 132-62.

Trim, J. (1977), *Report on some possible lines of development of an overall structure for a European Unit/Credit Scheme for foreign-language learning by adults*, Strasbourg 1977.

Trim, J. (ed.) (1981), *Modern languages (1971-1981)*, Strasbourg 1981.

Trudgill, P. (1974), *Sociolinguistics. An introduction*, Harmondsworth 1974.

Tucker, G., E. Hamayan, F. Genesee (1976), Affective, cognitive and social factors in second-language acquisition, *The Canadian Modern Language Review* 32, 1976, 214-26.

Turner, G. (1973), *Stylistics*, Harmondsworth 1973.

Turner, P. (1974), Why Johnny doesn't want to learn a foreign language, *The Modern Language Journal* 58, 1974, 191-6.

Upshur, J. (1979), Functional proficiency theory and a research role for language tests, in: Brière and Hinofotis (1979b), 75-100.

Vaid, J., F. Genesee (1980), Neuropsychological approaches to bilingualism: a critical review, *Canadian Journal of Psychology* 34, 1980, 417-45.

Valdman, A. (ed.) (1966), *Trends in language teaching*, New York 1966.

Valdman, A. (1968), Problems in the definition of learning steps in programmed foreign language materials, in: Mueller (1968a), 50-62.

Valdman, A. (1969), The limits of programmed instruction in foreign language acquisition, in: Newell, S. (ed.), *Proceedings of the third southern conference on language teaching, Atlanta, Febr. 1967*, Spartanburg, SC 1969, 41-54.

Valdman, A. (1975), Error analysis and pedagogical ordering. The determination of pedagogically motivated sequences, in: Corder, S., E. Roulet (eds.), *Some implications of linguistic theory for applied linguistics*, Brussels/Paris 1975, 105-26.

Valdman, A. (1978), Communicative use of language and syllabus design, *Foreign Language Annals* 11, 1978, 567-80.

Valdman, A., J. Walz (1975), *A selected bibliography on language learners' systems and error analysis*, Washington, DC 1975.

Valette, R. (1964), The use of the dictée in the French language classroom, *The Modern Language Journal* 48, 1964, 431-4.

Valette, R. (1977), *Modern language testing*, New York 1977.

Valette, R., R. Disick (1972), *Modern language performance objectives and individualization*, New York 1972.

Van Buren, P. (1974), Contrastive analysis, in: Allen and Corder (1974), 279-312.

Van Buren, P. (1976), Review of: Tomasz P. Krzeszowski, Contrastive Generative Grammar: Theoretical Foundations, Lódz 1974, *Interlanguage Studies Bulletin* 1, 2-3, 1976, 250-330.

Van Deth, J. (1979), *L'enseignement scolaire des langues vivantes dans les pays membres de la communeauté européenne: bilan, réflexions et propositions*, Brussels 1979.

Van Ek, J. (1970), *Het onderwijs in moderne vreemde talen. Problemen bij de leerstof-overdracht*, Gronigen 1970.

Van Ek, J. (1971), Linguistics and language teaching, *International Review of Applied Linguistics in Language Teaching* 9, 1971, 319-34.

Van Ek, J. (1976), *The Threshold Level for modern language learning in schools*, Strasbourg 1976. Also Groningen 1977.

Van Ek, J. (1978), The Unit/Credit System as a possible link between various forms of teaching, in: Freudenstein (1978a), 27-39.

Van Ek, J., L. Alexander (1975), *The Threshold Level in a European Unit/Credit System for modern language learning by adults*, Strasbourg 1975. Also Oxford 1980.

Van Ek, J., L. Alexander, M. Fitzpatrick (1977), *Waystage*, Strasbourg 1977. Also Oxford 1980.

Van Ek, J., P. Groot (1977), *Nota aanzet voor de ontwikkeling van een onderwijsleerplan moderne vreemde talen in het bijzonder met betrekking tot de taalvaardigheid*, The Hague 1977.

Van Els, T. (1977), 'The Threshold Level' as a specification of language learning objectives, *Interlanguage Studies Bulletin* 2, 3, 1977, 78–90.

Van Els, T. (1981), From foreign language needs to educational policy, *AILA Bulletin* 2(30), 1981, 48–61.

Van Els, T. (1983), Dutch foreign language teaching policy in a European perspective, *System* 11, 1983, 271–5

Van Meerem, L., A. Tordoir (1977), *Descriptieve analyse van leerboeken*, Amsterdam 1977.

Van Os, C. (1974), *Meinung gegen Meinung. Diskussionen über aktuelle Themen. Texte gesprochener deutscher Standardsprache 2*, München/Düsseldorf 1974.

Van Parreren, C. (1972), Lernpsychologische Gesichtspunkte beim Erwerb einer Fremdsprache, in: Goethe-Institut (ed.), *Beiträge zu den Fortbildungskursen des Goethe-Instituts für Deutschlehrer und Hochschulgermanisten aus dem Ausland 1972*, München 1972, 56–65.

Van Teslaar, A. (1963), Les domaines de la linguistique appliquée, *International Review of Applied Linguistics in Language Teaching* 1, 1963, 50–77.

Van Vlasselaer, J. (1972), Le structuro-global vis-à-vis des structuralismes, *Revue de Phonétique Appliquée* 21, 1972, 25–30.

Van Willigen, D. (1971), *Vreemde talen in het basisonderwijs*, Groningen 1971.

Vander Beke, G. (1929), *French word book*, New York 1929.

Verlée, L. (1954), *Basis-woordenboek voor de Franse taal*, Antwerpen/Amsterdam 1954.

Viëtor, W. (1882), *Der Sprachunterricht muss umkehren*, 1882. Reprinted in: Flechsig (1965), 155–72.

Vollmer, H. (1981), Why are we interested in 'General Language Proficiency'?, in: Klein-Braley and Stevenson (1981), 96–123.

Vollmer, H., F. Sang (1980), Zum psycholinguistischen Konstrukt einer internalisierten Erwartungsgrammatik, *Linguistik und Didaktik* 42, 1980, 122–48.

Von Elek, T. (1976), Experiments in teaching foreign language grammar by different methods: a summing-up of the research of the GUME/adults project, in: Nickel (1976), 353–63.

Von Elek, T., M. Oskarsson (1972a), An experiment assessing the relative effectiveness of two methods of teaching English grammatical structures to adults, *International Review of Applied Linguistics in Language Teaching* 10, 1972, 60–72.

Von Elek, T., M. Oskarsson (1972b), *Teaching foreign language grammar to adults: a comparative study*, Gothenburg 1972.

Von Elek, T., M. Oskarsson (1973a), *A follow-up study in teaching foreign language grammar*, Gothenburg 1973.

Von Elek, T., M. Oskarsson (1973b), *A replication study in teaching foreign language grammar to adults*, Gothenburg 1973.

Von Elek, T., M. Oskarsson (1975), *Comparative methods experiments in foreign language teaching: the final report of the GUME/Adults Project*, Gothenburg 1975.

Von Raffler Engel, W. (1973), Linguistique appliquée et apprentissage des langues: la place de la psychologie, in: Bibeau, G. (ed.), *Actes 3e colloque de l'ACLA*, Québec 1973, 35–60.

Von Walther, A. (1980), Sprachunterricht oder Geistesbildung? Bildungspolitische Einwirkungen auf das Schulfach Englisch im 19. Jahrhundert, *Die Neueren Sprachen* 79, 1980, 174–87.

Wächtler, K. (1974), Zur Einschätzung der amerikanischen Elemente im Bereich Linguistik und Englischunterricht, in: Nickel, G., A. Raasch (eds.), *Kongressbericht der 4. Jahrestagung der Gesellschaft für angewandte Linguistik*, Heidelberg 1974, 161–71.

Wadepuhl, W., B. Morgan (1934), *Minimum standard German vocabulary*, New York 1934.

Wall, W. (1958), The wish to learn: research into motivation, *Educational Research* 1, 1958, 23–37.

Walmsley, J. (1979), Phase and phase-sequence, *The Modern Language Journal* 63, 1979, 106–16.

Walsh, T., K. Diller (1981), Neurolinguistic considerations on the optimum age for second language learning, in: Diller (1981), 3–21.

Walter, G. (1979), *Englisch für Hauptschüler*, Königstein/Ts 1979.

Walter, G., K. Schröder (eds.) (1979), *Handbuch der Fachdidaktik. Fachdidaktisches Studium in der Lehrerbildung Englisch*, München 1979.

Wardhaugh, R. (1970), The contrastive analysis hypothesis, *TESOL Quarterly* 4, 1970, 123–30.

Wardhaugh, R., H. Brown (eds.) (1976), *A survey of applied linguistics*, Ann Arbor, Mich. 1976.

Warriner, H. (1980), Foreign language teaching in the schools-1979: focus on methodology, *The Modern Language Journal* 64, 1980, 81–7.

Weiand, H. (1978), *Film und Fernsehen im Englischunterricht. Theorie, Praxis und kritische Dokumentation*, Kronberg/Ts 1978.

Weinreich, U. (1953), *Languages in contact. Findings and problems*, New York 1953.

Weir, C. (1981), Reaction to the Morrow paper (1), in: Alderson and Hughes (1981), 26–37.

Weller, F. (1980), Skizze einer Entwicklungsgeschichte des Französischunterrichts in Deutschland bis zum Beginn des 19. Jahrhunderts, *Die Neueren Sprachen* 79, 1980, 135–60.

West, M. (1953), *A general service list of English words*, London 1953. rev. ed. 1969.

West, M., H. Hoffmann (1974), *Englischer Mindestwortschatz*, München 1974.

Westphal, P. (1979), Teaching and learning: a key to success, in: Phillips, J. (ed.), *Building on experience – Building for success*, Skokie, Ill. 1979, 119–56.

Whorf, B. (1941), Language and logic, *Technological Review* 43, 1941, 250–72.

Widdowson, H. (1968), The teaching of English through science, in: Dakin, J., B. Tiffen, H. Widdowson (eds.), *Language in education*, London 1968, 117–75.

Widdowson, H. (1975), Linguistic insights and language teaching principles, in: Gutknecht (1975a), 1–28.

Widdowson, H. (ed.) (1979a), *Explorations in applied linguistics*, London 1979.

Widdowson, H. (1979b), Notional syllabuses, in: Widdowson (1979a), 247–50.

Widdowson, H. (1979c), The communicative approach and its applications, in: Widdowson (1979a), 251–63.

Widdowson, H. (1980), Applied linguistics: the pursuit of relevance, in: Kaplan (1980), 74–87.

Wilkins, D. (1972a), *An investigation into the linguistic and situational content of the common core in a Unit/Credit System*, Strasbourg 1972.

Wilkins, D. (1972b), *Linguistics in language teaching*, London 1972.

Wilkins, D. (1974a), Grammatical, situational and notional syllabuses, in: Verdoodt, A. (ed.), *Applied sociolinguistics. AILA third congress Copenhagen 1972. Proceedings vol II.*, Heidelberg 1974, 254–65.

Wilkins, D. (1974b), Notional syllabuses and the concept of a minimum adequate grammar, in: Corder, S., E. Roulet (eds.), *Linguistic insights in applied linguistics*, Brussels 1974, 119–28.

Wilkins, D. (1974c), *Second-language learning and teaching*, London 1974.

Wilkins, D. (1975), A communicative approach to syllabus construction in adult language learning, in: Van Essen, A., J. Menting (eds.), *The context of foreign-language learning*, Assen 1975, 173-9.

Wilkins, D. (1976a), *Notional syllabuses*, London 1976.

Wilkins, D. (1976b), Notional syllabus: Theory into practice, *Bulletin CILA* 24, 1976, 5-17.

Willée, G. (1976), *Sprachlehrwerkanalyse mit Hilfe der elektronischen Datenverar-beitung*, Tübingen 1976.

Williams, R. (1976), Towards an education for Europe, *Modern Languages* 57, 1976, 1-6.

Windsor Lewis, J. (1971), The American and British accents of English, *English Language Teaching Journal* 25, 1971, 239-48.

Winitz, H., J. Reeds (1975), *Comprehension and problem solving as strategies for language training*, The Hague 1975.

Wipf, J. (1978), The preparation and use of non-photographic slides in the second-language classroom, in: Baker, R. (ed.), *Teaching for tomorrow in the foreign language classroom*, Skokie, Ill. 1978, 111-21.

Witkin, H., R. Dyk, H. Faterson, D. Goodenough, S. Karp (1962), *Psychological differentiation*, New York 1962.

Witkin, H., C. Moore, D. Goodenough, P. Cox (1977), Field-dependent and field-independent cognitive styles and their educational implications, *Review of Educational Research* 47, 1977, 1-64.

Witkin, H., P. Oltman, E. Raskin, S. Karp (1971), *A manual for the Embedded Figures Test*, Palo Alto 1971.

Wode, H. (1979), Operating principles and 'universals' in L1, L2, and FLT, *International Review of Applied Linguistics in Language Teaching* 17, 1979, 217-31.

Wode, H. (1981), *Learning a second language. 1. An integrated view of language acquisition*, Tübingen 1981.

Wolff, D. (1976), *Probleme des programmierten Fremdsprachenunterrichts*, Tübingen 1976.

Wong-Fillmore, L. (1976), The second time around: cognitive and social strategies in second language acquisition, unpubl. doctoral dissertation, Stanford University, Palo Alto 1976.

Wright, A., D. Betteridge, M. Buckby (1979), *Games for language learning*, London 1979.

Wulf, H. (1978), *Sprachlaborkursbuch: Programme im Englischunterricht; Technik, Erfahrungen und Empfehlungen*, Paderborn 1978.

Yorio, C. (1976), Discussion of E. Hatch and J. Wagner-Gough, 'Explaining sequence and variation in second language acquisition', *Language Learning*, special issue no. 4, 1976, 59-63.

Yorio, C., K. Perkins, J. Schachter (eds.) (1979), *On TESOL '79. The learner in focus*, Washington, DC 1979.

Yoshida, M. (1978), The acquisition of English vocabulary by a Japanese-speaking child, in: Hatch (1978), 91-100.

Zapp, F. (1975), Lernzielbestimmung und Leistungsmessung in ihrem bildungspolitischen und schulpraktischen Bezug, in: Hüllen *et al.* (1975), 7-15.

Zapp, F. (1976), Probleme der Fremdsprachenpolitik aus der Sicht des Fachverbandes Moderne Fremdsprachen, *Die Neueren Sprachen* 75, 1976, 269-74.

Zapp, F. (1977), Schulischer Fremdsprachenunterricht und europäische Integration, in: Hunfeld (1977), 226-32.

Zapp, F. (1978a), Fremdsprachenunterricht und Bildungsreform, *Neusprachliche Mitteilungen* 31, 1978, 129-30.

Zapp, F. (1978b), Planung des Fremdsprachenunterrichts in den Ländern der europäischen Gemeinschaft, in: Freudenstein (1978a), 215-28.

Zapp, F. (1979a), Forderungen ohne Förderungen. Internationale Forderungen zum Fremdsprachenunterricht und nationale Wirklichkeit, *Neusprachliche Mitteilungen* 32, 1979, 138-41.

Zapp, F. (1979b), *Foreign language policy in Europe. An outline of the problem*, Brussels 1979.

Zijlmans, S., H. Wesdorp (1979), Objectieve studietoetsen en hun effecten op talenonderwijs, *Levende Talen* 341, 1979, 271-87.

Zimmermann, G. (1979), Was ist eine 'Didaktische Grammatik'?, in: Kleine (1979), 96-112.

Zonder, S. (1978), *Psychologie und Sprachdidaktik*, Bochum 1978.

Index of subjects

Index of persons